Thirty-Five Years of Archaeological Research at Salmon Ruins, New Mexico

Volume Three: Archaeobotanical Research and Other Analytical Studies

Thirty-Five Years of Archaeological Research at Salmon Ruins, New Mexico

Volume Three: Archaeobotanical Research and Other Analytical Studies

edited by Paul F. Reed

Contributions by

Karen R. Adams
Eileen Bacha
Vorsila L. Bohrer
Dennis R. Danielson
John F. Doebley
Kathy Roler Durand
Stephen R. Durand
Arthur H. Harris
Maria A. Jordan
Maria M. Jordan
David L. Lentz
Sara Leroy-Toren
Karl J. Reinhard
Phillip H. Shelley
Howard N. Smith, Jr.
Laurie D. Webster
Stuart D. Wilson, MD
Thomas C. Windes

Center for Desert Archaeology, Tucson
and Salmon Ruins Museum, Bloomfield, New Mexico
2006

Center for Desert Archaeology
Tucson, Arizona 85705

Salmon Ruins Museum
Bloomfield, New Mexico 87413

ISBN 1-886398-54-2
$34.95

CONTENTS

VOLUME III: ARCHAEOBOTANICAL RESEARCH AND OTHER ANALYTICAL STUDIES

FIGURES

TABLES

Chapter 34

INTRODUCTION TO ARCHAEOBOTANICAL STUDIES AT SALMON PUEBLO

by Vorsila L. Bohrer and Karen R. Adams

Archaeobotanical research at Salmon Ruins had several primary goals. The foremost priority was to establish the economic basis on which the Salmon population existed. Documentation of the nature and distribution of the cultivated crops represents an important aspect of this objective. The evidence derives primarily from the macrofossil record, although portions of maize cobs and kernels have been recovered from flotation samples, and maize pollen has been extracted from sediments. In addition to the cultivated plants, native wild plants were also once an integral part of the economy of Salmon. The broad spectrum of utilized species was determined from a variety of sources, including macrofossils, flotation, pollen samples, and the analysis of coprolites (human feces).

A second goal of the archaeobotanical program was to contribute to the understanding of Salmon as a living community. The delineation of seven burned storerooms and their contents has revealed much about the lifestyle of the Secondary occupation inhabitants. Because the Primary (Chacoan) occupation lacked the type of catastrophic burning that left the contents of the storerooms so well preserved, Karen Adams initiated a pilot study to determine whether or not the pollen and flotation records provided hints as to the kinds of activities that took place on Primary floors. Adams discusses the results of this

study for Room 93W in Chapter 39 (see also K. Adams 1980). The distribution of maize pollen concerning evidence of plants of medicinal or ceremonial usage is explored in Chapter 42. In an effort to more fully identify the medicinal-ceremonial activities of Salmon's former inhabitants, we also studied the Salmon macrofossil record (also discussed in Chapter 42). The role that conifers played in trade is evaluated by Karen Adams in Chapter 40 (see also Windes and Bacha, Chapter 52).

A third goal was to delineate the nature of the environment in which the two Salmon residential groups lived. An initial survey of the juniper berry evidence suggested that the species composition of the juniper woodland may have differed in the past, but a careful study by David Lentz (Chapter 41; see also Lentz 1979) has revealed actual continuity in juniper species from ancient times to the present. Modern plant collections and other records of distribution also reveal that the former inhabitants of Salmon traveled extraordinary distances to procure timbers and other tree products. The coniferous tree-ring record also reveals climatic data that provide clues regarding the abandonment of Salmon in the late 1200s (see Chapter 40). Some of our modern plant collections contrast sufficiently with the prehistoric record to indicate that modern human activities may have altered the distribution of specific plants important to the ancient inhabitants of Salmon.

THE ARCHAEOBOTANICAL PROGRAM AT SALMON RUIN

Every archaeological site in the Southwest that yields archaeobotanical materials offers its own advantages depending upon (1) the techniques of excavation and sampling implemented, (2) the conditions of preservation, and (3) the nature of support for research and publication of results. Throughout the seven summers of excavation (1972–1978) a field ethnobotanist (Karen R. Adams) was on hand to consult and to encourage retention of all botanical

---

The core of this chapter was taken from the original 1980 Salmon report. It was modified to reflect the content of the nine following chapters that constitute the archaeobotanical portion of this report. More than two-thirds of the material is from the 1980 report; most of the remaining chapters were pulled from several sources, including published journal articles in *The Kiva* and *Journal of Ethnobiology*. Chapter 43 was developed from new synthetic work undertaken by Karen Adams, as part of the Center for Desert Archaeology's new Salmon Research Initiative, through partnership with Salmon Ruin Museum (K. Adams 2005; Reed, Chapter 1). One convention for these chapters—the term "archaeobotanical" is preferred over ethnobotanical these days. Therefore, most usages of "ethnobotanical" have been changed to archaeobotanical, except where the term ethnobotanical is part of a final title or actually refers to ethnobotanical research (with ethnographically known Native American groups) or field or laboratory studies.

materials in an orderly manner. A uniform method of archaeobotanical sampling for Salmon Ruin was developed for the first full year of excavation. Refinements in the original sampling plan were available in mimeographed form for excavators during the summers preceding actual publication (Bohrer and Adams 1977). Data recording forms were developed in conjunction with the early analysis of samples.

The methodological approach used by the Salmon Ruin Ethnobotanical Laboratory was discussed extensively by Bohrer and Adams in their 1977 publication *Ethnobotanical Techniques and Approaches at Salmon Ruin, New Mexico*. Additional methods are discussed, as appropriate, in the following chapters. Printouts of computerized data used in this study are archived at Salmon Ruins Museum. Unless otherwise stated, printouts are from the ethnobotanical file named DRUPE. Specific names of plants follow Kearney and Peebles (1960).

Identifying Ancient Plants

The Salmon archaeobotanical work relied on the premise that ancient plant parts could be identified by comparing them to modern plant specimens. Identification of prehistoric plant parts is most convincing when their traits overlap those of modern specimens and the two are indistinguishable. These identifications are strengthened when the available modern comparative collection is extensive enough to include closely similar taxa.

Most modern plants are identified on the basis of a series of characters, often emphasizing floral and fruiting structures. Archaeological specimens, on the other hand, frequently represent mere fragments of the total plant, and may lack the parts normally relied upon for confident identification. For example, delicate flowering parts may be too fragile to last hundreds of years in an archaeological site. Or, a prehistoric group might have selected for use only those parts of a plant not presently emphasized in modern taxonomies.

Because many of the plant parts recovered from ancient sites are not those generally used to identify living specimens, it was necessary to develop alternative methods to identify prehistoric materials. Individual parts (fruit, bark, wood) of modern plants can be studied with the aim of segregating a species or genus on the basis of unique morphological or anatomical traits. The use of multiple traits and well-documented modern variability in those traits together increases success in identification. In circumstances where modern species cannot be segregated on the basis of anatomy or morphology, ancient materials likewise cannot be segregated.

The need for accurate and current knowledge of modern specimens guided the archaeobotanical work at Salmon Ruin. During the summers of 1972–1977, when full-scale archaeological excavation was underway, ethnobotanical personnel made plant collections in the surrounding area to provide modern material, with plant specimens deposited in an accredited herbarium. At the same time, personnel described and tentatively identified the majority of macrofossils retrieved from the pueblo. As these preliminary identifications accumulated, it became clear that the collecting range of some modern comparative materials, such as conifers, would have to be broadened to include the distant mountains. Other identifications of Salmon Ruin plant materials were made in comparison to modern materials collected much closer to the ruin.

Interpreting Ancient Plant Usage

One of the underlying assumptions of our approach was that the individuals most familiar with the site and its history of excavation were best suited to study the ancient archaeobotanical record. Both Bohrer and Adams had the advantage of having been with the San Juan Valley Archaeological Project from its inception. Bohrer (the principal author) had the dual privilege of offering guidance to youthful catalogers of plant macrofossils while sharing in the most perplexing aspects of the botanical fragments. K. Adams played a similar role in guiding the analysis of the samples obtained by flotation. Bohrer accepts responsibility for the reliance upon archaeological context and interpretation. Any extensive research directing attention to similarities in usage in other archaeological sites or to historic Pueblo Indian usage in the Southwest must await integrative efforts that postdate this publication.

In all of our research illuminating the relationships between plants and people at Salmon Ruin we have attempted to look at each occupation as a separate entity; whenever the opportunity permitted we have compared and contrasted the occupations. Although Room 62W contained an unusual number of strata of moderate preservation, the frequent mixing of both occupations in these same strata blocked plans to make comparisons. The limited time available to evaluate the extensive database has also limited the extent of comparison between occupations.

Our methodology also made extensive use of the number of units in which a certain type of plant remains was found. For example, we employed the number of grids in which an item (corn pollen) was found in a room, the number of strata of equivalent preservation in which certain macrofossils turn up within a room, the number of strata throughout Salmon in which a given seed was recovered, and the number of rooms of a given type (storerooms) in which an item was present. Dashes in tables indicate that an item was not present. All of these comparisons provide a rough indication of the relative importance of one plant to another. We are aware of the pitfalls of such an approach and have discussed additional variables that may skew such estimates, as appropriate.

Additional discussion regarding archaeobotanical interpretation of pollen grains and charred seeds from archaeological sites is provided by K. Adams in Chapter 39.

Evaluating Conditions of Preservation at Salmon

The best conditions of preservation encountered at Salmon were indicated by stratigraphic units in which uncarbonized yucca fiber survived, either as part of a leaf or separate from it in the form of cordage or twine. Plant material in one stratigraphic unit either deposited in ashes or covered by ashes in Room 62W (L-2-7.1) exemplified the high level of preservation of materials such as yucca twine, leaf thongs, corn tassel fragments, scraps of cotton cloth, quids of grass, and feces.

So many plant materials have been preserved in association with yucca leaves and squash seeds that the two have been used as indicators of moderate preservation at Salmon. The yucca leaves typically lack most of their fibers and the squash seeds are generally thin and fragile. Twenty-three of 48 rooms exposed by excavation contained moderate levels of preservation in at least one stratigraphic unit. Because catalogers did not consistently record the presence of yucca fibers in the leaf interiors, the foregoing assessment may inadvertently include a few stratigraphic units of the best-preserved material.

Poor conditions of preservation are those in which the plant materials survived only by virtue of having been parched or carbonized; the items may have been preserved accidentally by carbonization when seeds were parched as part of food preparation. Only the smaller items were apt to be ground into a floor; larger items such as beans and piñon nut shells were easily picked up. Consequently trash deposits carry a wider size range of items than do habitation floors. A tabulation after three summers of cataloging macrofossils indicated that 43.8 percent came from trash and only 2.7 percent came from floors. Nevertheless, in both trash and floor stratigraphic units a variety of small seeds were recovered by flotation. The same units yielded abundant and well-preserved pollen, with few exceptions. Insuffi-

cient pollen came from stratigraphic units that either suffered a catastrophic fire or were redeposited from elsewhere. The loss of pollen from rooms quickly abandoned due to fire has been compensated by the recovery of many additional macrofossils. The collapse of burning roof rafters and the smothering of the fire by the falling adobe roof protected the contents. Secondary occupation plant remains from what are believed to be seven burned storerooms and from the Tower Kiva (Room 64W) have been preserved by such means.

The following nine chapters (35–43) describe and interpret the archaeobotanical record of Salmon Pueblo. In Chapter 35, Bohrer and Doebley describe cultivated plants. Chapter 36, by K. Adams, is an exploration of native, wild plant usage at Salmon. Doebley discusses plant remains from trash deposits in Chapter 37, and Bohrer reports on varied botanical remains and special contexts in Chapter 38. Adams's study of plant usage in Room 93W is presented in Chapter 39, and Chapter 40 focuses on conifer usage at Salmon. Lentz summarizes special research on junipers in Chapter 41. In Chapter 42, Bohrer explores ceremonial and medicinal plants at Salmon. Finally, K. Adams offers a summary and conclusions in Chapter 43.

The work of the Ethnobotanical Laboratory of Salmon Ruin was supported through the cooperation of many individuals. Rex K. Adams, Karen R. Adams, Daniel Landis, and David L. Lentz all played essential roles in the evaluation of the strata in which maize was found in quantity. The expertise that John Doebley acquired as a predoctoral student in maize evolution at the University of Wisconsin, combined with his earlier excavation and research experience at Salmon Ruin (1976), has altered the traditional role of a maize specialist from that of an outside investigator to one who has had close ties with the project. Through the unselfish help of Thomas W. Whitaker in identifying modern cucurbit material, Elizabeth Burgess-Terrel was able to relate the most durable characteristics of the modern seed to the archaeological seed remains at Salmon (1979). The last months of report preparation (in 1980), combined with the packing of archaeological plant material, offered special challenges. The organizational ability of Karen R. Adams and the thorough and cheerful manner in which Thomas E. Gee carried out storms of miscellaneous tasks have permitted the preparation of this report with unusual smoothness. To our several students who have tackled specific problems (Doebley 1976; Lentz 1979; Rose 1979a, 1979b) and to the numerous others who have aided us over the years (see our annual reports) we are grateful for the multitudinous and seemingly small steps taken that ultimately move the largest of tasks toward completion. For any reflections this report may contain of a larger sense of vision or purpose, we gratefully acknowledge the role of the late Cynthia Irwin-Williams, principal investigator.

ACKNOWLEDGMENTS

The work of the Ethnobotanical Laboratory of Salmon Ruin was supported through the cooperation of many individuals. Rex K. Adams, Karen R. Adams, Daniel Landis, and David L. Lentz all played essential roles in the evaluation of the strata in which maize was found in quantity. The expertise that John Doebley acquired as a predoctoral student in maize evolution at the University of Wisconsin, combined with his earlier excavation and research experience at Salmon Ruin (1976), has altered the traditional role of a maize specialist from that of an outside investigator to one who has had close ties with the project. Through the unselfish help of Thomas W. Whitaker in identifying modern cucurbit material, Elizabeth Burgess-Terrel was able to relate the most durable characteristics of the modern seed to the archaeological seed remains at Salmon (1979). The last months of report preparation (in 1980), combined with the packing of archaeological plant material, offered special challenges. The organizational ability of Karen R. Adams and the thorough and cheerful manner in which Thomas E. Gee carried out storms of miscellaneous tasks have permitted the preparation of this report with unusual smoothness. To our several students who have tackled specific problems (Doebley 1976; Lentz 1979; Rose 1979a, 1979b) and to the numerous others who have aided us over the years (see our annual reports) we are grateful for the multitudinous and seemingly small steps taken that ultimately move the largest of tasks toward completion. For any reflections this report may contain of a larger sense of vision or purpose, we gratefully acknowledge the role of the late Cynthia Irwin-Williams, principal investigator.

Chapter 35

CULTIVATED PLANTS FROM SALMON PUEBLO

by Vorsila L. Bohrer and John F. Doebley

Cultivated plants in general and maize in particular were economically important to both the Chacoan and Secondary occupations. The widespread presence of maize in flotation samples from Chacoan trash strata (10 of 13) compared with flotation samples from Secondary occupation strata (13 of 22) suggests greater emphasis on maize by the Chacoans. A survey of the content of Secondary storerooms suggests that beans may have ranked second only to corn; beans were recovered in six of seven storerooms. In a survey of the content of trash units, the frequency of squash seed exceeds the frequency of piñon shells, juniper seeds, outer onion bulb scales, yucca seeds, and chokecherry pits.

MAIZE FROM SALMON RUINS

The evolutionary history of maize (*Zea mays* L. ssp. *mays*) has been a subject of great controversy for the past 100 years. During part of this period (1940–1970) the Tripartite Hypothesis proposed by Drs. Mangelsdorf and Reeves (1939) appeared to resolve the controversy, and thus came to pervade the archaeological and botanical literature. According to this hypothesis maize is a domesticated form of a polystichous (many-rowed) wild maize, and teosinte (*Z. mays* L. ssp. *mexicana*), a close relative of corn, is the hybrid offspring of the polystichous wild maize and gamagrass (*Tripsacum*), a related but cytologically and morphologically much different grass.

In the past decade, however, considerable new botanical information has shed light on the origin of maize. Not only has the hypothesis of the hybrid origin of teosinte been put to rest after 40 years of often bitter argument, but teosinte has emerged as the direct ancestor of maize in the eyes of the bulk of the botanical community (Beadle 1939, 1972, 1980;

Langham 1940; Longley 1941; Darlington 1956; Miranda Colin 1966; Galinat 1971, 1988; Iltis 1979; DeWet and Harlan 1972; Kato 1975; Heiser 1979; Doebley and Iltis 1980). This topic, however, remains controversial (cf. Mangelsdorf 1974; Randolph 1976; Bird 1980).

With the rise of the view that teosinte is the direct ancestor of maize has come a shift in the emphasis placed upon certain aspects of maize research. One area of renewed interest is the elucidation of the initial transformation of the slender, distichous spike of teosinte into the massive, polystichous maize ear (Iltis 1979; Beadle 1972, 1980; Galinat 1971; Doebley and Iltis 1980; Allen and Iltis 1980). Other areas of current research have concentrated on determining which of the six allopatric taxa of teosinte the American Indians selected to produce the first cultivated maize and the degree to which each of these teosintes contributed to the past and present racial variability in maize through introgression. An understanding of the teosinte-maize transformation, of the extent of teosinte introgression, and of the initial place of maize domestication is essential not only for botanists and archaeologists working with maize remains from proto and early agricultural sites, but for any researchers working with prehistoric maize specimens. Only through an understanding of these issues can we begin to choose appropriate morphological characters for assessing primitiveness versus specialization, and thus place all archaeological maize in a phylogenetically coherent framework.

Because of its history of introgression from the wild teosintes, its diffusion into a wide variety of habitats from Canada to Argentina, and its central role in the cultures and religions of the American Indians, maize has come to vary as much as, if not more than, any cultivar ever produced by man. In Latin America alone this species contains well over 250 recognized races that differ in some very subtle, to other quite dramatic morphological, physiological, and genetic features. A large part of the morphological variability resides in the seed-bearing ear, the

---

This paper by Bohrer and Doebley was part of the 1980 Salmon report. It is more inclusive than the 1983 *Kiva* article by Doebley and Bohrer because it explains why certain maize measurements were taken and is more explicit regarding sample selection. For a more recent and updated discussion of corn evolution, see Wilkes (2004).

structure on which the Mexican and other American Indians directed the brunt of their intensive and remarkably successful selective pressures.

For the archaeologist this store of variability represents a valuable source of information that has often been employed in comparisons of different sites or different temporal horizons within a single site. However, the possibilities of addressing more penetrating questions concerning how cultural selection within a society affects maize variability in the archaeological record of a site have been scarcely considered. For example, within any one cultural group, direct or indirect social controls may determine what varieties of maize can be raised. Thus, at Zia Pueblo the cacique decides both the planting dates and the harvest dates of corn (Euler 1954:30). If a new variety of corn matures too early, it may be lost through failure of the cacique to sanction harvest. A given cultural group may also influence the amount of variability within any one variety. Ears used for ritual purposes whose kernels are later planted (Stevenson 1894:140–141) may be rigorously selected to meet certain cultural standards, as may the household supply of seed corn reserved for planting. Of course, variability due to the environment is a confounding factor, here as in many other situations, and must be considered separately from actual genetic variability.

We are fortunate that the study of maize from a large number of prehistoric sites in the southwestern United States has provided a model for the local evolution and diffusion of maize against which the variability at any particular site may be viewed. The general picture for the evolutionary history of maize in the Southwest, though not entirely clear, can be briefly summarized as follows. Initially, a form of maize related to the modern Chapalote of northwest Mexico entered the Southwest; this first introduction is usually dated to ca. 2300 BC (Mangelsdorf et al. 1967). In a recent critical review of the early occurrence of maize in the Southwest, Berry (1982) rejected this early date for maize at Bat Cave and other sites because of circumstances surrounding the methods of excavation and the carbon dating itself. He suggested the much more conservative date of ca. 500–750 BC or even ca. 300–100 BC. Whatever the time of its introduction, this Chapalote-like maize developed locally in the Southwest and probably gave rise to a number of local variants with 12 or 14 rows of grain (Galinat and Gunnerson 1963). Later, a second race of maize called Maize de Ocho entered the Southwest from Mexico. The time of its entry, initially placed at ca. AD 700 (Galinat and Gunnerson

1963), was later dated to ca. 38 BC (Galinat et al. 1970). Now, however, Galinat (personal communication) has reconsidered the identity of the ca. 38 BC specimens and suggests that they, and other early specimens of 8-row maize east of the Rockies, may be an 8-row relative of Nal-Tel, rather than Maize de Ocho sensu stricto.

After arriving in the Southwest, Maize de Ocho hybridized with the indigenous Chapalote-derived maize to produce a new hybrid variety called Pima-Papago. It has been suggested that the Pima-Papago hybrid developed early (Basketmaker II, ca. AD 300) and formed the basis for ancient Pueblo agriculture (Winter 1973). However, as most identifications are based on two measurements (row number and cupule width) that vary with the environment, we should not rush to discard the older idea that these hybrids did not figure prominently into Puebloan agriculture until after AD 700 (Galinat and Gunnerson 1963). If this is the case it would also explain the sudden drop in average row number from 12 to 10 during late Pueblo II (AD 100) times (Cutler 1966; Cutler and Meyer 1965) as Maize de Ocho spread from one site to the next.

Distribution of Maize Remains

Carbonized kernel and cob fragments of maize are common in flotation samples from Salmon Ruin. Their widespread distribution bears some relationship to usage, although variable methods of preparation may cause underrepresentation in the archaeological record. For example, boiled corn is less apt to carbonize and preserve than parched corn. All four Chacoan occupation floors examined (two with features and two without features) contained evidence of maize. Twelve of 22 floors utilized by the Secondary occupation produced diagnostic parts of maize, including two kiva floors (Room 6A, H-1-5.2 and Room 124A, H-1-6). Ten of 13 trash strata of Chacoan occupation and 13 of 23 strata of Secondary occupation contained maize. Flotation from trash represents a single sample (1 liter) from one stratigraphic unit, whereas floor flotation represents a variable number of 1 liter samples.

Our inventory of strata with more than six cobs revealed cob concentrations in 22 of 48 rooms exposed by excavation. Trash or roof stratigraphic units characteristically retained abundant maize cobs (Table 35.1) that are predominantly carbonized, although unburned degraded cobs have also been recovered. During the Secondary occupation, at least seven second-story floors (first-floor roofs) contained carbonized cobs and kernels when fire partially

Table 35.1. Distribution of maize samples of more than six cobs in stratigraphic units and rooms.

Stratigraphic Unit	Strata	Rooms
Structured and unstructured trash (C and M)	32	15
Roof-fall (F) and mixed roof-fall (N)	22	15
Occupational fill (G)	1	1
Pits (L)	3	3
Other (B, D, U)	3	2
Total	61	36

Based on D. Wilson's 4/28/78 inventory of 48 excavated rooms.

destroyed the contents of the storeroom. The slumping of the burning roofs and the dumping of the contents of the storerooms badly jostled the corn and the other items from their original stored positions. However, in Room 30W (H-1-4), a first-floor storage room, most cobs were found near the south wall, aligned parallel to it along the east-west axis in relatively horizontal positions. This is our only indication that ears were stacked for storage.

Some second-floor storerooms might also have retained whole ears of corn, judging from the attachment of some kernels to the cob. In addition, some kernels from Rooms 36W (F-1-15), 90W (F-2-9), and 119W (F-3-20) were carbonized except for the embryo. One wonders if the original location of the kernel on the cob protected the embryo from full carbonization in some instances. Concentrations of loose kernels came from numerous Secondary occupation strata, but only one Chacoan occupation deposit, which consisted of scattered sheet trash on the north side of the pueblo, held an abundance of kernels (Unit 2 BW, M-1-3).

Many other maize parts, in addition to cobs and kernels, have been revealed in the sediments of Salmon Ruin; for example one well-preserved stratigraphic unit of redeposited trash from Room 62W contained parts ranging from stalks to tassels (Table 35.2). From the empty, tied shucks, we may conclude that some ears were suspended from their tied husks. From the several stalks, we may judge that whole plants were sometimes brought to the pueblo. The range of preservation found in tassel fragments (see Table 35.2) points to dual possibilities: either some tassels were intentionally abraded or fragmented before discard, or their poor condition resulted from being churned in the trash. Evidence from pollen analysis supports an interpretation of deliberate abrasion (see Bohrer, Chapter 42). Aggre-

gates of prehistoric maize pollen can be duplicated experimentally only by crushing the immature anthers of modern Chapalote maize.

More evidence for the manner of maize utilization can be garnered from the content of feces and firepits, and from a study of kernel endosperm and metate morphology. Two human feces belonging to the Secondary occupation have small cob segments included in them. Our meager evidence of associated material (yucca leaf and insect bodies on one and squash seed in another) suggests that cobs were ingested at least in times of food shortage and perhaps more often. The Navajo have used ears when the silk first emerges and have ground mature cobs for food in times of famine within this century (Hill 1938:45–46). Small bits of burned cobs recovered from firepits at Salmon imply the additional use of cobs as fuel. The study of the nature of the starch granules in the endosperm of the kernel and its potential relationship to metate morphology in both occupations can be found in this maize discussion under "Analysis of Kernels."

Analysis of Cobs

As discussed in the introduction, one must appreciate the ancestral role of teosinte when attempting to construct an evolutionarily meaningful system of maize classification. This is especially true when studying archaeological cobs, for here an understanding of maize evolution mandates that considerable attention be devoted to the cupules. The cupules, which are nothing more than depressions in the rachis (axis) segments of the maize ear, once had the role of housing and protecting the teosinte seed from pests and predators, including humans. During the radiation of maize races, the cupules underwent remarkable changes in both form and function. They were collapsed, compressed, broadened, and flattened, and in some races molded into an impervious cylinder that both strengthened the cob and protected its vasculature from insects. Thus, these highly variable structures provide an important clue to the evolutionary link between teosinte and maize, and must be assigned considerable importance in any system of maize classification that purports to have an evolutionary basis. Much of the value of cupule characters to the maize taxonomist and archaeologist stems from the fact that they were rarely directly affected by the selective efforts of humans. Thus, they probably changed less rapidly than characters under stringent selection such as kernel shape or size, and should be useful in documenting relationships between races that differ greatly in general ear and kernel morphology.

Table 35.2. Examples of well-preserved maize parts.

Description	Record Key (Bot. Sample No.)
Stalk segment with 5 nodes present in 13 cm, cut at base with sharp instrument	(62W9002)
Stalk segment with 2 nodes present	51004
Two husks with small segment of peduncle attached, ends tied in knot	33874
Tassels with branches well preserved and numerous	(62W9037)
Two tassel segments bare of all spikelets	(62W9135)
Three florets of a tassel	(62W9127)
Many fragments of a tassel, all 5 cm or shorter; tips of spikelets are frayed, some rachis segments have spikelets removed entirely	33874

From Room 62W stratigraphic unit L-2-07.1 of mixed cultural affiliation, printout 3/27/79 Q6226-377. Unless otherwise noted in this and the following tables, printouts derive from the ethnobotanical file named DRUPE.

Nevertheless, operating under the Tripartite Hypothesis (Mangelsdorf and Reeves 1939; Mangelsdorf 1974), which dismissed the cupules as mere evidence of *Tripsacum*'s introgression into maize, the classification of Mexican maize races included no quantitative measurements of the cupule (Wellhausen et al. 1952). Anthropologists and botanists working with archaeological maize have, on the other hand, paid considerable attention to the cupule, as it was often the only organ of the maize plant reasonably well preserved in sites. Yet, their efforts have not been unified nor with some exceptions guided by an understanding of the teosinte-maize transition, because the anthropological community has for the most part and until quite recently acquiesced to the theory that maize evolved from the elusive polystichous wild maize and not teosinte (cf. Beadle 1972; Flannery 1973). For these reasons maize ear variability and the cupule in particular are the basis of this study, which aims to answer questions concerning cultural selection by the inhabitants of Salmon Ruin.

Materials and Methods

All strata containing maize were evaluated in an effort to identify those most closely matching the following criteria (Lentz 1978):

- The stratum contained at least 30 corn cobs.
- The stratum contained more than 30 sherds to indicate an occupational association with no contaminating sherds.
- The stratum contained no contradictory indicators of occupational association provided by the lithic or ceramic content.
- The stratigraphic unit was underlain by earlier strata and overlain by later materials. Usually the surrounding strata were of similar depositional association.
- Few or no signs of disturbance within the stratum.

After the strata were selected, they were segregated according to their cultural affiliation (Chacoan or Secondary), and then further subdivided by their stratigraphic type (roof, trash), location within the pueblo in space (southeast vs. northwest), in time (early vs. middle), and by presumed room function (ceremonial, living, storage). A series of 12 strata were then chosen that allowed comparison between and within the two major cultural groups occupying Salmon. Then, a sample of 30 cobs was picked from each of these 12 strata by means of a random numbers table. In cases where only 30 or fewer cobs were available from a particular stratum, an entire sample was taken.

This data set allowed comparisons of maize from ceremonial to nonceremonial rooms and maize in different periods within the Secondary occupation, as well as general comparisons between maize of Chacoan and Secondary occupations. Eight hypotheses were ultimately devised (Table 35.3).

Nine quantitative morphological traits of the maize ear and cupule were measured by the first author. Most of these traits have been employed previously by other researchers; thus, definitions for row number, rachis diameter, and cob diameter may be found elsewhere (Wellhausen et al. 1952). Similarly, Nickerson (1953) has described cupule width and glume width, and Bird (1980) defined rachis segment length. This leaves three characters used for the first time in need of definition. First, the cupule aperture width (Figure 35.1) represents in effect the total width of the cupule minus the width of the rachis flaps (cf. Bird and Bird 1980). In teosinte the rachis flaps are erect or turned slightly inward (Figure 35.2), so when measured in this plane they would be very narrow. In the evolution of maize the rachis flaps were turned outward and broadened so that the aperture has come to represent a smaller portion of the total cupule width than it does in teosinte.

Table 35.3. Hypotheses and questions tested with the maize sample from Salmon Ruin.

1. Does the maize used in the everyday lives of the occupants differ between the two occupations?
2. Chacoan occupation maize should be less variable than maize from the Secondary occupation.
3. Was there a change in maize between early and middle Secondary times?
4. Did maize from the northwest sector of Salmon differ significantly from the southeast sector in early Secondary and middle Secondary times?
5. Did ritual maize differ from everyday maize during the Chacoan occupation?
6. Did ritual maize differ from everyday maize during the Secondary occupation?
7. Are samples of maize from Chacoan and Secondary ceremonial rooms similar?
8. If Room 86 functioned as a ceremonial room, it should contain maize similar to that found in contemporary Kiva 64W.

Second, the cupule aperture height (see Figure 35.1) provides a measure of the degree of cupule compression. Whereas in teosinte (see Figure 35.2) the cupules are open (uncollapsed), in maize they are often nearly totally collapsed. This is probably the effect of both condensation of the internodes (cupules) and a strengthening of the attachment of the kernel to the cob, which resulted in the formation of the hard ridge composed of the bases of the lower glume and pedicel (glume-pedicel ridge; H.H. Iltis, personal communication; see Figure 35.1). Since in teosinte the cupule and lower glume hold the grain in place, there is no need for it to be strongly attached to the axis. Third, the cupule aperture depth is the distance from the level of the rachis flaps to the deepest point of the cupule on a line perpendicular to the long axis of the ear.

To ensure the most accurate measurement of these traits, all characters (with the exception of the rachis and cob diameter) were measured under a binocular microscope (10x) equipped with an ocular micrometer. Rachis and cob diameters, on the other hand, were measured using hand-held calipers.

Hotelling's T^2 test was used to determine whether samples are significantly different from each other. This is a multivariate extension of the univariate t-test, which incorporates all of the original variates in a single test. In addition to these T^2 tests, the program used (CANCOV; Kowal 1980) performed a multiple discriminant analysis for selected pairwise combinations of the 12 samples. This technique creates a synthetic variable, the discriminant score, which is computed by taking a weighted sum of the 12 original variates in such a way that it maximally separates the two samples.

When performing both the T^2 tests and the multiple discriminant analyses, the error matrix based on all 12 samples was used in each pairwise comparison; this provides a better estimate of the error variation. As these techniques require that each

specimen have a measurement for all characters; cobs for which some traits could not be measured were therefore excluded. Also, to keep the samples as large as possible, some characters that could not be measured on most cobs—all three kernel characters, glume width, and cob diameter—had to be excluded from the test.

After the T^2 test is performed and if the null hypothesis is rejected, one wants to know how each of the original variates contributed to the test statistic. One means of judging the contribution of the original variates is to look at their correlations with the discriminant scores from the multiple discriminant analysis. The larger the absolute value of the correlation, the better the character approximates the discriminant score. Further, if the correlations of the two characters with the discriminant scores have the same sign, then they contribute in the same way to the discrimination and T^2 test; that is, both characters are large in one sample and small in the other. If the correlations of two characters have opposite signs, then they contribute in opposite ways to the discrimination (when one character is large the other tends to be small).

Multinormality is one of the assumptions of Hotelling's T^2 test, so the data were checked for this condition by using normal probability plots. All samples were very near normal for all traits (with the exception of row number) when the data were log transformed. Row number most closely approached normality in the raw or untransformed state.

For this report 15 tests of significance using Hotelling's T^2 test were performed. When testing such a large number of hypotheses, it is necessary to adjust the level of significance (V) so that the experiment-wise significance level is not inflated. For example, if one does 20 tests at the V = .05 level, then the probability is that you will find a significant difference for one of these tests when in fact the difference is not significant. To correct for this problem,

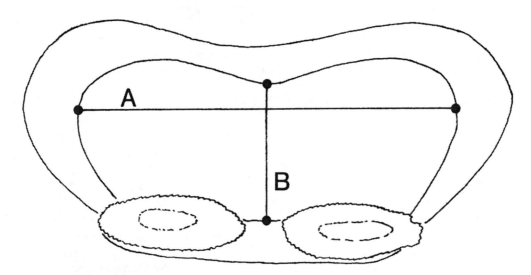

Figure 35.1. Diagram of a maize cupule. Line A indicates cupule aperture width. Line B indicates cupule aperture height.

the first author employed the Bonferoni Method, which merely involves testing at the $V/$(no. of test) level to obtain an experiment-wise significance level of V or less. Thus, to claim significance at the V = .05 level, one must observe $p \leq 0.00333$ (.05/15). This is a very conservative procedure.

In addition to testing for differences between the means, there was also a need to determine in some cases which samples were most variable. Unfortunately, no multivariate test has been designed to answer this question, and in the present case 119 univariate tests would be required to answer this question for all 15 pairwise comparisons—a number too large to be practical. For these reasons, the first author chose to present the average of the coefficients of variability of all traits for a sample. This average provides a measure of the amount of variability in the sample with all characters considered, and is free of discrepancies due to differences in the means or units of measurement.

Finally, the view taken here of the test statistics and significance levels is that these values are merely indicators of the degree of difference between two samples, and that the significance level is not a rigid boundary above and below which one must either accept or reject a particular hypothesis.

Maize from Non-Ceremonial Rooms
Temporal Variation

The first question addressed is whether or not the maize used in the everyday lives of the occu-

pants differed between the two occupations. To answer this question one can look at the difference between the two trash samples from each occupation. A comparison of Samples 2 and 8 from Room 91 and a comparison of Samples 3 and 9 from Room 100 seems best, as in each case the location of deposition is constant, but the cultural affiliation of the depositors differs. For both comparisons considerable dissimilarity is shown between the maize of the two occupations (Table 35.4). The correlations of the original variates to the discriminant scores (Table 35.5) for these two comparisons indicate that the two Chacoan occupation samples (Samples 2 and 3) have more rows of grain and narrower cupules than the Secondary occupation ones (Samples 8 and 9). For rachis diameter, however, the Chacoan period samples vary quite dramatically among themselves, as shown by the fact that the correlation for this character is negative for one comparison (3 vs. 9) and positive for the other (2 vs. 8; see Tables 35.4 and 35.5). Aperture height manifests the same trend as rachis diameter. Further, rachis segment length appears important in distinguishing the two samples from Room 100 but not from Room 91 (see Table 35.5).

These results suggest that the two Chacoan occupation samples (Samples 2 and 3) differ from each other—that is, variability exists within the initial occupation. A test of this hypothesis yields a probability of 0.00145, which though not as small as those from the two previous tests, is much smaller than the critical value of 0.00333, and thus supports the idea

Figure 35.2. A teosinte cupule with the glumes and grain removed.

that Samples 2 and 3 do not represent the same type of maize. The dissimilarity here principally involves rachis diameter, the sample from Room 100 having a much narrower rachis than the sample from Room 91 (see Tables 35.4 and 35.5). The explanation for this difference may reside in the fact that the sample from Room 91 (Sample 2) came from a stratum adjacent to an Intermediate period stratum. Thus, Sample 2 may express some influence from the Intermediate period, and may be atypical of Chacoan period maize.

Because the earliest construction at Salmon showed evidence that it was intended to be an integrated single structure from the very beginning, and because of the observation that the Secondary occupants tended to replace fallen walls with comparatively shoddy masonry on the decayed western end of the pueblo, it seems plausible that the Chacoan occupation exerted a stronger degree of social control over its members than the Secondary occupants did. This stronger social control should be reflected in stronger selection pressure toward an

ideal form of maize. In other words, Chacoan maize should be less variable than Secondary maize.

Thus, besides testing for differences between the sample means, a measure of the variability of each sample (average of the coefficients of variation) is also provided (see Table 35.4). These values indicate that the maize from both Chacoan trash samples is less variable than that from the Secondary trash samples. Unfortunately, as discussed above, no test of significance can be made on such multivariate measures of variability. In support of the indication that maize from the Secondary period trash samples varies more than from the Chacoan period, the univariate F-tests (not presented here) show the same trend.

The next hypothesis tested concerns differences between maize recovered from roof strata of early Secondary and middle Secondary times. The question is whether a change in maize took place over time within this one occupation. To test this hypothesis, we compared Sample 4 from Room 36 (early Secondary occuation) to Sample 5 from Room 37 (middle Secondary), and Sample 11 from Room 127 (early Secondary) to Sample 12 from Room 129 (middle Secondary).

Archaeological evidence indicates that the roofs of 36W (F-1-15) and 127W (F-1-4) were both destroyed by fire relatively early in the Secondary occupation. The roof of Room 36W apparently was partially destroyed by the fire that is roughly dated from the late 1100s to early 1200s. Subsequently there was time for 2–3 m of trash to accumulate on the fallen roof of 36W. Similarly, after the roof of 127W (F-1-4) burned and collapsed, there was time to form a floor over it and to remodel the room in other ways so that it served as a kiva during the latter part of the Secondary occupation.

Site-wide patterns of deposition in the Secondary period once again suggest that the two mid-Secondary stratigraphic units (37W, F-2-5 and 129W, F-1-8) are equivalent in age. The stratigraphic units in each room are preceded depositionally by earlier Secondary occupation strata characterized by Mesa Verde ceramics, and followed by Secondary stratigraphic units also containing Mesa Verde ceramics.

The tests for both of the above-mentioned comparisons (Samples 4 vs. 5 and 11 vs. 12) concerning variability between maize of the early and middle Secondary occupation indicate that there are differences (see Table 35.5). The major consistent differences seem to involve rachis diameter, rachis segment length, and cupule depth. The ratio of rachis diameter to rachis segment length is larger for the middle Secondary samples.

Table 35.4. A comparison of the means and coefficients of variation (CV) for maize from different occupations and localities within Salmon Ruin.

Sample No.	Room & Nature of Stratigraphic Unit	Total Cobs in Stratum	Row No. (CV:n)	Cupule Width (CV:n)	Aperture Height (CV:n)	Aperture Width (CV:n)	Cupule Depth (CV:n)	Rachis Segment Length (CV:n)
NON-CEREMONIAL								
Primary Occupation								
2	91W (C-8-22 & C-7-21) trash	30	11.9 (16.1:26)	6.6 (13.0:26)	0.90 (49.1:26)	4.0 (27.4:26)	1.7 (30.9:25)	3.9 (9.7:26)
3	100W (C-10-15, C-11-16, C-12-17, & C-13-18) trash	36	11.8 (20.3:24)	6.1 (12.5:24)	1.16 (42.9:23)	3.3 (28.6:22)	1.6 (31.4:22)	3.9 (11.6:24)
Secondary Occupation								
8	91D (C-3-17) trash	191	10.3 (16.0:30)	7.5 (21.8:30)	1.09 (42.9:30)	4.0 (31.4:30)	1.9 (43.0:30)	3.9 (12.6:30)
9	100W (N-1-3) roof	94	10.8 (12.5:30)	6.9 (20.0:30)	0.80 (35.2:29)	3.8 (29.9:28)	1.9 (43.4:30)	3.5 (11.9:30)
Early Secondary Occupation								
4	36W (F-1-15) storeroom	91	11.0 (16.4:30)	7.0 (15.6:30)	0.96 (35.5:29)	3.5 (24.1:29)	1.8 (36.0:30)	3.8 (10.4:30)
10	119W (F-3-20) storeroom	78	10.6 (17.8:28)	6.7 (13.6:28)	1.15 (34.0:28)	3.5 (24.3:28)	1.9 (38.9:27)	4.1 (12.0:28)
11	127W (F-1-4) storeroom rooftop	33	9.9 (14.2:27)	6.8 (13.1:27)	1.03 (54.4:27)	4.1 (26.9:27)	1.5 (30.9:27)	4.1 (11.0:27)
Middle Secondary Occupation								
5	37W (F-2-5) storeroom	30	10.6 (14.0:25)	6.3 (17.9:25)	0.92 (49.6:25)	3.4 (27.9:25)	1.9 (30.8:25)	3.5 (13.3:25)
12	129W (F-1-8, F-1-8.2, & F-1-8.3) storeroom	548	11.1 (13.9:30)	7.5 (18.6:30)	0.90 (46.8:30)	4.3 (27.7:30)	2.1 (30.2:30)	3.9 (12.7:30)
CEREMONIAL								
Primary Occupation								
1	81W (F-2-13) platform area	79	12.1 (15.5:30)	7.3 (21.5:30)	0.93 (45.2:30)	4.0 (27.4:30)	2.0 (41.7:30)	4.3 (11.7:30)
Secondary Occupation								
6	64W (F-1-6 & H-1-8) kiva bench and floor	51	11.7 (11.6:30)	6.8 (18.4:30)	0.76 (45.5:30)	3.5 (26.9:30)	2.1 (28.6:30)	3.8 (14.3:30)
7	86W (F-1-4) sq room with kiva-like features	30	10.9 (16.7:22)	7.2 (17.6:22)	0.76 (43.4:21)	3.7 (30.8:20)	2.0 (37.9:22)	4.1 (9.3:22)

Table 35.4 (continued)

Sample No.	Room & Nature of Stratigraphic Unit	Rachis Diameter (CV:n)	Cob Diameter (CV:n)	Glume Width (CV:n)	Kernel Length (CV:n)	Kernel Width (CV:n)	Kernel Thickness (CV:n)	Mean of CVs
NON-CEREMONIAL								
Primary Occupation								
2	91W (C-8-22 & C-7-21) trash	11.4 (16.5:26)	16.3 (11.0:9)	4.4 (15.2:11)	---	---	---	21.0
3	100W (C-10-15, C-11-16, C-12-17, & C-13-18) trash	9.3 (14.3:24)	14.5 (4.9:2)	4.5 (14.1:7)	---	---	---	20.1
Secondary Occupation								
8	91D (C-3-17) trash	10.1 (20.2:30)	13.9 (17.3:28)	5.3 (15.8:29)	8.6 (8.24:2)	7.4 (15.8:2)	4.7 (0.31:2)	24.6
9	100W (N-1-3) roof	10.3 (22.0:30)	14.1 (18.9:22)	4.8 (18.3:25)	---	---	---	23.6
Early Secondary Occupation								
4	36W (F-1-15) storeroom	9.1 (14.9:30)	13.3 (13.8:8)	5.3 (8.6:17)	8.8 (10.4:2)	8.5 (2.7:2)	5.1 (28.3:2)	19.5
10	119W (F-3-20) storeroom	9.4 (18.1:28)	14.8 (11.6:6)	5.0 (12.6:18)	9.4 (0:1)	8.3 (0:1)	4.1 (0:1)	20.3
11	127W (F-1-4) storeroom rooftop	9.2 (18.1:27)	13.6 (11.0:11)	4.9 (10.3:22)	8.4 (24.8:3)	7.8 (19.3:3)	5.27 (2.2:3)	21.1
Middle Secondary Occupation								
5	37W (F-2-5) storeroom	9.6 (10.9:25)	12.9 (13.1:9)	4.4 (11.0:19)	---	---	---	20.9
12	129W (F-1-8, F-1-8.2, & F-1-8.3) storeroom	11.2 (16.3:30)	15.6 (16.2:24)	4.8 (15.4:28)	---	---	---	22.0
CEREMONIAL								
Primary Occupation								
1	81W (F-2-13) platform area	12.2 (25.1:30)	16.7 (16.9:16)	5.1 (14.8:25)	---	6.8 (0:1)	4.6 (0:1)	24.4
Secondary Occupation								
6	64W (F-1-6 & H-1-8) kiva bench and floor	9.8 (15.8:30)	14.7 (12.5:20)	4.7 (16.9:22)	8.5 (0:1)	---	3.9 (0:1)	21.2
7	86W (F-1-4) sq room with kiva-like features	10.9 (20.2:22)	16.1 (14.7:9)	5.0 (17.6:15)	8.4 (38.6:2)	8.0 (30.5:2)	4.5 (26.0:2)	23.1

Table 35.5. Correlations of the original variates to the discriminant scores and T² statistics with their associated significance levels probabilities under the null hypothesis of no difference between the samples for each of the 15 comparisons.

Original Variate	Samples Compared							
	2 vs. 8	3 vs. 9	2 vs. 3	4 vs. 5	11 vs. 12	4 vs. 11	5 vs. 12	1 vs. 2
Row number	0.614	0.422	0.073	0.156	-0.468	0.519	-0.264	0.082
Cupule width	-0.376	-0.515	0.363	0.275	-0.293	-0.074	-0.770	0.470
Rachis segment length	-0.037	0.486	0.047	0.566	0.305	-0.373	-0.661	0.888
Cupule depth	-0.042	-0.221	0.078	-0.108	-0.595	0.407	-0.218	0.262
Rachis diameter	0.444	-0.353	0.800	-0.193	-0.675	-0.024	-0.644	0.257
Aperture width	0.020	-0.339	0.479	0.076	-0.131	-0.391	-0.643	-0.003
Aperture height	-0.272	0.488	-0.407	0.118	0.155	0.018	0.037	0.074
T²	5.217	4.046	3.446	4.339	5.100	3.094	3.085	1.726
Probability	0.000012	0.000294	0.001450	0.000134	0.000017	0.003637	0.003720	0.102449
Error degrees of freedom	48	44	40	47	50	49	48	48

Original Variate	Samples Compared						
	1 vs. 3	6 vs. 8	6 vs. 9	1 vs. 6	6 vs. 7	7 vs. 8	7 vs. 9
Row number	0.114	0.553	0.503	0.131	0.274	0.369	0.166
Cupule width	0.602	-0.301	-0.091	0.163	-0.232	-0.116	0.151
Rachis segment length	0.565	-0.235	0.43	0.641	-0.533	0.27	0.905
Cupule depth	0.224	0.273	0.226	-0.136	0.171	0.146	0.027
Rachis diameter	0.869	-0.055	-0.168	0.594	-0.469	0.415	0.32
Aperture width	0.428	-0.265	-0.226	0.247	-0.183	-0.124	-0.014
Aperture height	-0.321	-0.545	-0.203	0.262	0.045	-0.688	-0.221
T²	4.645	5.066	2.848	6.736	3.079	2.930	3.025
Probability	0.000058	0.000017	0.006835	0.000000	0.003777	0.005552	0.004346
Error degrees of freedom	45	53	52	53	44	44	43

In summary, strong evidence can be found for temporal change in the maize from nonceremonial rooms at Salmon Ruin. The Primary period maize tended to have more rows of grain and narrower cupules than maize of the final occupation. If Sample 2 from Room 91 represents the Intermediate period, then maize of this time may have been characterized by a narrower rachis than Primary period maize. Maize of the final occupation appears to have been more variable. Also, maize from the middle portion of the final period has a wider rachis, shorter rachis internodes, and deeper cupules than maize from the early portion.

Spatial Variation

There seems to be good evidence of temporal change in maize; one might also expect spatial variation in maize at the site, as clans or lineages in separate sections of the ruin may have maintained distinct forms of maize. Within the Secondary period, samples 4, 5, 11, and 12 can be used to ask if maize from the northwest sector of Salmon Ruin differed significantly from the southeast in early Secondary (36W vs. 127W) and mid-Secondary (37W vs. 129W) times. In each of the two comparisons the samples are from the same time period (early and middle Secondary, respectively), but at opposite ends of the site. For both of these comparisons, the T^2 tests show no significant differences between the samples (see Table 35.5). Thus it appears that no evidence exists to support the hypothesis that separate lineages maintained distinct varieties of maize at Salmon Ruin during the Secondary occupation.

Maize from Ceremonial Rooms

If the occupants used distinctive varieties of maize for rituals, or selected particular variants for ritual use from within the same variety of maize used in everyday activities, then these varieties or variants might be represented in samples from ceremonial rooms for each period. Only one room with maize (81W) seems to have had a ceremonial function during the earliest occupation. Several lines of evidence point to the unusual (ceremonial) nature of this room as well as Room 82W in Chacoan times. Room 82W originally opened onto the plaza through a T-shaped doorway and then connected to 81W by a T-shaped doorway to the north. The proximity to the Tower Kiva (64W) and the linkage of 81W with 82W suggests some ritual importance. Room 82W has an unusual number of pits and hearths, the apparent remains of an altar in the northwest corner, a partial room partition, the vestiges of milling bin platforms, and a high level of intrusive (trade) ceramics and

high percentages of corn pollen and corn pollen aggregates (Rose 1979a). The adjacent Room 81W, besides having a T-shaped door connection with 82W, also shares the high level of intrusive ceramics. No comment can be given on the pollen from the floor because it has not been analyzed. A wooden and adobe platform appears to have extended over much of the floor with indications from the northwest corner that a variety of plant material once occupied the platform. The sealing of the doors with masonry during Chacoan times (sometime after AD 1116) also indicates a special nature. Room 81W was not used afterward as a ground floor habitation of any kind, but some trash entered the room. Judging by the angle of repose of the earliest mounds against the southeast walls, holes in that sector of the ceiling first served as points of minor entry.

The described archaeological evidence suggests that the maize recovered from Room 81W was ceremonial in nature. Thus, for the Chacoan occupation we can address the question of whether or not ritual maize differed from everyday maize by comparing Sample 1 from ceremonial Room 81W to Samples 2 (Room 91) and 3 (Room 100) from Chacoan period trash deposits. The results from these two tests indicate that Sample 3 (Room 100) differs greatly from the ceremonial room maize, whereas Sample 2 (Room 91) does not. It would be difficult to claim on this basis that this ceremonial room contained a distinct variety of maize, unless the similarity between maize from it and that from Room 91 can be otherwise explained.

The reader should recall that this same sample (Sample 2) from Room 91 previously posed difficulties in interpretation when contrasted with the other Chacoan period trash sample (Sample 1). Whether Sample 2 with its large cobs, similar in some ways to those from ceremonial Room 81W, represents cobs grown under particularly good environmental circumstances or as previously suggested registers the morphological effects of the Intermediate time period remains unclear.

Turning to the final occupation, the same questions can be addressed—whether or not maize from a Secondary kiva (Room 64W, Sample 6) differs from maize found in the Secondary trash strata of Rooms 91 (Sample 8) and 100 (Sample 9). Here, as with the Chacoan period, the evidence for the presence of a ritual maize variety is ambivalent. Whereas one trash sample (Sample 8) shows clear differences from kiva maize, the other sample (Sample 9) does not (see Table 35.5).

To help clarify these ambiguous results, we may approach the question of identifying ritual maize from a different angle. A comparison of the Chacoan occupation ceremonial room sample (Sample 1) with the Chacoan trash samples (Samples 2 and 3) shows that all characters except aperture height and width are positively correlated with the discriminant score (see Table 35.5). This indicates that the Chacoan period ceremonial room contained ears with more rows of grain, larger cupules, and a wider rachis, or ears that were generally larger than everyday maize. If this was a type of ritual or ceremonial corn, then perhaps the Primary occupants were selecting larger ears for this purpose.

The situation with the Secondary kiva samples is slightly different. Here again the kiva sample contains ears with more rows of grain on the average than any other Secondary samples. Comparison of the Secondary kiva sample (Sample 6) with the two Secondary trash samples (Samples 8 and 9) shows that the two trash samples differ from the kiva sample in a similar way (see Table 35.5). However, in contrast to the Chacoan period, the kiva sample ears are smaller for most characters (i.e. negative correlations), including cupule width, rachis width, and cupule aperture width and height. Thus, if the maize from the Secondary kiva sample represents a variety reserved for rituals, then it was perhaps a type with smaller ears but more rows of grain than everyday Secondary maize.

Assuming for the moment that Chacoan and Secondary occupation ceremonial rooms both contained ritual corn, we may ask whether or not these two samples are the same or at least similar. To answer this question we compared Samples 1 (ceremonial Room 81W) and 6 (Room 64W). Table 35.5 shows that the difference between these two samples is very large. If these two samples represent ritual corn maintained by the two groups of occupants, then the type of ritual corn grown by each group was very different. The Chacoan maize ears have larger measurements for all traits except cupule depth than the Secondary occupation kiva maize, as shown by the correlations between the original variates and the discriminant scores.

Within the Secondary occupation, a number of architectural features point to 86W, a large square room, as having a ceremonial function. The room has traces of two earlier Secondary occupation floors that were circular and hence kiva-like. The final floor had a central hearth deflector. By then, or even perhaps earlier, the south T-shaped door had been modified into a ventilator and the north door filled with masonry. The several wall niches and the single slab metate set into position in the northwest corner of the room may be significant, as the only other one of

a similar nature is found in Kiva 6A as a milling bin wall remnant. Further, of the 18 oversized square rooms like 86W in the Secondary occupation, 10 can be identified as sharing kiva-like features or having actually been modified into circular kivas. Six of the remaining eight have not been sufficiently excavated to determine their nature.

If Room 86W functioned as a ceremonial room it might produce maize similar to that found in a contemporary circular kiva (Room 64W). A comparison of the samples from these two rooms gives a probability (p = .003777) slightly larger than the critical value (.00333), indicating that these samples do not differ from one another. Thus, we might conclude that Room 86W contained maize like that from the kiva (Room 64W). The trend here, however, parallels the comparison of the kiva (Room 64W) with the two trash samples (8 and 9); that is, the kiva sample has smaller ears with more rows of grain than the sample from Room 86W (see Tables 35.4 and 35.5). This cautions us to look more closely. A comparison of Room 86W with the two Secondary trash samples (Samples 8 and 9) yields probabilities larger than the critical value in both instances, suggesting that the sample from Room 86W does not differ from these samples either. Thus, the evidence fails to either accept or reject the hypothesis that the maize from Room 86W is a ritual type.

In summary, the evidence for the occurrence of ritual corn in ceremonial rooms at Salmon Ruin is somewhat ambiguous. In both occupations the ceremonial room samples have the most rows of grain. Although the Chacoan cobs from ritual locations are large compared to the other Chacoan cobs, the situation is just the opposite during the final period, with the smallest cobs coming from the kiva (Room 64W).

Comparison With Other Sites

As discussed in the introduction, prior to Pueblo II times (ca. AD 900) maize from most sites in the region had about 12 rows of grain (Cutler 1966; Cutler and Meyer 1965). At this time, perhaps as a result of the hybridization of the older 12-rowed Chapalote-like race with the 8-rowed Maize de Ocho race, the average row number reported for maize from most Pueblo II and Pueblo III sites dropped to about 10 (Cutler 1966; Cutler and Meyer 1965). In line with this trend, maize from Northern San Juan sites of the Pueblo III period (AD 1100–1300) has about 10 rows of grain (Table 35.6); the overall average for the Mesa Verdean occupation at Salmon Ruin (10.77) is similar. However, unlike most Pueblo II sites, the two Chacoan ones listed in Table 35.6 have maize with more (about 12) rows of grain.

Table 35.6. Number of rows of grain of maize from Puebloan sites.

Site	Period	Row Number	Reference
Chaco			
Chaco Canyon, Talus unit	1025–1125	12.05	Cutler & Meyer 1965
Pueblo Bonito	919–1250	11.59	Judd 1954
Mesa Verde			
Step House	PIII	10.00	Cutler & Meyer 1965
Long House	PIII	9.62	Cutler & Meyer 1965
Mug House	PIII	9.46	Cutler & Meyer 1965
Jug House	PIII	9.58	Cutler & Meyer 1965

Likewise the overall average row number for maize of the Chacoan occupation at Salmon Ruin is 11.9.

Perhaps the Chacoans never fully accepted Maize de Ocho, and continued instead to use the maize handed down from their Basketmaker ancestors. The fact that the shape and general appearance of the cupule differs greatly between Chacoan (narrow open cupules) and Secondary (broad collapsed cupules) maize suggests that mere environmental variability does not account for the difference in row number between the Chacoan and Secondary occupations at Salmon Ruin. In fact, it is cupule shape that distinguishes Maize de Ocho; it has wide cupules like the maize from the Secondary occupation (Galinat and Gunnerson 1963; Galinat 1970).

Analysis of Kernels

The kinds of starch found in the endosperm of maize kernels were first described by Sturtevant (1899). The endosperm of the pop-corns is dominated by hard, corneous starch. Upon heating, the accumulated steam explodes the kernel. The flint corns have soft starchy endosperm enclosed by a corneous layer that varies in thickness in different varieties. The dent corns possess a corneous endosperm at the sides of the kernel and the soft starchy endosperm extends to the summit. The starch in the summit of the kernel shrinks upon drying and forms a dent in the tip.

The change in the predominant form of metates at Salmon from trough in the Chacoan occupation to slab in the Secondary occupation (Shelley, Chapter 47) indicates that the manner of maize preparation differed (Table 35.7). Pop-corn kernels tend to slip and bounce when first crushed by a mano. Thus, the concave trough form of metate was perhaps better adapted to serve as the initial crushing anvil for kernels with hard, translucent starch. If the trough metate was more common in the Chacoan occupation, perhaps either pop or flint corns were also more

common than in the Secondary occupation.

To test the above hypothesis, a random sample of 125 kernels was selected from a series of kernels laid on each of 500 numbered compartments in a grid work. The process was repeated until a total of four subsamples of 125 grains each was accumulated. Only one Chacoan stratigraphic unit (2BW, M-1-3) furnished enough kernels to be selected in such a manner, whereas four Secondary storeroom floors provided diverse sources of kernels for sampling (Table 35.8). Each 125-kernel subsample was then randomly assigned a letter of the alphabet, so the researcher did not know which occupation each sample belonged to.

Modern specimens of pop, flint, and flour corn were parched in order to produce material of known origin for comparison. Flour corn was easily carbonized in the process. However, 2-year-old commercial popcorn and New England flint more than 8 years old retained enough moisture to partially pop the kernels instead of carbonizing them. These somewhat expanded grains showed how a flint kernel might sometimes be misclassified if it expanded upon heating to mimic the carbonized texture of the flour corn.

Carbonized grains were classified using several criteria. Prehistoric and modern burned flour corn looked porous and often reflected light as if it were a crystalline substance. It was also more subject to accidental pulverization on breakage than the kernels with corneous endosperm. Prehistoric carbonized pop-corn kernels were extremely fine grained in sectional view, as were modern uncarbonized kernels.

Table 35.7. Metate morphology.

Occupation	Trough	Slab	Unclassified
Chaco (n = 32)	75%	22%	3%
Secondary (n = 48)	21%	77%	2%

Table 35.8. Maize kernel composition frequencies for Primary and Secondary occupations.

Room	Stratigraphic Unit	Record Key No.	Kernel Type			Total
			Flour	Pop	Flint	
Primary Occupation						
2BW	M-1-3	73550	32	85	2	119
		76826	29	78	9	116
		73548	35	82	—	117
		73554	34	90	—	124
		Subtotal	130	335	11	476
Secondary Occupation						
30W	F-1-2					
	G-1-3	—	57	57	—	114
36W	F-1-15	76407	19	47	—	66
		76411	14	10	—	24
		76421	9	6	9	24
90W	F-2-9	56308	12	119	—	131
119W	F-3-20	40880	65	53	2	120
		Subtotal	176	292	11	479

Frequently the prehistoric broken grains showed abundant, hard, jagged edges. A few grains were still so hard that they needed to be broken with a mortar and pestle. Some already had a fissured surface, which caused them to fall apart before or during examination. Kernels that crumbled prematurely under pressure could not always be examined for the shift in texture that is characteristic of flint corn. Intact, carbonized flint corns retained the fine-grained outer cap and coarse center that was recognizable in modern unburned material. Flint grains that failed to hold together were probably misclassified as pop-corn. Whenever possible a representative fragment of each kernel was saved.

Although the results were informative, they did not tabulate as smoothly as first envisioned. Because of the crumbling that occurred between sample selection and examination, only about 477 kernels from each occupation (see Table 35.8) could be classified instead of 500. Due to the uncertainties in recognizing prehistoric flint from pop, the percentages should be considered together. In the Chacoan occupation 72.7 percent of the kernels were either pop or flint and 27.3 percent were flour; several kernels were classified as dents. In the Secondary occupation 63.3 percent of the kernels were either pop or flint and 36.7 percent were flour. The Room 90W sample differs from the trends shown in the other three Secondary samples, because it is almost completely pop-corn (see Table 35.8). If one omits this room from the calculation of percentages, the proportion of flour corn (48%) to pop and flint (51%) is more nearly equal for the Secondary occupation. In any case, the proportion of flint corn recovered from a burned storeroom may appear deceptively higher than what was originally stored there. Flour corns might be utilized first because of their inferior storage qualities in comparison to flint or pop. The time of year each storeroom burned is unknown.

Dishes using boiled corn, such as hominy, might have been common during the Chacoan occupation. Corn might also have been popped prior to being crushed to meal using the metate; such methods of corn preparation have been documented at Zuni (Cushing 1920; Stevenson 1915). In contrast, various forms of mush, pudding, or bread might have been made more regularly from flour corn by the Secondary occupants. The greater difficulty in crushing the flinty kernels either before or after popping could account for a greater proportion of trough metates in the Chacoan occupation than in the Secondary. The results of the kernel study also strengthen the argument that Maize de Ocho influenced the crop of the Mesa Verdean occupation (see "Analysis of Cobs"), because this 8-rowed corn was believed to possess a floury endosperm (Galinat and Campbell 1967:12) whereas the earlier Chapalote has smaller flinty kernels.

Maize Summary

Trash and roof strata generally retained abundant maize cobs, although kernels and fragments of cobs commonly also formed part of flotation samples at Salmon Ruin. Ten of 13 trash strata of the Chacoan occupation and 13 of 23 trash strata of the Secondary occupation contained maize. Seven first-floor roof strata were in actuality the floors of the second-story rooms that were utilized for storage by the final occupation. Stalks, husks, tassels, and pollen were also recovered.

Nine quantitative traits of the maize ear were used to make comparisons of a general nature between maize of the Chacoan and Secondary occupations, maize from ceremonial and nonceremonial rooms, maize from different sectors of the pueblo in a given time period, and maize in different periods of the Secondary occupation. The measurements consisted of row number, rachis diameter, cob diameter, cupule width, glume width, rachis segment length, cupule aperture width, cupule aperture height, and cupule aperture depth. These last three measures are defined in this study for the first time.

Samples of carbonized kernels from each major occupation were classified as having pop, flint, flour, or dent types of endosperm. The equivalence of their appearance to uncarbonized kernels was established by reproducing the carbonized condition in known flint and dent types. Pop types could not be carbonized without exploding the kernel, so we relied upon observations of the texture of the unburned kernel. Four coded subsamples of 125 kernels each from both occupations (500 kernels per occupation) were classified.

We used a multivariate extension of the univariate t-test that incorporates all of the cob variables into a single test, known as Hotelling's T^2, to determine whether two samples of cobs are significantly different. When the null hypothesis was rejected, the correlations of the original variates to the scores from the multiple discriminant analysis were examined. When it was necessary to determine which samples were most variable, the coefficients of variability for all traits of a cob sample were summed and compared to the values for other cob samples.

The maize used in the everyday lives of the two occupations shows considerable dissimilarity. The two Chacoan occupation cob samples have more rows of grain and narrower cupules than the Secondary occupation. Variability among the Chacoan occupation cob samples is shown in rachis diameter. However, the Chacoan trash samples show less within-sample variability than the Secondary trash samples, as measured by the sums of the coefficients of variability for all traits. In the Chacoan occupation 72.7 percent of the kernels were either pop or flint and 27 percent were flour. In the Secondary occupation 63.3 percent of the kernels were pop or flint and 36.7 percent were flour.

The indication that the Chacoan occupation used more pop and flint kernels is corroborated by the prevalence of basin-shaped metates, which gather the kernels together during the initial crushing stage. Similarly, the use of more of the easily crushed flour corn during the Secondary occupation was accompanied by an apparent increase in slab metates. Because the kernel study was derived primarily from remains from burned storerooms, there may be a bias because pop and flint types might have been retained in the storeroom longer due to their superior storage qualities.

Samples of maize from the early and middle Secondary occupation indicated major consistent differences, which seem to involve rachis diameter, rachis segment length, and cupule depth. Maize from the middle portion of the final occupation has a wider rachis, shorter rachis internodes, and deeper cupules than maize from the early part of the same period. In contrast, no differences in spatial distribution of maize in Salmon Ruin could be seen for the early portion of the Secondary occupation.

The evidence for the use of ritual corn in ceremonial rooms at Salmon is ambiguous. The ceremonial room samples from both occupations have the most rows of grains; the Chacoan occupation cobs are large compared to other cobs of the same period. The situation is just the opposite for samples from the final period, with the smallest cobs coming from the Tower Kiva (Room 64W). Furthermore, Room 86W with kiva-like features had maize apparently no different from that in everyday use. If ritual maize was present, it was only weakly differentiated from its contemporary nonritual forms.

The maize from the Chacoan and Secondary occupations is strongly differentiated, with earlier Chacoan period samples having more cobs that resemble the flinty, Chapalote-related variety common in the Southwest before the introduction of the floury-kerneled Maize de Ocho. Maize de Ocho apparently entered the Southwest at or before the Chaco era, so the first occupants of Salmon might have been reluctant to accept it. Evidence from the Secondary occupation, in the form of an increase in floury kernels, a lower average row number, and different cupule configuration suggests that the later inhabitants had fewer reservations concerning the growing and use of Maize de Ocho.

BEANS

Beans (*Phaseolus vulgaris*), which were recovered in 21 of 48 rooms exposed by excavation (Table 35.9), came almost exclusively from the Secondary occupation. Two types of stratigraphic units—trash and

Table 35.9. Distribution of beans in stratigraphic units and rooms. Some rooms may have beans in more than one stratum type.

Stratigraphic Unit	Strata	Rooms
Structured and unstructured trash (C and M)	14	10
Roof-fall (F) and mixed roof-fall (N)	15	12
Occupational fill (G) and floor surface (H)	3	3
Pits (L)	3	2
Total	35	27*

roofs—produced more than 80 percent of the macrofossil evidence of beans. Two roofs (Rooms 100W and 127W) apparently served as outdoor preparation areas. Six of the roofs in which beans were found might better be termed second-story floors than first-story roofs, with all foodstuffs recovered representing part of the content of fire-gutted storerooms (see Bohrer and Adams, Chapter 38). Only three floors had beans: H-1-5 in Room 31B, G-1-3.7/H-1-4 in Room 94W, and H-1-8 in the Tower Kiva (64W). Many items were left in situ in the kiva when a conflagration destroyed it.

The stratigraphic units from which beans were recovered do not unequivocally belong to the Chacoan occupation. The three potentially Chacoan strata from which they have been recovered contain evidence of contamination from the Secondary occupation in the form of Mesa Verde Black-on-white sherds. Two strata in 62W (C-2-7 and C-37-37) consist of Chacoan trash that has been redeposited by the Secondary occupation, including broken pottery from the Secondary occupation, so it is quite possible that some of the plant remains in the trash are also from the Secondary occupation. The trash unit in 84W (C-1-5) apparently resulted from trash spilling through the south doorway from Room 85W; about 3 percent of it is contaminated with Secondary occupation sherds. The roof stratigraphic unit immediately above it (N-2-4) is definitely from the Secondary occupation; some admixture from that unit is expectable.

Beans were typically recovered as burned cotyledons about 1.5 cm long or as fragments. Some charred beans exhibit portions of cotyledons exfoliated in partially curled strips (Rooms 64W and 91W). Some beans from 64W are still enclosed in their pods. The pods in one lot (64W 1161) followed the contours of the seeds so closely that there were sharp constrictions between seeds. Pod fragments con-

tained seeds of sufficient size to be fully mature, so an immature green bean can be ruled out. Nor is it obviously a mature pod of the Hopi green bean, type C11 (cf. Kaplan 1956); the author's collection of pods from that variety do not hug the outline of the mature bean as closely as the prehistoric material. Three other beans from the Tower Kiva floor are only 9 mm long (64W1158), but the elevated margin of the testea around the hilum of these small beans matches that of *Phaseolus vulgaris* (Kaplan 1956:205), and they are still within the size range of *P. vulgaris*. Although the variability in size of beans grown in the Secondary occupation may have potential varietal significance, all of the beans from Salmon Ruin can be classified as the common bean, *Phaseolus vulgaris*.

SQUASH

Squash (*Cucurbita* sp.) remains were recovered from 23 of 48 rooms exposed by excavation. Trash and roof stratigraphic units often retained evidence of squash (Table 35.10). Because squash remains are exceptionally well represented in trash strata in Room 62W, probably more than 70 percent of all squash remains are from trash. There is no evidence of squash in the flotation samples, presumably because squash residues are large and can be picked from the sediments by hand. Four near-floor contexts from the Chacoan occupation (33W, G-1.5-14.5; 43W, G-1-16; 62W, G-1-40; and 82W, G-1-23) and one from the Secondary occupation (64W, H-1-8) provided evidence of squash.

Squash was recovered most frequently as uncarbonized exocarp (ring) and seeds, although peduncles and vegetative parts were observed. Hard, smooth pieces of exocarp several millimeters thick are common in the assemblage, but some pieces exhibit small bumps or knobs (Table 35.11). The flower scar end of the rind is often well preserved; the interior shows a raised mark like a three-

Table 35.10. Distribution of squash seeds in stratigraphic units and rooms, except 62W. Some rooms may have beans in more than one stratum type.

Stratigraphic Unit	Strata	Rooms
Structured and unstructured trash (C and M)	14	11
Roof-fall (F) and mixed roof fall (N)	9	6
Occupational fill (G) and floor surface (H)	5	5
Pits (L)	6	5
Other (B, D)	3	3
Total	37	30*

Table 35.11. Aberrant squash (*Cucurbita*) rind from the Secondary occupation at Room 62W.

Description	Record Key or Sample No.	Stratigraphic Unit
Brown exocarp (rind) with exterior roughened by small bumps	33701	C-4-9
Exocarp 0.1–0.2 cm thick, some bumps	33108	C-22-22
Exocarp 0.1–0.4 cm thick, surface with bumps and ridges	51003	C-22-22
Exocarp fragments with knobs on exterior	62W9220	L-2-7.1

bladed airplane propeller. The mark probably represents scar tissue formed on the carpel sutures, but the particular configuration may possess value as a varietal indicator. Seeds often appear thin and fragile, with splitting and warping along suture lines. The curvilinear strip that emphasizes the margin of the seed is often rough and frayed. In spite of this, more than 300 seeds were sufficiently intact and undistorted to be measured (Burgess-Terrel 1979). In general, peduncle preservation was so poor that it was difficult to determine the original morphology. A few peduncles were unusually small and delicate. Pieces of tendril dried into tight corkscrews and a segment of the vine constitute only token vestiges of the vegetative portion of the plant (Table 35.12).

Observations on the condition of seeds, exocarp fragments, and peduncles provide data that have bearing on how squash was prepared for eating and storage. Each occupation exhibits evidence suggesting that at least some seeds were removed from the fruit en masse and subsequently discarded. After more than 700 years, a cluster of about six seeds still adheres to itself in a shingle-like arrangement, and another clump of seeds remains aligned in stacks cemented by a brown matrix (Table 35.13). In fact, the large amount of squash seeds recovered from trash gives the impression that seeds were frequently regarded as waste products. We have observed no teeth mark impressions on seeds or minced seed coats that might indicate deliberate seed consumption. However, several feces show that whole squash seeds occasionally journeyed through the digestive tract and were preserved unaltered (see Bohrer and Adams, Chapter 38).

Some hard-shelled squash fruits were roasted whole. A peduncle with the exocarp still attached was carbonized on the exterior only (Salmon Record Key 33468, Burgess-Terrel 1979:77), indicating that the peduncle was removed from the roasted fruit. In addition, we have numerous pieces of smooth exocarp that are burned only on the exterior. The presence of unburned peduncles and exocarp suggests other methods of preparation as well.

The archaeological record also contains some evidence that squash was dried for storage. Several broken segments of what appears to be turns in a coil of squash (with some squash seeds embedded) were recovered. In addition, we have an uncarbonized slice of flesh from near the flower scar end of the fruit, and another piece of dried flesh only 1.5 cm in diameter but bearing a central hole, as if it were a slice prepared for drying upon a cord (see Table 35.13).

Some of the hard-shelled squash may have been used as containers—one piece of exocarp was recovered with a hole in it (Burgess-Terrel 1979:78). Such a hole might have been one of a pair drilled on each side of a crack to accommodate a cordage tie, as is done to repair cracked pottery. It is possible that such a hole might have been created by insect activity, but if so, it is the only example that we have observed to date. A hard-shelled *Cucurbita pepo* fruit used as a container has been illustrated by Cutler and Whitaker (1961:481) from Glen Canyon on the Colorado River.

All of the well-preserved squash seeds have been identified as *Cucurbita pepo* (Burgess-Terrel 1979). Relatively sophisticated statistical techniques such as discriminant analysis and principal component analysis were first tested on measurements of modern seeds of *Cucurbita* species and cultivars and then applied to 301 prehistoric seeds from 10 rooms at Salmon. The discriminant analysis of prehistoric seeds resulted in all seeds being assigned to *C. pepo*; principal component plots indicated that the prehistoric seeds were in closest association with the *C. pepo* seeds. Comparison of the prehistoric and modern *C. pepo* dispersion patterns indicates a prehistoric dispersion pattern that had some degree of overlap with the modern *C. pepo* cultivars Connecticut Field and Small Sugar. However, the majority of prehistoric seeds were probably a subspecific type or types not represented by modern analogs (Burgess-Terrel 1979: 104).

Table 35.12. Examples of well-preserved vegetative parts of squash (*Cucurbita*) from Room 62W.

Description	Record Room Key No.	Stratigraphic Unit
Deeply fluted stems with oversize xylem vessels discernible, Primary occupation	79498	G-1-40
Curled tendril of vine, mixed cultural affiliation	33022	C-22-22 C-24-24
Curled tendril of vine, mixed cultural affiliation	52822	C-22-22, C-23-23, C-24-24, L-2-7.1

Based on printouts 3/27/79 Q6226-377 and 1/13/80 70 EMCR 34-13.

Table 35.13. Methods of squash (*Cucurbita*) preparation.

Description	Room	Record Key or Sample No.	Strat. Unit	Occupation
Cluster of more than 6 seeds adhering to one another in a shingle-like arrangement.	81W	44208	F-2-13	Primary
Seeds in stacks cemented by brown dried matrix.	62W	55743	C-26-26, C-27-27	Secondary
Dried coil of mesocarp (flesh) in fragments; some squash seed fragments embedded.	62W	62A9411	C-2-6.9	Secondary
Uncarbonized slice of fruit from near flower scar end, 0.24 cm thick; 0.9 cm diameter. One side embossed with trilete mark, other side less pronounced indentation.	62W	53598	C-24-24	Secondary
Slice of dried mesocarp (flesh) 1.5 cm max. in diameter with central hole 0.5 cm in diameter.	62W	79519	G-1-40	Primary
Exocarp (rind) fragments, some with burned exterior floral scars present.	81W	77201	F-2-13	Primary
Exocarp (rind) fragments, many carbonized on exterior surface.	62W	75643	C-27.7-27.7	Secondary
Exocarp (rind) fragments, some partially carbonized on exterior surface.	62W	75165	C-27.6-27.6	Secondary
Exocarp (rind) fragment, 0.1–0.2 cm thick, with round perforation.	62W	53758	C-20-20	Secondary

GOURDS

If gourds (*Lagenaria siceraria*) were actually raised by the inhabitants of Salmon, they left behind only the most tenuous evidence. The heavy use of a hard-shelled squash for food left many exocarp fragments that are easily confused with that of cultivated gourd. Only one fragment, a narrow tubular piece 0.5 cm in diameter at the small end and 1 cm at the large end, seems to have the unique shape of a dipper gourd handle. The specimen (Record Key 80155) was recovered in a Chacoan occupation stratigraphic unit from Room 62W (G-1-40). No gourd seeds were recovered at any time during excavation, so the dipper gourd fragment may have been a trade item.

COTTON

Cotton (*Gossypium hirsutum*) was known to the inhabitants of Salmon but it seems unlikely that it was cultivated locally. Small pieces of cloth and segments of cordage have been recovered from Room 62W in stratigraphic units that consist of Chacoan trash redeposited by the Secondary occupants. The Secondary trash may be intermixed, so the cultural affiliation of the unit is uncertain. However, the cloth is definitely cotton, as the distinctive ribbon-like seed hairs were easily recognized with a magnification of 100x. In addition, carbonized cloth fragments from both Chacoan and Secondary occupation contexts appear to be cotton. Notably lacking are cotton seeds, bolls, and other vegetative portions of the plant that could have been carried into Salmon by cultivators. Parched cotton seed was considered edible in much of the Southwest (Bohrer 1977), and one might therefore expect to recover accidentally carbonized seeds. Carbonized seeds should have been preserved despite the vagaries of preservation, which could easily destroy evidence of bolls or vegetative parts. Cotton cordage and woven goods apparently arrived as a trade item in both the Chacoan and Secondary occupations, just as certain kinds of pottery did. Distinctive methods of manufacture and design often allow pottery to be traced to its place of manufacture, but the small and frequently charred pieces of cotton cloth provide no similar clues.

AMARANTH

Since the recovery of a cultivated, white-seeded form of amaranth (cf. *Amaranthus hypochondriacus*) in a cliff dwelling in south-central Arizona (Steen et al. 1962:107), archaeologists have been hoping to find additional evidence from other sites. However, two factors have blocked the recovery of such evidence. The distinctive white seed coat that readily identifies amaranth as a cultigen becomes blackened by the very same carbonization process that preserves the seed, and also its white seed coat is relatively thin, compared to the wild, dark-seeded species, so it is more susceptible to degradation. The evidence described here is all that is currently available regarding the presence of the cultivar at Salmon: (1) Room 4A (B-2-3), Sample 4A005 (Secondary occupation), at 5.2 m below datum. The item has the appearance of a thin, translucent seed coat. The area where the embryo was once located is tightly wrinkled in a ring, and interior tissue is absent. (2) Room 102C (C-2-24), Sample 102C4100 (Chacoan occupation). This sample consisted of one white, whole Cheno-Am seed with a thin coat. The embryo has apparently collapsed and the coat hugs the groove the embryo once filled. Single instances of a poorly preserved seed coat in only two strata do not currently provide reliable enough evidence to confirm this cultivar's presence.

Chapter 36

NATIVE (WILD) PLANTS FROM SALMON PUEBLO

by Karen R. Adams

Poor conditions of preservation produce plant materials that have survived mainly by virtue of having been carbonized or lightly parched; such conditions can be found in strata throughout Salmon Pueblo. The bits of charcoal and seeds that have been preserved retain certain identifying characteristics that indicate an unusually broad sample of economic activity throughout Salmon Pueblo during both occupations. These materials were consistently concentrated through flotation analysis until the resultant mixture of charcoal and seeds became a dry, compact, light-weight sample that was easily stored or analyzed as part of a larger research design (Bohrer and Adams 1977:37).

In total, 216 flotation samples representing 64 separate locations from both Primary and Secondary deposits at Salmon Ruin were examined (Table 36.1). Of the 64 locations, 28 were discrete room floors and 36 were individual trash units. Only strata of clear cultural affiliation were selected for this study, because samples from culturally mixed units tell an equally mixed story in the laboratory. To be chosen for analysis, a floor had to be well preserved, easily recognized during excavation, undisturbed by rodents or roots, and adequately sampled. A further qualification was that the floor must not be overlain by trash, due to the possibility that material thrown into the room after abandonment might blur the record of actual room activities. All six Primary floors and 11 of 22 Secondary floors examined in this study were unburned (Table 36.2); many were protected by a fine covering of noncultural fill. The remaining 11 Secondary floors burned when their overhead roofs caught fire and collapsed directly onto the floors in Secondary times.

Flotation samples from floors were obtained by carefully scraping the occupation surface to obtain seeds and debris that had been ground in during use. A floor flotation sample represents 1 liter of sed-

iment from a single square meter, and the number of samples from any given floor ranges from 1 to 17. Therefore, when a taxonomic item has been noted as present on a floor, the item could represent the search through a variable number of samples. The greater the number of floor samples searched, the higher the probability of finding a rare item. Trash samples, on the other hand, represent one liter of debris selected from a single location within a trash stratum, except in rare cases where two samples were taken. Relative to each other, floor samples are apt to represent a longer period of deposition than trash samples, revealing items that became ground into the occupation surface while the room was in use. Trash samples probably represent a more limited period of plant use, relating to shorter segments of time between routine chores such as floor sweeping or hearth cleaning. The flotation method employed at Salmon (Bohrer and Adams 1977:37) essentially precludes any laboratory-induced opportunity for postexcavation mixing of sediments. The criteria for seed identification are listed in the "Guide to Learning Prehistoric Seed Remains from Salmon Ruin, Bloomfield, New Mexico" (Bohrer and Adams 1976).

Table 36.1. Number and range of flotation samples examined from Primary and Secondary floor and trash strata.

Strata Type	No. of Strata	No. of Samples	Range of Samples per Stratum
Primary			
Floor	6	45	1–15
Trash	13	16	1–2
Secondary			
Floor	22	129	1–17
Trash	23	25	1–2

Based upon CONURE printouts 3/21/80 7OETable 213 and 3/26/80 7OETable 459, and hand tallies of flotation data on the following floors not entered into the computer: Rooms 6A H-1-5.2; 51W H-1-5; 56W H-1-5; 58W H-1-8; 101W H-1-9; and 124A H-1-6/I-1-7.

This chapter was taken entirely from the 1980 Salmon report, with editing.

Table 36.2. Burned and unburned floors examined in flotation study.

	Unburned		Burned	
	Room	Floor	Room	Floor
Primary				
	30W	H-2-12	None	None
	31W	H-2-11	—	—
	56W	H-1-5	—	—
	89W	H-1-8	—	—
	93W	H-5-33	—	—
	101W	H-1-9	—	—
Secondary				
	6A	H-1-5.2	4A	H-1-6/I-1-7
	51W	H-1-5	7A	I-1-4
	58W	H-2-11	30W	H-1-4
	92A	H-1-9	31A	H-1-5
	93W	H-1-14	31B	H-1-5
	93W	H-2-22	57W	H-1-8
	96W	H-1-5	58W	H-1-8
	123A	I-1-6	62A	I-1-6
	123W	I-1-2	64W	H-1-8
	124W	H-2-9	124A	H-1-6/I-1-7
	127A	H-1-5/I-1-6	128W	H-1-3.5

Based upon field file printout 2/11/79 ROOFREX 36.

THE CASE FOR ECONOMIC USE

Seeds recovered from flotation samples can be evaluated from a number of perspectives to establish the likelihood that they were eaten by humans; a much stronger case is made when independent lines of evidence converge (Bohrer 1981). An effort was therefore made to consider numerous pathways by which a given specimen may have become incorporated into flotation samples, as well as to determine both the condition and the archaeological context of the prehistoric remains. Though not used here, other potentially valuable lines of evidence to support ancient use of a plant as food include ethnographic and archaeological analogy.

Pathways that can lead to introduction of a seed into an archaeological stratum are many. They can be transported by rodents or ants, travel on someone's clothing, or fall from weedy plants actually growing within the confines of a pueblo or an archaeological excavation, and of course there could have been purposeful human introduction. If most of the avenues of incidental incorporation can be logically eliminated, the case for intentional use by man is strengthened. For example, at Salmon Ruin areas of obvious root penetration or rodent disturbance were deliberately avoided when collecting flotation

samples; rodent feces in the samples were rare, which confirms that most of the strata sampled were undisturbed by burrowing creatures. No large nests belonging to harvester ants were encountered in the surrounding area or on the site itself. However, the occasional recovery in flotation samples of what appeared to be ant heads and appendages leaves open the possibility that ants carried some seeds into Salmon strata.

The morphological and physiological characteristics of a seed influences the likelihood that it might travel on a person's clothing or in an animal's fur. Seeds with barbed or awned appendages or those whose coat becomes mucilaginous when wet would be apt to be incidentally carried into a dwelling. Therefore, all seeds recovered from Salmon Ruin were considered in terms of their morphology and known physiological properties.

The normal habitat of plants was also evaluated as a pathway for seeds to enter the archaeological record. Weedy species that thrive in disturbed ground could opportunistically exploit prehistoric trash middens, paths leading to and from a pueblo, and abandoned rooms without roofs, and thus naturally leave seeds in ancient strata. Nonweedy plants such as perennials, water-loving species, and those requiring very special growing conditions would be less likely to become established within the boundaries of a town. All specimens in Salmon flotation samples were considered in light of their natural plant habitat, and some plants such as the water-loving Cyperaceae (sedge family) were easily dismissed as unlikely to have grown at the pueblo proper. Others required careful scrutiny of the archaeological field notes to help determine the possibility of accidental introduction. For example, it would be quite reasonable to expect that some trashy strata may have accumulated in abandoned rooms whose roofs had been either dismantled or burned. Weedy annual plants such as tansy-mustard (*Descurainia*) might have flourished in the full sunlight and decaying refuse of these locations, contributing fresh seeds to the growing pile of debris.

To explore this possibility, all trash middens were reviewed to determine whether there had been a roof over the room when the trash was being deposited. Only three roofs (in Rooms 56W, 119W, and 130W) are known to have burned and collapsed during the Primary occupation; the rest apparently remained intact over rooms until Secondary times. Because none of the Primary trash flotation samples examined in this study were selected from any of the three burned Primary rooms, all Primary trash samples likely came from darkened rooms not conducive to weedy plant growth. In Secondary times, however, 19 of the 23 unburned trash strata examined in this study were from rooms in which the roof had either burned or been dismantled before trash deposition occurred. Weedy plants growing on these sunlit middens might have deposited seeds in the accumulating debris. A midden fire could have burned some of these seeds, complicating the record by making them virtually indistinguishable from seeds that had been prepared by humans near a hearth. Field notes, however, indicate that none of the trash middens appeared to have burned, so the parched or carbonized seeds found in these 19 uncovered, unburned Secondary trash strata must have been burned prior to incorporation in the deposits, and are not from weedy growth on middens. Unparched or uncarbonized seeds, however, probably represent actual plant growth on the middens.

Carbonization is frequently used by archaeobotanists as evidence that people prepared a resource near a fire, but recognition of carbonization by laboratory workers is not always a simple matter. Light-colored seeds present no problem, but burning is quite difficult to recognize on seeds that are naturally black. Sometimes naturally black seeds such as Cheno-Am or purslane exhibit a warped appearance, and when their contents are partly extruded it is relatively easy to see that they have been burned. At other times the exterior gives few clues, and an entire seed must be broken in half to view a carbonized interior. Because the seed may be destroyed in the process, this step is sometimes omitted and the seeds are therefore not described as carbonized.

Parching is even more difficult to observe in ancient specimens. Parching can involve very short contact with heat—just enough to drive out moisture, but perhaps not enough to darken a seed coat. Naturally black, tan, or brown seeds may exhibit no visible signs of parching. Also, it is not known to what degree normal discoloration due to centuries of degradation may mimic the effects of parching.

When the condition of a prehistoric seed provides no recognizable evidence of human use, other data such as pollen samples and prehistoric context can sometimes be revealing. Pollen samples from the same locations as flotation samples can shed their own light on prehistoric plant use, and have been cited in this study when available. The archaeological context often strongly suggests that a particular resource was employed. For example, seeds in hearths probably represent accidents of food preparation or food offerings to deities, trash piles reveal items that are frequently discarded, foodstuffs in storerooms hint at what was kept for the future, and seeds recovered in fecal remains provide direct evidence of consumption. Wherever feasible, context is relied upon in providing grounds for economic use. Parched or carbonized seeds found on burned floors of the Secondary occupation (see Table 36.2) indicate either human preparation of the items or accidental charring during roof destruction by fire. Because of the possibility of dual interpretations, then, seeds recovered from burned floors have not been used in this study to establish method of preparation.

Seeds recovered from flotation samples are classified as being widespread, common, or rare according to arbitrarily recognized gaps in the frequency of their occurrence in 64 separate floor and trash strata (Table 36.3). We assume that seeds found again and again in flotation samples from both floor and trash units were widely used in prehistory. The broad distribution of Cheno-Am in 63 of 64 strata, and purslane in 50 of 64 strata, suggests that these were plants employed repeatedly by Salmon residents. Taxa that are less ubiquitous and yet are present in 23–35 of the 64 separate locations examined are designated as commonly occurring in prehistory. This includes the six plant families Gramineae, Cruciferae, Cactaceae, Euphorbiaceae, Solanaceae, and Cyperaceae, plus one disseminule of unknown

Table 36.3. Occurrence of wild plant taxa in 64 strata as derived from flotation analysis.[1]

Taxon[2]	Primary Occupation		Secondary Occupation		Total[3] Strata (n = 64)
	Floors (n = 6)	Trash (n = 13)	Floors (n = 22)	Trash (n = 23)	
WIDESPREAD					
Hybrid: Cheno-Am*	6 [4]	13 [4]	22 [5]	22 [9]	63
Portulacaceae					
Portulaca, including *P. retusa* type (purslane)	6 [2]	9 [3]	17 [2]	18 [5]	50
COMMON					
Gramineae					
Muhlenbergia (Muhly grass)	—	—	1 [1]	—	
Oryzopsis hymenoides type* (Indian ricegrass)	2 [1]	1 [1]	4 (floret) [0]	5 (bract, floret, inflorescence, lemma [4]	
Paniceae, including Panicum type	—	1 [0]	6 (floret) [1]	3 [0]	
Sporobolus (dropseed)	1 [0]	—	2 [0]	6 [6]	
Undetermined	2 (floret) [0]	5 [2]	9 (bract, callus, floret, lemma, spikelet [2]	8 [7]	
All Gramineae					35
Cruciferae					
Descurainia, including *D. obtuse* type (tansy-mustard)	5 [1]	3 [0]	17 (valve) [2]	5 [1]	30
Cactaceae					
Echinocereus, including *E. Fendleri* type (hedgehog)*	3 [0]	1 [0]	11 [0]	8 [2]	
Opuntia (Platyopuntia) (prickly pear)	—	—	1 [0]	—	
*Sclerocactus**	1 [0]	—	—	—	
Undetermined	—	—	5 (areole, spine) [1]	—	
All Cactaceae					26
Euphorbiaceae					
Euphorbia glyptosperma type (spurge)	4 [2]	6 [2]	7 [2]	9 [0]	26
Solanaceae					
Physalis, incl. *P. longifolia* type seeds and berries (groundcherry)	3 [1]	1 [1]	13 [4]	9 [3]	26
Unknown					
Tule Springs unknown	3 [0]	6 [5]	9 [3]	7 [4]	25
Cyperaceae					
Carex (sedge)	—	—	—	3 [2]	
Eleocharis montana type (spike-rush)	1 [0]	—	—	—	
Scirpus, including *S. acutis* type (bulrush)	1 [0]	1 [0]	5 [1]	5 [1]	
Undetermined	2 [1]	—	6 [1]	2 [0]	
All Cyperaceae					23

Table 36.3 (continued)

| Taxon[2] | Primary Occupation | | Secondary Occupation | | Total[3] Strata (n = 64) |
	Floors (n = 6)	Trash (n = 13)	Floors (n = 22)	Trash (n = 23)	
RARE					
Capparidaceae					
Cleome, including *C. serrulata* type (Rocky Mtn. beeweed)	2 [0]	1 [1]	6 [0]	4 [1]	
Polanisia type (clammy-weed)	—	1 [0]	1 [0]	1 [1]	
Undetermined	—	1 [0]	—	3 [0]	
All Capparidaceae					20
Loasaceae					
Mentzelia albicaulis type (stick-leaf)	2 [1]	1 [0]	12 [3]	3 [2]	18
Chenopodiaceae					
Cycloloma atriplicifolium type (winged-pigweed)*	1 [0]	1 [1]	3 [0]	7 [0]	
Suaeda, including *S. suffrutescens* type (seep-weed)*	1 [0]	—	1 [0]	—	
All Chenopodiaceae					13
Aizoaceae					
Trianthema portulacastrum type*	2 [0]	2 [1]	4 [1]	3 [0]	11
Anacardiaceae					
Rhus trilobata (squawbush)	—	1 [1]	—	6 [5]	7
Compositae					
Verbesina type (crown-beard)	—	—	1 [0]	—	
Undetermined	1 [0]	1 [0]	4 [0]	1 [0]	
All Compositae					7
Malvaceae					
Sphaeralcea, including *S. parviflora* type (globe mallow)	—	—	4 [0]	—	
Undetermined	—	—	2 [0]	2 [1]	
All Malvaceae					7
Unknown					
#8066	—	1 [0]	—	6 [0]	7
Juncaceae					
Juncus, including *J. Cooperi* type (rush)	1 [0]	—	5 [0]	—	6
Leguminosae					
Desmodium (tick-clover)	—	—	—	1 [1]	
Papilionoideae (bean subfamily)	—	—	1 [0]	—	
Undetermined	—	—	1(pod) [0]	1 [0]	
All Leguminosae					4
Polygonaceae					
Polygonum, including *P. Sawatchense* type (knotweed)*	—	1 [0]	1 [0]	2 [1]	4
Unknown					
#8063	—	—	1 [0]	2 [0]	3

Table 36.3 (continued)

Taxon[2]	Primary Occupation		Secondary Occupation		Total[3] Strata (n = 64)
	Floors (n = 6)	Trash (n = 13)	Floors (n = 22)	Trash (n = 23)	
Labiatae					
Salvia reflexa type (Rocky Mountain sage)	—	—	—	1 [0]	1
Nyctaginaceae					
Allionia	—	—	1 [0]	—	1
Plantaginaceae					
Plantago (Indian-wheat)	—	—	1 [0]	—	1
Sauraceae					
Anemopsis californica type (yerba-mansa)	—	—	—	1 [0]	1
Unknown					
Catkins	—	—	—	1 [1]	
Zygophyllaceae					
Kallstroemia	—	—	1(fruit) [0]	—	1

[1] Actual number of flotation samples examined is 215. Number of individual samples from a stratum ranges from 1 to 17. Based upon CONURE printouts 3/21/80 7OETable 213 and 3/26/80 7OETable 459, and hand tallies of flotation data records on the following floors not entered into the computer: Rooms 6A H-1-5.2; 51W H-1-5; 56W H-1-5; 58W H-1-8; 101W H-1-9; and 124A H-1-6/I-1-7.

[2] Items in this table are reproductive disseminules such as seeds, achenes, caryopses, or stones. Additional parts observed in limited numbers are noted in parentheses.

[3] Some strata contain more than one taxon; the final column (Total Strata) sums to less than its subunits.

*Seed or grain types with naturally black coats.

[ ] indicates the number of separate unburned strata in which specimens were listed as "some or all parched or carbonized."

affiliation. Common occurrence of a plant is considered to reflect relatively regular acquisition as a food product; medicinal or ceremonial plants would not be expected to be found in more than a third of the locations examined. Numerous plant taxa that occur in less than 20 of the 64 separate stratigraphic units have been labeled as rare, and so are not discussed in this report. Such plants may owe their low frequency to more than one explanation, such as infrequent use, presence of seed coats extremely susceptible to degradation, prehistoric preparation technique or lack of it, or incidental introduction into the pueblo. The distribution of taxa unique to either the Primary or Secondary occupation (Table 36.4) reveals that many rare specimens were recovered in only a single Salmon Ruin stratum.

Cheno-Am

Cheno-Am (*Chenopodium/Amaranthus*) seeds are ubiquitous in Salmon Ruin strata (see Table 36.3), being found in 63 of 64 locations examined. All six Chacoan floors and all 22 Chacoan trash strata sampled produced Cheno-Am seeds. Likewise, all 22 Secondary floors, and all but one of 23 Secondary trash middens contained Cheno-Am, which repre-

sents undoubtedly the most widespread seed types recovered in flotation samples at Salmon Ruin.

Cheno-Am has acquired its name because two separate plant families (goosefoot and amaranth) have genera with seeds that closely mimic each other in appearance. For example, seeds of some *Chenopodium* and *Amaranthus* are similar in size (many average 1.0–1.5 mm), round to slightly ovoid in shape, and black in color. They differ in surface texture, in the unilateral presence of a central calyx scar in *Chenopodium*, and in a distinct rim around most *Amaranthus* seeds (Bohrer and Adams 1976). Barbs or appendages to ensure transport are absent. Although the differences between seeds of the two genera facilitate separating them in modern populations, degraded archaeological specimens, including those distorted by fire, frequently lack the subtle characteristics that distinguish the taxa. Therefore, the custom has been to group all such prehistoric specimens into a category labeled Cheno-Am. Fortunately, the wild plants share many habitats and responses to growing conditions, and have been used by people in ways so similar that discussing them together is reasonable.

Most plants in the Cheno-Am group are annuals that thrive in sunny, disturbed habitats (Kearney and

Table 36.4. Flotation evidence of plant taxa unique to each occupation; derived from Table 36.3.

Taxon	Present in Separate Trash or Floor Strata (n = 19)
Primary Occupation	
Eleocharis montana type	1
Sclerocactus	1
Secondary Occupation	
Malvaceae	4
Sphaeralcea, including *S. parviflora* type	4
Carex	3
Unknown #8063	3
Leguminosae	2
Allionia	1
Anemopsis californica type	1
Desmodium	1
Kallstroemia	1
Muhlenbergia type	1
Opuntia (Platyopuntia)	1
Papilionoideae	1
Plantago	1
Salvia reflexa type	1
Verbesina type	1
Unknown catkins	1

Peebles 1960:251, 265), so they are frequently referred to as weeds. These plants often exhibit a "shifting" seasonality (Bohrer 1975d), being able to sprout over a long period of the frost-free season when enough moisture has fallen. Also, while going to seed on lower branches, upper branches may be just coming into flower, fostering simultaneous pollen and seed production on individual plants. Numerous species of both *Chenopodium* and *Amaranthus* grow in the San Juan Valley today (K. Adams 1976).

The likelihood that many of these Cheno-Am type seeds were accidentally introduced into Salmon strata is considered low for a number of reasons. First, careful sample selection served to minimize the possibility of rodent or root disturbances, and no harvester ant nests were seen in the local area. Second, the relatively hard, smooth-coated seeds are not likely to naturally catch on sandals, clothing, or animal fur, reducing the chance that they would be incidentally carried into a dwelling. Third, although prehistoric Secondary trash middens could have provided a habitat for normally weedy plant growth, 10 of the 22 deposits with Cheno-Am seeds either had a roof overhead during the accretion of the midden, or contained parched or carbonized seeds in otherwise unburned debris. However, 12 Secondary

trash strata contained unburned Cheno-Am seeds, and because these middens are known to have been open to sunlight in prehistory, their Cheno-Am remains may have resulted from weedy growth on middens. Finally, although archaeological disturbance from 1970 to 1978 did encourage growth of goosefoot and amaranth plants around the fringes of the archaeological site, modern seeds were easily recognized by their shiny seed coat, undamaged appearance, and lack of carbonization of the embryo and endosperm. On the rare occasions when a modern seed had become mixed in an ancient deposit, their presence simply supplemented, rather than changed, the record of Cheno-Am seed distribution.

The condition of many of the prehistoric Cheno-Am seeds and their locations within the pueblo converge to suggest that these plants served as food for Salmon residents. For example, 8 of 19 unburned Primary strata contained Cheno-Am type seeds that were noticeably parched or carbonized, and 14 of 45 unburned Secondary strata also contained seeds altered by fire. Many of these parched or burned seeds probably reflect preparation of the resource for consumption or storage. Parching renders a seed brittle, thus allowing it to be easily crushed when ground to flour; parching also drives out moisture, preventing seeds from becoming rancid or moldy if kept for any length of time. Modern Puebloans sometimes state that toasted seeds taste better (Underhill 1954:55–56).

The contexts within which Cheno-Am remains were recovered at Salmon provide evidence that the seeds were an important food. Cheno-Am seeds excavated from a hearth on one Primary floor (Room 93W, H-5-33) are thought to represent accidental parching, where some seeds spilled into the fire (K. Adams 1980:28–30; see also Chapter 39). Seeds found elsewhere in Room 93W, plus in another room (101W, H-1-9) also thought to have been Primary occupation living quarters, may have fallen to the floor during meals. Clumped *Chenopodium* pollen grains in these two rooms probably owe their presence to human transport of plants or seeds into the room for two reasons: clumped grains of wind-pollinated species are unlikely to travel far on air currents, and the harvesting process is apt to inadvertently include immature clumped pollen grains, as both seeds and pollen can be found simultaneously on a single plant. Seeds recovered from every one of the 13 Primary trash strata could have been waste from daily dinner preparation or consumption. Cheno-Am seeds and clumped *Chenopodium* pollen grains embedded in Primary floors containing no features of any kind (30W, H-2-12; 56W, H-1-5;

and 89W, H-1-8) may indicate locations where foodstuffs were stored.

A variety of contexts show that the Cheno-Am group constituted important food in Secondary times. Fourteen *Amaranthus* seeds found beneath an overturned quartzite metate in one room (93W, H-1-14) were probably dislodged from the pores of the grinding stone, and thus represent the residue of seeds ground into flour (K. Adams 1980:21; see also Chapter 39). Clumped *Chenopodium* or Cheno-Am pollen grains accompanying Cheno-Am seeds on two floors and in their associated hearths (Room 93W, H-1-14 and H-2-22) imply purposeful gathering of the plants (K. Adams 1980:26, 30; see Chapter 39); their presence in these living quarters implies that they were eaten there. Consumption of Cheno-Am seeds during Secondary times is documented by fecal remains. Cheno-Am remains recovered from the 10 Secondary trash strata mentioned earlier provide solid evidence that these seeds were regularly discarded. The storage of *Chenopodium* type seeds in Secondary times is indicated by the recovery of more than 65 ml of concentrated, carbonized seeds from a burned Secondary roof (90W, F-2-9) suspected of serving as a storage location. Many of these seeds, united by a fine-grained matrix of unknown nature, were actually fused to the interior surface of a large corrugated ceramic sherd. Secondary occupants appear to have gathered enough Cheno-Am seeds to store them in Room 90W right along with the harvest of cultivated crops. Cheno-Am seeds and clumped pollen grains recovered from four floors without features (51W, H-1-5; 57W, H-1-8; 58W, H-1-8; and 58W, H-2-11), and seeds from another suspected storeroom (119W, F-3-20), provide additional evidence that the resource was stored at Salmon. Cheno-Am seeds and clumped pollen grains were also identified on two Secondary kiva floors (6A, H-1-5.2 and 124A, H-1-6). In 6A, seeds were highly concentrated in a milling bin feature (over 1000 estimated), but were sparse (less than 20) in other areas in the room. One explanation for Cheno-Am evidence in kivas could be that the plants were considered important enough to be part of sacred rites, and therefore served a religious function at Salmon. On the other hand, kivas may have been used for nonceremonial purposes at various times, and the plant record could reflect a dual picture of both religious and nonreligious activities. The highly tentative identification of one or possibly two white-coated Cheno-Am seeds from Salmon may reveal the cultivation of this plant (see Chapter 35).

Judging from their widespread distribution, the unlikely incidental introduction of the majority of seeds, their carbonized condition, and numerous highly suggestive archaeological contexts, it appears that plants in the Cheno-Am category were a frequent dietary item for Salmon residents in prehistory. Those qualities that cause man to bemoan the weedy nature of goosefoot and amaranth plants today are the very same qualities that permitted Salmon residents to repeatedly harvest the plants as food. Because they are opportunists, they sprout new seedlings after each summer rain in what may seem like endless numbers to modern gardeners. Salmon housewives, however, would have been able to harvest greens for spinach and mature seeds for mush or flour throughout most of the frost-free season, as long as drought did not prevail. Disturbed habitats occur both naturally (arroyo and river edges, talus slopes) and as a result of human activities (pathways, trash heaps, cultivated garden plots), undoubtedly providing many locations within walking distance of the pueblo where wild goosefoot and amaranth plants appear to have been abundant enough that some of their seeds could even be set aside in storerooms.

Purslane

Purslane (*Portulaca*), including seeds of *P. retusa*, occurs almost as frequently in Salmon Ruin strata as Cheno-Am (see Table 36.3). Every one of six Primary floors and 9 of 13 Primary trash strata contained purslane seeds, as did 17 of 22 Secondary floors, and 18 of 23 Secondary trash strata. In total, 50 of the 64 strata examined contained evidence of purslane.

Purslane is a small, more or less succulent plant that can generally be found in late summer months (Kearney and Peebles 1960:290). Many of the Southwest species are annuals, including *Portulaca retusa*. All of the Arizona species prefer full sunlight, and are often found growing on plains and mesas. These plants derive moisture from the normally predictable summer or fall rains, but should the rains be either inappropriately timed or meager in amount, stands of purslane could be much reduced in density. The weedy behavior of purslane in modern gardens can probably be attributed to an abundance of available moisture, and naturally prolific stands were likely confined to relatively moist settings. These plants produce small (average 0.50–1.00 mm) black seeds that do not normally adhere to clothing or animal fur. Often the seeds will continue to mature even after the succulent plant has been picked.

The possibility that some of the purslane seeds were introduced accidentally in either ancient or modern times is slim. For example, precautions were taken to avoid areas where rodents or roots could have provided tunnels for mixing prehistoric and modern specimens. Also, although the plants may have grown in sunny open areas around the pueblo in prehistory, their relatively smooth seeds would not be apt to cling to sandals or clothing. However, some of the unburned purslane seeds recovered from 11 Secondary trash strata not covered by roofs in prehistory may have come from plants growing on the open middens themselves. (The seven remaining Secondary trash strata either contained obviously parched or carbonized seeds, or were covered by a roof in prehistory.) Finally, the disturbance caused by recent archaeological excavations probably did not contribute modern purslane seeds to ancient deposits because a search for *Portulaca* species near the ruin was unsuccessful. Only the purportedly introduced *Portulaca oleracea* has been found, a number of miles to the west (K. Adams 1976). Heavy domestic grazing in the Southwest in historic times probably drastically reduced the size of the purslane population (Bohrer 1978: 14).

The evidence that purslane was eaten at Salmon Pueblo takes a variety of forms. Samples from floors and trash of the Primary occupation, and from two unburned floors and five unburned trash deposits of the Secondary period, had seeds that appeared to be either parched or carbonized. Many of these seeds were likely toasted near a fire prior to eating or storage. Some of the seeds with no evidence of parching or burning may owe their presence in the pueblo to the use of the *Portulaca* plant itself, rather than its seeds. A succulent purslane plant picked to be used as spinach greens may possess mature capsules. Furthermore, if it were to be kept for even a few days in a pueblo room, rapidly maturing seeds could fall to the floor, leaving a record of the plant's presence.

The locations at which many of the prehistoric purslane specimens were found clearly suggest that the plant provided food throughout the pueblo's history. During Primary times, seeds were brought into a household area (93W, H-5-33) and deposited both on the floor and in the hearth (K. Adams 1980: 53; see Chapter 39). They were also found in another room (101W, H-1-9) where Primary residents are thought to have lived. Seeds recovered in 9 of 13 Primary trash strata probably represent waste from frequent preparation or consumption. Specimens found on a Primary floor without any features (56W, H-1-5) may reflect storage of the seeds in a featureless room.

The Secondary residents also carried purslane seeds or plants into living quarters. In Room 93W (H-1-14) seeds were recovered from the floor and within the fire hearth, as well as in association with a quartzite metate that was most likely used to grind them (K. Adams 1980:53; see Chapter 39). That the Secondary residents actually ate *Portulaca* seeds is documented by inclusions in fecal remains. Seeds in 7 of 23 trash strata are considered solid evidence that purslane was frequently part of the waste that found its way into trash heaps; seeds in 11 trash strata could represent actual growth of *Portulaca* plants on the middens themselves. The presence of purslane seeds in rooms with no architectural features (51W, H-1-5; 57W, H-1-8; 58W, H-1-8; and 58W, H-2-11) tentatively indicates their storage, as does the recovery of a single seed in a burned room (119W, F-3-20) thought to represent a storage area. The excavation of more than 900 *Portulaca* seeds from one Secondary kiva (6A, H-1-5.2) feature (a milling bin) as well as from 7 of 17 floor samples in another Secondary kiva (124A, H-1-6) suggests a possible sacred use for this plant. This interpretation is supported by the recovery of purslane seeds with an animal skull on yet another Secondary kiva floor (Sample 94W2080).

It seems surprising that purslane seeds are so well documented as a frequent food item in Salmon Ruin strata. Today it is not a resource that humans can depend upon every year, as erratic summer moisture often thwarts its growth. What is equally intriguing is the fact that a fall-ripening native seed crop could be so abundant. Perhaps the plants were regularly encouraged in garden plots, providing a bonus crop for the hard work of cultivation. Or perhaps domesticated crops were regularly inadequate to sustain Salmon residents, forcing them to rely on native resources. Whatever the explanation, *Portulaca* appears to have been a very frequently gathered resource at Salmon Pueblo.

Grass

At Salmon Ruin, occupants of both Primary and Secondary times knew the grass (Gramineae) family. At least four separate genera, plus a number of unidentified specimens, have been recognized in ancient deposits (see Table 36.3). Although any one particular genus has not been found in more than 12 strata, various grass grains and parts have been recovered in 35 of the 64 floor and trash strata examined. Grasses are therefore considered to have been common in the prehistoric Salmon diet.

The grass family contains most of the major cultivated plants in the world, such as maize, wheat, barley, and rice; grasses also contribute significantly to the diet of domesticated animals. Of 91 genera of grasses documented as occurring in Arizona (Kearney and Peebles 1960:70), at least 26 currently grow in the San Juan Valley (K. Adams 1976).

There is much variety in growth habit and seasonality within the grass family. Some grasses are annual plants, whose density in any given year may be closely linked to current climatic conditions. With abundant moisture, thousands of annual grass grains can germinate to produce a large crop of new harvestable grains. Other grasses are perennials, whose vigor and ability to set fruit are also tied to fluctuating weather. If conditions are too dry, a perennial grass may conserve moisture by producing few grains, or not fruiting at all. Grasses also differ in seasonality. Those that break dormancy and undergo significant vegetative growth in the spring or fall are considered cool season grasses, whereas others that wait until the hot summer months to initiate growth are known as warm season grasses. People at Salmon would benefit in the late spring when newly mature cool season grass grains offered a food resource, and again in the summer when warm season grasses could fill a void while the cultivated crops matured. Success at harvesting grasses derives partly from their variability; in any given frost-free season at least some species will have optimum conditions for fruit set, and hence be harvestable.

The methods that grasses have evolved to help ensure grain (caryopsis) planting have implications for their ease of harvest, as well as for the likelihood of accidental introduction into the pueblo. For example, some grass grains are closely enveloped by adhering bracts that do not release their cargo until it has been planted in the ground. The grains of muhly (*Muhlenbergia*), for example, are tightly enclosed in bracts (palea and lemma) that taper to a rather bristly point. Although such an arrangement increases the chances that the grain can bore into the ground, people and animals find it difficult to remove these sharp adherent appendages. Other grasses, such as dropseed (*Sporobolus*), release individual grains from the bracts when mature, thus permitting a harvester to accumulate an amount of pure grain relatively easily. Grains that fall easily from their surrounding bracts would take less effort to harvest, and would perhaps be more attractive as a food, compared to others that require removal of the bracts (Flannery 1965:1252). At the same time, grasses with barbs or bristles would be more likely to accidentally travel into a pueblo on someone's sandals or in an animal's fur.

With regard to the presence of muhly (*Muhlenbergia*), the possibility of accidental introduction must be considered. Only one Secondary floor (Kiva 6A, H-1-5.2) revealed this grass type (see Table 36.3), and the grain itself is usually enclosed within bracts bearing a minute bristle, so one could postulate that the grass was accidentally carried into the pueblo on sandals or clothing. However, its burned condition lends support to the contrary idea that the grain was prepared for consumption or storage by holding it near a fire. A ceremonial use of the plant is also possible because this Secondary floor also happened to be in a kiva. Because different species of *Muhlenbergia* are quite varied in plant habit and seasonality (Kearney and Peebles 1960), one cannot speculate further on a grass classifiable only to genus.

Although accidental introduction of some of the Indian ricegrass (*Oryzopsis hymenoides*) type grains into Salmon strata cannot be completely ruled out, the evidence for such an occurrence is relatively weak. For example, of five unburned Secondary trash strata with ricegrass remains, only one that was open to sunlight in prehistory contained unburned specimens. The remaining four strata all had seeds that evidenced parching or burning. The Navajo method of removing the grains by holding the entire plant over a fire (Castetter 1935:28) would explain the presence of a variety of carbonized reproductive parts in these Secondary trash deposits, as it would also explain the recovery of a single bract in a hearth on a Primary floor (K. Adams 1980:44; see Chapter 39). Also, even though *Oryzopsis* grains may remain loosely enclosed within adherent bracts, the absence of barbs would tend to rule out incidental transport of the seed on humans or animals. Other positive evidence for the use of ricegrass at Salmon consists of its recovery on a few Primary floors, where accidents of food preparation or eating might be recovered, and from trash middens attributable to the Primary occupation. A ricegrass seed retrieved in association with other plant materials from a room (119W, F-3-20) used for storage in Secondary times poses the possibility that the resource was occasionally set aside for future use. Ricegrass, which is available in the late spring, could have provided an important seed crop if stored foodstuffs had been depleted the previous winter. In addition, its grain size is relatively large (ca. 4 mm), making it an especially attractive food.

Grains of the Paniceae grass family, including *Panicum* type, have been identified in one Primary strata and nine Secondary locations (see Table 36.3). Unlike the muhly and ricegrass remains, Paniceae grains were recognized as parched or carbonized in only one stratum (unburned Secondary floor, 58W, H-2-11). Without more evidence that might imply human processing of the grains near fire, these remains in Salmon Ruin are not easily interpreted. Many species of *Panicum* grow in open ground, some preferring disturbed waste places (Kearney and

Peebles 1960:136), so presumably the specimens recovered from Secondary trash may have come from plants growing directly upon the middens. Perhaps the other grains were carried into the rooms when grass stems were used in the manufacture of domestic goods; the independent recovery of concentrations of carbonized Gramineae stems in three of seven suspected Secondary storerooms (see additional discussion below) shows that grass was brought in for some domestic purpose. Modern Tewas make brooms from *Panicum* to sweep metates and metate boxes (Robbins et al. 1916:64). Such a practice could introduce *Panicum* seeds into a food processing area, and yet not reflect a food use at all. *Panicum* grass has not been located in the surrounding area in recent years (K. Adams 1976), but it is not known if this is a long-standing absence.

Dropseed (*Sporobolus*) is a genus of annual and perennial grasses in which the tiny grain is actually free from the bracts that surround it (Kearney and Peebles 1960:112). Compared to other grasses which are tightly enclosed in enveloping structures, dropseed was probably easier to harvest. Although grasses with free-falling grains may cost less in energy to harvest and prepare than those that require additional work to render them edible, one must keep in mind that dropseed grains are very small (ca. 1 mm) and would still require more time to gather than larger-seeded resources such as ricegrass. Hopis therefore gave extra attention to dropseed in times of famine when other foods were less available (Whiting 1966:66). One factor that could occasionally offset the disadvantage of small seed size is the pioneer role that some members of this genus play in plant succession. Areas temporarily uninhabitable by competing vegetation might foster dense stands of dropseed grass, and thus make harvest of the concentrated resource more attractive.

The dropseed specimens found in Secondary deposits at Salmon Ruin very likely represent a food resource, as six separate unburned trash middens contained grains that had been parched or burned (see Table 36.3). The recovery of one unburned *Sporobolus* grain on a single Primary floor, however, does not provide unequivocal evidence that the Primary inhabitants also made use of this grass type. The fact that the dropseed grains from Salmon strata are unidentified as to species precludes speculation on season of acquisition, as various species of the genus mature from April through October in the Southwest (Kearney and Peebles 1960:113–114).

Although unidentified grass reproductive structures from Salmon may shed little light on specific plant choice, and may offer no clues as to season(s) of harvest, their very presence implies reliance on a variety of grasses. A plant family providing food for millions today in the form of cultivated crops played a dual role in prehistory by furnishing many wild and one cultivated species (maize) at Salmon. Unidentified grass specimens from two of five Primary strata evidenced parching or burning, as did those found in two unburned Secondary floors and seven of eight Secondary trash middens (see Table 36.3). The presence of varied parts on Secondary floors could reflect preparation of the grasses within the rooms themselves, rather than in some outdoor location such as the plaza or wherever the grains were harvested.

Tansy-Mustard

Tansy-mustard (*Descurainia*) has been identified in 30 of 64 separate strata from Salmon Ruin (see Table 36.3). Some of the specimens appear to closely match modern examples of *Descurainia obtusa*. Five Primary floors and three Primary trash strata revealed tansy-mustard seeds, as did 17 Secondary floors and five Secondary trash middens. Tansy-mustard appears to have been commonly sought at Salmon by both groups of residents.

Descurainia plants are annual herbs that appear in the spring and grow mainly in open ground (Kearney and Peebles 1960:349). As a cool season annual, tansy-mustard generally flowers and fruits within a relatively short time, producing seeds during the cool spring months. It is an erratic seed producer, however, restricted in many years by low rainfall to producing a meager seed crop. But in years when moisture is adequate, abundant stands of tansy-mustard can be found in open, sunny areas. The plants have been observed growing both on and around the Salmon site in recent years. The seeds of tansy-mustard are tiny (0.80–1.00 mm), relatively smooth, light yellow-orange in color, and easily harvested by bending the plants over a container and shaking the stems.

Tansy-mustard can be an aggressive weed in years when moisture is adequate, so the plants probably grew in and around the pueblo in prehistory, especially considering that many of the recovered seeds were not apparently parched or carbonized. One might be tempted to suspect that the majority of seeds of Primary affiliation were not purposefully brought in by people, were it not for the fact that they were recognized on five separate floors. The relatively smooth seeds would not be likely to cling to people or animals, so the seeds on Primary floors are probably from food use. Likewise, tansy-mustard seeds on 17 separate Secondary floors were also probably carried in by humans for consumption; the parched or carbonized specimens on two unburned Secondary floors (6A, H-1-5.2 and 96W, H-1-5) may reflect food preparation. Seeds in three Primary trash strata presumably did not grow in the middens themselves, because roofs covered the rooms during trash deposition. Seeds not obviously parched or burned from three Secondary trash strata without overhead roofs could owe their presence to plants growing on open middens during prehistory. In total, however, the overall distribution at Salmon suggests that most tansy-mustard seeds were used by humans. Modern seeds from plants that grew on the site in the 1970s were easily recognized by laboratory personnel; such seeds displayed undamaged coats and an even, yellow-orange color, and were sometimes accompanied by the very fragile mustard pod known as a silique.

A heavy native seed crop in the spring might bring welcome relief from winter food stress. In years when tansy-mustard bore abundantly, one could harvest large amounts of the free-falling seeds by walking through dense patches with collecting vessels. However, tansy-mustard is not at all reliable in the arid Southwest, and perhaps for this reason it is surprising to find it so frequently in Salmon stratigraphy. One wonders whether winters were regularly difficult times for people, forcing them to rely on native spring crops at every opportunity.

Cactus

Cacti (Cactaceae) were common at Salmon in prehistory. Seeds and other cacti parts were recovered from 26 of 64 strata examined, representing both the Primary and Secondary occupations (see Table 36.3). *Echinocereus*, occurring in 23 stratigraphic units, seems to have been frequently employed, whereas the remains of Platyopuntia, *Sclerocactus*, and other unknown types are less common.

Cacti are succulent perennials that are well adapted to the arid Southwest. They range from the very large and conspicuous saguaro (*Carnegia gigantea*) of southern Arizona and California, to the low ground-hugging hedgehog (*Echinocereus*). These plants are so well adapted to the vicissitudes of desert weather that they are rarely overcome by drought, and often seem to flower and fruit under the most adverse of conditions. Cacti flowers have brightly colored petals to attract pollinating insects, and the plants produce heavy, sticky pollen that can easily cling to an insect's body. The formation of fruit in the cactus family is such that the flower parts, including pollen-bearing stamens, sit above

the development fruit; thus the possibility exists that the heavy pollen may fall onto the fruit below, and be retained on its surface. The fruits of cacti can be divided into two main categories, based on the character of the ovary wall. Some cacti have fleshy, sweet tissue surrounding the seeds, thus making the fruit highly attractive to both animals and humans. Hedgehog and some species of prickly pear (Platyopuntia) are just a few of the taxa in this family that have these juicy fruits. Other cacti such as *Sclerocactus* and *Opuntia polyacantha* (a type of prickly pear) have dry fruit, in which the loose seeds rattle around, that are far less appealing as food. *Echinocereus*, *Opuntia polyacantha*, and *Sclerocactus* have all been found growing near Salmon Ruin in recent years (K. Adams 1976).

Hedgehog

Most of the cactus seeds identified in Salmon flotation samples appear to belong to the fleshy-fruited genus *Echinocereus* (including *E. fendleri*; see Table 36.3). Three Primary floors, one Primary trash midden, 11 Secondary floors, and eight Secondary trash deposits contained hedgehog seeds. Some of the seeds closely matched modern specimens of *E. fendleri*, which has been observed growing nearby (K. Adams 1976). Because cacti are very slow growing perennial plants, often taking years to reach reproductive maturity, it is highly unlikely that any of the cactus seeds in Salmon Ruin were introduced incidentally due to plants growing in or around the town. Their recovery at Salmon probably relates to food use, though not necessarily of the seeds themselves, as the hard seeds may have been discarded while the sweet fruit flesh was retained.

Pollen data strengthen this interpretation. The normally insect-pollinated *Echinocereus fendleri* type pollen grains have been recovered from two Primary floors and five Secondary floors, generally as one or two grains from any single square-meter area. The 15 grains in a 1 m grid along the north wall in a Secondary featureless floor (58W, H-2-11) constitute an especially high concentration. Perhaps dried hedgehog fruit was stored there, as the Hopi have been known to store fruit dried in the spring for sweetening (Whiting 1966:85). If fleshy fruits were split open to dry still-retained, shriveled-up flowers at their apex, pollen might be deposited in the room in which storage occurred. Or perhaps the blossoms themselves were carried into this room to be stored, because cactus petals can be eaten. Another possibility might be that edible stems brought in as food could serve to transport pollen from flowers.

Prickly Pear

Flotation evidence alone provides a very weak argument that prickly pear fruit was brought into the pueblo. Just a single Secondary stratum (58W, H-2-11) contained one unburned seed, and its poor condition precluded a determination whether it represented a fleshy or dry-fruited species. However, both the macrofossil and fecal records provide additional evidence that Salmon inhabitants brought in and ate the fruits of a fleshy-fruited prickly pear. Today, only a dry-fruited species (*Opuntia polyacantha*) grows in the region (K. Adams 1976). The Secondary residents also brought young prickly pear vegetative pads into the Tower Kiva (64W9001), and into other rooms as well. These pads were all preserved when parts of the pueblo caught fire; it is possible that if other cactus pads were carried into the pueblo, and not similarly carbonized, they eventually disintegrated and left no record of their use. A single Platyopuntia pollen grain was recovered from one Primary featureless floor (30W, H-2-12) and one also came from a Secondary featureless floor (58W, H-2-11). Perhaps the pollen traveled in on vegetative parts, which could have been dusted with pollen grains when the plant was in flower. Taken as a unit, the plant evidence reveals that prickly pear was at least an occasional resource for Salmon residents.

Sclerocactus

At present, only the Primary occupation has produced any evidence of *Sclerocactus* use, and the evidence is minimal (see Table 36.3). A single seed was found on a featureless floor (89W, G-1-7/H-1-8), as were two accompanying pollen grains. These plant remains suggest that on at least one occasion, the dry fruit was brought to the pueblo. Today one member of this genus has been observed in the surrounding area (K. Adams 1976).

Indeterminate

Unidentifiable cacti remains from Salmon Ruin include seeds and some other parts, such as areoles and a spine. These items came entirely from Secondary floors, and appeared to be parched or carbonized in three of five strata. Their presence serves basically to reinforce the interpretation that various cacti were exploited by Salmon residents.

Discussion

Cacti are very dependable as food in the desert. Their succulent nature permits them to flower and fruit with regularity, and their reproductive capacity is thus less closely tied to a given season's moisture than is fruit set in weedy annuals or nonsucculent perennials. Not only could humans regularly depend upon cacti fruit, but in all seasons of the year the naturally evergreen cactus vegetative pads or joints would be available, with the tender young pads produced in the spring being especially desirable. Prickly pear pads and cholla buds were used by Salmon residents. Fleshy-fruited types of cacti probably provided a more sought-after edible than their dry-fruited relatives, and it is not surprising to see that at Salmon the sweet juicy fruits of hedgehog and Platyopuntia were gathered frequently. Seeds of the dry-fruited *Sclerocactus* were also brought to the pueblo. The recovery of additional cacti parts confirms that the cactus family was no stranger to the residents of Salmon Pueblo.

Spurge

At Salmon Ruin, spurge (*Euphorbia glyptosperma*) seeds have been recovered from both Primary and Secondary strata. Four of six Primary floors and 7 of 22 Secondary floors contained spurge seeds, some with evidence of parching or burning. This seed type was also recognized in numerous trash strata from both occupations (see Table 36.3). Spurge type seeds have been recovered from 26 of the 64 separate strata examined in this study, suggesting that they were common in the pueblo.

Many spurges are low-growing, prostrate, weedy annuals that can often be found growing in waste places and disturbed areas; *Euphorbia glyptosperma* is no exception (Richardson 1978:68). No spurge has been collected recently in the San Juan Valley of New Mexico (K. Adams 1976), but in many of the Plains states it can be found in almost every type of habitat available. It forms seeds as early as June in Texas (Correll and Johnston 1970:977) and Arizona (Kearney and Peebles 1960:520), and as late as October in central New Mexico (specimen with University of Arizona accession no. 217575). The seeds of *E. glyptosperma* can adhere to passing animals because their seed coats become mucilaginous when wet; after a rainstorm or particularly heavy dew, these ground-level plants growing in the paths of wandering animals are likely to disperse many seeds by adherence. Many spurges are poisonous, but others are not (K. Adams 1980; Chapter 39). It is unknown whether various parts of *E. glyptosperma* contain toxic substances.

Because spurges are weedy, the recovery of apparently unparched and unburned seeds in eight Secondary trash strata not covered by protecting roofs may reflect incidental introduction. The plant may well have flourished at the pueblo as a weed, contributing some seeds to the archaeological record. Perhaps some unburned seeds on floors were carried in on sandals after a rain. However, these explanations cannot account for all of the Salmon spurge evidence. For example, the burned condition of seeds in four Primary and two Secondary strata implies that someone held the plants near a fire. Parched or carbonized seeds from one Primary featureless floor (56W, H-1-5) may represent spills from storage. The presence of more than 800 parched or carbonized spurge seeds in a milling bin feature of a Secondary kiva (6A, H-1-5.2), and from nowhere else within that room, strongly implies that people brought in the concentrated seed for a specific purpose. Burned seeds also came from a Primary habitation room (101W, H-1-9). This evidence reflects food use of spurge by Salmon residents; one would not expect a plant that served mainly medicinal or ceremonial needs to occur so frequently. Supporting this interpretation are two ecological factors. First, as a weedy annual plant growing in waste places, spurge would presumably be capable of producing large quantities of seeds that could be harvested. Also, if the plant is available from June through October, as an opportunist it could sprout new seedlings after each new rain and thus provide continually maturing seeds for a number of months.

At present, both archaeological and ecological evidence converge to suggest that in prehistory a weedy spurge of broad seasonal amplitude was eaten by Salmon residents. However, it is presently unknown whether *Euphorbia glyptosperma* is one of the poisonous spurges. For that reason, the final chapter on this seed type may not yet be written. Even if this species, or certain parts of it, are found to contain toxic substances, one cannot rule out the possibility that the Salmon occupants knew a way to prepare it that rendered the poison harmless.

Groundcherry

Like the cactus and spurge plants, groundcherry (*Physalis*, including *P. longifolia*) seems to have been common at Salmon. Groundcherry remains came from both the Primary and Secondary occupations, for a total representation in 26 of 64 strata (see Table 36.3); 4 of 19 Primary strata and 22 of 45 Secondary strata revealed groundcherry remains. A number of groundcherry seeds and berries have been labeled *Physalis longifolia* type, although other seeds may represent other groundcherry species.

The genus *Physalis* is composed of annual or perennial herbs that occupy a diversity of habitats (Kearney and Peebles 1960:754–755). *Physalis longifolia* has been observed growing near Salmon along modern irrigation ditches (K. Adams 1976), though it has also been found elsewhere in the Southwest in dry habitats such as prairies, plains, and deserts (Correll and Johnston 1970: 1390). This species is a perennial, and often spreads by creeping rootstocks or a deep rhizome (Kearney and Peebles 1960:754; Correll and Johnston 1970:1390). The many-seeded, smooth, edible berries, which generally mature by early July near Salmon Ruin, resemble tiny tomatoes enclosed in papery bracts (calyx), and are reminiscent of Japanese lanterns.

It is not known whether some of the unburned groundcherry seeds recovered from four Secondary trash strata open to sunlight in prehistory may have originated from plants growing on the middens. Recent observations in the San Juan Valley have not found groundcherry to be particularly weedy in nature (K. Adams 1976), and the fact that perennials have a much longer life cycle than annuals might tend to discourage perennial establishment in a trash heap regularly blanketed by new loads of debris. The chances of accidental transport of the relatively heavy groundcherry fruit to the pueblo seem remote, as the berry containing the seeds is rather large and smooth, inside its nonadherent papery calyx.

The evidence that groundcherry was eaten in prehistory is based upon its distribution in floor and trash strata of both occupations, as well as upon the parched or carbonized condition of some of the specimens in otherwise unburned strata. The burned condition seems somewhat puzzling, however, when one considers the difficulty in, or reason for, parching a tiny tomato. It seems that these fruits should be eaten whole, or perhaps split in half to dry in the sun, instead of being processed near a fire. One interpretation is that some of the burned groundcherry remains from hearths on two Secondary habitation floors in Room 93W (H-1-14 and H-2-22) were food offerings to gods; modern puebloans have been known to offer bits of food to their deities by tossing these bits into the fireplace before eating (K. Adams 1980:54–55; see Chapter 39). Likewise, a Primary habitation floor (101W, H-1-9) contained parched or carbonized groundcherry seeds. Burned seeds and berries recovered from the hearth and seeds from the floor of a Secondary kiva (6A, H-1-5.2) suggest a religious use. The presence of burned seeds on two unburned Secondary featureless floors (51W, H-1-5 and 58W, H-2-11) and one Primary featureless floor (89W, H-1-8/I-1-9) may reflect storage of groundcherry in prehistory, or some other use we fail to recognize. The fact that groundcherry was actually eaten has been documented in fecal remains from the Secondary occupation.

The archaeological record indicates that ground-cherry was rather commonly harvested by both Primary and Secondary occupants of Salmon Pueblo. The Salmon residents were probably able to find groundcherry plants in the area regularly, although whether the plants were restricted to moist habitats as in modern times is unknown. If *Physalis* had become established in prehistoric agricultural fields, farmers working the soil with digging sticks might break creeping rootstocks, and actually foster an increase in abundance, thus reaping an extra reward for one's agricultural labors.

Tule Springs Unknown

A disseminule labeled Tule Springs Unknown[*] is evident in 25 of 64 separate strata at Salmon Ruin; for this reason it is considered common in ancient strata. The item has never been clearly established as having a floral or faunal nature. It has been suggested that this disseminule may represent some type of termite or ant feces (K. Adams 1980:56), but this should be considered a working hypothesis only. The fact that some of the specimens have been burned is consistent with such an interpretation, if wood carried to the pueblo as firewood were infested with insects. To shed light on this problem, insect nests found in juniper (*Juniperus*) logs should be examined for associated material, as a preliminary study revealed that juniper was burned in a number of Salmon fire hearths. However, such an explanation would not account for all of the evidence at Salmon. For example, the recovery of parched or carbonized Tule Springs Unknown disseminules on unburned floors without hearths (Primary floors 30W, H-2-12; 56W, H-1-5; Secondary floor 58W, H-2-11) does not readily explain how the disseminules were burned. More than 300 Tule Springs Unknowns altered by fire came from a Primary habitation room (101W, H-1-9). Such evidence promotes the explanation that this item was a food resource at Salmon. Broad distribution of other items on floors and in trash of both occupations has been interpreted to imply food use at Salmon Pueblo; the Tule Springs Unknown is likewise broadly distributed. Specimens that reveal parching or carbonization may reflect a preparation step. Other explanations may eventually be advanced, but at present the best interpretation seems to be that it served as a food resource of some sort.

---

[*]Editor's note. After this chapter was written, the Tule Springs Unknowns were identified as termite fecal pellets (Adams 1984). Since these items are no longer interpreted as a food, the remainder of this chapter has been adjusted accordingly.

Sedge

Although individual members of the sedge (Cyperaceae) family have been identified in few Salmon strata, together sedge representatives appear in 23 of 64 locations examined in this study (see Table 36.3). Three genera and two species have been recognized, including *Carex*, *Eleocharis montana* type, and *Scirpus acutus* type. Specimens labeled as Cyperaceae could presumably represent any number of genera. *Scirpus* is the most frequently occurring taxon, found on one of the six Primary floors and 5 of the 22 Secondary floors, as well as in trash from both occupations. Some of these seeds were thought to closely match modern specimens of *Scirpus acutus*. Seeds labeled as Cyperaceae were identified on Primary and Secondary floors and in limited Secondary trash units. *Eleocharis montana* type and *Carex* disseminules came from a Primary floor and three Secondary trash locations, respectively.

Sedges are water-loving plants generally found along riverbanks or in other moist places (Kearney and Peebles 1960:145–164). *Scirpus*, *Eleocharis montana*, and *Carex* are all perennial members of this family, and species of *Scirpus* and *Eleocharis* have recently been located along nearby banks of the San Juan River (K. Adams 1976). The achenes of these plants are generally triangular, often with a smooth or slightly reticulate coat. As plants of water-saturated habitats, they would be more likely to regularly produce flowers and fruits than some of their terrestrial neighbors. The generally inconspicuous flowers of Cyperaceae are well adapted to wind pollination.

Accidental introduction of Cyperaceae achenes into Salmon Pueblo is rather unlikely; the lack of suitable wet habitats on and around the edges of the pueblo would discourage growth of the plants. Also, the rather slick achenes have no accompanying appendages that ensure transport by adhesion to man or animals. Therefore, sedge disseminules were likely brought into Salmon Ruin by humans.

The evidence that sedges were eaten by Salmon residents is best represented by the *Scirpus* remains. They are from a Primary floor and trash unit, as well as five Secondary floor and trash deposits (see Table 36.4). *Scirpus* achenes were designated as burned in three separate unburned strata; these specimens may reflect prehistoric preparation of the seeds for storage or consumption. Achenes recovered from a Secondary habitation floor (93W, H-1-14) suggest a food use, whereas those found on an unburned Secondary featureless floor (51W, H-1-5) may indicate storage. Achenes found in trash would be expected to represent items spilled during food preparation or consumption. The recovery of three *Scirpus acutus* type achenes in the niche of a Secondary kiva (124A, H-1-6/I-1-7) may reflect the use of sedge in medicinal or ceremonial rites. Small amounts of *Scirpus* pollen identified from various locations at Salmon (K. Adams 1980:38; K. Adams, Chapter 39; Doebley 1976:31) may be due entirely to the natural action of breezes.

Carex achenes were recovered from three Secondary trash strata; they had been burned in two of the strata. Cyperaceae stems have been identified from Salmon Ruin (Sample 037W2024), so the achenes may have been accidentally carried into the pueblo with the raw materials needed for making household goods (Doebley 1976:30). Such an explanation does not account for the burned condition of the specimens, however. An alternative explanation would be that *Carex* was carried to Salmon as food, and achenes burned during preparation eventually became part of trash deposits in Secondary times. The *Eleocharis montana* type specimen, which came from a single Primary habitation floor (101W, H-1-9), is by itself weak evidence for the use of this particular resource. Coupled with the unidentified sedge remains, however, one envisions that a number of members of the Cyperaceae, in addition to *Scirpus* and *Carex*, were known by Salmon residents.

Nine centuries ago, streambanks along the nearby San Juan River probably provided ideal habitats for the Cyperaceae to thrive, just as they do today. Members of this family likely offered a dependable yearly seed resource, as long as no significant lowering of the river occurred. For Salmon occupants, such dependability in an often undependable arid climate would undoubtedly have been important.

Summary

Numerous lines of evidence converge to indicate that seeds of both goosefoot/amaranth (Cheno-Am) and purslane were used repeatedly for food by Salmon residents of the Primary and Secondary occupations. These seed types were widely distributed in flotation samples, and many of the specimens were recognized as parched or carbonized in otherwise unburned strata. The presence of these taxa in a number of specific archaeological contexts, such as room floors, trash, and fecal remains, seems highly suggestive of food use. Also, the likelihood of either prehistoric or modern accidental introduction was deemed low except in the Secondary trash strata open to sunlight during accretion. Plants in the Cheno-Am group are weedy opportunists, and in drought-free years abundant stands would occur in disturbed habitats surrounding a pueblo. As long as the rains came, new seedlings would sprout, providing greens, and mature seeds would be harvestable for food throughout the summer. It seems that Cheno-Am seeds were abundant enough to be set aside in a corrugated vessel in at least one storeroom at Salmon. The high frequency of purslane seeds in Salmon strata is somewhat puzzling, as this is not a resource that humans could depend upon today; erratic moisture regimes in the arid Southwest cause wide yearly fluctuations in abundance. Its seeds generally do not mature until the early fall. But in years of inadequate cultivated crops, Salmon residents could possibly have relied upon this fall-ripening native plant.

A number of taxa are not as ubiquitous in Salmon strata as Cheno-Am and *Portulaca*, yet similar lines of evidence suggest common use. Included in this group are grasses (Gramineae), tansy-mustard (*Descurainia*), cacti (Cactaceae), a spurge (*Euphorbia glyptosperma* type), groundcherry (*Physalis*), and members of the sedge (Cyperaceae) family. For some of these taxa, seeds recovered from Secondary trash middens open to sunlight during midden buildup are considered possible incidental introductions. In the bulk of the remaining cases, however, evidence such as the archaeological context(s), the parched or carbonized condition of the specimens, and their common distribution in a variety of strata types provides strong evidence of intentional use by Salmon residents. Among the grasses, Indian ricegrass (*Oryzopsis hymenoides*) and dropseed (*Sporobolus*) seem to have been brought often to the pueblo as food. Indian ricegrass grains were recovered from floors and found burned in trash, and also came from a possible storeroom. The relatively large size of this grain type would heighten its usefulness as a late spring native crop, especially if food stores had been depleted during winter months. The ricegrass specimens appearing parched or carbonized in six separate Secondary trash strata are the best evidence that this grass was eaten at Salmon. Evidence is only tentative that muhly was used in Secondary times, and the recovery of unburned Paniceae grains may relate to a use other than food. The presence of unidentified grass parts, plus bracts of Indian ricegrass, hints that some of the grass grains may have been threshed from accompanying chaff within the pueblo itself. That tansy-mustard (*Descurainia*) provided a spring-ripening food can be seen in the broad distribution of its seeds in Salmon Ruin, coupled with the parched or carbonized condition of specimens in unburned strata. However, tansy-mustard is like the purslane in that it seems somewhat undependable.

Again, it is surprising that what we regard as an unreliable native resource was so common in Salmon strata.

Various cacti were also eaten in prehistory. Fleshy hedgehog fruits were brought into the pueblo by Primary and Secondary occupants, and some seeds were discarded in trash deposits or became ground into room floor surfaces. *Echinocereus* pollen on seven floors also attests to the use of this genus. Seeds of a fleshy-fruited prickly pear (Platyopuntia) were eaten, and presumably vegetative pads were eaten too. A dry-fruited *Sclerocactus*, and perhaps other unidentified Cactaceae, add to the list of cacti known to Salmon residents. Although transport by adherence may have been partly responsible for the presence of some of the seeds of the normally poisonous spurge family in Salmon strata, there is evidence that *Euphorbia glyptosperma* type seeds were eaten. Whether this particular plant, or its seed, is poisonous to humans is not known. However, the broad distribution of this seed type on floors, a high seed concentration in a kiva milling bin, and the parched or carbonized condition of many specimens in otherwise unburned strata, all converge to suggest that people purposefully brought the resource to the pueblo for food. The naturally weedy habit of this plant could allow it to provide abundant seeds under favorable conditions.

Groundcherry (*Physalis*) fruit was common in the pueblo throughout its history. The plants were probably locally available in prehistory, as they are today, perhaps even fostered by soil disturbance in agricultural fields. The broad distribution of groundcherry seeds and a few berries on floors and in trash strata of both occupations implies food use, and the recovery of seeds in fecal remains provides confirmation. However, the parched or carbonized condition of some of the specimens is not as easily understood. Rather than reflecting a preparation technique, these burned specimens may represent food offerings to deities. Finally, it seems that members of the water-loving sedge (Cyperaceae) family were also known in prehistory. *Scirpus* was eaten, stored, and possibly used as a medicinal or ceremonial item. *Carex* was also eaten, as were other members of the sedge family. These plants prefer to grow in water-logged habitats, and the banks of the San Juan River would have been ideal for their growth. As riparian taxa, they may have been quite dependable from year to year.

Variety is a key characteristic of the native plants brought to Salmon Pueblo by its residents. Native plant foods ranged from the dependable perennial cacti to the fickle tansy-mustard and purslane, so closely dependent on seasonal moisture. Plants spanned the frost-free growing season, beginning with the spring-ripe tansy-mustard and stretching to the fall-ripe purslane. In the summers of drought-free years, opportunistic plants such as those in the Cheno-Am group provided edible greens with each new rain of the summer, as well as a continual supply of maturing seeds. Hedgehog cactus offered large fleshy fruits, just as the tiny seeds of purslane, tansy-mustard, and dropseed were gathered. The ancient residents of Salmon Pueblo capitalized on the variety offered by surrounding native plants, and relied upon many of them to a great extent for subsistence.

Chapter 37

PLANT REMAINS FROM TRASH DEPOSITS AT SALMON PUEBLO

by John F. Doebley

The study of archaeological plant remains from a site can contribute to our understanding of its former occupants in several ways.* The identification of remains provides a partial inventory of plants once useful in fulfilling the nutritional, medicinal, ceremonial, and material cultural needs of the inhabitants. In addition, analyses of temporal and spatial distributions of plant remains may provide insights regarding changes in plant use through time and the location of activity areas within the site.

In an effort to gain such insights about the prehistoric inhabitants of Salmon Ruin, we conducted a study of some of the plants they left behind. Salmon Ruin is a large Puebloan site (three stories, estimated 250–300 rooms) located in the San Juan River valley in northwestern New Mexico, about 75 km north of Chaco Canyon. Dendrochronological dates reveal that the inhabitants erected Salmon Ruin between AD 1088 and 1094. Further, architectural and pottery styles suggest that construction of the pueblo took place under the influence of Chacoan peoples. However, by the early thirteenth century changes in pottery types and architectural modifications indicate both a waning of Chacoan influence and the emergence of new ties to the Mesa Verde area about 80 km to the north. In the late thirteenth century this second tradition at Salmon Ruin ended with abandonment, and the site was never reoccupied.

This chapter summarizes a 1976 study of plant remains (primarily seeds) recovered by water flotation of soil samples from trash deposits (Doebley 1976). The results include a partial inventory of plants once useful to the inhabitants, an assessment of the most widely used plants of those recovered, and a look at the changing nature of plant use through time at the site.

METHODOLOGY

The flotation samples used in this study were processed using procedures outlined by Bohrer and

Adams (1977). All material recovered from water flotation was examined under a binocular microscope (12–60x) and plant remains present were identified and recorded. The identification of taxa rested primarily on comparisons with local modern materials for which voucher specimens have been deposited in the University of Arizona Herbarium. Several publications were also employed in identification (Hermann 1970; Martin and Barkley 1961; Musil 1963).

Forty-one flotation samples from trash were selected to represent several kinds of known spatial and temporal variation at the site. Thus, samples represented rooms and the plaza area, different room types such as kivas and habitation rooms, interior rooms and rooms opening into the plaza, and all time periods. Since variation introduced by rodents transporting plant materials was unwelcome, rodent-disturbed areas were avoided.

After identifying the plant materials, the next step was to determine, if possible, how they came to be deposited at the site. Seeds that are modern in appearance, or members of taxa known to be post-Columbian (modern) introductions to the New World (for example, *Sisymbrium altissimum*, tumble mustard) may be considered contaminants. Carbonized, crushed, or parched seeds, on the other hand, are more likely to owe their presence to a cultural activity such as plant processing.

Seeds of unknown age and unaltered condition are difficult to interpret. When such seeds are randomly distributed between the cultural strata and the noncultural overburden that blankets the site, or are limited to the latter, they may be assumed to be contaminants. If, however, they occur exclusively or almost so in occupational strata, as do the seeds of *Physalis*, *Scirpus*, *Descurainia*, and *Euphorbia glyptosperma* at Salmon Ruin, then they may be treated as prehistoric (Bohrer and Adams 1977; Gasser 1979). Considering such seeds as prehistoric seems justified because if the wind blew these specimens into the ruin (as "seed rain"), one would expect them to be well represented not only in the cultural strata, but

* Reprinted (with minor editing) with permission from *The Kiva* 46(3):169–187, 1981.

in the noncultural overburden as well. Further, logic predicts that a seed rain would deposit all types of easily transported disseminules, including some without known ethnographic uses. Yet, in the flotation samples discussed here, nearly 100 percent of the seeds identified have known archaeobotanical uses, with the exception of a few modern contaminants. For these reasons it seems likely that most of these seeds are in fact cultural artifacts. The situation is undoubtedly different at other sites (Gasser 1979; Kirkpatrick and Ford 1977).

Even after plant remains have been identified as prehistoric, one still needs to be as certain as possible that they were recovered from their final prehistoric place of deposition and that they have not been redeposited within the site due to excavation or rodent activity. This consideration holds especially true when tabulating comparisons between the two major occupations. For this reason plaza samples, which contain many recognizable modern contaminants and thus could also contain unrecognizable ones (redeposited prehistoric seeds), were excluded from such comparisons. Samples from rodent-disturbed areas were avoided, although some rodent-disturbed areas were inadvertently sampled, as indicated by apparent rodent feces in 17 of 41 samples. These 17 samples contain no recognizable contaminants, so rodents were apparently not introducing foreign plant material. Perhaps the rodents occupied the ruin at the same time people did, and subsisted on the garbage discarded by these people. Ancient Pueblo towns are known to have had rodent occupations contemporary with human ones (Kelley 1975:83).

Having established which plant materials are probably bona fide archaeological specimens, one can infer the prehistoric use of these remains by considering four kinds of information: (1) the condition of the specimen may indicate its use (for example, items may have been carbonized while cooked or parched for storage); (2) the context in which the specimen was found may provide insights as to how it was employed (for example, items found in trash strata should be waste products); (3) analogies drawn from historically known uses may be suggestive of the role the plant played in prehistory; and (4) analogies drawn from known uses at other archaeological sites may be employed.

RESULTS

The number and condition of each taxonomic entity are listed by flotation sample in Table 37.1. Two terms used in this table require explanation.

The first is "Cheno Am," a hybrid category that combines the two genera *Chenopodium* and *Amaranthus*, whose seeds are often difficult to distinguish. The second term is "type," which informs the reader that the item resembles the taxon named, but may also resemble other taxa (Bohrer and Adams 1977:69). Such an item may be so similar to modern comparative material of the same taxonomic category that it cannot be distinguished. However, because of the considerable overlap in seed morphology between some groups, one should not assume that the type represents that taxon alone.

DISCUSSION

Interpretation of Use

As previously mentioned, the prehistoric role of the remains can be inferred by considering condition, context, and historically and archaeologically known uses. Applying these sources of information, I have inferred (where possible) uses for the plant remains recovered (Table 37.2). As space limitations do not allow a discussion of the reasons for the suggested function of each taxon, an abstracted reason or reference accompanies Table 37.2. A more detailed discussion of the reasons for each interpreted use may be found elsewhere (Doebley 1976).

The inferred function for most taxa is as food. This is not surprising, as the majority of these taxa are represented by seeds and fruits (achenes), which contain stored nutrients intended to nourish the developing plant embryo. Humans, of course, may intervene and reap the benefits of these stored nutrients for themselves. Furthermore, ethnobotanical reports give the impression that although roots, flowers, pollen, and stems may play a variety of roles in a culture, seeds are employed almost exclusively as food (Cook 1930; Robbins et al. 1916; Stevenson 1915; Swank 1932; Whiting 1939).

Another important point is that the taxa shown in Table 37.1 ripen at different times of the growing season. Some, such as *Oryzopsis hymenoides, Descurainia,* and *Mentzelia albicaulis,* mature their seeds in the late spring or early summer. Others, including *Cleome, Chenopodium* and *Physalis,* generally grow abundantly from July through August, although these three genera, in addition to *Amaranthus, Cycloloma,* and *Yucca baccata,* may continue to produce seeds and fruits late into the fall. This suggests that wild plant gathering was an activity of considerable economic importance and not merely a means for these agricultural people to survive during times of scarcity (Hill 1938).

Table 37.1. Plant remains recovered by flotation from Salmon Ruin. Unless otherwise specified all taxa are represented by disseminules (seeds, achenes, caryopses, or nutlets) or parts thereof. Scientific names follow Kearney and Peebles (1960).

Room or Plaza Area Room Sample Number	6W[1] 24	6W 33	30W 1028	30W 1033	30W 1035	31W 1040	31W 1045	31W 1047
Amaranthus type	1	–	–	–	–	1	–	–
Anemopsis californica type	–	–	–	–	–	–	–	–
Boraginaceae unknown (involucre)	–	–	–	–	–	–	–	–
Capparidaceae unknown	–	–	–	–	–	–	–	–
Carex type	–	–	–	–	–	–	–	–
Cheno Am	2C	21C	7C	10C	4	121CD	58CD	4D
Chenopodium type	–	–	–	–	–	–	7	–
Chenopodium watsonii type	–	–	–	–	–	frag	–	–
Cleome	–	–	–	–	–	–	–	–
Compositae unknown	–	–	–	–	–	–	–	–
Cryptantha (involucre)	–	–	–	–	–	–	–	–
Cucurbita	–	–	–	–	–	–	–	–
Cycloma atriplicifolium type	–	–	–	–	2	–	–	–
Cyperaceae unknown	–	–	–	–	–	–	–	–
Descurainia type	–	1	–	–	–	2	–	–
Desmodium type	–	–	–	–	–	–	–	–
Echinocereus fendleri type	–	–	–	–	–	–	–	–
Euphorbia glyptosperma type	–	–	–	–	–	–	–	–
Gramineae unknown	–	–	2C	1C	–	–	–	–
Juniperus	–	–	–	–	–	–	–	–
Leguminosae unknown	–	–	–	–	–	–	–	–
Lycium	–	–	–	–	–	–	1	–
Malvaceae unknown	–	–	–	–	–	–	–	–
Mentzelia albicaulis type	–	–	–	–	–	–	1	–
Oryzopsis hymenoides type	1C	–	–	–	–	–	–	–
Paniceae (tribe)	–	–	–	–	–	–	–	–
Physalis type	1C	1CD	–	–	–	–	–	–
Pinus edulis (testa)	–	–	–	–	–	–	–	–
Polanisia	–	–	–	–	–	–	–	–
Polygonum type	–	–	–	–	–	–	–	–
Polygonum persicaria type	–	–	–	–	–	–	–	–
Portulaca	1	2CD	–	–	–	31D	12D	1C
Prosopis pubescens type	–	–	–	–	–	–	–	–
Prunus	–	–	–	–	–	–	–	frag
Rhus trilobata type	1C	–	–	–	–	–	–	–
Salsola kali (leaf)	–	–	–	–	–	–	–	–
Salvia reflexa type	–	–	–	–	–	–	–	–
Scirpus acutus type	–	–	–	–	–	–	9CD	–
Sisymbrium altissimum type	–	–	–	–	–	–	–	–
Solanaceae unkonown	1	–	–	–	–	–	–	–
Sporobolus type	–	–	–	–	–	–	–	–
Trianthema portulacastrum type	–	–	–	–	–	–	–	–
Yucca baccata	–	–	–	–	–	–	–	–
Zea mays[2]	–	2C	–	–	–	3C	1C	2C
Undetermined disseminules	–	–	–	–	–	–	–	–
Number 1	–	–	–	–	–	–	–	–
Number 2	–	–	–	–	–	–	–	–
Number 3	–	–	–	–	–	–	–	–
Number 8036	–	1C	1C	1C	1	6C	–	44P
Number 8063	–	–	–	–	–	–	–	–
Number 8066	–	–	–	–	–	–	–	–
Unknowns	–	–	–	–	–	–	–	–
Ovary	–	–	–	–	–	–	–	–
Pistil	–	–	–	–	–	1	–	–
Floral parts	–	–	–	–	–	–	–	–
Total number of wild taxa (excluding contaminants)[3]	5	5	3	3	3	6	5	4

Table 37.1 (continued)

Room or Plaza Area Room Sample Number	33W 2038	93W 21	93W 22	93W 1025	93W 1029	101W 2046	All Rooms
Amaranthus type	–	–	–	–	–	–	2
Anemopsis californica type	–	–	–	–	–	–	0
Boraginaceae unknown (involucre)	–	–	–	–	–	–	0
Capparidaceae unknown	–	–	–	–	–	1	1
Carex type	–	–	–	–	–	–	0
Cheno Am	3D	4CD	8CD	4CD	73CD	23CD	342
Chenopodium type	4	–	–	–	–	–	11
Chenopodium watsonii type	–	–	–	–	–	–	F
Cleome	–	–	–	1C	–	–	1
Compositae unknown	–	–	–	–	–	–	0
Cryptantha (involucre)	–	–	–	–	–	–	0
Cucurbita	–	–	–	–	–	–	0
Cycloma atriplicifolium type	–	–	–	–	–	–	2
Cyperaceae unknown	–	–	–	–	–	–	0
Descurainia type	–	–	–	–	–	2	5
Desmodium type	–	–	–	–	–	–	0
Echinocereus fendleri type	–	–	–	–	–	–	0
Euphoria glyptosperma type	–	1P	9	32	70D	–	112
Gramineae unknown	–	1C	1C	–	1C	–	6
Juniperus	–	–	–	–	–	–	0
Leguminosae unknown	–	–	–	–	–	–	0
Lycium	–	–	–	–	–	–	1
Malvaceae unknown	–	–	–	–	–	–	0
Mentzelia albicaulis type	–	–	–	–	–	–	1
Oryzopsis hymenoides type	–	–	–	–	–	–	1
Paniceae (tribe)	–	–	–	–	–	–	0
Physalis type	–	–	–	–	–	–	2
Pinus edulis (testa)	–	–	–	–	–	–	0
Polanisia	–	–	–	–	–	1D	1
Polygonum type	–	–	–	–	–	–	0
Polygonum persicaria type	–	–	–	–	–	–	0
Portulaca	7	1	–	1D	140CD	16	196
Prosopis pubescens type	–	–	–	–	–	–	0
Prunus	–	–	–	–	–	–	F
Rhus trilobata type	–	–	–	–	–	–	1
Salsola kali (leaf)	–	–	–	–	–	–	0
Salvia reflexa type	–	–	–	–	–	–	0
Scirpus acutus type	–	–	–	–	–	–	9
Sisymbrium altissimum type	–	–	–	–	–	–	0
Solanaceae unknown	–	–	–	–	–	–	1
Sporobolus type	–	–	–	–	–	–	0
Trianthema portulacastrum type	–	–	–	–	–	12CF	12
Yucca baccata	–	–	–	–	–	–	0
Zea mays	–	1C	–	1C	1C	–	11
Undetermined disseminules	–	–	–	–	–	–	–
Number 1	–	–	–	–	–	–	0
Number 2	–	–	–	–	–	–	0
Number 3	–	–	–	–	–	–	0
Number 8036	–	–	–	–	–	7	61
Number 8063	–	–	–	–	–	–	0
Number 8066	1C	–	–	–	–	–	1
Unknowns	–	–	–	–	–	–	–
Ovary	–	–	–	–	–	–	0
Pistil	–	–	–	–	–	–	1
Floral parts	–	1	–	–	1	–	2
Total number of wild taxa (excluding contaminants)	3	4	3	4	5	6	19

Table 37.1 (continued)

Room or Plaza Area Room Sample Number	6W 4	6W 6	6W 12	0.54 1015	0.54 1024	0.58333 2016	0.58333 2019	0.66667 2011
Amaranthus type	–	–	–	–	–	–	–	–
Anemopsis californica type	–	–	–	–	–	–	–	–
Boraginaceae unknown type	–	–	–	–	1M	–	–	–
Capparidaceae unknown	–	–	frag	–	–	–	–	–
Carex type	–	–	–	–	–	–	–	–
Cheno Am	5CD	7CD	3CD	–	8CD	1D	9D	7D
Chenopodium type	–	–	–	–	–	–	–	–
Chenopodium watsonii type	–	–	–	–	–	–	–	–
Cleome	–	–	–	–	–	–	–	–
Compositae unknown	–	–	–	–	–	–	–	–
Cryptantha (involucre)	–	–	–	1M	–	–	–	–
Cucurbita	–	–	–	–	–	–	–	1
Cycloma atriplicifolium type	–	–	–	–	–	–	–	–
Cyperaceae unknown	2C	–	–	–	–	–	–	–
Descurainia type	–	–	–	–	–	1	–	–
Desmodium type	–	–	–	–	–	–	–	–
Echinocereus fendleri type	–	–	–	–	–	1D	5	–
Euphorbia glyptoperma type	–	–	–	–	56	2	2	–
Gramineae unknown	–	–	4C	3C	1C	–	1C	–
Juniperus	–	–	–	–	–	–	–	–
Leguminosae unknown	–	–	–	–	–	–	–	–
Lycium	–	–	–	–	–	–	–	–
Malvaceae unknown	–	–	–	–	–	–	–	1
Mentzelia albicaulis type	1C	–	–	–	–	–	–	–
Oryzopsis hymenoides type	–	–	–	–	–	–	1C	–
Paniceae (tribe)	–	–	–	–	–	–	–	–
Physalis type	–	–	–	–	–	–	–	–
Pinus edulis (testa)	–	–	–	–	–	–	–	–
Polanisia	–	–	–	–	–	–	–	–
Polygonum type	–	–	–	–	–	–	–	–
Polygonum persicaria type	–	–	–	–	–	–	1D	–
Portulaca	–	–	1	–	23D	–	6D	2
Prosopis pubescens type	–	–	–	–	–	–	–	–
Prunus	–	–	–	–	–	–	–	–
Rhus trilobata type	1C	–	–	–	–	–	–	1D
Salsola kali (leaf)	–	–	–	–	–	–	–	–
Salvia reflexa type	–	–	–	–	–	–	–	–
Scirpus acutus type	–	–	–	–	–	–	–	–
Sisymbrium altissimum type	–	–	–	–	–	–	1M	–
Solanaceae unknown	–	frag	–	–	–	–	–	–
Sporobolus type	–	1C	–	–	–	–	–	–
Trianthema portulacastrum type	–	–	–	–	–	1D	–	–
Yucca baccata	–	–	–	–	–	–	–	–
Zea mays	15C	frags	88C	17C	2C	–	–	–
Undetermined disseminules	–	–	–	–	–	–	–	–
Number 1	–	–	–	–	–	–	–	–
Number 2	–	–	–	–	–	–	1C	–
Number 3	–	–	–	–	–	–	–	–
Number 8036	–	1C	–	–	2C	–	–	–
Number 8063	–	–	–	–	–	–	–	1
Number 8066	–	–	–	–	–	–	–	–
Unknowns								
Ovary	–	–	–	–	–	–	–	–
Pistil	–	–	–	–	–	–	–	–
Floral parts	–	–	–	–	–	–	–	–
Total number of wild taxa (excluding contaminants)	4	4	4	1	5	5	7	5

Table 37.1 (continued)

Room or Plaza Area Room Sample Number	17P 2010	33W 1002	36W 2007	36W 2013	37A 1022	37W 1022	37W 2036	37W 2042
Amaranthus type	–	–	1	–	–	1	–	–
Anemopsis californica type	–	–	–	–	–	–	1D	–
Boraginaceae unknown type	–	–	–	–	–	–	–	–
Carex type	1C	–	2C	–	–	–	–	–
Cheno Am	3C	109D	14C	40	66CD	28C	10D	23D
Chenopodium type	–	–	–	–	–	–	–	–
Chenopodium watsonii type	–	–	–	–	–	–	–	–
Cleome	1DF	–	–	–	–	–	1	–
Compositae unknown	–	–	–	–	2	–	–	–
Cryptantha (involucre)	–	–	–	–	–	–	–	–
Cucurbita	–	–	–	–	–	–	2	–
Cycloma atriplicifolium type	–	2	–	–	–	–	15D	3
Cyperaceae unknown	–	–	–	–	–	–	–	–
Descurainia type	–	–	–	–	–	–	–	1C
Desmodium type	–	–	–	1	–	–	–	–
Echinocereus fendleri type	–	1	16F	–	–	–	–	–
Euphorbia glyptoperma type	1	–	–	–	–	–	–	–
Gramineae unknown	–	1C	–	–	–	–	–	–
Juniperus	–	–	–	–	–	–	–	–
Leguminosae unknown	–	–	–	–	–	–	–	–
Lycium	–	–	–	–	–	–	–	–
Malvaceae unknown	1	–	–	–	1C	–	–	–
Mentzelia albicaulis type	–	–	–	–	–	–	–	–
Oryzopsis hymenoides type	–	–	15CDF	9C	12CD	–	–	–
Paniceae (tribe)	–	–	frags	frags	–	–	–	–
Physalis type	1	2D	–	6CD	–	–	1	1
Pinus edulis (testa)	–	–	–	–	–	–	–	–
Polanisia	–	–	–	–	–	–	–	–
Polygonum type	–	–	–	–	–	–	1	–
Polygonum persicaria type	–	–	–	–	–	–	–	–
Portulaca	1	4D	1	1	3C	2	1	–
Prosopis pubescens type	–	–	–	–	–	–	–	–
Prunus	–	–	–	–	–	–	–	–
Rhus trilobata type	–	–	2CD	–	–	–	1	–
Salsola kali (leaf)	–	–	–	–	–	–	–	–
Salvia reflexa type	–	–	2C	–	–	–	–	–
Scirpus acutus type	–	1	–	4	–	4	1	–
Sisymbrium altissimum type	16M	–	–	–	–	–	–	–
Solanaceae unknown	–	–	3	–	–	–	–	–
Sporobolus type	1C	–	–	–	–	–	–	–
Trianthema portulacastrum type	–	–	4	–	–	–	–	–
Yucca baccata	–	–	–	1C	–	1C	–	–
Zea mays	1C	–	–	1C	1C	–	1C	–
Undetermined disseminules	–	–	–	–	–	–	–	–
Number 1	–	–	–	–	–	–	–	–
Number 2	–	–	–	–	–	–	–	–
Number 3	–	–	–	–	–	–	–	–
Number 8036	–	1C	–	–	–	–	1	–
Number 8063	–	1	2	–	–	–	1	–
Number 8066	–	3	–	1	3	–	5	–
Unknowns	–	–	–	–	–	–	–	–
Ovary	–	–	–	–	–	–	–	–
Pistil	–	–	–	–	–	–	–	–
Floral parts	–	–	–	–	–	–	–	–
Total number of wild taxa (excluding contaminants)	8	10	12	8	7	4	11	5

Table 37.1 (continued)

Room or Plaza Area Room Sample Number	58W 2037	62A 21	62W 1151	62W 1154	62W 2092	93W 19	93W 1002	93W 1008
Amaranthus type	–	–	–	2	–	–	–	–
Anemopsis californica type	–	1	–	–	–	–	–	–
Boraginaceae unknown type	–	–	–	–	–	–	–	–
Capparidaceae unknown	–	–	–	–	–	–	frag	–
Carex type	–	–	–	–	–	1C	–	–
Cheno Am	269D	21CD	7C	52	97D	3CD	29CD	9FCD
Chenopodium type	3	–	–	1	–	–	–	–
Chenopodium watsonii type	–	–	–	–	–	–	–	–
Cleome	–	–	–	1	1F	–	–	–
Compositae unknown	–	–	–	–	–	–	–	–
Cryptantha (involucre)	–	–	–	–	–	–	–	–
Cucurbita	–	–	–	1F	1F	–	–	–
Cycloma atriplicifolium type	6D	1	–	3D	32DF	–	–	–
Cyperaceae unknown	–	–	–	1C	–	–	–	–
Descurainia type	3	–	–	–	–	–	3	–
Desmodium type	–	–	–	–	–	–	–	–
Echinocereus fendleri type	9D	–	1C	1F	1	–	–	–
Euphorbia glyptoperma type	1	1	–	–	–	–	–	1
Gramineae unknown	–	1C	1C	1C	–	1C	2C	–
Juniperus	–	–	1	5	–	–	–	–
Leguminosae unknown	–	–	–	1	–	–	–	–
Lycium	–	–	–	–	–	–	–	–
Malvaceae unknown	–	–	–	–	–	–	–	–
Mentzelia albicaulis type	5C	2	–	–	–	–	–	–
Oryzopsis hymenoides type	–	–	–	2C	13C	–	–	–
Paniceae (tribe)	–	–	–	–	–	–	frags	–
Physalis type	6	2DF	2C	8C	10	–	–	1CD
Pinus edulis (testa)	–	–	–	frag	–	–	–	–
Polanisia	–	–	–	–	–	–	–	–
Polygonum type	–	–	–	–	–	–	–	–
Polygonum persicaria type	–	–	–	–	–	–	–	–
Portulaca	41D	3C	–	8	40	2D	30	1C
Prosopis pubescens type	–	–	–	–	–	–	frags	–
Prunus	–	–	–	–	–	–	–	–
Rhus trilobata type	–	–	4CD	–	–	–	–	–
Salsola kali (leaf)	–	–	–	–	–	–	1M	–
Salvia reflexa type	–	–	–	–	–	–	–	–
Scirpus acutus type	1	–	–	–	–	–	1	–
Sisymbrium altissimum type	–	–	–	–	–	–	–	–
Solanaceae unknown	–	–	–	–	–	–	–	–
Sporobolus type	–	1C	1C	–	–	–	1C	–
Trianthema portulacastrum type	–	–	–	–	–	–	–	–
Yucca baccata	–	–	–	–	–	–	–	–
Zea mays	1C	–	17C	–	1C	–	–	1C
Undetermined disseminules	–	–	–	–	–	–	–	–
Number 1	–	1	–	–	–	–	–	–
Number 2	–	–	1	–	–	–	–	–
Number 3	–	–	–	–	–	–	–	–
Number 8036	1	1	–	1C	–	–	–	–
Number 8063	2	–	–	–	–	–	–	–
Number 8066	–	5	–	9	2	–	–	–
Unknowns	–	–	–	–	–	–	–	–
Ovary	–	–	–	–	–	–	1	–
Pistil	–	–	–	–	–	–	–	–
Floral parts	–	–	–	–	–	–	–	–
Total number of wild taxa (excluding contaminants)	11	11	7	13	9	4	10	3

Table 37.1 (continued)

Room or Plaza Area Room Sample Number	93W 1015	93W 1017	119W 1043	All Rooms	All Samples, Except Room 62 & Plaza Area
Amaranthus type	–	–	1	5	3
Anemopsis californica type	–	–	–	2	1
Boraginaceae unknown type	–	–	–	1	0
Capparidaceae unknown	–	–	–	frag	frag
Carex type	–	–	–	4	3
Cheno Am	31CD	5C	40CD	896	691
Chenopodium type	–	–	–	4	3
Chenopodium watsonii type	–	–	–	0	0
Cleome	–	–	–	4	1
Compositae unknown	–	–	–	2	2
Cryptantha (involucre)	–	–	–	1	0
Cucurbita	–	–	–	5	2
Cycloma atriplicifolium type	–	1	–	63	27
Cyperaceae unknown	–	–	–	3	2
Descurainia type	3	–	78CD	89	88
Desmodium type	–	–	–	1	1
Echinocereus fendleri type	–	–	–	37	28
Euphorbia glyptoperma type	1D	6	–	71	9
Gramineae unknown	–	–	–	16	4
Juniperus	–	–	–	1	0
Leguminosae unknown	–	–	–	1	0
Lycium	–	–	–	0	0
Malvaceae unknown	–	–	–	3	2
Mentzelia albicaulis type	–	–	–	8	6
Oryzopsis hymenoides type	–	–	–	52	36
Paniceae (tribe)	–	–	–	frags	frags
Physalis type	–	–	–	40	17
Pinus edulis (testa)	–	–	–	frag	0
Polanisia	–	–	–	0	1
Polygonum type	–	–	–	1	1
Polygonum persicaria type	–	–	–	1	0
Portulaca	6CD	–	2C	178	95
Prosopis pubescens type	–	–	frags	frags	frags
Prunus	–	–	–	0	0
Rhus trilobata type	–	–	1C	10	5
Salsola kali (leaf)	–	–	–	1	1
Salvia reflexa type	–	–	–	2	2
Scirpus acutus type	–	–	–	12	12
Sisymbrium altissimum type	–	–	–	17	0
Solanaceae unknown	–	–	–	3	3
Sporobolus type	–	1C	–	6	3
Trianthema portulacastrum type	frags	–	–	5	3
Yucca baccata	–	–	–	2	2
Zea mays	–	–	2C	148	110
Undetermined disseminules	–	–	–	–	–
Number 1	–	–	–	1	0
Number 2	–	–	–	1	0
Number 3	–	–	–	1	0
Number 8036	–	–	–	8	4
Number 8063	–	–	–	6	5
Number 8066	–	–	–	28	22
Unknowns	–	–	–	–	–
Ovary	–	–	–	1	1
Pistil	–	–	–	0	0
Floral parts	–	1	–	1	1
Total number of wild taxa	5	4	5	34	28
(excluding contaminants)	–	–	–	–	–

[1]C = some carbonized, D = some damaged, F = some fragments, M = modern in appearance, P = some parched. W = whole rooms, A = rooms within rooms, P = plaza test pits. [2]*Zea mays* represented by kernels, cupules, and embryos. [3]Totals count only taxa that could not be listed twice; thus, if both *Cleome* and Capparidaceae unknowns, or both *Chenopodium* and Cheno Am are listed in a sample, only one is added to the total.

Table 37.2. Suggested uses of plants recovered from Salmon Ruins.

Taxon	Common Name	Suggested Use	Reference
Amaranthus	Pigweed	Food	Swank 1932:26
Anemopsis californica	Yerba-mansa	Unknown	n/a
Boraginaceae	Borage family	Contaminant	Modern appearance
Capparidaceae	Caper family	Food	Swank 1932:37,62
Carex	Sedge	Food	Bohrer 1970:417
Chenopodium	Goosefoot	Food	Harrington 1967:69
Chenopodium watsonii	Goosefoot	Food	Doebly 1976:46
Cleome	Spider flower	Food	Swank 1932:37
Compositae	Sunflower	Food?	n/a
Cryptantha	Borage family	Contaminant	Modern appearance
Cucurbita	Squash, wild gourd, pumpkin	Food	Stevenson 1915:67
Cycloma atriplicifolium	Winged pig-weed	Food	Stevenson 1915:67
Cyperaceae	Sedge family	Food	Bohrer 1970:417
Descurainia	Tansy-mustard	Food	Found under metate, Room 93
Desmodium	Tick clover	Unknown	n/a
Echinocereus fendleri	Hedgehog cactus	Food	Swank 1932:42
*Euphorbia glyptosperma**	Spurge	Food	Doebly 1976:26
Gramineae	Grass family	Food	Whiting 1939:18
Juniperus (berries)	Juniper	Food	Swank 1932:50
Leguminosae	Bean family	Unknown	n/a
Lycium	—	Food	Whiting 1939:89
Malvaceae	Mallow family	Unknown	n/a
Mentzelia albicaulis	Stick leaf	Food	Smith 1973
Oryzopsis hymenoides	Indian ricegrass	Food	Whiting 1939:18
Paniceae	Panic grasses	Food	Fry 1975
Physalis	Groundcherry	Food	Robbins et al. 1916
Pinus edulis	Piñon pine	Food	Stevenson 1915:70
Polanisia	Clammy-weed	Food	Swank 1932:62 &37
Polygonum	Knotweed	Food	Harrington 1967:198
Polygonum persicaria	Knotweed	Food	Harrington 1967:198
Portulaca	Purslane	Food, ceremony	Harrington 1967:89 Found on animal skull on kiva floor, Room 94
Prosopis pubescens	Screwbean mesquite	Food	Castetter and Bell 1942:64
Prunus	Plum, cherry	Food	Swank 1932:63
Prunus serotina	Chokecherry	Food	Swank 1932:63; Doebley 1976:58
Rhus trilobata	Squawbush	Food	Cook 1930:27
Salsola kali	Russian thistle	Contaminent	Post-Columbian introduction
Salvia reflexa	Sage	Food, medicine	Castetter and Bell 1951:195 Whiting 1939:91
Scirpus acutus	Bulrush	Food	Wetterstorm 1986
Sisymbrium altissimum	Tumble-mustard	Contaminent	Modern appearance; post-Columbian introduction
Solanaceae	Potato family	Unknown	—
Sporobolus	Dropseed	Food	Whiting 1939:66
Trianthema portulacastrum	—	Food	Bohrer 1970
Yucca baccata	Banana yucca, detail	Food	Swank 1932:75; Stevenson 1915:72
Zea mays	Maize, corn	Food, ceremony	Whiting 1939:67

*Previously identified as Bahia type and listed as such in Doebly (1976).

The Recognition of Widely Used Taxa

Examining the number of rooms and plaza test pits where each taxon occurs provides an indication of which taxa occur most frequently (Table 37.3). Frequent occurrence suggests regular use by inhabitants, so the taxa that appear in a large portion of the 13 rooms and four plaza test pits sampled should be the ones used most commonly. However, some frequently used plants (such as leafy greens and boiled squash) may have escaped detection due to poor preservation.

As shown in Table 37.3, Cheno Am and wild grasses occur frequently at the site. This corresponds well with the assessment of several wild grasses as staples among the Hopi (Whiting 1939:18) and the quantitative importance of chenopodiaceous and grass seeds among the Gosiute of Utah (Chamberlin 1911:31)

Another common taxa, *Portulaca*, has been attributed little importance as a food in the historic ethnobotanical literature, but such literature may not accurately portray the situation of 800 years ago. Although native species of *Portulaca* are rare in the Southwest today (possibly due to overgrazing), they may have been much more abundant prehistorically, and could have been a highly attractive resource for gathering (Bohrer 1978). Perhaps *Portulaca* held a position of greater importance in the prehistoric diet than in the historic diet of Southwest Indians; indeed, seed and plant collecting in general may have been a more important activity in the past for all Pueblo Indians, as it was for the Jemez (Cook 1930: 20).

Maize, unexpectedly, ranks below some small-seeded grains (see Table 37.3). Excavation methods may have artificially lowered the rate of recovery of maize in the rooms; easily visible cobs and kernels are generally removed from the stratum by excavators and do not become part of the flotation sample. Also, maize may have been prepared in ways that would be unlikely to leave archaeological remains (for example, boiling). Because these variables are not accounted for in Table 37.3, the presence of maize may be artificially lower when compared to the remains of other taxa.

Changing Patterns of Wild Plant Use Through Time

At the time of this research, based on ceramic evidence, the archaeologists at Salmon Ruin had defined two major periods of occupation: a primary occupation by people of Chacoan affiliation, and a final occupation by people affiliated with Mesa Verde in Colorado (Irwin-Williams 1975). A third ceramic complex dating between the two major periods was identified, but it was not included in this study. Thus, the 41 flotation samples examined for this report were assigned to one of the two major periods based on an analysis of painted pottery types and their various strata of occurrence. Comparing the evidence for wild plant use from the two major occupations should show any changes in the pattern of use. Change through time can be seen by examining the mean number of taxa per flotation sample, as well as the total number of taxa associated with each occupation. When interpreting the total number of taxa per time period (see Table 37.1), the fact that the final occupation has been more heavily sampled must be considered.

Table 37.1 shows that the pattern of plant use differs between these two periods. First, when the areas of best and least preservation (Room 62 and the plaza) are excluded, the final period contains more taxa (28 vs. 19), despite the fact that it has only three more samples (17 vs. 14). Second, the mean number of taxa per sample is larger for the last period (6.53 with Room 62 and the plaza excluded) than for the first (4.21). A two-sided Wilcoxon rank sum test shows that differences as great or greater than those between these two means could be obtained by chance only 5 percent (p = 0.05) of the time. Finally, *Echinocereus fendleri*, which occurs in 6 of the 17 rooms and plaza test pits sampled, appears only in association with the last period, suggesting that it was more commonly, if not exclusively, used during the last period. In general it appears that the final occupants of the site used a larger number of wild plant species, or that they used the same species more regularly.

Four steps were taken to minimize the possibility that the difference in the pattern of plant use was an artifact of the research methods or some noncultural variable. First, the soil was checked to see if differences in pH could have produced differential preservation; the two periods were similar (averaging 7.5). Second, samples from areas with unusually good or poor preservation (Room 62W and the plaza) were not used unless equally represented in all time periods. Third, samples were chosen to represent all areas of the site and different room types. This should reduce the likelihood of sampling error by ensuring that each period is represented by more or less the same variety of trash types. And fourth, samples containing many recognizable contaminants (many plaza samples) were excluded, as they might also contain unrecognizable ones.

Table 37.3. Occurrences of plant taxa at Salmon Ruin (ranked by frequency).

Taxon	Number of Rooms and Plaza Test Pits (n = 17)
Cheno Am	17
Portulaca type	16
All wild grasses	12
Zea mays	11
Undetermined disseminule 8036*	10
Physalis type	9
Descurainia	8
All Capparidaceae	7
Euphorbia glyptosperma type	7
Rhus trilobata type	7
Sporobolus type	6
Echinocereus fendleri type	6
Undetermined disseminule 8066	6
Oryzopsis hymenoides type	6
Mentzelia albicaulis type	5
Cleome	5
Undetermined disseminule 8063	4
Cucurbita	4
Carex type	4
Trianthema portulacastrum type	3
Anemopsis californica type	3
Paniceae	3
Yucca baccata type	2
Prosopis pubescens type	2
Malvaceae	2
Polygonum type	2
Polygonum persicaria type	1
Juniperus	1
Pinus edulis	1
Polanisia	1
Chenopodium watsonii type	1
Compositae unknown	1
Salvia reflexa type	1
Leguminosae unknown	1
Desmodium type	1
Prunus	1
Lycium	1
Undetermined disseminule 1	1
Undetermined disseminule 2	1
Undetermined disseminule 3	1

*Bohrer and Adams (1977:191)

In addition to the present work, other evidence supports the conclusion that the final occupants relied to a greater degree on wild plants. A study of juniper use at Salmon Ruin (Lentz 1979; Lentz, Chapter 41) revealed that the ratio of cucurbit to juniper seeds was significantly higher during the Chacoan occupation than during the final occupation. This corresponds well with the general picture of wild plants playing a more important role during the final occupation at Salmon Ruin.

Although noncultural explanations (such as sampling error) for the observed increase in wild taxa during the final occupation cannot be completely dismissed, some cultural explanations may be proposed. To explain why a change in plant use would have occurred it is important to understand the major use for the plants involved. From Table 37.2 it is clear that the seeds of most of these taxa could have been used as food; any change in their frequency should therefore reflect a change in subsistence activities. What cultural event can explain a change in wild plant food use at Salmon Ruin? At least three explanations can be proposed. First, the change could simply reflect differences in cultural preference between the earlier and later occupants regarding wild plant foods. Cultural differences are reflected for example in architectural styles, construction techniques, extensiveness of trade relationships, and utilization of room space (Irwin-Williams 1975; Pippin and Irwin-Williams 1972). Thus, it seems reasonable to expect differences in how they used wild plants. However, evidence from coprolite studies (Stiger 1977) shows that the occupants of Mesa Verde increased the number of wild plant species they ate from AD 1100 to 1250, as did the people of Salmon Ruin. This suggests that the ancestors of the Mesa Verde occupants of Salmon Ruin, like their relatives at Mesa Verde and the Chacoans of Salmon Ruin, used fewer species of wild plants around AD 1100. Therefore, mere cultural differences between the primary (Chaco) and final (Mesa Verde) people at Salmon Ruin seem not to explain the observed trend in plant use.

Second, the change in wild plant use could reflect a decrease in either agricultural productivity or other resources such as a few highly prized wild plant species, forcing a reliance on a greater number of wild plant species during the second occupation. Schoener (1971), in an article on feeding strategies of non-food-producing animals, suggested that the lower the total abundance of food, the larger the variety of items consumed. Thus, an increase in the number of wild species represented in the archaeological record may be one possible response when humans are faced with lower available amounts of their normal foodstuffs. Indeed, several authors have noted increases in the exploitation of wild plant and animal species as a response to increasing aridity (Euler et al. 1979:1096). Such a decrease in agricultural productivity or in other resources could have been caused by environmental deterioration in the Salmon Ruin vicinity. Tree-ring data from nearby Mesa Verde show wet conditions without significant dry periods during the early to mid 1100s, followed by a series of dry periods at AD 1170, 1218, 1237, and 1276 (Fritts et al. 1965:1200). Other geological, botanical, archaeological, and zoological information summarized in two recent review articles strongly supports this interpretation of greater aridity during the time of the second occupation at Salmon Ruin (Bryson 1980; Euler et al. 1979). Thus, there is some evidence for drought stress, which could have precipitated the observed increase in the number of wild plant species utilized at Salmon Ruin.

In addition to this climatic evidence, a study of Puebloan coprolites (Stiger 1977, 1979) revealed that although the amount of maize and the number of wild plant species consumed increased in the thirteenth century, the use of squash, piñon nuts, beeweed, and purslane decreased (cf. Fry and Hall 1975). It is of interest that both squash and piñon trees are especially susceptible to drought, the latter often aborting their seeds if they do not receive sufficient moisture (Adams, Chapter 40; Bohrer 1975d). Maize, on the other hand, can show less sensitivity to a decline in moisture, especially the drought-resistant varieties grown in the Southwest at this time (Galinat and Gunnerson 1963). Thus, the explanation that environmental deterioration along with other factors played a role on the changing subsistence pattern at Salmon Ruin seems plausible.

Finally, the observed change in subsistence strategy at Salmon Ruin could have resulted from human destruction of arable land, creating an imbalance between population and resources (Stiger 1977, 1979). The effects of environmental disturbance by the Puebloans very likely contributed to the eventual decline of these people on the Colorado Plateau, especially when coupled with a decrease in effective moisture, as well as other factors (Adams, Chapter 40; Euler et al. 1979; Fritts et al. 1965).

CONCLUSIONS

1. Thirty-eight identified taxa of wild plants were found in trash strata at Salmon Ruin, indicating the gathering of wild plants from spring through late fall during both periods of its occupation.

2. Cheno Am and grasses probably played important roles in the inhabitants' economy, as they have among certain historic Southwest Indian groups.

3. *Portulaca* seems to have had an important role in the occupants' economy, although no evidence could be found that it played such an important role in recent times.

4. The number of wild plant species used appears to have increased at Salmon Ruin during the last period of its occupation as compared to the first period.

5. No evidence could be found that noncultural variables (such as differential preservation) biased the findings of increased wild plant use, but these variables cannot be completely dismissed.

6. Suggested explanations for the increased wild plant use include cultural differences between the people of the two occupations, and a decline in agricultural productivity or certain key wild resources caused by drought and perhaps human environmental disturbance. The latter hypothesis appears to be strongly supported by both environmental and archaeological data.

ACKNOWLEDGMENTS
My thanks go to Karen Adams, Rex Adams, Everett Frost, Hugh Iltis and the University of Wisconsin Herbarium, Cynthia Irwin-Williams, and most especially to Vorsila Bohrer for help with virtually every aspect of this work.

Chapter 38

OTHER BOTANICAL REMAINS AND SPECIAL CONTEXTS AT SALMON

by Vorsila L. Bohrer and Karen R. Adams

Cultivated plants in general and maize in particular seem to have had major economic importance in both occupations at Salmon. Although maize ranked high for both, the widespread presence of maize in flotation samples from Chacoan trash strata (10 of 13) compared with flotation samples from Secondary occupation strata (13 of 22) may be indicative of greater agricultural emphasis on this crop during Chacoan times. A larger number of samples from the Chacoan occupation would be desirable.

Two additional studies provide some indication of the importance of agricultural crops. One, a survey of the content of Secondary occupation storerooms, suggests that beans may have ranked second only to corn; beans were recovered in six of seven storerooms. In the other study, a survey of the contents of trash units of moderate preservation, the presence of squash seed exceeds the frequency of macrofossils of piñon shells, juniper seeds, outer onion bulb scales, yucca seeds, and chokecherry (*Prunus*) pits. However, piñon was present in almost as many stratigraphic units (49 of 53), so at least in terms of widespread usage, it approached squash.

A study of the ratio of squash seed to juniper seed completed by Lentz (Chapter 41) indicated that the difference between occupations in ratios (16.12 for Chaco and 3.59 for Secondary) is significant at the 99 percent level. The higher ratio of squash seed in Chacoan occupation strata in relation to juniper could be viewed as evidence of greater emphasis on agriculture, although other cultural variables might also have created such results. For example, the differential consumption of immature squash fruits (seeds and all) by one occupation or the differential export of juniper berries by the other would also affect the ratios significantly (see Lentz, Chapter 41).

Juniper berries, cholla buds, young prickly pear pads, and squawbush (*Rhus trilobata*) berries apparently were all stored during Secondary times, but we

do not know how they compared in importance. The uneven preservation of the disparate evidence, or the possibility that diagnostic parts (i.e. seeds of yucca) were consumed instead of discarded, complicates any answers. We know that buffalo berry (*Shepherdia argenta*), juicy red prickly pear fruits (Platyopuntia), wild crabapples (*Crataegus*), and hackberries (*Celtis* sp.) furnished variety to the diet. Because they are recovered so much less frequently, their role in home consumption might seem less apparent.

The importance of small seeds and grains recovered by flotation techniques can best be evaluated by size range and not in relation to other consumables (K. Adams, Chapter 39). The study by K. Adams on the constancy of recovery of certain taxa from room floors and trash provides the necessary data. Of the smaller native seeds, the *Chenopodium* and *Amaranthus* taxonomic group (Cheno-Am) and *Portulaca* (purslane) were almost ubiquitous.

The interpretation of archaeological evidence for yucca utilization is complicated by the multiplicity of known historic uses for the genus (Bell and Castetter 1941), the presence of both broad-leaf (*Yucca baccata*) and narrow-leaf species, and the utilization of the leaves in two different ways. The common recovery of the thick, mature seeds (cf. *Yucca baccata*) in many strata of Room 62W attests to use of the fruit. We have no pollen evidence for use of the flowers, or evidence for use of stalks or immature fruits. The recovery of segments of yucca fiber cordage and the observation of yucca fibers protruding from human feces indicate that the leaf fiber was employed for cordage and the leaf pulp was used for food at least occasionally. One historic Tewa reference calls attention to the baking and eating of leaves by travelers when other provisions were not available (Robbins et al. 1916:50). The fact that human feces found at Salmon seldom retain a distinct form, and the susceptibility of the fibers to decay, deters any attempt to classify the frequency of each kind of use. Similarly, inadequate preservation has made it impossible to unambiguously separate steps in fiber or cordage

---

This chapter was taken entirely from the 1980 Salmon report, with editing.

manufacture from those associated with simple decay. We do know that split green strips of yucca leaf served as temporary ties.

Some unique epidermal tissue with distinct fibrous knobs proved to be of the thickened stem or heart of yucca. Because the tissue could be reproduced by "crock-pot" roasting, it is tempting to interpret the prehistoric material as evidence that yucca hearts were roasted for food; the historic precedent for such activity is found with both the Cochiti (Lange 1959:148) and the San Juan Paiutes (Kelly 1964:171). But using epidermal tissue to confirm consumption of yucca hearts may be unjustified, because it is not known whether degradation over time of the soft tissue of yucca hearts duplicates the physical appearance of having been roasted. The recovery of small-diameter, fibrous yucca hearts that have been split longitudinally is also relevant to this problem. Perhaps this represents a better condition of preservation than the aforementioned. Or perhaps we are seeing the basal stem of the narrow-leaf type of yucca, which may have had its own separate uses.

During the several summers of cataloging macrofossils under the author's supervision, the presence of the taproot of yucca was never noted; the root may have been pounded to a pulp and swished in water to make a detergent for hair washing in the manner of modern Southwest Indians (Bell and Castetter 1941:54–55)—the process would leave no recognizable residue.

There is a variety of evidence for use of the vegetative parts of other plants. The frequent occurrence of clumps of Cheno-Am pollen grains on floors could indicate use of those plants for greens, up to and including the flowering stage (as well as use of seeds that bear a dusting of pollen; Bohrer 1972:26). The recovery of occasional grains of purslane (*Portulaca*) pollen may indicate that those plants were used as greens as well. The male flowers of squash could have been used in soups, stews, or dumplings (Beaglehole 1937:68; Hughes 1972:25) although the pollen could have traveled on an old flower at the apex of a mature pumpkin or squash brought home. Seeds of Rocky Mountain beeweed (*Cleome serrulata*) were consumed; the young plants might also have been eaten as greens (as practiced by modern Puebloans). The roots or rhizomes of water-loving plants such as sedge or cattail (monocotyledon rhizomes occur in Room 62W) might have been part of the diet. Still other carbonized and more degraded pieces of root 1 cm or more in diameter recovered from storerooms or trash may have once figured in the diet. In fact, all of these items might have contributed to the finely minced vegetal material that

comprises the bulk of the human fecal remains from Salmon, as well as the varied content of fibrous quids.

At times the great variety of cultivated and wild plant food narrowed to a monotonous trickle of a few relatively unpalatable items. Some fiber quids examined under a 100x microscope reveal from the still-clinging epidermal tissue that they are composed not of corn husks or leaves but of native grass (Salmon Record Key 4546); quids of yucca leaves may also represent the residue from such emergency sustenance. The organic matrix of some preserved human feces contains shreds of juniper bark, small pieces of maize cobs, fragments of fiber and epidermis of yucca, and not much else.

FIVE PLANTS FROM MODERATELY PRESERVED STRATA IN ROOM 62

The best conditions of preservation were found only rarely at Salmon Ruin. What has been well preserved is of a fortuitous nature and not representative of the prehistoric numbers or distribution of plants. Conditions of moderate preservation are indicated by the presence of squash seeds and yucca leaves, as described above. Moderately preserved strata can be found in 23 of the 48 rooms exposed by excavation. Especially noteworthy is Room 62W, in which 53 of the 119 strata qualify as being moderately preserved. With such a large number of strata having the potential of yielding data, a preliminary tabulation of presence or absence of five macrofossils was undertaken, with the knowledge that any variability in the content of different strata could not be attributed to a change in location within the site.

The choice of macrofossils to be used in the tabulation was governed by several factors. All had to represent residue from plants of well-known economic importance as described in ethnobotanical references or ethnographies. In addition, each had to be variably present in the different strata. Because each macrofossil was found in association with yucca leaves and squash seeds and in some combination with the other four macrofossils, it was apparent that all five macrofossils were equally resistant to decay. Table 38.1 provides data on these plants. The macrofossils were the outer bulb scale network of onion (*Allium*), juniper seeds (*Juniperus osteosperma*), piñon nut shells (*Pinus edulis*), chokecherry pits (*Prunus*), and the thick seeds of yucca (cf. *Yucca baccata*).

The trash in Room 62W was a combination of the waste initially produced by the Secondary occupants and their activity in clearing Chacoan trash from other locations and redepositing it in this room. Because Secondary pottery is so frequently identifiable

Table 38.1. Occurrence of five food plants in Room 62W strata showing moderate preservation.

Stratum. Unit	Onion Bulb Scale	Juniper Seed	Piñon Nutshell	Chokecherry Pit	Yucca Seed
C-2-7	x	x	x	x	x
C-2.5-7.5	x	x	x	–	–
C-3 -9	–	–	–	–	–
C-4- 9	x	x	x	x	–
C-20-20	x	–	x	–	–
C-20.5-20.5	x	x	x	–	–
C-21-21	x	–	x	–	–
C-21.3-21.3	–	–	x	–	–
C-21.5-21.5	x	x	x	–	–
C-22-22	x	x	x	x	x
C-22.3-22.3	x	x	x	–	x
C-22.4-22.4	x	x	x	–	–
C-23-23	x	x	x	–	x
C-23.3-23.3	–	x	–	–	x
C-23.5-23.5	x	x	x	–	x
C-24-24	x	x	x	–	x
C-24.2-24.2	–	x	x	–	x
C-24.7-24.7	–	x	x	–	–
C-24.8-24.8	–	x	–	–	-
C-25-25	–	x	x	–	x
C-25.5-25.5	x	x	x	–	x
C-25.7-25.7	x	x	x	–	x
G-1-40	x	–	–	–	–
L-2-7.1	x	x	x	x	x
C-26-26	–	x	x	–	x
C-26.1-26.1	–	x	x	–	x
C-26.2-26.2	–	x	x	x	–
C-26.6-26.6	x	x	x	–	x
C-26.7-26.7	x	x	x	x	–
C-26.8-26.8	x	x	x	–	x
C-27-27	–	x	x	–	–
C-27.3-27.3	x	x	x	–	–
C-27.5-27.5	x	x	x	–	–
C-27.6-27.6	–	x	x	–	x
C-27.7-27.7	x	x	x	–	–
C-27.8-27.8	–	x	–	–	–
C-27.9-27.9	x	–	x	–	–
C-28-28	–	x	x	–	–
C-28.7-28.7	x	x	x	–	x
C-29-29	–	x	x	–	–
C-29.1-29.1	–	–	–	–	x
C-29.3-29.3	–	x	x	–	–
C-29.5-29.5	–	x	x	–	–
C-30-30	x	x	x	x	–
C-30.3-30.3	x	x	x	–	x
C-30.5-30.5	x	x	x	–	x
C-31-31	x	x	x	x	–
C-32-32	x	–	x	–	–
C-33-33	x	x	x	–	x
C-34-34	x	x	x	–	x
C-35-35	x	x	x	x	x
C-36-36	x	x	x	–	x
Total strata	34	43	48	8	26

*Based on printout 3/27/79 Q6226-377 and 3/30/79 Q6227-147.

in redeposited trash, it is impossible to be certain whether other inclusions are also of this nature. Consequently the tabulation of presence or absence of selected plant material creates a general picture of utilization rather than one specific to one occupation.

It is possible that the frequency of each item (see below) in the entire set of 53 stratigraphic units expresses the geographic availability, reliability, and taste preferences of the gatherers. The evidence that onion, juniper, and broad-leaf yucca grew in the immediate area is discussed below in "Changing Distributions of Plants Through Time." The documentation of the presence of juniper in a close radius of Salmon in modern and prehistoric times is provided by Lentz (Chapter 41) and K. Adams (Chapter 40). The evidence that piñon was not common in the immediate area of Salmon prehistorically is discussed by K. Adams (Chapter 40).

Geographic availability is one matter, and the reliability of each species for bearing edible parts in a given season is another. Wild onions in the modern Salmon area grew too sparsely to speculate about their reliability. Those observed on a sandy mesa-top overlooking the Puerco Valley (southeast of Salmon Ruin) were abundant and obvious in a spring following heavy winter moisture. During a drought year, the same onion population was much reduced by wind erosion and rodent exploitation. In addition, partial dormancy and lack of vigor of the drought-stressed population greatly reduced its visibility. The junipers in the vicinity of Salmon produced a berry crop of some kind every year that excavation was in progress. Chokecherries, occupying riverbank habitats, were probably highly reliable crops. A good crop of piñon nuts probably depends on the same factors as the production of wide growth rings—primarily moisture in either winter (Fritts 1965) or spring (Rose et al. 1981). Fruit formation in broad-leaf yucca is also dependent on stored reserves built up over several years; under normal growth conditions, a plant does not produce fruit in consecutive years (Wallen and Ludwig 1978:419).

The high frequency of recovery of piñon and the low frequency of chokecherry may reflect differences in taste. The heavy use of piñon runs counter to its erratic seed production at a distance from Salmon (K. Adams, Chapter 40). The low frequency of chokecherry pits may indicate a lack of popularity, for they seem to have been both available and reliable. Perhaps, however, we are misled in the archaeological record by the infrequent recovery of intact, recognizable pits. The Plains Indians (Gilmore 1977:36), the northern Paiutes (Kelly 1932:99), and the Navajos

(Bailey 1940:288–289) pounded chokecherries to a pulp, pits and all.

The frequency of use of onion, juniper, and yucca may have been governed by other factors besides taste, such as reliability or efficiency in gathering and processing (cf. Schoener 1971). When onions are available, their (former) density permitted easy gathering. More yucca may have actually been gathered than is indicated by the seed record alone. Additional late-maturing fruits might have been gathered and processed for winter storage outside of Salmon Ruin while people were out gathering piñon nuts (see Bandelier, April 4, 1882 in Lange 1959 for typical methods of preparation); some seeds would thus have been discarded away from Salmon. Another possibility is that some seeds escaped the archaeological record by being ground into meal, following a pattern described for the Papago (Castetter and Underhill 1935:23), or eaten with the fruit, as at Zuni (Stevenson 1915:72). Yucca fruit utilization has persisted among many Puebloans into modern times (Bell and Castetter 1941:9–14). Yucca fruit ranks close to piñon nuts in modern popularity, despite the availability of commercial foods.

The size of the stratigraphic unit in Room 62 could have played an important role in determining whether these foods were present. Eleven of 18 stratigraphic units in which all but chokecherry were recovered were defined largely on stratigraphic scale diagrams; thus the inclusion of all four subsistence items might be a result of the size and volume of the material represented. Within a series of 10 small stratigraphic units formed in the cavity between Mounds Two and Four (C-27.7-27.7 to C-29.9-29.9; see Table 38.1), the absence of a single item could be reasonably attributed to the limited size of the unit. However, the consistent lack of onion bulb scale network and yucca seeds in particular (rather than juniper or piñon) in these strata suggests that other cultural factors are more important than sample volume. Perhaps the taste of piñon and the reliability of juniper led to their continued popularity and use.

The presence of quids composed of tangled masses of flat fibers in 6 of 10 small strata, as mentioned above, is especially interesting. Subsequent investigation of the remains from 6 of 10 extensive stratigraphic units also revealed quids, although only two are specifically described as flat fibers. Flat fibers might conceivably represent anything from juniper bark, grass leaves, or flattened squash "strings" to remnants of the prickly pear vascular system. Thus, the consumption of relatively coarse vegetal material appears to have been common. We avoided tabulation of quids composed of fibers that were round in cross-section because such fibers might have been produced when making twine or rope from yucca, as well as having been an emergency food (Robbins et al. 1916:50–51).

SECONDARY OCCUPATION STORAGE ROOMS AND ROOF TOPS

A number of Secondary occupation roof units (F and N coded strata) were partially preserved when the burning roof timbers collapsed and the falling adobe smothered the fire, subsequently protecting any carbonized plant remains mixed in the debris. Many of the roof strata along the back or long axis of the pueblo came from rooms with evidence of walls projecting into a second story. The stratigraphic position of the roof stratum within a given room also sometimes suggests that a second-story floor (first-floor roof) has collapsed onto the floor below, as in Rooms 37W and 84W (Figure 38.1). However, it is often difficult to separate second-story floor stratigraphic units from the second-story roof (as well as third-story remains) when both have collapsed in a jumble on the surface below.

To distinguish plant materials that belonged to burned roof strata, an inventory was made of the rooms whose burned roofs had unburned stratigraphic units above and below (Table 38.2). The unburned nature of the trash that was eventually deposited on top of a burned, collapsed roof demonstrates that the trash does not belong to the roof stratigraphic unit. Some error in judging the proper association remains possible; for example, a burning roof may have ignited trash deposited in an abandoned room below. Or when a fire occurred, an unknown quantity of plant material may have been drying on a rooftop or was perhaps suspended from the rafters below. Despite these complications, the inventory reduces the problem of recognizing plant materials that did not originally belong to that stratigraphic unit. For the purposes of the following discussion, the plant material is assumed to have belonged to the second-story floor (in some cases, material may have come from third-story floors). Also, whereas fire impacts all plant remains, it may leave no lasting mark upon pottery or lithics; counts may be inflated by intrusive material from another depositional unit.

As shown in Tables 38.3 and 38.4, certain upper-story floors are characterized by the presence of maize cobs, kernels, beans, other plant remains, lithics, and abundant pottery, which suggests a storage function. The tables include Rooms 37W and 84W, which have burned stratigraphic units below them, to demonstrate the close similarity in content to other suspected storerooms. The amount of plant material actually consumed by the flames is unknown, as is the time of year when each storage room burned, so plant material was inventoried by presence rather than quantity recovered. In contrast, the actual numbers of pottery and lithic items are listed in Table 38.4. The ceramic counts in this table may exceed counts given in Table 38.2, which is based on total pottery used in factor score analysis; the computer program eliminated the rarer types of painted pottery in the count.

The storerooms were not all contemporary. Analysis of stratigraphic positions and relationships has determined that 36W (F-1-15) belongs to the early Secondary occupation whereas 37W (F-2-5) and 129W (F-1-8) belong to a later period (mid Secondary).

The most consistently recovered plant items were cultivated maize and beans. Maize was found in all seven rooms and beans in six. The broad distribution of these two cultigens in storage rooms reflects a reliance on agriculture. The only wild food item represented in more than two rooms was Cheno-Am. However, there is evidence for storage of juniper, piñon, lemonade berry fruit, young prickly pear pads, and cholla buds. The presence of tubers is of special interest, as their role in prehistoric pueblo subsistence is virtually unknown because of their perishable nature. Because small carbonized seeds in roof strata could be confused with the same items discarded in superimposed trash (Doebley 1976), only concentrations obvious to excavators were recorded. The one from Room 90W is particularly interesting because it came from a storeroom container. More than 65 ml of carbonized Cheno-Am seeds (some referable to *Chenopodium*) were recovered in association with three sherds from a large corrugated vessel; seeds were fused to the interior of one large sherd.

Raw materials for many other uses, ranging from coils of smooth bark to grass stems and yucca leaves, were evidently kept in storerooms. The finding of traces of basketry beside fused maize kernels suggests that some finished goods served as containers. Pieces of textile, matting, netting, twine, and vegetal thongs may have played a role in organizing storage, or they may have been stored for their own value. The Hopi custom of washing corn kernels to eliminate contamination by rat urine during storage (Harvey 1970:62) indicates that rodent droppings in a storeroom would not be unusual. The presence of

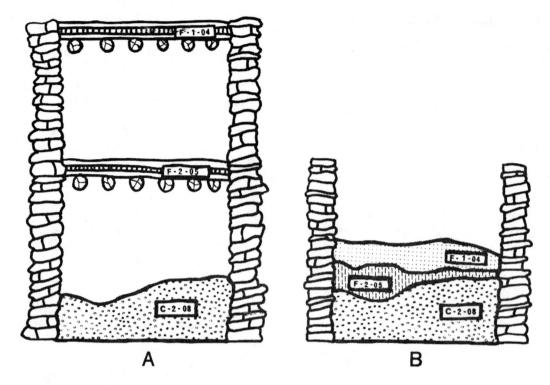

Figure 38.1. Schematic diagram through a vertical section of two stories at Salmon as it might appear (a) during occupation and (b) following the collapse of both roofs.

feces that resemble those of humans in size and shape seems more of a puzzle. The Hopi sometimes save dog manure in order to sprinkle a mixture of water and manure over young corn plants to repel rats and rabbits (Harvey 1970:61); one can only speculate on the otherwise enigmatic presence of fecal material in a storage room.

At least one storeroom was located on the ground floor. Room 30W had maize cobs stacked along the south wall of a floor (H-1-4) and aligned parallel to it along an east-west axis. Evidently beans were also stored there, as one was found mixed with the burned kernels of corn. The burned roof-fall (F-1-2) was mixed in with the stored items.

Two ground-floor rooftops of Secondary occupation rooms (100W and 127W) evidently served as outdoor processing areas as well as storage (Table 38.5). The many lithic artifacts from the Room 100W rooftop with potential use in plant processing were described by Yingst (1977). The plant contents of both roofs were distinguished from the stratigraphic units above and below by their singularly burned condition. A comparison of Table 38.3 with Table 38.5 reveals that the plant taxa recovered from the roof resemble those found on storage room floors. Cultigens like maize, beans, and squash, and wild

foodstuffs such as cholla buds, juniper berries, and winged pigweed seed all had a place on the rooftop. Such foodstuffs would likely be present according to the season in which they were gathered and processed. All but the cholla buds would normally be mature in the fall. Cholla buds may have been stored on the rooftop in covered pottery jars.

DIETARY COMPONENTS IN
FECAL REMAINS

A large amount of finely minced amorphous organic fecal material was recovered. This can be attributed perhaps to an extremely loose human bowel movement, or perhaps to postdeposition conditions of moderate preservation, which could have melted some of the fecal material into a shapeless mass. Discrete feces were observed infrequently; the rarity of single, recognizable feces contributed to the assumption that the bulk of the fecal matter was of human origin. Any study of diet based on such feces has limitations. Whenever possible it has been verified that the fibers and seeds were deeply embedded in the fecal matrix rather than sticking to the surface; in a few instances, seeds had already been removed and placed in vials.

Table 38.2. Distribution of plant remains and ceramics from burned Secondary roofs sandwiched between unburned strata (NA = not analyzed).

Room	Stratigraphic Unit			>6 Cobs	Maize Kernels	Beans	Other Macrofossils	No. of Sherds
	Roof	Above	Below					
7A	F-1-2	A-1-1	B-1-3	–	–	–	No record	48
11W	F-1-3	C-1-2	G-1-2	–	–	–	*Zea mays* kernels, Spermatophyte stems & possible basket	NA
30A	F-1-3	B-1-2	H-1-4	–	–	–	No record	472
33A	F-1-3	B-1-2	H-1-4	–	–	–	No record	NA
33C	F-1-5	C-1-7	G-1-6	–	–	–	No record	749
33W	F-2-9	I-1-8	C-2-10	x	x	–	See Table 38.3	651
36W	F-1-15	M-1-14	L-7-15.1	x	x	x	See Table 38.3	601
43W	F-1.5-6	B-3-5	L-1-6.5	x	x	x	Basketry, *Cucurbita* exocarp, *Cucurbita* peduncle, dicotyledon stem, human hair, 2-ply string, *Phragmites* stem, yucca twine and leaves, *Xanthium saccharatum* fruit	467
51W	N-1-4	B-2-3.5	B-2-4.5	–	–	–	*Zea mays* shank	164
59W	F-1-3	B-1-2	H-1-3.1	–	x	–	*Zea mays* kernels	138
59W	F-1-3	B-1-2	H-1-3.1	–	x	–	*Zea mays* kernels	138
82W	F-1-3	B-1-2	C-1-4	–	–	–	No record	3
83W	F-1-3	B-1-2	C-1-4	–	–	–	No record	5
89W	F-1-3	B-1-2	B-2-4	–	x	–	*Xanthium saccharatum* fruit	114
90W	F-2-9	C-3-8	C-3-10	x	x	x	See Table 38.3	864
98W	F-1-4	E-1-3	B-1-5	–	–	–	No record	NA
100W	N-1-3	B-1-2	C-1-4	x	x	x	See Table 38.3	706
101W	F-1-4	E-1-3	B-2-5	–	–	–	No record	NA
118W	F-1-3	B-1-2	E-1-4	–	–	x	*Phaseolus* seed	22
118W	F-2-5	E-1-4	F-2-5.1	x	x	–	Nothing burned	25
119W	F-3-20	L-5.5-19.5	B-5-21	x	x	–	See Table 38.3	415
123A	F-1-3	B-1-2	C-1-4	–	–	–	No record	45
127W	F-1-4	C-1-3	C-2-4.5	x	x	x	See Table 38.3	1530
129W	F-1-8	E-1-7	F-1-8.1	x	x	x	See Table 38.3	1407

Table 38.3. Content of seven burned storerooms of the Secondary occupation.

Plant Classification	Room and Stratigraphic Unit *						
	33W F-2-9	36W F-1-15	37W F-2-5	84W N-2-4	90W F-2-9	119W F-3-20	129W F-1-8
Cultivated Crops							
Zea mays (maize)	kernels	cobs, kernels,	cobs, kernels,	cobs, kernels,	cobs, kernels,	cobs, kernels,	seed, cobs, kernels, tied husks
Phaseolus vulgaris (bean)	–	seed	seed	seed	seed	seed	seed
Cucurbita (squash)	seed	ring	rind	–	–	–	seed, rind
Wild Foods–Small Disseminules							
Chenopodium/Cheno-Am	–	–	–	–	seed on sherd	seed	seed
Cleome	–	–	–	–	–	seed	–
Cycloloma	–	seed	–	seed	–	–	–
Oryzopsis	–	–	–	–	–	florets	–
Portulaca	–	–	–	–	–	seed	–
Wild Foods–Large Items							
Cylindropuntia (cholla)	–	stem, seed	–	bud	–	–	bud
Platyopuntia (pr. Pear)	–	seed	–	pad	–	–	–
Pinus edulis (piñon)	nut	–	–	–	–	–	–
Juniperus (juniper)	–	berries	–	–	seed	–	seed
Rhus (squawbush)	–	–	–	pit	–	pit	–
Unknown	tuber	tuber	–	–	–	–	legume pod (1.0 x 0.4 cm)
Raw Material							
Juniperus	shredded	–	bark	frayed bark	–	twig	twig w/leaves and bark
Gymnosperm	wood	wood	–	–	–	–	–

Table 38.3 (continued)

Plant Classification	Room and Stratigraphic Unit *						
	33W F-2-9	36W F-1-15	37W F-2-5	84W N-2-4	90W F-2-9	119W F-3-20	129W F-1-8
Raw Material (continued)							
Monocotyledon	–	–	–	tissue, stems	–	–	leaves, quid
Gramineae (grass)	stems	stems	stems	–	–	–	evenly cut stems
Phragmites (reed grass)	stem bundle	stem	–	stem	–	–	–
Cyperaceae (sedge)		–	–	–	–	–	–
Yucca	–	leaf bundle	leaves	–	–	broad leaf	heart w/most leaves cut
Dicotyledon	coiled bark; cf. alder, aspen, birch, etc.	smooth bark; cf. alder, aspen birch, etc.; fiber bundle	smooth bark; cf. alder, aspen, birch, etc.; leaf obvate	branch wood; ring porous	–	–	wood
Finished Items							
Juniperus	–	–	–	–	–	–	twigs and leaves
Yucca leaf	knot leaf	knot	leaf knot	–	–	–	leaves cut at base
Unknown	–	braided fiber	cordage	2-ply twine	–	–	2-ply twine
Unknown	plaited mat	textile	–	–	–	–	–
Unknown	net: 1 knot per 5 mm	–	–	–	–	–	matting with corn kernels
Miscellaneous							
Feces	4x2x1.5 cm	3x2.5x1.5 cm	–	rodent	–	rodent	7x2.5x2.5 cm
Xanthium (cocklebur)	–	–	–	–	fruit	–	fruit
Decorated/Utility Sherds	484/423	191/545	220/251	203/355	247.618	21/431	373.1055

Based upon printout 7/9/78 LISTSORT 2.
*The stratigraphic units in Rooms 37W (F-2-5) and 84W (N-2-4) are included for comparison even though the units below them have burned as well.

Table 38.4. Lithic and ceramic contents of seven burned storerooms of the Secondary occupation.

Classification	Storerooms						
	33W F-2-9	36W F-1-15	37W F-2-5	84W N-2-4	90W F-2-9	119W F-3-20	129W F-1-8
LITHIC CLASSIFICATION							
Manuports							
Ornaments	1	1	12	1	6	–	3
Pigment	3	–	9	–	13	–	4
Shaped stone slab	6	34	14	1	22	3	12
Modified stone	7	10	12	–	14	1	14
Unmodified stone	53	14	9	41	55	3	15
Mealing bin wall	–	1	–	–	–	–	–
Pecked/Ground Stone							
Metate	4	1	2	3	–	–	1
Mortar	1	1	–	–	–	–	1
Lapstone/palette	1	2	1	–	–	1	1
Mano	9	7	10	–	1	3	6
Abrader, grooved	1	–	–	–	–	–	–
Abrader, ungrooved	–	1	–	–	–	–	3
Polishing stone	2	2	2	–	–	–	4
Chopper uniface	1	2	2	1	–	–	5
Chopper biface	4	3	7	–	1	–	3
Axe, grooved	–	–	2	1	–	–	–
Axe, notched	2	–	2	–	–	–	–
Grinding stone	3	3	10	1	10	1	1
Smoothing stone	5	–	9	–	1	1	–
Lightning stone	–	–	1	–	–	–	–
Tchamahia	2	–	–	1	–	1	1
Sculpture	1	–	–	–	–	–	–
Polished stone	5	–	2	–	2	–	2
Ground stone, other	16	2	4	4	5	3	16
Ground stone, indeterm.	16	6	15	2	7	3	17
Composite Implements							
Core- chopper	1	–	3	–	–	–	2
Core-pounder	2	1	2	–	–	–	–
Chopper-pounder	3	2	4	–	1	1	5
Pounder-abrader	4	1	3	–	1	–	1
Chopper-abrader	3	–	4	1	–	–	3
Composite, other	5	4	3	–	–	–	3
Core-chopper-pounder	–	–	–	–	1	–	1
Core-pounder-abrader	–	1	2	–	1	–	1
Core-abrader	–	1	2	–	–	1	–
Fossil	–	–	1	–	–	–	–
Concretion	–	–	1	–	1	–	–
Axe-maul, grooved	–	1	2	1	–	–	–
Axe-maul, notched	–	1	1	–	–	–	–
Hammerstone	2	–	6	–	1	1	1
Cores							
Exhausted cores	2	–	3	–	–	–	1
Core rejuvenation flake	1	–	–	–	–	–	–
Core, other	14	4	11	–	1	–	1
Flake Implements							
Retouched w/projection	1	1	–	–	–	–	2
Retouched w/o projection	3	–	–	–	1	–	2

Table 38.4 (continued)

Classification	Storerooms						
	33W F-2-9	36W F-1-15	37W F-2-5	84W N-2-4	90W F-2-9	119W F-3-20	129W F-1-8
Non-retouched w/ projection	14	–	1	–	–	–	3
Non-retouched w/o projection	95	1	34	3	5	2	63
Non-retouched, notched	3	–	–	–	–	–	1
Bifacially Retouched Implements							
Projectile point	10	–	4	1	4	1	6
Knife	2	–	1	1	–	1	–
Drill	–	1	–	–	–	–	–
Biface, other	1	–	–	–	1	–	–
Debitage	597	174	314	43	72	15	541
CERAMICS							
Utility	423	545	251	355	618	431	1055
Decorated	484	191	220	203	247	21	37?

Based upon printouts (Lithics)4/2/8070 ECXTAB56;4/7/8070 EZXTAB374; and7/14/8070 EVORSI C313966.

Table 38.5. The plant content of two rooftops of the Secondary occupation.

Plant Classification	Room and Stratum	
	100W, N-1-3	127W, F-1-4
Cultivated Crops		
Maize	cobs	cobs
	kernels	kernels
	peduncle	—
	tassel	—
	knotted leaves	—
Beans	seed	seed
Squash	rind	—
	peduncle	—
Wild Foods		
Atriplex patula (cf.)	seed	—
Cycloloma (winged pigweed)	seed	—
Cylindropuntia (cholla)	bud	bud
Juniperus (juniper)	berry	—
Raw Materials		
Juniper	bark	—
Grass	stems	—
Yucca	caudex or crown	—
Finished Items		
Yucca	thong	—
Unknown	cordage	coiled basket
Waste Products		
Feces	5 x 2.5 x 2 cm	—

Based upon printout 7/9/78 LISTSORT 2.

Pollen analysis of fecal material produces limited results, as obtaining pollen from the interior of a flattened fecal deposit can be impossible. Seeds and vegetal matter definitely identified as remnants of feces can be assumed to have passed through a digestive tract. At best, we can consult the record of seed inclusions in feces from appropriate entries on the Compound Materials Form (see Bohrer and Adams 1977:96–97). The tabulated results for each occupation are given in Tables 38.6 and 38.7.

The seeds included in the recovered feces actually represent only a small fraction of the prehistoric diet; unfortunately the finely minced organic matrix remains unstudied. Feces of domestic ruminants and small rodents are studied using a series of microscope slides made of epidermal tissue of known plant species found within the grazing range of the animal. Such a technique has only recently been applied to prehistoric human feces (Stiger 1977:9); any similar study at Salmon would necessitate the preparation and analysis of reference slides of epidermal tissue. The vegetal content of diet can therefore be inferred only from the analysis of the larger plant remains, the flotation samples, and the pollen samples from floors and trash.

CHANGING DISTRIBUTIONS OF PLANTS THROUGH TIME

Changes in the abundance of annuals since prehistoric occupation are especially difficult to assess because the emergence of modern plants may be closely linked to yearly weather conditions. However, 6 years of plant collecting while Salmon Ruin was being excavated (K. Adams 1976) minimized this source of error. Prehistoric annuals such as purslane (*Portulaca*) and spurge (*Euphorbia glyptosperma*), which were consumed regularly for subsistence, surely must have been common enough to be gathered by many families. Even those species less commonly recovered, like winged pigweed (*Cycloloma atriplicifolium*), whitestem blazingstar (*Mentzelia albicaulis*), and horse purslane (*Trianthema portulacastrum*), probably had an important place in the economy. Pigweed (*Cycloloma*) was recovered from two storeroom floors, a rooftop area, and a corrugated vessel on the floor (H-1-5) of Room 127W. Although the other two annuals lack comparable evidence for mass preparation and storage, they were recovered in approximately the same total frequency, from 11 to 18 strata in a total of 65. Indeed, *Mentzelia albicaulis* may have actually been used more commonly than indicated, as the fragile seed coat seems vulnerable to degradation. It is more difficult to evaluate the annuals from Salmon whose

presence was rare in the archaeological record (1 in 65 cases), such as windmills (*Allionia*), spiderling (*Boerhaavia*), caltrop (*Kallstroemia*), and lanceleaf sage (*Salvia reflexa*); Salmon crew members collected the last two genera only. Presumably the first two genera are even more rare today.

The distribution or abundance of present-day perennial species can be established more easily than the annual species because their above-ground parts persist from year to year. Perennials used regularly as food prehistorically were presumably common enough to have been gathered by many families. Examples from Salmon include piñon nuts (*Pinus edulis*), juniper berries (*Juniperus osteosperma*), banana yucca (*Yucca baccata*), chokecherry (*Prunus virginiana*), and wild onion (*Allium*). Juniper is no problem, as it is common in the vicinity today (Lentz 1979). Piñon woodlands were probably not particularly close in prehistory but were nevertheless exploited for their crops of nuts (K. Adams, Chapter 40).

The piñon woodland may also have served as the source area for the fruits of banana yucca, as the species currently grows on Pinon Mesa near Farmington, New Mexico. However, it is conceivable that banana yucca formerly grew closer to Salmon; it grows as low as 2000 feet in elevation in central Arizona (Benson and Darrow 1954:67), although it is restricted to the margins of the desert washes, as in the Jornada range in southern New Mexico (Wallen and Ludwig 1978:410). The Navajo living in Canyon del Muerto and Canyon de Chelly found it advisable to protect yucca from the inroads of livestock (Hill 1938:37). The failure to provide protection for the plant near Salmon may have led to its local extinction.

Modern efforts to collect chokecherry and wild onion in the vicinity of Salmon Ruin have brought limited results. One specimen of chokecherry was collected near Farmington and two of *Allium macropetalum* were found near Salmon. The recovery of these latter two specimens should be credited to the diligence and enthusiasm of the collector, Mary Blankenhorn, rather than to any degree of commonness of the species in the natural environment today. One could not garnish a single meal for a family of four with the amount of wild onions currently growing in the vicinity.

Perennials whose inedible parts were not regularly discarded in trash at Salmon should not necessarily be regarded as having been rare in prehistoric times. Examples of less common prehistoric fruits would be hackberry (*Celtis*), hawthorne (*Crataegus*), buffalo berry (*Shepherdia argentea*), and the fleshy-fruited prickly pear. Several alternative explanations

Table 38.6. Dietary components observed in fecal remains from Primary (Chacoan) and mixed occupations.

Taxon and Description	Record Key No.	Room	Stratum	Occupation*
Pieces of black seed coats, possibly Cheno-Am	33469	62W	C-2.5-7.5	Mixed
Cleome (beeweed) seeds	33472	62W	C-2.5-7.5	Mixed
At least two seeds of *Cucurbita* (squash)	76573	62W	L-2-0.1	Mixed
Cucurbita seed	53446	62W	C-26.2-26.2	Mixed
Juniperus bark inclusions with charcoal flecks	78942	62W	C-36-36	Mixed
Platyopuntia (prickly-pear) seeds with prominent comma mark	76642	62W	C-30-30 C-31-31 C-33-33 C-34-34 C-35-35 C-36-36	Mixed Mixed Mixed Mixed Mixed Mixed
Rhus trilobata (squawbush) stone	28948	62W	C-2-7	Mixed
Carbonized hollow berry with nutlet of *Crataegus saligna* or *C. chrysocarpa* (hawthorn)	79482	62W	G-1-40	Primary
Juniperus twigs oriented longitudinally in matrix, appear partly roasted	75871	81W	F-2-13	Primary
Four *Shepherdia argentea* (buffalo berry) seeds	75871	81W	F-2-13	Primary

Based upon printouts 3/30/79 Q6227-147 and 1/13/80 70 EMCR 34-13.

Table 38.7. Dietary components observed in fecal remains from the Secondary occupation at Salmon.

Taxon and Description	Record	Room	Stratigraphic Unit
Chenopodium (goosefoot) seed	54976	62W	C-34-34
Chenopodium seed	78936	62W	C-34-34
Cleome (beeweed) seeds	75167	62W	C-27.65-27.65
Cucurbita (squash) seed with *Zea mays* (maize) cupules	76683	62W	C-26.8-26.8
Juniperus stems	75163	62W	C-26.67-26.67
Juniperus bark, embedded deep in fecal matrix	78936	62W	C-34-34
Juniper bark shreds in fecal matrix	78936	62W	C-34-34
Vegetal material, *Juniperus* bark *Yucca* leaf epidermis bumpy *baccata* type	78936	62W	C-34-34
Portulaca (purslane) seeds	76679	62W	C-27.8-27.8
Physalis (ground cherry) seeds	75163	62W	C-26.67-26.67
Rhus (squawbush) stone	33783	62W	C-2.5-7.5
Rhus stones	76643	62W	C-26.8-26.8
Zea mays cob fragments	76643	62W	C-26.8-26.8
Zea mays cob fragments smaller than a dime, *Yucca* leaf, bone fragments, insect bodies	76643	62W	C-26.8-26.8
Cucurbita seed, *Zea mays* cob cupules	76683	62W	C-26.8-26.8
Insect parts	76643	62W	C-26.8-26.8

Based upon printout 3/30/79 Q6227-147 and Ethnobotanical Laboratory Progress Report 1977-1978 by Karen R. Adams.

should be considered: (1) the fruits may not have been popular, (2) the fruits were eaten as snacks away from home, or (3) the seeds were swallowed or pulverized beyond recognition. The distribution of these species has likely changed since prehistoric times.

The one modern collection of hackberry was in Farmington Glade, 21 km from Salmon; it seems improbable that prehistoric people would have traveled that distance to bring hackberry fruits back to Salmon. The single prehistoric stone must have been from a locally growing tree. It is known that people find young hackberry leaves edible (Irvine 1961:419), and it is likely that domestic livestock do too, which suggests a possible reason for the diminution of the species; domestic animals seldom reject forage palatable to people.

Hawthorne and buffalo berry, which have potential value as browse for domestic animals, both tend to occupy riverine habitats, which have now been invaded by Russian olive (*Eleagnus angustifolia*). Hawthorne should grow in canyons, on riverbanks, and at valley margins above 5000 feet in elevation (Harrington 1964:296)—generally in many of the locations where one now finds Russian olives. Attention has been drawn, in the eastern United States, to the contrast in the natural versus browsed growth form induced by domestic livestock. Buffalo berry can still be found by a diligent search near the San Juan River not far from Salmon, but so many Russian olives now dominate riverbank habitats that the buffalo berry population has doubtless been reduced. In

addition, the translation of the Navajo name for *Shepherdia rotundifolia* as "sheep food" (Wyman and Harris 1951: 32) may be indicative of grazing as a factor in the reduced visibility of the genus.

The literature provides almost no insight as to why the juicy-fruited prickly pear might have disappeared from the vicinity of Salmon. Although dry-fruited forms of prickly pear grow nearby today, no fleshy-fruited species have been observed. The seeds of dry-fruited species differ morphologically from the fleshy-fruited ones, so the assessment of the archaeological record is probably accurate. Private ownership of prickly pear patches by the Navajo in Canyon del Muerto and Canyon de Chelly perhaps indicates one reason: the recent practice began in order to protect the cactus against the inroads of livestock (Hill 1938:23).

All of the foregoing indicates that the plant composition of many habitats has changed considerably since prehistoric times. Of all the habitats that plants prefer, the ones near permanent water seem to have been most deeply affected by historic human activity. The banks and marshes of the San Juan River have been heavily grazed and frequently modified for agricultural use. Chokecherry, hawthorne, buffalo berry, and hackberry might once have been present in greater abundance. The introduced Russian olive dominates modern riverbank locations. Yerba mansa is not at all conspicuous in the vicinity today, and may be absent, although cattail (*Typha*), sedge (*Cyperaceae*), and reedgrass (*Phragmites communis*) still persist in varying amounts.

Chapter 39

AN ARCHAEOBOTANICAL STUDY OF ROOM 93W AT SALMON PUEBLO

by Karen R. Adams

In the late 1800s, as the first white settlers came to the San Juan Basin of northwestern New Mexico, they wrote in their diaries of a virgin land of tall waving grass ... thick grass which reached to the stirrups of a horseback rider (Cornelius 1933) ... and of a valley rich in natural resources. They wrote of beautiful scenery, of great rock masses seen across wide fertile valleys, and they called the country one of the garden spots of the world (San Juan Times 1894a). Here these pioneers would settle, as other travelers had stopped and stayed centuries before.

When Peter Salmon migrated from Indiana and decided to permanently settle in the San Juan Basin in 1877, he set down roots in a land already rich in history, for this area had known the arrival and departure of many groups of Native Americans hundreds of years previously. Here, in a land of prominent mesas, rolling hills, and lush valley bottoms, all who entered must have recognized the potential for making a home. A variety of plant and animal resources accompanied a growing season long enough to allow cultivated crops to mature in the fertile valley soils. The permanent San Juan River was undoubtedly a major attraction, providing a sure source of water for both humans and animals.

Prehistoric people had made their livelihood in the valley by growing crops, gathering native plant foods, and hunting wild game; Peter Salmon and his neighbors chose to fatten thousands of sheep, goats, and cattle on the great expanse of grass in the San Juan Basin. When participating in round-ups, the stockmen of the 1800s were impressed by the pueblo ruins, many of enormous size and architectural complexity. As additional settlers came to the region, many of these ancient towns went under the plow, or came to harm in other ways. But Peter Salmon's son George, spurred by the concerns of his wife, protected for future generations a large ruin on his property, known as the Salmon Ruin.

This chapter is a reproduction, with minor editing and a modified title, of a separate publication by Karen Adams (*Pollen, Parched Seeds, and Prehistory*) in 1980 for Eastern New Mexico University's Contributions to Anthropology series.

Salmon Ruin is situated on a low terrace along the north bank of the San Juan River, about 3.5 km (2 miles) west of the town of Bloomfield, New Mexico. On a clear day one can stand on the highest point of the ruin, and looking across rolling plains, see the top of Angel Peak, more than 32 km (20 miles) to the southeast. To the north, higher river terraces partially obstruct the view of the horizon. The river location, coupled with the rolling topography to the south and terraces to the north, offers an advantageous position for exploiting plant and animal resources on numerous landforms. At an elevation of 1662 m (5450 ft), the site is easily within walking distance of open juniper woodland, sage-grassland, and river vegetation.

Salmon Pueblo served as home to at least two groups of ancient inhabitants. Chaco Canyon people living 75 km (47 miles) to the south either built or directed the construction of the three-story pueblo around AD 1090. Salmon's ties to Chaco are clearly seen in its fine Chaco-style architecture, pottery, and carefully conceived town plan. After Chacoan influence waned at Salmon in the mid-1100s, for reasons yet unclear, a group of people with different cultural affiliations moved into the structure. These people remodeled many rooms and left pottery suggesting that they were connected to or traded with people from the Mesa Verde region. When this second group left in the late 1200s, the pueblo was never occupied again.

When the last occupants of Salmon Pueblo departed, they left behind more than a magnificent architectural structure; they also left behind a subtle record of their daily activities. Archaeologists prize ancient trash mounds for the information they retain about prehistoric life. A more revealing record of activities can sometimes be found in a room that was hurriedly abandoned, because artifacts may remain in their original position until excavation uncovers them. Some of the antiquities recovered at Salmon Ruin are pottery vessel fragments (some distinctly associated with each of the major occupations), stone tools and the chips discarded during tool manufacture, and bones remaining from numerous dinners of wild game. Plant remains offer their own unique view of the daily lives of the Salmon occupants, revealing much about ancient diet and other facets of living. Sometimes when pottery and stone tool fragments are sparse in a room, plant parts provide essential clues to former activities.

Plant remains occur in a variety of forms at archaeological sites, and size has proven to be a convenient way to distinguish them. The largest plant remains are termed macrofossils. Corn cobs, squash seeds, and juniper berries are easily seen during excavation. In contrast, microfossils such as pollen grains and tiny seeds are hidden from the human eye in soil and adobe. At Salmon, hundreds of these tiny plant fragments provide a better understanding of the prehistoric activities of ancient Puebloans.

POLLEN

Pollen grains are extremely tiny spores that carry the male genes of flowering plants to the unfertilized eggs. While traveling through a pine forest in June, one can sometimes see gusts of wind-released, fine yellow dust coming from fingernail-sized cones on the pine branch tips. This dust is actually composed of millions of pollen grains. How can something so small as pollen help the archaeologist?

Pollen employs two primary modes of transportation. Plants such as pines, grasses, and ragweeds, with inconspicuous flowers, produce pollen that can easily travel on the wind. Wind-borne pollen is small, sleek, and designed to float in the air (Figure 39.1). Large amounts of such pollen are necessary to ensure pollination because air currents provide a less dependable means of transport from one plant to another than insects. In contrast to wind-carried pollen, plants with bright, showy conspicuous flowers (e.g., cholla cactus and cultivated squash) produce pollen that is carried from the male to female organs by insects (Figure 39.2). This pollen is heavy, sticky, adapted to cling to insect bodies, and not likely to be transported very far from the parent plant under natural conditions.

Excavators routinely collect small bags of dirt (6 tablespoons) from select areas (see Bohrer and Adams 1977), hoping to find enough preserved pollen grains to tell a story. These pollen samples are brought to permanent laboratory facilities where the dirt undergoes processing to extract pollen. Trained personnel use harsh chemicals such as hydrochloric, hydrofluoric, and nitric acid and other procedures to dissolve the dirt particles until virtually nothing remains but the exteriors of the pollen grains, or

exines. The exines are generally distinct from one plant type to another, and can normally be identified by a pollen analyst. The analyst routinely counts and identifies the first 200 grains seen on a microscope slide, and the sample is then ready for interpretation.

The relative amounts of each pollen type in a sample is examined for clues to whether it may have been deposited naturally or brought in by humans. The pollen from insect-pollinated plants that normally produce low amounts of heavy, sticky pollen might not be expected to show up in a pueblo unless the plant or its pollen was deliberately carried in by humans, or unless the plant grew there after abandonment. Low percentages of wind-borne pollen could be accounted for by the action of natural breezes, but high amounts should be examined carefully in light of the archaeological context before being dismissed as naturally introduced pollen rain.

Interpretation is undoubtedly the most difficult step. After determining which pollen types were likely to have entered a prehistoric site with the help of humans, suggestions on how the plant might have been used are sought in historic accounts of Southwest groups. For example, if high amounts of a wind-carried pollen occur frequently with prehistoric milling stones, the literature may reveal that the pollen was used in recent times to bless household work areas, or the plant may have provided seeds for food that could thus have carried in pollen grains. Relying on ethnographic studies from the 1880s for assistance in interpreting ancient plant remains assumes a traditional link between past and

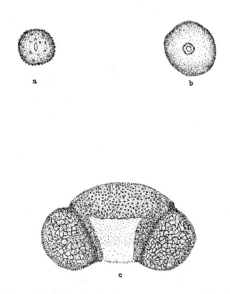

Figure 39.1. Wind-carried pollen types, magnified 1000x: (a) ragweed (*Ambrosia acanthicarpa*), (b) grass (*Bouteloua gracilis*), (c) ponderosa pine (*Pinus ponderosa*).

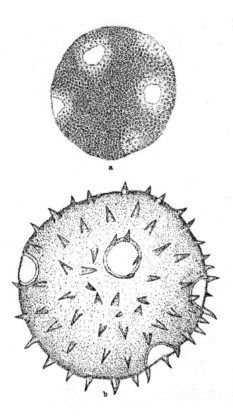

Figure 39.2. Insect-carried pollen types, magnified 1000x: (a) cholla cactus (*Opuntia whipplei*), (b) squash (*Cucurbita pepo*).

SEEDS

Seeds are the compact and self-sufficient carriers of embryonic flowering plants. Within a protective outer case, a seed has stored nutrients that sustain the new plant before it can begin extracting food and moisture from the soil. They are often high in protein and carbohydrates, and can provide a palatable and abundant source of energy for humans.

Heavy or repeated use of seeds increases the probability that they may become lost in the rooms of a pueblo. For example, the more poppy seeds I toast, the better chance there is for spilling some of them on the floor and having a few lodge in inaccessible locations, such as beneath the stove. In prehistory, many seeds were extremely small, and could easily have become ground into an adobe floor, or come to rest for centuries in a room corner.

Seeds can also enter a pueblo in unplanned ways. For example, seeds with a rough or barbed surface may accidentally cling to clothing or sandals. Rodents, both prehistoric and modern, have been known to store caches of seeds in pueblo niches. Digging by archaeologists inadvertently encourages weedy plant species to grow near excavations, allowing modern seeds to drift into ancient rooms now open to the modern air.

Excavators routinely collected a liter (approximately a quart) of dirt from the same select areas in Salmon where pollen samples were taken (Bohrer and Adams 1977), hoping that minute seeds in the dirt would complement the archaeobotanical story unveiled by the pollen study. In the field laboratory, personnel removed the seeds from the dirt by sprinkling the sample into a bucket of water. The dirt sinks to the bottom, while the seeds and other plant materials, which are very light because of air trapped within the cellular structure, float on the water's surface; hence the process is termed "flotation." After being skimmed off with a fine mesh strainer, the floated plant remains are dried indoors for about 12 hours. The seeds are then sorted from the other plant debris with the aid of a low-power binocular microscope, preparatory to identification.

Although 200 grains are routinely counted in a pollen sample, in a flotation sample the technician counts and identifies all seeds present. The number of seeds recovered can fluctuate widely, from a single specimen to many hundred. Each flotation sample is a standard size of 1 liter to facilitate comparisons of seed density.

There are a number of considerations in interpreting seed frequencies, such as how the seeds may have been deposited in the first place, the signifi-

present. Salmon Ruin was once a pueblo, so references about modern pueblo peoples are generally consulted, as well as writings on nonpueblo groups. Changes in the use of plant resources in the Southwest have probably occurred over the centuries, but often the prehistoric evidence seems consistent with modern uses. The archaeological context is always very important to any explanation.

Though not discussed here, other interpretations of pollen data are also of archaeological value; pollen records are not limited to reconstructing the relationships between plants and cultural groups. For example, in biostratigraphic analysis, pollen values are used as clues to the temporal relationships between deposits found in different parts of a site; such a study can sometimes confirm or deny chronological interpretations made on the basis of geological or ceramic studies (Hill and Hevly 1968). Pollen values can also help in estimating the kinds of vegetation patterns and climatic conditions that existed at the time a site was occupied (Bohrer 1972; Gish 1976; Hevly et al. 1978; Schoenwetter 1974). Often the pollen record at an archaeological site can fulfill more than one function.

cance of seed size, and the fact of differential preservation. Seeds growing in abundance nearby, or those most easily separated from accompanying chaff, might represent parts of daily meals. Other preferred seeds, restricted in season or abundance, may be gathered only occasionally. But suppose for example that someone toasted both common and rare seed types for dinner one day, and then spilled the rare seeds around the hearth. Some of these seeds might easily be trampled into the surface of the floor, to be secured centuries later in an archaeologist's flotation sample. The higher frequency of the rare seed type on this floor might lead the analyst to erroneously believe that the rare type was used more heavily.

One way to partially circumvent this kind of dilemma is to rely more on the general archaeological picture than on specific seed frequencies. A common assumption is that the seeds used more frequently in prehistory would be those most often spilled. Common seed types employed by many households are likely to show up repeatedly in the archaeological record; rarely used types are not expected to occur as often. The archaeobotanist generally attempts to interpret seed frequencies from a particular room in light of many samples from many rooms.

Another problem in dealing with the meaning of seed frequencies concerns the number of seeds recovered in relation to their size. Whereas 300 goosefoot seeds might nearly disappear in the bottom of a thimble, one piñon nut might fill it entirely. One piñon nut might be considered significantly less important, numerically, than 300 goosefoot seeds. One method of dealing with the interpretive distortion caused by size variation is to consider only similar-sized seeds. This seems especially important because small seeds are more likely to be lost upon a dirt floor than larger seeds. If spilled, larger seeds can be rather easily returned to the parching pot or swept up with a coarse broom, whereas tiny seeds may elude even the most fastidious housekeeper. The record of use of larger seed types in a prehistoric pueblo may therefore be underrepresented.

Both natural and cultural factors can play a role in seed preservation. Like other floral structures, seeds vary from plant to plant in their basic shapes and strengths. For example, goosefoot (*Chenopodium* sp.) has a fairly durable seed coat that frequently preserves entirely, whereas the multifaceted, thin-walled stickleaf (*Mentzelia albicaulis*) seed crushes easily under pressure. Stickleaf seeds may naturally not preserve as well as goosefoot seeds, regardless of how extensively each resource was exploited. Furthermore, cultural habits such as how seeds are prepared for consumption or other uses can be critical to

archaeological preservation. For example, mild parching, a method long employed in the Southwest to dry seeds and thus preserve food supplies, greatly lessens the probability that seeds might decay, while increasing the possibility that the slightly toasted seed coats may be recovered at some future time. On the other hand, beans boiled all day in a stew pot are likely to turn to mush and lose all identifying characteristics. Although finding one lone bean on a floor might be indicative of rare use, it more likely reflects preparation techniques.

This report covers only three floors at Salmon Ruin, and trends in seed frequencies recognized now could undergo future revision. However, seed evidence from broadly distributed trash samples at Salmon (Doebley 1976; Chapter 37) lends support to archaeological interpretation. Additional information, such as the condition of the prehistoric specimens, their archaeological context, the use of the plants by modern Southwest groups, and observations concerning living plants, was also used to evaluate the prehistoric pollen and seed records.

ROOM 93W: DETECTIVE WORK IN A FREQUENTLY RENOVATED ROOM

For Sherlock Holmes, understanding the history of Room 93W at Salmon Ruin would have been a cinch. Even for Watson, it could only have been classed as "elementary." Because the room's stratigraphic sequence was easy to follow, and because both Chaco and Mesa Verde related people had chosen to live in it, Room 93W was a great setting for a study of plant microfossils.

Room 93W is located in the east-central section of the pueblo (Figure 39.3). Rectangular in outline, it measures approximately 7 m (21 ft) east-west and 2.6 m (8 ft) north-south. It had been renovated repeatedly; we found at least seven distinct floor surfaces (Figure 39.4). No other room has as many well-defined floors. For this report, the floors are numbered consecutively from the top down, in the order they were encountered in excavation.

There is evidence of other modification in 93W in addition to the unusual number of floors. For example, Floor 7 appears to extend below the east wall of the room, suggesting prehistoric activities in a long narrow passage prior to the actual enclosure of space that formed Room 93W. Also, a number of wall niches have been filled in and plastered shut, and at least twice during its history the roof collapsed. One roof fell onto Floor 4, and sometime later Floor 3 was constructed above the fallen roof and other debris. The second, and apparently last, roof over 93W collapsed while the room was being used

Figure 39.3. Aerial view of Salmon Pueblo, showing Room 93W.

for trash disposal during the latter part of Salmon's history. This roof can be seen sandwiched between trash loads in Figure 39.4. No evidence of raging fire has been observed in Room 93W, although other rooms at Salmon Ruin experienced such intense fire that the plaster on their walls melted and fused.

As at many prehistoric Southwest sites, ceramics were used for chronological studies. The Chacoans and later San Juan inhabitants at Salmon each employed distinct pottery types; see Table 39.1 for complete sherd data. Lithic artifact data used to infer how lithics were used in each room are available in Table 39.2. According to ceramic analysis, based on their associated early pottery types or on stratigraphic placement in the room, Floors 1 and 2 were evidently used during the later Mesa Verdean occupation, and Floors 4, 5, 6, and 7 were part of the earlier Chacoan occupation. Floor 3 is sandwiched between the two distinct ceramic traditions of the pueblo, but because no diagnostic sherds were found, its cultural affiliation remains unknown. The choice of Floors 1, 2, and 5 for microfossil analysis was based on the time period each floor represented, and the similarity of architectural features. On the basis of ceramic or stratigraphic evidence, Floors 1 and 2 (Mesa Verdean) and Floor 5 (Chacoan) were judged to represent the two culturally distinct occupations of the pueblo. In addition, each of the floors had a cen-

trally located hearth, which produced plant microfossils as well as comparative samples of microfossils from the floor area around the hearths. The current restricted sampling plan will not reveal activities occurring much beyond the hearth areas. Additional pollen and flotation analysis could include samples from a broader area than is represented here.

Floor 1

The uppermost floor (Floor 1) in Room 93W consisted of thick, hard-packed adobe and sand with a smooth, even surface. Localized rodent disturbance accompanied trash deposition, judging from the evidence of burrowing into trash and the edge of the adjacent north floor. Major features on the floor include a circular hearth, several metates, and numerous stone artifacts (Figure 39.5). The hearth, located slightly east of center in the room, measured approximately 63 cm (24 inches) in diameter and 7–10 cm (2.75–4 inches) in depth. It was constructed of shaped sandstone slabs and blocks, fitted well with adobe mortar. Prehistoric charcoal and ash filled the interior.

Ninety-eight lithic items on Floor 1 (see Table 39.2) were interpreted as representing food processing, tool maintenance (i.e. keeping tools sharp), and tool manufacture (Cameron 1975). The large quartzite metate southwest of the hearth showed evidence

Table 39.1. Ceramic series sherd counts from floors in Room 93W.

Provenience and Ceramic Series (Salmon field notes designations in parentheses)	Sherd Count	Estimated No. of Probable Vessels
Floor 1 surface (H-1-14) and associated hearth (L-1-15.5)		
Chuska corrugated jar	1*	1
San Juan Series		
Black-on-white bowl, carbon paint	1	1
Black-on-white jar, carbon paint	1	1
Corrugated jar	6 (2*)	5
Plain gray jar or bowl	11*	4
Plain white jar	2	1
Red ware jar	2	2
White Mountain Red Ware bowl	1	1
Total	25	16
Floor 1 adobe matrix (I-1-15)		
Chuska corrugated jar	7	1
Cibola plain white jar	1	1
San Juan Series		
Black-on-white bowl, carbon paint	1	1
Black-on-white jar, carbon paint	1	1
Black-on-white ladel handle, carbon paint	1	1
Corrugated jar	66	45
Mancos bowl	3	3
Mancos bowl with corrugated exterior	1	1
Mancos jar	1	1
McElmo bowl	1	1
Mesa Verde bowl	3	3
Plain gray bowl or jar	20	15
Plain white bowl	5	5
Plain white jar	8	8
Tsegi Orange Ware Series		
Medicine Black-on-red	1	1
Tusayan Black-on-red	1	1
Total	121	89
Floor 2 surface (H-2-22)		
Chuska corrugated jar	1	1
San Juan corrugated jar	6	4
Total	7	5
Floor 2 adobe matrix (I-2-23)		
Chuska corrugated jar	3	3
San Juan Series		
Black-on-white bowl, carbon paint	3	3
Corrugated jar	10	10
Mancos bowl	1	1
Mancos jar	1	1
Mesa Verde bowl	6	5
Mesa Verde jar	3	1
Plain white bowl	1	1
Plain white jar	3	3
Plain white unknown form	1	1
White Mountain Red Ware		
St. John's Black-on-red bowl	1	1
Unidentified black-on-red bowl	1	1
Total	34	31
Floor 4 surface (H-4-28)		
Chuska corrugated jar	3	3
Cibola Series		
Chaco pitcher	4	1(?)
Plain white jar	1	1
San Juan Series		
McElmo jar	2	2
Plain gray jar	1	1
Unidentified red ware bowl	1	1
Total	12	9

Table 39.1 (Continued)

Provenience and Ceramic Series (Salmon field notes designations in parentheses)	Sherd Count	Estimated No. of Probable Vessels
Floor 5 surface (H-5-33) and associated hearth (L-6-35)		
Chuska corrugated jar	1*	1
Forestdale (?) smudged red bowl	2	1
San Juan corrugated jar	1*	1
Total	4	3
Floor 5 adobe matrix (I-5-34)		
Chuska corrugated jar	1	1
Cibola plain white jar	1	1
San Juan Series		
Black-on-white bowl, carbon paint	2	2
Black-on-white jar, carbon paint	1	1
Mesa Verde bowl	1	1
White Mountain Red Ware		
Wingate Black-on-red bowl	1	1
Total	7	7

*Sherds found in the hearth.

Table 39.2. Lithic artifact counts from floors in Room 93W.

Function	Floor 1*	Floor 2	Floor 5
Grinding I	6	4	–
Grinding II	7	–	–
Pounding/chopping	10	6	–
Fine tool	22	12	–
Core	1	1	–
Debitage	48	11	1
P & O	4	–	–
Total	98	34	1

Explanation of lithic functions (arbitrary groupings based on ethnographic data and accepted archaeological typology).

Grinding I	Milling bin walls, metates, manos, a pestle. Inferred function is plant food processing.
Grinding II	Shaped stone slabs, miscellaneous ground stone items. No inferred function.
Pounding/chopping	Hammerstones, chopper-uniface, chopper-biface, core-chopper-pounder, chopper-pounder. Inferred functions are tool manufacture and/or plant food preparation.
Fine tool	Non-retouched flakes (utilized flakes) with and without projection. Inferred functions are scraping, cutting, and perforating.
Core	Core material. Inferred function is tool manufacture.
Debitage	Waste flakes. Inferred functions are tool manufacture, tool use, and tool maintenance.
Pigments/ornaments	Pigment material (kaolin) and shell ornaments.

Abstracted from Cameron (1975).
*Salmon Ruin field note designations: Floor 1 (H-1-14/I-1-15), Floor 2 (H-2-22/I-2-23), Floor 5 (H-5-33/I-5-34).

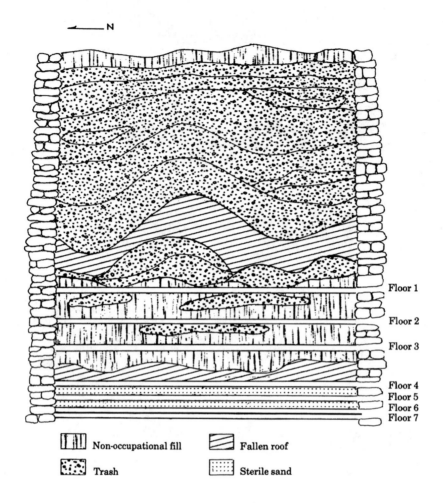

Figure 39.4. Schematic profile of Room 93W, showing stratigraphy; not to scale.

of more than one function. The flat, striated surface appears to have been employed for grinding, but the same face also shows the surface sharply pitted by blows. Perhaps the pits represent upkeep; when the Cochiti wore smooth the surface of the grinding stone, they often had to roughen it by applying a series of intense blows with a hammerstone (Lange 1959:174). Because the metate was recovered with its abraded surface face down, a flotation sample taken beneath this surface probably reflects plant debris caught in the pitted areas during use, and dislodged when the stone was overturned prehistorically.

The pottery types from Floor 1 and its associated hearth spanned both Mesa Verde and Chaco times, even after sherds having ambiguous provenience (locational) data were eliminated. The 25 sherds (see Table 39.1) represent portions of 16 different vessels (Whitten 1977a). The same mixture of both early and late ceramic types was discovered in the trash strata both above the surface of the floor and below the adobe floor matrix. Considering that this was the last floor occupied, it is surprising that the two time periods are mixed together so consistently. Because Floor 2 directly below was built by people affiliated with the Mesa Verde group, Floor 1 should also relate to the Mesa Verde occupation.

Explaining large numbers of Chacoan sherds interspersed in the strata in and surrounding Floor 1 is a problem. Perhaps prehistoric habits relating to the movement of trash could account for such mixing. At Salmon, trash was occasionally deposited within abandoned rooms, while other parts of the pueblo were still occupied. The convenience of a nearby trash heap might outweigh any drawbacks to such a practice. Trash may have been deposited somewhere within the pueblo by the early Chacoan occupation and then later moved to Room 93W by the Mesa Verde inhabitants to provide bulk material for a smooth surface for Floor 1. When the Mesa Verde people abandoned Room 93W and used it

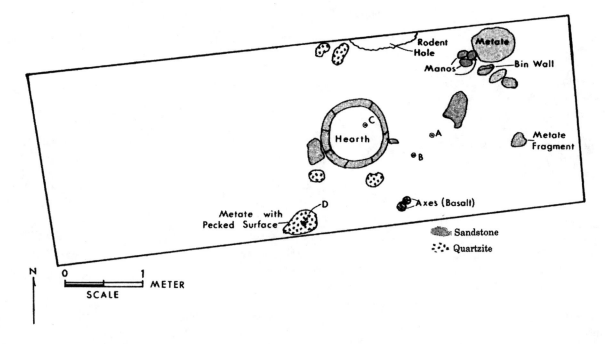

Figure 39.5. Ground plan of Floor 1, Room 93W: (a) pollen 0034, flotation 0028, (b) pollen 0035, flotation 0029, (c) pollen 0027, flotation 0023, (c) flotation 0280.

exclusively as a trash depository, again movement of old Chaco trash from elsewhere to this room could account for the Chaco sherds above the Mesa Verde floor.

Ceramic material recovered from the hearth consisted of only utility (everyday) plain gray and corrugated sherds, most burned on the exterior. These sherds may have broken during their use in hearth-related activities, such as cooking. The presence of only utility ware could indicate specialized activity; in contrast a practice such as brushing the floor sweepings into the hearth during daily cleaning might deposit both decorated and utilitarian pieces.

Eleven sherds were found on the floor surface; five came from the northeast corner of the room containing a sandstone metate and parts of a milling bin wall. If all of the sherds found in this corner were actually associated with milling activity, then a variety of pottery styles and types were used in that endeavor, including a corrugated vessel, a black-on-white jar, a black-on-white bowl, and a White Mountain Red Ware bowl. The latter, thought to have been imported to the Salmon pueblo, was blackened on the exterior, probably from burning. In historic times at Santa Ana Pueblo, "bowls" were used for parching corn (White 1942).

Pairs of pollen and flotation samples from three locations have been examined (see Figure 39.5), and in one location only a single flotation sample was evaluated (Table 39.3). Since trash was deposited on top of this floor when the room was abandoned, plant materials upon the floor surface near the hearth could represent either the time of occupation or the time following abandonment, or both. However, seeds and pollen found beneath the overturned quartzite metate with pecked surface, and within the surface of the hearth (fairly protected positions), are probably associated with the original room activities.

Floor 2

Floor 2 in Room 93W contained more sand and less adobe than Floor 1, and showed slightly deteriorating patches possibly indicative of needed improvement. Perhaps the prospect of repair was discouraging, for the floor was abandoned and Floor 1 was constructed directly above. Rodents had disturbed the north edge of Floor 2, as they had done in Floor 1. Features on this floor included a circular hearth as well as numerous large sandstone artifacts (Figure 39.6). The hearth, which dominates the center of the room, measured 8 cm (3 inches) deep. Constructed of shaped sandstone blocks and adobe, this

Table 39.3. Original data, pollen and flotation samples for Floor 1.

	Hearth[1]		Floor				Metate[2]
	Flotation 0023[3]	Pollen 0027	Flotation 0028	Pollen 0034	Flotation 0029	Pollen 0035	Flotation 0280
Amaranthaceae							
Amaranthus sp.	–	–	–	–	–	–	14[4]
Cactaceae							
Opuntia sp. (cholla)	–	–	–	1:0	–	–	–
Chenopodiaceae							
Atriplex sp.	–	–	–	–	–	–	3
Chenopodium sp.	–	–	2	–	–	23	1
Sarcobatus vermiculatus	–	1c	–	25:14[5]	–	12c	–
Cheno Am	11*	3	89	41:57c	21*	–	79
Compositae							
Ambrosia sp. type	–	–	–	9:8	–	9	–
Artemisia sp.	–	–	–	0:1	–	–	–
Long-spine pollen	–	–	–	2:3	–	6[6]	–
Verbesina sp.	–	–	–	–	1	–	–
Cruciferae							
Descurainia sp.	–	–	18	–	–	–	295*
Cupressaceae							
Juniperus sp.	–	–	–	0:1	–	–	–
Twigs/scale leaf	X*	–	X*	–	X*	–	–
Cyperaceae							
Scirpus sp.	–	–	2	3:1	–	–	–
Euphorbiaceae							
Euphorbia glyptosperma type	–	–	28*	–	–	–	8
Gramineae	–	–	1	1:0	–	1	–
Paniceae	–	–	–	–	1	–	–
Zea mays	–	2	–	8:7	–	37	–
Juncaceae							
Juncus sp. type	1*	–	3	–	–	–	–
Loasaceae							
Mentzelia albicaulis	–	–	1*	–	1*	–	1*
Pinaceae							
Pinus sp.	–	–	–	1:0	–	8	–
Polygonaceae							
Eriogonom sp.	–	–	–	1:0	–	1	–
Polygonom sawatchense type	–	–	4	–	–	–	–
Portulacaceae							
Portulaca sp.	1	–	12	–	–	–	15
Solanaceae							
Physalis sp.	1*	–	–	–	–	–	–
Typhaceae							
Typha sp.	–	–	–	–	–	2	–
Miscellaneous							
Black spherical items	–	–	X	–	–	–	X
Bud tips	–	–	–	–	X*	–	X*
Cuticular layer inside seeds	–	–	X	–	–	–	X
Feces	–	–	–	–	–	–	X
Insect segments, cocoons, larvae	–	–	X	–	–	–	X
Tule Springs Unknown	–	–	1	–	–	–	1*

Table 39.3 (Continued)

	Hearth[1]		Floor				Metate[2]
	Flotation 0023[3]	Pollen 0027	Flotation 0028	Pollen 0034	Flotation 0029	Pollen 0035	Flotation 0280
Unknown Disseminules							
8015	–	–	2	–	–	–	–
8033	–	–	2	–	–	–	–
8035	–	–	–	–	–	–	1
8038	1	–	–	–	–	–	–
Other and Unidentifiable	–	2	–	8:6	–	1	–
		n = 8		n = 200		n = 100	

[1]Salmon Ruin field note designations: Hearth (L-1-15.5), Floor (H-1-14/I-1-15).
[2]Quartzite metate with pecked surface (record key 6107).
[3]Flotation and pollen sample numbers all use prefix 093W.
[4]Flotation data are seeds or achenes, unless otherwise noted.
[5]In this report, pollen data recorded as (25:14) indicates that the pollen analyst (Dr. Vorsila Bohrer) counted 2 subsamples of 100 pollen grains each for a total 200-grain sample. The first number (25) corresponds to the first subsample of 100 grains, and the second number (14) corresponds to the second subsample of 100 grains. For this example, 25% and 14% respectively of pollen grains in the two subsamples belonged to *Sarcobatus vermiculatus*. Occasionally, the pollen analyst counted more or less than 200 grains; all total counts are therefore marked in the text (e.g., n = 215 or n = 8). Pollen samples containing few grains generally have percentages that are not meaningful for interpretation.
[6]Includes one *Helianthus* type.
X = present but not counted; * = some or all parched or carbonized; c = some clumped.

hearth also contained charcoal and oxidized sandstone from prehistoric use. The sandstone metate and associated bin wall in the northeast corner of the room projected above Floors 1 and 2, thus serving the occupants of both floors. The 34 lithic items from Floor 2 (see Table 39.2) were probably used to process food, or sharpen or produce tools (Cameron 1975). Although the lithic remains are less numerous than those on Floor 1, they are thought to have served the same purposes.

The ceramic materials on Floor 2 (see Table 39.1) consisted of six San Juan corrugated sherds and one trachyte-tempered corrugated sherd (Whitten 1977b). All but one of these sherds were localized southwest of the hearth, near a milling area. Five of the sherds had fire-blackened exteriors. The fact that all of the pottery on this floor represents corrugated vessels may prove typical of habitation rooms. At Broken K Pueblo in Arizona, Hill (1970) found that higher percentages of corrugated pottery were associated with kivas and habitation rooms, though storage rooms by comparison contained very low amounts of any pottery types.

Because the floor surface lacked painted pottery, the time of occupation could not be determined from ceramic evidence alone. Therefore, the pottery sherds from the adobe floor matrix itself were examined, revealing a high percentage of Mesa Verde type pottery sherds and a St. John's Black-on-red sherd (generally considered a late pottery type), coupled with the absence of any Cibola (Chacoan) type pottery. The floor was therefore likely built and used by people related to the Mesa Verdean culture.

Matched pairs of pollen and flotation samples from three locations were examined (see Figure 39.7); in a fourth location, only a pollen sample was analyzed (Table 39.4). These samples generally represent the area near the hearth. Only the single pollen sample from the western segment of the room may record evidence of nonrelated activities.

Floor 5

Unlike the hard-packed adobe surfaces of Floors 1 and 2, Floor 5 in Room 93W had a smooth undisturbed surface consisting of a very thin gray organic band, overlying 1–2 cm of clean, tightly packed yellow sand. In addition, sterile sand, purposefully brought in by the Salmon inhabitants, separated Floor 5 from the floors above and below it. A centrally located hearth measured 93 cm (63 inches) from east to west and 55–77 cm (21–29 inches) north to south; it descended 14 cm (5 inches) below the floor surface (Figure 39.8). The hearth was defined mainly by a heavy oxidation ring caused by repeated fires in its interior, and a few sandstone slabs were set around the rim in a loose fasion; two slabs appeared to be part of an earlier hearth wall. Only one piece of lithic debris was recovered from this floor (see Table 39.2), shedding no light on room use.

Floor surface and floor matrix pottery totaling 11 sherds (see Table 39.1) was used to date the time of occupation of Floor 5 (Whitten 1977c). A corrugated

Figure 39.6. Photograph of quartzite metate with pecked surface from Room 93W, Floor 1.

sherd with trachyte temper from the Chuska Valley, and two smudged red[1] bowl sherds from the floor surface indicate that the floor was occupied during the Chacoan portion of Salmon's history. Six of seven sherds imbedded in the floor matrix are also characteristic of the Chacoan occupation. A single Mesa Verde sherd associated with the floor matrix is of uncertain provenience. Supplementary evidence from the floor above (Floor 4) indicates that Floor 5 is probably Chacoan, as the later floor contained pottery types characteristic of the early part of Salmon's history (see Table 39.1).

Activities thought to occur on Floor 5 must be considered speculative due to the few sherds found and the single lithic item recovered. Two corrugated sherds from the hearth fill show evidence of exterior burning. Either they are pieces of original cooking vessels, or they were scorched when pieces were swept into the hearth. The two smudged red sherds may indicate a nonceremonial area; smudged red sherds at Kin Klesto in Chaco Canyon were located almost exclusively in rooms other than kivas (Vivian and Mathews 1964:65). However, the unit of analysis at Kin Klesto was "floor and fill above floor," so it is uncertain whether the red sherds related to room use or to trash deposition into the room after abandonment.

Four flotation samples and four pollen samples were taken from two contiguous 1 m areas (see Figure 39.8). Three pairs of these pollen and flotation samples came from within the hearth, and one pair represents the floor near the hearth (Table 39.5). The hearth on Floor 5 was apparently superimposed over a series of previously existing hearths associated with the floor below (Floor 6). In fact, pollen and flotation pairs B and C may represent the earlier hearths associated with Floor 6, as the excavators could not define the bottom of the hearth of Floor 5 (Figure 39.9). Taxa unique to samples B and C were noted in case there were potential differences in plant materials between lower hearth samples B and C and the upper hearth samples A; however, the discrepancy between lower and upper hearth samples consisted of only a grass floral part and an unknown seed, so the data from all hearth samples were combined.

PLANT REMAINS FROM THREE FLOORS IN ROOM 93W, THE SALMON RUIN

Twenty-seven plant genera were identified in the pollen flotation samples from the three floors in Room 93W. The following section, arranged alphabetically by plant family, examines the evidence and evaluates the potential story told by these minute plant parts.[2]

---

[1]Smudged red sherds at Salmon Ruin refer to a pottery ware with a plain red exterior and an intentionally blackened (or smudged) interior. This pottery type is apparently first fired in an oxidizing atmosphere and is then inverted, and the inside is subjected to a smoky, reducing atmosphere.

---

[2]All plants in the figures have been reduced in size by a third. The normal size of each seed is included in the sketches, often appearing as a small black dot.

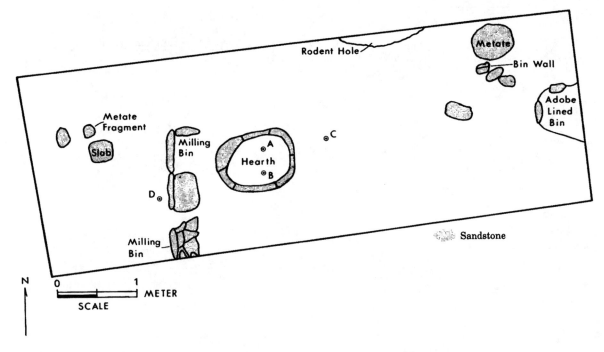

Figure 39.7. Ground plan of Floor 2, Room 93W: (a) pollen 0040, flotation 0032, (b) pollen 0038, flotation 0030, (c) pollen 0039, flotation 0031, (d) pollen 0031.

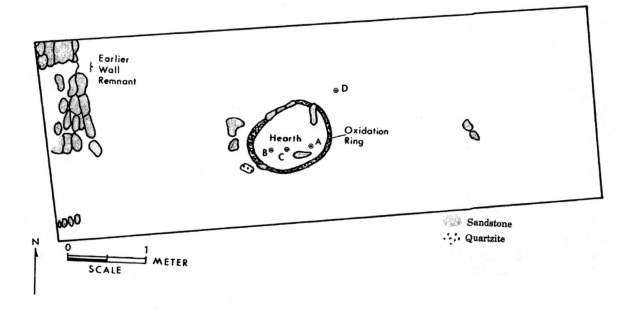

Figure 39.8. Ground plan of Floor 5, Room 93W: (a) pollen 0047, flotation 0039, (b) pollen 0050, flotation 0042, (c) pollen 0049, flotation 0041, (d) pollen 0051, flotation 0043.

Table 39.4. Original data, pollen and flotation samples for Floor 2.

	Hearth[1]				Floor		
	Flotation 0030[2]	Pollen 0038	Flotation 0032	Pollen 0040	Flotation 0031	Pollen 0039	Pollen 0031
Cactaceae							
Opuntia sp. (cholla)	–	2:0	–	–	–	1:1	–
Chenopodiaceae							
Chenopodium sp.	–	43:50c	–	–	–	44:54c	–
Sarcobatus vermiculatus	–	7:3	–	–	–	5:1	5:3
Cheno Am	1[3]	–	15*	–	–	–	54:41c
Compositae							
Ambrosia sp. type	–	8:7c	–	1	–	10:7c	11:9
Artemisia sp.	–	1:1	–	–	–	1:1	1:3
Low-spine prolate	–	–	–	–	–	–	1:2
Long-spine pollen	–	3:3c	–	–	–	3:1	0:3
Cucurbitaceae							
Cucurbita sp.	–	1:0	–	–	–	–	–
Cupressaceae							
Juniperus sp.	–	7:4c	–	–	–	2:2	0:1
Twigs/scale leaf	X*	–	X*	–	X*	–	–
Ephedraceae							
Ephedra nevadensis	–	0:1	–	–	–	0:1	1:1
Ephedra torreyana	–	3:1	–	–	–	3:1	1:1
Gramineae (floret)	1	3:2	–	–	–	4:2	1:1
Zea mays	–	3:1	1*	1	2*	11:13	1:1
Loasaceae							
Mentzelia albicaulis	–	–	1*	–	–	–	–
Malvaceae							
Sphaeralcea	–	–	–	1	–	–	–
Pinaceae							
Pinus sp.	–	17:21	–	2	–	5:11	7:4
Polygonaceae							
Eriogonom sp.	–	–	–	–	–	2:0	1:0
Solanaceae							
Physalis sp.	–	–	1*	–	–	–	–
Miscellaneous							
Black spherical items	–	–	X	–	–	–	–
Bud tips	X*	–	X*	–	–	–	–
Catkins	–	–	X	–	–	–	–
Feces	–	–	X	–	–	–	–
Insect segments, cocoons, larvae	–	–	–	–	X	–	–
Tule Springs Unknown	–	–	10*	–	–	–	–
Other and Unidentifiable	–	2:6	–	–	–	9:6	17:10
		n = 200		n = 5		n = 200	n = 181

[1]Salmon Ruin field note designations: Hearth (L-3-21), Floor (H-2-22/I-2-23).
[2]Flotation and pollen sample numbers all use prefix 093W.
[3]Flotation data are seeds or achenes, unless otherwise noted.
X = present but not counted; * = some or all parched or carbonized; c = some clumped.

Table 39.5. Original data, pollen and flotation samples for Floor 5.

	Upper Hearth Fill[1]		Floor		Lower Hearth Fill			
	Flotation 0039[2]	Pollen 0047	Flotation 0043	Pollen 0051	Flotation 0041	Pollen 0049	Flotation 0042	Pollen 0050
Cactaceae								
Opuntia sp. (cholla)	–	–	–	1:0	–	–	–	–
Capparidaceae								
Cleome sp.	1[3]	–	–	–	–	–	–	–
Chenopodiaceae								
Chenopodium sp.	2	–	4	–	2	–	–	–
Sarcobatus vermiculatus	–	2	–	3:1	–	–	–	–
Cheno Am	13	7c	1	60:52	5	2	12	–
Compositae								
Ambrosia sp. type	–	7	–	15:23	–	2	–	–
Artemisia sp.	–	–	–	1:0	–	–	–	–
Long-spine pollen	–	–	–	1:0	–	–	–	–
Low-spine prolate	–	1	–	10:3	–	–	–	–
Cupressaceae								
Juniperus sp.	–	–	–	2:1	–	–	–	–
Twigs/scale leaf	X*	–	–	–	X*	–	–	–
Cyperaceae	2	–	–	–	–	–	–	–
Ephedraceae								
Ephedra nevadensis	–	–	–	1:0	–	–	–	–
Ephedra torreyana	–	–	–	1:0	–	–	–	–
Gramineae	–	–	–	3:0	–	1	–	–
Oryzopsis hymenoides (lemma)	–	–	–	–	1*	–	–	–
Zea mays	1*	1	–	1:0	–	3	2*	–
Juncaceae								
Juncus cooperi type	22*	–	–	–	–	–	–	–
Pinaceae								
Pinus sp.	–	–	–	7:10	–	1	–	2
Polygonaceae								
Eriogonom sp.	–	1	–	1:1	–	–	–	–
Portulacaceae								
Portulaca sp.	64	–	1	–	1	–	–	–
Miscellaneous								
Bones	X	–	–	–	–	–	–	–
Bud tips	X*	–	–	–	–	–	–	–
Cuticular layer inside seeds	X	–	–	–	–	–	X	–
Feces	X	–	–	–	–	–	–	–
Insect segments	X	–	X	–	–	–	–	–
Unknown Disseminules								
8006	1	–	–	–	–	–	–	–
8007	1	–	–	–	–	–	–	–
8008	–	–	–	–	–	–	1	–
8012	1	–	–	–	–	–	–	–
8033	1	–	–	–	–	–	–	–
Other and Unidentifiable	–	–	–	6:11	–	1	–	–
		n = 19		n = 215		n = 10		n = 2

[1]Salmon Ruin field note designations: Upper Hearth Fill (L-6-35), Floor (H-5-33/I-5-34, Lower Hearth Fill (L-7-37).
[2]Flotation and pollen sample numbers all use prefix 093W.
[3]Flotation data are seeds or achenes, unless otherwise noted.
X = present but not counted; * = some or all parched or carbonized; c = some clumped.

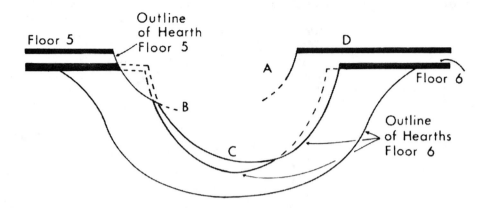

Figure 39.9. Cross-section (not to scale) through hearths on Floors 5 and 6: (a) pollen 0047, flotation 0039, (b) pollen 0049, flotation 0041, (C) pollen 0050, flotation 0042, (d) pollen 0051, flotation 0043.

AMARANTHACEAE-AMARANTH FAMILY
Pigweed (*Amaranthus*)

Many pigweeds are weedy annuals that thrive in disturbed habitats (Figure 39.10; Kearney and Peebles 1960:265). Agricultural fields and trash heaps are ideal for such opportunists, which exhibit a "shifting" seasonality (Bohrer 1975d:3). Young pigweed seedlings could be available as greens (like spinach) from late spring through fall, whenever the right growing conditions occur. In a particularly moist season, recently sprouted pigweed greens can be harvested repeatedly as new plants spring up with each rain. Later, the seeds would be ready in both summer and fall. Three native species of pigweed currently grow fairly close to Salmon Ruin.

The 14 pigweed seeds beneath the overturned quartzite metate on Floor 1 may indicate that the Salmon inhabitants ground these small seeds into a meal or flour, much as historic people did. The Zuni ground the seeds of *Amaranthus blitoides* S. Wats[3] with corn meal, added water, and then steamed the resulting dumplings (Stevenson 1915:65). The Acoma and Laguna Indians also ground the seeds of *Amaranthus* spp. for food (Swank 1932:26). The Papagos formerly also valued *Amaranthus palmeri* seeds (Castetter and Bell 1942:62).

Prehistoric people are also known to have used various pigweeds. *Amaranthus* sp. seeds were found by Bohrer (1973a:215) at Fresnal Shelter, dating 100 AD and earlier. Jones and Fonner (1954:94–95) identified pigweed seeds in Basketmaker II sites in south-

western Colorado, and Struever (1977:42) found them in a small pueblo constructed in the late 700s AD in Chaco Canyon. Wetterstrom (1976) also noted their presence at Arroyo Hondo, a pueblo near Santa Fe, New Mexico that was occupied between 1200 and 1400 AD. It is therefore clear that pigweeds have been a part of Southwest food resources for a very long time.

CACTACEAE – CACTUS FAMILY
Cholla (*Opuntia*)

Cholla cacti have round stems and are easily distinguished from the flat-padded prickly pear cacti of the Southwest deserts. Presently only one species of cholla grows around Salmon Ruin—the short, ground-hugging *Opuntia whipplei* Engelm. & Bigel. The tall, conspicuous cholla (*Opuntia imbricate*) of central and eastern New Mexico has not yet been found after 5 years of searching in the San Juan Valley.

Cholla offers a variety of edible parts; perhaps among the most relished parts were the flower buds, which form in spring. Historic groups have recognized the food value of the cholla buds, as the Pima ranked cholla buds third in predominance among ancient native foods (Castetter and Bell 1942:63), the Maricopa listed them as fourth in importance (Castetter and Bell 1951:201), and the Hopi ate them as well (Nequatewa 1943:19). Cholla joints (stems) were also eaten, but were apparently viewed as starvation food among some groups. The Hopi used the vegetative parts of *Opuntia whipplei* in the spring, and sometimes called the month of March the "cactus moon" because of food scarcity at this time (Whiting

---

[3]Notations following a scientific name, such as S. Wats, refer to the authority that originally described and published an account of the plant.

Figure 39.10. Pigweed (*Amaranthus* sp.) plant and seed, magnified 15x.

1966:86). The Acoma and Laguna also roasted the joints of *Opuntia imbricata* (as *O. arborescens* Engelm.) and ate them in times of famine (Swank 1932:55). Such "aseasonal" parts (Bohrer 1975d:3) would represent year-round reliable resources that were apparently not preferred in times of plenty. The fruits of cholla cactus, generally found in the fall, can also be eaten.

Cholla were sometimes used for purposes other than food. For example, a Zuni fraternity cared for a bed of *O. imbricata* (as *O. arborescens* Engelm.) about 3 miles from Zuni, gathering the plants from this particular bed to be used in whipping ceremonies of the fraternity (Stevenson 1915:95). The Hopi chewed or pounded and boiled the root of *O. whipplei* and took it in conjunction with globemallow (*Sphaeralcea* sp.) for diarrhea (Whiting 1966:86).

The occurrence of low frequencies of cholla pollen on floors in 93W (Table 39.6) may be due to chance, but the fact that these insect-pollinated grains are present on all three floors may indicate repeated prehistoric use. Cholla pollen has been recovered from washing the fruits and stems of modern cholla (Bohrer 1972:26), and it seems reasonable to assume that in prehistory these heavy, sticky grains may have entered 93W on various cholla parts brought in for use. Charred cholla buds have been recovered from the floor of the Tower Kiva (Room 64W). Additional rooms at Salmon need to be examined to further substantiate cholla use.

CAPPARIDACEAE – CAPER FAMILY
Rocky Mountain Beeweed (*Cleome*)

Rocky Mountain beeweed is a tall, impressive annual with showy purple flowers, often found growing in disturbed places such as roadsides and arroyo washes (Figure 39.11). The plant easily finds its way into cultivated fields today, as it probably did centuries ago. The present-day Hopi encourage *Cleome serrulata* Pursh. in their cornfields, ensuring a large supply of tender greens for the following spring (Whiting 1966:16).

Rocky Mountain beeweed, like the pigweed, is a plant of "shifting" seasonality. Its seeds lie ready throughout the growing season to germinate when conditions are favorable. In a particularly good growing season, beeweed greens could be available spring through fall, with seeds ready for harvest in the summer and fall. One species of beeweed (*Cleome serrulata* Pursh.) grows very near Salmon Ruin today.

A single *Cleome* seed in the hearth on Floor 5 of Room 93W may not seem like strong evidence for the use of Rocky Mountain beeweed, but trash samples from other locations at Salmon have also produced seeds of this plant (Doebley 1976:33). Excavators also recovered beeweed seeds from a burial (Sample 102W1018). *Cleome* sp. seeds found in human coprolites (feces) in Glen Canyon and Antelope House (Fry and Hall 1975:89) attest to their use as food by other Southwest prehistoric groups.

Young seedlings of *Cleome serrulata* Pursh. have frequently served as a potherb among modern Southwest groups, comparable to spinach (Castetter 1935:24; Elmore 1944:50). Young plants can also be boiled until thick and black to use as paint for pottery (Robbins et al. 1916:58–59; Stevenson 1915:82). Swank (1932:37) noted that the Acoma and Laguna gathered beeweed seeds in the fall and cooked them well, then dried the mixture on willow sticks for winter use. The concoction was later prepared for eating by cooking into mush. The Isleta ground the seeds to make flour for bread, but apparently this practice had faded by the early 1930s (Jones 1931:26).

Table 39.6. Cholla (*Opuntia* sp.) evidence from three floors in Room 93 W.

Floor No.	Location	No. of Seeds	No. of Pollen Grains
1	Floor	–	1 (n = 200)
2	Floor	–	2 (n = 200)
	Hearth	–	2 (n = 200)
5	Floor	–	1 (n = 215)

Figure 39.11. Rocky Mountain beeweed (*Cleome serru-lata*) plant and seed, magnified 6x.

The Sia (as Zia) of New Mexico also ate the seeds (White 1962:107).

CHENOPODIACEAE – GOOSEFOOT FAMILY

Saltbush (*Atriplex*)

Three fragile papery wings of a saltbush fruit were recovered from beneath the quartzite metate on Floor 1. The fruit itself was absent, so the wings may have blown in on the wind, but the location of this material seems inconsistent with such an explanation. It is perhaps coincidental that they have been found beneath a heavy grinding stone, and not elsewhere in the room. The seeds of a number of species of saltbush were ground into flour by groups in Utah, Arizona, and California (Palmer 1878:603). Perhaps the saltbush fruit constituted a food resource at Salmon as well, although the evidence is currently suggestive at best.

Goosefoot (*Chenopodium*)

Goosefoot gets its common name because its leaves take the general shape of a webbed goose's foot (Figure 39.12). Both annuals and perennials belong to this genus. Annual goosefoots, like many

pigweeds, are often plants of "shifting" seasonality, taking advantage of good growing conditions at any time between the last frost of spring and the first frost of fall. Thus, goosefoot leaves would be available for the cookpot for many months, and the seeds were available for flour or mush during the summer and fall seasons. The plants could be eaten by themselves, or used in conjunction with a number of other foods, as the Hopi did (Whiting 1966:74). Seven species of goosefoot have been collected in the San Juan Valley recently.

When mature, the tiny goosefoot seeds are easily shaken free from their enclosing bracts and collected with a beater basket. The Zuni and the Navajo collected the seeds (Standley 1911:458), and the Papago valued *Chenopodium murale* as well (Castetter and Bell 1942:62).

Some of the goosefoot seeds found in Room 93W (Table 39.7) were associated with a hearth and a metate, perhaps indicative that the seeds were processed prior to use. The Zuni ground the seeds of *Chenopodium leptophyllum* (Moq.) Nutt. with corn meal, added water, and steamed the mixture for consumption (Stevenson 1915:66). During transfer of seeds from collecting basket to metate to cookpot, some seeds could easily be spilled around the grinding stone and into the cooking fire. Perhaps the Salmon inhabitants prepared goosefoot seeds in much the same way as the historic Zunis.

The pollen grain evidence also suggests that goosefoot was brought in purposefully. Although goosefoot pollen is normally carried by the wind and could presumably occur naturally in high frequencies, the presence of clumps of pollen grains on Floor 2 implies another mode of transportation. Single pollen grains travel easily on air currents, but clusters are far less likely to float away from the parent plant. Clumped goosefoot pollen could have been brought to the pueblo clinging to winnowed seed, or enclosed in young flowers carried in for greens (see also the discussion of Cheno Am pollen).

Greasewood (*Sarcobatus vermiculatus*)

The man-sized greasewood (Figure 39.13) grew abundantly on the unexcavated ruin prior to 1970, and continues to grow there today. Since the pollen is naturally transported on the wind, no particular significance can be attached to the pollen grains found on the three floors in Room 93W (Table 39.8). However, a very high percentage of greasewood pollen (70%) was recovered in a ceramic bowl (Sample 102W1008) elsewhere at Salmon, indicating intentional collection of the flowers.

Figure 39.12. Goosefoot (*Chenopodium* sp.) plant and seed, magnified 17x.

Greasewood is not generally considered a food plant, but it has been employed in other ways by the Hopi of Arizona. The Hopi used the wood for rabbit sticks, planting sticks, arrows, and general construction, and as a chief kiva fuel (Whiting 1966:74). Wood scraps found at Salmon should be examined carefully for possible greasewood fragments.

Cheno Am (*Chenopodium-Amaranthus*)

The seeds of genera in two separate plant families (*Chenopodium* of the goosefoot family, and *Amaranthus* of the amaranth family) exhibit an amazing similarity, as do their pollen grains. Distinguishing between poorly preserved seed specimens of these two genera in the laboratory is nearly impossible, so an artificial grouping labeled Cheno Am is frequently utilized. Fortunately, documentation of the uses of both goosefoot and pigweed parallel each other to a great extent, making interpretation easier (see other sections of this report for some of these uses).

The ubiquitous distribution of Cheno Am seeds on all three floors of 93W (Table 39.9) may indicate heavy or repeated use. Doebley (1976:46) found Cheno Am seeds (and pollen) in trash samples from every room and plaza test pit he examined at Salmon

Ruin. The burned condition of a number of the seeds in Room 93W suggests that the Salmon people were preparing them near a fire, and perhaps accidentally dropped a few into the hot ashes. Surplus seeds destined for winter storage may have been toasted to stay the growth of mold or fungi. Brittle, heat-dried seeds easily crumble to flour under the pressure of the grinding stone. The more handling of Cheno Am seeds that occurred prehistorically, the more chances there were to drop some into the firepit or onto the floor.

The high percentages of Cheno Am pollen grains on all three floors (ranging up to 60%) are puzzling. Do they represent actual use of the pollen or plants by the inhabitants of Salmon, or were they transported onto the floor naturally by the wind? When pigweed and goosefoot plants begin pollination, large amounts of their pollen grains are dispersed into the air (Potter and Rowley 1960:15), and presumably could have drifted onto the floors in Room 93W. Evidence was found, however, to suggest that at least some of the Cheno Am pollen was brought in by humans. A clump of 15 Cheno Am pollen grains was recovered from Floor 1, and a number of clusters of goosefoot pollen grains were observed in the hearth and floor samples on Floor 2, in clumps of 2 to 30 grains. A single clump also came from the hearth of Floor 5. Since this pollen type generally travels as single grains on the wind, these clumps may have been brought in on winnowed goosefoot

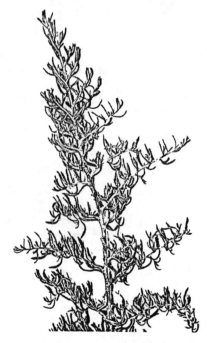

Figure 39.13. Greasewood (*Sarcobatus vermiculatus*) branch.

Table 39.7. Goosefoot (*Chenopodium* sp.) evidence from three floors in Room 93W.

Floor No.	Location	No. of Seeds	No. of Pollen Grains
1	Floor	2	23 (n = 100)
	Beneath quartzite metate	1	–
2	Floor	–	44:54 (n = 200)[1]
	Hearth	–	43:50 (n = 200)[1]
5	Floor	4	–
	Hearth	4	–

[1]Some clumped.

Table 39.8. Greasewood (*Sarcobatus vermiculatus*) evidence from three floors in Room 93W.

Floor No.	Location	No. of Seeds	No. of Pollen Grains
1	Floor	–	25:14 (n = 200)
			12 (n = 100)[1]
	Hearth	–	1 (n = 8)
2	Floor	–	5:3 (n = 181)
	Hearth	–	7:3 (n = 200)
5	Floor	–	3:1 (n = 215)
	Hearth	–	2 (n = 19)

[1]Some clumped.

Table 39.9. Cheno Am evidence from three floors in Room 93W.

Floor No.	Location	No. of Seeds	No. of Pollen Grains
1	Floor	110[1]	41:57 (n = 200)[2]
	Hearth	11[1]	3 (n = 8)
	Beneath quarzite metate	79	–
2	Floor	–	54:41 (n = 181)[2]
	Hearth	16[1]	–
5	Floor	1	60:52 (n = 215)[2]
	Hearth	30	9 (n = 29)[2]

[1]Some or all burned. [2]Some clumped

Table 39.10. Ragweed (*Ambrosia* type) evidence from three floors in Room 93W.

Floor No.	Location	No. of Seeds	No. of Pollen Grains	
			Low Spine	Low Spine Prolate
1	Floor	–	9:8 (n = 200)	–
			9 (n = 100)	
2	Floor	–	11:9 (n = 181)	1:2 (n = 181)
			10:7 (n = 200)	
	Hearth	–	8:7 (n = 200)[1]	–
			1 (n = 5)	
5	Floor	–	15:23 (n = 215)	10:3 (n = 215)
	Hearth	–	9 (n = 29)	1 (n = 19)

[1]Two clumps.

seed. The goosefoot plant can have both mature seeds and pollinating flowers on its stems at the same time, and flowers might be easily beaten into a basket along with the desired seeds. Thus both pollen and seeds would be brought into a room at the same time.

COMPOSITAE – SUNFLOWER FAMILY
Ragweed (*Ambrosia* type)

Pollen grains of ragweed are wind-borne, as most hayfever sufferers know. Ragweed grains in 93W (Table 39.10) could easily be dismissed as naturally introduced, except that two clumps of ragweed type[4] grains were observed on Floor 2. Because wind-borne pollen grains generally travel singly, these clumps may indicate prehistoric use of ragweed. Since the clumped grains were found only on one floor, further evidence from Salmon Ruin is needed to seriously document ancient ragweed utilization. Modern ethnographic literature generally remains mute regarding this plant. The low-spine prolate pollen grains resemble ragweed, and since they too are wind-borne, they may have been introduced naturally into Room 93W.

Sagebrush (*Artemisia*)

There are no more than eight sagebrush pollen grains associated with any floor (Table 39.11), and they could have been introduced by the wind, their natural mode transportation. No evidence exists for any other interpretation.

Crown-Beard (*Verbesina* type), Sunflower (*Helianthus* type), and Long-Spine Compositae

Many members of the sunflower family, such as the common roadside sunflowers (*Helianthus* sp.) and the crown-beard (*Verbesina* sp.), are pollinated by insects. These plants produce large, heavy pollen grains designed to cling to insect bodies and appendages to ensure plant cross-fertilization. The long-spine pollen and the crown-beard evidence from 93W (Table 39.12) have been combined for this discussion, as both belong to this group of insect-pollinated sunflowers.

Single grains of pollen from insect-pollinated plants are somewhat unlikely to travel far from the parent plant without the help of humans or animals; the likelihood that clumps of insect-pollinated grains will travel any distance on their own is zero. The recovery of one clump of three long-spine pollen

grains in the hearth of Floor 2 therefore strongly suggests intentional use by humans. For example, this pollen may have entered the room either on the flowers, or clinging to the winnowed seeds (achenes) of one of the species of sunflower. As an experiment, Bohrer (1972:26) washed some modern winnowed sunflower seeds (the seeds develop long after the flowers have shriveled) and found abundant pollen in the wash water. It seems that even though the flowering stage may be long past, the pollen can still cling to the seeds and become part of the archaeological record. Perhaps the crown-beard seed could have been the carrier of some of the long-spine pollen of Floor 1.

The precise identification of the plant(s) producing the long-spine pollen on floors in 93W is currently unknown, so it is difficult to know what plants to examine in the archaeobotanical literature for possible modern usage. Many insect-pollinated members of the sunflower family have served numerous economic needs among Southwest groups (Bohrer 1966:5). For illustrative purposes, uses for the common sunflower (*Helianthus* sp.) are given here, as one pollen grain was tentatively identified as this type in Room 93W. *Helianthus* sp. flowers have been employed by the Zuni in ceremonies (Stevenson 1915:93), by the Navajo for good luck in hunting (Vestal 1952:52), and by the Jemez and Hopi in dances (Cook 1930:24; Whiting 1966:97). The seeds were eaten by both the Navajos (Elmore 1944:87) and the Hopis (Whiting 1966:97).

CRUCIFERAE – MUSTARD FAMILY
Tansy Mustard (*Descurainia*)

Tansy mustard is a herbaceous annual of disturbed habitats, capable of producing abundant small reddish seeds in the spring or cool season (Figure 39.14). One of the first annual seed crops to mature, it may have played an important role in prehistoric food resources. Late winter and early spring were perhaps difficult seasons in years when the previous summer's crops were consumed and the bulk of the new year's native plant growth was just barely beginning. A large early crop of tansy mustard greens and seeds would have been welcome relief in times of food stress.

Despite the potential productivity of tansy mustard, however, it is not seen regularly in the spring. As a plant of "qualified" seasonality (Bohrer 1975d:3) it has to have just the right environmental conditions to produce abundant seeds. When the late winter and early spring ground moisture level is adequate a widespread crop of tansy mustard can be expected. When ground moisture is low, only a sparse crop

---

[4]The word *type* implies that the prehistoric specimen is morphologically similar to the modern species, but they may not be exactly alike.

Figure 39.14. Tansy mustard (*Descurainia* sp.) plant and seed, magnified 20x.

can be harvested. So although tansy mustard is an important cool season resource, it is not always dependable in the arid Southwest. Two species of tansy mustard grow in the San Juan Valley today; one (*D. sophia* L.) is a historical introduction.

The occurrence of tansy mustard seeds on Floor 1 in Room 93W (Table 39.13) may indicate deliberate prehistoric gathering and use of this resource. Seeds found beneath the quartzite metate may be residue from a batch that was ground into meal. Most of the seeds appeared parched and deflated under the microscope. Doebley (1976:51) found tansy mustard seeds, some parched and some carbonized, in 8 of 17 rooms and plaza areas sampled at Salmon Ruin; they might represent a prehistoric food resource.

A strong tradition of exploiting tansy mustard seed was found among nonpueblo groups. The Pima parched and ground the seeds of tansy mustard, *Sophia pinnata* (Walt.) Britton., and mixed them with water to form a gruel of pinole (Russell 1975: 77). The Mohave and Yuma Indians used the small reddish seeds in a similar manner. The Maricopa

considered them to be the most important of the small seeds (Castetter and Bell 1951:191). In 1936 a Ramah Navajo woman was observed making a cake from the ground seeds of *Descurainia pinnata* (Walt.) Britton. (Vestal 1952:28), though this practice was rapidly dying out.

The only historic record of pueblo use of tansy mustard is among the Hopi, who ate the young plants as greens in the spring (Whiting 1966:77). It seems that in prehistory the seeds played a larger role in pueblo life, at least at Salmon Ruin and in Chaco Canyon (Struever 1977:52). The prehistoric record can also be cited to show that tansy mustard had both broad geographic coverage and time depth in prehistory. For example, tansy mustard seeds have been found in Basketmaker II sites near Durango, Colorado (Jones and Fonner 1954:95) dating to 100 AD, in Hohokam archaeological sites in southern Arizona dating between 1100 and 1200 AD (Bohrer 1970:419; Bohrer et al. 1969:3), and in Tularosa Cave in the Mogollon Culture Area (Cutler 1952:479).

CUCURBITACEAE – GOURD FAMILY

Squash, Pumpkin, Gourd (*Cucurbita*)

The cucurbit family includes the wild gourd *Cucurbita foetidissima* and cultivated species such as pumpkins. Five years of searching for the wild gourd in the San Juan Valley have produced no evidence of its presence there, even though the elevation is conducive to its growth (Kearney and Peebles 1960:822). However, casual observation indicates that the wild gourd does grow in New Mexico along roads or in other areas unexposed to grazing pressure. Since domestic grazing has been part of the San Juan Valley's history from the late nineteenth century (San Juan Times 1894b), wild gourd may have been an available resource prior to that time, although no seeds of the wild *Cucurbita* have been recognized among the Salmon macrofossils. Cultivated *Cucurbita* have been part of the Southwest's history since at least 300 BC (Cutler and Whitaker

Table 39.11. Sagebrush (*Artemisia* sp.) evidence from three floors in Room 93W.

Floor No.	Location	No. of Seeds	No. of Pollen Grains
1	Floor	–	1 (n = 200)
2	Floor	–	1:1 (n = 200)
			1:3 (n = 181)
	Hearth	–	1:1 (n = 200)
5	Floor	–	1 (n = 215)

Table 39.12. Additional Sunflower family (Compositae) evidence from three floors in Room 93W.

Floor No.	Location	No. of Seeds (Achenes)	No. of Pollen Grains (Long Spine)
1	Floor	1[1]	6 (n = 100)[2]
			2:3 (n = 200)
2	Floor	–	3:1 (n = 200)
			3:0 (n = 181)
	Hearth	–	3:3 (n = 200)[3]
5	Floor	–	1:0 (n = 215)

[1] *Verbesina* type.
[2] Includes one *Helianthus* type.
[3] One clump.

1961:471), and cultivated *Cucurbita pepo* seeds and peduncles have been identified at Salmon Ruin (Terrel 1979).

Although the fruits of the wild and cultivated cucurbits look quite different from one another, precise identification of the pollen grains remains difficult (Cutler 1966:21). Therefore, the single *Cucurbita* pollen grain (n = 200) in the hearth on Floor 2 may be either wild or cultivated. Because no seeds of the wild gourd have been recovered at Salmon, and because cultivated *Cucurbita pepo* appears to have played an important role in Salmon subsistence in prehistory, the pollen grain is likely from the cultivated plant.

In light of the historic use of cucurbit flowers, it is not unreasonable for a pollen grain to be recovered from a hearth. In fact, it might seem surprising that only one grain has been found, were it not for the fact that squash grains are relatively large and fragile, and degrade easily. The Hopi actually gathered the flowers of squash or pumpkin (*Cucurbita moschata* Duchesne) in the preparation of special foods (Whiting 1966:93), often boiling them with salt and grease (Beaglehole 1937:68). The Navajo cooked the blossoms by adding them to meat stew as a seasoning, sometimes preserving the flowers for later use by stringing them in the shade to dry (Bailey 1940: 289). Even today, gardeners of many cultures cook squash blossom pancakes for a change-of-pace breakfast.

CUPRESSACEAE – CYPRESS FAMILY
Juniper (*Juniperus*)

Juniper assumes many disguises for the casual observer. These common, scale-leaved evergreens that grow on mesas in the Colorado Plateau can appear to be bushy shrubs or large trees, sometimes

with several branching trunks, sometimes with a single straight trunk. One species of juniper, *Juniperus osteosperma* (Torr.) Little, grows abundantly around Salmon Ruin today.

The ethnographic record contains many references to juniper use that may help explain the evidence from 93W floors. The berries were known and eaten by groups all over the Southwest (Gallagher 1977:27–30, Harrington 1967:242–244). The fleshy blue fruit coat was eaten and the hard interior seeds were discarded. Such discarded seeds occurred in a variety of rooms and stratigraphic types at Salmon (Lentz 1979:50), generally in trash and pits. The absence of juniper seeds on floors in 93W may well reflect a prehistoric habit of disposing of food residue that is no longer useful.

In addition to the edible berries, the wood, leaves, and twigs have all served many needs among modern groups. The Cochiti used great quantities of the wood for firewood, corral fences, and fence posts. Dead wood at Cochiti belonged to the finder, but no living tree was supposed to be cut (Lange 1959:145). Hopi use of juniper for firewood and general construction parallels Cochiti use, as does their sentiment against cutting green juniper wood (Whiting 1966:62). Certain Hopi rituals, however, required green juniper leaves for a woman who has just had a child. Hopi men washed themselves with water in which juniper branch had been boiled when they returned from burying a corpse (Whiting 1966:62). The Zuni prescribed juniper leaf tea both before and after childbirth (Stevenson 1915:55). Ramah Navajo uses of juniper are also quite numerous (Vestal 1952:11–12). The Acoma and Laguna rubbed the green twigs of *Juniperus monosperma* (Engelm.) Sarg. On their moccasins to color them green. Larger twigs were used for basket frames, bent to shape by allowing them to remain in the sun, or for quicker bending, pushed in the hot ashes under a fire. The leaves were ground with salt and put in the ear to get bugs out (Swank 1932:48–49).

Table 39.13. Tansy mustard (*Descurainia* sp.) evidence from three floors in Room 93W.

Floor No.	Location	No. of Seeds	No. of Pollen Grains
1	Floor	18	–
	Beneath quartzite metate	295[1]	–

[1] All parched.

The juniper twigs and scale leaves (pieces of the broken twigs) found on floors and in the hearth in 93W (Table 39.14) have all been parched or carbonized. If the Salmon inhabitants brought the branches in as dead wood for a fire, the tender dry twigs would have been apt to completely burn up. Green twigs, on the other hand, might simply parch, due to the moisture trapped inside, leaving evidence in the form of the twigs and scale leaves. In fires of low intensity, they might even escape complete disintegration. A number of reasons can be offered for burning green juniper branches: a lack of dead wood in the surrounding area, a desire for a slow-burning, cooler fire, or burning the green juniper branches after having used them for some other purpose. At this time no particular hypothesis is supported by evidence from 93W. The fact that green branches were apparently brought in repeatedly throughout the history of the room may tell an intriguing story, when coupled with juniper evidence from other rooms at Salmon.

The low frequency of juniper pollen grains on all three floors could signify natural introduction, although a clump of six pollen grains in the hearth on Floor 2 suggests intentional transportation into the room. Although wind-pollinated juniper trees produce abundant pollen, the grains appear to preserve poorly in silty, alkaline soils (Potter and Rowley 1960:22). Thus, if many juniper pollen grains entered a room, through either natural or human-related means, the soil composition of Salmon pueblo might prevent us from knowing the whole story.

CYPERACEAE – SEDGE FAMILY
Bulrush (*Scirpus*) and other Cyperaceae

The Cyperaceae or sedge family contains many water loving members, including the bulrush *Scirpus* (Figure 39.15). Streambanks along the nearby San Juan River would provide ideal locations for these plants to thrive. As "true" seasonal plants (Bohrer 1975d:3), the bulrushes could provide a dependable

Figure 39.15. Bulrush (*Scirpus* sp.) seed, magnified 11x.

seed resource each fall, as long as no significant lowering of major streams occurred in the valley. For humans, such a plant is highly dependable as a resource in the same season, year after year. At the present time, five species of sedge, three of them bulrush, grow near Salmon Ruin.

The few seeds (achenes) on Floors 1 and 5 in Room 93W (Table 39.15) can be cautiously viewed as evidence that the Salmon occupants exploited the nearby riparian habitat of the San Juan River. Finding additional sedge seeds on other Salmon Ruin floors would support this claim. The pollen on Floor 1 may or may not have come in with the bulrush seeds; since sedge pollen is wind-borne, introduction could have been by natural means.

It is difficult to document the use of *Scirpus* achenes among recent Southwest groups, perhaps because some groups (the Hopi, for example) combine all "grass-like plants growing near water" (Whiting 1966:70), and do not themselves distinguish between sedge species. Or perhaps many of the Southwest ethnographies were written after the importance of sedge seeds had declined, as appears to have happened with tansy mustard (*Decurainia* sp.). Twelve of 14 Northern Paiute tribes were known to use achenes of *Scirpus acutis* Muhl. as food (Stewart 1941:428). Although the Acoma and Laguna apparently did not eat *Scirpus* sp. seeds, they knew this resource for its tender, raw shoots (Swank 1932: 68).

Bulrush seed use by prehistoric groups is more readily documented than among historic peoples. Doebley (1976:31) found bulrush (*Scirpus acutis* type) seeds and pollen in trash at Salmon Ruin, and Struever (1977:64) documented them at Chaco Canyon. Bohrer (1970:417) also found sedge seeds at Snaketown. Some of the more spectacular evidence comes from Lovelock Cave, a dry shelter near the Humboldt Sink in Nevada. There, parched bulrush (*Scirpus* sp.) and cattail (*Typha* sp.) seeds comprised over 90 percent of the seeds found in human coprolites (feces). Apparently the basic Paiute diet at Lovelock Cave changed little between 750 and 1800 AD, as the archaeological evidence indicates constant reliance on bulrush and cattail resources for that 1000-year period (Cowan 1967:22, 25).

EPHEDRACEAE – JOINT FIR FAMILY
Mormon Tea (*Ephedra nevadenses* and *E. torreyana*)

The pollen grains of Morman tea, a wind-pollinated plant, could be expected to appear in low frequencies in 93W (Table 39.16) without implying any special effort by humans to bring them into the

Table 39.14. Juniper (*Juniperus* sp.) evidence from three floors in Room 93W.

Floor No.	Location	No. of Berries	Twigs & Scale Leaves	No. of Pollen Grains
1	Floor	–	Present	1:0 (n = 200)
	Hearth	–	Present	–
2	Floor	–	Present	2:2 (n = 200)
		–	–	1:0 (n = 181)
	Hearth	–	Present	7:4 (n = 200)[1]
5	Floor	–	–	2:1 (n = 215
	Hearth	–	Present	–

[1]One clump.

Table 39.15. Bulrush (*Scirpus* sp.) and other Cyperaceae evidence from three floors in Room 93W.

Floor No.	Location	No. of *Scirpus* Seeds (Achenes)	No. of Cyperaceae Seeds (Achenes)	No. of Cyperaceae Pollen Grains
1	Floor	2	–	3:1 (n = 200)
5	Hearth	–	2	–

Table 39.16. Mormon tea (*Ephedra nevadensis* and *E. torreyana*) evidence from three floors in Room 93W.

Floor No.	Location	No. of Seeds	No. of *E. nevadensis* Pollen Grains	No. of *E. torreyana* Pollen Grains
2	Floor	–	1:0 (n = 200)	3:1 (n = 200)
			1:1 (n = 181)	1:1 (n = 181)
	Hearth	–	1:1 (n = 200)	3:1 (n = 200)
5	Floor	–	1:0 (n = 215)	1:0 (n = 215)

room. However, Morman tea stems have been identified in Salmon Ruin strata (K. Adams, Chapter 36), attesting to deliberate introduction of this resource, perhaps for tea.

EUPHORBIACEAE – SPURGE FAMILY
Spurge (*Euphorbia glyptosperma* type)

Common spurges are mostly weedy, annual or perennial herbs. They occur in grasslands, in pastures, along roadsides, and in waste places (Muenscher 1939:139). A number of species are widely distributed in western North America from Canada to Mexico (Kearney and Peebles 1960:520). Five species of spurge have been found near Salmon Ruin recently, two of them documented as poisonous.

By and large, members of *Euphorbia* are known to contain toxic substances in their sap which causes dermatitis in some people and severe poisoning if eaten in quantity (Harding 1974:116). When taken internally, spurges may produce swelling and burning about the eyes and mouth, accompanied by

abdominal pains, fainting spells, and emetic and purgative effects. Domestic grazing animals have been known to die from ingesting too much spurge-infested hay (Muenscher 1939:141). Toxicity is apparently not lost by drying the plants (Kingsbury 1964:189).

Because of the generally poisonous nature of *Euphorbia*, it is puzzling that seeds of *Euphorbia glyptosperma* type[5] (Figure 39.16) have turned up in Salmon Ruin deposits, and from a small pueblo in Chaco Canyon (Struever 1977:61, as *Bahia* type). Although these seeds closely match modern specimens of *E. glyptosperma* (Table 39.17), taxonomic similarities between plants of *E. glyptosperma* and *E. serpyllifolia* (Richardson 1978:72) are very strong, and may

[5]We are indebted to Mary B. Struever for pointing out the striking similarity between modern vouchered *E. glyptosperma* seeds and our prehistoric specimens. Use of the word *type* implies that the prehistoric specimen is morphologically similar to the modern species, but they may not be identical.

Figure 39.16. Spurge (*Euphorbia glytosperma* type) seed, magnified 21x.

lead to misidentification of either species, even though seeds of the two species should be distinguishable.

At Salmon Ruin, *E. glyptosperma* type seeds have been recovered in 19 of 38 rooms or plaza areas examined to date. And of a total of 45 flotation samples containing spurge seeds, 17 had specimens that appear to have been processed in some way.

On Floor 1 in Room 93W (Table 39.18), both the burned appearance of some of the spurge seeds and their location beneath the quartzite metate raised two questions: (a) are some *Euphorbia* species not poisonous, and (2) what might the presence of these seeds in Salmon pueblo imply?

Although many *Euphorbia* are known to contain toxic substances, a few species have been eaten by humans. One wonders how people distinguished the few nonpoisonous members from the many potentially lethal plants. Perhaps people knew how to prepare *Euphorbia* in such a way as to render the poison harmless. *Euphorbia buxifolia* has been dried and used for tea on the Bahama Islands, *E. serpens* is taken as a "refreshing beverage" by people in Paraguat, and *E. cinerea* and *E. didyma* (of North Borneo and the Philippine Islands respectively) are reported to have edible fruit (Altschul 1973:168, 169, 177).

Much closer to home, the Zuni method of utilizing the roots and leaves of *E. serpyllifolia* Pers. seems to give tacit recognition to its nontoxic properties. This information is of particular interest, as the plants of *E. serpyllifolia* are very similar in general appearance to *E. glyptosperma* (Richardson 1978:72), and could easily be confused in identification. The native term for *E. serpyllifolia* was translated to mean "mouth sweetened," which applies to the use of the roots in sweetening corn meal. A woman would place a small piece of the root in her mouth and let it remain there, taking it out only to sleep or eat. After two days, she removed the root and put as much freshly ground corn meal into her mouth as she possibly could, holding it there until the accumulation of saliva forced her to eject the mass. This process

was continued until the desired quantity of corn had been "sweetened" (Stevenson 1915:68). It has been suggested that the saliva, containing the enzyme diastase, changed the starch of the corn meal into sugar (Castetter 1935:29). Not only were the roots of *E. serpyllifolia* Pers. put in the mouth, but the Zuni also chewed the leaves for their pleasant taste (Stevenson 1915:68). A possibility exists that the prehistoric seeds at Salmon might have been introduced simultaneously with the roots and leaves when used in a manner similar to that of *E. seryllifolia* described for the Zuni.

Accidental introduction of spurge seeds to Salmon cannot be completely ruled out for two reasons. First, *E. glyptosperma* occupies a diversity of habitats (Richardson 1978:68), from prairies and valleys to disturbed locations along roadsides and in waste places. Such plants would be likely to grow around the edges of a village, where human activity might frequently disturb the ground. Second, when wet, the seeds of the prostate *E. glyptosperma* plant become mucilaginous, and if the species were abundant, the opportunity could exist for many seeds to be carried in on sandals after rain. Perhaps the seeds came in on grass used for roofing, pit lining, or bedding. Discarded sandals and grass are too degraded at Salmon Ruin to pursue these explanations, though neither would adequately account for the presence of the burned seeds in 93W.

The burned appearance of some of the spurge seeds on Floor 1 in Room 93W (and in other locations at Salmon) is not explained by the ethnographic record. On Floor 1 these seeds may have bounced out of a parching pot, whereas those found beneath the quartzite metate may be a part of the residue from a batch that was ground for meal. A search into the literature on food value revealed that members of the spurge family contain seeds with a significant amount of oil and protein, relative to many other plant families (Barclay and Earle 1974). Also, the widespread distribution of spurge seeds at Salmon implies frequent handling of the resource in prehistory, such as might occur with a common food item; a medicinal, ceremonial, or seldom-used food plant, for example, would not be expected to be so common in flotation samples at Salmon Ruin. The possibility remains that *Euphorbia* seeds were utilized as a food in prehistory.

GRAMINEAE – GRASS FAMILY

The grass family contains annual and perennial wind-pollinated members that mature at different times during the late spring through fall growing season. Grasses grow in a variety of habitats, and 37

Table 39.17. Characteristics of modern and prehistoric *Euphorbia glyptosperma* seeds.

Source	Sample Size	Length (mm)			Width (mm)			Shape	Remarks
		Mean	SD	Range	Mean	SD	Range		
Richardson 1978:68[1]	–	–	–	0.7–1.2	1.00[2]	–	–	Ovate	Ventral[3] facets concave, transversed by 3–5 prominent ridges; dorsal facets convex, transversed by 5–7 prominent ridges passing more or less through lateral (facet) margins.
Modern specimens[4]	30	1.18	0.05	1.0–1.3	0.56	0.05	0.41–0.68	Ovate	Ventrical facets concave, transversed by ≥ 3 prominent ridges; dorsal facets concave, also transversed by prominent ridges; lateral margins sometimes appearing undulating.
Prehistoric specimens, Salmon Ruin[5]	30	1.21	0.07	1.08–1.37	0.52	0.075	0.44–0.80	Ovate	Ventral facets concave, transversed by ≥ 3 prominent ridges; dorsal facets concave, also transversed by prominent ridges; lateral margins sometimes appearing undulating.

[1] Author provides no information in categories containing dashed lines.
[2] May not represent statistical mean.
[3] Ventral refers to the surface of the seed bearing the hilum which faces toward the central axis of the capsule.
[4] University of Arizona Herbarium Accession No. 217575, identified through the courtesy of G.A. Yatskievych.
[5] Derived from measurements of 10 seeds each from three large (n ≥ 310) homogeneous samples, numbers 6A0013, 90W0011, 92A0040.

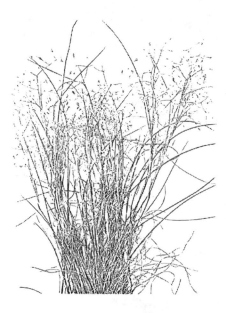

Figure 39.17. Indian ricegrass (*Oryzopsis hymenoides*) plant.

species have been recently documented on different landforms in the San Juan Valley. Included in this list of modern types are species whose seeds (caryopses) can be easily harvested from the enclosing bracts (e.g. dropseed or *Sporbolus*) or those whose seeds are difficult to dislodge with either parching or burning (e.g. Indian ricegrass). Grass seeds that require less work to harvest would seem most attractive as a food resource (Flannery 1965:1252).

Indian Ricegrass (*Oryzopsis hymenoides*)

Indian ricegrass flowers in May and early June in the San Juan Valley (Figure 39.17). This grass prefers sandy, disturbed habitats, and one can often see it growing today along roadsides or in arroyo margins near Salmon Ruin. Indian ricegrass seems to be a plant of "qualified" seasonality in central and northwestern New Mexico, implying that favorable growing conditions are necessary for an abundant spring harvest of seeds (Figure 39.18).

Table 39.18. Spurge (*Euphorbia glyptosperma* type) evidence from three floors in Room 93W.

Floor No.	Location	No. of Seeds	No. of Pollen Grains
1	Floor	28[1]	–
	Beneamth quartzite metate	8	–

[1]Six burned.

Because of its early maturity (June or early July), the seeds of this plant might have been quite important in times of food stress (Bohrer 1975b:199). Perhaps this suggestion is supported by Castetter (1935:27–28), who noted that the seeds of ricegrass (*Oryzopsis hymenoides* as *Eriocoma cuspidate* Nutt.) were used extensively by Indian groups, and by Whiting (1966:65), who found that the seeds were collected by the Hopi, particularly in times of famine. The Hopi not only used the seeds, but also named a clan after this grass. The Zuni ground the small black seeds to make bread (Castetter 1935:28).

A single burned lemma (a bract that helps protect the seed) in the hearth of Floor 5 (Table 39.19), coupled with Doebley's (1976:32) findings of carbonized ricegrass grains, florets, and bracts in trash at Salmon Ruin, may indicate that the Salmon occupants used this grass in a manner similar to the Navajo. The Navajo ate the seeds, and gave them a name that translates as "burnt off or burnt free." Castetter (1935:28) interpreted the name as referring to "the adhering chaff (palea and lemma) which can be removed only by burning at the time the edible seeds are cleaned. The Franciscan Fathers give the word *ndidlidi* (that which is scorched) for this species, so called because the seeds were collected by holding a bunch of the grass near the fire, the seeds falling to the base of a flat stone placed obliquely nearby." Jones (1938) and Bohrer (1975b:202) both give a fuller discussion of the former role of this and other cool-season grasses.

Grass (Gramineae) and Paniceae (Tribe of Grass Family)

The occurrence of two seeds belonging to the grass family on Floor 1 (see Table 39.19) poses particular difficulty in interpretation. Lack of detailed identification of these specimens prevents us from sorting through the ethnographic literature on grass for clues to prehistoric use. Neither the condition nor the context of the two seeds provides help. Both seeds lack association with any ground stone artifact, which might have indicated possible grinding, or with the hearth, which could have implied parching. These two seeds may have been parched just enough to preserve them, yet not enough that this condition was recognized by the laboratory technician that examined them.

Looking at grass seeds from nonoccupational fill (the blanket of soil that covered the pueblo after its abandonment) might clarify questions of preservation. If no unburned seeds are found in this natural overburden, one could possibly infer that parching is necessary to preservation, and the seeds in Floor 1

Figure 39.18. Indian ricegrass (*Oryzopsis hymenoides*) seed, magnified 10x.

were probably parched prehistorically. However, the problem still remains of just which kinds of grass were preserved.

Grass pollen, which is naturally wind-borne, might be expected to occur in low frequencies as part of the normal pollen rain, or alternatively, the pollen could perhaps have been carried into the room on winnowed grain (Bohrer 1972:26). The low frequency of grass pollen on the floors in Room 93W does not support the latter explanation.

Corn, Maize (*Zea mays*)

Corn, also known as *Zea mays*, is one of the cultivated crops grown by the Salmon inhabitants. Requiring moisture during critical stages of its life cycle, and a fairly long frost-free season of nearly 4 months, corn could be a resource of great abundance or frustration, depending on yearly growing conditions. Corn was grown by both the early Chacoan (Floor 5) and the later Mesa Verdean occupations (Floors 1 and 2). Prehistoric cobs of 8, 10, 12, and 14

rows have been recovered. Rooms containing concentrations of cobs with kernels intact indicate that the Salmon puebloans were able at times to store some for future use.

Documentation of corn use among modern pueblo tribes exists in abundance. Its importance as a food resource cannot be underestimated. A good crop could spell the difference between living or dying, between staying or migrating. Perhaps as a reflection of the importance and high status of this crop, corn pollen has been cited in the ethnographic literature in connection with ceremonies and use in burials. The Acoma, Laguna (Swank 1932:78), and Sia (Stevenson 1894:81) employed corn pollen as both medicine and prayer meal. In some way or other, corn appears in virtually every Hopi ceremony, as corn meal, as an actual ear of corn, or as a symbolic painting (Whiting 1966:67).

One floor pollen sample in 93W (Sample 93W 0035 on Floor 1) had an unusually high percentage (37%) of corn pollen in relation to other pollen types (Table 39.20). At another prehistoric pueblo (Arroyo Hondo), Bohrer (1986) has noted that records of corn pollen above 15 percent are likely to represent deliberate concentration by humans.

Are there certain daily habits of a puebloan that call for the disbursement of collected corn pollen? The Cochiti of New Mexico offer corn meal or corn pollen to the fire, and place it under the grinding stone in the house so that corn meal may be ground rapidly (Goldfrank 1927:68). No pollen sample was secured beneath the quartzite metate on Floor 1, but it is interesting to speculate whether high concentrations of corn pollen might have been there. Cochiti individuals also privately offer corn meal or corn pollen each morning to their many supernatural helpers (Goldfrank 1927:67–68). Such private prayers could occur anywhere within the pueblo, but were perhaps most likely in the home as the individual prepared for the day's events.

The high percentage of corn pollen in a sample on Floor 1 is cause for further speculation, when compared with the low corn pollen percentage found in a sample not more than a meter away. Perhaps the dramatic difference in percentages indicates two separate overlapping floor surfaces, imperceptible to the excavators. If the floor was resurfaced with adobe at some time during use, the two pollen samples might represent separate time intervals reflecting different uses of corn pollen.

The few corn pollen grains in other samples on Floors 1, 2, and 5 could owe their explanation to routine handling of ears of corn. Corn pollen may remain associated with kernels or husks even after

Table 39.19. Grass (Gramineae) evidence from three floors in Room 93W.

Floor No.	Location	No. of Seeds (Caryopses)	No. of Pollen Pollen Grains
1	Floor	2[1]	2(n = 300)
2	Floor	–	4:2(n = 200)
	Hearth	1[2]	1:1 (n = 181)
5	Floor	–	3:0 (n = 215)
	Hearth	1[3]	1(n = 10)

[1]One Paniceae type.
[2]Gramineae foret, bract that encloses seed.
[3]*Oryzopsis hymenoides* lemma.

the pollen-bearing structures and leaves are removed from the cob. When examining the wash water left over from rinsing modern cornhusks and kernels, Bohrer (1972:26) observed pollen grains in low amounts. Thus, a pueblo woman preparing a dinner of corn for her family could easily introduce a few pollen grains into the room.

Additional evidence for corn utilization in 93W includes cobs on Floor 1, a kernel, a cupule (a smaller division of the cob), and an embryo on Floor 2, and a kernel, cupule, and cob on Floor 5. Most have been either parched or carbonized. Corn kernels were frequently parched prior to storage, to prevent them from spoiling. Corncobs also make a handy fuel resource, especially on cold, snowy winter days when collecting firewood proves inconvenient.

JUNCACEAE – RUSH FAMILY
Rush (*Juncus*)

One would be likely to find members of the rush family along banks and meanders of the San Juan River, for these perennial grasslike plants prefer locations where groundwater levels remain within reach. At the present time, at least seven species of rush (*Juncus*) grow near Salmon Ruin.

A search of the ethnographic literature on Southwest groups elicits very little information on rushes, and no reference to their use as food. Whether this reflects actual nonuse by puebloans, or a prominent gap in the ethnographical literature, remains unclear. The Hopi group together all grass-like plants growing near water, particularly those with round stems and leaves. Occasionally such plants were employed

in ceremonies because of their association with water (Whiting 1966:70).

Despite the lack of modern information on rushes, the presence of 22 burned rush (*Juncus cooperi* type) seeds or achenes (Figure 39.19) in the hearth of Floor 5 (Table 39.21) may indicate that they were being parched, perhaps prior to consumption or storage. This hypothesis is not supported by Doebley's (1976) examination of numerous trash samples from Salmon Ruin, but the small size of rush seeds (about 1 mm) may have reduced their chances of being swept from a floor and deposited in trash. Any interpretation would be more secure if, by the development of an exhaustive comparative collection of modern seeds, the full identity of these prehistoric specimens could be assured.

LOASACEAE – LOASA FAMILY
Stickleaf (*Mentzelia albicaulis*)

Stickleaf is an attractive plant, with delicate yellow petals and conspicuously white stems. It gets its name because fragments of the leaves and stems stick readily to clothing and animal hair (Kearney and Peebles 1960:564). As a plant of "qualified" seasonality, stickleaf could be an abundant, though undependable, spring resource.

Three years of activity searching for this plant in the San Juan Valley have produced rare sightings of living specimens. Much reduced in numbers in the present environment (Bohrer 1978), it has been labeled a "depleted" species. We suspect that before the influx of domestic grazing animals, the plant would have been much easier to find.

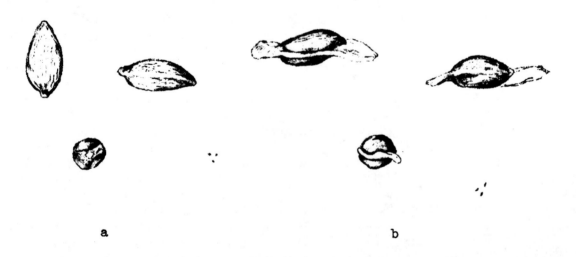

a   b

Figure 39.19. Rush (*Juncus cooperi*) seed, magnified 22x: (a) without wings, (b) with wings.

Table 39.20. Corn (*Zea mays*) evidence from three floors in Room 93W.

Floor No.	Location	Macrofossil Fragments (Cobs & Kernels)	No. of Pollen Pollen Grains
1	Floor	Present	37 (n = 100)
			8:7 (n = 200)
	Hearth	–	2 (n = 8)
2	Floor	2	11:13 (n = 200)
			1:1 (n = 181)
	Hearth	1	3:1 (n = 200)
			1 (n = 5)
5	Floor	–	1:0 (n = 215)
	Hearth	3	4 (n = 29)

Table 39.21. Rush (*Juncus* sp.) evidence from three floors in Room 93W.

Floor No.	Location	No. of Seeds (Achenes)	No. of Pollen Grains
1	Floor	3	–
	Hearth	1[1]	–
5	Hearth	22[2]	–

[1]Burned.
[2]*Juncus cooperi* type, all burned.

Table 39.22. Stickleaf (*Mentzelia albicaulis*) evidence from three floors in Room 93W.

Floor No.	Location	No. of Seeds	No. of Pollen Grains
1	Floor	2[1]	–
	Beneath quartzite metate	1[1]	–
2	Hearth	1[1]	–

[1]Burned.

Table 39.23. Pine (*Pinus* sp.) evidence from three floors in Room 93W.

Floor No.	Location	No. of Seeds	No. of Pollen Grains
1	Floor	–	9 (n = 300)
2	Floor	–	5:11 (n = 200)
			7:4 (n = 181)
	Hearth	–	17:21 (n = 200)
			2 (n = 5)
5	Floor	–	7:10 (n = 215)
	Hearth	–	3 (n = 12)

The stickleaf seeds (Figure 39.20) found in Room 93W (Table 39.22) have all been burned. When seeds are toasted near a fire, and not frequently stirred, some will carbonize. Seeds were often prepared for storage by parching, which served to drive out moisture and retard fungal growth. The same process also improves seed taste and makes the task of grinding seeds easier.

The single stickleaf seed beneath the quartzite metate on Floor 1 may imply that this resource was ground, although its presence there could also be purely accidental. Doebley (1976:56) found stickleaf in trash from Salmon Ruin, and suggested that it was used as food; ethnographic evidence favors such an interpretation. In his discussion of tribes along the United States–Mexico boundary, Torrey (1859:67) stated that "the oily seeds are pounded and used by the Indians as an ingredient of their Pinole mantica, a kind of cake." Fewkes (1896:20) noted that the Hopi parched the seeds and ground them into a sweet meal. Smith (1973:102) suggested that *Mentzelia albicaulis* Dougl. was a major component of the aboriginal Hualapai diet on the Arizona Plateau, and Stewart (1941:428) recorded that 13 of 14 Northern Paiute bands used the seeds for food.

Mentzelia albicaulis seeds have been found at other prehistoric sites. Cutler (1952:479) found them at Tularosa Cave, and 3 pounds of *Mentzelia* sp. were recovered from a pottery vessel in Cordova Cave in southwestern New Mexico (Kaplan 1963:354). They have also been found in Point of Pines Ruins in Arizona (Bohrer 1973b:431) and in Arizona BB:13:50, a Hohokam site south of Tucson (Bohrer et al. 1969:7).

MALVACEAE – MALLOW FAMILY
Globemallow (*Sphaeralcea*)

Although globemallow disperses its pollen with the help of insects, a single pollen grain in the hearth of Floor 2 (n = 5) in 93W constitutes tenuous evidence for use of this resource. The globemallow story must await examination of additional rooms at Salmon Ruin.

PINACEAE – PINE FAMILY
Pine (*Pinus*)

The low amounts of pine pollen in Room 93W (Table 39.23) could easily have been carried by wind from a distance, as the pollen is well suited to air transport (Hevly et al. 1965:130). Note the inflated bladders or balloons that apparently help it stay aloft (see Figure 39.1).

816	Karen R. Adams

Figure 39.20. Stickleaf (*Mentzelia albicaulis*) seed, magnified 14x.

POLYGONACEAE – BUCKWHEAT FAMILY

Buckwheat (*Eriogonom*) and Knotweed (*Polygonom sawatchense* type)

Knotweed and buckwheat both belong to the buckwheat family. The knotweed *Polygonom sawatchense* Small. commonly grows in dry pine woods at elevations of 5500–9500 ft (Kearney and Peebles 1960:248). Although we have not found this knotweed in the San Juan Valley recently, three other species of knotweed have been documented.

The four knotweed type seeds on Floor 1 (Table 39.24) are puzzling. Neither their condition nor their location is helpful to interpretation. A search of the literature revealed no known uses of this particular plant, though general knowledge of other knotweed species has been mentioned. For example, the Acoma and Laguna prepared a tea made from *Polygonom lapathifolium* L. for stomach problems (Swank 1932: 62). If the knotweed seeds on Floor 1 are residue from a food (such as a tea), perhaps further evidence from Salmon Ruin can be found to support this use.

The necessary restraint in interpreting the knotweed seeds also applies to the buckwheat pollen grains. Buckwheats may be either insect or wind pollinated, so their presence could have no significant relationship to human activities.

PORTULACACEAE – PORTULACA FAMILY

Purslane (*Portulaca*)

The succulent purslane sprawls close to the ground, absorbing its full share of moisture from the dry soil, thriving in uninterrupted sunlight (Figure 39.21; Kearney and Peebles 1960:290). Native purslane plants appear to be of "qualified" seasonality, with leaves available for the stewpot possibly in the summer (July), but more often serving as a leaf and seed resource in the fall. Favorable growing conditions are necessary to ensure an abundant crop; severe drought would reduce the purslane harvest substantially. No native species of purslane have

been found in the San Juan Valley recently, though one species introduced historically into the New World (*P. oleracea* L.) grows there today.

Purslane seeds were well represented in Salmon trash strata (Doebley 1976:58), covering an animal skull on a kiva floor (Sample 94W2080), and on Floors 1 and 5 in 93W (Table 39.25). The seeds in 93W were found in hearths and beneath a quartzite metate, in addition to the surface of the two floors. Taken together, this evidence suggests that purslane not only had widespread use in the pueblo, probably as a food resource, but was also of ceremonial significance.

Portulaca seeds and fleshy leaves have been gathered by various historic groups in the Southwest. The Navajo collected the seeds of *Portulaca* spp. (Elmore 1944:47), as did the Zuni (Standley 1911:458). The Hopi cooked the introduced purslane (*Portulaca oleracea* L.) plants as greens in a gravy (Whiting 1966:75), and the Acoma and Laguna employed it in making a medicinal tea (Swank 1932:63). The Zuni, Acoma, and Laguna may have used the native plants before the introduced purslane was available. Purslane seeds have also been recovered from a number of prehistoric sites in the Southwest (Bohrer 1978:13).

Figure 39.21. Purslane (*Portulaca* sp.) plant and seed, seed magnified 25x.

Table 39.24. Buckwheat (*Eriogonom* sp.) and knotweed (*Polygonom sawatchense* type) evidence from three Room 93W floors.

Floor No.	Location	No. of *P. sawatchense* Type Seeds	No. of *Eriogonum* Pollen Grains
1	Floor	4	2 In = 300)
2	Floor	–	2:0 (n = 200)
			1:0 (n = 181)
5	Floor	–	1:1 (n = 215)
	Hearth	–	1 (n = 19)

Table 39.25. Purslane (*Portulaca* sp.) evidence from three floors in Room 93W.

Floor No.	Location	No. of Seeds	No. of Pollen Grains
1	Floor	12	–
	Beneath quartzite	15	–
	Hearth	1	–
5	Floor	2	–
	Hearth	64	–

Table 39.26. Groundcherry (*Physalis* sp.) evidence from three floors in Room 93W.

Floor No.	Location	No. of Seeds	No. of Pollen Grains
1	Hearth	1[1]	–
2	Hearth	1[1]	–

[1]Burned.

SOLANACEAE – POTATO FAMILY
Groundcherry (*Physalis*)

Groundcherry plants are annual or perennial herbs (Figure 39.22) that produce small, edible berries encased in papery coverings, which give the berries the appearance of Japanese lanterns. The small berries resemble miniature tomatoes in look and texture; in fact the "tomatillas" that one can occasionally buy in the grocery store for preparing salsa are closely related. Groundcherry plants are also opportunists; under favorable growing conditions they could mature and provide a food resource from early summer through fall. Recently three species of groundcherry have been found growing in the San Juan Valley.

The groundcherry seeds in the hearths on Floors 1 and 2 (Table 39.26) are intriguing, because this resource is not parched among pueblo peoples today. This is not surprising, when one considers the difficulties that might arise in parching a tiny tomato. The Zuni did boil the fruit of *Physalis fendleri* A. Gray. in a small quantity of water and then crushed and used the mixture as a condiment (Stevenson 1915:70), so boiling the fruit might be one avenue for spilling some into the hearth. Other groups, however, such as the Acoma, Laguna, and Hopi, have used groundcherry fruits but make no reference to cooking them (Swank 1932:59; Whiting 1966:21).

If groundcherry fruits are not regularly prepared by a method that requires fire, what other explanation could there be for finding burned seeds in the hearth? White (1932:125) noted that the Acoma customarily offered a bit of food at mealtime to their deities and to Mother Earth, with prayer before eating. The morsel was then thrown into the fireplace. In a similar vein, Parsons (1970:24, 103) mentioned that at Taos, bits of all food eaten were dropped into a small pit within the house door for Earth Mother and Dirt Boy. Thus, offering bits of food to a deity could be one explanation for finding groundcherry seeds in each hearth on Floors 1 and 2. Accidental introduction is another possibility, though less likely, since Doebley (1976) found carbonized *Physalis* type seeds in 13 of 41 trash samples at Salmon Ruin.

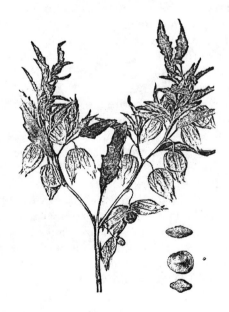

Figure 39.22. Groundcherry (*Physalis* sp.) plant and seed, seed magnified 9x.

TYPHACEAE – CATTAIL FAMILY
Cattail (*Typha*)

Cattail is a water-loving perennial, thriving along riverbanks and in marshy places. As a "true" seasonal plant, a cattail could be depended upon for pollen, seeds, and vegetative parts year after year, provided no significant lowering of the water table occurred. At least one species of cattail (*Typha latifolia* L.) grows today within half a mile of the Salmon Ruin, along the banks of the San Juan River.

The presence of two cattail pollen tetrads (naturally occurring groups of four adherent pollen grains) on Floor 1 (n = 100) poses an interpretive problem. In a modern study of natural pollen rain on the San Augustine plains of New Mexico, Potter and Rowley (1960:20) noted that the comparatively heavy cattail (*Typha latifolia*) tetrads were of low incidence away from the marshy areas where the plant grew. Apparently this species, though wind pollinated, is not able to dispel pollen far from its point of origin. Whether the pollen tetrads on Floor 1 were carried to the pueblo on the wind from the nearby river, or whether they were brought in by human use remains unknown.

Because it is possible that the cattail pollen was brought in by people, the ethnographic literature was examined for information on cattail use. The pollen itself has been used in ceremonies, as a coloring, and as a food. The Apaches and the Navajos employed *Typha* sp. pollen in ceremonies, though over the years the Navajo gradually replaced cattail pollen with corn pollen (Castetter and Opler 1936:36; Elmore 1944:24). In a secular vein the Pima made a yellow coloring from *Typha angustifolia* Linn. pollen (Russell 1975:161), and in southern Arizona the Cocopa, Maricopa, Mohave, and Yuma ate cattail pollen every year, despite the laborious collection and preparation necessary (Castetter and Bell 1951: 209–210).

Historic groups were not the only ones fond of cattail pollen as a food resource. According to human fecal evidence, the Paiutes of the Humboldt Sink in Nevada ate large amounts of cattail pollen, which they had probably prepared by baking in a pit (Heizer and Napton 1969:566). These people also relied on parched cattail seeds for more than a thousand years, while occupying Lovelock Cave between 750 and 1800 AD (Cowan 1967:25).

Perhaps direct use of the vegetative parts of the cattail plant (stems, leaves, roots) might lead to the introduction of pollen into a room. Pollen sifting down from the flowers could cling to stems and leaves beyond the pollinating season. In the South-west the Pima used the stems of *Typha angustifolia* Linn. as a foundation in basket making (Russell 1975:133), and Hopi children chewed the stems of *Typha angustifolia* L. the same way that children elsewhere chewed sugar cane (Whiting 1966:64). The Acoma and Laguna ate the roots and tender shoots of *Typha latifolia* L. with salt for food, and shook the ripened heads to simulate clouds in the rain dance (Swank 1932:73). All of these uses serve as potential avenues for cattail pollen to enter a room.

MISCELLANEOUS ITEMS

A number of miscellaneous items found on the floors could be only partly identified or are of unknown nature (Table 39.27). Although the presence of these items in Room 93W is not understood today, they may take on meaning in the future.

TULE SPRINGS UNKNOWN

The item known as "Tule Springs Unknown" has never been clearly established as having a floral or faunal nature (Figure 39.23). The same type item was found in both the Hay Hollow Site in east-central Arizona and the Tule Springs Site in southern Nevada (Bohrer 1972:22). Evidence from the Tule Springs site and a modern soil transect taken 12 miles from the Hay Hollow site implies that the unknown preferred a damp or mesic habitat (Bohrer 1972:23).

The Tule Springs Unknown, though low in frequency, is common at Salmon Ruin. A possible clue to the identification of this unknown came when an Eastern New Mexico University graduate student brought in some modern materials found in a termite nest in an old building in California. Except for a difference in size, these modern materials were a close morphological match to Salmon's Tule Springs Unknown. Were wooden roof beams plagued by termites 900 years ago, just as modern house foundations are now? Another explanation, still to be pursued, is that the Tule Springs Unknowns are ant feces, or droppings of some insect other than termites.

SYNTHESIS

Although Salmon housewives did not enjoy the convenience of a local grocery store, the proximity of native wild plants must have eased the burden of food gathering. Most of the resources brought into Room 93W can still be found in the surrounding area, although some (e.g. stickleaf) seem to have been depleted by heavy domestic grazing. None of the plant materials suggest trade or long journeys for acquisition. During the fourth month of the growing season, Salmon cooks roamed the land collecting

Table 39.27. Miscellaneous items from three floors in Room 93W.

Items	Floor No.	Location	Remarks
Black spherical bodies	1	Floor and beneath quartzite metate	Less than 1 mm diameter; tiny spores of mold or fungus?
	2	Hearth	
Bones	5	Hearth	Unidentified
Bud tips	1	Floor and beneath quartzite metate	Burned; whether flower or vegetative bud tips unclear. Young growth brought in repeatedly.
	2	Hearth	
	5	Hearth	
Catkins	2	Hearth	Unidentified; modern contaminents from nearby willow or cottonwood trees?
Cuticular layer inside seed coats	1	Floor and beneath metate	Possibly the eroded interior of Cheno Am seeds.
	5	Hearth	
Feces	1	Beneath quartzite metate	Size range (0.5–2.0 mm) suggests insect droppings. Insects eating food residue?
	2	Hearth	
	5	Hearth	
Insect segments, cocoons, larvae	1	Floor and beneath metate	Insects eating food residue?
	2	Floor	
	5	Floor	
Tule Springs Unknown	1	Floor and beneath metate	See text
	2	Hearth	All burned

plants that ranged from dependable to fickle. Numerous locations, including river banks, disturbed areas around well-trotted paths and around garden plots, rolling juniper hills, and gravel terraces, offered potential sources of food for the family larder.

Floor 1

Evidence on Floor 1 indicates that many meals of native plant foods were prepared in the room. Before the large quartzite metate south of the firepit was placed face down, it was used to grind a number of native seeds into flour. Seeds of tansy mustard (*Descurainia* sp.), pigweed (*Amaranthus* sp.), purslane (*Portulaca* sp.), Cheno Am (*Chenpodium-Amaranthus*) and possibly stickleaf (*Mentzelia albicaulis*) and spurge (*Euphoria glyptosperma* type) were prepared; the Cheno Am, stickleaf, tansy mustard, and spurge were parched near the hearth prior to grinding. One clustering of corrugated vessel fragments near the hearth suggests cooking, and the association of a variety of vessel types and the metate and milling bin in the northeast corner of the room also implies food preparation. While the women of the house parched seeds near the fire, reduced them to flour and perhaps boiled them into a simple gruel in plain

gray and corrugated ceramic vessels, other family members worked on keeping their stone tools in good repair. Someone even fashioned new stone tools while staying indoors, perhaps keeping warm around a fire of juniper (*Juniperus* sp.) boughs.

The very high (37%) percentage of corn (*Zea mays*) pollen on Floor 1 indicates that someone deliberately gathered and used it in concentrated form. Private prayers or corn pollen or corn meal offerings could account for this unusual abundance of corn pollen. The dramatic differences in corn pollen percentages in two closely spaced floor samples might

Figure 39.23. Tule Springs Unknown disseminule, magnified 23x.

indicate overlapping (though distinct) floor surfaces, although this was not apparent during excavation.

When the modern ethnographic record is mute, or when not enough pollen and seed evidence has accumulated in a context that clearly suggests the way they were used, explanations about prehistoric plant remains are tentative. Perhaps the single groundcherry (*Physalis* sp.) seed in the firepit of Floor 1 was an offering to a deity. Someone might have harvested rush (*Juncus cooperi* type) and bulrush (*Scirpus* sp.) seeds from the banks of the San Juan River, or accidentally brought them into the pueblo. And the presence of apparently unburned grass (Gramineae and Paniceae grains) and knotweed (*Polygonom sawatchense* type) seeds on Floor 1 is also unexplained. Even when modern ethnographic literature includes clear statements on the use of a plant, finding just the trace of its presence in a prehistoric site may not be enough to establish the certainty of use. The single cholla (*Opuntia* sp.) pollen grain, the cattail (*Typha* sp.) pollen tetrads, the long-spine Compositae (including *Helianthus* type) pollen grains, and the crown-beard (*Verbesina* sp.) seed on Floor 1 do not unquestionably imply human use.

Floor 2

Floor 2 also seems to have served as a locus for food preparation. Two separate forms of evidence in the hearth suggest that Cheno Am plants were prepared nearby. Clumped goosefoot pollen grains, which are not likely to travel on the wind, and burned Cheno Am seeds jointly support interpretation that someone handled these plants near the fire. The generally high frequency of goosefoot and Cheno Am pollen in the room further implies repeated use of this dietary component.

The hearth contained parched juniper twigs and young bud tips of an unknown plant, as well as several unique pollen types. Perhaps no dead wood was available to heat the home. Alternatively, someone might have needed a slow-burning fire for a special purpose. Maybe the juniper pollen, not likely to travel in bunches on the wind, came in on green juniper boughs. The Salmon children might have picked catkins (tree buds or blossoms) in the spring for food, as the Pima boys have been known to do (Russell 1975:69). The single *Cucurbita* sp. pollen grain in the hearth is probably from a cultivated squash, though pollen from the wild gourd looks very similar.

Both pollen and macrofossils tell us that cultivated corn was brought into the room. Corncobs were burned as fuel, at least occasionally. A mother

must have spent many a chilly morning and evening grinding meal for the family in the milling bin located so near the hearth, while her family eagerly smelled the parched corn, Cheno Am, and possibly stickleaf seeds she stirred by the fire. The man of the house sharpened and manufactured stone tools amidst the activity. When the family gathered for a meal, perhaps someone offered a groundcherry fruit to the fire.

Some plant microfossils on Floor 2 may have been naturally or accidentally introduced. Cholla pollen grains, clumped ragweed (*Ambrosia* sp.) pollen, long-spine sunflower (Compositae) pollen, and a grass (Gramineae) floret all fall into this category. More evidence must be accumulated to suggest the manner in which these resources may have been used.

Floor 5

Only the plant data indicated that food preparation occurred on Floor 5; four ceramic sherds and one piece of lithic debitage shed little light on room use. It appears that native seeds were frequently parched in this room. Corn was also brought in, and at least some of the cobs fed the hungry fire as well. The presence of burned rush seeds in the hearth suggests preparation for consumption, though historic groups are not known to eat them. The heavy scatter of Cheno Am seeds over this early floor may well be typical of all early floors, as Cheno Am remains were recovered in all eight Chacoan trash samples examined at Salmon Ruin (Doebley 1976). This indicates that the Chacoan occupants of the pueblo prepared many of the same meals as their Mesa Verde successors. The early inhabitants of the pueblo also knew the fall resource purslane, which might be rather undependable.

How some plants become part of the archaeological record cannot be explained with certainty. Two sedge (*Cyperaceae*) seeds found in the hearth could have been burned during food preparation, though the only ethnographic literature that substantiates this possibility concerns the Paiute. A Rocky Mountain beeweed (*Cleome* sp.) seed, an Indian ricegrass (*Oryzopsis hymenoides*) lemma, a cholla pollen grain, and sunflower long-grain pollen grain associated with Floor 5 could signify actual use, or could be the result of unintentional introduction; historic groups are known to have used them all. Burned juniper twigs showed up in the hearth of Floor 5, as they did on Floors 1 and 2. Green juniper boughs seem to have been commonly burned throughout Salmon's history.

Highlights of Room 93W

The combination of goosefoot, pigweed, and purslane seeds on floors in Room 93W is the same one that most often appears in trash discarded from a wide variety of locations at Salmon Ruin (Doebley 1976:103). It seems reasonable that common seed types used repeatedly by many households are likely to show up again and again in the archaeological record. Therefore, we believe that pigweed, goosefoot, and purslane were very common foods at Salmon Pueblo, as at other prehistoric sites. Because we know something of the growing habits of these species, it seems probable that their ubiquitous distribution was not only the result of cultural preference, but also came about due to their continued availability during the growing season.

Pigweed and goosefoot grow today as weeds in modern gardens, taking advantage of extra water and disturbed land. The Salmon occupants may have encouraged growth of these plants in their own garden plots, and searched for locations around the pueblo where natural conditions favored large stands. These shifting seasonal plants can be available over a long part of the frost-free growing season, and are ready as both greens and seeds prior to corn and other cultivated crop maturation. The case may have been different for purslane, which would bear abundantly during the fall harvest season provided enough moisture was available. Even so, the Salmon occupants used this resource throughout the pueblo's history.

As a result of investigating the plant remains, we know more about which seeds were ground into flour and which were prepared by parching near a fire. Salmon cooks ground the seeds of tansy mustard, pigweed, purslane, goosefoot, and stickleaf, while sometimes parching the pigweed, goosefoot, tansy mustard, and stickleaf seeds beforehand. We can offer well-formed guesses on just what ingredients were prepared in the pottery vessels. Flour ground from corn and tiny seeds of native plants provided many a meal for the pueblo occupants.

Inhabitants of all three floors in Room 93W burned green juniper boughs in the hearths, or at least brought in green juniper branches for some purpose. They all cultivated corn, as evidenced by macrofossils or pollen. A squash pollen grain was recovered from Floor 2. Occupants of Floors 1 and 5 may have exploited habitats of high ground water, as suggested by the sedge, rush, and possibly cattail remains.

In sum, during both major occupations of the pueblo (Chaco and Mesa Verde), Room 93W was used for various aspects of native and cultivated plant food preparation. The most probable explanation for the burned seeds in the hearths of each floor and on the surface of Floors 2 and 5 would be food preparation; some of the plant remains on Floor 1 may have been deposited with trash thrown into the room after abandonment. Grinding stones on Floors 1 and 2 were used to pulverize many small seeds of native plants. The virtual lack of corn kernels, cobs, and juniper seeds on these floors may be due to the ease in sweeping or picking up such larger objects; discarded cobs and juniper seeds are abundant elsewhere in trash heaps at Salmon Ruin. People probably shared the plants that the earth provided with their deities, or so it seems from the concentration of what many would call corn "prayer meal" on Floor 1, and from the apparent presence of ground-cherry offerings to the fire on Floors 1 and 2. Although no known ethnographic record of food use has been found for spurge seeds, their presence on Floor 1 and their general ubiquity in trash strata (many apparently parched) suggests that this seed was a source of flour and food in prehistory. Although most spurges are poisonous, some exceptions are known, and it seems that the Salmon inhabitants knew of a nonpoisonous type. Also, it appears that tansy mustard and perhaps sedge seeds played a larger role in prehistoric life than in modern times. More than seven centuries ago, the occupants of Salmon pueblo flourished in the San Juan Valley in New Mexico. Like Peter Salmon and his descendants, they took from the land's rich stock of resources, and they prospered for many years.

Chapter 40

PINES AND OTHER CONIFERS FROM SALMON PUEBLO

by Karen R. Adams

The ancient pueblo of Salmon Ruin in northwestern New Mexico sits on a terrace just north of the San Juan River, surrounded by diverse topography (Figure 40.1). Mountain ranges intersperse with broad plateaus and valleys, three permanent rivers grace the landscape, and flora and fauna show corresponding diversity. On a clear day one can stand on the highest point of the pueblo and see 30 km to the southeast across rolling plains to the top of Angel Peak. To the north, layers of gravel terraces partially obstruct the view of the horizon. At an elevation of 5450 feet (1661 m), the predominant local vegetation type is Utah juniper (*Juniperus osteosperma*) woodland, with grama (*Bouteloua*) and galleta (*Hilaria*) grasses predominating (Morain et al. 1977). Sagebrush (*Artemisia*) and riverine vegetation are both locally common.

The building and remodeling history of Salmon Ruin has been reconstructed via dendrochronology, archaeomagnetic sampling, architectural studies, and ceramic typology. Late in the eleventh century, a group of people with ties to Chaco Canyon to the south carefully planned and built a multiroom pueblo, perhaps assisted by local San Juan Valley inhabitants. This period of Chacoan occupation lasted at least until around AD 1120–1125, when many occupants left the pueblo. For the next few decades, both architectural modifications and new construction slowed, yet stratigraphic continuity in a few rooms suggests some use of Salmon Pueblo during this "Intermediate" period. This chapter treats the Intermediate as a separate period in the history of Salmon, following the original chronology of Rex Adams (1980); Paul Reed's revised chronology has the Early Secondary period beginning at the end of the Chacoan occupation, at AD 1120–1125.

This paper was originally written in 1979 by Karen R. Adams. It was subsequently added to the ethnobotanical section for the 1980 Salmon Final Report. Adams reworked the paper for the new Salmon Report, and the updated version is presented here.

The Secondary occupants made Salmon their home until the late AD 1280s or 1290s (Reed, Chapter 8).

The total amount of materials recovered archaeologically from the Secondary occupation at Salmon Ruin far exceeds that left by the earlier Chacoans. At least three factors could account for this difference. First, the Chacoans occupied the pueblo for only 50 years, relative to a much longer period for the Secondary folks. Second, it appears that the Secondary group may have reused materials originally acquired by the Chacoans, such as roof beams and stone tools. Reuse of other objects may not be directly observable, yet still contributes to the relative difference in bulk of remains associated with the two occupations. Third are the cultural differences associated with how groups discard trash—although the Chacoans occasionally used abandoned rooms within the pueblo for trash deposit, the Secondary occupants left numerous rooms filled to the top with all types of debris.

Plant materials were especially well preserved in Salmon deposits. This chapter focuses solely on evidence for conifer use by Salmon occupants during the Pueblo's entire history. Conifers are typically needle-bearing and evergreen trees or shrubs of temperate climates. In the Southwest, conifers are often the most abundant trees on the landscape, projecting well above other vegetation.

To understand the role that conifers played in prehistory in the San Juan Valley, identifications of ancient specimens had to be as accurate as possible. To facilitate this goal, modern conifers growing in northwestern New Mexico and southwestern Colorado (Table 40.1) were gathered and described, providing the means to view variability within and between species and their parts. Dichotomous keys developed on the basis of distinguishable traits in modern conifer parts furnished a critical tool for identifying the ancient conifer specimens from Salmon Ruin (K. Adams 1979:7–46). Other published reports on conifer part identification were also consulted (Chang 1954; Harlow 1931; Shaw 1914).

Figure 40.1. Aerial view of Salmon Pueblo.

Table 40.1. Conifer species encountered in northwestern New Mexico and Southwestern Colorado today.

Typical Habitat	Common Name	Species
High Mountain	Alpine fir	*Abies lasiocarpa*
Corkbark fir	*Abies lasiocarpa* var. *arizonica*	
Dwarf juniper	*Juniperus communis*	
Engelmann spruce	*Picea engelmannii*	
Blue spruce	*Picea pungens*	
Limber pine	*Pinus flexilis*	
Mid-Low Mountain	Spruce-fir	*Abies concolor*
Alligator bark juniper	*Juniperus deppeana*	
Rocky Mountain juniper	*Juniperus scopulorum*	
Ponderosa pine	*Pinus ponderosa*	
Douglas fir	*Pseudotsuga taxifolia*	
High Plateau	One-seeded juniper	*Juniperus monosperma*
Utah juniper	*Juniperus osteospserma*	
Piñon pine	*Pinus edulis*	

Nomenclature follows Kearney and Peebles (1960).

Stratigraphic position and diagnostic ceramic sherds in Salmon Ruin strata together suggest cultural affiliation for associated plant remains. In this study, conifer materials recovered with Chaco, Escavada, and Gallup Black-on-white ceramic types (Franklin 1975) are considered Chacoan in affiliation, and those associated with Mesa Verde Black-on-white pottery (Breternitz et al. 1974:45–46) belong to the Secondary occupation of the pueblo. Conifer remains associated with McElmo type pottery are considered to belong to the Intermediate period, and those recovered with a mixture of diagnostic sherds are labeled "mixed cultural affiliation."

The conifer assemblage discussed in this chapter was recovered from Salmon between 1973 and 1977 with two exceptions. First, tree-ring specimens discussed include those excavated in 1972 and sampled from the site in the 1960s. Second, some conifer remains from the 1978 season are discussed when they offer additional insights. Most conifer remains recovered during excavation in 1971 and 1972 have yet to be examined. Taxonomy in this chapter conforms to *Arizona Flora* (Kearney and Peebles 1960).

An examination of the list of conifer macrofossils preserved at Salmon reveals that the Chacoan and Secondary groups both used many of the same materials (Table 40.2). Both cultural groups also used the same species of juniper for seeds (Lentz 1979, 1984; Lentz, Chapter 41), grew the same species of squash (*Cucurbita pepo*) in their gardens (Terrel 1979), and gathered many of the same wild plant foods (Doebley 1976, 1981; Doebley, Chapter 37). Conifers

provided food, fuel, household items, medicinal and ceremonial materials, and construction timbers.

USE OF CONIFERS FOR FOOD
Piñon

Piñon nuts and juniper berries were eaten by both Chacoan and Secondary people. Storage of these resources also seems likely, as does the use of immature nut crops and bark during times of food shortage. Conifer evidence also provides insights into season(s) of gathering.

In the Southwest, piñon nuts generally ripen after agricultural crops have been harvested. If the growing conditions of two consecutive years have been satisfactory, the piñon crop can be bountiful. More often, however, the immature nuts abort in long dry spells, or succumb to fungal insect attacks (Zarn 1977:25). Perhaps the need for ritual arose because of the uncertainty of a piñon harvest. In ceremonies among the Zia, the Koshairi have used magic to encourage abundant harvest of a number of cultivated and wild crops, including piñon (White 1974:145).

When the piñon harvest was good, the high-fat nuts were gathered by many modern groups (Watt and Merrill 1975:46), such as the Zia (White 1974: 107), Cochiti (Lange 1959:145), Acoma and Laguna (Swank 1932:60–61), Isleta (Jones 1931:37), Hopi (Nequatewa 1943:18), Zuni (Stevenson 1915:70), Santa Clara, and Navajo (Castetter 1935:40–41). People from Isleta collected enough nuts to store them for the coming winter (Jones 1931:37).

Table 40.2. Conifer macrofossil presence in rooms and strata at Salmon Ruin, organized by occupation

Taxon and Part	Chacoan		Intermediate		Secondary		Mixed Affiliation	
	Room	Strata	Room	Strata	Room	Strata	Room	Strata
Abies concolor or Pseudotsuga bark	–	–	–	–	–	–	62W	trash
Ephedra stems	–	–	–	trash	–	–	62W	trash, pit
Juniperus osteosperma/monosperma								
bark cordage	33W	roof	–	–	36W	trash	–	–
bark 'needle'	–	–	36W	trash	–	–	–	–
coiled bark	–	–	–	–	62W	trash	62A	trash
layered bark	–	–	–	–	62W	trash	–	–
pot rest/burden ring	–	–	–	–	59W	trash	62W	trash
toilet paper	–	–	–	–	62W	trash	–	–
twig bundle	–	–	–	–	129W	roof*	–	–
twisted bark	–	–	–	–	127W	roof*	–	–
Juniperus scopulorum bark/wood	–	–	–	–	–	–	62A	trash
Picea engelmannii bark scale	101W	trash	–	–	36W	trash	130W	foot drum
Picea pungens bark scale	–	–	–	–	–	–	90W	trash
cf. *Picea*								
bark scale	84W	trash*	–	–	–	–	–	–
female cone scale	–	–	–	–	–	–	43W	roof
Pinus edulis								
female cone scale	33W	roof	–	–	36W	trash	62A	trash
	81W	roof*	–	–	62W	trash	62W	trash*
twig with fascicle	–	–	–	–	62W	pit	–	–
Pinus ponderosa								
bark section	–	–	–	–	102B	burial pit	62A	trash
	–	–	–	–	–	–	62W	trash*
needles	–	–	–	–	–	–	33W	roof
	–	–	–	–	–	–	62W	trash
Pinus ponderosa or *P. edulis* twig	–	–	62W	trash	–	–	–	–
Pinus female cone scale	33W	roof*	–	–	–	–	–	–
Pinus or *Picea* bark scale	33W	roof	37W	trash*	–	–	–	–
	129W	trash*	–	–	–	–	–	–
	31W	fill	–	–	–	–	–	–

* most of strata was burned; This table excludes piñon (*Pinus edulis*) nutshells reported in Table 40.3, charred conifer wood from hearths reported in Table 40.4, and juniper (*Juniperus osteosperma*) berries and seeds reported by Lentz (1979, Chapter 41, this volume).

Single-leaf piñon (*Pinus monophylla*) nuts were also of great interest in other areas. Foraging Shoshonean groups would take the entire family into the hills to spend many days gathering piñon nuts (Lowie 1968:203 [1924]), sometimes traveling long distances to get there. The semisedentary Owens Valley Paiute in northern Nevada would walk more than 14 miles to a piñon camp (Steward 1933:241, map 2), frequently camping there through the winter months if the harvest was good. There were two seasons for piñon collection among the Kawaiisu of California . The first, most important season was late summer–early fall (July and August), when the immature cones remained tightly closed around the nuts and had to be roasted to loosen their nuts. A second (minor) gathering occurred in September, when the cones had opened and their nuts were dispersing naturally (Zigmund 1981).

Numerous hunting and gathering groups preferred the first method of picking the closed cones just before maturity and roasting them to loosen the nuts. The Southern Paiute (Stuart 1945:155), Southeastern Yavapai (Gifford 1932:208–209), Northeastern and Western Yavapai (Gifford 1936:255), and possibly additional groups (Palmer 1878:594–595) all followed this practice. One cannot help but wonder if these nomadic groups harvested immature nut crops as a matter of necessity, rather than preference, perhaps because they were more frequently burdened by food shortages than sedentary, agricultural people were.

Although hunters and gatherers often focused on immature nut crops, other groups waited until the nuts were free from their cones before harvesting. Navajos were especially proficient at hand picking the nuts from the ground. Another method of gathering was to spread cloths beneath the trees and shake the nuts free by beating the branches with a stick. Sometimes brooms were used to sweep the nuts into piles. One of the fastest methods was to rob a pack-rat nest, where up to 30 pounds of nuts could often be found (Castetter 1935:40–41).

Regardless of harvesting method, piñon nuts were often roasted because parching rendered the hull brittle and allowed it to be easily removed. At the same time the fat in the kernel was set free, making it more digestible and preventing it from becoming rancid and moldy if stored (Palmer 1878:595). Toasted nuts were also thought to taste better (Underhill 1954:55–56).

Hundreds of piñon nuts and nutshell fragments have been recovered from more than half the 48 excavated rooms representing both Chacoan and Secondary occupations (Table 40.3). Modern experi-

ments on piñon nuts have shed some light on the various processing methods: piñon nuts were roasted in a coffee can over a gas flame until parched or carbonized, and then were cracked with a mortar and pestle to remove the nutmeats, and raw nuts were cracked with a mortar and pestle or with the teeth. Raw nutshells have light-colored interiors and brown exteriors; parching noticeably darkens the interior of the nutshell, but not the exterior. Charring results in interior and exterior blackening and extremely brittle nutshells. Piñon nuts cracked with mortar and pestle produce relatively small segments of nutshells, with half or less of the shell remaining, and nuts cracked with the teeth result in larger (half or more) nutshell fragments.

A 20 percent sample of the ancient specimens was chosen to document amount of nutshell present, discoloration, and unusual traits. This sample included both large (greater than half) and small (less than half) nutshell fragments. The Salmon inhabitants of both major occupations apparently cracked piñon nuts with their teeth and shelled some of them on a hard grinding surface. Internal darkening on the majority of ancient nutshells indicates that most of the nuts were parched. However, it is possible that internal discoloration could result naturally from prolonged burial in the earth, or it could reflect depositional environment. The presence of a few nutshells with light-colored interiors suggests that some piñon nuts were consumed raw. A small number of nutshells had irregular holes with tapered edges, an effect produced by rodents when gnawing their way through a tough nut, as opposed to the clean breaks characteristic of nutshells cracked with human teeth or pestles. Finally, the recovery of a bent and collapsed piñon nutshell fragment suggests that a thin, flexible shell with immature nut was harvested and carried to the pueblo during the Chacoan occupation.

The recovery of whole piñon cones in an archaeological site might imply that piñon trees were near enough to bring the entire cones in for processing. However, the presence of individual cone scales cannot likewise be considered. The uncarbonized female cone scales recovered in three rooms at Salmon (see Table 40.2) could have been accidentally collected during piñon nut harvests when trees were shaken to loosen the nuts, or when a scattered nut crop was swept up from beneath a tree. The same explanation might also apply to the piñon twig recovered from the Secondary occupation.

Although excavations uncovered no recognizable caches of piñon nuts at Salmon Ruin, some evidence exists that indirectly implies ancient storage of

Table 40.3. Distribution of piñon (*Pinus edulis*) nuts at Salmon Ruin with more than half the shell present.

Room Number	Chacoan	Intermediate	Mixed Secondary	Cultural Affiliation
4A	–	–	3	–
31W	1	–	9	–
33W	65	–	6	–
36W	–	1	70	–
37W	–	–	9	–
43W	35	–	55	–
57W	1	–	1	–
58W	–	–	1	–
59W	–	–	14	–
60B	–	–	16	–
62A	–	–	–	19
62W	75	118	874	258
64W	–	1	25	–
67W	–	–	4	–
82W	–	2	9	–
84W	8	–	3	–
89W	–	–	4	–
91A	–	–	1	–
97W	8	–	5	–
98W	2	–	–	–
100W	–	1	2	–
101W	6	–	–	–
118W	–	–	5	–
127W	–	–	37	–
129W	–	–	2	–
Totals	201	123	1155	277

this resource. For example, most of the piñon nuts appear to have been parched, and parching is a step that often precedes storage. The presence of a parched piñon nutshell associated with other food-stuffs stored on a roof of Room 33W (F-2-9) supports this suggestion. Also, rodent-gnawed nutshells could have succumbed to such damage while in storage. A few piñon nutshells with evidence of parching or burning and gnawing may represent a nut cache prepared by humans for storage but subsequently raided by rodents.

Piñon nut use spans broad temporal and geographic horizons in the ancient Southwest. The earliest evidence of piñon nuts is from Bat Cave, a Mogollon cultural tradition site in west-central New Mexico (Smith 1950:165), dating to perhaps 2300 BC (Mangelsdorf et al. 1967:17). There, hundreds of piñon (*Pinus edulis*) nutshells comprised one of the most abundant plant remains recovered. Other early piñon nuts and cone fragments have been found at Fresnal Shelter (Bohrer 1973a:211), representing the Jornada branch of the Mogollon (2000 BC–AD 100) in south-central New Mexico. Large numbers of piñon nutshells and cones were also preserved at Tularosa

and Cordova Caves in west-central New Mexico (Cutler 1952:478; Kaplan 1963:351) dating 300 BC–AD 1200.

Outside of the Mogollon area, piñon (*Pinus* cf. *monophylla*) nutshells dating from Basketmaker III–developmental Pueblo times have been recovered from a cave in Zion National Park, Utah (Jones 1955:197). Also in Utah, a pottery jar in a Pueblo I site at Alkali Ridge (Jones 1946:331) contained about a pint of charred piñon nuts. In Arizona, carbonized piñon nuts dating to the eleventh and twelfth centuries AD have been retrieved from trash mounds at Winona Village–Ridge Ruin sites near Flagstaff (McGregor 1941:261). Piñon nuts were also consumed at Betatakin, a Pueblo III Kayenta site in northeastern Arizona (Judd 1931:66).

Piñon nuts contributed to the ancient diet seven centuries ago in the Mesa Verde area of southern Colorado (Rohn 1963:10), as well as at Pueblo Bonito and Pueblo del Arroyo in Chaco Canyon, New Mexico (Judd 1954:61, 1959:125). Aztec Ruins, 15 km north of and contemporaneous with Salmon Ruin, revealed piñon nuts dating to the AD 1200s (Richert 1964:30), and nut cones, shells, and cone scales were also recovered from Guadalupe Ruin, a Chacoan-related town approximately 80 km south of Chaco Canyon in New Mexico (Pippin 1987:267).

Utah Juniper

Utah juniper berries, available in most years, are perhaps more dependable in the Southwest than piñon nuts. Many modern groups ate juniper berries, either alone or with other foods. The Cochiti considered them of some importance, sometimes boiling them until soft before eating (Lange 1959:146). The Jemez ate the berries, either raw or cooked, and at Hopi they were served with fresh piki bread (Nequatewa 1943:18). At Zuni the fruits were gathered and ground into meal, which was then made into cakes. The Tewa ate fruits of more than one species of juniper, either fresh or heated; the heated fruit was considered more palatable (Castetter 1935:31–32). The Acoma and Laguna gathered the berries and mixed them with chopped meat, which they sometimes roasted in a cleaned deer stomach. In times of plenty the berries often served as a seasoning, but when food was scarce they were relied upon heavily (Swank 1932:49–50). Juniper berries have also served as an emergency food during times of famine for the Hopi (Whiting 1939:21).

Various lines of evidence indicate that Utah juniper berries were eaten by both Chacoan and Secondary occupants at Salmon Pueblo (Lentz 1979, 1984; Lentz, Chapter 41). Three carbonized berries were recovered in direct association with fire hearths, probably representing cooking. Seventy-six trash strata produced juniper seeds, likely places for the discard of food residue. Seven carbonized seeds located on a bench in the Tower Kiva (Room 64W) accompanied food cultigens and grinding stones. Eight roof strata containing juniper seeds were possible locations where juniper cones were air-dried. Finally, a strong co-occurrence was observed between juniper seeds and berries and other food items in a number of strata. Perhaps the high value of juniper as a food product at Salmon is revealed by the fact that eight burials were accompanied by juniper seeds; apparently juniper was considered an important enough food to sustain the deceased on their final journey.

Not only did juniper berries serve as food at Salmon, but they also appear to have been stored with other foodstuffs. In two-story rooms 36W (F-1-15) and 90W (F-2-9), the roofs burned simultaneously and fell onto unburned debris, subsequently becoming covered with unburned material. Any items associated with roof stratigraphy in the two rooms can be recognized due to their unique carbonized condition among unburned strata. Burned food items associated with roofs in these two rooms included juniper berry or seed remains, maize (*Zea mays*) cob and kernel fragments, and beans (*Phaseolus vulgris*); one possible explanation for such an association of food items would be roof storage.

The use of juniper berries in prehistory is also known from other sites in New Mexico. Juniper seeds were recovered at both Tularosa and Cordova Caves in west-central New Mexico (Cutler 1952:478; Kaplan 1963:352), as well as in Bat Cave (Smith 1950:166). In south-central New Mexico, burned and unburned juniper seeds and fruits were found in Fresnal Shelter (Bohrer 1973a:211), and in north-central New Mexico a charred juniper berry was retrieved from a pit house (Ford 1968a:239). In western New Mexico, Cutler identified juniper berries from Higgens Flat Pueblo (1956:181).

Elsewhere in the Southwest, juniper berries and seeds were found beneath some of the clay floors at Mug House in the Mesa Verde area of Colorado, although there was no direct evidence that these were eaten in prehistory (Rohn 1971:257). Carbonized juniper seeds have also been found at the Carter Ranch site in eastern Arizona (Cutler 1964:234), as well as in a cave in Zion National Park in Utah (Jones 1955:197).

Immature Piñon and Juniper Parts

Conifer evidence suggests that the ancient inhabitants of Salmon Pueblo may have experienced food shortage at various times. For example, the recovery of four burned piñon female cone scales, one scale with its immature nutshell still adhering, poses the intriguing possibility that the Salmon residents picked the not-quite-mature cones in the early fall and roasted them to loosen the nuts (Figure 40.2). The potential significance of this evidence must be viewed against two factors—the potential success of the cultivated plant harvest and the life cycle of the piñon tree. Cultivated corn and squash would usually be at their peak in late summer or early fall, and could conceivably require many days of harvest activity by many people. Consequently, few would have time to concentrate on gathering wild plants.

If the corn or squash harvest were meager, however, individuals would presumably be out searching the area for alternative wild plant edibles, such as piñon nuts. But piñon nuts were not always reliable resources. In the early fall of its second year of growth, a piñon cone bends back its scales and releases the mature nuts. However, when cones are

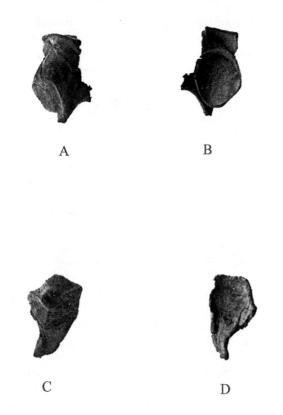

A   B

C   D

Figure 40.2. Prehistoric *Pinus edulis* female cone scales, Salmon Ruin; (a) dorsal view, Room 62W, Record Key No. 76650; (b) ventral view of same cone scale, with immature nutshell still adhering; (c) dorsal view, Room 62W, Record Key No. 76585; (d) ventral view, same cone scale.

immature, no amount of beating will loosen their seed cargo, and roasting them becomes necessary. As noted above, many hunting and gathering groups appear to have harvested and roasted immature cones (Gifford 1932:208–209, 1936:255; Palmer 1878: 594–595; Stuart 1945:155; Zigmund 1981). If the sedentary Salmon community experienced food stress in the late summer or early fall, hungry individuals would recognize the practical advantages of harvesting an immature piñon crop. The additional recovery of a bent and collapsed immature nutshell fragment from Room 81W lends support to the hypothesis that immature nuts were harvested.

In another part of New Mexico, one carbonized piñon pine cone scale dated to AD 1775–1250 was found in Saltbush Pueblo in Bandelier National Monument (Ford 1974:79). The author has implied that this female cone scale could have resulted from collecting piñon cones before they were completely mature; he further commented that pueblo groups today sometimes collect immature cones if the crop of nuts is expected to be mediocre, and competition

with rodents and birds for the nuts could therefore be keen. Such activity indicates that people are taking no chances in sharing the crop with animals, presumably because they have a real need for real food.

The possibility of food stress at Salmon is supported by the recovery of both juniper bark and yucca (*Yucca*) leaf epidermis from within a coprolite from the Secondary occupation (Room 62W, stratum C-34-34). Juniper bark and yucca leaves are relatively low in nutrition and palatability, having served mainly as famine foods among modern groups (Castetter 1935:32; Robbins et al. 1916:50). The real advantage of these plant parts is that they represent very reliable plant resources, available throughout the year. In situations of food shortage, the bark of the juniper and the leaves of the always-green yucca plant could fill empty stomachs despite their relative lack of palatability.

CONIFER DATA AND SALMON'S SEASON(S) OF OCCUPATION

Food remains from ancient sites can sometimes indicate the probable season of occupation, if the harvested parts are relatively restricted in availability during the growing year. For example, some cool-season grasses such as Indian ricegrass (*Oryzopsis hymenoides*) and six-weeks fescue (*Festuca octoflora*) mature in the spring, so their presence in an archaeological record would imply spring residence in that area. Other plants such as pigweed (*Amaranthus*) and goosefoot (*Chenopodium*) can grow throughout the frost-free season, so their recovery from a site is not as helpful in providing estimates of specific season of habitation.

Even when a particular season of occupation is strongly suggested by the plant record, one cannot easily speculate on how long after that season the people remained. People may store plant products so that some foods last throughout the year (Adams and Bohrer 1998); evidence of such storage may therefore be conservatively interpreted to suggest habitation of an area for at least one season following the time of normal harvest.

In this study, piñon and juniper specimens suggest early fall occupation of Salmon Pueblo. Evidence includes burned piñon cone scales, one with its immature nutshell still adhering. Unfortunately, the group that brought them to the pueblo is unknown, as these scales were recovered from strata of mixed cultural affiliation. Also indicative of early fall residence is the presence of a bent and collapsed piñon nutshell fragment of Chacoan affiliation, whose condition implies that an immature nut was harvested.

Piñon and juniper evidence also points to winter occupation. For example, many of the piñon nutshells of both Chacoan and Secondary affiliation appear parched, a step needed for long-term storage (Palmer 1878:595); a parched piñon nutshell was recovered from the roof of a room (33W, F-2-9) where other foodstuffs were stored. The presence of rodent gnaw marks on nuts of Chacoan affiliation provides additional evidence of long-term storage, if rodents raided a storage area following harvest. Other evidence of winter occupation at Salmon includes the presence of juniper berries in two suspected food storage areas (36W, 90W). Supplemental evidence of fall and possibly winter occupation of Salmon Pueblo includes remains of tansy mustard (*Descurainia*), stickleaf (*Mentzelia albicaulis*), Indian ricegrass, onion (*Allium*) bulb scales, and cholla (*Cylindropuntia*), all indicating that the pueblo was inhabited in the fall or early winter. Likely the pueblo was also occupied during the summer, when Cheno-Am seeds, groundcherry (*Physalis longifolia* type) fruit (K. Adams 1980; Adams, Chapter 39), and squaw-bush (*Rhus trilobata*) fruit (Doebley 1976:39, 1981; Chapter 37) all ripen.

CONIFERS AS FUELWOOD

A small study of charcoal within Salmon Ruin hearths (Rossi 1977) revealed that conifers constituted a firewood of choice for both Chacoan and Secondary occupants (Table 40.4); charred juniper wood was preserved in seven of eight hearths. Modern groups at Cochiti (Lange 1959:145–146) frequently burned juniper in hearths, people at Acoma and Laguna liked it when a steady, even fire was desired (Swank 1932:48–49), and at Isleta juniper wood was chosen because it produced a very hot fire (Jones 1931:32–33). Navajo groups also appreciated its pleasant odor and clear smoke (Bailey 1940:273).

The recovery of *Pinus* charcoal from a single Chacoan hearth poses interpretive difficulty. If piñon trees grew nearby in prehistory, it is reasonable to expect that dead wood would have been carried in for fuel, as modern Tewa groups do (Robbins et al. 1916:41). But the single instance of pinewood from this study of Salmon hearths seems dubious grounds for assuming that piñon was locally available. Another possibility would be that the Chacoans burned leftover ponderosa (*Pinus ponderosa*) beam fragments when constructing the pueblo. Clearly, more analysis is needed to document fuel choice through time.

Two pieces of ponderosa pine bark were recovered in trash containing ceramic sherds of both Secondary and mixed cultural affiliation (see Table 40.2); one of these bark sections was charred (Figure 40.3). Any ponderosa pine roof timbers brought to Salmon and debarked after their arrival at the pueblo would provide this fuel or tinder source.

The presence of microscopic flecks of burned Douglas fir wood on at least two floors at Salmon Ruin raised the question as to whether the species served as firewood. Five out of seven pollen samples from Floor H-2-12 in Room 30W (Chacoan occupation) and five out of eight pollen samples from Floor H-2-11 in Room 58W (Secondary occupation) exhibited the presence of Douglas fir wood fly ash (characterized by tracheids with spiral thickening and bordered pits). If Douglas fir wood were burned as fuel in a firepit, fly ash escaping from the hearth could have become embedded in an adobe floor. Since neither floor in 30W or 58W had a hearth of its own, presumably fly ash would have had to enter

A

B

Figure 40.3. Prehistoric charred *Pinus ponderosa* bark, Salmon Ruin: (a) top view, Room 62W, Record Key No. 28890; (b) side view, same specimen.

Table 40.4. Charred conifer wood identified in Salmon hearths (Rossi 1977). Secondary features represent reuse of Chacoan hearths. Limited nonconifer wood was also recovered from Secondary hearths.

Wood Type	Chacoan		Secondary	
	Room Number	Feature Number	Room Number	Feature Number
Juniperus	20P	4	151W	101
	92W	46	151W	102
	94W	4	—	—
	101W	9	—	—
	123B	7	—	—
Pinus	6W	25	—	—

from another section of the pueblo. However, the current evidence implies that Douglas fir was not regularly burned in Salmon hearths; the small pilot study of charcoal from eight firepits revealed no Douglas fir specimens. Other explanations to account for the presence of Douglas fir wood fly ash on floors at Salmon must therefore be considered. Perhaps pueblo roof rafters of Douglas fir burned at various times in prehistory. Tree-ring studies have revealed that the Chacoans carried in some Douglas fir beams during the major construction of the pueblo. Salmon excavations identified only two roofs (130W and 56W) that might have burned during the Chacoan occupation; both are somewhat distant to have contributed fly ash to the floor of 30W (Figure 40.4). However, currently unexcavated rooms south of Room 30W may in the future reveal additional burned roofs that could potentially account for the fly ash deposited in Chacoan times. During the Secondary period, widespread conflagrations caused numerous roofs to be destroyed. Fly ash produced by burning in many sectors of the pueblo could then have drifted onto the floor in Room 58W.

Another explanation for the presence of Douglas fir wood fly ash on Salmon floors might be deliberate use in ceremonies. Ash is used for many rites among modern Puebloan groups (Bunzel 1932:506; Laski 1958:42; Ortiz 1969:54; Parsons 1929, 1939; White 1932:73). Ashes are especially associated with magic and witchcraft, and as a means to ward off disease or calamity. (For a full discussion of the use of ash in exorcism among pueblo groups, see Parsons 1939)

Because of widespread modern Puebloan use of ash in a variety of contexts, it seems reasonable to infer that these practices occurred at Salmon. Although juniper has filled modern ash needs (Whiting 1939:62), one wonders whether other trees might be used as well. Among the modern Tewa, Douglas fir branches are disposed of very carefully when their

use in certain ceremonies is over (Robbins et al. 1916:42–43). Perhaps some of the Douglas fir wood fly ash on floors in Salmon resulted from ritual disposal of Douglas fir branches into the fire, and then subsequent spreading of the ash in various purification or sacred rites. Just as likely might be deliberate placement of "fir" branches into the fire, as has been documented at Acoma to bring rain in summer and snow in winter (Paytiamo 1932:156).

The recovery of clumps of maize pollen from Floors 30W and 58W strengthens the argument that ceremonial activities may have occurred in these two rooms. Maize pollen clumps were observed in all nine pollen samples from 30W and in seven of eight pollen samples from 58W. Clusters of maize pollen may well represent the gathering of immature tassels (Bohrer 1981). Since modern Puebloans are known to gather maize pollen for medicinal or ceremonial use (Parsons 1939; Robbins et al. 1916:97; Swank 1932: 78), ancient pollen aggregates may well have carried the same significance.

CONIFERS AS HOUSEHOLD ITEMS: JUNIPER

Shredded juniper bark was gathered to construct a variety of household items at Salmon, rivaled only by yucca leaves as a widely used material for daily household needs. To understand why juniper bark might be an attractive resource, it is necessary to review how bark functions on a tree. In general, the bark of a tree provides a rather impenetrable shield against fungal attack, insulates the tree from extremes in temperature, and serves as a waterproof covering. Such highly desirable qualities could be valuable. For example, a bark lining in an underground storage pit would be likely to resist fungal infiltration, moderate fluctuating soil temperatures, and keep dampness out. Juniper bark has apparently been used to line storage bins at numerous southwestern sites (Breternitz 1960:26–27). As clothing or

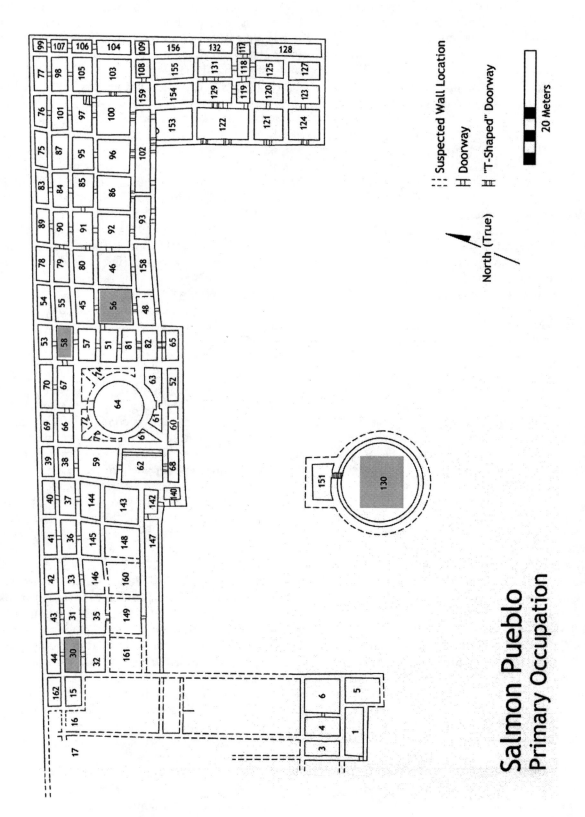

Salmon Pueblo
Primary Occupation

Suspected Wall Location

Doorway

"T-Shaped" Doorway

North (True)

20 Meters

Figure 40.4. Map of Salmon Ruins showing rooms (highlighted) discussed in text.

bedding, bark would offer insulation as well as repelling moisture. When used in roof construction, bark could provide the insulation necessary for a warmer winter and a cooler summer habitation.

Although these qualities are shared by most types of bark, bark often forms inelastic plates that would be difficult to maneuver in a storage pit, or uncomfortable to sleep upon. Two types of juniper—Utah juniper and one-seeded juniper (*Juniperus monosperma*)—provide an outstanding exception. Their bark can be detached from the tree in long, loose, strips (Figure 40.5), it bends easily without breaking, and it can be shredded to form a soft, pliable material. A quality that is both desirable and undesirable is the flammability of juniper bark. Although it could serve as a match for starting a fire, it could also easily catch fire from hearth sparks, especially if used as a layer of roofing.

At Salmon, juniper bark was fashioned into cordage, pot rests or burden rings, roofing material, and toilet paper, and was used in other undetermined ways as well. The fact that masses of shredded but otherwise unmodified juniper bark were recovered from 24 of 48 excavated rooms at Salmon, spanning both major cultural occupations, suggests the extent of its ancient utility.

The Chacoan and Secondary occupants of Salmon Pueblo used juniper bark as cordage, as indicated by the following examples (see Webster, Chapter 46, for more discussion). The Secondary occupants left two unburned 2-yarn strands of juniper bark cordage in the trash in Room 36W (see Figure 40.5). The 2-yarn cordage was made by first twisting narrow strips of juniper bark to the left to form two separate Z-twist yarns, and then twisting these two yarns together to form single strands of rather loose cordage. Two additional single Z-twist yarns, averaging 5 cm in length, accompanied the cordage. One yarn is nearly 1 cm in width and displays very even and uncharred ends, and the other is less than 0.3 cm in width and has frayed, irregular ends. The Chacoan occupants left a short (3 cm) unburned 2-yarn strand of juniper bark cordage associated with a roof in Room 33W. This cordage was made in the same way as that recovered from the Secondary occupation trash in Room 36W. Two narrow (1 mm) strips of juniper bark were twisted into Z-twist yarns, and then twisted together again to form a strand of loose cordage.

Juniper bark cordage could be used in fashioning breech clouts, skirts, mats to sleep on, dolls, and fiber blankets, much as modern Paiutes did (Kelly 1964; Palmer 1878:594; Stewart 1941:38). Unfortunately, no larger fragments have been preserved to indicate any such use at Salmon. The cordage in the roof of Room 33W might have been used to secure something from the rafters to dry. Other materials have also been recovered at Salmon, such as yucca knots and cotton (*Gossypium*) cordage and cloth, broadening the understanding of the species used to make domestic goods in prehistory. The cotton was likely traded into the pueblo, as processed cotton lint but no weaving tools have been found.

The use of juniper bark cordage in the Southwest extends back to at least the Basketmaker II period (ca. 1900 years). Juniper bark cordage with a Z-twist has been recovered from Basketmaker II through Pueblo age deposits in a cave in Zion National Park (Jones 1955:186) and in a Basketmaker Cave in Kane County, Utah (Nusbaum 1922). An S-twist cordage has been identified from Basketmaker III sites (date range AD 46–324) near Durango, Colorado (Jones and Fonner 1954:105).

A trash stratum in Room 59W of Secondary affiliation yielded a partially burned and broken circular ring of juniper bark (Figure 40.6). Relatively thin layers of bark were looped into a circle approximately 9 cm in diameter, with a 3 cm hole in the center; no evidence remains as to how the bark was originally secured to form the ring. The outer edge of the ring is 1.4 cm thick, tapering to 0.3 cm at the inner edge. The ring appears compact in the center, and much degraded, with cement-like soil permeating its structure. Such thorough incorporation of dirt may have occurred when the item was used as a pot rest on an adobe floor; round-bottomed ceramic pots do not sit well on a flat floor, but they stand upright in a supporting ring (Cushing 1886:503). The pressure of a ceramic pot resting on the ring may have forced adobe into its fibers during use.

Secondary trash strata in Room 62W also yielded a similar, though not completely identical, circular artifact of juniper bark. This artifact consists of strips of shredded bark that have been coiled together to form a ring 11 cm in diameter and 4 cm high, with a 5 cm diameter hole in the middle. After the first circular loop was completed, the free end was extended about halfway around the coil and presumably secured, although no method of holding the coil together can be observed. Unlike the circular ring from Room 59W, this one has not been burned, nor was dirt ground into its structure. Rather than serving as a pot rest on an adobe floor, perhaps this artifact functioned as a burden ring for balancing round-bottomed ceramic vessels upright on someone's head. If daily trips were made to the San Juan River to carry water, burden rings may have made the job easier.

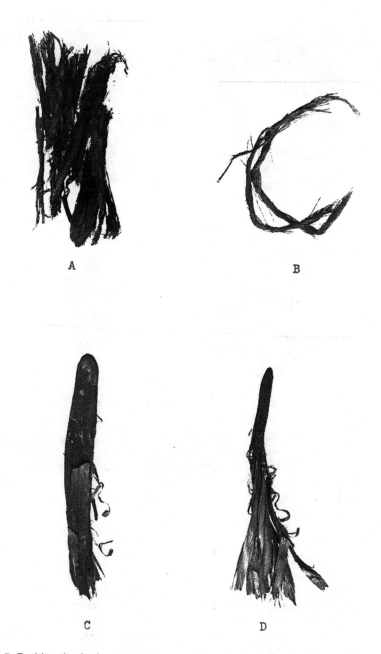

Figure 40.5. Prehistoric *Juniperus osteosperma/monosperma* bark artifacts, Salmon Ruin: (a) shredded, unmodified bark, (b) bark cordage, Room 36W, Record Key No. 33685, (c) bark needle top view, Room 36W, Record Key No. 76371, (d) bark needle side view.

A third circular juniper artifact was also found in trash in Room 62W, but the cultural affiliation of the stratum is unknown (see Figure 40.6). Thin shredded strips of bark have been gathered into a single coil 12 cm in diameter and 3 cm thick, with a 5 cm diameter hole spanning the center. Only the ends of a few strips of the bark are visible; the remaining ends have been concealed in the body of the ring, evidently by taking pieces of shredded bark not more than 1.5 cm thick and at least longer than the circumference of the ring, and wrapping them around the circle, sealing off loose ends in passage. Two narrow (0.4 cm) strips of juniper bark remain as evidence of how the ring was secured. They appear to have been wrapped at right angles to the length of the coil to hold it together. The fact that the ring is not penetrated with soil leaves open the possibility that this ring also functioned as a burden ring. Juniper bark

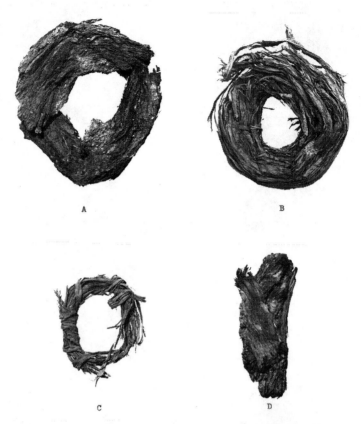

Figure 40.6. Prehistoric *Juniperus osteosperma/monosperma* bark artifacts, Salmon Ruin: (a) bark pot rest, Room 59W, Record Key No. 30577, (b) bark burden ring, Room 62W, Record Key No. 33904, (c) coiled bark, Room 62A, Perishable No. 199, (d) layered bark, Room 62W, Record Key No. 76648.

pot rests or burden rings have been recovered in other nearby archaeological sites in the Southwest. They were found in the large pueblos of the Mesa Verde area in southwestern Colorado (Rohn 1963:8) as well as in Mesa Verde affiliated strata in the Aztec Ruins complex north of Salmon (Richert 1964:23).

A coiled juniper bark artifact much smaller than the three just discussed was found in trash of mixed cultural affiliation in Room 62A. Shredded juniper bark has been coiled into a circle 6 cm in diameter and 1.25 cm thick, with a 4 cm diameter hole in the center. The coil is fastened by a single strand of juniper bark wrapping, which forms a loose spiral around the bark ring. Parallel portions of the spiral are spaced approximately every 2 cm apart. At one place, however, several closely spaced wraps can be seen, and a loose end of the tying strand sticks out from beneath these multiple wraps. Passing the tying strand under a number of closely spaced wraps could secure it against future unraveling. This artifact is not thought to represent a pot rest or burden ring because its thinness (1.25 cm) would essentially

give no support to a ceramic vessel. Perhaps it is a raw material bundle that was to be used in the manufacture of cordage.

Trash in Room 62W attributed to the Secondary occupation produced two segments of layered bark. In the first one, two fragments of multiple, compact layers of bark are irregularly aligned to one another and joined to form one item 11 x 3.5 x 2 cm (see Figure 40.6). One fragment has a smooth surface; it may have had its origin where bark joins wood (near cambium) on a juniper tree. The other bark fragment is oriented 22¡ from the perpendicular plane of the first piece, and is firmly attached to it. The item is frayed at the edges, burned in places, and has dirt ground throughout its structure.

Perhaps this piece of dirt-encrusted, charred juniper bark was once incorporated in a roof that eventually burned. Shredded juniper bark served as a layer in the construction of at least one well-preserved Chacoan roof at Salmon Pueblo (Figure 40.7). In that room (60A) the sequence of roof construction appears to have been as follows: at least

A

B

Figure 40.7. *Juniperus osteosperma/monosperma* bark as a layer in roof of Room 60A, Salmon Ruin: (a) side view of roof, with thick layer of adobe sealing all lower layers, (b) top view of *Juniperus osteosperma/monosperma* bark layer.

five wooden timbers (vigas) of up to 20 cm diameter were placed across the north-south axis of the room, and secured into wall sockets to form the main roof supports. Directly above these vigas, smaller trunks or tree limbs (latillas) of 5–8 cm diameter were spaced 5–8 cm apart in an east-west orientation. Above these latillas a continuous layer of small-diameter (< 2.5 cm), closely spaced willow twigs was arranged, this time in a north-south alignment. At

this point in construction, adobe appears to have been pushed between the larger wooden vigas from the bottom, making contact with the two upper sets of large and small latillas. Above the small willow latillas a thick layer of adobe was packed, upon which shredded juniper bark was layered. Above the juniper bark was another layer of adobe, forming the floor surface upon which activities of the second story could take place. Should such a roof have collapsed at Salmon, layered, compact, adobe-encrusted juniper bark, like the piece from the trash in Room 62W, would have been released.

Although Chacoan occupants used layered juniper bark in the roof of Room 60A, they apparently varied the materials of roof construction in other rooms; juniper wood slats appear to have been used, rather than shredded bark, in at least three rooms (101W, 98W, 67W). Juniper bark was used in the construction of Puebloan roofs elsewhere in the Southwest. Ancient pueblos in Chaco Canyon (Judd 1931: 9), the large towns of the Mesa Verde in southwestern Colorado (Rohn 1963:6), and the Aztec Ruins complex 15 km north of Salmon (Richert 1964:9) all incorporated juniper bark into roof construction.

The second fragment of layered bark is also from Secondary occupation trash in Room 62W. This piece of naturally compact juniper bark appears twisted into a semicircle and overlain by another segment of naturally compact bark; overall dimensions are 3 x 2.5 x 0.5 cm. A juniper twig lies sandwiched horizontally between the two pieces of bark. A survey of modern juniper trees has produced no natural examples of such an arrangement of bark and twig. Perhaps this item is the remains of a juniper bark basket constructed with juniper twigs as supports. The inhabitants of Acoma and Laguna used juniper twigs for basket frames, bending them to shape by allowing them to remain in the sun or by pushing them into hot ashes (Swank 1932:48–49). Flexible strips of juniper bark were woven between the juniper stick frames to form the body of the basket.

Among its other uses, juniper bark appears to have served as toilet paper for Salmon's Secondary occupants. Masses of juniper bark were recovered in association with abundant human coprolites in Room 62W, sandwiched among the coprolites in a manner that clearly suggested toilet paper. A search of the modern ethnographic literature has revealed that other soft, flexible materials such as sand sagebrush (*Artemisia filifolia*) and fringed sagebrush (*Artemisia frigida*) have been used by Navajos (Elmore 1944:81), but this is one sector of modern ethnobotany that has received little attention.

The "Intermediate" period between the Chacoan and Secondary occupations of Salmon Pueblo produced an unusual juniper bark item in the trash in Room 36W (see Table 40.2). A long (7.5 cm) and narrow (consistently 0.9 cm wide) strip of juniper bark shows two distinctly different ends. One end is formed of naturally compact layers of bark that taper to a symmetrical blunt point, with slight charring around the perimeter, and the opposite end displays layers of bark that have been separated, appearing as

a series of flat ribbons splayed open. At the frayed end, all the layers of bark terminate at the same place and show slight charring (see Figure 40.5). The condition of this item supports an interpretation that it served as a sewing tool. A compact, fire-hardened end on a strip of juniper bark could provide a convenient "needle" to weave the remaining strip through other layers of bark. When the strip was satisfactorily incorporated into an item, the needle could be detached quickly by singeing off the compact end. These used needles would then be discarded.

Five segments of twisted juniper bark were recovered together in a roof stratum from Room 127W. Although the roof was constructed in AD 1105–1106 during the Chacoan occupation, the Secondary occupants used the room extensively, and may have been responsible for bringing these items to the pueblo. One short (7 cm), fairly thick (2.5 cm) section of shredded bark appears closely twisted into a Z-twist. On both ends of the item the individual strands of bark terminate simultaneously, and show slight evidence of charring at the very tips. The four remaining fragments likewise have even, often slightly charred ends, suggesting that fire quickly seared through the bark. Of these, all are narrow (not greater than 1.25 cm), and two (5 and 10 cm long respectively) have been twisted into a Z-twist. The third fragment (23 cm long) shows little evidence of having been twisted, although it has been coiled into two overlapping loops. The bark layers of the fourth piece (10 cm long and consistently 1.25 cm wide) are naturally compact at one end and loosely frayed at the other.

The twisted segments of fire-seared juniper bark may have resulted from a number of different uses. For example, the twisted bark may have been used for ceiling construction; twisted bundles of juniper bark were thought to have been used in building at least one ancient ceiling at Pueblo Bonito (Judd 1964: Plate 61). Or, the twisted bark may have been used as a rope, to tie plant materials to the roof as storage or to dry in the warmth of the room. That this roof served as a food storage location is supported by the recovery of food items such as a cholla bud, a bean, and maize cobs and kernels. Whether used in roof construction or as a rope to tie something to the rafters, the bark may have become singed when the roof burned. A third explanation may be that the twisted seared bark served as a torch or slow match at Salmon, as has been observed among modern Tewa (Robbins et al. 1916:39) and Hopi (Whiting 1939:62) people. Juniper bark torches or matches appear also to have been used in prehistory, at Tonto

National Monument (Bohrer 1962:83) and at nearby Aztec Ruins (Morris 1919:62).

CONIFERS USED IN MEDICINE AND CEREMONY

It appears that conifers and the closely allied Mormon tea (*Ephedra*) served Salmon occupants in medicinal or ceremonial ways. In modern southwestern literature, it is often difficult to separate distinctly medicinal uses of a plant from those of a purely ceremonial nature. Often medicines may be given to a patient during a ceremony, and some rite may have a healing function. Medicine and ceremony blend quite harmoniously among southwestern groups today; they may well have done the same in prehistory.

Spruce Bark Scales

The spruce (*Picea*) evidence in Salmon Ruin is rare, but it derives from both major occupations. Blue spruce (*Picea pungens* type) and Engelmann spruce (*Picea engelmanni*) bark scales (Figure 40.8) have been identified in trash strata believed to belong to the Chacoan and Secondary occupations respectively, as well as in trash strata of unclear cultural affiliation. A single unburned Engelmann spruce bark scale, also of unclear cultural affiliation, has been recovered from the foot drum of the Great Kiva (Room 130W).

Because no construction beams from Salmon Pueblo have been identified as spruce, the presence of spruce bark scales may not relate to construction needs. The recovery of the Engelmann spruce bark scale in the foot drum of the Great Kiva strongly suggests ceremonial use; perhaps the planking of the foot drum was made of spruce wood. The remaining spruce bark scales at Salmon do not directly confirm this suggestion, because they were recovered in Secondary trash deposits. However, their proximity to ceremonial structures may indirectly reflect a ceremonial use. Assuming that trash was not transported far within the pueblo, the Chacoan blue spruce-type bark scales from trash in Room 101W, and the cf. *Picea* bark scale in trash in Room 84W, may have originated in a nearby row of unusually large, square rooms (46W, 56W, 86W, 92W, 96W, 100W). These large rooms have been suspected of serving more than one function for the Chacoan people. For example, Room 100W appears to have been used mainly as a habitation room, although late in its history rare bird types such as macaw and waterfowl were kept there. The adjacent Room 96W functioned first as a habitation, then as a kiva during the closing portion of the Chacoan occupation. In addition, Rooms 86W and 92W have features usually

Figure 40.8. Probable medicinal or ceremonial conifer evidence at Salmon Ruin: (a) *Juniperus osteosperma/monosperma* twig bundle, Room 129W, Record Key No. 56117, (b) *Picea pungens* type bark scale, Room 90W, (c) *Picea engelmanni* type bark scale, Room 130W (Great Kiva) foot drum, Record Key No. 73043.

associated with ceremonial rooms, such as a subfloor ventilator shaft in 86W and a floor vault in 92W. Perhaps spruce gathered for ceremonies in these large rooms became part of trash deposited in nearby areas. Likewise, the *Picea engelmanni* bark scales found in the trash in Room 36W, dating to the Secondary occupation, might have originated in the kiva in Room 33C, one room west.

If spruce bark scales at Salmon represent ancient ceremonial needs, some corroboration can be found in the modern ethnographic literature. Although no

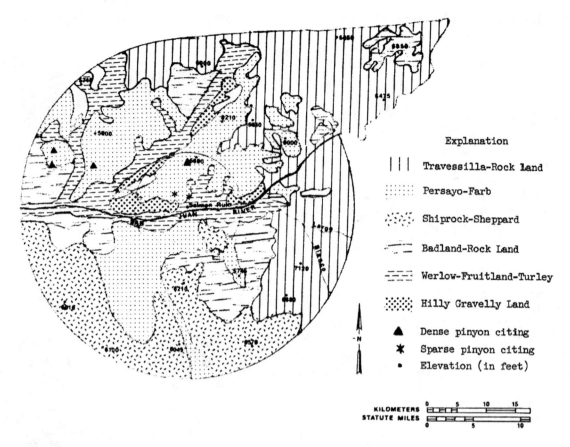

Figure 40.9. Predominant soil associations surrounding Salmon Ruin; small circle radius = 9.6 km; large circle radius = 29 km; elevations given in feet (adopted from Maker et al. 1973).

direct mention of the use of spruce bark or wood has been located, it is significant that spruce twigs and foliage have occasionally been documented among modern people as serving religious needs. At Santa Ana, hunters made an emetic out of spruce leaves and twigs when preparing to hunt big game (White 1942:287), and the Ramah Navajo used spruce (*Picea engelmanni* Parry) as a ceremonial emetic (Vestal 1952:12). The modern pueblos of Sandia, San Juan, San Ildefonso, Santa Clara, Jemez, Cochiti, Santo Domingo, and Zia (representing Tiwa, Tewa, Towa, and Keresan language groups, respectively) apparently all visited a shrine 3465 m (11,400 ft) high on the Jemez Plateau, where a particularly tall tree was encircled by eight small mounds of stone (Douglass 1917:358). Both the elevation and growth form (Douglass 1917; Figure 40.9) suggest that the tree was an Engelmann spruce.

Modern Tewa-speaking Puebloans have been known to carefully dispose of ceremonial paraphernalia away from the pueblo (Robbins et al. 1916:42–43). One cannot know whether such a practice was standard in prehistory among other Puebloan

groups as well, but if it was, the spruce bark scales in trash at Salmon Pueblo seem contradictory. Possibly a few bark scales escaped into the trash in spite of the best efforts to dispose of them properly.

Juniper

A neatly wrapped bundle of juniper twigs from the roof of a Secondary occupation room (Room 129) implies that the twigs were purposefully gathered and perhaps stored for later use (see Figure 40.8). The presence of juniper twigs or scale leaves in 87 of 210 (40%) broadly distributed flotation samples documents the widespread use of juniper boughs at Salmon. Historically, family medicine resources always included juniper twigs; many pueblos gave a tea of juniper sprigs to a mother just after childbirth, and often for a period of time afterward. The Zia (White 1974:200, 202), Cochiti (Lange 1959), Zuni (Stevenson 1915:55), Santa Ana (White 1942:165), Navajo (Bailey 1940:290), Tewa (Robbins et al. 1916:40), Hopi (Whiting 1939:62), and Isleta (Jones 1931:32–33) all followed this practice. Among the Acoma and Laguna the twigs were chewed or a tea was prepared and used as an emetic. Juniper twig tea served as a general cure-all—as a laxative, a cure for diarrhea, and a stomach tonic. When ground with salt, the leaves were put in the ear to get bugs out (Swank 1932:48–49). At Hano, the leafy twigs were toasted and then bound tightly over a bruise or sprain to reduce pain and swelling (Robbins et al. 1916:40). The Ramah Navajo used the twigs of Rocky Mountain juniper (*Juniperus scopulorum*) as a cold remedy, as a gastro-intestinal aid, and as protection from witches and enemies (Vestal 1952:12). Perhaps the bundle of ancient twigs from Salmon served one of these many purposes, or filled a domestic household need, as among the Acoma and Laguna, who rubbed green juniper twigs on their moccasins to color them green (Swank 1932:48–49).

Six juniper seeds were recovered close together in the roof-fall of the Tower Kiva (64W); each seed had two holes bored at opposite ends (Lentz 1979:82). Although juniper seeds are prey to insect infestation, and may have one hole drilled through their surface by insects seeking food, rarely would two natural holes be expected (Lentz 1979:51–52, 1984; Lentz, Chapter 41). Therefore, the six seeds with two holes may represent an ancient necklace. Although a juniper seed necklace could easily represent an item of personal adornment, as among modern Hopis (Whiting 1939:63) and Navajos (Elmore 1944:18), its location in the Tower Kiva may signify that it served in some medicinal or ceremonial rite.

Ponderosa Pine

Two groups of ponderosa pine needles from mixed cultural contexts were recovered at Salmon. The modern use of needles only hints at possible reasons for their presence in the ancient pueblo. The needles were procured for winter ceremonies in recent years at Hano by a runner who was dispatched to acquire some ponderosa branches to supply the needles for prayer feathers (Robbins et al. 1916:41, as *Pinus brachyptera*). The Hopi also tied the needles to prayer sticks to bring cold weather, and smoked the needles ceremonially (Whiting 1939:63). The Ramah Navajo took a decoction of the needles as a medicine for colds and fever (Vestal 1952:13–14).

Ponderosa pine bark is rare in the Salmon Ruin archaeological remains. The Secondary occupants may have used it to line a burial pit in Room 102B; however, this suggestion should be considered tentative, as only a single segment of ponderosa bark has been recovered from this burial pit. One cannot know whether additional bark has since degraded, or whether this was the only piece incorporated into the burial. Elsewhere in the Southwest, ponderosa pine bark has been excavated from storage pits at Grasshopper Ruin in Arizona (Bohrer 1975a), at Fresnal Shelter in south-central New Mexico (Bohrer 1973a:211), and in a Pueblo II structure in north-central New Mexico (Ford 1968a:251).

Mormon Tea

A number of *Ephedra* stem segments have been identified from ancient trash and a large pit in a room (62W) containing exceptionally well preserved plant material. Mixtures of ceramic sherds representing both Chacoan and Secondary cultural groups accompanied all the stems, so it is impossible to say which group (if not both) used this plant. *Ephedra* is a plant closely allied to the conifers.

Many southwestern groups have found uses for Mormon tea in recent times, often for medicinal purposes. Among the pueblos, the stems were sometimes boiled and given as a medicine to cure a variety of ailments. The Acoma and Laguna found it an effective cough medicine (Swank 1932:42), the Isleta used it as a skin lotion (Jones 1931:28), and the Zuni (Stevenson 1915:49) and Hopi (Whiting 1939:63) made it into a tea for treating syphilis. Seminomadic groups such as the Paiute and Shoshone of Nevada (Hocking 1956:160) also made extensive use of Mormon tea in treating various disorders. It is a reasonable assumption that the ancient Salmon inhabitants had similar knowledge of the plant. Mormon tea stems were also recovered from Aztec Ruins, north of Salmon (Morris 1919:63).

CONIFERS USED FOR ROOFING TIMBERS

Roof timbers excavated from Salmon Ruin during the years 1972–1977 have been identified by the Laboratory of Tree-Ring Research. Salmon inhabitants chose a wide variety of conifer trees (Douglas fir, ponderosa, juniper, piñon, spruce-fir, and spruce) for construction, along with some nonconifer types (cottonwood and scrub oak). Modern ethnographic literature sheds light on roof timber preferences, and how large beams were obtained historically. The record of construction timber choice at other southwestern sites verifies that Salmon groups were not alone in relying on conifers in prehistory.

Ponderosa Pine

The length, strength, and even trunk diameter of the stately ponderosa pine make it an excellent choice for pueblo roof supports. Ponderosa pine timbers were used extensively for roof beams by the Chacoan builders of Salmon Pueblo. The Secondary occupants, on the other hand, appear not to have cut new ponderosa beams during their stay.

Historic ethnographies provide insight into the methods used to acquire large building beams. At Cochiti, people cut ponderosa trees in the autumn and piled them in a secluded spot to dry for a year, as dry logs were lighter and easier to handle (Lange 1959:146), especially when transported for any distance. In the mountains east of the pueblo of Isleta, large decaying ponderosa stumps were formerly cut with instruments having blades approximately 4 cm wide. Shallow incisions on the stumps suggested that much labor was required to cut down a tree, prior to being transported 19–24 km to the pueblo (Jones 1931:37). Difficulties related to acquiring large beams were likely shared by ancient and modern peoples. The Chacoan inhabitants of Salmon may have relied upon the San Juan River for transportation of their large beams from mountain areas, or perhaps they undertook the difficult task of carrying them overland. Elsewhere in prehistory, ponderosa beams were used to construct ancient pueblos in Chaco Canyon (Bannister 1964) and Mesa Verde (Hayes 1964). "Large pine beams" comprised the majority of roof supports in the West Ruin at Aztec National Monument (Richert 1964:13). Recent chemical analysis of ancient roof timbers and modern source areas suggests that the Chuska and San Mateo Mountains northwest and southeast of Chaco Canyon, respectively, provided the canyon with conifer building timbers (English et al. 2001).

Juniper

Both Utah juniper and Rocky Mountain juniper have trunks that can be used for construction, as roof supports. Rocky Mountain juniper is especially suitable for this purpose, as it grows faster than most southwestern junipers (Little 1950: 23) and produces logs large enough to be valuable to the lumber industry (Lamb 1971:16). Chacoans made some use of juniper beams (though the species is not known) during the major building effort at Salmon Pueblo, and the Secondary occupants relied almost exclusively on juniper for roof repair. At Aztec National Monument, 19 km to the north and built shortly after Salmon Pueblo, juniper wood was also the predominant Secondary timber choice in the East Ruin (Richert 1964:13). In other areas of the Southwest, juniper timbers were used in the construction of roofs at Tonto National Monument in Arizona (Bohrer 1962:81) as well as in many of the large pueblos at Mesa Verde, Colorado (Rohn 1963:7).

Spruce-Fir

Of the three kinds of true fir found in northwestern New Mexico and southwestern Colorado today,

only spruce-fir (*Abies concolor*) has been identified at Salmon Ruin. Three roof beams tentatively identified as *Abies concolor* were incorporated into two roofs (60W, 62W) southwest of the Tower Kiva (64W) by the Chacoans. Additional roof beams of spruce-fir appear to have been cut sometime during the late AD 1000 period of intense Chacoan building activity, but no secure cutting dates are available for these specimens.

Douglas Fir

Both Chacoan and Secondary occupants at Salmon used Douglas fir in roof construction, though the Secondary record of use consists of only one securely dated roof beam. Elsewhere in the Southwest, Mesa Verdeans in southern Colorado sought Douglas fir for pueblo building (Rohn 1963:7).

Piñon

Modern ethnographic literature does not mention that piñon served building needs in recent times. Because of the rather short trunk and uneven growth of this tree, piñons do not generally make suitable beams for construction. Only piñon beams were used in the construction of Salmon Pueblo. Elsewhere in the ancient Southwest, however, piñon was apparently used more extensively in housing. At Tonto National Monument in south-central Arizona, piñon timbers were secured as roof beams, even though such a practice required a considerable amount of effort (Bohrer 1962:81). Residents of the Mesa Verde area of southern Colorado also made use of piñon timbers in roof construction (Rohn 1963: 7). Both citations are interesting from the standpoint that people will obviously cut down trees that represent potential future food resources.

CONIFER AVAILABILITY

To assess whether conifers were readily accessible to Salmon occupants of either the Chacoan or Secondary occupations, two assumptions were made. First, if a conifer exhibits a wide variety of parts and a generally broad distribution in strata at Salmon Ruin, then the resource was easily obtainable in prehistory, probably growing relatively near the pueblo. Alternatively, conifers exhibiting few parts and restricted distribution in Salmon could have been either locally available but rarely chosen to satisfy daily needs, or not locally available and only rarely acquired.

Second, the dominant plant species present in modern plant communities does not differ significantly from those of the ancient plant communities. For example, spruces today rarely grow in the same plant community with Utah juniper. The intermingling of these species would likewise not be expected to have been common during the period of Salmon occupation. This assumption does not extend to the species composition and density of smaller shrubs and herb components of plant communities, which may be significantly altered now due to historic animal grazing. Based on this reasoning, conifers recovered from Salmon range from those locally obtainable in the twelfth through thirteenth centuries, to those growing perhaps as distant as 80 km, as discussed below.

Juniper

Both the variety of parts and their widespread distribution at Salmon Ruin suggest that juniper was readily available. For example, both the Chacoan and Secondary groups used juniper beams in roof construction. Juniper wood was also burned in seven of eight ancient hearths examined in a pilot study (see Table 40.4). Shredded juniper bark occurred in 24 of 48 excavated rooms, and juniper bark cordage, pot rests or burden rings, toilet paper (see Table 40.2), roofing material (see Figure 40.7), and other bark items likely represent a variety of domestic uses. Juniper twigs and scale leaves have been identified in 87 of 210 widely distributed flotation samples, suggesting that branches were frequently carried into the pueblo. Supporting this possibility was the recovery of a juniper twig bundle (see Figure 40.8) and a juniper seed necklace, each thought to have been used in some medicinal or ceremonial way. Finally, numerous lines of evidence reveal that juniper berries were frequently eaten in prehistory at Salmon (Lentz 1979, 1984; Lentz, Chapter 41).

Utah juniper was most likely the locally available juniper nine centuries ago, based on the identification of all the juniper seeds and berries as *Juniperus osteosperma* (Lentz 1979:34, 1984; Chapter 41). Today Utah juniper grows vigorously and abundantly within a 10 km radius of Salmon Ruin (Lentz 1979:18, 1984; Chapter 41) and is often the dominant tree on the gently rolling hills and plateau areas of the region; no other juniper has been recognized within this local area. A stand of one-seeded juniper (*Juniperus monosperma*) has been observed approximately 45 km south of Salmon Ruin (Lentz 1979, 1984; Chapter 41). Rocky Mountain juniper seems to grow even farther from the ruin, and is often restricted to distant mountainous locations.

Piñon

The record of piñon use at Salmon Pueblo consists mainly of widespread nutshells (see Table 40.3).

Such evidence cannot automatically be considered indicative of locally growing piñon trees, because nuts lend themselves to efficient transport over great distances (Lightfoot 1979:331). Therefore, additional evidence must be evaluated to determine how far away these trees may have grown in prehistory. At Salmon, the presence of one positively identified piñon twig, a few piñon cone scales, several piñon construction beams, and pine wood in one of eight fire hearths together are not considered sufficient to imply locally available piñon trees. On the contrary, the absence of piñon bark and whole cones and the lack of piñon twigs and hearth fuel indicate that piñon trees probably grew some distance from Salmon Pueblo in prehistory. The archaeological evidence suggests that piñon was rare in the local area in the past, and modern vegetation patterns seem to provide confirmation. Today piñon trees are located very sparsely within 8 km of Salmon Ruin (Table 40.5), becoming abundant at this distance only northeast of the pueblo. The elevation and soils of the Salmon area (see Figure 40.9) are well within the range of other piñon stands in Colorado (Kelly 1970: 126). For whatever reason(s), piñon is scarce today in the local Salmon Ruin area, and was probably scarce in the past as well.

Ponderosa Pine

The evidence of ponderosa use at Salmon Pueblo consists mainly of construction timbers. The Chacoans used numerous ponderosa beams for pueblo building. Rare parts recovered include bark and needles. No positively identified ponderosa pine wood was identified in Salmon fire hearths. Today ponderosa pines have been located 34 km southwest of Salmon Ruin, growing on alternating shale and sandstone beds. They do not grow locally with Utah juniper. In fact, one must travel more than 80 km north and east to the mountains of southern Colorado to find ponderosa forests. This species has been observed to grow occasionally as low as 1915 m, but it attains full vigor and abundance between 2128 and 2736 m in mountainous areas. Ponderosa pine can grow in a variety of soil types (Table 40.6), so its current restriction to areas above 2128 m suggests that a cool, moist habitat is of prime importance. Potentially, ponderosa trees could grow in cool north-facing canyon environments nearer to Salmon than is presently observed.

Douglas Fir

The only Douglas fir parts positively identified from Salmon Ruin strata are roof beams, the majority of which derive from the Chacoan occupation; no

Table 40.5. Location and setting of piñon (*Pinus edulis*) in central and northwestern New Mexico.

Landform	Substrate	Elevation (m)	Location
Steep colluvial slope, N-NE facing	Basalt	2109	Rio Puerco, NM
Steep colluvial slope, NW facing	Shale	2103	South of Bloomfield, NM
Shallow colluvial slope	Sandstone	1884	Navajo Dam, NM
Shallow colluvial slope, N facing	Limestone	2103	Clines Corners, NM
Shallow and steep colluvial slopes	Sandstone and shale	1763	Aztec, NM
Steep colluvial slope, N facing	Shale	1824	Rio Puerco, NM
Mesa edges	Sandstone	1824	Rio Puerco, NM

Table 40.6. Location and setting of ponderosa pine (*Pinus ponderosa*) in central and northwestern New Mexico, and southwestern Colorado.

Landform	Substrate	Elevation (m)	Location
Shallow colluvial slope	Basalt and colluvium	2401	Rio Puerco, NM
Shallow colluvial slope, N facing	Shale	2188	South of Bloomfield, NM
Steep colluvial slope, E facing	Igneous granite	2687	Sangre de Cristo Mountains, NM
Steep colluvial slope, S facing	Gravels and shales	2419	La Plata Mountains, CO
Shallow colluvial slope	Sandstone and shale	1915	34 km southwest of Salmon Ruin, M

other Douglas fir parts have been recognized. Today Douglas fir grows 80 km from Salmon Ruin in the 2128–3192 m mountain ranges of southern Colorado. Douglas fir trees grow on sandstone bedrock, igneous granite, and a gravelly valley bottom, attesting to its ability to occupy a diversity of parent materials. The presence of Douglas fir in mountain regions today may be more dependent on the cool, moist conditions prevalent there than on the specific character of the soil. Presumably, protected locations near the pueblo may have also fostered Douglas fir stands in prehistory.

Spruce-Fir

Evidence of spruce-fir use at Salmon derives solely from Chacoan use of roof timbers; the Secondary group appears not to have utilized this species at all. Spruce-fir can be found 80 km from Salmon today in lower mountain reaches starting around 2128 m, often growing with ponderosa pine and Douglas fir. Although spruce-fir has been observed in a variety of habitats (USDA 1974:170), its restriction to elevations above 2128 m indicates that a cool, moist regime is necessary for it to do well.

No recognizable parts of corkbark fir (*Abies lasiocarpa* var. *arizonica*), alpine fir (*Abies lasiocarpa*), or limber pine (*Pinus flexilis*) have been recovered to date as evidence that the Salmon occupants of either Chacoan or Secondary affiliation used these species in the past. Today these high mountain firs and limber pine are often found growing above 2432 m at a distance of more than 80 km.

Spruce

Both the Chacoan and Secondary Salmon inhabitants acquired bark scales of spruce, though the evidence is quite limited in amount and distribution. Today a trip of more than 80 km to high mountain regions above 2432 m would be required to find spruce. Blue spruce prefers to grow in moist sites, such as along mountain streams and around boggy areas (Harrington 1964:28; Kelly 1970:125; Lamb 1971:10), and Engelmann spruce prefers very high elevations, above 2500 m. Salmon Ruin, at an elevation of 1640 m, is currently unsuitable as a spruce habitat.

Mormon Tea

Mormon tea is included in this report because of its close affinity to conifers. Two-leafed stem segments of *Ephedra* have been recovered from limited Salmon strata (see Table 40.2), suggesting occasional ancient use. One two-leafed species (*Ephedra cutleri*) has been seen in modern times growing 16 km south of Salmon Ruin.

DISCUSSION

This study suggests that juniper trees probably grew near Salmon Pueblo in the twelfth and thirteenth centuries, and that Utah juniper was locally available nine centuries ago, just as it is today. Other conifers, recovered in limited locations and represented by fewer parts, are considered to have grown some distance from the pueblo via analogy to modern vegetation distributions. Except for easily transportable nutshells, piñon parts occurred in relatively restricted distribution in Salmon strata. Today piñon does not grow within 8 km of the site, and it seems that it was also some distance from Salmon Pueblo in prehistory. Construction beams represented the only part of ponderosa pine occurring with frequency in Salmon strata, so ponderosa pines probably did not grow nearby the pueblo in prehistory. The limited recovery of Douglas fir (*Pseudotsuga*), spruce-fir, and spruce parts indicates that they also grew some distance from the pueblo.

The history of construction and occupation of Salmon Pueblo seems remarkably coincident with paleoenvironmental conditions of the eleventh through late thirteenth centuries. A recent composite reconstruction of paleoenvironmental indicators for the central Mesa Verde region northwest of Salmon Pueblo suggests the following (Van West and Dean 2000). First, the AD 1000–1130 period was excellent for farmers because of aggrading floodplains, rising regional alluvial water tables, favorable local and regional climatic conditions, a fairly wide dryland farming belt, and high crop production. This period was especially favorable because precipitation was also trending upward and moisture was fairly predictable for agriculturalists. Assuming these favorable conditions also applied to the San Juan River valley approximately 70 km to the southeast, it may be no coincidence that Salmon Pueblo was successfully established by Chacoans during this favorable interval. The paleoenvironmental indicators then point to an extended period of unfavorable conditions between AD 1130 and 1180, when alluvial water tables were depressed, floodplains were degraded by stream channel entrenchment, a persistent drought ensued, precipitation trended downward slightly, and agricultural productivity was markedly reduced (Van West and Dean 2000). It is perhaps not surprising that the population of Salmon Pueblo experienced a lull, tree-cutting stopped, and possibly only a portion of the pueblo was occupied. Subsequently, a second favorable period with characteristics similar to the first one spanned the years AD 1180–1250, when the Secondary occupants appear to have occupied and remodeled Salmon Pueblo. Finally, a second major period of unfavorable conditions from AD 1270 to 1300 included greatly reduced agricultural productivity, disruption of a long-standing pattern of seasonal precipitation, and reduction in spatial variability of environments across the northern Southwest.

Within this three-century-long reconstruction, two hinge points occurred. These were times when two or more paleoenvironmental indicators changed to the detriment of agriculturalists—in AD 1130 and in AD 1275. Both represent times of change for which existing subsistence and social systems were unprepared (Van West and Dean 2000). For the hinge point of AD 1275, the ancient plant record indicates that the Secondary inhabitants relied to a greater extent on wild plants in relation to cultivated foods (Lentz 1979:92, 1984; Lentz, Chapter 41), and included a greater diversity of wild plant foods in their diet (Doebley 1976, 1981; Chapter 37) than the Chacoans did.

Abandonment and the Conifer Evidence

If one accepts the argument advanced here that the distribution of conifers in relation to Salmon Pueblo in prehistory was similar to the regional distribution observed today, it is reasonable to suggest similarities between the climatic regime then and now. This conclusion, however, obscures the importance of short-term temperature or precipitation fluctuations that could potentially cause economic hardship to an ancient population. For example, in a 2–3 year period of abnormally low precipitation, long-lived junipers might remain basically unchanged in density in an area, even though branches might die back and some seedlings fail. On the other hand, short-lived herbs and grasses might be considerably reduced in density in response to the same dry, hot, or cold conditions. Although a prolonged period of drought might be needed before impact on the local juniper woodland was felt, only a short segment of below-average moisture might be required to radically suppress reproduction in both wild annual plants and cultivated crops. And it was the cultivated (Terrel 1979) and wild herbaceous plants (Doebley 1976, 1981; Chapter 37) that provided a significant portion of foods in prehistory. Some set of events necessitated that some Salmon occupants resorted to eating juniper bark and immature piñon nuts. How often this occurred cannot be easily determined.

Conifer Use by Chacoan and Secondary Inhabitants

The ancient record of conifer use has permitted a glimpse of the similarities and differences between the Chacoan and Secondary groups that lived at Salmon (Table 40.7). Both groups used juniper beams for construction and relied upon piñon nuts and Utah juniper berries for food. Shredded juniper bark fulfilled many household needs, and both groups brought juniper firewood to the pueblo. The two groups may also have obtained some of the same items for religious purposes, as indicated by the recovery of spruce bark scales in contexts attributable to each occupation. Although Douglas fir wood was used by both groups, the very limited nature of the Secondary sample of Douglas fir roof beams does not clearly imply a shared preference with the Chacoans for this timber type.

Differences in the use of conifers between Chacoan and Secondary occupants relate primarily to choice of construction timbers; only the Chacoan builders used spruce-fir timbers (but identification is tentative). Perhaps more significant was the use of ponderosa pine beams solely by the Chacoans. Not one of the 58 roofing timbers associated with the Secondary occupation was of ponderosa; rather, juniper was the main choice. Such a preference for juniper beams by the Secondary inhabitants might reflect their social organization. Perhaps only the Chacoans had the necessary social organization to engage in mountain expeditions for nonjuniper roof beams (Irwin-Williams 1977:74–75). Although the Secondary builders used at least one Douglas fir beam in construction, they possibly acquired it locally or retrieved it from the San Juan River. Because the species of juniper wood gathered by the Secondary group is unknown, it remains possible that they sought the mountain-growing *Juniperus scopulorum* that grows some distance from the pueblo.

Conifer Use and Ancient Trade

The fact that Salmon Pueblo was constructed under heavy influence of Chaco Canyon to the south raises the issue of transport and exchange of goods between the two areas. Perhaps one of the reasons Salmon was established was to provide certain items to Chaco Canyon communities. Alternatively, lithic and ceramic items manufactured from nonlocal resources have been identified in Salmon deposits, so the pueblo may have been the recipient of goods in a trade network. These issues are explored here in relation to conifer resources.

Exporting Piñon Nuts to Chaco Canyon

Numerous piñon nutshells and a few cone scales at Salmon together suggest routine use of piñon nuts in prehistory. Further, the recovery of burned piñon cone scales suggests that the Salmon occupants themselves occasionally went to piñon stands to harvest and process immature cones. Perhaps Salmon residents at times supplied Chaco Canyon with piñon nut harvests. Piñon nutshells have been recovered in Chaco Canyon sites (Judd 1954:61; Struever 1977:79–80), and Lightfoot (1979:331) has calculated that the highly nutritious nuts could be efficiently transported up to 90 km on foot. The 64 km distance between Salmon and Chaco falls well within this range.

Ecological as well as archaeological data have been considered to evaluate the likelihood that Chaco Canyon pueblos received piñon nuts from the Salmon area. First, scattered piñon trees grow in Chaco Canyon today (Struever 1977). Both the average 1900 m elevation and the alternating sandstone and shale sediment type of the canyon seem able to support extensive piñon stands elsewhere in the state (see Table 40.6). Second, the presence of piñon pine charcoal fragments in four trash deposits at Chetro Ketl (Bannister 1964:152) suggests that piñon was once common enough in Chaco Canyon to be regularly burned in ancient hearths. The pack-rat midden evidence (Betancourt and Van Devender 1981) and a model of the long-term effects of fuelwood harvests on piñon-juniper woodlands (Samuels and Betancourt 1982) together suggest that a piñon-juniper woodland in Chaco Canyon was overused and reduced to desertscrub by the Chacoans. If this occurred, at times the need for receiving piñon nuts from distant communities such as Salmon may have been large, despite the fact that Salmon Pueblo residents likely had to walk some distance (8 km) to harvest piñon nuts in quantity.

Exporting Ponderosa Pines to Chaco Canyon

Numerous ponderosa pine beams were harvested between AD 861 and 1124 for the construction of Chaco Canyon pueblos (Bannister 1964). Archaeologists have puzzled over whether such tall pines grew abundantly in the Chaco area in prehistory (Vivian and Mathews 1964:7) or whether beams were transported overland from some outlying areas. Any beams used prior to AD 1088, the start of Salmon's major construction period, would not have been provided by Salmon occupants. After Salmon was built, such Chaco Canyon sites as Kin Bineola (with

Table 40.7. Summary of conifer uses through time at Salmon Pueblo.

Conifer	Chacoan	Intermediate	Secondary	Mixed Affiliation
Abies concolor				
Wood	Construction	—	—	—
Juniperus osteosperma				
Berries	Food	—	Food	—
Juniperus osteosperma / monosperma				
Shredded bark	Household needs	—	Household needs	—
Twigs	—	—	Medicine, ceremony	—
Juniperus scopulorum				
Bark/wood	—	—	—	Unknown
Juniperus				
Wood	Construction, firewood	—	Construction, firewood	—
Picea engelmannii				
Bark scales	—	—	Medicine, ceremony	Medicine, ceremony
Picea pungens				
Bark scales	Medicine, ceremony	—	—	Medicine, ceremony
Pinus edulis				
Female cone scales	Food residue	—	Food residue	—
Twigs	—	—	Food residue	—
Nutshells	Food residue	Food residue	Food residue	Food residue
Wood	Construction	—	—	—
Pinus ponderosa				
Bark	—	—	Medicine, ceremony	Household needs
Needles	—	—	—	Medicine, ceremony
Wood	Construction	—	—	—
Pinus				
Wood	Firewood	—	—	—
Pseudotsuga				
Wood	Construction	—	Construction	—
Ephedra (nonconifer)				
Stems	—	—	—	Medicine, ceremony

ponderosa beams dating AD 1111–1124), Kin Ya'a (AD 1084–1106), Kin Kletso (AD 1049–1124), and Pueblo del Arroyo (AD 1052–1103) could all have been recipients of beams transported from the Salmon area. A wide "North Road" connecting Chaco Canyon with the San Juan valley, possibly in use AD 1050–1150 (Morenon 1975), may have served as the overland transportation route.

However, the case for transport of large ponderosa beams from Salmon Pueblo to Chaco Canyon is weak. The Salmon area is unsuitable to ponderosa pine growth today, and the nearest abundant ponderosa stands are nearly 80 km away. The limited presence of ponderosa pine needles and bark in Salmon deposits indicates that these trees did not grow near the pueblo in prehistory. If Salmon was providing ponderosa pine beams for Chaco Canyon pueblos, trips to and from mountain regions would have first been required to harvest timbers, followed by overland trips of about 65 km to Chaco Canyon.

The Chaco Canyon region may have offered suitable ecological conditions for at least some ponderosa pine growth in prehistory. That neither the elevation nor the soils are prohibitive to ponderosa tree growth there is confirmed by historic records of remnant stands (Judd 1954:2; Vivian 1972:16–17).

Also, the decayed remains (including great snaglike roots) of a large pine in a courtyard of Pueblo Bonito indicate that a pine grew on the valley floor in AD 1017 (Judd 1954:2). Also, Judd (1954:2) thought that some of the ponderosa timbers in Pueblo Bonito were not carried vary far, commenting that "fragments (of logs) unearthed during the course of our excavations were invariably straight-grained, clean and smooth. They had been felled and peeled when green; they showed no scars of transportation."

Judd likewise noted no transportation scarring or chafing on ceiling beams in nearby Pueblo del Arroyo (1959:128). If these timbers had been transported a long distance overland from Salmon, some evidence of the trip would be expected to show up as gouges and nicks in the wood of the beams. It also seems that if green logs were used, as Judd suggested, the hardship of carrying them overland would be substantially increased due to their heavy water content. Recent chemical studies of ancient spruce and fir beams from Chaco Canyon pueblos suggest that they may have come from mountains to the south (San Mateo Mountains) and west (Chuska Mountains), but not from the east (San Pedro Mountains; English et al. 2001).

Although the possibility exists that Salmon was a recipient of conifers in an ancient trade network, it is unlikely. Like modern Isleta builders who traveled 24 km for their roof beams (Jones 1931:37), Salmon inhabitants probably obtained their own construction timbers, via a large and organized Chacoan work force. Individual or small groups of traders would be less likely to obtain and deliver quantities of construction beams within a short time or over a long distance. Likewise, although piñon nuts have been traded among modern pueblo peoples (Robbins et al. 1916:41; Underhill 1954:55–56), this study suggests that the Salmon occupants traveled to stands to fulfill their own needs, at least occasionally.

Ancient and Modern Puebloan Use of Conifers

Sometimes what is known of modern Puebloan traditions from oral histories can be extended back into prehistory with the aid of archaeological evidence. Resources gathered in recent times were also used nine centuries ago. For example, modern Puebloans use juniper wood as roof beams and firewood, the bark for numerous domestic needs, the twigs for tea, and the berries for food—all practices documented at Salmon Pueblo. Also, historic records document that Puebloan people eat piñon nuts, drink Mormon tea, and build with ponderosa pine beams. The ancient Puebloan inhabitants of Salmon did likewise. In these instances, traditional uses for

conifers span several centuries. On the other hand, some evidence for conifer use at Salmon contrasts with modern uses. Douglas fir and spruce-fir roof timbers both fall into this contrasting category, as discussed below. Also, although spruce seems to have been regarded as ceremonially important among both modern and ancient peoples, the parts used do not coincide.

Although Douglas fir beams were carried to Salmon Pueblo as construction material, modern ethnographic literature offers another perspective on its use. Modern groups rarely use Douglas fir for domestic purposes; rather it generally serves a sacred purpose. Because of this apparent dichotomy, the ethnographic literature is briefly summarized here.

In mythology, the Zia (White 1974:116) and Cochiti (Lange 1959:146) believed it was a Douglas fir tree that spanned the gap between the lower and upper worlds, permitting the Koshairi and all the people to ascend to earth. In ceremonial life, Cochiti and many neighboring pueblos listed Douglas fir as the most important plant. Twigs were carried by dancers, were used as collars for Katsina masks, and often adorned dancers' hands and feet (Lange 1959: 467–511; Robbins et al. 1916:42–43; Swank 1932:64; Whiting 1939:63). Occasionally the entire tree would be carried to a pueblo ceremony, as at Isleta (Jones 1931:41). Prior to a basket dance, the Santa Clara of New Mexico brought whole young trees to the pueblo and set them up in a plaza to appear as if they had grown there (Robbins et al. 1916:42–43).

A measure of the need for Douglas fir branches or trees can perhaps be expressed in the distance people would travel to find them, or by the trouble taken to secure them. A distance of 19 km had to be covered by Isletans in search of this tree (Jones 1931:41). At Hano, where Douglas fir was needed for almost all of the winter dances, a fast runner had to be sent some miles to the hills to get the necessary parts (Robbins et al. 1916:42–43). The Hopi of Second and Third Mesas apparently traveled 56 km for Douglas fir branches (Whiting 1939:63).

It is unclear why Douglas fir, specifically, is such an important ceremonial conifer tree among modern pueblos. Other evergreens, such as juniper and piñon, can often be more easily obtained than Douglas fir, so it is not just an "evergreen" that is needed for certain occasions, but a very specific one. Sometimes the more available piñon (Mathews 1887: 464) or juniper (Whiting 1939:63) will be substituted in a sacred rite, but Douglas fir still retains its position as the sacred tree. The role of Douglas fir in mythology attests to a longstanding recognition of this tree as more important than most among Puebloan groups, but the reasons for this esteem are unknown.

Although the disparity between modern and ancient use of Douglas fir may be real, two other reasons could potentially account for this observed difference. First, the ethnographic record may overlook the use of Douglas fir in construction, even though other construction beam choices have received comment by a number of authors (Jones 1931: 37; Lange 1959:146; Swank 1932:61; Whiting 1939:63). Second, it is possible that prescribed methods of disposal of ceremonial paraphernalia may make the ancient record appear empty. In modern Tewa-speaking pueblos, when ceremonies were over, Douglas fir branches were often disposed of with reverence, rather than being carelessly tossed away. Branches worn or carried by dancers at Santa Clara were always thrown into the river when the dance had concluded, and at Hano they were thrown from the edge of the mesa or dropped in some appropriate place among the rocks (Robbins et al. 1916:42–43). Such practices, if carried out in prehistory, would prevent many Douglas fir branches from ever becoming part of the archaeological record. The Douglas fir wood fly ash recovered from two floors (one Chacoan and one Secondary) at Salmon Ruin may owe its origin to deliberate burning of the branches, or to ritual disposal of Douglas fir branches in the fire, and then to subsequent use of the ash in various purification or sacred rites.

If the identification of ancient spruce-fir timbers is correct, the Chacoan inhabitants of Salmon used spruce-fir as roof beams in two rooms (60A, 62W) during Salmon's construction. Modern southwestern groups, though, have been known to use fir mainly for medicinal needs (Train et al. 1941:30 in Moerman 1977:1). Some groups also gather it for decorations, as a hot tea (Swank 1932:24), and for making pipe stems and treating cuts (Robbins et al. 1916:38). No mention can be found of its use in building construction, at least in recent times.

The presence of an Engelmann spruce bark scale in a foot drum of the Great Kiva (Room 130W), and the location of additional spruce bark scales in trash strata not far from ceremonial or suspected ceremonial rooms, is interpreted to reflect a ceremonial use of either the planking or bark in prehistory. Although spruce has also served in some ceremonial way among modern southwestern groups, the parts of the tree used seem to have been different. In recent times spruce twigs and foliage have been used by both the Santa Ana (White 1942:287) and the Rama Navajo (Vestal 1952:12) in various ceremonial rites. Modern Keresan, Tiwa, Tewa, and Towa-speaking Puebloan groups venerated an Engelmann

spruce tree at a shrine on the Jemez Plateau (Douglass 1917:358; photo identification by K. Adams).

CONCLUSIONS

Many of the conifers growing in northwestern New Mexico and southwestern Colorado today were also present 900 years ago, providing resources for the ancient inhabitants of Salmon Pueblo. Juniper, piñon, ponderosa, Douglas fir, spruce, and probably spruce-fir were all brought to the pueblo for a range of uses.

Conifers were a substantial food source for Salmon's occupants, as clearly seen in the piñon nut and juniper seed evidence. Hundreds of whole piñon nutshells from more than half the excavated rooms indicate that both Chacoan and Secondary occupants ate piñon nuts. Modern experiments suggest that people cracked the nuts with their teeth and also cracked them on a hard surface. The recovery of four burned piñon female cone scales and one bent and collapsed (immature) nutshell fragment implies that some nuts were collected while immature. This suggests food shortage, when people did not wait for a nut crop to mature. Piñon nuts were parched, likely for long-term storage.

Utah juniper berries furnished a food resource throughout Salmon's history. Evidence for this includes carbonized berries in hearths, carbonized seeds in association with food cultigens and grinding stones, widespread distribution of seeds in trash strata, a strong co-occurrence of juniper seeds and berries with other known food items, and the likelihood that juniper berries were stored with other foods. The recovery of juniper bark in coprolites from the Secondary occupation strongly suggests food stress at Salmon Pueblo, when bark must have been one of the few items available to fill empty stomachs.

Piñon and juniper food remains shed light on fall and winter seasons of pueblo occupation. Early fall occupancy is implied by the presence of four burned piñon cone scales, one with its immature nutshell still adhering. A bent and collapsed piñon nutshell fragment reflects harvest of an immature piñon crop. Two types of evidence suggest that people may have remained in the pueblo into the winter months. First, parched piñon nutshells from both Chacoan and Secondary strata indicate that the nuts may have been stored for some time after the fall harvest, some eventually succumbing to rodent raiding. Second, the recovery of a parched piñon nutshell and juniper berries in probable storage areas is suggestive of storage following the fall harvest.

A preliminary examination of charcoal from

eight hearths indicates that juniper wood constituted a common fuel choice through time. Seven of the eight hearths reveal that the last fires built by both Chacoan and Secondary groups were of juniper. Assuming that people would choose fuels from available resources in the local area, juniper was a consistent choice. Pine wood and nonconifer wood were burned occasionally, and ponderosa pine bark may also have served as a hearth fuel or tinder. Fly ash from Douglas fir wood may represent roof burning, deliberate addition of branches to a fire, or ritual burning of wood following ceremonies.

Shredded juniper bark served a wide range of domestic needs for the Salmon inhabitants. The Chacoans used the bark as cordage and in roof construction. The Secondary occupants used it for cordage, pot rests or burden rings, and toilet paper. Unmodified juniper bark recovered in half the excavated rooms at Salmon, representing both Chacoan and Secondary groups, likely reflects juniper bark's utility.

For medicinal or ceremonial purposes, Engelmann spruce bark or planking was installed in the foot drum of the Great Kiva (130W), and Engelmann spruce or blue spruce type bark was also used in other sacred locations. Mormon tea stems and a juniper twig bundle perhaps served as teas. A Utah juniper seed necklace was likely worn during some rite. Ponderosa pine trees provided needles for prayer or medicine, as well as bark for the lining of a burial pit. Both Chacoan and Secondary groups brought in spruce bark, although juniper twigs and ponderosa bark are preserved only from the Secondary occupation. The ponderosa needles and Mormon tea stems are of mixed cultural affiliation.

The identification of hundreds of roof timbers from numerous Salmon Ruin rooms revealed that conifers were chosen consistently when construction beams were required. The Chacoans relied heavily on ponderosa pine and juniper; to a lesser extent they used Douglas fir, possibly spruce-fir, and a single piñon beam. The Secondary occupants used juniper, although they also acquired at least one Douglas fir beam.

Cutting dates obtained from more than 300 conifer samples provide data on the construction history of Salmon Pueblo. Trees were cut and brought to the pueblo during several different episodes from AD 1068 to 1263. Ponderosa pine and juniper beams were stockpiled during the major phase of Chacoan construction in the late AD 1080s. There is no correlation between species use and room size, room type, or room location. During the Intermediate period of Salmon's history, no new trees were cut and carried

to the pueblo, but the Secondary occupants reused beams from the Chacoan period and cut a large number of juniper trees to reroof the Great Kiva in the spring of AD 1263.

The archaeobotanical record provides information on the relative availability of conifers to Salmon Pueblo in prehistory. The variety of juniper parts (wood, bark, twigs, berries) recovered, coupled with their widespread distribution in strata of both Chacoan and Secondary affiliation, suggests that local conditions in prehistory promoted juniper growth near the pueblo. Furthermore, Utah juniper was probably the nearby species nine centuries ago, just as it is today. Other conifers, recovered in limited locations and represented by fewer parts, were interpreted to have grown some distance from the pueblo, similar to the situation at present. For example, the nature of piñon material in Salmon strata indicates that piñons grew some distance from the pueblo. The recovery of piñon nutshells, a few female cone scales, and a single twig together suggests that people traveled to stands to harvest the nuts. The small number of piñon construction timbers implies that these trees did not grow nearby, similar to today. The even more limited recovery of parts of ponderosa pine, spruce-fir, Douglas fir, and spruce, coupled with the fact that none of these trees grow commonly with Utah juniper today, implies that all were resources quite distant from Salmon Pueblo in prehistory. At present, an 80 km trip is required to reach significant stands of these conifers.

Evidence of the former distribution of conifers provides a general view of climate in the San Juan valley 900 years ago. Generally, the climate prevailing during Salmon's occupation may have been much like that which is observed today, since Utah juniper appears to have been the locally dominant conifer tree then, as now. However, periods of low or unpredictable precipitation probably caused hardship to Salmon occupants. That there was at least occasional food stress is suggested by the fact that Salmon residents resorted to eating juniper bark and to gathering immature piñon nuts. Paleoenvironmental indicators suggest an especially severe period for farmers around the time the Chacoans moved out, and during the Intermediate phase. Likewise, the Secondary abandonment of the town around AD 1280 appears linked to significant paleoenvironmental changes.

The types of conifers used and the ways they were used by Salmon Pueblo groups are remarkably similar. Juniper served both Chacoan and Secondary groups as construction beams, firewood, and food, and for other domestic purposes as well. Piñon provided nuts throughout the pueblo's history. The two groups appear to have obtained some of the same items for religious needs, as indicated by the recovery of spruce bark scales in strata from both occupations.

The fundamental difference in conifer use between Chacoan and Secondary occupations is reflected in the record of construction timbers. Tentatively identified spruce-fir beams were procured solely by the Chacoans. More striking is the record of ponderosa pine timbers, one of the most popular species cut by the Chacoans for building purposes, yet not used at all by the Secondary occupants for roof repair. Perhaps the apparent Secondary preference for juniper beams reflects either a less well organized work force or cultural choice. The same pattern of timber use also appears in nearby Aztec Ruins, where juniper again appears to have been the consistent choice of its later occupants.

The idea that Salmon did not regularly provide piñon nuts or ponderosa beams to Chaco Canyon to the south rests on an understanding of the habitats and ancient plant materials from both regions. For example, at Chaco neither elevation nor substrata appear completely restrictive to piñon or ponderosa growth. At Salmon, the ancient record implies that the pueblo was not necessarily in a superior position to acquire either piñon or ponderosa resources to negotiate exchanges. Recent chemical analyses suggest that some of the large conifer building timbers for Chaco Canyon were transported from mountains to the west and south of the canyon.

Whether Salmon received conifer construction beams or food in an ancient trade network is uncertain. It seems reasonable to conclude that the sheer bulk of conifer roof timbers required to build the pueblo might have been procured by an extensive, organized work force from Salmon, rather than by traders. Likewise, the presence of burned, immature, piñon female cone scales in trash strata at Salmon may indicate that the inhabitants gathered and roasted the not-quite-mature nuts themselves, perhaps to alleviate food stress. Other nuts could have arrived at Salmon via trade.

In some respects, conifer use through the centuries has remained the same. Certain practices that have been observed in this century among modern southwestern groups appear also to have prevailed at Salmon in the past. For example, the extensive use of juniper spans nine centuries, including use of the wood for construction and firewood, the bark for many household items, twigs for tea, and the berries for food. Piñon nuts provide food today, as they did centuries ago. Likewise, ponderosa pine beams have been sought for ages in house construction. The closely allied Mormon tea furnished tea both in prehistory and in recent times.

Other evidence from Salmon Ruin seems to deviate from the modern use of conifers, although historic literature may simply be incomplete. For example, although Douglas fir served the Salmon inhabitants as a construction material, today it fulfills many ceremonial needs. Certain Tewa-speaking groups have been observed to carefully dispose of ceremonial paraphernalia away from the pueblo at the close of a ceremony. Such a practice in prehistory might preclude retrieval of these plant materials by an archaeologist. Also, spruce-fir provided roof beams in prehistory, but today no mention can be found of its use in building construction. Rather, medicinal or ceremonial needs are often met by this species or related species.

Finally, spruce bark scales from Salmon Ruin pose an interpretive problem. The presence of one bark scale in a foot drum of the Great Kiva, coupled with others in close proximity to suspected ceremonial locations, suggests that spruce planking or bark served a ceremonial function in prehistory. Yet today, only twigs and foliage are gathered. If the ancient bark scales do relate to ceremonial usage, they may document uses for spruce wood not practiced or recorded historically.

Chapter 41

UTAH JUNIPER CONES AND SEEDS FROM SALMON PUEBLO

by David L. Lentz

More than 1600 juniper cones and seeds were unearthed during extensive archaeological excavations at Salmon Ruins.* These abundant plant remains provide evidence of the use of juniper cones by the prehistoric inhabitants of Salmon Ruin. Information on juniper taxonomy, regional topography, plant ecology, and ethnographic accounts of traditional Southwest Native American plant use practices are integrated to provide a greater understanding of this archaeobotanical evidence.

Salmon Ruins, a prehistoric Puebloan site 16 km east of Farmington in the northwest corner of New Mexico, is on the eastern side of the Colorado Plateau and is just north of the San Juan River floodplain. Elevations in the area range from 1900 m at the river to 2200 m on the higher escarpments above the site.

The dwelling at the multicomponent site, which was built in the late eleventh century AD, was first inhabited (Primary occupation) by Anasazi groups associated with the Chaco Canyon cultural manifestation (Irwin-Williams 1975). The E-shaped, pueblo-style edifice (Figure 41.1) was later inhabited and partially modified by another group, the Mesa Verde Anasazi (Secondary occupation) in the thirteenth century. The occupations were identified by pottery styles associated with early and late stratigraphic levels.

PLANT ECOLOGY

Above the floodplain to the north and south of the San Juan River valley are ancient terraces that have been carved out of the plateau by the westward-flowing river. The principal plant community of the terrace has been variously described as pigmy forest (Woodbury 1947), piñon-juniper woodland (Howell 1941; Randles 1949; Zarn 1977), and juniper-piñon savanna (Daubenmire 1943). Visual dominants

of the community are, as some of the names suggest, piñon (*Pinus edulis*) and juniper (*Juniperus* spp.), the latter being much more numerous. *Juniperus osteosperma* (Utah juniper) was the only representative of its genus found within 10 km of Salmon Ruin. A small stand of *J. monosperma*, one-seed juniper, was located 15 km to the southeast of the site, but other juniper species that might have been expected in the region, such as alligator juniper (*J. deppeana* Steud.) or Rocky Mountain juniper (*J. scopulorum* Sarg.), were not observed despite intensive botanical surveys. Approximately 50 percent of the land area within 10 km of Salmon Ruin is covered with piñon-juniper woodland, or what might more accurately be called Utah juniper woodland with a few small stands of piñon mixed in.

JUNIPER SEED IDENTIFICATION

Reference seeds from modern junipers were collected to compare with the ancient seeds from Salmon Ruin. Since almost all of the Salmon Ruin seeds were round in cross-section, alligator and Rocky Mountain junipers were excluded as possible species of origin because they usually have two or more seeds per cone (Kearney and Peebles 1960; Little 1950), resulting in distinctive flattened areas, or facets, on their seeds. Utah and one-seed junipers usually have one seed per cone and are isodiametric. Morphologically, the latter two species have seeds that are quite similar, although Utah juniper seeds tend to be larger than one-seed juniper seeds.

To determine the species of the Salmon seeds, maximum length and width measurements for modern one-seed and Utah junipers were compared to those of the unbroken ancient seeds. Seed length and width were multiplied together, forming an index, to accentuate the size differences and simplify the data (Table 41.1). A Turkey-Kramer pairwise comparison (Sokal and Rohlf 1969) of the three populations listed in Table 41.1 reveals highly significant differences (P < 0.01) among all three groups. Nevertheless, the seeds from Salmon Ruin must be

---

*Reprinted, with permission, limited editing, and a revised tittle, from the *Journal of Ethnobiology* 4(2):191–200, 1984.

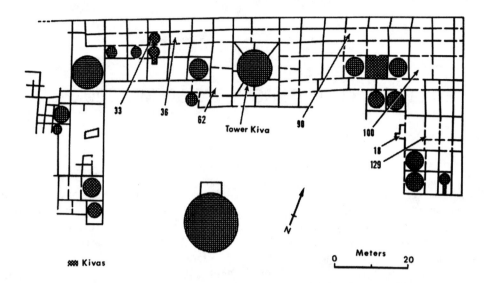

Figure 41.1. Floor plan of Salmon Ruin showing selected rooms containing juniper seed macrofossils. Room numbers are referred to in the text; juniper (*J. scopulorum* Sarg.) was not observed despite intensive botanical surveys. Within 10 km of Salmon Ruin are approximately 156 km (50% of the land area) covered with piñon-juniper woodland, or what might more accurately be called Utah juniper woodland with a few small stands of piñon mixed in.

from at least one of the species represented in the comparison. The frequency polygons of the three seed populations (Figure 41.2) reveal the similarities between the Utah juniper curve and the Salmon juniper seed curve, especially at the lower ends. If there were a number of one-seed juniper seeds in the Salmon seed collection, the curve of the latter would take on a bimodal configuration, the variance would be increased, and seeds would appear in the strictly one-seed size range. However, this was not the case.

Although the Salmon seed-size index mean is larger than the mean for modern Utah juniper seeds, this disparity can be explained. The modern seeds were collected during a dry year, 1977, with 33.3 mm lower than average rainfall (U.S. Department of Commerce 1977). The preceding year was even drier, with an 81.3 mm rainfall deficit (U.S. Department of Commerce 1976). In this arid region, even a small drop in rainfall has substantial ramifications as precipitation averages only 264 mm per year. The seed size of the modern junipers was thus probably adversely affected. The juniper seeds from Salmon were collected over many years and undoubtedly reflect a closer approximation to the true population mean. The durable nature of the seeds combined with the xeric conditions of the region can account for the preservation of these plant artifacts.

ETHNOGRAPHIC SOURCES AND ARCHAEOBOTANICAL INTERPRETATION

Most traditional Southwest Native Americans use juniper cones for food, medicine, or ornamentation. The extensive ethnographic literature on the use of juniper cones is outlined in Table 41.2. If plant use practices of present-day Native American are similar to those of the past, ethnographic information can aid in the interpretation of archaeobotanical data.

Table 41.3 contains data from several Salmon Ruin stratigraphic units, illustrating the kinds of activities with which juniper cones were associated as suggested by the ethnographic literature. The units were selected on the basis of their stratigraphic integrity, favorable preservation, and absence of rodent disturbance. By selecting strata according to these criteria, the modifying effects of postdepositional factors have been minimized.

Modern Southwest Native Americans often cook juniper cones by boiling or roasting them; the prehistoric Salmon Ruin inhabitants seem to have done the same. More than 200 of the juniper cones and seeds found at the site were carbonized (Figure 41.3). Several trash strata in Room 62 contained carbonized and uncarbonized juniper seeds, as well as other plant macrofossils, embedded in matrices of ash.

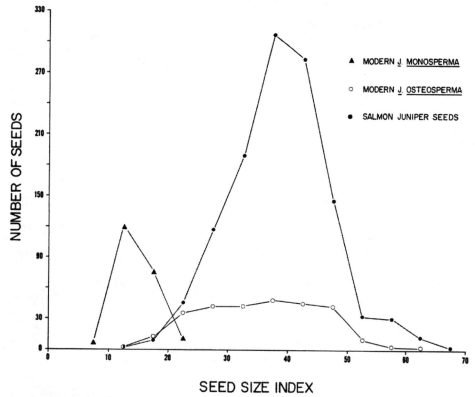

Figure 41.2. Graph showing frequency polygons for three juniper seed populations; seed index = length in mm x width in mm.

These units represent redeposited hearth refuse. Since juniper seeds are regarded as waste products according to ethnographic sources, it should not be surprising to find the seeds in prehistoric midden deposits. Indeed, Room 62 contained 53 trash strata, of which 43 include juniper seeds. Many of the juniper seeds found at Salmon Ruin are uncarbonized, indicating consumption of fresh cones by the prehistoric inhabitants in patterns similar to those revealed in the ethnographic literature.

Ethnographic sources show that juniper cones are sometimes sun dried (Gallagher 1977) and stored for winter use (Vestal 1952). One Secondary rooftop (Room 100) at Salmon Ruin with juniper remains evidently served as an outdoor processing area (Bohrer and Adams, Chapter 38). Also, juniper seeds were discovered in three burned storerooms (36, 90, and 129), indicating that the inhabitants may have kept some in reserve.

Juniper seeds were also found on an activity surface in the Tower Kiva (Room 64), suggesting that they may have been used for ceremonial purposes. Kivas are traditionally rooms where rituals are practiced (Vivian and Reiter 1960), so oftentimes associated artifacts have ceremonial significance.

Five burials at the site contained juniper seeds and cones; all of the burials were enveloped by matting, or the remains thereof, ensuring that these strata were discrete units. Stratum L-1-11.5 in Room 33, for example, showed evidence of a grave offering with two cones found adjacent to the body inside of what was left of the surrounding matting of the inhumation. In the Southwest, food offerings were often placed in proximity to the deceased (Bohrer and Adams 1977) to provide nourishment for the long journey after death (Parsons 1939).

Figure 41.3. Utah juniper cones and seeds. From left to right: modern cone, modern seed, carbonized cones from Salmon Ruin, seed from Salmon Ruin.

Table 41.1. Size index (length x width, in mm) for sample population of juniper seeds.

	Juniperus monosperma (modern collection)	*J. osteosperma* (modern collection)	Juniper Seeds from Salmon Ruin
Mean	14.75	35.5	38.65
Standard deviation	2.98	9.74	8.12
Median	14.28	36	65.91
Minimum value	6.21	10.4	13.69
Maximum value	23.37	63	66
Number of seeds counted	210	283	1180

Table 41.2. Use of juniper cones and seeds by Southwest Native Americans.

Group	*Juniperus* Species	Use	References
Hopi	*J. osteosperma*	Cones baked with piki bread, seeds used as beads for necklaces	Whiting 1939
Tanoan Pueblo (Jemez)	*J. scopulorum*	Cones eaten fresh or stewed	Cook 1930
Tanoan Pueblo (San Juan)	*J. communis* *J. monosperma*	Cones eaten fresh	Ford 1968b
Tanoan Pueblo (Isleta)	*J. deppeana*	Cones boiled then eaten	Jones 1931; Castetter 1935
Tanoan Pueblo (Santa Clara)	*J. monosperma*	Cones eaten fresh or heated in an open pan over a fire, decoction in water used as remedy for internal chills and as a diuretic	Robbins et al. 1916
Tanoan Pueblo (Santa Clara)	*J. monosperma*	Cones eaten fresh	Hough 1931
Tanoan Pueblo (San Ildefonso)	*J. monosperma*	Cones eaten fresh (?)	Robbins et al. 1916
Keres Pueblo (Sia)	*J. monosperma* *J. scopulorum*	Cones eaten fresh or cooked	White 1945
Keres Pueblo (Cochiti)	*J. monosperma*	Cones eaten fresh or baked, tea used as tonic after childbirth	Castetter 1935
Keres Pueblo (Acoma, Laguna)	*J. monosperma*	Cones eaten fresh or mixed with chopped meat and roasted	Swank 1932 Castetter 1935
Western Apache	*Juniperus* spp.	Cones an important wild food	Goodwin 1942
Western Apache	*J. osteosperma*	Cones eaten fresh, stored in sealed baskets	Basso 1969
Western Apache	*J. monosperma*	Cones eaten fresh, seeds spat out, beverage derived from dried cones mixed with water, cones sun dried and stored for winter	Gallagher 1977
White Mountain Apache	*J. monosperma* *J. osteosperma* *J. occidentalis*	Cones boiled before eating	Reagan 1929
San Carlos Apache	*Juniperus* spp.	Cones boiled before eating	Hrdlicka 1908
Northern and Southern Tonto	*Juniperus* spp.	Cones eaten fresh	Gifford 1940
Navajo	*J. monosperma* *J. osteosperma*	Cones eaten fresh, boiled juice used as a cure for influenza, as a source of green dye; seeds used as beads for necklaces	Elmore 1943
Ramah Navajo	*J. monosperma* *J. deppeana*	Cones eaten fresh, boiled, roasted use and also stored for winter	Vestal 1952
Gosiute	*J. osteosperma*	Cones eaten after boiling	Chamberlin 1911
Southern Paiute	*J. osteosperma*	Trees sampled for sweetest cones; cones crushed on a metate, seeded, then eaten.	Kelly 1964

Table 41.3. Selected strata from Salmon Ruin containing juniper seeds and cones.

Room	Number of Juniper Remains	Strati-graphic Unit	Archaeological Context	Occupational Component	Use / Interpretation	Associated Macrofossils
18P	2s	L-1-8	Burial; juniper seeds next to the skull	Secondary	Grave offering	Yucca leaves
33W	2k	L-1-11.5	Burial	Primary	Grave offering	Brush of monocotyledon leaves; arrow shaft
36W	2ck	F-1-15	Burned store room	Secondary	Stored food	Zea mays cobs and kernels; Phaseolus vulgaris seed; Cucurbita rind; Cycloloma seed; Opuntia spp. stems and seeds; Phragmites stems; Yucca leaf bundle
62A/W	784s 68k 8sc	43 strata	Trash	Primary and Secondary	Discarded food remains	Zea mays cobs and kernels; Cucurbita seeds and rinds; Pinus edulis testa; Allium bulb scales; Prunus pits; Yucca seeds and leaves; Xanthium fruits; Opuntia spp. stems and seeds; other plant remains
64W Tower Kiva	7cs 1ck	H-1-8	Burned floor	Secondary	Food, ceremonial or medicinal use	Zea mays cobs; Phaseolus pods; Curcurbita rinds and seeds; Mentzelia albicaulis seeds; Yucca leaves; Pinus edulis testa; basketry
90W	2s	F-2-9	Burned store room	Secondary	Food or food refuse	Zea mays cobs and kernels, Phaseolus vulgaris seed; Chenopodium seed; Xanthium fruit
100W	1ck	N-1-3	Outdoor processing or storage area, burned rooftop	Secondary	Food	Zea mays cobs, kernels, tassel, peduncle, knotted leaves; Phaseolus vulgaris seed; Cucurbita rind and peduncle; Atriplex seed; Opuntia bud; Cycloloma seed; Yucca cordage
129W	1ck	F-1-8	Burned store room	Secondary	Food	Zea mays kernels, cobs, and tied husks; Phaseolus vulgaris seed; Cucurbita seeds and rinds; Xanthium fruit; Chenopodium seeds; Opuntia bud; monocotyledon leaves (quid); grass stems, evenly cut; Yucca stem heart, leaves, twine, matting

*plaza test trench, c = carbonized, s = seeds, k = seeds with cone parts attached.

DISCUSSION

Because of the numerous juniper remains found in a variety of archaeological contexts at Salmon Ruin, it seems apparent that the cones were a part of the prehistoric subsistence pattern of those early inhabitants. Although is seems likely that juniper cones were not a staple for the Salmon Ruin Anasazi, their supplementary role should not be disregarded. Studies comparing plant remains from the Primary and Secondary occupations indicate an increased reliance on wild foods, such as juniper, by the latter occupation (Doebley 1981; Doebley, Chapter 37; Lentz 1979).

Utah Juniper cones have been shown to contain 7.5 percent reducing sugar (Yanovsky and Kingsbury 1938) and a comparable amount, 10.66 percent, has been shown for the bread of *J. occidentalis* Hook, with 5.69 percent protein and 17.87 percent starch (Palmer 1871). Heat of combustion tests on Utah juniper cones from the Salmon Ruin area reveal the presence of 5.3 kcal/gr in strobilus material (minus the seeds), or 6.5 kcal/cone. Combine this with the estimated 488 mill cones produced within a 10 km radius of Salmon (Lentz 1979) during the relatively dry year of 1977, and a substantial, reliable resource appears to have been readily available.

In addition to its nutrient contents, juniper cones contain volatile oils, resins, and other chemicals with irritant properties (Claus et al. 1970). Cooking ameliorates the taste of juniper cones by driving off many of the unpleasant compounds. Another cultural adaptation for reducing the effects of irritants has been recorded for the Southern Paiutes (Kelly 1964), who sample different trees until they find ones with the sweetest taste, that is, with lower irritant contents. Similar methods would have allowed the prehistoric inhabitants of Salmon Ruin to have exploited the juniper cone crop with fewer ill effects.

The agricultural subsistence base of the prehistoric inhabitants of Salmon Ruin was probably precarious, but the drought-resistant juniper crop was always available, even during lean years. In addition to the ceremonial uses of juniper cones and seeds, the prehistoric inhabitants of Salmon Ruin could rely on nutrients in abundance from the surrounding juniper woodland.

ACKNOWLEDGMENTS

This paper is based on a Master's thesis completed at Eastern New Mexico University, with Dr. Vorsila L. Bohrer as chairperson. I wish to thank her, as well as Ms. Karen R. Adams, Dr. Robert R. Haynes, Dr. C. Earle Smith, Jr., and Ms. Vicki L. Young for their editorial comments. Also, I would like to thank the late Dr. Cynthia Irwin-Williams for providing funds; Ms. Jo Smith, San Juan County Archaeological Research Center, Salmon Ruin, for lending juniper macrofossils; and Dr. Mercedes Hoskins, New Mexico State University, who determined the caloric values for Salmon Ruin area juniper strobiles.

Chapter 42

CEREMONIAL AND MEDICINAL PLANTS FROM SALMON PUEBLO

by Vorsila L. Bohrer

When religious activity pervades all aspects of life, even the most ordinary events may carry a deep spiritual meaning. Although planting corn may seem to be a purely secular task, it represented part of a continuing ritual in the life of the Navajo farmer (Hill 1938), and doubtless also to some of his earliest instructors, the Pueblo Indians themselves (Cushing 1920:167–216). When religion and medicine are closely integrated in a society, the plants or material culture that may have been rich in meaning or strong in healing properties may be difficult to differentiate.

A high percentage of maize pollen in a sample may be indicative of ancient medicinal or ceremonial activity. Collecting maize pollen by tapping the tassel into a container should result in no maize aggregates (Bohrer 1980a). Some of our strongest evidence for ceremonial usage derives from observations of maize pollen aggregates on the floors of Salmon Ruin. Several methods of collecting pollen from two varieties of maize were attempted in order to identify the conditions under which maize aggregates were formerly released from the tassel (Bohrer 1980a). Only the immature tassels of the Chapalote variety of maize released pollen aggregates that survived the acetolysis treatment used to prepare modern reference materials. Modern Puebloans are known to gather maize pollen for medicinal or ceremonial use, and ancient maize pollen aggregates are thought to carry the same significance.

MAIZE POLLEN AGGREGATES

In stratigraphic units related to the Chacoan occupation, maize pollen aggregates have been recovered from floors with and without features (Table 42.1) and from two of three trash samples. The most intense medicinal or ceremonial activity would likely be evidenced by the presence of maize pollen aggregates in almost all sampled grid squares in a room floor. According to this criterion, such activities were evident on the floors of 30W and 89W. These rooms are located on the distal ends of the long axis of the pueblo (Figure 42.1). In addition, Room 62W, near

the centrally located Tower Kiva, seems also to have been a focus of medicinal or ceremonial activity. The least amount of such activity apparently took place on the featureless floor of 56W and on a floor with a hearth (101W, H-1-9), which may have been a habitation floor. This first-floor room had another floor above it and was located far to the rear of the pueblo, making access quite indirect.

In stratigraphic units belonging to the Secondary occupation, maize pollen aggregates have been recovered from floors without features (see Table 42.1) and in 12 of 23 separate trash units. Two superimposed habitation floors from 93W were free of maize pollen aggregates (K. Adams 1980; Chapter 39). Medicinal or ceremonial activity seems to have been widespread on three floors without features (in Rooms 57W and 58W), all near the Tower Kiva; these three floors yielded a broad distribution of maize pollen aggregates. Samples from the Tower Kiva itself yielded no pollen, probably because of the intense fire in the room. The two other kivas, usually regarded as ceremonial areas, were less informative. However, one should note that the aggregates of maize pollen in the slab-lined bin of Kiva 6A may be residue from grinding maize tassels on the metate that presumably occupied the bin. The bin yielded small seeds that are normally prepared by parching and grinding (see ÒPlants from Kivas,Ó below). The presence of maize pollen aggregates in trash may be due to discard of the floor sweepings enriched with maize pollen from ceremonial locations. Evidently disposal habits in regard to maize pollen were quite similar for both occupations.

Two of our best examples of Primary ceremonial rooms (30W and 62W), identified by widespread maize aggregates, have pollen percentages above 80 percent. The sample from Primary floor H-2-11 of Room 31W, with 83 percent maize pollen content, might qualify as a ceremonial room by analogy. The floor of Room 31W had numerous chopping tools and bones scattered upon it; quite likely the products of hunting had been divided here. Whether these

Salmon Pueblo

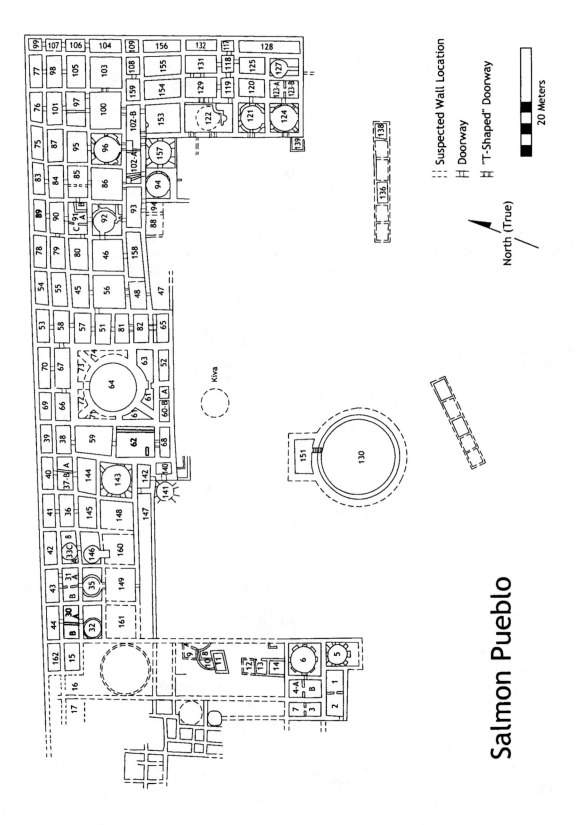

Figure 42.1. Map of Salmon Ruin showing rooms (shaded) with considerable evidence of maize pollen aggregates.

Table 42.1. Maize pollen aggregates from floors and features.

Floors	Maize Pollen Clumps Present	Number of Pollen Samples w/ Maize Pollen	Total Number of Pollen Samples	Highest Frequencies of Maize Pollen	Location of Sample(s) w/ Highest Frequencies and Remarks
FLOORS WITH FEATURES					
Primary					
93W, H-5-33	0	3	4	4/11	Lower hearth fill (one floor sample only: 1/215 maize)
101W, H-1-9	1 clump of 2 grains in 1 sample	7	7	30/200	Doorway
Secondary					
93W, H-1-14	0	3	3	37/100	Southeast floor, near hearth
93W, H-2-22	0	4	4	24/200	Center of floor
FLOORS WITHOUT FEATURES					
Primary					
30W, H-2-12	9	9	10	170/200 176/200 164/200	Northeast corner Southeast corner North wall
56W, H-1-5	1	4	4	71/200	Northeast corner
62W, H-1-41	8	8	8	166/200	Northwest corner
82W, H-2-24	4	7	84	84/200 86/200	Wall hearth Northeast pit
89W, H-1-8/G-1-7	4	4	4	69/200	North wall
Secondary					
51W, H-1-5	3	6	63	85/200	East-central section
57W, H-1-8	3	4	4	53/200	South wall
58W, H-1-8	5	5	5	166/200	Northeast corner
58W, H-2-11	7	8	8	103/200	North wall
SECONDARY KIVA FLOORS					
6A, H-1-5.2	1	5	6	94/200	Milling bin
124A, H-1-6	3	9	10	120/200	Northeast sector

butchering tools were abandoned close to the time of pollen deposition cannot be determined. However, if corn pollen and artifact deposition were synchronous, the pollen may represent residue from certain rituals that preceded butchering the meat. For example, at Zia Pueblo the war chief visited the homes of successful hunters to sprinkle the antelope with maize pollen. The next day the game is brought to the ceremonial house, where it is eventually divided between cult societies (Stevenson 1894: 120).

PLANTS FROM KIVAS

A variety of seeds of economic importance to the inhabitants of Salmon Ruin have been recovered from three kiva floors belonging to the Secondary occupation; they represent all kiva floors investigated to date. The prevalence of subsistence items in the Secondary kivas serves as a reminder that what we would normally call secular aspects of life were expressed in the kiva as well as the sacred. The ultimate interpretation as to whether the act of eating is sacred or secular rests in the mind of the partaker. We have only burned seeds as evidence.

During the Secondary occupation either seed grinding or storage took place in Kiva 6A within the walls of what has been termed a milling bin. The true function of the bin is not certain because no grinding stone was found in place. The use of the bin to store seeds seems unlikely as one of the bin slabs is mortared into place at an angle of close to 45 degrees, providing little protection from rodents (Figure 42.2). As Table 42.2 illustrates the scarcity of seeds in liter samples of soil from various other grids in the kiva floor contrasts with the concentration of seeds in the bin area (Figure 42.3). The concentration of Cheno-Am and tansy-mustard seed is 100 times greater in the bin area than at other locations on the floor, and heavy concentrations of purslane (*Portulaca retusa*), *Mentzelia albicaulis* type, and *Euphorbia glyptosperma* type were unique to the bin. Exceptionally high concentrations of maize pollen (47%) in conjunction with a maize pollen aggregate were recovered from the bin, with just a token number of kernels. The next highest concentration of pollen was from a wall niche on the far side of the kiva. The concentration of maize pollen in the bin might be

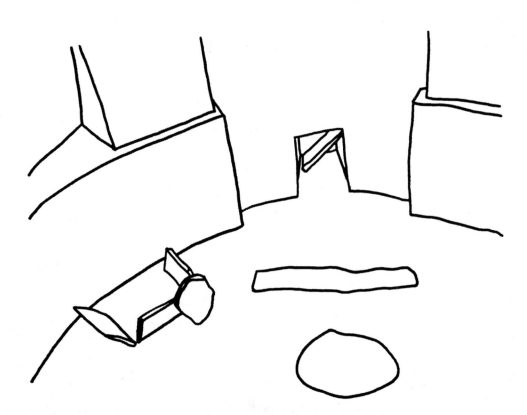

Figure 42.2. Partial drawing of the Room 6A kiva, Floor H-1-05.2, looking south. The firepit and deflector occupy the central part of the figure and the walls to the bin can be seen on the left.

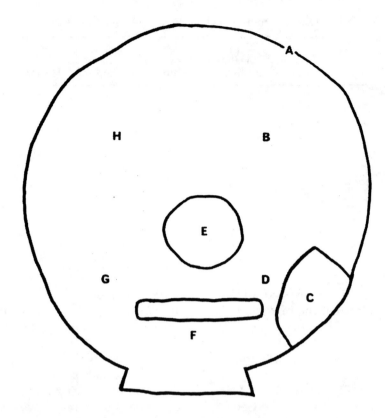

Figure 42.3. Floor diagram of the Room 6A kiva (H-1-05.2). Letters designate where pollen and flotation samples were obtained. A is a wall niche; the oblong shape between F and E is a deflector.

explained either as a religious offering or as representing the area where maize tassels were lightly ground to release their pollen.

Other Secondary occupation kivas, such as 124A (H-1-6) and 64W (H-1-8), also carry a broad spectrum of small edible seeds. All of the seed types from the kiva milling bin in 6A, with the exception of groundcherry (*Physalis*), have been recovered from beneath the metate on the habitation floor (H-1-14) of Room 93W (K. Adams 1980:77–79; see Chapter 39). This lends greater credence to the theory that a grinding stone once occupied the bin.

When a devastating fire precipitated the swift abandonment of the Tower Kiva (64W), the remains of a number of food plants were left on the floor, including ears of maize, beans in pods, squash rind, cholla (*Cylindropuntia*) buds, young prickly pear stems or joints, piñon nuts, and juniper berries. Young prickly pear joints and cholla buds are available in the spring and piñon nuts and juniper berries in the fall. The same dichotomy is noticeable in seeds recovered from the same floor by flotation (Table 42.3), as whitestem blazingstar (*Mentzelia albicaulis*) is found in spring and purslane in late summer or fall. It is by no means clear which items were stored and

which were fresh, but the food in the kiva clearly represents several seasons of gathering.

PLANTS FROM OTHER CONTEXTS

Much evidence would be overlooked if one were to restrict a discussion of medicinal or ceremonial plants to only those recovered in kivas (Table 42.4). Foremost is a series of objects that carry traces of red or pink stain from stratigraphic units of unknown cultural affiliation in Room 62W. Among items represented are broken pieces of peeled sticks of diffuse porous wood a centimeter or less in diameter, yucca leaves, and young prickly pear pads.

Some of our small cardboard boxes carried bands of red paper around their rims, so the possibility was considered that rain might have caused the red paper to fade and stain the contents. However, because Room 62W was composed of extremely complex stratigraphic units containing unusually good preservation, extraordinary care was expended in sorting the plant material in the field and boxing it in a suitable manner, and the entire crew working in the room protected the strata and the excavated materials with tarps whenever rain threatened; also, one of the excavators (Daniel Landis) remembers

Table 42.2. Number of seeds in a 1 liter sample from a kiva floor (Room 6A, H-1-5.2), Secondary occupation.

Plant Classification	NE Sector	In Mealing Bin	Near Mealing Bin	North of Deflector	In Hearth	SW Sector	Wall Niche
Cheno-Am	1	1249	17	1	1	1	5
Descurainia obtuse type (tansy-mustard)	–	114*	–	–	–	–	–
Euphorbia glyptosperma type	–	892*	–	–	–	–	–
Gramineae (grass)							
Festucoideae floret	–	–	1	–	–	–	–
Zea mays kernels	–	1*	1*	–	–	–	–
Muhlenbergia type grain	1*	–	–	–	–	–	–
Physalis seeds	–	1*	1*	3	2*	–	–
Physalis berries	–	–	–	3	–	–	–

*Indicates some degree of parching or carbonization present.

removing the pink-stained prickly pear pads directly from the stratum. The idea that the pink stain resulted from modern processing of the material was therefore rejected.

An explanation for the objects stained pink has not been developed. Although the small prickly pear pads must have been gathered while young and succulent, evidently they were not considered edible after they received the pink coloration. The find represents one of the few instances of seemingly edible plant parts being discarded. As the coloration evidently carried some significance beyond normal edibility, it could well have some bearing on ritual.

Another item discarded in the trash is a stick whose tip had been fashioned in the shape of the letter ñCî by taking a forked shoot, cutting away one branch, and flattening the other on the inside so it could be bent. Similar sticks were recovered from Pueblo Bonito (Judd 1954:269). Hooked or bent sticks form part of ceremonial events, although the sticks may vary from pueblo to pueblo or from ceremony to ceremony. Many references to pueblo uses have been assembled by Judd (1954:269).

The trash contained several examples of reed cigarettes in varying stages of degradation (see Table 42.4). One well-preserved specimen still retains the dottle in the burned portion of the tube, by means of the bent distal edge of reed used to extinguish it. Modern use of reed cigarettes by Puebloans invariably occurs in a ceremonial context (Steen et al. 1962: 87); the tradition could have been carried forward from prehistory.

Deposited in the trash of Room 100W is a small, painted, canteen-shaped jar (see Table 42.4). The heat that caused the black design to oxidize to a reddish hue perhaps also caused the carbonization of the seeds within. The jar contained charred seeds of

squash (*Cucurbita*) and winged pigweed (*Cycloloma atriplicifolium*), as well as maize pollen (five of six observations). The extracted pollen was too low in density to count 100 grains.

Small canteen-shaped jars are not normally used for cooking, nor is it usual to alter the coloration of the design by placing them in the fire. Although the broken rim piece may have been an accident, it also might have been an intentional act to release the essence within it, which might have been thought to have health and life-giving properties (Cushing 1920: 315). Pueblo Indians believe that upon death the spirit no longer partakes of regular food, but only the odor or smoke of prepared food. The Zuni say that whenever food is put into the fire and burned, the ghosts eat it (Parsons 1939:302). When the departed eats in such a manner, the spirit becomes light, like a cloud person. Perhaps archaeologists found the residue from such a meal, offered to a departed spirit. There was no direct association with a burial, but there were several burials nearby.

Table 42.3 Carbonized seeds or fruits from the floor of the Tower Kiva (64W) obtained by flotation.

Name	Sample
Cheno-Am seed	64W0031
Chenopodium (goosefoot)	64W0035
Cleome (Rocky Mtn. beeweed)	64W0035
Descurainia (tansy-mustard)	64W0044
Euphorbia glyptosperma type	64W0043 & 64W0044
Mentzelia albicaulis type	64W0044
Papilinoideae	64W0044
Physalis (groundcherry)	64W0035
Portulaca (purslane)	64W0031
Sphaeralcea (globe mallow)	64W0035

Table 42.4 Medicinal-ceremonial plant evidence.

Description	Record Key or (Bot. Sample No.)	Room Stratum	Phase*
Dicotyledon twigs, fragmented and peeled with all ends broken and the wood stained pink; 0.6–1.1 cm diameter; diffuse porous anatomy	76639	62W, C-30.5-30.5	M
Dictoyledon twigs, fragmented with all ends formed by breakage. Wood stained pink; diffuse porous anatomy.	53440	62W, C-30-30 and C-31-31	M
Dicotyledon wood stained pink	28980	62W, C-2-7	M
Platyopuntia (prickly pear) young stems (pads) from 2 x 2 to 3 x 3.5 cm; some are stained pink	76642	62W, C-30-30 and C-31-31	M
Platypountia young stems stained pink	53480	62W, C-30-30	M
Platyopuntia young stems with average size of 3 x 4 cm; stained pink	78936	62W, C-34-34	S
Platyopuntia young stems	78940	62W, C-34-34	S
Yucca leaves, some stained pink	53758	62W, C-20-20	S
Dicotyledon diffuse porous wooden artifact of sickle shape	33027	62W, L-2-7.1 and C-22-22	M
Phragmites communis (reed grass) nodal segments of stem about 3 cm long, many burned at one end; one has hand-finished end and pierced septum with dottle retained in burned interior	50457	62W, L-2-7.1	M
Phragmites communis stem burned at one end, septum pierced, 3.1 x 1.0 cm.	(62W9178)	62W, C-2-7	M
Phragmites communis longitudinally split stem carbonized at end close to node, 1.7 cm long; no way to know if septum is pierced	75647	62W, C-27.9-27.9	S
Anemopsis californica (yerba mansa) seed	(37W2036)	37W, C-2-8	S
Anemopsis californica seed	(62A0021)	62W, C-2-8	S
Kallstroemia fruit	(30W0020)	30W, H-1-4	S
Kallstroemia fruit	(121W0001)	121W, test trench	S
Small jar (canteen; inventory no. 269), chipped constricted orifice, highly oxidized Mancos B/w, contained charred *Cucurbita* (squash) seed, charred fruit and seeds of *Cycloloma atriplicifolium* (winged pigweed), corn pollen in soil from interior (sample 100W1043); no burial association	56291	100W, C-1-4	S

Based upon Doebley 1976, Rose 1979, K. Adams , Chapter 40; and printouts 3/4/79 Flotcode 13, 3/15/79 Q67129 YC-259, 3/27/79 Q6226-377, 3/30/79 Q6227-147.

*M = mixture of occupations, S = Secondary occupation.

No portion of either caltrop (*Kallstroemia*) or yerba mansa (*Anemopsis californica*) has a reputation for edibility by people of the Southwest. Dried yerba mansa leaves, ground to a powder, can be used on open sores (Swank 1932:26–27) and the Pima have used an infusion of the fragrant roots to treat ailments (Kearney and Peebles 1960). Caltrop is valued as a medicinal plant at San Ildefonso Pueblo and by New Mexicans of Spanish descent (Curtin 1947:68). Although either species may grow in locally dense patches, the seeds or fruits carry little morphological adaptation to accidental transport by humans. The low frequency of recovery of these two species (in 4 of 272 flotation samples) is in line with expectations of a low frequency of recovery for a medicinal plant. One would not expect to recover it as often as an item used for food.

Other items of potential medicinal or ceremonial interest include such things as burned groundcherry seeds, Mormon tea (*Ephedra*), spruce bark scales, and juniper twig bundles (see K. Adams, Chapter 36, for interpretive details).

WHEN FOOD BECOMES CEREMONY

The chewing of *Euphorbia serpyllifolia* (common name spurge) root to stimulate saliva flow in order to accumulate chewed corn meal in a bowl for a sweet pudding is a unique reference (Stevenson 1915:68). Cushing (1920:300) indicated that both mastication and fermentation were involved in Zuni production of their sweet pudding delicacy, but did mention prior chewing of the *Euphorbia* root. Because *Euphorbia serpyllifolia* is related in morphology to *E. glyptosperma*, a seed type identified by Adams in flotation in unburned rooms (Adams, Chapters 36 and 39), the singular ethnographic reference is of particular interest.

More than 800 burned or parched seeds of *Euphorbia glytosperma* type were recovered from Salmon in several contexts: (1) a milling bin (Feature 1) in the Secondary occupation Kiva 6A; (2) two Secondary occupation floors, including floor H-1-4 in Room 93W (28 seeds, 6 burned) and eight seeds from beneath a quartzite metate on the same floor; (3) a Primary habitation room (101W, H-1-3); and (4) a Primary featureless floor (56W, H-1-5) and two Primary trash deposits.

Pearl Beaglehole (1937) has provided the best discussion of the numerous Hopi recipes that make use of a sweet sauce created by masticating corn meal. For corn beverages, she mentioned a medicinal corn meal drink made simply with water. For Hopi courtship and wedding ritual, Mary-Russell Colton's (1933) description of a maiden's cake and a bride's cake made with the addition of the aforementioned sweet sauce places the two cakes in the realm of ceremony as much as food. Colton (1933) also described a maize drink served along with piki bread to men in the kiva made of white corn meal that has been boiled, dried, parched, and ground, and which supposedly tasted like malted milk. This hardly sounds like the medicinal drink referred to by Beaglehole. The special flavor of the "malted" corn drink suggests that it could have been served in Mesa Verde mugs in prehistory. If it were possible to trace the context of all three comestibles archaeologically, all would probably be recognized for their role in both food and ceremony.

An analogy to the potential use of the *Euphorbia* root in daily life and in ceremony might be the use of *Euphorbia glyptosperma* type seeds at Salmon Ruin. The toasted seed may have been used as a symbolic flavoring added to dishes made of corn meal that were used in everyday life but also in ceremonial contexts. If there were toxins in the seeds, as Adams suggests, they might have been dissipated by the heat of parching. People detoxify many seeds by parching, roasting, or heating, including some in the *Euphorbia* family and genus (Johns 1988: Table 1).

Chapter 43

ARCHAEOBOTANICAL SUMMARY AND CONCLUSIONS

Karen R. Adams

Cultivated plants were of major economic importance to both the Chacoan and Secondary occupants of the Salmon great house. Both groups grew maize, beans, and squash in their fields. They also gathered a wide range of wild plants available throughout the growing season, using most as food. Failure or low productivity of cultivated plants may explain the widespread remains of Cheno-Am and *Portulaca* seeds, along with grass grains, cactus seeds, tansy mustard seeds, reproductive parts of sedge and other riparian taxa, and many other wild food resources. A comparison of the two occupations suggests that the Chacoans ate more maize and fewer wild plants than the Secondary inhabitants. This overview provides no direct information on potentially important food resources such as leafy greens or other vegetative plants that are unlikely to have been preserved in the archaeological record.

CULTIVATED CROPS
Maize

Zea mays cobs, cupules, ears, husks, kernels, pollen, stalks, and tassels were all recovered at Salmon Ruin. The studies of Salmon Ruin maize (Bohrer and Doebley, Chapter 35; Doebley and Bohrer 1983) provide a good overview of its presence and use. Carbonized kernels, cobs and cupules were frequently recovered in flotation samples, suggesting regular use. Maize samples of more than six cobs occurred in 22 of the 48 rooms studied, primarily in trash and roof-fall. Although a number of Secondary occupation second-story floors or first-floor roofs contained associated maize when the roofs burned and collapsed, only one burned first-story storage room (30W) clearly contained maize cobs, which were aligned parallel to the south wall in a relatively

horizontal position, as ears would be if stacked in storage. A single stratigraphic unit of redeposited trash in Room 62W preserved stalks and tassels, and the presence of empty tied husks suggests that maize ears were once braided together by their attached husks. The presence of whole stalks implies that plants were sometimes cut and carried to the pueblo. It seems likely that tassels were abraded to remove pollen for use in some rooms, including those adjacent to the Tower Kiva, where numerous examples of aggregated maize pollen and high concentrations of maize pollen were identified. Two human coprolites from the Secondary occupation contained embedded small cob segments, suggesting that the cobs were eaten in times of food scarcity, similar to a reported ethnographic practice (Hill 1938:45–46). The repeated recovery of cob fragments and cupules from firepits implies the use of leftover cobs as fuel.

Squash

Cucurbita seeds, rind (exocarp) fragments, dried flesh, peduncles, and vine tendrils were all preserved in Salmon deposits (Bohrer and Doebley, Chapter 35; Burgess-Terrell 1979). Most of these were recovered as macrofossils, visible to excavators, and virtually none of them were identified in flotation samples. In one study of trash units of moderate preservation (Bohrer, Chapter 38), the presence of squash seeds suggested a relatively high ranking as a food source, exceeding the frequency of piñon nutshells, juniper seeds, onion bulb scales, yucca seeds, and chokecherry seeds. Trash and roof units most often retained squash evidence, along with four Chacoan floors and one Secondary floor. The bulk of evidence was recovered as seeds and uncharred exocarp (rind).

Modern *Cucurbita* provided the basis for identifying the Salmon *Cucurbita* (Burgess-Terrell 1979). Prior to a detailed study of whole *Cucurbita* seeds (n = 84) associated with the Chacoan occupation and whole seeds (n = 168) from the Secondary occupation, Burgess-Terrell had used principal component

---

This chapter was taken entirely from the Salmon synthetic volume, in a paper titled "Subsistence and Plant Use Among the Chacoan and Secondary Occupations at Salmon Ruin," by Karen R. Adams (2005).

and discriminant analyses to develop a systematic method of separating three modern domesticates (*Cucurbita pepo*, *C. moschata*, and *C. argyrosperma*, as *C. mixta*) and one wild cucurbit (*C. foetidissima*), using detailed seed measurements.

When applied to the Salmon seeds, the results suggested that all but a single seed of both occupations belonged to *Cucurbita pepo*. Also, it appears that more than one variety of this squash was grown, and they differed to some degree from the two modern varieties of *Cucurbita pepo* (Connecticut Field pumpkin and Small Sugar) included in this study. Seven *Cucurbita pepo* peduncles (stems) were also identified, some of them burned or partially burned.

Coupled with burned *Cucurbita* rind charred on the exterior but not the interior, it seems that mature squash fruits were occasionally roasted whole, a known ethnographic preparation method for this species of squash (Castetter and Bell 1942:190). Other uncharred rind fragments suggest other preparation methods. The ethnographic record also suggests that although seeds of some squash varieties were eaten, those of *Cucurbita pepo* rarely were, due to their comparatively small stored food value (Castetter and Bell 1951:114). This helps explain the presence of squash seeds in the Salmon trash record, where it seems that squash seeds were often removed from their fruit and discarded. Two clusters of squash seeds still clumped together were removed in bulk from the fruit. However, the presence of squash seeds in coprolites (Bohrer, Chapter 38) reveals that the seeds were in fact eaten, at least occasionally. Segments of curved dried squash flesh from Room 62A/62W reveal that the practice of drying *Cucurbita* has considerable time depth in the American Southwest. When comparing squash seeds of both occupations within a well-preserved room (62W), the fruits were considered to be similar, suggesting continuity of use of this variety of squash through time.

Beans

Evidence of domesticated common beans (*Phaseolus vulgaris*) in 21 of 48 rooms belongs almost exclusively to the Secondary occupation (Bohrer, Chapter 38). Three potential Chacoan strata with common beans exhibited evidence of contamination with Secondary occupation trash. More than 80 percent of the bean evidence was preserved in trash and roof strata, and two roofs (100W and 127W) apparently served as outdoor preparation areas. Beans were typically recovered as burned cotyledons (seed halves), although others were preserved whole, or were even still in their pods. The presence of beans in six of seven Secondary occupation storerooms

suggests that beans may have ranked second to maize in importance of cultivated plants.

Gourd

Clear evidence of *Lagenaria* use comes only from the Chacoan occupation (Bohrer and Doebley, Chapter 35). A single fragment of rind from Room 62W has the unique shape of a dipper gourd handle. Since no gourd seeds were ever recovered, this most likely represents a trade item.

Cotton

Gossypium fiber, cordage, and textile fragments were found in very limited amounts, indicating that cotton was known to the Salmon inhabitants (Bohrer and Doebley, Chapter 35). Small pieces of cloth and cordage segments were preserved in Chacoan trash in Room 62W and in Secondary occupation contexts. Notably lacking are the cotton seeds, bolls, and other parts of the cotton plant that would suggest cultivation in the area. If people had access to cotton seeds, they likely would have parched some for consumption. Evidence for weaving cotton cloth appears to be very restricted in the San Juan Basin, relative to the Kayenta, Hohokam, Sinagua, and Salado regions to the south (Webster, Chapter 46). Webster reports that imported cotton fiber may have been woven in limited amounts in the Chacoan ritual core of the pueblo in Room 81W, where four weaving tools were found. However, she thinks that most of the textile production focused on *Yucca* (yucca) baskets, sandals, and mats, and on turkey-feather blankets and rabbit fur robes. Some cotton cloth may also have been acquired in trade.

Amaranth

Two single instances (one Chacoan, one post-Secondary) of poorly preserved seed coats only hint that the domesticated grain amaranth (cf. *Amaranthus hypochondriacus*) may have been in use at Salmon (Bohrer and Doebley, Chapter 35). However, this is not considered reliable evidence to indicate a cultivated amaranth.

Cholla

The case for cholla bud use begins with evidence of charred cholla (*Opuntia* sp.) flower buds from the floor of the Tower Kiva (64W), and cholla pollen in trash strata. The presence of cholla pollen on all Chacoan and Secondary floors of Room 93W suggests its use through time (K. Adams 1980 and Chapter 39). Evidence for cholla management is primarily based on pollen grains, associated with Chacoan occupation rooms (31W and 93W), that do not conform to the range in size of pollen of modern cholla plants growing in the area. Possible explanations are trade for a variety of cholla that grew elsewhere, or local cultivation of cholla plants incapable of growing in the area without human attention.

WILD PLANTS AS FOODS

Most items on the long list of reproductive plant parts recovered from Salmon Ruin strata were likely used as food. This suggests that wild plant gathering was a regular activity of considerable economic importance, and not merely a means for these agricultural people to survive times of food scarcity (Doebley 1976, 1981, and Chapter 37). K. Adams (Chapter 36) has provided a broad overview of wild plant use at Salmon in a study of 216 flotation samples from 28 room floors and 36 trash units. Only floors that were well preserved, undisturbed by rodents or roots, adequately sampled, and not overlain by trash were included in the analysis. All six Chacoan floors studied were unburned, as were 11 of 22 Secondary floors. Thirteen Chacoan trash strata and 23 Secondary trash strata were included.

Evidence for subsistence use included condition (charred or not), nature of associated pollen evidence, context, and association with other known foods. Each taxon was also evaluated for the likelihood of incidental introduction into the Salmon community. Widespread and common taxa were associated with both Chacoan and Secondary occupations, and rare taxa were most often associated only with the Secondary occupation.

Widespread

Cheno-Am and *Portulaca* seeds recovered from 50 or more of the 64 locations studied (K. Adams, Chapter 36) represent plants of disturbed habitats—such as fallow agricultural fields and trash heaps—that are able to produce quantities of both greens and seeds. Cheno-Am and *Portulaca* seeds were also found in nearly all trash samples examined from a separate study of 17 rooms and plaza test pits (Doebley 1976:103; Doebley, Chapter 37) and from three habitation floors within Room 93W (K. Adams 1980 and Chapter 39). Charred Cheno-Am seeds adhering to the interior of a large corrugated sherd in storage on a roof (Room 90W) suggests occasional storage of the seeds (K. Adams, Chapter 36), and their presence in human coprolites indicates consumption (Bohrer, Chapter 38). The frequency of clumps of Cheno-Am pollen grains on floors could indicate that young *Chenopodium* or *Amaranthus* plants in the flowering stage were harvested as greens (Bohrer, Chapter 38).

Common

In 23–35 of the 64 locations studied by K. Adams (Chapter 36), the following taxa were commonly encountered—grass grains (*Muhlenbergia*, *Stipa hymenoides* as *Oryzopsis hymenoides*, Paniceae/*Panicum*, and *Sporobolus*), tansy mustard seeds (*Descurainia*), seeds of various cacti (*Echinocereus*, *Opuntia*, and *Sclerocatus*), spurge seeds (*Euphorbia glyptosperma*), groundcherry seeds (*Physalis*/*P. longifolia*), and reproductive parts of a number of riparian resources (Cyperaceae, *Carex*, *Eleocharis montana*, *Scirpus*/*S. acutus*).

In his separate trash study, Doebley (1976, 1981, and Chapter 37) also noted that wild grasses were recovered (n = 12) more often than maize (n = 11). He pointed out that the Hopi have long considered grasses to be among the most important of wild foods, with *Stipa hymenoides* and *Sporobolus* being chief in importance (Whiting 1939:18). Doebley's study also identified the rest of the common resources recognized by K. Adams (Chapter 36). A look at plant remains from three Room 93W floors (K. Adams, Chapters 36 and 39) was clearly able to associate widespread and common seeds associated with metates as indicating grinding (tansy mustard, pigweed, purslane, goosefoot, stickleaf), and seeds recovered from within hearths as suggesting parching prior to consumption (tansy mustard, pigweed, goosefoot, stickleaf).

Both piñon (*Pinus edulis*) nuts and juniper (*Juniperus osteosperma*) berries (cones) may have been common foods, although the evidence at Salmon Pueblo is contradictory. Few plants rank higher for energy return (1200–1700 kilocalories) per hour of labor than piñon nuts (Barlow 2002: Figure 5), and the digestible portion of juniper berries provides 5200–5500 kilocalories per kilogram, enough to suggest the presence of fat (Lentz 1979:112). At Salmon, however, no evidence of either resource was found in 216 flotation samples from 64 separate floor and midden locations (K. Adams, Chapter 36) or in additional midden samples analyzed by Doebley (1976 and Chapter 37), unless the very best and worst conditions of preservation are included. In contrast, parched piñon nuts or nutshell fragments were preserved as macrofossils in more than half (25 of 48) of excavated rooms (K. Adams, Chapter 40), and juniper (*Juniperus osteosperma*) berries (cones) were frequently recovered in conjunction with fragile squash seed evidence (Lentz 1979 and Chapter 41). More than 80 percent of 53 well-preserved strata in Room 62W contained evidence of both piñon and juniper (Bohrer, Chapter 38). The fact that they are both routinely absent from floors may be due to their larger size, making them easy to retrieve when spilled. That they are routinely absent from flotation samples within middens suggests that under relatively poor conditions of preservation, they degrade. It appears that both size and preservation conditions can notably influence the recovery of piñon and juniper remains.

Rare

Reproductive parts of a long list of plants were recovered from 1 to 20 of the 64 locations studied; many of these were present only in deposits of the Secondary occupation (K. Adams, Chapter 36). The case for the use of vegetative parts of plants is weak, but such use could have included young goosefoot, pigweed and purslane greens, squash flowers, young beeweed plants, roots/rhizomes of riparian plants such as sedge or cattail, other roots, wild grass leaves and yucca leaves as quids, juniper bark, prickly pear pads, and maize cobs (Bohrer, Chapter 38).

TWO WILD FOODS OF SPECIAL INTEREST

An intensive study by Lentz (1979 and Chapter 41) focused on the more than 1600 juniper seeds and cones (berries) found in stratified trash, pits (including burials), roof-fall, and other locations. Morphometric comparisons with modern *Juniperus* species reveal that they are all seeds of *Juniperus osteosperma*, the local juniper in the region. Seeds and cones were both charred and uncharred, some had insect borer holes, and some were likely carried in by rodents in prehistory (Doebley 1976:98) or recently. However, the majority of them were considered cultural, and were interpreted as food, based on their presence in 76 stratified trash strata in association with other foods, in burned store rooms of the Secondary occupation, and in collapsed roof strata where they were either drying on the rooftops or being processed there—a common location for milling by the Secondary occupants. Seven charred juniper seeds on the bench in the Tower Kiva (64W) were associated with maize, several other cultigens, and grinding stones. Juniper was also used as a funerary item, for adornment, and to satisfy a medicinal or ceremonial need.

In an effort to understand the potential contribution of juniper cones to the Salmon diet, Lentz (1979) made estimates of the available juniper woodland within 6 miles; the caloric value of juniper cones minus the indigestible component, which ranged between 5200 and 5500 kcal/kg; and the caloric requirements of a population of 300 individuals, assuming an average daily need of ~2430 kcal. He determined that the juniper woodland could reason-

ably be expected to provide 52 percent of the required kilocalories per year for 300 occupants of the Salmon community. The fact that juniper remains did not occur routinely in flotation samples from floors and middens may be due to the size and preservation issues discussed above, which may together prevent an accurate estimate of the role of juniper berries in the diet.

The presence of spurge (*Euphorbia glyptosperma*) seeds in conjunction with other foods in Room 93W and in trash deposits (K. Adams, Chapters 36 and 39; Doebley 1976) suggests that it was a food in prehistory. Spurge remains were also recovered within a milling bin in Secondary occupation Kiva 6A, but not in sediments from around the bin. These findings are surprising, given the generally poisonous nature of spurge plants, yet are supported by its association with other known foods, the contexts in which the seeds were recovered, and limited ethnographic references (K. Adams 1980 and Chapters 36 and 39). Bohrer (Chapter 42) has compiled additional ethnographic literature speculating that toasted spurge seeds were formerly used as a flavoring or symbolic flavoring added to dishes made of corn meal for use in both everyday life and ceremony. Parching, roasting, and heating are all known detoxification methods, including for some members of the spurge family and genus (Johns 1988: Table 1).

COMPARISON OF CHACOAN VS. SECONDARY SUBSISTENCE

Cultivated Crops

The presence of maize in 77 percent of flotation samples from Chacoan trash (10 of 13 strata) compared with 57 percent of flotation samples from Secondary trash (13 of 23 strata) suggests greater agricultural reliance on maize during the Chacoan period, although a larger sample is needed to demonstrate statistical significance (Bohrer and Doebley, Chapter 35; Doebley and Bohrer 1983). This difference is important because it is clear that the Secondary occupants gathered a wider variety of wild plants, as discussed below.

In addition to recognizing maize as an important subsistence resource, maize ear variation was studied to examine the social behavior of the Salmon inhabitants (Bohrer and Doebley, Chapter 35; Doebley and Bohrer 1983). Multivariate statistical analyses of a number of cob and cupule traits for 12 samples of 22–30 specimens each revealed a number of interesting differences:

1. Maize of the Chacoan occupation at Salmon averaged 11.9 rows per ear, similar to some Pueblo II

Chacoan sites (Cutler and Meyer 1965; Judd 1954) and greater than the average row number of Secondary occupation maize at Salmon (10.77 rows/ear) and other Pueblo III sites on Mesa Verde (~10 rows/ear; Cutler 1966; Cutler and Meyer 1965). Differences in the shape and general appearance of Chacoan maize cupules (narrow, open cupules) versus Secondary cupules (broad, collapsed cupules) also suggest differences in maize varieties, with the Secondary maize being more like maize de ocho, an 8-rowed, wide-cupule maize (Galinat and Gunnerson 1963; Galinat 1970) introduced into the northern Southwest sometime after AD 900.

2. Maize recovered from nonceremonial rooms of the Chacoan occupation exhibits features dissimilar to that of comparable rooms of the Secondary occupation; for example, Chacoan maize had more rows of kernels and narrower cupules than Secondary maize.

3. Maize morphology appears to have changed over time during the Secondary occupation. Maize from roof strata of the early Secondary period showed significantly differences in rachis diameter, rachis segment length, and cupule depth, as well as the ratio of rachis diameter to rachis segment length, compared to later Secondary maize.

4. Early Secondary maize from nonceremonial contexts in the northwest and southeast sectors of the pueblo are similar, revealing no evidence to suggest that separate lineages maintained distinct maize varieties.

5. Maize from a Chacoan ceremonial room (81W) had more rows of kernels and were generally larger ears than everyday Chacoan maize;

6. Maize from a Secondary ceremonial room (64W) also had more rows of kernels but had generally smaller ears than everyday Secondary maize.

7. If the maize types recovered from Chacoan (81W) and Secondary (64W) ceremonial rooms represent ritual maize, then the differences between them are large.

8. A study of kernel endosperm texture (flour, flint, or pop) revealed the proportion of maize types for both occupations to be similar—Chacoan had 27.3% flour and 72.7% pop/flint and Secondary had 36.7% flour and 63.3% pop/flint. This supported expectations that the trough metates (75%) most often used by Chacoan occupants were better suited to crushing kernels with hard, translucent starch, but contradicted expectations that the predominance of slab metates (75%) used by the Secondary occupants would have been better suited for grinding soft floury kernels. Postcontact practices such as parching or popping maize kernels prior to grinding, or

preparing maize dishes via boiling, suggest that other factors may have been operating between the two Salmon occupations with regard to maize kernel preparation.

Wild Foods

Studies comparing plant remains between the Chacoan and Secondary occupations have indicated an increased reliance on wild foods, including drought-resistant juniper berries, by the Secondary occupants (K. Adams, Chapter 36; Doebley 1976 and Chapter 37; Lentz 1979 and Chapter 41). In Doebley's study of flotation and pollen samples from 41 trash strata chosen to represent both spatial and temporal variation, the Chacoan occupants utilized 19 wild plants, versus 28 by the Secondary occupants. After samples from the best (Room 62W) and poorest (plaza) preserved locations were removed from consideration, the mean number of wild plant taxa (4.25) in flotation samples from trash (n = 14) of the Chacoan occupation was also lower than such taxa (6.53) in trash samples (n = 17) of the Secondary occupation (Doebley, Chapter 37). A two-sided Wilcoxon rank sum test produced a 95 percent probability that the results were produced by a mechanism other than chance. Although the same trend was seen in the mean number of cultural plant taxa per pollen sample in trash, small sample size weakened the pollen results. Noncultural explanations for these trends, such as differential preservation conditions and differential soil pH, were reviewed and dismissed as unlikely to have affected these values (Doebley 1976).

Doebley considered cultural explanations to be more likely to account for these differences (1976). For example, it is reasonable that two groups of individuals with different backgrounds and lifestyles would also have different preferences for food. However, such an explanation is difficult to test with this data set alone, as it requires a regional examination of archaeobotanical records. Another possibility that Doebley considered was that a decrease in agricultural productivity led to an increased reliance on wild foods by the Secondary occupants. In this case, one might expect that plants growing farther from the community would necessarily increase in presence (e.g. piñon nuts or broad-leaf yucca fruits), but this did not occur. Nor was there a strong preference by Secondary occupants for perennial resources over annual resources, similar to Hopi preferences when crops failed (Doebley 1976:88). However, an unfavorable climatic period between AD 1270 and 1300, including a long drought, lowering water tables, and stream entrenchment, most likely did affect the agricultural productivity of the Salmon folks in a negative way (Van West and Dean 2000). These climatic difficulties, coupled with increasing population pressure in the late 1200s, together would explain why the Secondary occupants experienced an increased reliance on wild foods.

Lentz also tested the hypothesis that the Secondary occupants relied more on wild foods than the Chacoans did (1979:83–92). He examined the ratio of domesticated *Cucurbita* seeds to wild juniper seeds for eight primary strata (16.12) and 11 Secondary strata (3.59). A chi-square test indicated that the difference is significant at the 99 percent level, supporting Doebley's (Chapter 37) suggestion of a heavier reliance on wild foods later in time. K. Adams's large study of 216 flotation samples from trash and well-preserved floors of both occupations revealed that 15 plant taxa were recovered only in Secondary occupation strata, many of them likely foods. Finally, although it appears that the Chacoans relied less on piñon nuts (found in only 9 rooms) than the Secondary occupants did (found in 22 rooms), the original study (K. Adams, Chapter 40) made no estimate of relative stratum preservation, which may have skewed these results.

Elsewhere in the region, a study of coprolites at Mesa Verde revealed an increase in the amount of maize and the number of wild plants consumed during the AD 1200s (Stiger 1977, 1979). At Antelope House, the use of squash, piñon nuts, beeweed, and purslane decreased in the same period (Fry and Hall 1975). Squash and piñon nuts are both particularly susceptible to drought. A separate study of coprolites at Salmon Ruin (Reinhard, Chapter 44) focused on parasites and their relation to health.

DIETARY COMPONENTS IN HUMAN COPROLITES

Direct evidence of food consumption preserved in human coprolites from Rooms 62W and 81W confirms a number of Chacoan and Secondary occupation food choices (Bohrer, Chapter 38). The following list must be considered incomplete, as it does not include identification of epidermal tissues that might reveal consumption of young leafy greens or underground parts such as roots and tubers. Chacoans consumed hawthorn (*Crataegus*) fruit, partly roasted juniper twigs, and buffalo berry (*Shepherdia argenta*) seeds. They may also have consumed beans, beeweed (*Cleome*) seeds, squash seeds, juniper bark, prickly pear seeds, and lemonade berry (*Rhus aromatica*) seeds. Secondary occupants also ate squash, beeweed, and lemonade berry seeds, along with goosefoot, purslane, and groundcherry seeds.

Coprolites also provide information on the general health of Salmon inhabitants (Reinhard, Chapter 44). Salmon coprolites lacked giardia (*Giardia lamblia*, see Chapter 45), likely because the nearby water sources included the flowing San Juan River and other smaller drainages. The low prevalence of pinworm infection among the Secondary occupation at Salmon may have been due to people living in open second-story rooms with adequate air currents, and to the use of specific rooms as latrines (e.g. 62W), which could have slowed or stopped the spread of parasites among the population.

SECONDARY STORAGE ROOMS OR ROOFTOPS

Seven burned Secondary occupation roofs, sandwiched between unburned strata, were considered prime locations to study burned associated plant remains (Bohrer, Chapter 38). These were characterized by the presence of maize cobs and kernels, beans, squash, a diversity of wild foods, raw plant materials (wood, bark, stems), finished items (leaf knots, plaited mat fragments, cordage, textile fragments), lithics, and ceramic sherds. Altogether these assemblages suggest that these rooms functioned as storage rooms. The most consistently recovered plant items were cultivated maize and beans. Wild foods in storage included Cheno-Am seeds, the fruits of lemonade berry (*Rhus aromatica*, as *R. trilobata*), juniper fruit and seeds, piñon nuts, prickly pear pads, and cholla flower buds. Unidentified tubers indicate the use of underground plant parts that are rarely preserved in the archaeobotanical record. Raw materials in storage included coils of smooth bark, grass stems, and yucca leaves. Basketry fragments in association with fused maize kernels suggest a storage container. Pieces of textile, matting, netting, twine, and braided fiber were either parts of storage containers or items in storage. The presence of rodent feces suggests rodent problems with stored materials. A storeroom on the ground floor (30W) contained maize cobs stacked along the south wall of a floor, next to the wall. Beans were also in storage there when a roof burned and fell onto the stored crops during the Secondary occupation. Two other ground-floor rooftops of the Secondary occupation (100W and perhaps 127W, although it was probably two stories high) served as outdoor processing areas as well as storage. The plant inventory of these two outdoor locations is quite similar to that of the interior storage rooms discussed above (e.g. maize, beans, squash, cholla flower buds, and juniper berries). Perhaps cholla flower buds were in storage in a vessel, as they are the only food product in this assemblage available in the springtime, and all other foods identified there ripen in the fall.

PLANT REMAINS ASSOCIATED WITH KIVAS

Interest in the types of activities that occur in kivas or other recognized ceremonial rooms is high. Plant remains can comprise evidence for either ceremonial or everyday usage of plants, such as food preparation. The evidence for ceremonial use of maize pollen in blessings is considered first (Bohrer, Chapter 42). Two Chacoan nonkiva ceremonial rooms (30W and 62W) produced maize aggregates and maize pollen percentages above 80 percent. Two Secondary kiva floors (6A, 124A) did not yield broadly distributed maize pollen aggregates, although aggregates in a slab-lined bin in Kiva 6A may be residue of grinding maize tassels on a metate within the bin. Some ceremonial activities with maize were also associated with nonkiva locations, including Chacoan rooms with features (93W, 101W) and without features (30W, 56W, 62W, 82W, 89W), and Secondary rooms with features (93W) and without features (51W, 57W, 58W). Some of these rooms (51W, 57W, 58W, 62W) are close to the Tower Kiva (64W), which did not preserve pollen due to destruction by an extremely intense fire.

A variety of seeds of economic importance were preserved on three Secondary occupation kiva floors (Rooms 6A, 64W, and 124W), suggesting that secular aspects of life occurred in these locations (Bohrer, Chapter 38). Whether this food was consumed during special ceremonies cannot be determined. Within Kiva 6A, seeds were concentrated in and near a milling bin with the grinding stone removed. There, the concentration of Cheno-Am and tansy mustard seeds is 100 times greater than elsewhere on the kiva floor, and heavy concentrations of purslane, stickleaf, and spurge seeds are unique to the bin area. These remains accompany a high concentration (47%) and presence of maize pollen aggregates within the bin, perhaps where maize tassels were also ground to remove the pollen. Most of the seed types from this milling bin area were also recovered from beneath the metate on a habitation floor of Room 93W (K. Adams 1980 and Chapter 39), lending support to the notion that the former grinding stone was also used to grind food.

The two other Secondary kivas (64W and 124W) preserved a broad spectrum of small seeds that are regarded as foods. When the fire precipitated the swift depopulation of the Tower Kiva (64W), many food plants were burned on the floor. Among these were maize ears, beans in pods, squash rind, tansy mustard seeds, stickleaf seeds, cholla flower buds, young prickly pear pads, bee weed seeds, purslane seeds, piñon nuts, and juniper seeds. These clearly reflect more than one season of gathering.

SUMMARY

Drawn from many studies and reports, the plant record of Chacoan and Secondary occupants of Salmon Ruin is rich in detail and insight. Despite the fact that the relative recovery of Secondary materials was significantly higher than that of plant remains of the Chacoan period, multiple seasons of systematic archaeological sampling of macrofossils, flotation, and pollen samples have provided a comparative basis for viewing subsistence and other uses of plants through time.

The basis of subsistence for both occupations appears to have been their own agricultural efforts to grow maize, beans, and squash. Maize of the two occupations differed in notable ways. Gourd containers may have been traded in, along with limited amounts of cotton fibers and cloth. Chacoans may have managed a type of cholla plant, or traded for its fruit. Wild plant gathering was a regular activity, particularly of weedy plants that grew in cultivated fields and other disturbed locations. Grass grains, cactus fruit, piñon nuts, and juniper berries were also among the gathered resources, along with many others. The long list of foods spans nearly all the seasons of the year, except winter, when plant products such as juniper berries, cactus pads, and tree bark could still be found.

A comparison of foods between the Chacoan and Secondary occupations reveals some differences. The Chacoans utilized maize more often, and sought fewer wild plants. Coprolite preservation reveals that during the Secondary occupation, people were eating corn cobs, juniper bark, and yucca leaves—none of them particularly nutritious, but filling. A shortage of maize and an increasing reliance on wild plants and less-preferred foods may have been one result of a late thirteenth century environment that became less predictable and dependable for maize farmers.

In addition to subsistence, plants served many other needs. Juniper seeds were used as adornment, a range of conifer and some nonconifer trees were sought as roofing elements, piñon and juniper were burned regularly for cooking, heating, and light, juniper bark served many household needs, and yucca leaves were fashioned into such things as baskets, mats, and sandals. It appears that maize pollen was used in ritual contexts, as was cattail pollen. Food placed in jars perhaps constituted offerings to departed spirits. Many items (peeled sticks, yucca leaves, prickly pear pads, and perishable artifacts) with remnants of pink or red staining may also relate to ritual needs. Juniper twigs in many contexts could have been routinely used in medicinal ways.

The storage habits of Secondary occupants are known from a number of burned storage locations. Maize and beans were present most often, along with weed seeds and many seeds and fruits of perennial plants. Coils of bark, grass stems, and yucca leaves in storage suggest materials for later construction of textiles, matting, twine, and braided fibers. In one case, maize was stacked along the south wall of a Secondary period ground floor.

Kivas contained evidence of both ceremonial activities and everyday life. Maize pollen aggregates can only be explained by the intentional gathering of maize pollen. Charred seeds considered to represent economic resources on three Secondary occupation kiva floors indicate secular use of the structures. When the Tower Kiva (64W) burned at the end of the Secondary period, plants in storage reflected more than one season of gathering, and represented many of the foods found in nonceremonial contexts and in middens.

Most of the plant materials of both occupations of Salmon Pueblo were available locally, or possibly within a day's journey. Some, such as the large conifer roof elements, clearly required a trip and

some effort. The range of plant parts of juniper trees strongly suggests that a juniper woodland surrounded the pueblo; piñon trees likely were not as abundant. Plants obtained through trade included cotton, gourds, screwbeans, and a rare form of cholla cactus that has not been found in the local area in modern times. Salmon farmers may have, in turn, traded maize for these nonlocal resources.

The question of final Puebloan depopulation seems a complex one. Inter or intrapueblo stresses were likely responsible for the final Tower Kiva fire that caused numerous deaths. The plant record suggests that final pueblo depopulation was related in part to difficulties in acquiring maize, either because the environment had become unpredictable or perhaps because the productivity of fields had declined due to a few centuries of use. One result seems to have been the increased use of wild plants, some of them of low nutritional value. The possibility that these subsistence differences related to social or political influences, or simply to differences in food preferences between the Chacoan and Secondary occupations, cannot be ruled out. These explanations require inclusion of multiple archaeological data sets in addition to plant remains, and a regional comparative framework of subsistence and plant use information from contemporary great house and post–great house communities.

Chapter 44

COPROLITE ANALYSIS FROM SALMON RUINS: THE SAN JUAN OCCUPATION

by Karl J. Reinhard, Sara LeRoy-Toren, and Dennis R. Danielson

Fry (1977) was the first researcher to use coprolite analysis to investigate ancestral Pueblo (Anasazi) subsistence. Minnis (1989) and Reinhard (1992, 1996) later used Fry's approach to identify regional Pueblo dietary variation. However, Reinhard (1996) found that coprolites from Salmon Ruin did not provide the same quality of data as coprolites from other sites from other regions. Initially, Reinhard (1992) suggested that preservation conditions limited the recovery of plant macrofossils. Since that time, however, the methods applied to Salmon Ruin coprolites have been refined to include phytolith analysis (Danielson 1993), starch granule analysis (presented here), pollen concentration analysis (Reinhard et al. 2006), and new macrobotanical analysis (presented here). These new analytical methods show that Salmon Ruin coprolites are in fact well preserved, and they represent a different cuisine and food processing strategy than previously described for ancestral Puebloans.

MATERIALS AND METHODS

The coprolite sampling strategies at Salmon (Reinhard 1996) were devised to include many defecations by separate humans. Only one Salmon latrine (Room 62) was sampled, but it was a very large, stratified deposit of coprolites; thousands of these were excavated and curated. A coprolite sample was taken from each alternate 10 cm level in alternate 1 m grids (Reinhard 1996).

Ultimately, 112 coprolites from Room 62 were selected for parasitological and macrofloral analysis (Reinhard 1996). Twenty of these were also analyzed for phytolith content (Danielson 1993). Reinhard et al. (2006) analyzed the pollen from 26 coprolites, and LeRoy-Toren analyzed the macrobotanical remains from 24 small fragments that had been retained in 1988 for future analysis. Starch granule, pollen, and other microscopic analyses of these 24 coprolites is ongoing.

Pollen and Starch Granule Processing

In the last decades, a new method of presenting pollen data has been devised (the pollen concentration method) that allows calculation of the approximate number of pollen grains per unit measure of coprolites. In a review of this method, Maher (1981) presented methods for calculating the numbers of pollen grains per gram of sediment using the following formula: Pollen concentration =

$$\frac{(no.\ pollen\ grains\ /\ no.\ marker\ grains) \times no.\ marker\ grains\ added}{weight\ or\ volume\ of\ sediment}$$

In this analysis, the weight of the coprolite sample was used to calculate the numbers of pollen grains per gram of coprolite (pg/gc).

Using Puebloan coprolites from New Mexico, Utah, and Arizona, Reinhard (1993) compared very limited chemical processing to extensive chemical processing. Equal results were achieved with both extremes. The coprolites described here were processed using extensive chemical treatments.

Most Salmon Ruin coprolites provided 1 g fragments to study, but some fragments were only 0.75 g or 0.5 g. The samples were rehydrated in 0.5% trisodium phosphate for 48 hours. After rehydration, macroscopic remains were screened from the microscopic remains and the microscopic residues were washed three times in distilled water. The sediments were treated in approximately 40% hydrochloric acid. After three distilled water washes, the sediments were left for 24 hours in approximately 70% hydrofluoric acid. The samples were washed repeatedly in distilled water until the supernatant was clear. Then after three water washes and one glacial acetic acid wash, the residues were treated with a 20 min acetolysis bath at 100°C. After another glacial acetic acid wash, the samples were then washed repeatedly in distilled water until the supernatant was clear. Finally, the sediments were treated in 0.5% KOH for 2 min and washed in distilled water three times. The samples were then transferred to 1 dram vials and stored in glycerine. At least 200 grains were counted for each sample, and up to 1000 grains were counted for some samples. Single pollen grains and pollen aggregates were counted and tabulated.

Many maize pollen grains were fragmented, broken, or shredded; this was consistent with grains described by Bryant and Morris (1986) that were associated with grinding stones. We counted broken maize grains separately to determine whether there was significance in this observation. Only maize annuli were counted for the fragmented maize grains.

Twenty of the pollen preparations were scanned for starch granules. One slide from each sample was scanned for the presence or absence of starch. Maize starch granules were identified by phase contrast analysis and comparison to starch granule reference collections.

Phytolith Recovery

Phytolith processing followed the procedures given in Danielson and Reinhard (1998). One-gram fragments from each coprolite were rehydrated in 0.5% trisodium phosphate and rinsed with distilled water. Each sample was then placed in a 600 ml glass beaker and immersed in 50% hydrogen peroxide. Then about 20 mg of potassium dichromate were added to the beaker, resulting in a violent reaction that digested most of the coprolite matrix, leaving only the inert structures of silica and calcium oxalate; the extraction of phytoliths from coprolites is very destructive and dangerous. An attempt was made to count 200 phytoliths per sample. Phytoliths were identified based on comparison to phytolith reference collections of Colorado Plateau native plants.

Macroscopic Analysis

The analysis of 112 coprolites 20 years ago was disappointing (Reinhard 1988a, 1992, 1996). Relatively few had identifiable remains, and the coprolites simply did not disaggregate in the standard rehydration solution during the standard 48–72 hour rehydration period. A surprisingly small amount of residue was retained on the 300 μm mesh that separated macroscopic from microscopic remains. Reinhard (1992) thus concluded that the coprolites were poorly preserved.

Reinhard, LeRoy-Toren, and Reinhard's graduate student Dorsey-Vinton later conducted another analysis of coprolites from Chile (Reinhard and LeRoy-Toren, n.d.; Dorsey-Vinton 1997), which led to the discovery that the methods developed in North America were not very successful in the

recovery of dietary components from cultures who processed their foods extensively. Armed with this knowledge, Reinhard and LeRoy-Toren began re-examining the residues. Twenty-four small coprolite fragments were rehydrated for a minimum of 120 hours in 0.5% trisodium phosphate, and the samples were thoroughly disaggregated with a magnetic stirrer. The residue was screened and the macroscopic residues were examined. The unprocessed microscopic residues are still being studied at this writing.

RESULTS

Starch granules were present in 19 of the 20 coprolites examined; the granules are consistent with maize. Phytoliths were rare compared to other Anasazi sites. Only 7 of the 20 coprolites contained sufficient phytoliths to make a 200 count (Table 44.1). All seven of these were dominated by calcium oxalate phytoliths of the Agavaceae and Cactaceae. Silica phytoliths were identified from the Chenopodiaceae, Amaranthaceae, Poaceae, Fabaceae, and Cucurbitaceae families. Agavaceae (consistent with *Yucca*) phytoliths were present in 10 coprolites. Cactaceae (consistent with *Opuntia*, prickly pear) phytoliths were present in nine coprolites. Cheno Am (consistent with Chenopodium and Amaranthus) phytoliths were present in nine coprolites. Phytoliths identifiable only to the family Fabaceae were found in four coprolites, but no phytoliths from *Phaseolus* were found. Squash (*Cucurbita pepo*) phytoliths were found in one coprolite. Ten coprolites contained phytoliths of various types of grass.

Pollen was abundant in all 26 samples (Tables 44.2 and 44.3). The pollen concentrations of some taxa—Asteraceae, Brassicaceae, Cheno Am, *Cleome*, broken maize, whole maize, *Opuntia*, and wild Poaceae—exceeded 10,000 pg/gc. In addition, cultivated *Cucurbita* pollen was present in low concentrations, perhaps indicating human consumption of this taxon.

The macroscopic analysis showed that relatively few of the Salmon Ruin coprolites contain macroscopic residues larger than 300 μm. The mean sample weight for the coprolite fragments was 0.69 g, and the mean residue weight was 0.28 g. Therefore, on the average 59 percent of the sample passed through the screen. As much as 90 percent of some samples or as little as 30 percent of others passed through the screen. Despite this, 22 of 24 coprolites contained identifiable macroscopic remains, which is a better return than the previous analysis (Reinhard 1992).

Sample 24 was of particular interest, because initially it was not clear whether it was in fact a cop-

Table 44.1. Phytolith percentages from Salmon Ruin (n = 20). The numbers are percentage expressions of the total count for each coprolite. The total phytoliths counted are also presented.

Taxa	Coprolite									
	1	2	3	4	5	6	7	8	9	10
Yucca	0	0	0	0	0.5	0	0	0	34	0
Cactaceae	0	0	0	0	0	0	0	0	46	0
Cheno Am	0	0	0	0	0	0	0	0	20	0
Festucoid	0	0	47	0	0.5	0	0	0	0	0
Panicoid	100	0	0	0	0	0	0	0	0	0
Other grass	0	0	0	0	0	0	0	0	0	0
Fabaceae	0	0	53	0	0	0	0	0	0	0
Cucurbita pepo	0	0	0	0	0	0	0	0	0	0
Unidentifiable	0	0	0	0	99	0	0	0	0	0
Total count	1	0	17	0	20	0	0	0	215	0

(Table 44.1, continued)

Taxa	Coprolite									
	11	12	13	14	15	16	17	18	19	20
Yucca	4	86	81	47	88	85	95	9	0	0
Cactaceae	52	0	13	13	2	1	2	83	4	0
Cheno Am	44	0	5	38	2	5	3	8	51	0
Festucoid	0	5	0.4	0.5	8	4	0	0	41	0
Panicoid	0	9	0	0	0	0	0	0	2	9
Other grass	0	0	0	0.5	0	0	0	0	0	0
Fabaceae	0	0	0	0.5	0	5	0	0	1	0
Cucurbita pepo	0	0	0	0	0.5	0	0	0	0	0
Unidentifiable	0	100	0	0	0	0	0	0	0	0
Total count	273	55	228	207	179	221	239	208	74	0

rolite. It was composed of squash seeds adhered in a fibrous matrix; it might have been a deposit of seeds cleaned out of a squash and thrown away. The analysis revealed small animal bone fragments as well as the seeds, which is consistent with coprolites that sometimes contain fragmented rodent or lagomorph bone. Therefore, it is likely that whole squash seeds were eaten.

Cheno Am flour was present in five coprolites in the form of finely ground seeds—this was a new find. Apparently more thorough rehydration and disaggregation released these small particles more efficiently than in the past. Another five coprolites contained whole *Chenopodium* seeds. Therefore, people were eating the seeds or fruits of this plant.

Bark was found in two coprolites—this was also a new find. Another new discovery was *Helianthus* achenes in two coprolites. It is apparent that *Physalis* fruit was eaten because seeds and/or fruit skin (pericarp) consistent with *Physalis* were found in four coprolites. In one of these, only ground *Physalis* seeds were found, indicating that the whole fruits were eaten and that in some cases the fruits or just the seeds were processed. The fruits of *Echinocereus* were also eaten as indicated by the presence of its seeds in one coprolite.

Maize was evident in various forms including pericarp fragments, husk, and silk. Nine coprolites contained maize remains. This value is slightly lower than in Reinhard's previous study (1992).

Table 44.2. Pollen concentration values (number of pollen grains per gram of coprolite, pg/gc) for 26 coprolites from Salmon Ruin.

Taxa	Coprolite								
	1	2	3	4	5	6	7	8	9
Apiaceae	–	–	–	285	–	–	3,800	–	–
Artemisia	6,270	1,524	276	–	–	–	–	–	–
Asteraceae HS	1,425	–	69	–	7,600	–	–	1,221	–
Asteraceae LS	7,695	1,368	622	1700	–	1,256	–	–	–
Brassicaceae	285	–	–	–	–	–	30,400	–	–
Carex	285	–	–	–	–	–	–	–	–
Cheno Am	7,695	80,256	8,291	3705	273,600	2,511	–	1,221	–
Cleome	855	9,576	967	62,415	53,200	1,216,000	3,750,600	–	–
Cucurbita	–	–	–	–	–	–	–	407	–
Ephedra	–	456	–	–	–	–	–	407	–
Equisetum	–	–	–	–	–	–	–	–	–
Eriogonum	–	–	–	–	–	–	–	–	–
Fabaceae	–	–	–	–	–	–	–	–	–
Juniperus	4,560	456	69	570	–	–	–	–	–
Ligulaflorae	285	–	–	–	–	–	–	–	–
Liliaceae	–	–	–	–	–	–	7,600	–	–
Maize broken	855	1,814	2,902	855	5,145,200	11,300	–	814	589,650
Maize whole	1,425	3,192	898	855	1,725,200	25,111	–	407	711,511
Opuntia	–	–	–	–	–	7,533	–	401,850	–
Pinus	3,420	1,368	484	–	–	–	–	407	–
Plantago	–	–	–	–	–	2,511	3,800	–	–
Poaceae	1,710	912	207	1,140	592,800	–	–	–	–
Polemonium	–	–	–	–	–	–	–	–	–
Quercus	–	–	–	–	–	1,256	–	–	–
Rhus	–	–	–	–	–	–	–	–	–
Rosaceae	–	–	–	–	–	–	–	–	1,310
Sarcobatus	855	–	–	–	–	–	–	–	–
Salix	–	–	–	–	–	–	–	–	–
Shepherdia	–	456	–	–	–	–	–	–	–
Sphaeralcea	–	–	–	–	–	–	–	–	–
Typha	–	–	–	–	–	–	–	–	–
Unknown	7,125	456	–	–	–	–	–	407	–
Unidentifiable	23,085	912	1,244	–	1,520	–	3,800	–	–

(Table 44.2, continued)

Taxa	Coprolite								
	10	11	12	13	14	15	16	17	18
Apiaceae	–	–	–	–	224	–	–	–	–
Artemisia	–	–	–	1,382	224	570	283	–	–
Asteraceae HS	39,086	200,018	814	–	2,235	570	50,122	80	1,322
Asteraceae LS	–	–	2,443	1,382	5,141	1,140	2,073	400	330
Brassicaceae	–	–	–	–	–	950	188	240	–
Carex	–	–	–	–	–	–	–	–	–
Cheno Am	19,542	5,182	4,071	6,909	7,153	2,850	5,276	2,720	1,487
Cleome	6,364,457	29,018	56,593	1,355,561	5,365	78,470	4,522	–	133,165
Cucurbita	–	–	–	–	–	–	660	320	–
Ephedra	–	–	–	–	–	–	–	–	–
Equisetum	–	–	–	–	–	190	–	–	–
Eriogonum	–	–	–	–	447	–	–	–	–
Fabaceae	–	–	–	–	–	2,470	–	–	–
Juniperus	–	–	–	–	–	–	–	–	–
Ligulaflorae	–	–	–	–	–	–	–	–	–
Liliaceae	–	–	–	–	–	190	–	240	–
Maize broken	39,086	133,691	6,921	–	3,129	8,852	471	6,640	–
Maize whole	45,600	664,309	1,629	–	10,059	48,590	565	5,280	–
Opuntia	–	–	–	8,291	–	40,280	–	–	–
Pinus	–	–	2,036	–	2,459	190	848	80	330
Plantago	–	–	–	–	–	–	–	–	–
Poaceae	–	2,073	1,221	9,673	5,812	1,520	848	80	165
Polemonium	–	–	–	–	–	–	–	–	–
Quercus	–	–	–	–	447	–	–	–	–
Rhus	–	–	2,443	–	224	–	188	–	–
Rosaceae	–	–	–	–	–	–	–	–	–
Sarcobatus	–	1,036	–	–	447	570	94	634	496
Salix	–	–	–	–	1,788	190	94	–	–
Shepherdia	–	–	–	–	–	–	–	–	–
Sphaeralcea	–	–	–	–	224	190	–	–	–
Typha	–	–	407	–	–	–	–	–	–
Unknown	–	–	–	–	2,235	950	–	–	330
Unidentifiable	6,514	–	3,257	1,382	2,012	3,420	565	480	496

(Table 44.2, continued)

Taxa	Coprolite							
	19	20	21	22	23	24	25	26
Apiaceae	–	156	–	–	–	442	–	–
Artemisia	–	156	–	–	2,974	442	–	–
Asteraceae HS	3,257	312	–	633	3,635	–	–	–
Asteraceae LS	–	937	–	1,267	11,896	2,209	–	950
Brassicaceae	–	–	–	–	–	442	–	1,900
Carex	–	–	–	–	–	–	–	–
Cheno Am	8,686	1,249	–	4,433	8,922	5,744	80,108	9,500
Cleome	1,060,743	11,556	2,926,000	20,266	42,296	412,251	1,472,757	931,000
Cucurbita	1,086	2,811	–	–	–	–	–	–
Ephedra	–	–	–	633	1,322	–	–	–
Equisetum	–	312	–	–	330	–	–	–
Eriogonum	–	–	–	–	–	–	–	–
Fabaceae	1,086	–	–	633	–	–	–	–
Juniperus	–	–	–	–	–	–	–	–
Ligulaflorae	–	–	–	–	–	–	–	–
Liliaceae	–	312	–	–	330	–	–	–
Maize broken	1,086	5,153	9,500	51,933	661	5,744	–	950
Maize whole	1,086	937	–	53,200	6,278	6,186	–	–
Opuntia	–	156	–	–	–	–	–	–
Pinus	1,086	156	–	–	18,835	1,326	–	1,900
Plantago	–	–	–	–	–	–	–	–
Poaceae	–	156	76,000	633	12,557	3,977	–	1,900
Polemonium	–	–	–	–	330	–	–	–
Quercus	–	–	–	–	661	–	–	–
Rhus	–	–	–	–	–	442	–	–
Rosaceae	–	–	–	–	–	–	–	–
Sarcobatus	5,429	468	–	–	2,643	3,535	6,162	950
Salix	–	–	–	–	330	–	–	–
Shepherdia	–	–	–	–	–	–	–	–
Sphaeralcea	–	–	–	–	–	–	–	–
Typha	2,171	–	–	–	–	–	–	–
Unknown	–	–	–	–	5,948	–	–	–
Unidentifiable	1,086	2,342	4,433	–	8,591	5,744	3,081	1,900

Table 44.3. Descriptive pollen statistics for Salmon Ruin coprolites.

Pollination	Taxa	Mean pg/gc	Std Dev	No./26	Max Conc.
Anemophilous	*Artemisia*	552.3	1,349.0	10	6,270
	Asteraceae LS	1,646.5	2,723.3	17	11,896
	Cheno Am	21,196.6	55,516.6	23	273,600
	Equisetum	32.0	92.9	3	330
	Juniperus	660.5	1,804.5	10	8,261
	Maize broken	231,815.7	1,008,883.4	22	5,145,200
	Maize total	336,925.3	1,348,019.0	22	6,870,400
	Maize whole	127,396.9	374,700.8	20	1,725,200
	Pinus	1,343.3	3,684.8	15	18,835
	Poaceae	27,437.9	36116,264.0	19	592,800
	Sarcobatus	763.0	1,418.2	13	6,162
	Typha	99.2	430.0	2	2,171
Entomophilous	Asteraceae HS	12,015 .4	40,193.0	16	200,018
	Brassicaceae	1,327.1	5,944.1	7	30,400
	Cleome	769,139.7	1,489,134.7	23	6,364,457
	Cucurbita	203.2	590.3	5	2,811
	Opuntia	17,619.6	78,780.6	5	401,850
	Rhus	126.8	483.0	4	2,443

Note: No./26 is the number of coprolites positive for the specified taxon out of 26 total.

Finally, resin was encountered in one sample. After rehydration, this appeared as a soft, amber-colored, adherent nodule. It looks like tree sap.

DISCUSSION
Starch and Phytoliths

Starch shows how much cultivated maize was eaten, and calcium oxalate phytoliths show how much "starvation food" (yucca leaf bases and prickly pear pads) was consumed. Silica phytoliths indicate the consumption of both cultivated and noncultivated plants.

In general, phytoliths are the most abundant microfossil type in Southwestern coprolites (Reinhard and Danielson 2005). The San Juan Salmon phytolith data can be compared to two other Pueblo sites and an Archaic site on the Colorado Plateau.

Calcium oxalate phytoliths are ubiquitous in coprolites from Dust Devil Cave (n = 17), an Archaic site near Navajo Mountain, Utah. Yucca and/or prickly pear phytoliths are present in every coprolite, and 200 phytolith counts were easily obtained from every sample (Danielson 1993). Reinhard (1985) identified the source of the Agavaceae phytoliths as yucca (*Yucca*). There were also silica phytoliths in the coprolites from the bean family, the grass family, and the Chenopodiaceae or Amaranthaceae families. *Chenopodium* seed and grass seed from the genus

Sporobolus (dropseed) were common foods at Dust Devil Cave (Reinhard 1985).

Pueblo coprolites also contain phytoliths, but they do not make up the high volume of fecal residue as commonly seen in Archaic coprolites. About 10–20 percent of the volume of Archaic coprolites is composed of phytoliths, whereas phytoliths make up less than 10 percent of the volume of Pueblo coprolites.

The phytoliths from the Pueblo site of Bighorn Sheep Ruin in Grand Gulch, Utah contained calcium oxalate and silica phytoliths. All tested coprolites from this site (n = 20) contained abundant phytoliths, with 200 counts achieved for all samples. Identifiable phytoliths were present in 19 coprolites, and one coprolite contained phytoliths of an unknown plant. Calcium oxalate phytoliths from yucca were found in 12 of 20 coprolites. Calcium oxalate phytoliths from prickly pear were found in 10 of 20 coprolites. Fourteen coprolites contained calcium oxalate crystals from one or the other, or both of these plants. Silica phytoliths were present in all coprolites and were more abundant than calcium oxalate phytoliths in 18 samples. Silica phytoliths were from the Chenopodiaceae, Amaranthaceae, Poaceae, Fabaceae, and Cucurbitaceae families. These include cultivated squash (*Cucurbita pepo*) and cultivated bean (*Phaseolus vulgaris*).

All coprolites from Antelope House in Canyon de Chelly, Arizona contained abundant phytoliths; 23 of 25 contained calcium oxalate phytoliths. All coprolites from this site produced 200 counts. Phytoliths of yucca and/or prickly pear were nearly ubiquitous in these samples. However, silica phytoliths were also abundant. Calcium oxalate phytoliths dominated in only nine coprolites. Silica phytoliths were present in 22 coprolites from the same plant families as those for Bighorn Sheep Ruin.

Phytoliths were comparatively rare in Salmon Ruin coprolites. Only 7 of 20 contained sufficient phytoliths to make a 200 count—all were dominated by calcium oxalate phytoliths of yucca and/or prickly pear. Silica phytoliths were encountered from the Chenopodiaceae, Amaranthaceae, Poaceae, Fabaceae, and Cucurbitaceae families. In summary, relative to other Pueblo sites, there was more maize and less "starvation" food eaten during the San Juan occupation of Salmon Ruin. Maize was clearly important in the Salmon Ruin diet, as shown by the presence of maize starch granules in 95 percent of the coprolites.

Pollen Data

The pollen concentration data from Salmon Ruin were compared with a similar analysis of Antelope House (Reinhard et al. 2006); this was the first study to demonstrate the importance of pollen concentration in comparing Pueblo diet and cuisine from different sites. Pollen-rich foods were eaten at both sites, but Antelope House's PIII inhabitants ate more wild foods whereas Salmon inhabitants ate more maize, especially ground maize flour. Pollen and spore-producing organs from standing-water, aquatic plants were common at Antelope House. The concentrations of Typha and Equisetum pollen grains ranged in the tens of millions pg/gc. In contrast, broken maize is more common in Salmon Ruin remains. The highest total concentration of maize, including broken grains and whole grains, was 6,870,400 (pg/gc) at Salmon Ruin compared to a maximum of 3,803,800 pg/gc for Antelope House. In general, pollen grains from maize are more common in Salmon Ruin coprolites, as seen in the higher mean (336,925.3 pg/gc) relative to the mean of 153,832.8 pg/gc for Antelope House. The means of whole maize pollen abundance are very similar for the sites; however, four coprolites from Salmon Ruin exceeded 100,000 pg/gc as opposed to one from Antelope House. The near statistically significant chi-square value for the difference in broken maize pollen is amplified by the pollen concentration data (Table 44.3). Both the mean and maximum pg/gc values are higher for Salmon

Ruin. Broken maize pollen grains come from grinding stones and signal the consumption of corn. This indicates that stored, dried maize was more important in the Salmon diet and that Salmon was more reliant on maize.

Antelope House Puebloans consumed more wild plant taxa than Salmon Ruin Puebloans did. The mesic taxa Typha and Equisetum are very important in documenting dietary differences in the coprolite samples. The mean concentration values of Equisetum spores (7354.7 pg/gc for Antelope House vs. 32 pg/gc for Salmon Ruin) and maximum concentration values (159,000 pg/gc for Antelope House vs. 330 pg/gc for Salmon Ruin) support the significant chi-square analysis. These data verify the macrofloral analysis, which indicated that Equisetum strobili was a part of the Antelope House diet. A mean value of 3,884,875 pg/gc and a max value of 101,000,000 pg/gc clearly show that Typha pollen was also consumed at Antelope House. The lower mean of 99.1 pg/gc and maximum of 2171 pg/gc for Salmon Ruin possibly reflect consumption of pollen with drinking water.

Cleome is the most ubiquitous noncultivated dietary pollen type found in Puebloan coprolites (Martin and Sharrock 1964; Williams-Dean 1986; Aasen 1984). Cleome is an insect-pollinated genus that does not occur in coprolites as part of natural contamination from the ambient environment. The mean pg/gc value is greater at Salmon Ruin than at Antelope House, and more Cleome values were above 100,000 pg/gc for Salmon Ruin. Therefore, Cleome is nearly ubiquitous in coprolites from both sites, but has greater concentrations at Salmon Ruin.

Cucurbita and Opuntia buds and/or flowers were prehistoric Puebloan foods that were perhaps exploited to different degrees in different environments. They are obviously seasonal foods and therefore would be eaten only in the spring. After the fruits of the plant form, the pollen grains are gone. Therefore, eating cultivated squash flesh or prickly pear fruit does not introduce pollen into the digestive tract. These types are insect pollinated and do not occur as ambient contamination from the natural environment. In this analysis, neither type was very ubiquitous in Antelope House or Salmon Ruin coprolites. Only three Salmon Ruin coprolites and five Antelope House coprolites have relatively high values of Cucurbita and Opuntia.

The data indicate that both high-spine and low-spine Asteraceae were background and dietary pollen sources. With regard to pollination, low-spine grains are primarily anemophilous whereas high-spine grains tend to be entomophilous; both types occur in a majority of the samples. Usually, the concentrations for these types are under 20,000 grains per gram, but Salmon Ruin produced high numbers of high-spine Asteraceae pollen, at 40,000, 50,000, and 200,000 gp/gc. These higher values suggest that foods rich in Asteraceae pollen were eaten at Salmon, whereas Antelope House produced only one high value for low-spine Asteraceae, at 376,200 pg/gc. Bohrer (1981) showed that sunflower seeds carry high-spine Asteraceae pollen. The source of the low-spine Asteraceae pollen is unknown.

Chenopodium and *Amaranthus* seeds were eaten at almost all Puebloan sites (Reinhard 1992), including Antelope House and Salmon Ruin, as shown by phytolith analysis (Danielson 1993). The high concentrations of Cheno Am pollen in some coprolites from both sites show that foods rich in Cheno Am pollen were part of the diet at both sites; however, the majority of coprolites have lower concentrations of less than 10,000 pg/gc. These lower values are probably the result of ingestion of ambient pollen in air, drinking water, or food contaminated with anemophilous pollen.

Piñon pine, juniper, and/or sumac (*Rhus*) nuts were also eaten at Salmon Ruin (Reinhard 1992, 1996). The Salmon Ruin nuts were fragmented, apparently by a grinding implement, and it is not yet clear whether the nuts are from *Juniperus* or *Rhus*. There are some high-pollen values for *Juniperus*, which might suggest that the nuts are juniper, but *Juniperus* is a prolific wind-borne pollen type so the high values could be from natural pollen rain. Juniper bark was noted in the field in association with Salmon Ruin coprolites.

Poaceae macrofossils, excluding maize, were found in both Antelope House and Salmon Ruin coprolites (Reinhard 1992, 1996). These included seeds of noncultivated grasses and glumes from grass spikelets. Most of the pollen concentration values of wild Poaceae were low and consistent with what might be ingested with water, air, or contaminated food. However, the high values noted from both sites might signal the consumption of foods rich in Poaceae pollen.

In general, there was a relationship between the total pollen content of the coprolites and the number of plant taxa represented in the coprolites. Coprolites with the highest overall pollen concentration values had the fewest number of plant taxa represented by the pollen, whereas coprolites with relatively low pollen concentrations tended to have the largest number of pollen types. This is best seen in the data from Salmon Ruin. The coprolites that contained in excess of 1,000,000 grains per gram generally had an

average of 5.2 taxa identified in the pollen counts. Coprolites with less than 10,000 grains per gram had an average of 11.9 taxa identified in the counts. This trend is also apparent in the Antelope House counts. The coprolites that contained in excess of 1,000,000 grains per gram had an average of 3.7 taxa identified in the pollen counts, and those with less than 10,000 grains per gram had an average of 13.8 taxa identified in the counts. The types that are less likely to appear in higher counts are wind-pollinated, nondietary types. Therefore, it appears that when large amounts of pollen-rich foods are eaten, the ambient pollen becomes infrequent relative to dietary types. This is identical to the pattern previously reported by Reinhard et al. (2002). Therefore, the likelihood of finding the more dilute ambient types is lessened in pollen-rich coprolites.

In summary, the San Juan occupants of Salmon Ruin ate more maize, and especially ground maize flour, than the people at Antelope House. *Cleome* was a major spice for both sites but more was eaten at Salmon Ruin. More high-spine Asteraceae pollen was eaten at Salmon Ruin, and wild grass pollen (Poaceae) was more common in high concentrations at Salmon Ruin. Prickly pear fruits and squash flowers were occasionally eaten at both sites.

Macroscopic Remains

The macroscopic analysis here is very different from the previous analysis (Reinhard 1992). The previous analysis was successful in recovering large dietary components such as nuts and bean seed coats from 5.0 g coprolite samples. The previous analysis was not successful in the recovery of smaller remains such as ground foods. In this analysis, refined recovery techniques allowed identification of very small dietary components (Table 44.4). Taken together, these analyses provide a good survey of San Juan Salmon Ruin foods (Table 44.5).

The data for Cheno Am from both analyses show that *Chenopodium* and *Amaranthus* were important food sources. The importance of these foods is emphasized in the second analysis because ground seed fragments were recovered. Ten coprolites (42%) of the second study contained *Chenopodium* or ground Cheno Am seed. The implication is that *Chenopodium* and *Amaranthus* were harvested, possibly stored, and ground in a manner that we usually associate with maize. Indeed, independently of pollen and starch granule analysis, Cheno Am is as numerically common as maize.

Maize was the second major source of carbohydrate at Salmon Ruin. It is interesting that cupules, husk, and silk were observed in the second analysis.

Table 44.4. Macroscopic observations and weights from Room 62 coprolite samples.

Lab No.	Stratum	Sample wt/ Macro wt	Seed/Plant Parts	Bone
1-33781	C-2-7	1.07/0.34 g	*Helinathus* achenes (1 whole, 1 partial); *Chenopodium* fruit (1 partial); *Zea mays* pericarp, cupulea	1 fragment
2-33781-2	none	1.60/1.33 g	*Zea mays* husk fragment; charcoal	None
3-54147	none	1.43/0.57 g	< 1% *Zea mays*; *Physalis* pericarp	None
4-53458	C-31-31; C-30-30	0.71/0.50 g	Cactus pad spine receptacle	None
5-78941	C-35-35	1.53/0.61 g	Piñon seed, adherent golden orange resin	None
6-78940	C-33-33	0.70/0.20 g	Parched plant epidermis; ground Cheno Am	None
7-76575	C-27-27	0.32/0.03 g	*Physalis* seed, partial	None
8-76652	C-31-31	0.60/0.18 g	*Chenopodium* seed, 1 whole, many ground, apparently parched; 1 whole *Physalis* seed	None
9-76568	C-24-24	0.43/0.17 g	Ground *Zea mays*; charcoal	None
10-53446	C-26-26	0.53/0.08 g	*Zea mays* cupules	None
11-75170	C-29-29	0.81/0.23 g	Whole and ground *Chenopodium*; white fibers; charcoal	None
12-75163	C-26.67-26.67	0.33/0.07 g	Ground *Chenopodium* seed; ground *Physalis* seed; *Helianthus* achene; small black (0.5 mm) obsidian flakes; fibrous material; possible fruit pericarp; charcoal	None
13-76653	C-30.3-30.3	0.34/0.16 g	Ground Cheno Ams, no whole seed found; woody material, small bark pieces	None
14-78935	C-26-26	0.49/0.13 g	3–5 whole *Chenopodium* seeds; primarily ground Cheno Am seed	None
15-32957	C-2.5-7.5	0.70/0.31 g	Small amount ground Cheno Am; *Zea mays* silk and husk	None
16-78974	C-23.5-23.6	0.11/0.03 g	Grass bracts	None
17-76643	C-27-27	1.23/0.39 g	~90% ground Cheno Am; 4 intact *Echinocereus* seeds	None
18-76651	C-31-31	0.60/0.15 g	Ground Cheno Am	None
19-33782	C-2.5-7.5	0.57/0.14 g	Curved, dark brown seedcoat; charcoal	None
20-53470	C-29.3-39.3	0.41/0.07 g	Nothing identifiable	1 mammal
21-76657	C-34-34	0.86/0.05 g	Nothing identifiable	9 mammal
22-32929	C-2-7	0.93/0.12 g	8–10 pieces of woody plant tissue, bark	None
23-76674	C-27.7-27.7	0.62/0.10 g	Finely ground plant material including woody fragments and epidermis	3 mammal
24-78942	C-36-36	1.69/0.84 g	~15 squash seeds, relatively intact, size 1.0–1.2 cm	3 mammal

Note: Sample wt/Macro wt is the original weight of the unprocessed sample followed by the weight of macroscopic remains recovered after rehydration and screening through a 300-micrometer mesh. For example, 1.07/0.34 means that the original dry weight was 1.07 gm and the dry weight of macroscopic remains larger than 0.3 mm recovered from the original sample was 0.34 g.

The discovery of silk helps to explain the high pollen concentrations of whole maize. Clearly, silk was consumed as a food source. The discovery of maize husk in two coprolites in this study suggests that Salmon Ruin's inhabitants chewed the husks of maize, perhaps in the same manner as yucca quids. Maize kernels were eaten both fresh and ground. Up to 43 percent of coprolites contain macroscopic evidence of maize.

Fruits of several wild plants were eaten, including prickly pear and *Echinocereus* cacti. More commonly, *Physalis* fruits were eaten.

The greatest dietary distinction of the San Juan Salmon Ruin diet relative to other Puebloans is the reliance on conifers. Piñon pine nuts were present in 4–6 percent of the coprolites. What are probably cracked juniper nuts (initially identified as *Rhus* by Reinhard, in 1992) are present in 23 percent of the

Table 44.5. Comparison of macroscopic plant parts from the 1992 Salmon Ruin study and the current study. The values represent the percentage of coprolites that contained the taxa.

Taxa	1st study (Reinhard 1992)	2nd study (this analysis)
Amaranthus	6	0
Bark	0	8
Cheno Am	0	21
Chenopodium	14	21
Charcoal	–	21
Cleome	2	0
Cucurbita	0	4
Cycloloma	1	0
Descurainea	4	0
Fiber	–	4
Fruit pericarp	0	8
Echinocereus	1	4
Helianthus	0	8
Juniperus / Rhus	23	0
Opuntia	1	0
Phaseolus	10	0
Physalis	1	17
Pinus	6	4
Portulaca	6	0
Resin	0	4
Zea	43	38

coprolites. The resin found in one coprolite might reflect a dietary or medicinal use of conifers. Therefore, conifers provided an important source of nutrition.

Salmon coprolites contain more *Phaseolus vulgaris* (bean) seeds than most other Puebloan sites. Ten percent of coprolites analyzed by Reinhard (1992) contained beans. Only Hoy House and Inscription House have a higher frequency of beans (Stiger 1977; Fry and Hall 1986).

Relative to other Puebloan coprolites, the occurrence of fiber from yucca and prickly pear is rare. This also makes Salmon Ruin distinct. Although ethnographically these are considered starvation foods, these plants were quite common in the prehistoric Puebloan diet, as also observed by Minnis (1991). However, in a component analysis of the dietary residues from 180 Antelope House coprolites, yucca occurred only in the absence of maize and wild foods available in the summer and fall. This suggests that at least yucca leaf bases and prickly pear pads were cold season foods, eaten

primarily in the absence of other foods. The low occurrence of these "starvation" foods indicates either that the San Juan inhabitants had a better year-round source of stored foods, or that the winter diet is not well represented in Salmon Ruin latrines.

The seeds of *Cleome*, *Descurainea*, and *Portulaca* found at Salmon may have been used as spices. *Cucurbita*, *Cycloloma*, and *Helianthus* were relatively rare food sources. Charcoal was also found in several coprolites, indicating that parching was one way of preparing food.

Bark is very difficult to identify, especially when only small fragments are found. It is likely that the bark reflects a medicinal use as opposed to a food source.

CONCLUSION

In general, when researchers discuss the ancestral Pueblo diet, the terms "dependent" or "reliant" are often used with regard to certain foods, especially maize. But the coprolite data show a remarkable diversity of foods used by Puebloans. The success of Puebloan communities on the Colorado Plateau is likely based on a "reliance on diversity." The San Juan coprolites from Salmon Ruin illustrate this (Table 44.6).

Certainly maize was an important food at Salmon Ruin. However, maize plants produced a diversity of foods—leaf quids, pollen-rich silk, fresh kernels, and ground flour. Because of the diversity in the ways that maize was eaten, maize remains were found in all types of study except for phytolith analysis.

Cheno Am greens (*Chenopodium*, *Amaranthus*, and related species) provided another important source of diversity in the diet. Cheno Am use is evident in macroscopic, pollen, and phytolith remains. These plants were an important source of greens, storable seeds, and flour.

The analysis also shows that *Opuntia* cactus provided many different foods. Pollen analysis shows that buds and flowers were a food source. Seeds show that fruits were eaten, and the phytolith analysis shows that pads, or perhaps fruits, were eaten. *Echinocereus* cactus fruits were also eaten. The most important fruit in the San Juan diet was *Physalis*, which was probably eaten like modern tomatoes and/or tomatillos.

The frequency of probable juniper nuts indicates that juniper berries were a frequent food, which is unique among Puebloan coprolites studied so far. Conifer nuts and perhaps resin were also eaten. One in five coprolites contained conifer nuts.

Table 44.6. Plant remains from analyses presented in this report compared with the previous study at Salmon Ruins (Reinhard 1992).

Taxa	Macro	Starch	Phytolith	Pollen	Reinhard '92
Asteraceae bud, flower, seed, foliage	–	–	–	38	–
Asteraceae–*Helianthus*	8	–	–	–	–
Bark	4	–	–	–	–
Brassicaceae bud, flower, seed, foliage	–	–	–	8	–
Brassicaceae–*Descurainea* fruit, seed	–	–	–	–	4
Charcoal	21	–	–	–	–
Cheno Am bud, seed, foliage, flour	–	–	40	54	–
Cheno Am flour	21	–	–	–	–
Cheno Am–*Amaranthus* fruit, seed	–	–	–	–	6
Cheno Am–*Chenopodium* fruit, seed	21	–	–	–	14
Cheno Am–*Cycloloma* fruit, seed	–	–	–	–	1
Cleome bud, flower	–	–	–	88	–
Cleome fruit, seed	–	–	–	–	2
Conifer? resin	4	–	–	–	–
Conifer–*Juniperus* nuts	–	–	–	–	23
Conifer–*Pinus* nuts	4	–	–	–	6
Cucurbita bud, flower	–	–	–	19	–
Cucurbita pulp	–	–	5	–	–
Cucurbita seed	4	–	–	–	–
Echinocereus fruit	4	–	–	–	1
Fabaceae pod, foliage	–	–	20	–	–
Fabaceae–*Phaseolus* seed	–	–	–	–	11
Fiber	4	–	–	–	–
Opuntia bud, flower	–	–	–	19	–
Opuntia fruit	–	–	–	–	1
Opuntia fruit, pads	–	–	45	–	–
Physalis fruit	13	–	–	–	1
Physalis? fruit pericarp	8	–	–	–	–
Poaceae bud, flower, seed	–	–	–	23	–
Portulaca fruit, seed	–	–	–	–	6
Yucca leaf bases	–	–	50	–	–
Zea	38	95	–	77	43
Zea flour	–	–	–	85	–
Zea silk, husk	9	–	–	–	–

Cultivated squash was eaten in a diversity of ways. However, it was a relatively rare food at Salmon. The phytolith analysis shows that pulp was eaten, and the pollen analysis shows that flowers were eaten. Finally, the macroscopic analysis shows that seeds were occasionally eaten as well.

Beans were also important. Bean seed coats were present in 11 percent of the coprolites. However, phytoliths from Fabaceae plants are present in 20 percent of the coprolites. Therefore, Salmon exhibits the highest documented Puebloan consumption of beans.

The main spice in the Salmon Ruin San Juan diet was *Cleome* flowers and buds. The pollen concentration analysis shows that this was nearly ubiquitous, and probably dietary. A high prevalence of *Cleome* pollen is a cuisine feature that is shared with other sites. However, pottery making may have been a potential source of pollen contamination; Hopi potters interviewed by Reinhard in 1977 indicated that carbon pottery paint is made from *Cleome*. It would be very interesting to examine the pollen content of paint made from *Cleome*. Spices of lesser importance were *Cleome* fruits or seeds, *Portulaca* seeds, and Brassicaceae (mustard) seeds or foliage.

Seven coprolites (35%) produced yucca phytoliths exceeding 10 percent of the total phytolith count, indicating consumption of yucca leaf bases. No yucca pollen or seeds were observed in the coprolites, so it appears that only leaf bases were part of the diet.

Finally, nondomestic grass seeds and sunflower family plants were eaten as well.

PERSPECTIVES FOR FUTURE RESEARCH

Armelagos (1994) presented three goals for paleonutrition study: (1) identification of the prehistoric "menu" meaning a list of foods available, (2) defining "diet" meaning the frequency of relative consumption of foods on the "menu," and (3) determining the nutritional profile of the "diet."

With regard to Salmon Ruin, the first goal has been achieved by analysis of food remains excavated from the site. Table 44.7 provides a list of the many food plants available at Salmon Ruin. The second goal can best be achieved by coprolite analysis because the actual foods consumed in prehistory are evident in the feces. However, this goal is only partly achieved for Salmon Ruin. The main dietary components such as maize, Cheno Am, pine, and juniper have been recovered and quantified, but many minor menu items discovered in the ruin have not been found in the coprolites. Of the 61 plant food taxa found in the ruin, only 20 have been found in the coprolites. Therefore, 67 percent of the "menu" has not been found in the "diet."

The coprolites from Salmon Ruin must be the focus of more intensive work to fully define the San Juan occupation diet and nutrition. To that end, a more diverse sample of 200 coprolites could be analyzed. This analysis should include pollen concentration study, phytolith extraction, refined macroscopic analysis of large coprolite fragments, and ancient DNA analysis of chloroplast sequences following the method of Poinar et al. (2001). Only through such analysis will the diet finally be known, to lay the foundation for reconstruction of Salmon Ruin paleonutrition.

Table 44.7. List of dietary plant genera identified from Salmon Ruin derived from K. Adams (2005) compared to list of taxa recovered from Salmon Ruin coprolites.

Taxon	Part(s) found in Salmon Excavation	Use	Part(s) found in Salmon Coprolites
Allionia	Pollen	Food?	–
Allium	Bulb scale	Food	–
Amaranthus	Seed	Food	Seeds and flour
Ambrosia	Pollen	Unknown	–
Anemopsis	Seed	Medicine	–
Artemisia	Pollen	Unknown	–
Asteraceae HS	Pollen	Food	Pollen
Asteraceae LS	–	Food	Pollen
Cactaceae	All taxa, all parts	Food	–
Carex	Achene	Food	–
Celtis	Seed	Food	–
Cheno Am	Embryo, seed	Food	Pollen, phytoliths, seeds from buds, greens, and fruits
Chenopodium	Pollen, seed	Food	Seeds and flour
Cleome	Seed	Food	Seeds and pollen from buds, flowers
Crataegus	Berry, nutlet	Food	–
Cucurbita	Pollen	Food	–
Cucurbita pepo	Fruit flesh, rind (pericarp), peduncle, seed, vine tendril	Food	Seeds, pollen, and phytoliths from pulp and flower
Cycloloma	Seed	Food	Seed
Cylindropuntia	Pollen	Food	–

Table 44.7 (continued)

Taxon	Part(s) found in Salmon Excavation	Use	Part(s) found in Salmon Coprolites
Cyperaceae	Pollen	Food	–
Descurainia	Seed	Food	Seeds and Brassicaceae pollen from buds and flowers
Desmodium	Seed	Unknown	–
Echinocereus	Seed	Food	Seed from fruit
Eleocharis	Achene	Food	–
Ephedra	Stem	?	–
Eriogonum	Achene, pollen	Food?	–
Euphorbia	Seed	Food	–
Helianthus	Pollen	Food	Achenes
Juncus	Achene	Food	–
Juniperus	Berry (cone), seed	Food	Pollen and seed
Kallstroemia	Seed	Medicine	–
Lycium	Seed	Food	–
Mammillaria	Pollen	Food	–
Mentzelia	Seed	Food	–
Paniceae	Bract	Food	–
Phaseolus vulgaris	Cotyledon, pod, seed	Food	Seed coats
Physalis	Seed	Food	Seeds and skin from fruits
Pinus	Nut, nutshell (testa), cone	Food	Nutshells
Plantago	Seed	Food	–
Platyopuntia	Pollen	Food	Pollen, phytoliths, and seeds from buds, pads, and fruit
Poaceae	All taxa, all parts	Food	Pollen
Polanisia	Seed	Food	–
Polygonum	Achene	Food?	–
Portulaca	Seed	Food	Seed
Prosopis	Seed	Food	–
Prunus	Drupe	Food	–
Rhus aromatica	Stone (seed)	Food	–
Salvia reflexa	Seed	Food, medicine	–
Sarcobatus	Pollen	Unknown	–
Scirpus, S. acutus	Achene	Food	–
Shepherdia argentea	Seed	Food	–
Sphaeralcea	Pollen	Food	–
Sporobolus	Caryopsis	Food	–
Stipa hymenoides	Bract, caryopsis, floret	Food	–
Suaeda	Seed	Food	–
Trianthema	Seed	Food	–
Typha	Pollen	Food	–
Verbesina	Achene	Food	–
Xanthium	Involucre	Food?	–
Yucca sp.	Fruit, leaf, seed	Food	Phytoliths from leave bases
Zea mays	Cupule, cob, embryo, kernel, stalk, pollen, tassel	Food	pollen, tassel, husk, flour

Chapter 45

COPROLITE ANALYSIS FOR *GIARDIA LAMBLIA* AT SALMON RUINS

by Stuart D. Wilson, Maria M. Jordan, and Maria A. Jordan

Giardia lamblia is a freshwater protozoan whose habitat is temperate climates worldwide. It is widely distributed and very prevalent as a human intestinal parasite. In 1978, U.S. State Health laboratories reported that giardia was the most frequently reported pathogenic parasite identified in human fecal specimens (Smith and Gutierrez 1991). In New Mexico, the Department of Health reported 241, 300, and 284 cases in 1991, 1992, and 1993, respectively (Gallaher and Vold 1993, 1994). The majority of cases were reported from Bernalillo County, but San Juan County in New Mexico has averaged nine cases per year from 1984 through 1992 (Maggi Gallaher, personal communication 1992 and 1993). Although not proven, it is reasonable to assume that, in the absence of modern sanitary conditions, infestation by this organism may not have been uncommon in prehistoric Anasazi peoples in this same area of northern New Mexico. However reasonable this assumption may be, the hypothesis is complicated by a paucity of archaeoparasitological documentation showing that this organism or any protozoan parasite did in fact exist in prehistoric populations.

In his comprehensive review article, Reinhard (1990) specifically noted that "the preservation of protozoa has not yet been demonstrated in any North American study" of prehistoric parasitism. Shortly thereafter, Faulkner (1991) identified *Giardia intestinalis* (*lamblia*) in one of eight human coprolites recovered from Big Bone Cave excavations in Tennessee. He was able to achieve this unique finding through the use of an immunofluorescent assay, which employed a monoclonal antibody (detection reagent) specific for the antigenic cyst wall of *Giardia*. By way of explanation, such assays employ a marker (a specific, "purified" antibody) that attaches itself to the parasite's outer surface (antigen). This attachment is confirmed by a secondary marker, which is

joined to the antibody. This second marker is recognizable under the microscope because it fluoresces when exposed to a light source with a specific wavelength. This fluorescence is an indirect indicator that the specific antibody has combined with the specific antigen, thus identifying the parasitic cyst wall. This technology was not routinely employed in earlier studies because it has only recently become commercially available.

During the 1970s excavation of Salmon Ruins, 112 coprolites with different proveniences were recovered from several latrine areas (Reinhard 1988b; Reinhard et al. 1987). Only 12 of these specimens (11%) demonstrated parasites, and these were all reported as *Enterobius vermicularis* (pinworm); no protozoan parasites were identified. Based on the hypothesis that *Giardia lamblia* organisms might reasonably have existed in this population, a sample of the Salmon Ruin coprolites was restudied by the immunofluorescent technique using a specific monoclonal antibody label.

MATERIALS AND METHODS

An initial survey of coprolite material was conducted on samples acquired from multiple levels of a single, fully excavated room (Room 62) that was used as a latrine during a period estimated to span AD 1200 and 1275. Thirty-three coprolites that Reinhard had analyzed using traditional methods were included in this preliminary study. This limited sample was evaluated to assess the likelihood of giardia infestation at this Anasazi site.

A 5 g sample was separated from each of the 33 coprolites. Rehydration employed a 0.5% trisodium phosphate solution, with immersion of each sample in the solution for a minimum of 48 hours. After 24 hours, Pen-Fix was added to each rehydrating coprolite to retard microbial growth. The mixed specimens were screened with distilled water through 300 and 180 µm mesh brass geological sieves. Screened fluid was centrifuged for 2 minutes at 2000 rpm in 50 ml capped plastic conical test tubes. After decanting

Reprinted with permission (and minor editing) from *Of Pots and Rocks: Papers in Honor of A. Helene Warren*, 1995, Archaeological Society of New Meixco.

the supernatant, each specimen was preserved in 20 ml of 10% sodium acetate buffered neutral formalin (a solution of formaldehyde with methanol). Sedimentation for 4 hours was accomplished after adding 5 ml of ethyl acetate. After sedimentation, the plug at the top of the conical tube was loosened with an applicator stick and the supernate was decanted. The sediment was resuspended by gently tapping the bottom of the tube.

The MerIFluor kit with controls was provided in commercial form by Meridian Diagnostics of Cincinnati, Ohio. This kit employs an FITC-labeled monoclonal antibody (detection reagent) specific for the cyst wall of formalin-fixed giardia. Following the manufacturer's recommended procedure (MerIFluor 1991), a drop of each resuspended specimen was applied to the treated slide and spread well over the surface, being careful not to scratch the slide surface. Both positive and negative control specimens were applied in the same manner. After air drying for 30 minutes, the detection reagent and eriochrome black counterstain were added to each well. Following light-protected incubation in a humidified chamber for 30 minutes, slides were rinsed with buffer solution and drained of excess fluid. After adding a cover slip with formalinized buffered glycerol as the mounting medium, slides were scanned at 100–200x magnification using fluorescent microscopy with a mercury lamp. One or more cysts with apple-green fluorescence and characteristic morphology would represent a positive test.

This immunofluorescent method has been shown to be highly specific for giardia cysts. According to the manufacturer, the sensitivity and specificity for giardia in stools are both 100 percent. In clinical trials preparatory to the release of the kit for commercial purposes, a wide variety of protozoa, helminthes, bacteria, yeast, and fungi did not cross-react with the antibody or demonstrate nonspecific fluorescence. However, it should be noted that the Meridian Diagnostics kit for giardia also contains a second monoclonal antibody for Cryptosporidium species. This organism is an opportunistic protozoan parasite found in the bowels of humans whose immune systems are damaged from defending against chronic infection. Such immunologically compromised people are either born with the deficiency or develop it as part of a disease process. Although its presence was sought as part of this study, it is unlikely that examples would be identified in the presumed immunocompetent (normal immune response) prehistoric Native American.

RESULTS

No *Giardia lamblia* organisms were conclusively identified in any of the 33 samples of typical coprolite material. Controls for *Giardia lamblia* did give appropriate positive fluorescence with the procedure. Although these coprolites were recovered from multiple levels in the one room, the small number of samples analyzed represents less than a statistically significant sample population of coprolites deposited over time at this site.

DISCUSSION

Infection with *Giardia lamblia* is enteric, principally involving the small intestine. The organism has been documented in both sporadic endemic and epidemic infestations. Although person-to-person and, rarely, food transmissions have been demonstrated, the most common source of infestation is from contaminated water; transmission by water contamination has been implicated as the principal source of most large outbreaks in modern times (Smith and Gutierrez 1991). Incidence of infection is more prevalent in areas where local water supplies are not protected with adequate public health measures (Owen 1993). Obviously, prehistoric habitation sites did not utilize such measures, thus creating and perpetuating opportunities for endemic infestation of the population.

Only about half of exposed individuals become infected. Factors favoring infection include youth, malnutrition, bacterial overgrowth in the upper small bowel, and impaired immunological defenses. These factors may operate in a synergistic manner to enhance the parasite's pathogenicity or ability to cause infection. Infestation with the organism is asymptomatic in most patients, but those with symptoms exhibit varying degrees of fatigue, nausea, vomiting, anorexia, postprandial distress, abdominal cramps, diarrhea, and weight loss. Some individuals, especially children, may develop a malabsorption syndrome with significant complications: steatorrhea (excess of fat in stools); reduction of serum carotene, vitamin B12, and foliate; and impairment of D-xylose excretion (Monroe 1995). Children may exhibit growth retardation. Chronic fallout from these disease effects can be debilitating and may result in significant modification of a person's ability to cope with environmental challenges.

The implications of symptomatic infections for prehistoric populations are significant. In societies where a high degree of physical competence was necessary for survival, the competitive edge would go to the healthy individual. When marginal circumstances existed in the environment and malnutrition prevailed, the effects of even limited disease on a culture could have been quite significant. Protozoan infections are known to have had adverse effects in modern populations. The motivation to cope and compete could reasonably be expected to suffer as the incidence of disease complications increased. Moreover, it has been well documented that helminthic (intestinal worm) infestations were more prevalent in sedentary groups than in more transient and mobile prehistoric hunter-gatherers of the Southwest (Reinhard et al. 1987); similar findings have been documented in twentieth-century primitive societies (Chernela and Thatcher 1989). It may therefore be reasonable to assume that this same phenomenon could have operated in regard to protozoan infections, creating an imbalance between adversaries. Thus, the defense capabilities and subsistence strategies of more sedentary peoples with predominantly agricultural traditions may have been compromised relative to those of the mobile, marauding aggressors with dominant hunter-gatherer traditions.

Although the preliminary results of this initial sample did not demonstrate giardia organisms, the test sample of the total coprolite population that could be presumed to have been deposited at this site over the time of occupation was small. The test sample was also limited to only one of the identified latrine rooms at the site. It would be appropriate to study additional samples from other rooms to conclusively disprove the hypothesis in a statistically meaningful way. Regardless of the ultimate results, it is apparent that a new technical standard in archaeoparasitological studies has been established. Whether *Giardia lamblia* is or is not ultimately demonstrated in the Salmon Ruins coprolites, it is no longer necessary to limit future studies of coprolite and contaminated soil material to traditional, less-sensitive methods of protozoan parasite identification. Commercial kits are now available that permit application of monoclonal antibody technology by immunofluorescent techniques for the identification of three protozoan enteric parasites, including *Entamoeba histolytica* (amebiasis). In areas where modern endemic infections occur or where environmentally appropriate conditions existed in prehistoric times, it would be appropriate to subject all materials to immunofluorescent techniques to identify not only *Giardia lamblia*, but *Entamoeba histolytica* as well.

ACKNOWLEDGMENTS

The authors express their appreciation to the San Juan County Archaeological Research Center and Library at Salmon Ruin and specifically to David E. Doyel, former executive director, who made coprolite materials available for this study, and to Larry L. Baker, current executive director, for his continued encouragement of this project.

Chapter 46

WORKED FIBER ARTIFACTS FROM SALMON PUEBLO

by Laurie D. Webster

More than 1100 fragments of worked fiber artifacts were collected or recorded during excavations at Salmon Pueblo. Large assemblages of perishable artifacts are rarely preserved at open archaeological sites, but some of the massive Chacoan great houses provide an exception to this rule. At Salmon, Aztec, and several sites in Chaco Canyon, the thick standing walls, intact ceilings or roof-fall, and deep deposits of well-drained sandy fill have preserved literally thousands of worked perishable artifacts. Although preservation at Salmon was not as extensive as at Pueblo Bonito or the West Ruin at Aztec, the Salmon assemblage is large and diverse, and provides a valuable perspective on the rich ritual and craft traditions of the Middle San Juan region from the late eleventh through the thirteenth centuries.

This description and basic interpretation of the worked fiber artifacts from Salmon includes all of the worked fiber artifacts from the site—cordage, knots, mats, baskets, pot rests, sandals, twined blankets, and woven fabrics—but not leather, hide, or wooden artifacts. I hope that another researcher will take on the study of these other artifacts.[1]

PREVIOUS RESEARCH

During the original Salmon project in the 1970s, no analysis was planned or completed on the perishable artifacts (Irwin-Williams and Shelley 1980). Late in the project, however, a basic analysis of the "manipulated fiber" artifacts was undertaken by Gayle Potter, then a graduate student researcher at New York University. A few other students also contributed to this analysis. This work resulted in the

creation of a manipulated fiber database, which was made available to me. Potter (1981) discussed some of the textile and basketry data from mortuary contexts in her unpublished master's thesis, which examined social differentiation at Salmon during the Secondary occupation. Bohrer and Adams (see Chapter 38) referenced a few of the worked fiber artifacts from Salmon in the archaeobotanical report. Otherwise, the Salmon worked fiber assemblage has been completely overlooked by researchers since the 1970s excavations. Neither Kate Peck Kent (1983) nor Lynn Teague (1998) mentioned Salmon in their synthetic overviews of Southwestern textiles, nor is it referenced in recent Southwestern basketry studies (e.g., Adovasio and Gunn 1986).

PROJECT METHODOLOGY

Analysis was conducted at the Salmon Ruins Museum over an 8-week period during the summer and fall of 2003. In addition to not having to move these fragile collections, working at the site allowed me to consult the Salmon archives as needed for contextual and photographic information. Given the fragmentary and disturbed condition of the assemblage, this information proved invaluable.

I made a concerted effort to trace the artifacts to their original field contexts and to identify those that had been assigned a significant artifact (SA) number in the field. Significant artifact numbers, or occasionally feature numbers, were assigned to artifacts that the excavators deemed to be of particular importance, including artifacts recorded and mapped as part of mortuary and floor assemblages. These significant artifact and feature numbers are currently the closest analogues we have to field numbers at Salmon, linking selected objects with their field records and archaeological contexts. During the original Salmon excavations, Record Key (RK) numbers were assigned to individual 1 x 1 m units, feature areas, and other provenience units. These numbers were computerized and designed to track work completed at the site. RK numbers were used in many of the

---

[1]In 2003, I was invited by the Center for Desert Archaeology to analyze the diverse worked fiber assemblage from Salmon Pueblo. My analysis was conducted with Center support as part of the Salmon Research Program, through partnership with Salmon Ruins Museum (P. Reed 2002; see Chapter 1, this report). I have also compared fiber artifacts from Salmon, Aztec, and Chaco Canyon for the 2005 Salmon synthetic volume.

individual analytic databases created during the original Salmon Project. Unfortunately, a master computer index file with all the RK numbers was apparently never created. As a result, a complete RK database does not exist, severely limiting the utility of RK numbers as a tracking method. Instead of trying to use RK numbers to track artifacts, the SA and features numbers were used. In addition, Field Specimen (FS) numbers were assigned to all artifacts (as described below).

A detailed analysis form was completed for each object or batch of objects. Categories of information collected for each object include artifact type, provenience, construction technique or weave structure, element composition, element density, raw material, dimensions, and condition; this information was transferred to an Excel database. Color slides were taken of approximately 250 objects, including a sample of the cordage and knots, and most of the baskets, textiles, and miscellaneous objects. Photographs and analysis sheets generated by the study will be archived at the Salmon Ruins Museum. Most of the analysis did not require the use of additional magnification, but a few objects were examined under a dissecting microscope at 30x magnification and some fibers were identified under a light microscope at 100x.

Vorsila Bohrer's identifications for the worked fiber specimens have yet to be incorporated into my analysis because of problems linking the sample numbers from the two data sets. This is regrettable because her plant identifications are certainly more reliable than mine. The only other analysis performed on the assemblage was X-ray fluorescence spectrometry, a non-destructive technique used to identify the red hematite pigment on three red-stained artifacts. The analysis was conducted at the University of Arizona in January 2005 by Dr. Nancy Odegaard, conservator at the Arizona State Museum, and Dr. David Smith, professor in the Department of Chemistry, using a Niton Xli 700 Series handheld X-ray fluorescence spectrometer.

A new FS catalog number was assigned during anaysis to each worked fiber artifact, beginning with FS 80,001. Catalog numbers had been assigned inconsistently during the original project; someimes a single number was assigned to a batch of objects, other times multiple numbers were assigned to pieces of a single object. To maintain comparability between the old and new numbering systems, I assigned the new FS catalog numbers to the same original samples. However, in discussing the assemblage I have tried to "reconstruct" the original artifacts as much as possible, and all catalog numbers pertaining to a given object are provided in the accompanying tables.

The updated database includes all worked fiber artifacts housed at the Salmon Ruins Museum and all fiber artifacts discovered in the field and referred to in the field records, but for one reason or another not collected. The original manipulated fiber database contained 482 records; the updated database contains 596. I consider these 596 catalog records to represent the remains of 918 unique objects (914 worked fiber objects and 4 weaving tools), including 104 unique batches of cordage (299 cordage fragments) and 595 knots—these two categories constitute 76.5 percent of the worked fiber assemblage— and 64 mats (60 plaited, 4 twined or sewn), 34 baskets (8 plaited, 26 coiled), 3 plaited pouches, 33 pot rests or coils of raw materials, 34 sandals (13 twined and 21 plaited, the latter including a looped turkey-feather shoe-sock), 15 twined robes, 10 batches of cotton cloth, 10 unidentified plaited objects (mats, sandals, baskets, or pot rests), and 12 miscellaneous fiber objects (Table 46.1). The original manipulated fiber database also contained entries for 20 "mats" that I believe to represent the remains of roof thatch or other unworked plant material. I have excluded these materials from Table 46.1 and from the artifact discussions, but their new FS catalog numbers are provided in Table 46.45 at the end of the chapter.

I have reclassified the temporal associations assigned to several of the artifacts in the original manipulated fiber database from Secondary to Primary. These designations were derived from the original stratigraphic level codex developed by Rex Adams. Under this system, a stratum was identified as Primary, Intermediate, or Secondary based on a variety of criteria—for trash deposits, usually the proportion of ceramic sherds. For example, if 30 percent of the sherds from a given trash deposit were attributed to the Primary occupation and 70 percent to the Secondary occupation, that stratum was classified as predominantly Secondary and all non-ceramic artifacts from that stratum were also identified as Secondary. Unfortunately, this system failed to account for the highly mixed nature of many of the deposits. If 30 percent of the sherds in a particular trash deposit dated to the Primary occupation, then it is reasonable to assume that a proportion of the other artifacts in that stratum might also date to the Primary occupation. I consider this to have been the case for a number of the fiber artifacts. In addition, Paul Reed is in the process of reassessing most of the Salmon strata for temporal assignments (Reed, Chapter 12). Many of the so-called Intermediate strata have been reassessed as Mixed Primary and Secondary, and do not actually reflect mid-1100s dating.

I used the following criteria to reassess the temporal designations for several objects. If comparative evidence from Chaco, Aztec, or other perishable assemblages suggested that a particular style of object might date to the late 1000s or early 1100s, and if the ceramic rough counts for that stratum at Salmon corroborated this possibility, then I tentatively reclassified the artifact. If I was unable to corroborate my hunch with ceramic data (as was the case with the well-preserved trash deposit from Room 62W), I classified the stratum as culturally mixed, but did not assign a new temporal designation. I discuss these specific changes in greater detail in the room and artifact sections.

DISTRIBUTION AND TEMPORAL ASSOCIATION OF THE WORKED FIBER ARTIFACTS

Table 46.1 provides the room distribution for the 914 worked fiber artifacts and 4 weaving tools from Salmon. Forty-three room contexts, including subdivided rooms, are represented. The greatest number of fiber artifacts for all periods came from Room 62W, located adjacent to and southwest of the Tower Kiva. This unusually large, special-use room was used during the Primary occupation, then modified during the Secondary occupation and subsequently served as a trash dump. Vast quantities of worked fiber artifacts and unworked plant materials were preserved within this room in a deep, well-drained midden of ashy soil. More than 500 worked fiber artifacts (57% of the assemblage) came from this one room alone. Unlike most fiber artifacts from other rooms at Salmon, these artifacts are mostly unburned, some contributing important information about the use of pigments at Salmon. Unfortunately, the trash deposits in this room were highly mixed, making it difficult or impossible to distinguish Primary and Secondary materials from stratigraphic or ceramic evidence alone.

Other rooms that produced significant quantities of perishables are scattered throughout the pueblo. Rooms located in the second row from the back wall, originally two or three stories high, are especially well represented in the sample. Catastrophic burning is the reason for much of this preservation, as many of the rooms with perishables also experienced one or more burn events (e.g., Rooms 64W, 129W).

Primary Assemblage

The original manipulated fiber database assigned 67 fiber artifacts to the Primary occupation. My reassessment resulted in the identification of 82

objects from definite or well-supported Primary contexts (Table 46.2). This excludes objects from the problematic, culturally mixed trash strata in Room 62W; many of these probably also date to the Primary occupation. Figure 46.1 shows the distribution of all probable Primary perishable artifacts at the site. One important concentration of Primary worked fiber artifacts occurred in Rooms 61A, 62W, and 81W, the area surrounding the Tower Kiva, which appears to have served as the ritual core of the pueblo. The best-preserved and best-dated Primary assemblage came from Room 61A, the interstitial fill of the southwest corner of the Tower Kiva. This deposit included two plaited ring baskets, three pot rests or coils of basketry material, a red-colored twined sandal, and an unknown textile that was not collected. Because these items were placed during kiva construction around AD 1090, and with the discovery of similar perishable deposits in Chaco Canyon, I have interpreted this deposit as an intentional ritual offering (see "A Possible Ritual Cache of Fiber Artifacts" at the end of this chapter). Room 81W, another specialized room southeast of the Tower Kiva, contained an internal platform or rack and a range of unusual, well-preserved objects, including an important assemblage of Primary occupation weaving tools.

In addition to a small assemblage of Primary artifacts from a Primary trash midden, many of the other fiber artifacts from Room 62W probably also date to the Primary occupation. Bohrer (Chapter 35) expressed a similar sentiment in regards to the archaeobotanical remains from that room. Unfortunately, the only way to demonstrate this archaeologically would be to directly date the artifacts. Based on comparisons with artifacts from known Primary contexts at Salmon, I think that most if not all of the twined sandals, coils or raw materials, red-stained artifacts, and miscellaneous objects from Room 62W trash probably date to the Primary (or early Secondary?) occupation. Many of the finely plaited sandals probably also date to this period. After the Aztec and Chaco fiber assemblages are studied in depth, we will have a better understanding of the types of artifacts used in Chacoan great houses during different periods.

Primary worked fiber artifacts also came from a number of smaller rooms. The room with the most diverse Primary assemblage was 33W, where the perishables-rich, late Primary burial 33W012 was found. Another Primary burial, 100W302, also contained evidence of a red-stained mat. I discuss these mortuary patterns in greater detail at the end of the chapter. Other rooms containing Primary fiber arti-

Table 46.1. Distribution of worked fiber artifacts and weaving tools at Salmon Pueblo.

Room	Cordage	Knots	Plaited Mats	Sewn/ twined Mats	Plaited Ring Baskets	Plaited Pouches	Coiled Baskets	Pot Rests & Coils[1]	Plaited Sandals & Shoe-Sock	Twined Sandals & Tump-bands	Twined Fur or Feather Robes	Cotton Cloth	Un-identified Plaited Objects	Misc. Fiber Objects	Weaving Tools	Total Objects
4A	1	3	1	–	–	–	–	–	–	–	–	–	–	–	–	5
30W	1	2	–	–	–	–	1	–	1	–	–	–	–	–	–	5
31A	1	–	–	–	–	–	–	–	–	–	–	–	–	–	–	1
31W	–	–	1	–	1	–	1	–	–	1	–	–	–	–	–	4
33B	1	–	3	–	–	–	1	–	1	–	–	–	–	–	–	6
33C	–	2	–	–	–	–	–	–	–	–	–	–	–	–	–	2
33W	–	7	4	1	–	–	–	–	1	–	1	1	–	1	–	16
36W	7	7	3	–	2	–	4	2	–	–	–	–	1	–	–	26
37W	2	9	1	–	–	–	2	3	2	–	–	–	–	1	–	20
43W	7	12	9	1	–	2	3	4	3	1	4	3	–	1	–	50
58W	–	–	–	–	–	–	1	–	–	–	–	–	–	–	–	1
59W	2	2	–	–	4	–	–	–	–	–	–	–	–	–	–	4
60B	–	–	–	–	1	–	–	1	–	–	–	–	–	–	–	1
61A	–	–	–	–	2	–	–	3	–	1	–	–	–	1	–	7
62A	–	2	2	–	1	–	1	1	1	–	–	–	–	–	–	8
62B	–	–	–	–	1	–	–	–	1	–	–	–	–	–	–	2
62W	46	417	5	–	2	–	3	11	8	6	–	3	5	5	–	511
64W	8	5	3	–	–	1	3	4	–	–	–	1	–	1	–	26
67W	–	3	–	–	–	–	–	–	–	–	–	–	–	1	–	4
81W	1	10	–	1	–	–	–	1	–	–	–	–	–	–	4	17
82W	1	–	–	–	–	–	–	–	–	–	–	–	–	–	–	1
84W	4	4	–	–	–	–	–	–	–	–	1	–	–	–	–	9
88W	–	–	1	–	–	–	–	–	–	–	–	–	–	–	–	1
90W	–	1	–	–	–	–	–	–	–	–	–	–	–	–	–	1

Table 46.1 (continued)

Room	Cordage	Knots	Plaited Mats	Sewn/twined Mats	Plaited Ring Baskets	Plaited Pouches	Coiled Baskets	Pot Rests & Coils[1]	Plaited Sandals & Shoe-Sock	Twined Sandals & Tump-bands	Twined Fur or Feather Robes	Cotton Cloth	Un-identified Plaited Objects	Misc. Fiber Objects	Weaving Tools	Total Objects
91A	–	1	–	–	–	–	–	–	–	–	–	–	–	–	–	1
91W	–	2	–	–	–	–	–	–	–	–	–	–	–	–	–	2
93W	–	–	1	–	–	–	–	–	–	–	–	–	–	–	–	1
97A	–	8	1	–	–	–	–	–	–	–	–	–	–	–	–	9
97B	–	–	1	–	–	–	–	–	–	–	–	–	–	–	–	1
97W	–	1	5	–	–	–	–	–	1	–	2	–	–	–	–	9
98W	–	2	–	–	–	–	–	–	–	–	–	–	–	–	–	2
100W	3	8	1	–	–	–	1	1	1	–	–	–	–	1	–	16
101W	–	2	–	–	–	–	1	1	–	2	–	–	1	–	–	7
102W	–	–	1	–	–	–	–	–	–	–	–	–	–	–	–	1
118W	–	2	–	–	–	–	–	–	–	–	–	–	–	–	–	2
119W	–	–	–	–	–	–	–	1	–	–	–	–	–	–	–	1
121W	–	–	1	–	–	–	–	–	–	–	–	–	–	–	–	1
122W	–	–	2	–	–	–	–	–	–	–	–	–	–	–	–	2
123B	1	–	1	–	–	–	–	–	–	–	1	1	–	–	–	4
127B	–	–	1	–	–	–	–	–	–	–	–	–	–	–	–	1
127W	–	1	6	–	–	–	2	–	–	2	5	1	–	–	–	17
129W	18	82	1	–	–	–	1	–	1	–	1	–	3	–	–	107
130W	–	–	1	–	–	–	–	–	–	–	–	–	–	–	–	1
Unkn.	–	–	4	1	–	–	–	–	–	–	–	–	–	–	–	5
Total	104	595	60	4	8	3	26	33	21	13	15	10	10	12	4	918

[1]Includes pot rests and coils of plant materials.

Table 46.2. Distribution of worked fiber artifacts and weaving tools from known or strongly suspected Primary contexts. (Table excludes objects from culturally mixed trash deposits in Room 62W, which contain an unknown quantity of Primary materials.)

Room	Type of Deposit	Cordage	Knots	Plaited Mats	Sewn/ twined Mats	Plaited Ring Baskets	Coiled Baskets	Plaited Pot Rests & Coils	Twined Sandals & Shoe-Sock	Sandals & Tump-bands	Twined Robes	Un-identif. Plaited Objects	Cotton Cloth	Misc. Fiber Objects	Weaving Tools	Total
31W	Fill, roof-fall	–	–	1	–	–	–	–	–	1	–	–	–	–	–	2
33W	Burial 33W012, trash	1	4	3	1	–	–	–	1	–	1	–	1	1	–	13
36W	Lithic scatter	–	–	2	–	–	–	–	–	–	–	–	–	–	–	2
37W	Post-occ fill	–	–	–	–	–	–	1	–	–	–	–	–	–	–	1
43W	Lithic scatter, fill	–	1	–	–	–	–	2	1	1	–	–	–	–	–	5
61A	Interstitial space of Tower Kiva	–	–	–	–	2	–	3	–	1	–	–	–	–	–	6
62W	Fill, trash, burial	4	1?	–	–	1	–	2	–	–	–	1	–	–	–	8
81W	Fill, roof-fall	1	10	–	1	–	–	1	–	–	–	–	–	–	4	17
84W	Trash	–	3	–	–	–	–	–	–	–	1	–	–	–	–	4
97W	Trash, log feature, floor	–	1	2	–	–	–	–	1	–	–	–	–	–	–	4
98W	Floor surface	–	1	–	–	–	–	–	–	–	–	–	–	–	–	1
100W	Burial 100W302, trash	–	1	1	–	–	–	–	–	–	–	–	–	1?	–	3
101W	Trash, fill	–	2	–	–	–	–	2	–	1	–	–	–	–	–	5
127W	Roof-fall, Burial 127W147	–	–	–	–	–	–	–	–	2	1	–	1?	–	–	4
129W	Trash, roof-fall	1	–	–	–	–	1	–	1	–	1	3	–	–	–	7
Total		7	23	9	2	3	1	11	4	6	4	4	2	2	4	82

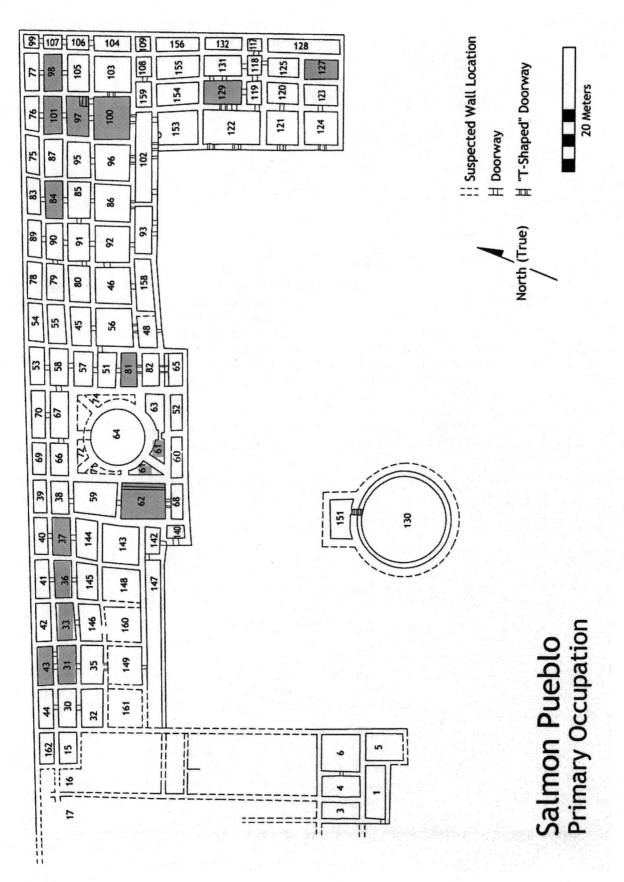

Salmon Pueblo
Primary Occupation

Suspected Wall Location
Doorway
"T-Shaped" Doorway

North (True)

20 Meters

Figure 46.1. Map of Salmon showing Primary distribution of worked fiber artifacts.

facts were 31W, 36W, 37W, 43W, 84W, 97W, 98W, 101W, 127W, and 129W. Burned room 129W produced a particularly rich and diverse assemblage of perishables believed to date to the Primary period.

My identification of the artifacts in Table 46.2 as Primary, rather than Primary-Intermediate or Intermediate, follows the revised Salmon chronology (P. Reed, Chapter 12). In the new chronology, "Intermediate" has been replaced by Early Secondary to reflect the continuity seen at Salmon in the mid-late 1100s. Excavators identified a few items as Intermediate-Secondary in the original Salmon perishable database, but none as Intermediate alone. Although we are no longer using the term Intermediate, I frequently cite the excavators' original field designations of "Intermediate" artifacts in my discussion and chapter tables.

Distinguishing between Primary and early Secondary perishable artifacts is problematic. Strong similarities can be seen between many of the Primary artifacts from Salmon and those recovered by Earl Morris from "Chacoan" contexts at the West Ruin of Aztec, which park archaeologist Gary Brown (personal communication 2004) considers to date to the McElmo phase, extending into the 1130s, if not later. Thus, at least some of the Salmon artifacts that I refer to here as Primary could conceivably date well into the twelfth century at Salmon, past the period when the Chaco leadership may have moved to the East Ruin of Aztec (ca. AD 1115–1120), according to the interpretations of Paul Reed (personal communication 2004). To deal with this fuzzy line between the Primary and Secondary periods, I use the term "early Secondary" as a substitute for "Intermediate" to characterize artifacts—such as the twined sandals—that appear to represent a Primary (i.e., Chacoan) technology that continued into the mid or even late twelfth century.

Secondary Assemblage

The majority of the assemblage appears to date to the Secondary occupation; Figure 46.2 shows the distribution of Secondary artifacts at the site. In addition to the culturally mixed trash deposit in Room 62W, substantial quantities of Secondary fiber artifacts were recovered from Rooms 30, 31, 33, 36, 37, and 43 in the northwest part of the pueblo, Room 64W (the Tower Kiva) in the center, Rooms 97, 100, and 101 in the northeast, and Room 127 in the southeast. Virtually all of these rooms were burned, resulting in the extensive preservation of carbonized remains. A mid-thirteenth-century fire in the Tower

Kiva preserved a wide range of ceremonial items in place, including a plaited pouch, pot rests, baskets, and the matting over the foot drums. Matting was also found in association with the floor vaults of Room 130W, the Great Kiva.

DISTRIBUTION OF WORKED FIBER ARTIFACTS
Southwest Sector

The preservation of perishables in the southwest section of the pueblo was poor. Only one excavation context, a Secondary burial in remodeled single-story Room 4A, furnished evidence of worked fiber remains (Table 46.3). Burial 4A002, an adult male, was wrapped in a 2/2 (?)-twill plaited mat finished with an intricate selvage (Feature 4A007=FS 80,003 and 80,004, Figure 46.3). The knotted ties (FS 80,001) found with the burial are probably the remains of cords used to secure the mat around the body. The body had been placed into a slab-lined pit that was covered with wood beams and a second layer of matting (Feature 4A005=FS 80,002). Associated ceramics included a Mesa Verde mug, a Mesa Verde Black-on-white bowl, and a corrugated vessel.

Northwest Sector

Perishables were recovered from six three-story rooms in the northwest part of the pueblo: 30W, 31 (A and W), 33 (B, C, and W), 36W, 37W, and 43W. (Identification of these rooms as three-story follows from Paul Reed's (Chapters 4 and 8) reinterpretation of Salmon's size and layout. Excavators identified this section as two-story.) These rooms are all in the second row from the back wall, except for Room 43W, which is along the back wall. All except Room 36W were excavated down to the Primary floor. An intense fire destroyed this part of the pueblo during the Secondary occupation, preserving extensive deposits of carbonized perishable remains in the trash and fallen roof debris. Much of this is domestic trash, but significant quantities of perishables, some unburned, were also preserved as mortuary offerings with burials in Rooms 33, 36, and 43.

Room 30W

This room produced a small assemblage of burned and unburned perishables (Table 46.4). An unburned, finely plaited sandal (FS 80,007) was recovered from what excavators called Secondary/ Intermediate trash, and the circular base of a carbonized coiled basket (FS 80,005) was found in roof-fall debris (Figure 46.4). Attributed to the Secondary occupation, this basket has a two-rod-and-bundle

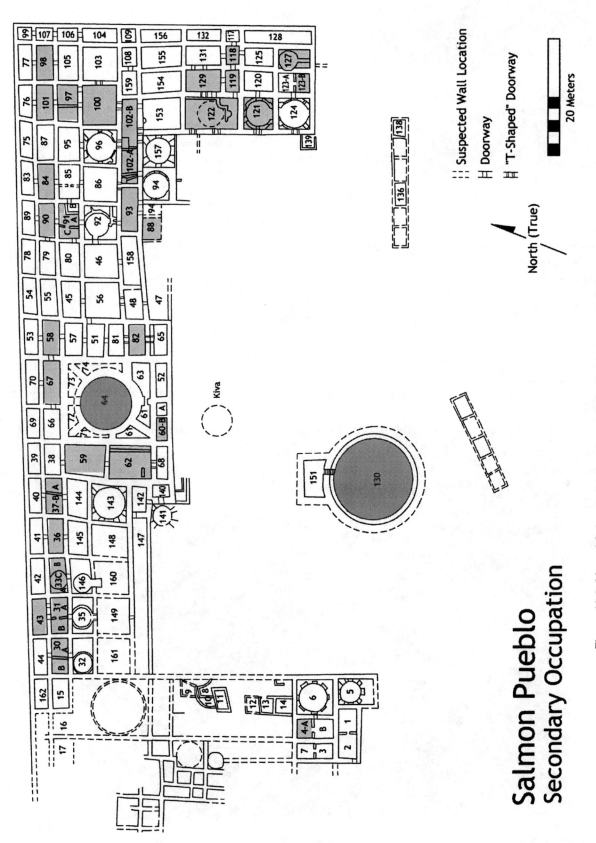

Salmon Pueblo
Secondary Occupation

Figure 46.2. Map of Salmon showing Secondary distribution of worked fiber artifacts.

Figure 46.3. Room 4A, in situ view of plaited mat Feature 4A007 (FS 80,003 and 80,004) with Burial 4A002.

foundation and was originally at least 19 cm in diameter. When found, the base was fused to a sandstone slab (FS 80,010) that was probably lying on the roof or floor of an upper-story room when the ceiling collapsed (Figure 46.5).

Rooms 31A and 31W

Room 31A yielded only a few bits of cordage and some possible matting (Table 46.5). Room 31W, however, produced several worked fiber artifacts, including a deteriorated plaited mat worked in 2/2 (?) twill (FS 80,015) from Primary fill. Objects tentatively attributed to the Secondary occupation include a large rim section of a 3/3-twill plaited ring basket (Feature 31W008=FS 80,013, see Figure 46.62c) and a large steep-sided coiled basket with a two-rod-and-bundle foundation (SA 31W011=FS 80,479). When found, the basket was lying upside down in a pit (Feature 31W017) that had been dug into unstructured trash on the roof (Figure 46.6). Roof-fall also produced a fragment of a twined sandal or tumpband (FS 80,014). Although excavators classified the artifacts in this stratum (F-1-06) as Secondary, more than half of the sherds were identified in the rough sort as Chaco, Escavada, Gallup, Mancos, or McElmo Black-on-white. I believe this twined object dates to the Primary occupation as well.

Excavators also described a "mat" of unwoven cedar bark (SA 31W012) in association with a burial found in this room (Feature 31W013). Evidently this matting was not collected.

Rooms 33B, 33C, and 33W

Worked fiber artifacts were associated with two Secondary burials in Room 33 (Table 46.6). Burial 33B001, a richly furnished, multiple burial of three

Figure 46.4. Room 30W, in situ view of carbonized basket base (FS 80,005) and corn in roof-fall.

Table 46.3. Distribution of perishable artifacts in Room 4A.

Feature Number	Feature Type	Stratum	Occupation	Object Type	Fea./Artifact (SA) No.	New FS Cat. No.
004A002	Burial	B-4-8	Secondary	Yucca or hide cordage; 2 yucca square knots	–	80,001.1, 80,001.2
004A002	Burial	B-4-8	Secondary	1 yucca square knot + fragment of yucca leaf (remains of upper mat; remainder not recovered)	Feature 004A005	80,002
004A002	Burial	B-4-8	Secondary	Lower plaited mat with intricate selvage	Feature 004A007	80,003, 80,004

Table 46.4. Distribution of perishable artifacts in Room 30W.*

Context	Stratum	Occupation	Object Type	Fea./Artifact (SA) No.	New FS Cat. No.
Roof/roof-fall	F-1-02	Secondary	Impression of coiled basket on sandstone slab	–	80,010
Occupational fill	G-1-03	Secondary	Coiled basket base	–	80,005
Occupational fill	G-1-03	Secondary	Yucca cordage	–	80,009
Occupational fill	G-2-08	Secondary	Disarticulated remains of mat	–	80,006
Unstructured trash	M-1-06	Secondary/Intermediate	Plaited sandal?	–	80,007
Unstructured trash	M-1-06	Secondary/Intermediate	2 yucca square knots	–	80,008

*All artifacts lack feature associations.

Table 46.5. Distribution of perishable artifacts in Rooms 31A and 31W.

Room	Feature Number	Context	Stratum	Occupation	Object Type	Fea./Artifact (SA) No.	New FS Cat. No.
031A	–	Occupational fill	G-1-04	Secondary	Yucca cordage	–	80,011
031A	–	Mixed	Mixed	Unassigned	Remains of mat?	–	80,012
031W	–	Roof-fall	F-1-06	Primary/early Secondary	Twined sandal or tumpband	–	80,014
031W	–	Pit fill	L-1-07	Secondary	Plaited ring basket	Fea. 031W008	80,013
031W	–	Fill	L-3-12.2	Primary	Plaited mat	–	80,015
031W	031W017	Pit in trash on roof	L-1-03.5	Secondary?	Coiled basket	SA 031W011?	80,479

Figure 46.5. Room 30W, impression of coiled basket FS 80,005 on sandstone slab (FS 80,010) from roof-fall.

individuals, was accompanied by a coiled basket with a two-rod-and-bundle, bunched (?) foundation (FS 80,016, see Figure 46.65b) and two 2/2 diagonal-twill plaited mats (Feature 33B006=FS 80,017 and 80,018). Excavators also recovered a bowstring of sinew or yucca (Feature 33B007=FS 80,020) from one (SA 33B002) of the two full-sized bows with Skeleton 2. Other offerings with this burial included several wooden arrows and at least six decorated ceramic vessels, including a St. Johns Polychrome bowl.

The other burial in this room, Feature 33B002, was an infant. The child was associated with a wooden cradleboard and a 2/2 twill-plaited mat (FS 80,019, Figure 46.7). In addition to these mortuary-related perishables, the heel end of an unburned, finely plaited yucca sandal (FS 80,021, see Figure 46.83a) was found in the roof-fall of this room.

Only one fiber artifact, a yucca square knot, was found in Room 33C (Table 46.6). Room 33W produced one of the most important burials at Salmon, an elderly male (Feature 33W012) interred on what excavators identified as a Primary/Intermediate contact surface. Irwin-Williams (Chapter 16) identified this individual as a possible "bow priest." The burial was associated with several layers of wrappings, including a cotton plain-weave blanket (FS 80,023.3 and 80,030.3, Figure 46.8), a twined fur (or feather?) robe (SA 33W023 and botanical samples 33W2020 and 33W2021), a finely woven 2/2 twill-plaited mat (SA 33W019), and an exterior mat woven in 2/2 twill plaiting with intentional shifts (SA 33W 011; see Table 46.6 for FS numbers, Figure 46.9). A small twig bundle (botanical sample 33W2024=FS 80,032.2) was tied around the neck. Excavators recorded a 3.5 cm-wide plaited "strap" (SA 33W021= FS 80,026 and 80,027, see Figure 46.58d) extending from the knee

Figure 46.6. Room 31W, in situ view of coiled basket SA 31W011 (FS 80,479) upside-down in roof trash.

Table 46.6. Distribution of perishable artifacts in Rooms 33B, 33C, and 33W.

Room	Feature Number	Context	Stratum	Occupation	Object Type	Fea./Artifact (SA) No.	New FS Cat. No.
033B	033B001	Burials (three)	L-1-03	Secondary	Coiled basket	–	80,016
033B	033B001, SKEL 2	Burials (three)	F-1-03	Secondary	Plaited mat	Fea. 33B006	80,017
033B	033B001, SKEL 2	Burials (three)	L-1-03	Secondary	Cordage from bow	Fea. 33B007	80,020
033B	033B001, SKEL 3	Burials (three)	L-1-03	Secondary	Plaited mat	–	80,018
033B	033B002	Burial	C-1-12	Secondary	Plaited mat	–	80,019
033B	–	Roof-fall	F-1-03	Secondary	Plaited sandal	–	80,021
033C	–	Structured trash	C-1-07	Secondary	1 yucca square knot	–	80,022
033W	033W012	Burial	L-1-11.5	Primary (late?)	Cotton plain-weave cloth	–	80,023.3, 80,030.3
033W	033W012?	Feature fill	L-1-11.5	Primary (late?)	2 yucca square & granny knots	–	80,035
033W	033W012	Burial	L-1-11.5	Primary (late?)	Twig bundle	Bot. sample 33W2024	80,032.2
033W	033W012	Burial	L-1-11.5	Primary (late?)	Exterior plaited mat	SA 33W011	80,023.1, 80,030.1, 80,032.1
033W	033W012	Burial	L-1-11.5	Primary (late?)	Interior plaited mat	SA 33W019	80,024, 80,025, 80,033.1
033W	033W012	Burial	L-1-11.5	Primary (late?)	"Strap" or selvage of plaited mat	SA 033W021	80,026, 80,027
033W	033W012	Burial	L-1-11.5	Primary (late?)	Reed blind	SA 033W022	Not found
033W	033W012	Burial	L-1-11.5	Primary (late?)	Twined robe	SA 033W023; + bot. samples 033W2020, 033W2021	80,023.2, 80,028, 80,029, 80,030.2, 80,031 80,033.2, 80,034
033W	–	Structured trash	C-3-12	Primary	Plaited sandal	–	80,041, 80,042
033W	–	Roof-fall	F-2-09	Secondary/ Intermediate	Plaited mat	–	80,036
033W	–	Roof-fall	F-2-09	Secondary/ Intermediate	1 hide (?) square knot	–	80,037
033W	–	Roof-fall	F-2-09	Secondary/ Intermediate	2 yucca square knots	–	80,038, 80,039
033W	–	Roof-fall	F-3-13	Primary	1 yucca square knot	–	80,040
033W	–	Occupational fill	G-1.5-14.5	Primary	1 yucca or cedar bark square (?) knot	–	80,043

Figure 46.7. Room 33B, in situ view of plaited mat (FS 80,019) with infant Burial 33B002.

to the neck of the individual. This strap closely resembles the intricate selvages found on many plaited mats at Salmon, and could be the selvage from the exterior mat. However Keith Adams, who excavated the burial, remembers it as a separate strap (personal communication 2003).

One of the most richly furnished burials at Salmon, burial 33W012, was also associated with several other perishable artifacts, including a "reed blind" (SA 33W022, not located), a large wooden bow, nine or more reed arrows, two carved and painted wooden prayer sticks, a grass brush, and a wooden rabbitstick. (As noted, I did not examine the wooden artifacts.) The field map and the significant artifact form for the reed blind indicate that the blind was rolled up when found (Figure 46.10). It is intriguing to speculate that this might have been a reed cylinder or quiver similar to examples found at Aztec Ruins and Chaco Canyon. I discuss this object in greater depth in the discussion of twined reed mats.

Figure 46.8. Room 33W, in situ view of cotton plain-weave textile (FS 80,023.3 and 80,030.3) with Burial 33W012.

Room 33W also produced a few non-mortuary-related perishables, including an unburned, finely plaited yucca sandal (FS 80,041 and 80,042, see Figure 46.83b) associated with Primary trash and pieces of carbonized 3/3-twill plaited matting (FS 80,036, see Figure 46.57f) from what excavators identified as Secondary/Intermediate roof-fall.

Room 36W

Room 36W produced a diverse assortment of perishables (Table 46.7). The only artifact from an identified Primary context is the deteriorated remains of what excavators described as a mat (Feature 36W028=FS 80,055), now a mass of disarticulated plant material (yucca?). The mat was associated with a Primary lithic scatter (Features 36W028 and 36W031).

A Secondary burial in this room (Feature 36W 003) also contained faint evidence of matting, but none survived. The only worked fiber artifact recovered from this burial is the remains of deteriorated cordage (FS 80,044), fused to the surface of a tapered wooden object. The latter might be the digging stick mentioned in the burial report.

Trash and burned roof deposits produced the remains of nine baskets and pot rests. Four of these are coiled baskets. Two (FS 80,049 and 80,050) are dated to the Secondary occupation have two-rod-and-bundle foundations. FS 80,066 and 80,067 were two miniature coiled baskets recovered from what excavators called Secondary/Intermediate structured trash. I was unable to locate either miniature basket, although it is known that they were collected, because they were examined by an unidentified analyst in 1977. It is unfortunate that neither could be located, because miniature baskets have an intriguing association with ritual and mortuary contexts at Pueblo Bonito and Aztec, and one was found with burial 43W005 at Salmon.

This room also produced the remains of two plaited ring baskets and fragments of another plaited basket or pot rest (FS 80,054), all dated to the Secondary occupation. The first ring basket (SA 36W044 and botanical sample 36W4018=FS 80,045) was recovered from a trash deposit above the burned roof. It is woven in 2/2 twill and includes a section of the wooden ring. The second basket (SA 36W049 and SA 36W056 and botanical sample 36W4142= FS 80,047, 80,048, and 80,052) is the remains of a large plaited ring basket with a diamond-twill design, recovered from burned roof-fall (Figure 46.11, see also Figure 46.62e, f).

Two, and perhaps three plaited pot rests were also found in this room, all dated to the Secondary

Figure 46.9. Room 33W, in situ view of exterior plaited mat SA 33W011 (FS 80,023.2 and others), wooden artifacts, and projectile point with Burial 33W012.

occupation. SA 36W048 (FS 80,046, see Figure 46.71a, b) is a nearly complete, carbonized pot rest of the truncated form worked in 2/2 plaiting. It was associated with burned roof-fall, as was botanical sample 36W4182 (FS 80,053), the probable remains of another 2/2-plaited pot rest. FS 80,054, also 2/2 plaited,

might be yet another example. All of these plaited artifacts were recovered from the upper fill or burned roof deposits. The plaited baskets and pot rests and at least one coiled basket (FS 80,049) were probably lying on the roof or floor of an upper-story room when this section of the pueblo burned.

A diverse assortment of worked fiber artifacts, most dated to the Secondary occupation, was recovered from the burned roof-fall, trash, and floor of Room 37 (Table 46.8). The deteriorated remains of a coiled basket (SA 37W081=FS 80,069) and plaited mat (SA 37W083=FS 80,070) were found directly on the Secondary floor (Figure 46.12). Two coiled pot rests or coils of basketry raw materials, SA 37W075 (FS 80,068, Figure 46.13) and SA 37W077 (not found), were found in trash deposits, some mixed with burned roof-fall. Excavators identified the B-2-11 stratum in which FS 80,068 was found as postoccu-

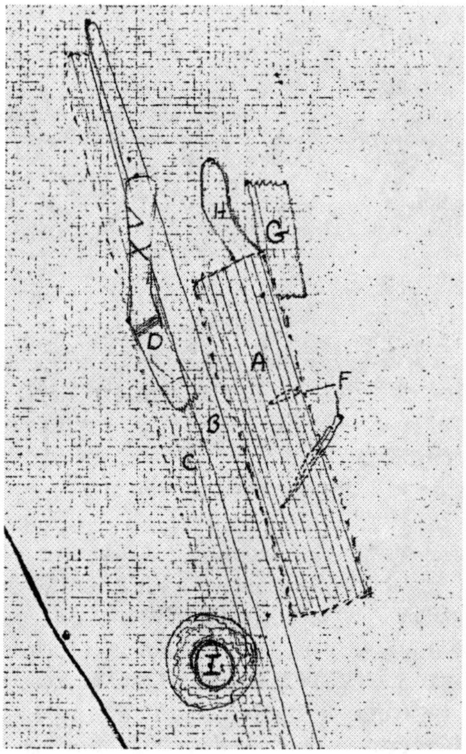

Figure 46.10. Room 33W, detail of field sketch showing rolled-up blind SA 33W011 and other artifacts with Burial 33W012.

Figure 46.11. Room 36W, in situ view of plaited ring basket SA 36W049 (FS 80,047 and others) in burned roof-fall.

Table 46.7. Distribution of perishable artifacts in Room 36W.

Feature Number	Context	Stratum	Occupation	Object Type	Fea./Artifact (SA) No.	New FS Cat. No.
036W003	Burial	L-1-05.5	Secondary	Traces of cordage	–	80,044
036W029	Lithic scatter	C-25-04.5	Primary	Mat? (mass of plant material)	Fea. 036W028?	80,055
036W031	Lithic scatter	C-6.2-08.2	Primary	Mat? (mass of plant material)	Fea. 036W032	Not found
–	Post-occupational fill	B-1-02	Secondary	Plaited basket or pot rest	–	80,054
–	Structured trash	C-3-05	Secondary	Remains of plaited mat?	–	80,056
–	Structured trash	C-3-05	Secondary	Coiled basket	Bot. sample 036W2039	80,050
–	Structured trash	C-13-19	Secondary/ Intermediate	5 yucca square knots	–	80,059
–	Structured trash	C-14-20	Secondary	Mat? (mass of plant material)	–	80,064
–	Structured trash	C-15-21	Secondary/ Intermediate	Yucca cordage	–	80,057
–	Trash and roof-fall	C-15-21	Secondary/ Intermediate	1 yucca square knot	–	80,062
–	Structured trash	C-15-21	Secondary/ Intermediate	Mat? (mass of plant material)	–	80,063
–	On burned roof	F-1-15	Secondary	Plaited pot rest	SA 036W048	80,046
–	Roof-fall	F-1-15	Secondary	Plaited pot rest?	Bot. sample 036W4182	80,053
–	Roof-fall	F-1-15	Secondary	1 yucca square knot	–	80,061
–	Roof-fall	F-1-15	Secondary	Yucca cordage	–	80,065
–	Unstructured trash	M-1-14	Secondary	Cordage	Bot. sample 036W4046	80,051
–	Unstructured trash	M-1-14	Secondary	Plaited ring basket	SA 036W044 and bot. sample 036W4018	80,045
–	Unstructured trash	M-1-14	Secondary	Yucca cordage	–	80,058, 80,060
–	On burned roof	N-1-13	Secondary	Plaited ring basket	SA 036W049, SA 036W056, bot sample 036W4142	80,047, 80,048, 80,052
–	Roof-fall	N-1-13	Secondary	Coiled basket	SA 036W058	80,049
–	Structured trash	N-1-13	Secondary/ Intermediate	2 baskets	–	80,066, 80,067

pational fill and attributed to the Secondary occupation. However, 86 percent of the sherds in the ceramic rough sort are Escavada, Gallup, or Mancos B/w, and I have tentatively reclassified this artifact as Primary. Secondary trash deposits also produced a 2/2-plaited pot rest (FS 80,072) and the probable remains of two finely plaited sandals worked in 2/2 diagonal-twill plaiting (FS 80,073.2 and 80,071). Fragments of a coiled basket with a two-rod-and-bundle foundation (FS 80,073) and an assortment of yucca cordage and yucca ties were also found in this room.

Room 43W

Room 43W produced one of the largest perishable assemblages at Salmon, as well as some of the most richly furnished burials at the site (Table 46.9).

Never remodeled during the Secondary occupation, the room was used instead for burials (Reed, Chapter 8). Table 46.9 provides the FS catalog numbers for the mortuary artifacts from this room. Additional fiber artifacts were preserved in the burnt roof-fall of this room.

Burial 43W003. This well-preserved, adolescent female was wrapped in a twined feather (?) robe (SA 43W039) and a large, coarsely woven 2/2-twill plaited mat with an intricate-selvage border (SA 43W030 and SA 43W032). Excavators noted a resemblance between the selvage on this mat and the "straps" reported from other burials (e.g., 33W012). A second 2/2-plaited mat (SA 43W031), finer in weave, was also found. Figure 46.14 shows both mats prior to excavation. An elliptically shaped

Table 46.8. Distribution of perishable artifacts in Room 37W.

Context	Stratum	Occupation	Object Type	Fea./Artifact (SA) No.	New FS Cat. No.
Post-occupational fill	B-2-11	Primary?	Coiled pot rest or raw materials; tied with red yucca square knot	SA 037W075	80,068.1, 80,068.2
Structured trash	C-2-08	Secondary?	Coiled pot rest or raw materials	SA 037W077	Not found
Structured trash	C-2-08	Secondary	Plaited pot rest	–	80,072
Structured trash	C-2-08	Secondary	2 yucca or cedar bark square knots	–	80,073.1
Structured trash	C-2-08	Secondary	Plaited sandal?	–	80,073.2
Structured trash	C-2-08	Secondary	Coiled basket	–	80,073.3
Structured trash	C-2-08	Secondary	Remains of mat?	–	80,074.1
Structured trash	C-2-08	Secondary	Yucca cordage	–	80,074.2
Structured trash	C-2-08	Secondary	3 yucca square knots	–	80,075, 80,076, 80,079
Structured trash	C-3.5-11.5	Secondary	Disintegrated knot	–	80,082
Structured trash	C-4-10	Secondary	2 yucca square (?) knots	–	80,078, 80,083
Structured trash	C-4-10	Secondary	1 yucca square knot	–	80,081
Structured trash and roof-fall	F-2-05	Secondary	Plaited sandal?	–	80,071
Structured trash and roof-fall	F-2-05	Secondary	Stick wrapped with yucca leaf	–	80,077
Roof-fall	F-2-05	Secondary	Yucca cordage	–	80,080
Floor surface	H-1-13	Secondary	Coiled basket	SA 037W081	80,069
Floor surface	H-1-13	Secondary	Plaited mat	SA 037W083	80,070

plaited pouch (SA 43W041, see Figure 46.68a, b) containing organic plant material was found beneath one shoulder and next to the head. Fragments of matting (SA 43W031) found north of the skull are probably additional pieces of this pouch; one appears to be the mouth opening. Excavators suggested that this pouch might have served as a pillow.

Burial 43W005. This burial of a child less than 12 years in age was accompanied by multiple layers of burial wrappings and a rich assortment of offerings. The latter included a plaited pouch, a small coiled basket, and two possible miniature arrows. Most of these objects became carbonized as a result of a localized fire. Excavators noted similarities between this burial and 33W012, the "bow priest" burial.

The child was wrapped in a large twined turkey-feather robe (SA 43W008 and SA 43W010, see Figure

Figure 46.12. Room 37W, in situ view of plaited mat SA 37W083 (FS 80,070) on floor.

Figure 46.13. Room 37W, in situ view of coil of sumac (?) twigs SA 37W075 (FS 80,068) in trash deposit.

Table 46.9. Distribution of perishable artifacts in Room 43W.

Feature Number	Context	Stratum	Occupation	Object Type	Fea./Artifact (SA) No.	New FS Cat. No.
043W003	Burial	L-2-07.5	Secondary	Coarse plaited mat with intricate selvage	SA 043W030 (body of mat), SA 043W032 (selvage)	80,085, 80,087, 80,159.1
043W003	Burial	L-2-07.5	Secondary	Finely plaited mat (some fragments part of pouch)	SA 043W031	80,159.
043W003	Burial	L-2-07.5	Secondary	Twined fur or feather robe	SA 043W039	80,086
043W003	Burial	L-2-07.5	Secondary	Plaited pouch	SA 043W041	80,084, 80,159.3
043W005	Burial	L-1-06.5	Secondary	1 yucca square knot	–	80,110
043W005	Burial	L-1-06.5	Secondary	Cotton plain weave cloth	Bot. sample 043W2062 from SA 43W007	80,096
043W005	Burial	L-1-06.5	Secondary	1 incomplete yucca knot	Bot. sample 043W2087	80,109
043W005	Burial	L-1-06.5	Secondary	Fine and coarse plaited mats with intricate selvages	SA 043W004	80,088, 80,089.1, 80,090.2, 80,091.1
043W005	Burial	L-1-06.5	Secondary	Plaited pouch	SA 043W006	80,092, 80,093
043W005	Burial	L-1-06.5	Secondary	Cotton plain weave cloth with possible weft-wrap openwork	SA 043W007	80,090.3, 80,091.2, 80,094, 80,095, 80,096, 80,097.1
043W005	Burial	L-1-06.5	Secondary	Twined feather robe	SA 043W008, SA 043W010, SA 043W015 (header cord)	80,089.2, 80,090.1, 80,091.3, 80,091.4, 80,097.2, 80,098, 80,099, 80,100, 80,101, 80,102, 80,103, 80,104.1, 80,105, 80,106, 80,108
043W005	Burial	L-1-06.5	Secondary	Fine plaited mat	SA 043W011	80,104.2
043W005	Burial	L-1-06.5	Secondary	Small coiled basket with opening	SA 043W012	80,107
043W019?	Burial or roof-fall	S-2-06.6	Secondary	Coiled (?) pot rest	SA 043W022	Not found
043W019	Burial	F-1.5-06 (formerly L-3-6.6)	Secondary	Coiled basket	SA 043W025	80,112, 80,113, 80,114
043W019	Burial	F-1.5-06, S-2-06.6 (formerly L-3-6.6)	Secondary	Twined feather robe	SA 043W026, SA 043W040	80,115, 80,117.1, 80,118, 80,123, 80,124, 80,125
043W019	Burial	F-1.5-06, S-2-06.6 (was L-3-6.6)	Secondary	Blind (threaded wood slat "curtain")	SA 043W027	80,116, 80,120.2

Table 46.9 (continued)

Feature Number	Context	Stratum	Occupation	Object Type	Fea./Artifact (SA) No.	New FS Cat. No.
043W019	Burial	S-2-06.6 (formerly L-3-6.6)	Secondary	Plaited mat	SA 043W028	80,117.2, 80,119, 80,120.1, 80,121, 80,122
043W042	Lithic scatter	G-1-10	Primary	Twined sandal	SA 043W050	80,127
043W042	Lithic scatter	G-1-10	Primary	Plaited sandal	SA 043W071	80,126
043W057?	Near burial	F-2-07	Secondary	Coiled basket containing bone awl	SA 043W055	80,128
043W057	Burial	F-1.5-06	Secondary	Cotton plain weave cloth	–	80,139
043W057	Burial	F-2-07, L-4-06.7	Secondary	2 plaited mats (upper mats)	SA 043W059, SA 043W060; also bot from top of mug (SA 043W065) assoc with burial	80,129, 80,130, 80,131, 80,132, 80,160, 80,485.1, 80,485.2
043W057	Burial	L-4-06.7	Secondary	6 yucca square knots	SA 043W066	80,133, 80,134, 80,135
043W057	Burial	F-2-07, L-4-06.7	Secondary	Twined fur or feather robe	SA 043W069	80,136, 80,137.1, 80,138, 80,140.1, 80,143
043W057	Burial	L-4-06.7	Secondary	Lower plaited mat	SA 043W070	80,137.2, 80,140.2, 80,141, 80,142
043W057	Burial	L-4-06.7	Secondary	Thick twined object	–	Not found, but visible in field photo
–	Post-occup. fill (trash)	B-4-09	Primary	Remains of bent wood knot (not analyzed)	–	80,158
–	Post-occup. fill (trash)	B-4-09	Primary	Coiled pot rest or yucca raw materials	SA 043W018	80,145
–	Post-occup. fill (trash)	B-4-09	Primary?	Coiled (?) pot rest	SA 43W017	Not found
Assoc w/ 043W003?	Unstructured trash/ roof-fall	F-1.5-06	Secondary	Plaited pot rest	SA 043W013	80,111, 80,144
–	Unstructured trash/ roof-fall	F-1.5-06	Secondary	Yucca cordage	Bot sample 043W2061	80,146
–	Roof-fall	F-1.5-06	Secondary	Plaited sandal	–	80,147
–	Roof-fall	F-1.5-06	Secondary	Yucca cordage	–	80,148, 80,149, 80,150, 80,155
–	Roof-fall	F-1.5-06	Secondary	Cotton plain weave cloth	Related to 80,139?	80,151
–	Roof-fall	F-1.5-06	Secondary	Plaited sandal or mat	–	80,152
–	Roof-fall	F-1.5-06	Secondary	1 yucca square knot	–	80,153
–	Roof-fall	F-3-08	Secondary	1 hide or yucca square knot	–	80,156
–	Contact between strata	S-2-06.6	Secondary	Feather cordage tied in square knot	–	80,154.1, 80,154.2
–	Contact between strata	S-2-06.6	Unassigned	Yucca cordage	–	80,157

Figure 46.14. Room 43W, in situ view of two plaited mats SA 43W030-43W032 (FS 80,085 and others) with Burial 43W003.

46.76a-d) and a finely woven cotton plain-weave blanket that might have been decorated in weft-wrap openwork (SA 43W007; see discussion in analysis section, also Figure 46.73a-c). The body had been placed into a pit that was lined with a coarsely woven 2/2-twill plaited mat, bordered with a 3–4 cm wide intricate selvage (SA 43W004). A finely woven 2/2-twill plaited pouch (43W006, see Figure 46.68c) was found beneath the head, and might have served as a pillow. The pouch was filled with a thick mass of plant remains, including corn tassels, juniper twigs, and unidentified seeds (SA 43W009). A small coiled basket (SA 43W012, see Figure 46.67e) was found next to the skull. Only a small section of the base was recovered. This basket appears to have been made with a bundle foundation, and it has a conspicuous 0.5 cm diameter hole at the center. Unfortunately, no in situ photos were found to help determine its original size and shape.

Excavators described a yucca ornament (SA 43W 015) near the right arm of the burial. My analysis identified this as part of the header cord from the twined robe. The possible miniature arrows (not analyzed) had been placed above the tibia on top of the cloth wrapping.

Burial 43W019. This burial of an adult female was not as well preserved as the other burials in this room, but it nevertheless was accompanied by a wide range of wrappings and perishable objects. The burial had been interred on an upper-story floor, which collapsed when the room burned, incinerating the body and funerary goods. Excavators questioned the association of some of these objects, noting that some of them may have been lying on the roof (or the upper-story floor) when the ceiling collapsed, rather than intentionally placed with the burial.

The body was wrapped in a twined feather robe (SA 43W026 and 43W040) and a large plaited mat woven in 2/2 and 3/3-twill plaiting (SA 43W028, Figure 46.15, see also Figures 46.57f, 76e, f). Other perishable artifacts associated with the burial or found nearby in the burnt roof-fall included a coarsely woven coiled basket with a two-rod-and-bundle foundation (SA 43W015, see Figure 46.65c), a coiled pot rest (SA 43W022, not located), and a "wood slat curtain" made of willow elements threaded together (SA 43W027, Figure 46.16). This latter object was of indeterminate size, but was originally at least 22 cm wide and 36 cm long. As noted, it is possible that the coiled basket and wood slat curtain were originally associated with the upper-story floor, rather than the burial.

Burial 43W057. A rich assemblage of burial wrappings accompanied this burial of an adult female. The body had been covered with soil and debris before the room burned. This insulated the matting from the fire, allowing some of it to survive in an unburned state. Although now extremely frag-

Figure 46.15. Room 43W, detail of field sketch showing plaited mat SA 43W028 (FS 80,117.2 and others) and framework of twined robe SA 43W026 and 43W040 (FS 80,115 and others) with Burial 43W019.

mentary, both the mats and the twined robe were remarkably well preserved (albeit minus the fur or feathers) when uncovered during excavation.

The body was wrapped in a twined fur or feather robe (SA 43W069, Figure 46.17, see also Figure 46.77a). Two small fragments of cotton cloth (FS 80,139, see Figure 46.73d) found among the robe fragments are probably the remains of an inner cotton blanket. The body had been placed into a pit lined with a 3/3-diagonal twill mat with an intricate

selvage (SA 43W070, see Figure 46.58f), then covered with two overlapping plaited mats, one woven in 2/2 twill, the other 3/3, both with intricate selvages (SA 43W059 and SA 43W060, Figures 46.18 and 19, see also Figures 46.57d, 58b, c, e). An unidentified twined (?) object, visible in several field photos but not collected or described in the burial report, was found near the feet (Figure 46.20). This could be the remains of a twined bag or perhaps a coarse sandal. A rabbit stick had been placed on the body. A small, well-preserved basket bowl with a two-rod-and-bundle foundation (SA 43W055), containing the tip of a bone awl, was found near the burial and may have been associated (Figures 46.21 and 22, see also Figure 46.65d).

Figure 46.16. Room 43W, in situ view of coiled basket SA 43W025 (FS 80,112-80,114), lower, and portion of wood slat curtain SA 43W027 (FS 80,116 and 80,120.2), upper, in roof-fall. Possibly associated with Burial 43W019.

Figure 46.17. Room 43W, in situ view of framework of twined robe SA 43W069 (FS 80,136 and others), left, and other artifacts with Burial 43W057.

Figure 46.18. Room 43W, in situ view of two overlapping mats SA 43W059 and 43W060 (FS 80,129 and others) covering Burial 43W057.

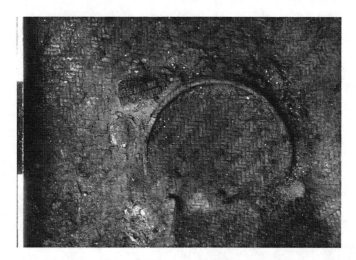

Figure 46.19. Room 43W, detail of large 3/3-plaited mat SA 43W059 and 43W060 (FS 80,129 and others) covering ceramic bowl with Burial 43W057.

Figure 46.20. Room 43W, in situ view of unidentified twined (?) object (not collected) with Burial 43W057.

Figure 46.21. Room 43W, in situ view of well-preserved basket bowl SA 43W055 (FS 80,128) found near south wall. Possibly associated with Burial 43W057.

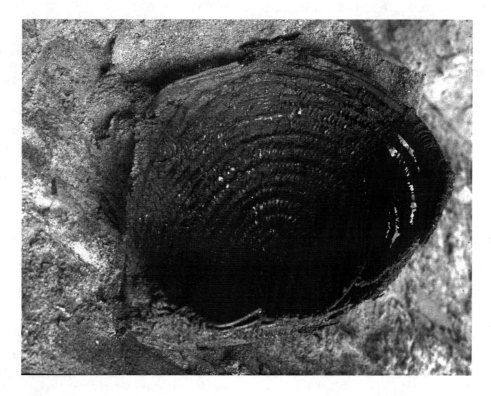

Figure 46.22. Room 43W, different in situ view of basket bowl SA 43W055 (FS 80,128).

In addition to this large assemblage of mortuary artifacts, Room 43W also produced perishable artifacts from the floor, trash, and roof-fall. The remains of two unburned sandals, one twined (SA 43W050= FS 80,127, see Figure 46.79c) and the other plaited (SA 43W071=FS 80,126), were recovered from an organic matrix associated with a Primary lithic scatter, Feature 43W042. Two coiled pot rests or coils of basketry raw materials (SA 43W017, not located, and SA 43W018=FS 80,145) were also found in a Primary trash level in this room.

Figure 46.23. Room 43W, in situ view of truncated pot rest SA 43W013 (FS 80,111 and 80,144) in roof-fall.

Other perishable artifacts, most from burned roof-fall, are attributed to the Secondary occupation. In addition to the usual assortment of yucca cordage and knots, the roof-fall yielded a 2/2-twill plaited pot rest of truncated form (SA 43W013=FS 80,111 and 80,144, Figure 46.23, see also Figure 46.71c), the remains of a finely woven 2/2-twill plaited sandal (FS 80,147, see Figure 46.83d), a finely woven 2/2-twill plaited sandal with intentional shifts (FS 80,152, see Figure 46.84a, b), and fragments of cotton plain-weave cloth (FS 80,151). The latter could be related to the cloth from burial 43W057.

The Tower Kiva and Surrounding Rooms: The Ritual Core of the Pueblo

Some of the most interesting fiber artifacts at Salmon came from the Tower Kiva and adjacent rooms. The interstitial space of the Tower Kiva (Room 61A) produced an unburned assemblage of Primary perishables. Other Primary artifacts were recovered from the deep unburned trash deposits in Room 62W. The only assemblage of weaving tools found at Salmon, dated to the Primary occupation, also came from this area of the pueblo (Room 81W).

Fiber perishables dated to the Secondary occupation were recovered from rooms 58W, 59W, 60B, 62A, B, and W, 81W, and 82W. Hundreds of fiber artifacts came from Room 62W alone. One of the best in situ assemblages of perishables at the site was found in the Tower Kiva (Room 64W), where an important assemblage of Secondary perishable artifacts was preserved on the burnt bench and floor.

Room 58W

This room produced only one worked fiber artifact—the remains of a coiled basket with a two-rod-and-bundle, bunched foundation (SA 58W019=FS 80,161, see Figure 46.65e and Table 46.10). The basket was lying on the floor, and was probably crushed by roof-fall when the structure burned. Although only the base remains, its shape suggests that it was part of a large, steep-sided conical basket (or perhaps a plaque), at least 15 cm in diameter.

Room 59W

Excavators collected large quantities of plant materials from Room 59, which they described as an extensive layer of willow and juniper "matting" located between two layers of trash strata (Features 59W001 and 59W007, Table 46.11). I was unable to find any evidence of weave structure in this material, and believe it to be thatching, rather than woven matting. The only other worked fiber artifacts from this room are a few pieces of yucca cordage and knots.

Room 60B

One worked fiber artifact, a coiled bundle of juniper bark possibly used as a pot rest (FS 80,178), was recovered from the roof surface of Room 60B, a small, remodeled, plaza-facing room south of the Tower Kiva (Table 46.12). This Secondary artifact may have been sitting on the roof when the structure burned.

Room 61A— Tower Kiva Interstitial Space

Excavations in the southwest interstitial space of the Tower Kiva (Room 61A) produced a small but important and well-preserved assemblage of Primary perishable artifacts (Table 46.13). The assemblage includes the probable remains of two plaited ring baskets with different rim constructions (Features 61A012=FS 80,179 and 61A013=FS 80,180.1 and .2, Figure 46.24, see also Figure 46.63b-d), a finely woven twined sandal colored red with hematite (Feature 61A023=FS 80,182, Figure 46.25, see also Figure 46.80), and three pot rests or coils of raw materials (Features 61A014 and 61A017, not located, and 61A025= FS 80,181). Feature 61A017 is a coil of sumac (?) twigs (Figure 46.26), and Feature 61A025 (FS 80,181) is a coil of juniper bark bound with yucca cordage (Figure 46.27, see also Figure 46.70d); these objects may have been deposited as a ritual offering during initial kiva construction. (This possibility is discussed, together with similar deposits from Chaco Canyon, in greater depth at the end of the chapter.)

Table 46.10. Distribution of perishable artifact in Room 58W.

Feature Number	Context	Stratum	Occupation	Object Type	Fea./Artifact (SA) No.	New FS Cat. No.
–	Floor surface	H-2-11	Secondary	Large conical coiled basket	SA 058W019	80,161

Table 46.11. Distribution of perishable artifacts in Room 59W.

Feature Number	Context	Stratum	Occupation	Object Type	Fea./Artifact (SA) No.	New FS Cat. No.
–	Structured trash	C-1-04	Secondary	Mat?	–	80,175
–	Structured trash	C-1-04	Secondary	2 yucca square knots	–	80,176
–	Structured trash and contact betweem strata	C-2-05, S-1.4-05.4	Secondary	Mat?	Feature 059W001	80,162, 80,163, 80,164, 80,165, 80,166, 80,167, 80,168, 80,169, 80,170, 80,171, 80,172
–	Roof and backfill	E-1-03	Secondary/ Post-Secondary	Yucca cordage	–	80,177
–	Roof-fall	F-1-03	Secondary	Yucca cordage	–	80,174
–	Contact between strata	S-1.4-05.4	Secondary	Mat?	Feature 059W007	80,173

Table 46.12. Distribution of perishable artifact in Room 60B.

Feature Number	Context	Stratum	Occupation	Object Type	Fea./Artifact (SA) No.	New FS Cat. No.
–	Roof surface	E	Secondary	Coiled pot rest	–	80,178

Table 46.13. Distribution of perishable artifacts in Room 61A (interstitial space of Tower Kiva).

Context	Stratum	Occupation	Object Type	Fea./Artifact (SA) No.	New FS Cat. No.
Interstitial space	D-1-02	Primary	Plaited ring basket (two rods)	Feas. 061A012, 061A013	80,179, 80,180.1
Interstitial space	D-1-02	Primary	Plaited ring basket (single rod)	Fea. 061A013	80,180.2
Interstitial space	D-1-02	Primary	Pot rest	Fea. 061A014	Not found
Interstitial space	D-1-02	Primary	Twined sandal, colored red	Fea. 061A023	80,182
Interstitial space	D-2-03	Primary	Coiled pot rest or raw materials (juniper bark)	SA 061A025	80,181
Interstitial space	D-2-03	Primary	Coiled pot rest or raw materials (sumac?)	Fea. 061A017	Not found
Interstitial space	B-1-02	Secondary?	Textile	Bot sample TX/61A-1	Not found

Figure 46.24. Room 61A, in situ view of plaited ring baskets Features 61A012 and 61A013 (FS 80,179 and 80,180) in interstitial fill of Tower Kiva.

Figure 46.25. Room 61A, in situ view of red-stained twined sandal Feature 61A023 (FS 80,182) in interstitial fill of Tower Kiva.

Figure 46.26. Room 61A, in situ view of coil of sumac (?) twigs Feature 61A017 (not located) in interstitial fill of Tower Kiva.

Figure 46.27. Room 61A, in situ view of coil of juniper bark Feature 61A025 (FS 80,181) in interstitial fill of Tower Kiva.

Another textile, not described in the field records or located during analysis, was reportedly collected as a botanical sample from the upper fill of this room. This textile was from a different stratum and was probably not part of the original Primary cache.

Rooms 62A, 62B, and 62W

Room 62, an unusually large room adjoining the Tower Kiva to the southwest, produced the largest assemblage of worked fiber artifacts at Salmon (Table 46.14). Much of this perishable material has not been burned, and some is surprisingly well preserved. Small quantities of perishables were recovered directly from Primary and Secondary floors. However, most of the material from this room was recovered from deep trash deposits interpreted by excavators as Secondary structured or redeposited trash.

Several perishable artifacts were recovered from the Secondary floor surface of Room 62A. These were part of a general artifact scatter that included corrugated and McElmo Black-on-white ceramics. Two baskets were found: a large plaited ring basket woven in 2/2 twill with some 3/3 shifts (Feature 62A004=FS 80,183, see Figure 46.62b) and a large coiled basket, possibly of conical form, associated with burnt corn and feathers (SA 62W042=FS 80,184 and 80,185, Figure 46.28, see also Figure 46.66a). Other objects on the floor included a plaited pot rest (SA 62A053=FS 80,188) found near a scatter of sherds (Figure 46.29), and the remains of plaited mats (SA 62SA031=FS 80,186 and SA 62A043=FS 80,187). Excavators also reported a finely plaited sandal or mat (SA 62A030) from the floor, but this item was not found during analysis.

The fragmentary remains of two fiber artifacts were found in Room 62B: a 2/2 plaited sandal (FS 80,192.1) and a coiled basket with a one-rod foundation (FS 80,192.2, see Figure 46.67b). Both were associated with Secondary trash.

Room 62W produced the largest assemblage of worked fiber artifacts at the site. Primary perishables were recovered from two strata: G-1-40, an in situ deposit of Primary occupational fill, and CT-45-45, a Primary structured trash deposit. The occupational fill (G-1-40) produced the deteriorated remains of a plaited mat, basket, or sandal (FS 80,335) and a coil of pine needles (?) bound crosswise with yucca strips (botanical sample 62W5055=FS 80,225, see Figure 46.70a). The latter probably served as a pot rest or a bundle of raw materials. Perishables recovered from Primary structured trash include a coil of juniper bark, possibly used as a pot rest (FS 80,332, see Figure 46.70f), and the probable remains of a plaited ring basket colored red with hematite (FS 80,325, see Figure 46.62a). Also found was some yucca cordage, possibly colored red and yellow.

According to the field records, an infant burial (62W122) was found in stratum G-1-40. I was unable to find any additional information about the burial or locate the perishable artifacts—cotton cloth, matting, braided hair—reportedly associated with it. No Primary burials were reported from this room (see Espinosa, Chapter 15). However, the G-1-40 stratum into which the burial was laid was a Primary stratum, so a Primary attribution seems possible.

The vast majority of perishable artifacts from Room 62W came from 2 meters of stratified trash sandwiched between the Primary strata of Room 62W and the Secondary floor of Room 62A. Excavators originally identified this trash deposit as an ash

pit (Features 62W002 and 62W063) and later as redeposited trash. Virtually all of the fiber artifacts recovered from these C- and L-strata midden deposits were classified by excavators as Secondary redeposited trash. However, based on the ceramic rough sort and on stylistic comparisons with other Primary assemblages, I view these deposits as highly mixed, and believe that many of the artifacts date to the Primary occupation.

The C-level strata are dominated by carbon-painted (McElmo/Mesa Verde?) sherds, so much of the materials from these deposits probably dates to the Secondary occupation. In contrast, the deep l-2-07 trash deposit is dominated by Escavada, Gallup, and Mancos Black-on-white sherds; therefore many of the fiber artifacts from this level probably predate the Secondary occupation. Still, all of these levels have been churned up by rodents, so it is impossible to date these objects from their stratigraphic levels alone. I have characterized the cultural affiliation of these contexts as "mixed" in lieu of the excavators' original "Secondary (redeposited)" designation, which I consider misleading.

Cordage and knots constitute the largest proportion of fiber artifacts recovered from these trash strata. Nearly all of the cordage and knots are yucca, and nearly all of the knots are square knots. Some of the cordage is wrapped with rabbit fur or turkey feathers (see Figure 46.53c, d). Some of the yucca cordage and knots appear to be stained red or yellow. Small quantities of cotton yarn and some yucca 3-strand braids were also found (see Figure 46.53e).

Other materials recovered from these trash deposits include woven cotton cloth, sandals, baskets, mats, and pot rests or coils of raw material. Two pieces of cotton plain-weave cloth were found (FS 80,199.1 and 80,209, see Figure 46.73e). The deposits also produced six twined sandals, some with decorated soles (FS 80,272, FS 80,210, FS 80,212.1, botanical sample 62W2066=FS 80,223, FS 80,262, and FS 80,294, see Figure 46.79b, d). Nine objects are probably the remains of finely plaited sandals (SA 62W082=FS 80,200, FS 80,212.2, FS 80,217, FS 80,267.1, FS 80,271.2, FS 80,291, FS 80,310, FS 80,312, FS 80,321, see Figure 46.83c, e, f). Three of these sandals are colored red, and one is nearly complete (Figure 46.30, see also Figure 46.84c-e). A small selvage fragment (FS 80,205.2, see Figure 46.86c, d) could be the selvage from a plaited sandal, basket, or other object.

Baskets include the remains of a plaited ring basket (FS 80,232, see Figure 46.62d) and another plaited basket or mat (botanical sample 62W2024=

Table 46.14. Distribution of perishable artifacts in Rooms 62A, 62B, and 62W.

Room	Feature Number	Context	Stratum	Occupation	Object Type	Fea./Artifact (SA) No.	New FS Cat. No.
062A	–	Structured trash	C-2-07	Mixed	1 yucca square knot	–	80,189
062A	–	Redeposited trash	F-1-04	Secondary	Plaited ring basket	Fea. 62A004	80,183
062A	–	Floor surface	F-1-04, H-2-05.5	Secondary	Coiled basket	SA 062W042, bot sample 062W1034?	80,184, 80,185
062A	–	Floor surface	H-2-05.5	Secondary	Plaited sandal?	SA 062A030	Not found
062A	–	Floor surface	H-2-05.5	Secondary	Plaited mat	SA 062A031	80,186
062A	–	Floor surface	H-2-05.5	Secondary	Mat (?)	SA 062A043	80,187
062A	–	Floor surface	H-2-05.5	Secondary	Plaited pot rest?	SA 062A053	80,188
062A	–	Unknown	X-1-10	Secondary	1 yucca square knot	–	80,190
062A, 062W	–	Structured trash	C-2-07	Mixed	1 yucca square knot?	–	80,191
062B, 062W	–	Structured trash	C-2-06.9	Mixed	Plaited sandal?	–	80,192.1
062B, 062W	–	Structured trash	C-2-06.9	Mixed	Coiled basket	–	80,192.2
062W	062W002	Redeposited trash	C-2-07	Mixed	1 juniper bark & 17 yucca square knots	–	80,193
062W	062W002	Redeposited trash	C-2-07	Mixed	Intricate selvage from plaited mat	–	80,196
062W	062W002	Redeposited trash	C-2-07	Mixed	1 yucca knot, unidentified	–	80,197
062W	–	Structured trash	C-2-07	Mixed	Plaited basket or mat, colored red?	Bot sample 062W2024	80,220
062W	–	Structured trash	C-2-07	Mixed	Yucca cordage	Bot sample 062W2025	80,221.1
062W	–	Structured trash	C-2-07	Mixed	Cotton yarn	Bot sample 062W2025	80,221.2
062W	–	Structured trash	C-2-07	Mixed	1 yucca knot, incomplete	Bot sample 62W2025	80,222
062W	–	Structured trash	C-2-07	Mixed	44 yucca square knots	–	80,229, 80,233, 80,234, 80,235, 80,238, 80,239, 80,250, 80,251, 80,252, 80,253, 80,256, 80,257.1, 80,267.2, 80,268
062W	–	Structured trash	C-2-07	Mixed	Plaited ring basket	–	80,232
062W	–	Structured trash	C-2-07	Mixed	Plaited mat, basket, or ties?	–	80,236
062W	–	Structured trash	C-2-07	Mixed	Yucca cordage	–	80,243, 80,257.2, 80,259
062W	–	Structured trash	C-2-07	Mixed	Plaited sandal?	–	80,267.1
062W	–	Structured trash	C-2.5-7.5	Mixed	Twined sandal	Bot sample 62W2066	80,223

Table 46.14 (continued)

Room	Feature Number	Context	Stratum	Occupation	Object Type	Fea./Artifact (SA) No.	New FS Cat. No.
062W	–	Structured trash	C-2.5-7.5	Mixed	12 yucca square knots	–	80,226, 80,246, 80,248, 80,258, 80,265, 80,328
062W	–	Structured trash	C-2.5-7.5	Mixed	1 sumac or willow square knot	–	80,237.1
062W	–	Structured trash	C-2.5-7.5	Mixed	Coil of raw mat (sumac or willow)?	–	80,237.2
062W	–	Structured trash	C-3-08	Mixed	1 yucca square knot	–	80,247
062W	–	Structured trash	C-4-09	Mixed	4 yucca square knots	–	80,241, 80,264
062W	–	Structured trash	C-5-10	Mixed	24 yucca square knots	–	80,269
062W	–	Structured trash	C-5-10	Mixed	Plaited mat	–	80,270
062W	–	Structured trash	C-20-20	Mixed	2 yucca square knots, 1 yucca overhand knot, yucca ties colored red	–	80,260
062W	–	Structured trash	C-20-20	Mixed	Wrapped wood (axe handle?)	–	80,274
062W	–	Structured trash	C-20-20	Mixed	3 yucca square knots	–	80,282, 80,303
062W	–	Structured trash	C-20-20	Mixed	6 yucca square knots, colored red and/or yellow?	–	80,298, 80,307
062W	–	Structured trash	C-20-20	Mixed	Coiled pot rest or raw materials (sumac)?	–	80,331
062W	–	Structured trash	C-20-20	Mixed	1 yucca knot, incomplete	–	80,333
062W	–	Structured trash	C-20.5-20.5	Mixed	4 yucca square knots, 2 colored red	–	80,309
062W	–	Structured trash	C-21-21	Mixed	2 yucca square knots	–	80,308
062W	–	Structured trash	C-22-22	Mixed	4 yucca square knots	–	80,281, 80,297, 80,300
062W	–	Structured trash	C-22-22	Mixed	Plaited sandal, colored red	–	80,291
062W	–	Structured trash	C-23-23	Mixed	2 yucca square knots, colored red and/or yellow?	–	80,305
062W	–	Structured trash	C-24-24	Mixed	Yucca cordage	–	80,289
062W	–	Structured trash	C-24-24	Mixed	2 yucca square knots	–	80,292
062W	–	Structured trash	C-24.2-24.2	Mixed	1 yucca square knot	–	80,293
062W	–	Structured trash	C-24.2-24.2	Mixed	Coiled pot rest (juniper bark)	–	80,317
062W	–	Structured trash	C-26.2-26.2	Mixed	Coiled conical basket	Bot sample 062W5053	80,224
062W	–	Structured trash	C-26-26	Mixed	1 yucca square knot	–	80,273
062W	–	Structured trash	C-26-26	Mixed	1 yucca square knot, colored red and/or yellow?	–	80,334
062W	–	Structured trash	C-27.5-27.5	Mixed	Pot rest? (juniper bark)	–	80,316.1
062W	–	Structured trash	C-27.5-27.5	Mixed	58 yucca square knots	–	80,316.2, 80,320
062W	–	Structured trash	C-28-28	Mixed	4 yucca square knots	–	80,327
062W	–	Structured trash	C-29-29	Mixed	Plaited mat or basket	–	80,276

Table 46.14 (continued)

Room	Feature Number	Context	Stratum	Occupation	Object Type	Fea./Artifact (SA) No.	New FS Cat. No.
062W	–	Structured trash	C-29-29	Mixed	Plaited sandal, basket, or mat, colored red?	–	80,312
062W	–	Structured trash	C-29-29	Mixed	5 yucca square knots	–	80,319
062W	–	Structured trash	C-30-30	Mixed	Willow square knot?	–	80,315
062W	–	Structured trash	C-30.3-30.3	Mixed	Coiled pot rest (juniper bark)	–	80,318
062W	–	Structured trash	C-30.4-30.4	Mixed	Coiled pot rest (juniper bark)	–	80,326
062W	–	Structured trash	C-33-33	Mixed	Plaited sandal	–	80,321
062W	–	Structured trash	C-34-34	Mixed	Coiled pot rest (juniper bark), tied w/ yucca sq knot	–	80,330.1 80,330.2
062W	–	Structured trash	CT-45-45	Primary	Yucca cordage	–	80,322
062W	–	Structured trash	CT-45-45	Primary	Yucca cordage, colored red and/ or yellow?	–	80,323
062W	–	Structured trash	CT-45-45	Primary	Plaited ring basket (?), colored red	–	80,325
062W	–	Structured trash	CT-45-45	Primary	Coiled pot rest or raw materials (juniper bark)	–	80,332
062W	–	Occupational fill	G-1-40	Primary	Coiled pot rest or raw materials (pine needles)	Bot sample 062W5055	80,225
062W	–	Occupational fill	G-1-40	Primary	Plaited mat, basket, or sandal	–	80,335
062W	062W122	Infant burial	G-1-40?	Unknown (Primary?)	Cotton cloth	SA 062W113	Not found
062W	062W122	Infant burial	G-1-40?	Unknown (Primary?)	Mat	SA 062W115	Not found
062W	062W122	Infant burial	G-1-40?	Unknown (Primary?)	Braided hair (or yucca?)	SA 062W116	Not found
062W	–	Structured trash	L-1-7.1	Mixed	Yucca cordage	–	80,311
062W	062W063	Redeposited trash	L-2-07	Mixed	Plaited sandal	SA 062W082	80,200
062W	062W002	Redeposited trash	L-2-07	Mixed	4 yucca square knots	–	80,201, 80,231.2, 80,290
062W	062W002	Redeposited trash	L-2-07	Mixed	1 yucca knot, incomplete	–	80,202
062W	062W063	Redeposited trash	L-2-07	Mixed	52 yucca square knots, 4 incomplete yucca knots, 3 colored red	–	80,204.1
062W	062W063	Redeposited trash	L-2-07	Mixed	Yucca cordage tied in square knot	–	80,204.2
062W	062W063	Redeposited trash	L-2-07	Mixed	1 corn husk square knot	–	80,204.3
062W	062W063	Redeposited trash	L-2-07	Mixed	Twined sandal	–	80,210
062W	–	Structured trash	L-2-07	Mixed	Yucca cordage, some feather- and hide- wrapped	–	80,231.1
062W	–	Structured trash	L-2-07	Mixed	Wooden knot, incompete	–	80,275
062W	–	Structured trash	L-2-07	Mixed	Plaited sandal	–	80,310
062W	062W002	Redeposited trash	L-2-07.1	Mixed	10 yucca square knots, colored red and/or yellow?	–	80,194, 80,296, 80,301

Table 46.14 (continued)

Room	Feature Number	Context	Stratum	Occupation	Object Type	Fea./Artifact (SA) No.	New FS Cat. No.
062W	062W002	Redeposited trash	L-2-07.1	Mixed	123 yucca square knots	–	80,195, 80,205.1, 80,206, 80,211, 80,215, 80,216, 80,227.1, 80,240, 80,249, 80,277, 80,278, 80,280, 80,283, 80,284, 80,285, 80,299, 80,304, 80,313, 80,329.1
062W	062W002	Redeposited trash	L-2-07.1	Mixed	Yucca cordage	–	80,198, 80,227.3, 80,255, 80,288, 80,295
062W	062W002	Redeposited trash	L-2-07.1	Mixed	Cotton plain-weave cloth, tied in sq knot	–	80,199.1
062W	062W002	Redeposited trash	L-2-07.1	Mixed	Feather-wrapped cordage	–	80,199.2, 80,203.1
062W	062W002	Redeposited trash	L-2-07.1	Mixed	Yucca cordage, colored yellow?	–	80,203.2
062W	062W063	Redeposited trash	L-2-07.1	Mixed	Selvage of plaited sandal or basket?	–	80,205.2
062W	062W063	Redeposited trash	L-2-07.1	Mixed	Yucca (?) cordage	–	80,207
062W	062W063	Redeposited trash	L-2-07.1	Mixed	Yucca cordage, some hide-wrapped	–	80,208.1
062W	062W063	Redeposited trash	L-2-07.1	Mixed	Cotton yarn	–	80,208.2, 80,219.2, 80,242.2, 80,244, 80,245.1
062W	062W063	Redeposited trash	L-2-07.1 ?	Mixed	Cotton plain-weave cloth	–	80,209
062W	062W063	Redeposited trash	L-2-07.1	Mixed	Twined sandal	–	80,212.1
062W	062W063	Redeposited trash	L-2-07.1	Mixed	Plaited sandal?	–	80,212.2
062W	062W063	Redeposited trash	L-2-07.1	Mixed	4 yucca granny knots	–	80,213
062W	062W063	Redeposited trash	L-2-07.1	Mixed	30 yucca square knots, 2 colored red	–	80,214
062W	062W063	Redeposited trash	L-2-07.1	Mixed	Plaited sandal?	–	80,217
062W	062W063	Redeposited trash	L-2-07.1	Mixed	Yucca cordage, some wrapped in feather or fur, 2 with overhand knots	–	80,218.1, 80,218.2
062W	062W063	Redeposited trash	L-2-07.1	Mixed	Yucca 3-strand braid	–	80,218.3
062W	063W062	Redeposited trash	L-2-07.1	Mixed	Yucca cordage, some hide- wrapped	–	80,219.1
062W	–	Structured trash	L-2-07.1	Mixed	1 yucca overhand knot	–	80,227.2
062W	–	Structured trash	L-2-07.1	Mixed	Coil of raw material (sumac or willow basketry splints)?	–	80,227.4
062W	–	Structured trash	L-2-07.1	Mixed	Unique plaited object	–	80,228

Table 46.14 (continued)

Room	Feature Number	Context	Stratum	Occupation	Object Type	Fea./Artifact (SA) No.	New FS Cat. No.
062W	–	Structured trash	L-2-07.1	Mixed	Coiled conical (?) basket	–	80,230
062W	–	Structured trash	L-2-07.1	Mixed	Yucca cordage, some wrapped in feather and fur	–	80,242.1
062W	–	Structured trash	L-2-07.1	Mixed	Feather ornament	–	80,245.2
062W	–	Structured trash	L-2-07.1	Mixed	2 yucca knots, incomplete	–	80,254
062W	–	Structured trash	L-2-07.1	Mixed	8 yucca square knots, 1 colored red	–	80,263
062W	–	Structured trash	L-2.07.1	Mixed	Ball of yucca 3-strand braided cordage	–	80,266
062W	–	Structured trash	L-2-07.1	Mixed	Intricate selvage from plaited mat	–	80,271.1
062W	–	Structured trash	L-2-07.1	Mixed	Plaited sandal?, stained red	–	80,271.2
062W	–	Structured trash	L-2-07.1	Mixed	2 twined sandals	–	80,272, 80,294
062W	–	Structured trash	L-2.07.1	Mixed	2 willow (?) square knots	–	80,279
062W	–	Structured trash	L-2-07.1	Mixed	Yucca (?) cordage	–	80,286
062W	–	Structured trash	L-2-07.1	Mixed	Coil of raw material? (willow or sumac twigs)	–	80,287
062W	–	Structured trash	L-2-07.1	Mixed	Plaited mat	–	80,302
062W	–	Structured trash	L-2-07.1	Mixed	Wrapped wood (remains of hoop?)	–	80,306
062W	–	Structured trash	L-2-07.1	Mixed	Yucca cordage	–	80,314
062W	–	Structured trash	L-2-07.1	Mixed	4 yucca chains	–	80,329.2
062W	–	Backfill	P-0-00	Unassigned	1 yucca square knot	–	80,261
062W	–	Backfill	P-0-00	Unassigned	Twined sandal	–	80,262
062W	–	Unknown	Unknown	Unassigned	Coiled basket	–	80,324.1
062W	–	Unknown	Unknown	Unassigned	1 yucca square knot, colored red?	–	80,324.2
062W?	–	Unknown	Unknown	Unknown	Square knots assoc. with 2 wrapped sticks	–	80,486.1; could be 80,213?
062W?	–	Unknown	Unknown	Unknown	Unidentified willow knot	–	80,486.2; could be 80,197?
062W?	–	Unknown	Unknown	Unknown	Yucca (?) cordage	–	80,486.3
062W?	–	Unknown	Unknown	Unknown	4 yucca square knots	–	80,486.4
062W?	–	Unknown	Unknown	Unknown	Bundle of yucca leaves tied in overhand knot	–	80,486.5

Note: The "mixed" designation in the occupation column is a term I created to describe the mixed nature of the deep trash deposits from this room. Excavators used the term "Secondary (redeposited)" to identify the cultural affiliation of most of these objects. Based on the ceramic rough sort and comparisons with fiber artifacts from other "Chacoan," sites, I believe many of these artifacts to date to the Primary occupation.

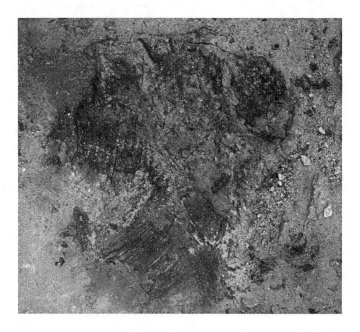

Figure 46.28. Room 62A, in situ view of carbonized remains of large coiled basket SA 62W042 (FS 80,184 and 80,185) on floor. Burnt corn fused to basket surface.

Figure 46.29. Room 62A, in situ view of plaited pot rest SA 62A053 (FS 80,188) on floor near sherd scatter.

Figure 46.30. Room 62W, in situ view of nearly complete plaited sandal SA 62W082 (FS 80,200) in trash deposit.

80,318, FS 80,326, FS 80,330.1, Figure 46.32, see also Figure 46.70e) and four of sumac or willow twigs (FS 80,227.4, FS 80,237.2, FS 80,287, FS 80,331, see Figure 46.70b, c). Although some of these may have served as pot rests, they also might represent bundles of raw materials stockpiled for craft production.

Finally, Room 62W produced several unique perishable artifacts, including a small yucca square or "doodle" worked in 1/1 plaiting (FS 80,228, see Figure 46.86e), four yucca chains for hanging corn or other plant materials (FS 80,329.2, see Figure 46.86f), and the remains of a feather ornament made using a weft-wrap technique (FS 80,245.2, see Figure 46.85d, e). Many of the items recovered from this room (the red-stained artifacts, the conical baskets, and the feather ornament, for example) probably served a ritual function. It is intriguing to speculate where this refuse might have come from. Some of these objects might have originated with Primary ritual activities performed in this special-function ceremonial room, whereas others might represent sweepings from adjoining rooms or the Tower Kiva.

Room 64W—Tower Kiva

Excavations in the Tower Kiva produced a large and diverse assemblage of carbonized fiber artifacts dated to the late Secondary occupation (Table 46.15). Associated with the floor, bench, foot drum, and

FS 80,220), the latter possibly colored red. Three coiled baskets with two-rod-and-bundle foundations were found (botanical sample 62W5053=FS 80,224, FS 80,230, FS 80,324.1). The first two of these were probably steep-sided conical baskets (Figure 46.31, see also Figure 46.66b, c). The midden also produced fragments of plaited mats, including two with intricate selvages (FS 80,196, FS 80,236, FS 80,270, FS 80,271.1, FS 80,276, and FS 80,302).

Nine coils of plant materials were also recovered: five of juniper bark (FS 80,316.1, FS 80,317, FS

Figure 46.31. Room 62W, in situ view of coiled basket Botanical Sample 62W5053 (FS 80,224) in structured trash.

Figure 46.32. Room 62W, in situ view of coil of juniper bark (FS 80,330.1) in structured trash.

roof-fall, most of these objects were probably abandoned in place when the kiva burned in a catastrophic fire, ca. AD 1290. This assemblage is significant not only for confirming a ritual role for certain classes of fiber artifacts, but also for contributing information about their ritual contexts of use.

Objects found on the floor include three plaited yucca pot rests (Feature 64W035=FS 80,337, SA 64W 089=FS 80,344, and SA 64W090=FS 80,345, Figures 46.33–36, see also Figure 46.71d, e). SA 64W089 probably supported a Mesa Verde Black-on-white jar found nearby. Also found were a yucca coiled (?) pot rest (Feature 64W012=FS 80,350, Figure 46.37), two plaited mats with intricate selvages (SA 64W098, not collected, and Feature 64W041=FS 80,338-80,340, Figure 46.38, see also Figure 46.57c), a tiny scrap of cotton cloth (FS 80,348), and two coiled baskets—one a basket base or plaque (SA 64W096=FS80,346, Figure 46.39) and the other possibly the remains of a steep-sided conical basket (Feature 64W011=FS 80,349, Figure 46.40, see also Figure 46.66d, e). Excavators speculated that the latter, found upside down, had fallen from the bench during the fire.

Fiber artifacts were also found in association with the foot drum (Feature 64W118), where a layer of 2/2-twill matting with an intricate selvage (SA 64W120=FS 80,341) lined the area beneath the planks (Figure 46.41). An unusual, semi-circular object of woven yucca (SA 64W086=FS 80,343, see Figure

46.86h), possibly the remains of a thick sandal or pad, was also found on top of a plank.

The bench produced an elliptical 2/2-twill plaited yucca pouch with a tapered mouth opening (Feature 64W013=FS 80,336, Figure 46.42, see also Figure 46.68d, e). The pouch was filled with a variety of plant materials, including corn tassels. It closely resembles the plaited pouch "pillows" found with burials 43W003 and 43W005 in Room 43W.

The burned roof-fall of the kiva also produced several perishable artifacts, including fragments of a coiled basket (FS 80,352 and FS 80,354) and some yucca cordage. The basket may have been lying on top of the roof when the structure burned.

Room 67W

Aside from a few yucca knots, the only noteworthy fiber artifact from this room is a modern piece of silk fabric woven in a 3/1 satin weave, probably the remains of a ribbon (FS 80,358, see Figure 46.85f and Table 46.16). Postdating the occupation of Salmon, it could have been left at the site by an early Native or Anglo visitor or perhaps by a member of Irwin-Williams' field crew.

Room 81W

Located adjacent to and directly east of the Tower Kiva, this special-use room produced the only evidence of loom weaving at Salmon Pueblo. Both

Table 46.15. Distribution of perishable artifacts in Room 64W (the Tower Kiva).

Feature Number	Context	Stratum	Occupation	Object Type	Fea./Artifact (SA) No.	New FS Cat. No.
064W004	Bench	H-1-08	Secondary	Plaited pouch	Fea. 064W013	80,336
064W118	Foot drum	F-1-06	Secondary	Yucca cordage tied in square knot	SA 064W057	80,342.1, 80,342.2
064W118	Foot drum	H-1-08	Secondary	Plaited mat with intricate selvage	SA 064W120	80,341
064W118	Foot drum	H-1-08	Secondary	Yucca plain-weave pad?	SA 064W086	80,343
–	Bench wall	Bench wall	Secondary	Yucca cordage, 1 piece tied in square knot	–	80,351.1, 80,351.2
–	Roof-fall	F-1-06	Secondary	Yucca cordage	–	80,347, 80,353, 80,355
–	Roof-fall?	F-1-06?	Secondary	Coiled basket	–	80,352
–	Roof-fall	F-1-06	Secondary	Coiled basket	–	80,354
–	Floor surface	F-1-06	Secondary	1 yucca knot, incomplete	–	80,356
–	Floor surface	H-1-08	Secondary	Plaited pot rest	Fea. 064W035	80,337
–	Floor surface	H-1-08	Secondary	Plaited mat with intricate selvage	Fea. 064W041	80,338, 80,339, 80,340
–	Floor surface	H-1-08	Secondary	Plaited pot rest	SA 064W089	80,344
–	Floor surface	H-1-08	Secondary	Plaited pot rest	SA 064W090	80,345
–	Floor surface	H-1-08	Secondary	Coiled basket base or plaque	SA 064W096	80,346
–	Floor surface	H-1-08	Secondary	Cotton plain weave cloth	–	80,348
–	Floor surface	H-1-08	Secondary	Coiled conical (?) basket	Fea. 064W011	80,349
–	Floor surface	H-1-08	Secondary	Coiled pot rest	Fea. 064W012	80,350
–	Floor surface	H-1-08	Secondary	Yucca cordage, 2 pieces tied in square knots	–	80,357.1, 80,357.2
–	Floor surface	H-1-08	Secondary	Plaited mat with intricate selvage	SA 064W098	Not found

Table 46.16. Distribution of perishable artifacts in Room 67W.

Feature Number	Context	Stratum	Occupation	Object Type	Fea./Artifact (SA) No.	New FS Cat. No.
–	Structured trash	C-4-10	Secondary	1 yucca square knot	–	80,361
–	Roof-fall	FC-2.5-05.5	Historic	Silk cloth (ribbon?)	–	80,358
–	Roof-fall	FC-2.5-05.5	Secondary	Bundle of yucca leaves, tied w/ overhand knot	–	80,359
–	Roof-fall	FC-2.5-05.5	Secondary	1 yucca square knot	–	80,360

Laurie D. Webster

Figure 46.33. Room 64W (Tower Kiva), in situ view of carbonized plaited pot rest Feature 64W035 (FS 80,337) and corn on floor.

Figure 46.34. Room 64W (Tower Kiva), in situ view of carbonized plaited pot rests SA 64W089 (FS 80,344), left, and SA 64W090 (FS 80,345), right, on floor.

Figure 46.35. Room 64W (Tower Kiva), detail of plaited pot rest SA 64W089 (FS 80,344) on floor.

Figure 46.36. Room 64W (Tower Kiva), detail of plaited pot rest SA 64W090 (FS 80,345) on floor.

Figure 46.37. Room 64W (Tower Kiva), in situ view of carbonized coiled pot rest Feature 64W012 (FS 80,350) on floor.

Figure 46.38. Room 64W (Tower Kiva), in situ view of carbonized plaited mat Feature 64W041 (FS 80,338-80,340) on floor.

Figure 46.39. Room 64W (Tower Kiva), in situ view of carbonized coiled basket base or plaque Feature 64W096 (FS 80,346) on floor.

this room and Room 82W to the south contained unusual Chacoan architectural features, including a platform or rack in Room 81W and an "altar-like" feature in Room 82W. Baker (2005) has reinterpreted this feature as being archaeoastronomical. These rooms also contained abundant in situ Chacoan deposits. These features suggest a non-domestic, ritual use of these rooms during the Primary occupation.

In addition to specialized forms of lithics and ceramics, Room 81W also produced large quantities of well-preserved perishable materials, including several wooden artifacts, a reed bundle, corn cobs on

sticks ("corn mothers"), and abundant plant food remains. Excavators described the northwest quadrant of this room as being particularly rich in perishable materials. From the field notes one gets the impression that this room rivaled Room 62W in preservation. Unfortunately, no worked fiber artifacts seem to have been collected. However, in fallen roof debris (stratum F-2-13), excavators found a concentration of three (or possibly four) wooden objects (SA 81W251, SA 81W 253, SA 81W354), which they identified as possible weaving tools (Figures 46.43 and 44). Only one of these (SA 81W253=WO80-000023, Figure 46.87a) was located during analysis. A sketch on the significant artifact form for SA 81W251 suggests that this was another small batten for use with a belt or backstrap loom (Figure 46.87b). The form for SA 81W354 describes that object as a flat piece of wood with a squared-off end (Figure 46.87c). Perhaps these items will be located when the wooden artifacts are finally studied in depth.

Excavators also recorded the presence of a small bowl with a rounded base near SA81W251 that they considered to be associated with the weaving tools. The bowl might have been used to support a spindle during the spinning process. When this bowl is located, it will be interesting to examine the interior for wear patterns.

Figure 46.40. Room 64W (Tower Kiva), in situ view of carbonized coiled basket Feature 64W011 (FS 80,349) on floor.

Figure 46.41. Room 64W (Tower Kiva), in situ view of carbonized plaited mat SA 64W120 (FS 80,341) associated with foot drum Feature 64W118.

Figure 46.42. Room 64W (Tower Kiva), in situ view of carbonized plaited pouch Feature 64W013 (FS 80,336) on bench.

Figure 46.43. Room 81W, in situ view of weaving tool concentration in fallen roof or platform debris.

Figure 46.44. Room 81W, in situ view of weaving batten SA 81W251 (not located) or SA 81W253 (WO80-23) in roof or platform debris.

In addition to these weaving artifacts, the field notes also mention a number of fiber perishables from this room (Table 46.17). None of these are listed in the original manipulated fiber database, so either they were not collected or their original field associations were lost. At least 10 yucca knots and four pieces of braided fiber cordage were observed, as well as the probable remains of a juniper-bark pot rest.

The field notes also report the presence of a bundle or mat of horsetail reeds (SA 81W341) in the northwest corner of this room. Although found in the same roof-fall stratum as the other perishable artifacts from this room, this reed bundle was reportedly situated close to the floor. No object with this SA number was found during analysis.

The original context of the weaving tools is open to question. Although the stratum in which they were found was described as "roof-fall" (F-2-13), Adams and Reed (Chapter 7) suggest that the room had a wooden platform. If that is the case, perhaps weaving activities might have been taking place on a raised platform in this room, or weaving tools were being stored there. Both interpretations support a ritual association for loom weaving at Salmon. Although no actual loom parts were found, the sizes of the battens correspond with the use of a belt or backstrap loom. As for the reed mat, it could have been laid out on top of the platform or incorporated into the platform structure as a decorative element.

Room 82W

Only one worked fiber artifact (and some roof thatching) was recovered from this specialized ceremonial room (Table 46.18). The fiber artifact is unique to Salmon. FS 80,362 (see Figure 46.53d) is a fragment of chocolate brown yarn spun from the hair of an unidentified animal, possibly dog or bison. It definitely is not rabbit hair, and based on its 6-ply configuration, I do not believe it to be wool from domesticated sheep. Recovered from roof-fall, this unburned yarn is from the Secondary occupation.

Northeast Sector

The preservation of perishables was not particularly good in this part of the pueblo. A few rooms contained carbonized perishables, but most of the materials from this section were unburned and highly deteriorated. Several rooms produced only one or two fragments. Worked fiber artifacts were recovered from rooms 84W, 88W, 90W, 91A and W, 93W, 97A, B, and W, 98W, 100W, 101W, and 102W. Most of these artifacts were dated to the Secondary occupation, but rooms 84W, 97W, 98W, and 101W

also produced some Primary fiber artifacts. Room 100 also contained a Primary burial with traces of perishables. The largest and most diverse assemblages were associated with four Secondary burials in Room 97 and the fill of Rooms 100 and 101, three interconnected rooms near the northeast corner.

Rooms 84W, 90W, and 91A and W

These possibly three-story, contiguous rooms are situated near the rear of the pueblo, roughly halfway between the east wall and the Tower Kiva. Although Rooms 84W and 90W were completely excavated, and Rooms 91 A and W partially so, they produced only a few yucca cords and ties (Table 46.19). Carbonized cordage (FS 368.1, see Figure 46.77b, c) from a structured trash deposit in Room 84W is the remains of a twined robe, probably Primary in age. An unburned Secondary knotted yucca tie (FS 80,372) from Room 90W has a slight orange cast, and might have been colored with hematite or yellow ocher.

Rooms 88W, 93W, and 102W

These three contiguous one-story rooms all face the plaza. Excavators described the latter two rooms as having been used for food preparation. All three of these unburned rooms produced the remains of matting dated to the Secondary occupation (Table 46.19). The mat from Room 88W was woven in 2/2 twill; those from Rooms 93W and 102W are too deteriorated to identify. The mat from Room 102W was evidently used to line the grave of burial 102W001.

Rooms 97A, 97B, and 97W

The only fiber perishables from Room 97A came from Secondary burial 97A1001. This burial of an elderly male contained the deteriorated remains of 2/2-twill plaited matting and some yucca square knots (Table 46.20).

Room 97B. One Secondary burial in this room, Feature 97B002, an adult male, contained traces of unburned plaited matting. Fragments were found above and below the body, indicating that this individual had been wrapped in the mat.

Room 97W, near the northeast corner of the pueblo, served as a milling room during the Primary occupation, and was later used for burials. A few Primary fiber artifacts were found (Table 46.20). A log feature (97W2007) in this room contained a lens of Primary trash that had been used to level the area for the milling bins. This trash deposit produced the remains of two unburned fiber artifacts: a plaited sandal (botanical sample 97W2017=FS 80,385, see Figure 46.83g), and a plaited mat with 3/1 floats (botanical sample 97W2020=FS 80,386). Deteriorated

Table 46.17. Distribution of perishable artifacts in Room 81W.

Feature Number	Context	Stratum	Occupation	Object Type	Fea./Artifact (SA) No.	New FS Cat. No.
–	Roof-fall	F-2-13	Primary	"Possible weaving stick"– wooden batten?	SA 081W251	Not found
–	Roof-fall	F-2-13	Primary	Small ceramic bowl with rounded base	SA 081W252	Not found
–	Roof-fall	F-2-13	Primary	"Loom tool" – wooden batten	SA 081W253	WO80-000023
–	Roof-fall	F-2-13	Primary	Reed bundle	SA 081W341	Not positively identified; could be 80,489?
–	Roof-fall	F-2-13	Primary	"Wood tool," found with other weaving tools	SA 081W354	Not found
–	Roof-fall	F-2-13	Primary	Coiled pot rest of juniper bark?	–	Not found
–	Roof-fall	F-2-13	Primary	10 or more yucca knots	–	Not found
–	Roof-fall	F-2-13	Primary	Braided cordage of yucca or bark	–	Not found

Table 46.18. Distribution of perishable artifacts in Room 82W.

Feature Number	Context	Stratum	Occupation	Object Type	Fea./Artifact (SA) No.	New FS Cat. No.
–	Roof-fall	F-2-17	Secondary	Dog or bison hair yarn?	–	80,362
–	Roof-fall	L-4-15.5	Secondary	Roof thatching?	–	80,363

Table 46.19. Distribution of perishable artifacts in Rooms 84W, 88W, 90W, 91A, 91W, 93W, 98W, and 102W.

Room	Feature Number	Context	Stratum	Occupation	Object Type	Fea./Artif. (SA) No.	New FS Cat. No.
084W	–	Structured trash	C-1-05	Primary?	Yucca cordage = remains of twined robe; 3 pieces tied in square knots	–	80,367, 80,368.1, 80,368.2, 80,369.1, 80,369.2
084W	–	Roof-fall	N-2-04	Secondary	Yucca cordage	–	80,364, 80,366, 80,370
084W	–	In wall	W-2-04	Secondary	Yucca cordage	–	80,365
088W	–	Floor surface	H-1-06	Secondary	Plaited mat	–	80,371
090W	–	Structured trash	C-2-07	Secondary	1 yucca knot, incomplete, colored red or yellow?	–	80,372
091A	–	Structured trash	C-4-18	Secondary	1 yucca square knot	–	80,373
091W	–	Structured trash	C-5-19	Intermediate/ Secondary	2 yucca square knots?	–	80,374
093W	–	Structured trash	C-4-06	Secondary	Remains of mat	–	80,375
098W	–	Floor surface	H-1-08	Primary?	1 yucca knot, incomplete	–	80,393
098W	–	Post-occup fill	B-1-05	Secondary?	1 yucca square knot	–	80,394
102W	102W001?	Burial	L-1-03.5	Secondary	Remains of mat?	Bot sample 102W1021	80,413

Table 46.20. Distribution of perishable artifacts in Rooms 97A, 97B, and 97W.

Room	Feature Number	Context	Stratum	Occupation	Object Type	Fea./Artifact (SA) No.	New FS Cat. No.
097A	097A1001	Burial	H-1-04	Secondary	Plaited mat	–	80,376, 80,377, 80,378.1, 80,379, 80,380.1, 80,381.1, 80,382.1, 80,383
097A	097A1001	Burial	H-1-04	Secondary	8 yucca square knots		80,378.2, 80,380.2, 80,381.2, 80,382.2,
097B	097B002	Burial	B-2-06	Secondary	Remains of plaited mat	–	80,384
097W	097W1006	Burial	N-1-03	Secondary?	Plaited mat	–	80,387.1
097W	097W1006	Burial	N-1-03	Secondary?	Cordage (twined robe?)	–	80,387.2
097W	097W1007	Burial	N-1-03	Secondary?	Plaited mat	–	80,388.1, 80,389.1
097W	097W1007	Burial	N-1-03	Secondary?	Remains of twined robe	–	80,388.2, 80,389.2
097W	097W2007	Log feature	D-1-11	Primary	Plaited mat	Bot sample 097W2020	80,386
097W	097W2007	Log feature	D-1-11	Primary	Plaited sandal	Bot sample 097W2017	80,385
097W	–	Structured trash	C-3-14.5	Primary	Plaited mat with intricate selvage?	–	80,392
097W	–	Artificial fill	D-1.5-11.5	Primary?	Remains of plaited mat	–	80,391
097W	–	Artificial fill	D-2-13	Primary	1 yucca square knot?	–	80,390

2/2-plaited matting (FS 80,391) and a yucca knot (FS 80,390) were also found in this Primary artificial fill. A Primary structured trash deposit in this room produced a deteriorated 2/2-twill plaited mat with a slight reddish cast (FS 80,392). Two Secondary burials in this room (Features 97W1006 and 97W1007) contained the remains of 2/2-twill matting and twined robes (Table 46.20).

Room 98W

Located at the northeast corner of the pueblo, this room produced only two unburned yucca knots, attributed to the Primary and Secondary occupations (Table 46.19).

Room 100W

This large, plaza-facing living room is connected to rooms 97W and 101W. The room was abandoned during the Primary occupation, then used for the disposal of Primary and Intermediate (early Secondary) trash. Although excavators described the presence of extensive trash deposits from these occupations, limited fiber artifacts were present, including two yucca knots (Table 46.21).

Room 100W contained one of the few Primary burials found at Salmon. This burial, Feature 100W 302, is unusual because rather than being interred in a prepared pit like most burials at Salmon, this individual was sprawled face-down in an unflexed position on a layer of Primary trash (Espinosa, Chapter 15; Irwin-Williams, Chapter 16). With the possible exception of a ceramic bowl found nearby, this burial was unaccompanied by grave offerings. However, traces of matting and red pigment on the surface of the skull indicate that a plaited mat once covered the head. Either this mat was stained red, like several others at the site, or hematite had been applied to the head. A red-stained grinding stone was also found in this room in stratum C-2-05, but it is not known if the stone has any relationship to the burial.

Irwin-Williams (Chapter 16) speculated that the interment of this individual spurred the abandonment of this room during the Primary occupation. The room appears to have retained a special function throughout the Salmon occupational sequence. Unlike most large front-facing rooms at Salmon, it was never remodeled or reused during the Secondary

Table 46.21. Distribution of perishable artifacts in Room 100W.

Feature Number	Context	Stratum	Occupation	Object Type	Fea./Artif. (SA) No.	New FS Cat. No.
100W014	No information	N-1-03	Secondary	Remains of cornhusk knot	–	80,395
100W302	Burial	S-1-13.5	Primary	Traces of matting and red pigment on cranium	–	Not collected
–	Structured trash	C-11-16	Primary?	1 yucca knot, incomplete	–	80,404
–	Structured trash	C-8-13	Intermediate?	1 yucca square knot	–	80,405
–	Roof-fall	N-1-03	Secondary	Plaited sandal?	–	80,396
–	Roof-fall	N-1-03	Secondary	Coiled basket	–	80,397
–	Roof-fall	N-1-03	Secondary	1 yucca square knot	–	80,398
–	Roof-fall	N-1-03	Secondary	1 yucca or cornhusk square knot	–	80,399
–	Roof-fall	N-1-03	Secondary	1 yucca square knot	–	80,400
–	Roof-fall	N-1-03	Secondary	1 yucca knot, incomplete	–	80,401
–	Roof-fall	N-1-03	Secondary	Yucca cordage tied in square knot	–	80,402.1, 80,402.2
–	Roof-fall	N-1-03	Secondary?	Coiled pot rest or raw materials? (yucca)	SA 100W002	80,484
–	Roof-fall/ Structured trash	N-1-03	Primary?	Yucca cordage artifact, mustard yellow color; altar tassel?	–	80,403
Unknown	Infant burial?	N-1-03, C-1-04.2	Secondary?	Blue and yellow cordage	–	Not found

occupation except for the disposal of trash. A macaw skeleton was found in the doorway between this room and Room 97W.

Room 100W was destroyed by fire late in the Secondary occupation (Adams and Reed, Chapter 7). Most of the perishables found in this room are attributed to burnt Secondary roof-fall. In addition to the usual array of yucca knots, this roof-fall produced one and perhaps two cornhusk knots (FS 80,395 and 80,399), a plaited sandal or mat (FS 80,396, see Figure 46.83h), and a coiled yucca-leaf bundle or pot rest (SA 100W002=FS 80,484). This stratum also produced an unburned yucca artifact (altar tassel?) made of cordage wrapped around a cordage core, still bright yellow in color (FS 80,403, see Figure 46.86a). The field notes also describe a Secondary infant burial (feature number unknown) from mixed trash and roof-fall that was accompanied by a Mesa Verde Black-on-white pot and some blue and yellow cordage (the latter not found during analysis). Given that this context seems to have been conducive to textile preservation, it is surprising that so few perishables were found or collected.

Room 101W

North of Room 97, west of Room 98, and one row in from the back wall of the pueblo, this multiple-story room was completely excavated. It produced a small but diverse assortment of unburned perishables (Table 46.22). Fragments of a twined

sandal (FS 80,411, Figure 46.79e) came from Primary occupational fill, and two yucca knots and a deteriorated yucca pot rest were found in Primary structured trash. The top of the roof (stratum C-1-06) produced three worked perishables attributed to the Secondary occupation: a thick and heavy twined sandal (SA 101W002=FS 80,406 and 80,407, see Figure 46.81b), a coiled basket with a one-rod foundation (SA 101W 003=FS 80,408, see Figure 46.67c), and the remains of a finely plaited sandal or mat (SA 101W004=FS 80,409).

Southeast Sector

Worked fiber artifacts were recovered from several rooms in this section: 118W, 119W, 121W, 122A, 123B, 127B and W, and 129W. The most diverse assemblages were found with burials in Rooms 123B, 127B, and 127W and in the burnt roof-fall of Room 129W.

Rooms 118W, 119W, 121W, 122A, and 122W

These rooms produced few worked perishables (Table 46.23). Excavations in Room 118W yielded only two yucca knots from the roof and fill. Secondary roof-fall in Room 119W produced one perishable artifact—an unburned plaited yucca pot rest woven in 2/2 twill (SA 119W046=FS 80,416, see Figure 46.71f). Secondary infant burial 121W033 in Room 121W was associated with a 2/2 (?)-twill plaited mat (SA 121W039 = FS 80,417-80,420, see Figure 46.57b), only fragments of which survived. In Room 122W, some fine 2/2-twill matting (FS 80,422) was found with adult male burial 122-1?; the stratigraphic record identifies this burial as Primary, but the database lists it as Secondary. Finally, Room 122A produced a collection of sticks that could be the remains of matting but more likely is roof debris.

Room 123B

Situated along the south wall of the pueblo, Room 123B contained a child burial (Feature 123B 005) with multiple layers of burial wrappings (Table 46.24). These wrappings, designated Feature 123B 004, included the remains of a cotton plain-weave blanket (FS 80,424.2, see Figure 46.74a, b), a twined rabbit-fur robe (FS 80,423 and 80,424.1), and a 2/2 (?)-twill plaited mat (FS 80,425-80,427). Thick yucca cords (FS 80,424.3) were used to secure the robe at the neck and ankles. Although only fragments of the robe were recovered, the twining framework was relatively intact when exposed in the field (Figure 46.45, see also Figure 46.77d). No other burial goods were found with this burial, which was identified by excavators as Intermediate/Secondary in age. Given that fur robes appear to be more characteristic of the early occupation at Salmon, an early Secondary attribution seems likely.

Figure 46.45. Room 123B, in situ view of framework of twined robe Feature 123B004 (FS 80,423 and 80,424,1) with Burial 123B005.

Rooms 127A and 127W

Located at the south end of the East Wing, Room 127 was used extensively for burials during the Secondary occupation. When this room was remodeled it became the interstitial space of a late Secondary kiva (Room 127A) and served as the burial place for an adult female, Feature 127B001. This individual was wrapped in a large, coarse 2/2-twill plaited mat (SA 127B003=FS 80,428-80,429), only traces of which were recovered (Figure 46.46 and Table 46.25).

Seven burials from Room 127W contained the remains of wrappings and other perishable artifacts (Table 46.25). Burial 127W055, an adolescent female, was associated with a carbonized 2/2-twill plaited

Figure 46.46. Room 127B, in situ view of plaited mat SA 127B003 (FS 80,428 and 80,429) with Burial 127B001.

Table 46.22. Distribution of perishable artifacts in Room 101W.

Feature Number	Context	Stratum	Occupation	Object Type	Fea./Artifact (SA) No.	New FS Cat. No.
–	On roof, structured trash	C-1-06, L-1-06	Secondary	Thick twined sandal	SA 101W002	80,406, 80,407
–	On roof, structured trash	C-1-06	Secondary	Coiled basket	SA 101W003	80,408
–	On roof, structured trash	C-1-06	Secondary	Plaited mat or sandal	SA 101W004	80,409
–	Structured trash	C-2-07	Primary?	2 yucca square knots	–	80,410
–	Structured trash	C-2-07	Primary?	Plaited (?) pot rest	–	80,412
–	Occupational fill	G-1-08	Primary	Twined sandal	–	80,411

Table 46.23. Distribution of perishable artifacts in Rooms 118W, 119W, 121W, 122A, and 122W.

Room	Feature Number	Context	Stratum	Occupation	Object Type	Fea./Artifact (SA) No.	New FS Cat. No.
118W	118W012	Roof	F-2-05.1	Secondary	1 yucca square knot	Bot sample 118W3022	80,414
118W	–	Rodent or root disturbance	U-2-10.5	Secondary?	1 yucca square knot	–	80,415
119W	–	Roof-fall	F-3-20	Secondary	Plaited pot rest	SA 119W046	80,416
121W	121W033	Burial	L-16-33	Secondary	Plaited mat	SA 121W039, Bot sample 121W2089	80,417, 80,418, 80,419, 80,420
122A	–	Feature fill?	L	Secondary	Remains of mat?	–	80,421
122W	122-1?	Burial	D-0-0	Primary or Secondary	Plaited mat	–	80,422

Table 46.24. Distribution of perishable artifacts in Room 123B.

Feature Number	Context	Stratum	Occupation	Object Type	Fea./Artifact (SA) No.	New FS Cat. No.
123B005	Burial	C-1-03	Intermediate/Secondary	Twined fur robe	Fea. 123B004	80,423, 80,424.1
123B005	Burial	C-1-03	Intermediate/Secondary	Cotton plain weave cloth	Fea. 123B004	80,424.2
123B005	Burial	C-1-03	Intermediate/Secondary	Yucca cordage (binding cords)	Fea. 123B004	80,424.3
123B005	Burial	C-1-03	Intermediate/Secondary	Plaited mat	Fea. 123B004	80,425, 80,426, 80,427

Table 46.25. Distribution of perishable artifacts in Rooms 127B and 127W.

Room	Feature Number	Context	Stratum	Occupation	Object Type	Fea./Artifact (SA) No.	New FS Cat. No.
127B	127B001	Burial	D-2-05	Secondary	Plaited mat	SA 127B003	80,428, 80,429
127W	127W055	Burial	L-1-08	Secondary	Plaited mat	SA 127W056	80,430, 80,431
127W	127W055	Burial	L-1-08	Secondary	Twined feather (?) robe	SA 127W091	80,432
127W	127W099	Burial	L-2-11.5	Secondary	Twined feather (?) robe	SA 127W100	80,433.2
127W	127W099	Burial	L-2-11.5	Secondary	Plaited mat	SA 127W100	80,433.1, 80,434
127W	127W106	Burial	L-6-16	Secondary	Coiled basket	SA 127W121	80,435
127W	127W106	Burial	L-6-16	Secondary	Mat	–	Not recovered
127W	127W106	Burial	L-6-16	Secondary	Twined robe?	–	Not recovered
127W	127W107	Burial	L-7-18	Secondary	Traces of mat	–	Not recovered?
127W	127W115	Burial	L-8-20	Secondary	Traces of mat	SA 127W120	Not recovered?
127W	127W115	Burial	L-8-20	Secondary	Twined feather robe	Bot sample 127W3032	80,436, 80,437.1, 80,437.2, 80,438
127W	127W126	Burial	L-12-26	Secondary	Coiled basket?	SA 127W137	Not found
127W	127W147	Burial	L-23-44	Primary?	Fur (?) robe	SA 127W154, Bot sample 127W4036	80,439
127W	127W147	Burial	L-23-44	Primary?	Plaited mat	SA 127W157, Bot sample 127W4042	80,440
127W	–	Roof-fall	F-1-04	Primary or Secondary	Cotton twill weave cloth	SA 127W053	80,441
127W	–	Roof-fall	F-1-04	Primary/ Intermed?	Twined sandal	SA 127W051	80,442
127W	–	Roof-fall	F-1-04	Primary/ Intermed?	Twined sandal or tumpband	–	80,443

mat (SA 127W056=FS 80,430 and 80,431) and a twined feather (?) robe (SA 127W091=FS 80,432). Other grave goods included a Mesa Verde Black-on-white bowl.

Burial 127W099, a child of undetermined sex, predated burial 127W055. It, too, was associated with a twined feather (?) robe (FS 80,433.2) and a large 2/2-twill plaited mat (SA 127W100=FS 80,433.1 and 80,434, Figure 46.47).

Infant burial 127W106 was wrapped in yucca matting (SA 127W112, probably not collected) and associated with the remains of a coiled basket with a two-rod-and-bundle, bunched (?) foundation (SA 121W121=FS 80,435). The basket was found near the head, leading excavators to suggest that the child's head might have been placed in the basket at the time of burial. Although neither collected nor mentioned in the burial report, a probable remnant of a twined robe is visible in the field photograph (Figure 46.48). Another infant burial found in this room, 127W107, was also associated with matting (not collected).

Traces of a 2/2-plaited mat (SA 127W120, not recovered) and a twined feather robe (botanical sample 127W3032=FS 80,436-80,438) were found with burial 127W115, an adolescent of undetermined sex. Burial 127W126, an adult female, was poorly preserved and lacked any evidence of wrappings, but a small woven object was preserved within the fill of a Mesa Verde Black-on-white bowl with this burial. This object (SA 127W137) was not located during analysis, but an in situ photo suggests the

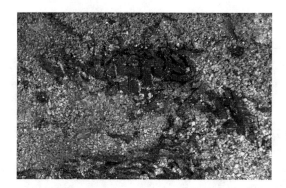

Figure 46.47. Room 127W, in situ view of plaited mat SA 127W100 (FS 80,433.1 and 80,434) with Burial 127W099.

remains of a two-rod-and-bundle coiled basket (Figure 46.49).

Finally, Feature 127W147, another infant burial and probably the earliest burial in this room, was associated with the deteriorated remains of a plaited mat of undetermined weave (SA 127W157 and botanical sample 127W4042=FS 80,440) and a twined fur (?) blanket (SA 127W154 and botanical sample 127W4036=FS 80,439). The burial record states that the body had been laid into a pit, which was partly lined or covered with an unidentified substance possibly colored with red ocher (botanical sample 127W4040). Excavators considered the pit to be associated with the H-3-24 adobe surface. Although it is identified in the database as a Secondary burial, this burial could in fact be quite early, given its position in the lowermost part of this room and the inclusion of a possible fur robe and red ocher. Moreover, Paul Reed has reinterpreted floor stratum H-3-24 as a Primary stratum. Accordingly, I have tentatively reclassified the mat and robe associated with this burial as Primary, rather than Secondary. It will be interesting to see what kinds of ceramics were associated with this burial (SA 127W133-127W136) when the ceramics are reunited with their SA numbers.

Figure 46.48. Room 127W, in situ view of plaited mat and framework of twined robe with Burial 127W106. Objects not recovered.

Besides these mortuary perishables, collapsed roof-fall in this room also produced three carbonized fiber artifacts. Although excavators classified this F-1-4 roof-fall stratum as Secondary, more than 30 percent of the sherds are Chaco, Mancos, or McElmo types (by ceramic rough count), suggesting that some of the fiber artifacts could be Primary in age. SA 127W053 (FS 80,441) is the remains of a large cotton blanket woven in 2/1 diagonal twill (Figure 46.50, see also Figure 46.74c-f). This is the only example of a loom-woven twill fabric from Salmon. Approximately 90 percent of the textile was recovered. Excavators thought they had encountered multiple fabrics, but this is probably due to the fact that this 2/1 weave structure produces two different faces—one with a diagonal-twill appearance, the other with a plain-weave. It is likely that this twill blanket was decorated with brown and/or red stripes, like examples known from other Southwestern sites. Also found in this roof stratum were fragments of a carbonized twined sandal (SA 127W051= FS 80,442, see Figure 46.79f) and another twined object that could be a sandal or a tumpband (FS 80,443, see Figure 46.81c). In my opinion, the twined objects most likely date to the Primary occupation, whereas the cotton cloth could be Primary or Secondary.

Room 129W

This two-story room was abandoned during the Primary occupation and used thereafter as a trash repository. It was twice destroyed by fire; most of the perishables from this room came from burnt roof-fall. A few perishables were also found in Primary and Intermediate (early Secondary) structured trash (Table 46.26). Artifacts from Primary trash include a 1/1-plaited mat or sandal (FS 80,459 and probably also 80,469, see Figure 46.86g), the only example of this basketry structure found at Salmon, and the disarticulated remains of another plaited object (FS 80,472), a sandal, basket, or mat that appears to have been colored red. The only artifacts attributed by excavators to the Intermediate occupation were some yucca knots.

A large assemblage of fiber artifacts was recovered from roof-fall stratum F-1-8. Although the excavators identified this roof-fall as Secondary, the tree-ring data suggest a Primary date for this roof (ca. AD 1090; Tom Windes, personal communication 2003). The sherds are mixed, with a large proportion of the ceramic rough sort consisting of Gallup, Escavada, and McElmo sherds. Given the ceramic and tree-ring evidence, I have tentatively reclassified the perishable artifacts from this stratum as Primary. In addition to a sizable collection of yucca cordage and

Table 46.26. Distribution of perishable artifacts in Room 129W.

Feature Number	Context	Stratum	Occupation	Object Type	Fea./Artifact (SA) No.	New FS Cat. No.
–	Structured trash	C-3-11	Intermediate/ Secondary?	1 yucca square knot	–	80,462
–	Structured trash	C-3-11	Intermediate/ Secondary	1 yucca square knot	–	80,466
–	Structured trash	C-22-30	Primary/ Intermediate	1 yucca square knot	–	80,465
–	Structured trash	C-23-31	Primary?	Plaited sandal, basket, or mat, colored red?	–	80,472
–	Structured trash	C-25-33	Intermediate/ Secondary	1 yucca square knot	–	80,458
–	Structured trash	C-32-39	Primary	Plaited mat, band, or sandal	–	80,459
–	No info	C-32-39 ?	Primary?	Plaited mat, band, or sandal	–	80,469; part of 80,459?
129W007	Burial	F-1-08	Secondary	Plaited mat	–	80,444
–	Roof-fall	F-1-08	Primary?	Coiled (?) basket	SA 129W005	Not recovered
–	Roof-fall	F-1-08.1	Primary?	Bundle of yucca 3-strand braided cordage	SA 129W008	80,446, 80,473
–	Roof-fall	F.1-08	Primary?	Yucca cordage, 2 pieces tied in square knots	SA 129W006, Bot sample 129W2060	80,447.1, 80,447.2
–	Roof-fall	F-1-08	Primary?	Yucca cordage	–	80,448, 80,449 80,450 80,451, 80,452, 80,453, 80,454, 80,455, 80,456, 80,457
–	Roof-fall	F-1-08	Primary?	Twined feather robe; 1 piece yucca cordage in sq knot	–	80,460.1, 80,460.2
–	Roof-fall	F-1-08	Primary?	Yucca cordage, some fur wrapped	–	80,461
–	Roof-fall	F-1-08	Primary?	8 yucca square knots	–	80,463, 80,464, 80,467, 80,471, 80,474
–	Roof-fall	F-1-08	Primary?	Yucca cordage	–	80,468
–	Roof-fall	F-1-08	Primary?	Yucca cordage, 3 pieces tied in square knots	–	80,470.1, 80,470.2
–	Roof-fall	F-1-08	Primary?	Plaited mat, basket, or sandal?	–	80,475
–	Roof-fall	F-1-08	Primary?	Shoe sock w/ plaited sole & looped turkey-feather upper	–	80,476
–	Roof-fall	F-1-08.2	Secondary (or Primary?)	5 yucca square knots	–	80,487
–	Roof-fall	F-1-08.4	Secondary (or Primary?)	4 yucca square knots	–	80,488
–	Unstructured trash	M-1-06	Secondary	48 yucca square knots, 7 incomplete yucca knots, 2 incomplete wooden knots	SA 129W002?	80,445

Figure 46.49. Room 127W, in situ view of coiled basket (?) fragments SA 127W137 (not located) in fill of ceramic bowl with Burial 127W126.

Figure 46.50. Room 127W, in situ view of carbonized cotton twill-weave fabric SA 127W053 (FS 80,441) in roof-fall.

ties, the roof-fall also produced the remains of a twined robe (FS 80,460), a plaited mat, basket, or sandal (FS 80,475), a coiled basket (SA 129W005, not recovered), and a bundle of 3-strand braided yucca (SA 129W008=FS 80,446 and probably 80,473, Figure 46.51, see also Figure 46.53f). It also yielded an artifact unique to Salmon: a carbonized shoe-sock with a 2/2-twill plaited sandal sole and a looped upper of turkey-feather cordage (FS 80,476, see Figure 46.85a). Both the shoe-sock and the 3-strand braided yucca compare favorably with Late Bonito or McElmo phase artifacts from Chaco Canyon (e.g., Mathien 2004: Figures 10–12; Pepper 1920: Figure 123). Finally, a Secondary disturbed burial in this room (129W 007) contained the remains of 2/2-plaited matting (FS 80,444).

Room 130W—Great Kiva

Conditions within this large, single-story structure were not conducive to the preservation of perishables. The only fiber artifact reported from the Great Kiva was the remains of plaited matting (botanical sample 130W4087=FS 80,477 and 80,478), which had been used to line the base of the foot drum (Feature 130W30, Table 46.27). Poorly preserved, these fragments appear to represent the remains of a 2/2-twill plaited mat. As noted, the foot drum in the Tower Kiva was also lined with matting.

OBJECTS FROM UNKNOWN PROVENIENCES

A few objects that were found unlabelled on exhibit or in the storeroom were assigned new catalog numbers (Table 46.28). Most of these are fragments of mats, but this category also includes a

relatively well preserved twined reed blind (FS 80,489). (See the section on twined mats.)

DESCRIPTIONS OF THE WORKED FIBER ASSEMBLAGE

Cordage

Roughly 300 fragments of cordage were recovered at Salmon. Many of these appear to be multiple fragments from larger strands. These fragments likely represent the remains of 104 original cordage objects (Table 46.29). Six (5.7%) of these items are cotton, one (1%) is animal hair, and the remaining 97 (93.3%) are yucca or a similar plant fiber. Nearly half of the cordage from Salmon came from the well-preserved trash deposit in Room 62W. Sizable assemblages were also recovered from Rooms 36W, 43W, 64W, and 129W (Figure 46.52). Because so much of the assemblage is from the culturally mixed trash deposit in Room 62W, it is not possible to compare the Primary and Secondary use of cordage at the site.

Spun and Plied Cordage

Figure 46.53a illustrates examples of cordage structures represented in the assemblage. The most common yucca cordage configurations at Salmon are 2s-Z and 2(2z-S)Z. These two constructions are essentially the same, except that in the former case, the S-spun strand is single ply (or the individual plies could not be seen), and in the latter case, the S-spun strand is plied. These two constructions constitute 65 percent of the yucca cordage in the assemblage, including all of the fur- and feather-wrapped

Table 46.27. Distribution of perishable artifact in Room 130W (Great Kiva).

Feature Number	Context	Stratum	Occupation	Object Type	Fea./Artifact (SA) No.	New FS Cat. No.
130W030	Foot drum	H-1-05	Secondary	Plaited mat	Bot sample 130W4087	80,477, 80,478

Table 46.28. Perishable artifacts of unknown provenience.

Feature Number	Context	Stratum	Occupation	Object Type	Fea./Artifact (SA) No.	New FS Cat. No.
Unknown	Unknown	No info	Unknown	Plaited mat	Unknown	80,480
Unknown	Unknown	No info	Unknown	Mat	Unknown	80,481
Unknown	Unknown	No info	Unknown	Plaited mat	Unknown	80,482
Unknown	Unknown	No info	Unknown	Plaited mat	Unknown	80,483
Unknown	Unknown	No info	Unknown	Twined mat	Unknown	80,489

Table 46.29. Cordage (quantities represent estimated number of unique cordage objects, not number of fragments).

Room	Context	Cotton								Yucca								Animal Hair 6z-S	Unkn.	Total
		Z	3z-S	6z-S	S or Z	2s-Z or 2(2z-S)Z	2s-Z* or 2(2z-S)Z	2(2s-Z)S	3(2s-Z)S	2[2(2z-S)Z]S	2[2(2z-S)Z]Z	3[2(2z-S)Z]S	2z-S	3z-S	4s-Z	3(2z-S)Z	3-strand braid			
4A	Burial	–	–	–	–	–	–	–	–	1	–	–	–	–	–	–	–	–	–	1
30W	Occ fill	–	–	–	–	–	–	–	–	–	–	–	–	–	–	1	–	–	–	1
31A	Occ fill	–	–	–	–	1	–	–	–	–	–	–	–	–	–	–	–	–	–	1
33B	Burial	–	–	–	–	1	–	–	–	–	–	–	–	–	–	–	–	–	–	1
36W	Burial	–	–	–	–	–	–	–	–	–	–	–	–	–	–	–	–	–	1	1
36W	Trash	–	–	–	–	2	1	–	–	1	–	1	–	–	–	–	–	–	–	5
36W	Roof-fall	–	–	–	–	1	–	–	–	–	–	–	–	–	–	–	–	–	–	1
37W	Trash	–	–	–	–	1	–	–	–	–	–	–	–	–	–	–	–	–	–	1
37W	Roof-fall	–	–	–	–	1	–	–	–	–	–	–	–	–	–	–	–	–	–	1
43W	Roof-fall	–	–	–	–	5	–	–	–	–	–	–	–	–	–	–	–	–	–	5
43W	Contact	–	–	–	–	–	2	–	–	–	–	–	–	–	–	–	–	–	–	2
59W	Roof-fall	–	–	–	–	–	2	–	–	–	–	–	–	–	–	–	–	–	–	2
62W	Burial	–	–	–	–	–	–	–	–	–	–	–	–	–	–	–	1	–	–	1
62W	Trash	3	2	1	4	18	10	–	–	–	–	–	1	2	–	–	2	–	1	44
62W?	Unknown	–	–	–	–	1	–	–	–	–	–	–	–	–	–	–	–	–	–	1
64W	Foot drum	–	–	–	–	1	–	–	–	–	–	–	–	–	1	–	–	–	–	2
64W	Roof-fall	–	–	–	–	3	–	–	–	–	–	–	–	–	–	–	–	–	–	3
64W	Bench	–	–	–	–	1	–	–	–	–	–	–	–	–	–	–	–	–	–	1
64W	Floor	–	–	–	–	2	–	–	–	–	–	–	–	–	–	–	–	–	–	2
81W	Roof-fall	–	–	–	–	–	–	–	–	–	–	–	–	–	–	–	1	–	–	1
82W	Roof-fall	–	–	–	–	–	–	–	–	–	–	–	–	–	–	–	–	1	–	1
84W	Wall	–	–	–	1	–	–	–	–	–	–	–	–	–	–	–	–	–	–	1
84W	Roof-fall	–	–	–	2	–	–	–	–	–	–	–	–	–	–	1	–	–	–	3
100W	Roof-fall	–	–	–	–	1	–	–	–	–	–	–	–	–	–	–	–	–	–	1
100W	Burial	–	–	–	–	–	–	–	–	–	–	–	–	–	–	–	–	–	2	2
123B	Burial	–	–	–	–	1	–	–	–	–	–	–	–	–	–	–	–	–	–	1
129W	Roof-fall	–	–	–	–	12	1	1	1	–	1	–	1	–	–	–	1	–	–	18
Total		3	2	1	7	52	16	1	1	2	1	1	2	2	1	2	5	1	4	104

*Fur or feather wrapped yucca.

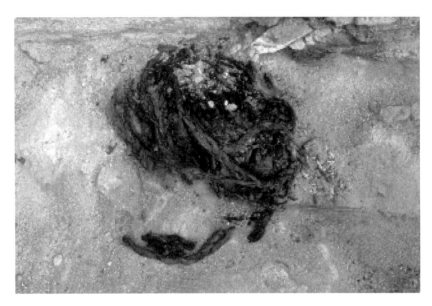

Figure 46.51. Room 129W, in situ view of carbonized bundle of braided yucca SA 129W008 (FS 80,446 and 80,473) in roof-fall.

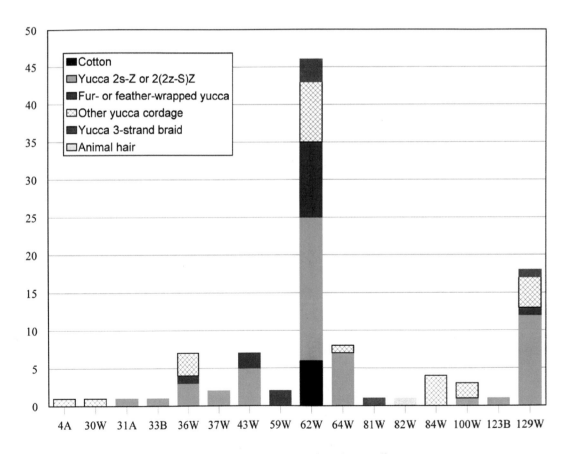

Figure 46.52. Distribution of cordage artifacts.

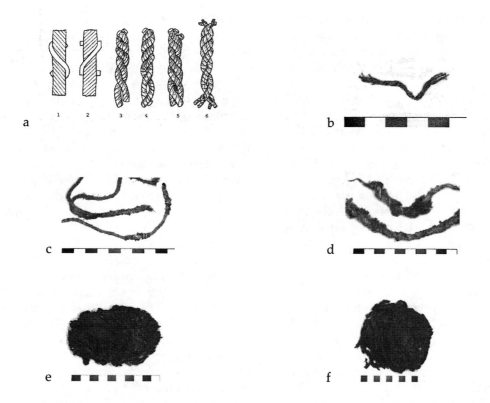

Figure 46.53. Cordage artifacts. (a) examples of cordage structures represented in the assemblage: 1) s-spun; 2) z-spun; 3) 2z-S; 4) 2s-Z; 5) 3z-S; 6) 2(2z-S)Z. (b) FS 80,362, 6z-S yarn spun from unidentified animal hair, Room 82W roof-fall. (c) FS 80,218, feather-wrapped yucca cordage with remains of wrapped quills, Room 62W trash. (d) FS 80,218, rabbit fur-wrapped yucca cordage with remains of fur pile, Room 62W trash. (e) FS 80,266, bundle of 3-strand braided yucca leaves, Room 62W trash. (f) FS 80,446 (SA 129W008), bundle of 3-strand braided yucca leaves, Room 129W roof-fall.

cordage. About 23.5 percent of the 2s-Z and 2(2z-S)Z yucca cordage (15.4% of the cordage assemblage) exhibits evidence of fur or feather wrapping. At least some of these strands are probably the remains of fur or feather blankets. In most cases, only remnants of the quill or hide wrapping is present (Figure 46.53c). However, some of the unburned cordage from Room 62W still retains its original rabbit-fur pile (Figure 46.53d). The bowstring from burial 33B001 (FS 80,020), a 2s-Z cord, could be yucca or sinew.

Most yucca cordage in the assemblage is either an unburned natural tan color or carbonized black. However, three strands from Room 62W appear to be colored with pigment. FS 80,323, attributed to the Primary occupation, contains fragments of fine 3z-S yucca (?) cordage and coarser 2s-Z yucca cordage, both colored a faint red. FS 80,203.2, from the culturally mixed trash stratum, is a fine 2s-Z yucca cord colored yellow. The field notes also describe blue and yellow cordage (not collected) from a Secondary infant burial in Room 100W. The colored artifacts from Salmon are discussed in greater depth at the end of the chapter.

Six examples of cotton cordage were recovered from the well-preserved trash deposit in Room 62W. Three are single-ply z-spun, two are plied 3z-S, and one is 6z-S. The single-ply strands could be disassociated warp or weft elements from deteriorated woven fabrics or untwisted plies from compound yarns.

The assemblage also contains one example of 6z-S animal hair yarn (FS 80,362, Figure 46.53b) recovered from the Secondary roof-fall of Room 82W. The source of the hair has not been identified, but its chocolate brown color suggests dog or bison hair. The hair was microscopically examined at 100x and does not appear to be human or rabbit hair. Although an intrusive deposit of historic sheep wool is possible, I suspect the 6z-S configuration is more typical of pre-contact yarns. As noted above, a 6z-S yarn of cotton was also recorded at Salmon.

Braided Cordage

The assemblage contains five objects of braided cordage. Two are mentioned only in the fieldnotes and evidently were not collected. One is described as braided hair (SA 62W116) from undated (Primary?) infant burial 62W122. The other is a braided cord of yucca or juniper bark (no SA number) from Room 81W Primary roof-fall.

All three braided cords that were collected appear to be made of yucca leaves. FS 80,218.3 is a yucca three-strand braid from Room 62W trash. The other two, FS 80,266 from Room 62W trash and FS 80,446 and 80,473 (SA 129W008) from Room 129W roof-fall (Figure 46.53e and f, see also Figure 46.51), are balls or bundles of 3-strand braided cords made with doubled yucca-leaf elements, one element stacked on top of the other. Excavators attributed these latter three objects to Secondary contexts. However, as previously discussed, I have reinterpreted the 62W trash deposit as mixed and the Room 129W roof-fall as Primary. Undated infant burial 62W122 appears to have been associated with Primary occupational fill. (The braided "hair" described with this burial might have been carbonized yucca, which preserves much better than hair.) Thus, it is not inconceivable that all five of these braided artifacts could date to the Primary occupation.

Regional Comparisons. A preliminary assessment of the literature identifies braiding as having been a popular means of making non-cotton rope and cordage at Chacoan sites. Pepper (1920: Figure 123) reported a thick, braided, coiled-up rope from the floor of Room 86 at Pueblo Bonito. Kent and Loehr (1974:17, 30, Chart 5) identified 11 fragments of 3-strand braids in the Gallo Cliff Dwelling assemblage from Chaco Canyon. Morris collected at least nine 3-strand braids of yucca, rush, or other plant material from the West Ruin at Aztec (Webster 2004). Additional examples have been reported from Antelope House (Magers 1986:266) in Canyon del Muerto and Mug House (Rohn 1971:239, Figure 284c) and Long House (Osborne 1980: 335, Figure 412) at Mesa Verde. To my knowledge, none of these braids were rolled up into bundles or balls like the two examples from Salmon.

Knots

The assemblage contains 595 knots; 408 were from the well-preserved trash midden in Room 62W. Another large collection (82 knots) came from Room 129W (Table 46.30). The vast majority of these knots (518) are knotted yucca-leaf ties, and many (64.1%) incorporate doubled or tripled elements. Most of these yucca ties probably served to bind architectural elements or to hang objects from walls or beams. Thirty-two knotted yucca ties from the culturally mixed trash deposit in Room 62W appear to have

been colored red or yellow. Knots also occur on yucca cordage, feather-wrapped cordage, corn husks, cedar bark bundles, sumac or willow twigs, hide (?) strips, and cotton cloth (Table 46.30).

Square knots were the most common knot structure at Salmon, representing 91.6 percent of the knot assemblage (Figures 46.54 and 55). The assemblage also contains six overhand knots (1%) and one granny knot (0.2%), the latter attributed to the Primary occupation. (These totals do not include the four yucca chains composed of overhand and square knots discussed at the end of the chapter; see Miscellaneous Worked Fiber Artifacts.) Forty-three knots are of unknown structure (unidentified, fragmentary, or not collected). If we consider only the 552 knots of known structure, then 98.7% of the knots from Salmon Ruin are square knots. Because overhand knots are themselves components (i.e., one half) of square knots, and many of the incomplete knots appear to be the remains of square knots, it is not inconceivable that, with the exception of the lone granny knot, virtually all knots at Salmon were square. Clearly, when it came to tying knots, the Salmon population had a very patterned way of doing things.

Mats

Plaited Mats

Plaited matting was the most common woven item at Salmon Pueblo, where examples were reported from at least 24 rooms (Figure 46.56). The remains of 60 plaited mats were identified in the assemblage or recorded in the fieldnotes (Table 46.31). Additional plaited fragments of unidentified form and function might also be the remains of mats (Table 46.32). Although a few mats were nearly intact when found (e.g. Figures 46.14 and18), most are now extremely fragmentary. More than half of these mats (35 mats, or 58.3%) served as mortuary wrappings, which probably contributed to their preservation. Rooms 43W and 127W, which contained multiple burials, also produced the largest number of mats. Plaited mats were also associated with roof-fall, floors, activity areas, and refuse deposits. Matting was recovered from both the floor and the foot drum of the Tower Kiva (Room 64W) and the Great Kiva (Room 130W).

Weave structure could be determined for only 40 of the 60 mats (Table 46.31). The other 20 mats were not collected, not located, or too deteriorated to analyze. Of the 40 identifiable mats, 34 (85%) were woven in 2/2 diagonal twill (Figure 46.57a-c), three (7.5%) in 3/3 diagonal twill (Figure 46.57d, e), two (5%) in either 2/2 or 3/3 twill, and one (2.5%) in a

Table 46.30. Knots.

Room	Context	Square Knots											Other Knots			Total
		Yucca leaf elements single	Yucca leaf elements paired	Yucca leaf elements triple	Yucca Cordage or fiber	Feather cordage	Cotton cloth	Hide?	Cedar bark	Sumac or Willow	Corn husk	Granny	Over hand	In- complete	Un- ident. knot	
4A	Burial	–	2	–	1	–	–	–	–	–	–	–	–	–	–	3
30W	Trash	–	2	–	–	–	–	–	–	–	–	–	–	–	–	2
33C	Trash	1	–	1	–	–	–	–	–	–	–	–	–	–	–	2
33W	Burial	1	–	–	–	–	–	–	–	–	–	1	–	–	–	2
33W	Roof-fall	1	3	–	–	–	–	–	–	–	–	–	–	–	–	4
33W	Occu. fill	1	–	–	–	–	–	–	–	–	–	–	–	–	–	1
36W	Trash	5	–	–	1	–	–	–	–	–	–	–	–	–	–	6
36W	Roof-fall	1	–	–	–	–	–	–	–	–	–	–	–	–	–	1
37W	Trash	2	4	2	–	–	–	–	–	–	–	–	–	1	–	9
43W	Burial	1	4	2	–	–	–	–	–	–	–	–	–	1	–	8
43W	Roof-fall	–	1	–	–	–	–	1	–	–	–	–	–	–	–	2
43W	Contact	–	–	–	–	1	–	–	–	–	–	–	–	–	–	1
43W	Post-occu. fill	–	–	–	–	–	–	–	–	–	–	–	–	1	–	1
59W	Trash	–	2	–	–	–	–	–	–	–	–	–	–	–	–	2
62A	Trash	–	2	–	–	–	–	–	–	–	–	–	–	–	–	2
62W	Trash	132	238	11	1	–	1	–	1	4	1	–	4	15	–	408
62W?	Unknown	2	4	–	–	–	–	–	–	1	–	–	1	–	1	9
64W	Foot drum	–	–	–	1	–	–	–	–	–	–	–	–	–	–	1
64W	Bench	–	–	–	1	–	–	–	–	–	–	–	–	–	–	1
64W	Floor	–	–	–	2	–	–	–	–	–	–	–	–	1	–	3
67W	Roof-fall	1	–	–	–	–	–	–	–	–	–	–	1	–	–	2
67W	Trash	1	–	–	–	–	–	–	–	–	–	–	–	–	–	1

Table 46.30 (continued)

Room	Context	Square Knots											Other Knots			Total
		Yucca leaf elements single	Yucca leaf elements paired	Yucca leaf elements triple	Yucca Cordage or fiber	Feather cordage	Cotton cloth	Hide?	Cedar bark	Sumac or Willow	Corn husk	Granny	Over hand	In-complete	Un-ident. knot	
81W	Roof-fall	–	–	–	–	–	–	–	–	–	–	–	–	–	10	10
84W	Trash	–	1	–	3	–	–	–	–	–	–	–	–	–	–	4
90W	Trash	–	–	–	–	–	–	–	–	–	–	–	–	1	–	1
91A	Trash	–	1	–	–	–	–	–	–	–	–	–	–	–	–	1
91W	Trash	2	–	–	–	–	–	–	–	–	–	–	–	–	–	2
97A	Burial	–	8	–	–	–	–	–	–	–	–	–	–	–	–	8
97W	Artificial fill	1	–	–	–	–	–	–	–	–	–	–	–	–	–	1
98W	Floor	–	–	–	–	–	–	–	–	–	–	–	–	1	–	1
98W	Post-occu. fill	1	–	–	–	–	–	–	–	–	–	–	–	–	–	1
100W	Unknown	–	–	–	–	–	–	–	–	–	–	–	–	1	–	1
100W	Roof-fall	–	2	–	1	–	–	–	–	–	1	–	–	1	–	5
100W	Trash	–	1	–	–	–	–	–	–	–	–	–	–	1	–	2
101W	Trash	–	2	–	–	–	–	–	–	–	–	–	–	–	–	2
118W	Roof	1	–	–	–	–	–	–	–	–	–	–	–	–	–	1
118W	Rodent disturbed	–	1	–	–	–	–	–	–	–	–	–	–	–	–	1
127W	Burial	1	–	–	–	–	–	–	–	–	–	–	–	–	–	1
129W	Trash	22	28	–	1	–	–	–	–	1	–	–	–	8	–	60
129W	Roof-fall	9	10	–	3	–	–	–	–	–	–	–	–	–	–	22
Total		186	316	16	15	1	1	1	1	6	2	1	6	32	11	595

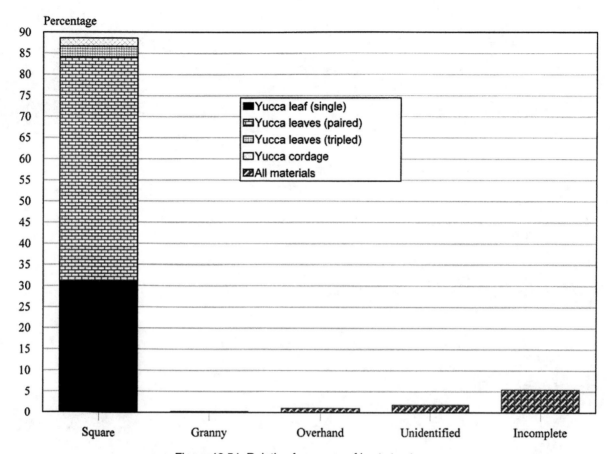

Figure 46.54. Relative frequency of knot structures.

patterned weave (Figure 46.57f). (Two other objects worked in 1/1 plaiting are discussed in the section Miscellaneous Worked Fiber Artifacts.) The patterned mat, from Secondary burial 43W019, has alternating narrow and wide elements and is woven with 2/2 and 3/3 principal intervals and intentional 2/5/2, 3/4/3, and 3/5/3 shifts (Figure 46.57f). A 2/2-twill mat from late Primary burial 33W012 might exhibit some intentional 2/3/2 shifts, or this could just reflect the disturbed and deteriorated state of the mat. Of the 15 possible Primary mats in the sample (including four from the mixed Room 62W trash deposit), six are woven in 2/2 diagonal twill and nine are too deteriorated to identify. Based on this less-than-perfect sample, there are no definite examples of 3/3 plaiting from Primary contexts. The Secondary assemblage is larger and more diverse, containing examples of 2/2, 3/3, and patterned weaves.

Most mats in the assemblage appear to have been made of flattened rush elements (*Scirpus* sp.).

Some of the finer mats may employ yucca elements, either narrowleaf yucca (*Yucca angustissima*) or wide *Yucca baccata* leaves cut into strips. The finest mat in the assemblage has a weave density of 4 elements per cm (elements 0.2 cm wide), and the coarsest has 1 element per cm (1 cm wide). For the fine mats, the average density and element width is 3.5 elements per cm (0.3 cm wide), and for the coarse mats, 2 elements per cm (0.5 cm wide). In general, the 2/2-twill mats in the assemblage are more coarsely woven than the 3/3-twill mats. However, some fine 2/2-twill mats were also found.

Selvage Finish

The selvages are missing on nearly two-thirds (71.7%) of the mats. Four (6.7%) mats have 90° self-selvages, and the remaining 13 (21.7%) have a decorative type of multiple self-selvage that J. M. Adovasio (1977:117, 148–152, Figures 160–163; see also Adovasio and Gunn 1986:349–360, Figures 160–187) refers to as an intricate selvage with twining (Figure 46.58a). The intricate selvages from Salmon

Table 46.31. Plaited mats.

Feature or Artifact (SA) No.	New FS Cat. No.	Room and Context	Occ	No. mats repres.	Body Weave Structure and Measurements							Selvage Finish			Comments
					2/2 twill	3/3 twill	2/2 or 3/3 twill	Pattern weave	Un-ident.	Number elements per cm	Avg. element width cm	Intricate selvage	90° self-selvage	Missing	
Fea. 4A007	80,003, 80,004	4A, burial 4A002	Sec	1	X?	-	-	-	-	1.5-2.0	0.6	X	-	-	Lower mat; jumbled up
-	80,015	31W, fill	Pri	1	X?	-	-	-	-	4.0?	0.25	-	-	X	Poor condition
Fea. 33B006	80,017	33B, burial 33B001, Skel 2	Sec	1	X	-	-	-	-	1.5	0.6	-	-	X	Coarse weave
-	80,018	33B, burial 33B001, Skel 3	Sec	1	X?	-	-	-	-	1.6	0.6	-	-	X	Tiny fragments only
-	80,019	33B, burial 33B002	Sec	1	X	-	-	-	-	2.5	0.4	-	-	X	Fine weave
SA 33W011	80,023.1, 80,030.1, 80,032.1	33W, burial 33W012	Pri	2?	X	-	-	?	-	2.0	0.5	-	-	X	Exterior mat; remains of two different mats? Possible 2/3/2 shifts
SA 33W019	80,024, 80,025, 80,033.1	33W, burial 33W012	Pri	1	X	-	-	-	-	3.0-3.5	0.3	-	?	-	Fine weave interior mat
SA 33W021	80,026, 80,027	33W, burial 33W012	Pri	0	-	-	-	-	X	-	-	X?	-	-	Excavators called it a "strap"; could be selvage to SA 33W011
-	80,036	33W, roof-fall	Sec/Int	1	-	X	-	-	-	4.0	0.3	-	-	X	Fine weave; carbonized
Fea. 36W028?	80,055	36W, lithic scatter 36W029	Pri	1	-	-	-	-	X	-	-	-	-	X	Remains of plaited mat? Deteriorated, covered large area
Fea. 36W032	N/A	36W, lithic scatter 36W031	Pri	1	-	-	-	-	X	-	-	-	-	X	Mat? (mass of plant material)
-	80,056	36W, trash	Sec	1	-	-	-	-	X	-	-	-	-	X	Remains of mat? Jumbled elements
SA 37W083	80,070	37W, floor	Sec	1	-	-	-	-	X	-	-	-	-	X	Field photo suggests 2/2 plaiting

Table 46.31 (continued)

Feature or Artifact (SA) No.	New FS Cat. No.	Room and Context	Occ	No. mats repres.	2/2 twill	3/3 twill	2/2 or 3/3 twill	Pattern weave	Un-ident.	Number elements per cm	Avg. element width cm	Intricate selvage	90° self-selvage	Missing	Comments
SA 43W030 (body of mat), SA 43W032 (selvage)	80,085, 80,087, 80,159.1	43W, burial 43W003	Sec	1	X	–	–	–	–	2.0–2.5	0.4–0.5	X	–	–	Large weave mat; "strap" is probably selvage of a coarse mat
SA 43W031	80,159.2	43W, burial 43W003	Sec	1	X	–	–	–	–	4.0	0.2	–	–	X	Fine weave; associated with plant remains
SA 43W004	80,088, 80,089.1, 80,090.2, 80,091.1	43W, burial 43W005	Sec	2	X	–	–	–	–	3.0	0.3–0.4	–	–	X	2 mats (1 fine, 1 coarse)
										2.0	0.5	–	–	X	
SA 43W011	80,104.2	43W, burial 43W005	Sec	1	X	–	–	–	–	3.0–3.3	0.25	–	–	X	Fine weave
SA 43W028	80,117.2, 80,119, 80,120.1, 80,121, 80,122	43W, burial 43W019	Sec	1	–	–	–	X	–	1.0–2.0	0.3–1.0	–	X	–	Alternating wide and narrow elements; 2/2 & 3/3 principal intervals with intentional shifts
SA 43W059, SA 43W060; also bot samp from mug (SA43W065)	80,129, 80,130, 80,131, 80,132, 80,160, 80,485.1, 80,485.2	43W, burial 43W057	Sec	2	X	X	–	–	–	2.0–2.5	0.4–0.5	X	–	–	2 upper mats, one 2/2 twill, other 3/3 twill; 3/3 one is finer; selvage has rounded corners
										3.5	0.3–0.4	X	–	–	
SA 43W070	80,137.2, 80,140.2, 80,141, 80,142	43W, burial 43W057	Sec	1	–	X	–	–	–	3.0–4.0	0.25	X	–	–	Lower mat; fragments of 2/2 twill mixed in from other mat
SA 62A031	80,186	62A, floor	Sec	1	–	–	X	–	–	2.0	0.5	–	–	X	Coarse weave; assoc w/ McElmo bowl
SA 62A043	80,187	62A, floor	Sec	1	–	–	–	–	X	–	–	–	–	X	SA form says twilled; assoc with corn
—	80,196	62W, trash	Mix	1	–	–	–	–	X	–	–	X	–	–	Selvage only; no body weave

Table 46.31 (continued)

Feature or Artifact (SA) No.	New FS Cat. No.	Room and Context	Occ	No. mats repres.	Body Weave Structure and Measurements							Selvage Finish			Comments
					2/2 twill	3/3 twill	2/2 or 3/3 twill	Pattern weave	Un-ident.	Number elements per cm	Avg. element width cm	Intricate selvage	90° self-selvage	Missing	
–	80,270	62W, trash	Mix	1	–	–	X	–	–	2.0	0.4	–	–	X	Deteriorated remains of mat
SA 62W115	N/A	62W, infant burial 62W122	Unkn	1	–	–	–	–	X	–	–	–	–	X	Not collected
–	80,271.1	62W, trash	Mix	1	–	–	–	–	X	–	–	X	–	–	Selvage only; no body weave
–	80,302	62W, trash	Mix	1	–	–	–	–	X	1.5	0.6-0.7	–	–	X	Probably coarse mat
SA 64W120	80,341	64W, foot drum 64W118	Sec	1	X	–	–	–	–	1.8	0.6	X	–	–	Coarse mat
Fea. 64W041	80,338, 80,339, 80,340	64W, floor	Sec	1	X	–	–	–	–	2.5	0.5	X	–	–	Coarse mat
SA 64W098	N/A	64W, floor	Sec	1	–	–	–	–	X	–	–	X	–	–	Not collected? Field photo shows intricate selvage with rounded corner
–	80,371	88W, floor	Sec	1	X	–	–	–	–	2.0	0.4-0.5	–	–	X	2 deteriorated frags
–	80,375	93W, trash	Sec	1	–	–	–	–	X	–	–	–	–	X	Probable remains of plaited mat
–	80,376, 80,377, 80,378.1, 80,379, 80,380.1, 80,381.1, 80,382.1, 80,383 97A1001	97A, burial	Sec	1	X	–	–	–	–	2.0	0.4-0.5	–	X	–	Deteriorated remains of mat
–	80,384	97B, burial 97B002	Sec	1	–	–	–	–	X	–	–	–	–	X	Tiny fragments; only traces found
Bot samp 97W2020	80,386	97W, log Feature 97W2007	Pri	1	–	–	–	–	X	–	–	–	–	X	Jumbled layers from flotation sample

Table 46.31 (continued)

Feature or Artifact (SA) No.	New FS Cat. No.	Room and Context	Occ	No. mats repres.	2/2 twill	3/3 twill	2/2 or 3/3 twill	Pattern weave	Un-ident.	Number elements per cm	Avg. element width cm	Intricate selvage	90° self-selvage	Missing	Comments
—	80,387.1	97W, burial 97W1006	Sec?	1	X	–	–	–	–	2.5	0.3-0.4	–	–	X	Folded; several layers represented
—	80,388.1, 80,389.1	97W, burial 97W1007	Sec?	1	X	–	–	–	–	2.5	0.4	–	–	X	Deteriorated remains of mat
—	80,391	97W, artificial fill	Pri?	1	X?	–	–	–	–	3.0	0.3	–	–	X	Loose elements only; 2 frags with weave
—	80,392	97W, trash	Pri?	1	X	–	–	–	–	–	–	?	X	–	Part of an intricate selvage? Elements have a slight reddish cast
—	N/A	100W, burial 100W302	Pri?	1	–	–	–	–	X	–	–	–	–	X	Traces of mat on cranium; notes say colored red; not collected
Bot samp 102W1021	80,413	102W, burial 102W001?	Sec	1	–	–	–	–	X	N/a	0.5	–	–	X	Probable remains of mat
SA 121W039, Bot samp 121W2089	80,417, 80,418, 80,419, 80,420	121W, burial 121W033	Sec	1	X	–	–	–	–	1.2-2.5?	0.4-0.8?	–	–	X	Soil impression of coarsely woven mat
—	80,422	122W, burial 122-1?	Pri m. or Sec,	2	X	–	–	–	–	3.0-4.0	0.3-0.4	–	–	X	Fine 2/2 mat fused to coarse unident. mat
			Sec,	–	–	–	–	–	X	–	–	–	–	X	
Fea. 123B004	80,425, 80,426, 80,427	123B, burial 123B005	Int/ Sec	1	X?	–	–	–	–	3.0-4.0	0.25-0.3	–	–	X	Fine weave
SA 127B003	80,428, 80,429	127B, burial 127B001	Sec	1	X?	–	–	–	–	2.0	0.5	–	–	X	Deteriorated remains of mat

Table 46.31 (continued)

Feature or Artifact (SA) No.	New FS Cat. No.	Room and Context	Occ	No. mats repres.	2/2 twill	3/3 twill	2/2 or 3/3 twill	Pattern weave	Un-ident.	Number elements per cm	Avg. element width cm	Intricate selvage	90° self-selvage	Missing	Comments
SA 127W056	80,430, 80,431	127W, burial 127W055	Sec	1	X	–	–	–	–	1.0-1.5	0.6-0.9	–	X	–	Coarse weave; assoc with Mesa Verde B/W bowl
SA 127W100	80,433.1, 80,434	127W, burial 127W099	Sec	1	X	–	–	–	–	4.0	0.25	–	–	X	Fine weave
SA 127W112	N/A	127W burial 127W106	Sec	1	X?	–	–	–	–	–	–	–	–	X	Not collected; field photo suggests 2/2 twill
–	N/A	127W, burial 127W107	Sec	1	–	–	–	–	X	–	–	–	–	X	Described as traces of mat; not collected?
SA 127W120	N/A	127W, burial 127W115	Sec	1	–	–	–	–	X	–	–	–	–	X	Described as traces of mat; not collected?
SA 127W157, Bot samp 127W4042	80,440	127W, burial 127W147	Pri	1	–	–	–	–	X	N/a	0.3	–	–	X	Disarticulated elements
–	80,444	129W, burial 129W007	Sec	1	X	–	–	–	–	3.0	0.3	–	–	X	5 small fragments
Bot samp 130W4087	80,477 80,478	130W, Foot drum 130W030	Sec	1	X?	–	–	–	–	–	–	–	–	X	Poor condition; one small section could be 2/2 twill
Unknown	80,480	Unknown	Unkn	1	X	–	–	–	–	2.0-3.0	0.3-0.5	X	–	–	Found in collections
Unknown	80,481	Unknown	Unkn	1	–	–	–	–	X	–	–	–	–	X	Found in collections
Unknown	80,482	Unknown	Unkn	1	X	–	–	–	–	1.8	0.6	–	–	X	Coarse weave; found in collections
Unknown	80,483	Unknown	Unkn	1	X	–	–	–	–	2.5	0.4	–	–	X	Found in collections

Table 46.32. Unidentified plaited objects (mats, sandals, baskets, pot rests).

Feature or Artifact (SA) No	New FS Cat. No.	Room and Context	Occ	Number Objects Repres.	Weave Structure					Selvage		Comments
					1/1 Plaiting	2/2 Twill Plaiting	Un-ident.	Number Elements per cm	Avg. Element Width cm	Self-selvage	Unknown or Missing	
–	80,054	36W, post-occup fill	Sec	1	–	X	–	4.0	0.2-0.3	–	X	Basket or pot rest
Bot samp 62W2024	80,220	62W, trash	Mixed	1	–	?	–	3.0	0.3	–	X	Basket or mat; weave jumbled up; colored red?
–	80,228	62W, trash	Mixed	1	X	–	–	1.0	0.6-0.9	180°	–	Unique plaited object; yucca-leaf elements folded to make a small square 2 elements wide and 4 layers thick
–	80,236	62W, trash	Mixed	1	–	–	X	N/a	0.4-0.6	–	X	Disarticulated elements; mat, basket, or ties?
–	80,276	62W, trash	Mixed	1	–	?	–	3.0	0.3	–	X	Several layers; basket or mat?
–	80,312	62W, trash	Mixed	1	–	X	–	3.0-3.5	0.3	–	X	Sandal, basket, or mat; colored red? Fine weave
–	80,335	62W, occup fill	Pri	1	–	–	X	2.5?	0.4?	–	X	Mat, sandal, or basket; very deteriorated
SA 101W004	80,409	101W, trash on roof	Sec	1	–	X	–	3.0	0.3-0.4	–	X	Mat or sandal; fine weave
–	80,459;	129W, trash probably 80,469	Pri	1	X	–	–	3.0	0.3	90°	–	80,459 is large fragment of mat, band, or sandal; square corner; seems too delicate for a sandal. 80,469 has only 4 interacting elements; these t suggest 1/1 plaiting; probably part of same object as 80,459
–	80,472	129W, trash	Pri?	1	–	–	X	N/a	0.2?	–	X	Disarticulated elements; sandal, basket, or mat?; leaves have a brick red cast
–	80,475	129W, roof-fall	Pri?	1	–	–	X	N/a	N/a	–	X	Mat, basket, or sandal?; Potter identified this as plaited; now just a mass of yucca (?) fiber

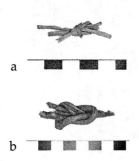

Figure 46.55. Knots. (a) FS 80,189, yucca leaves tied in square knot, Room 62A. (b) FS 80,279, willow (?) twig tied in square knot, Room 62W.

conform to Adovasio's (1977:117, 148–153) basic description of the technique. They were made by folding the terminal elements of a mat at an obtuse (130–150°) angle to the main body weave, then plaiting them with like elements for a desired distance before folding them back along the outer edge at a 90° angle. The elements were then plaited together again until they reached the inner edge of the border, at which time they were usually folded again at a 90° angle and clipped off (Adovasio 1977:117). In the simplest terms, the elements follow a path of zigzag-zig. At Salmon, these selvages were usually reinforced with single row of 2-strand twining, twined S-wise, worked in rush elements (Figure 46.58a). Figures 46.58b and 58c illustrate the upper and lower faces of one example.

The intricate selvages in the Salmon assemblage have rounded corners and average about 3 cm in width. These selvages occur on eight of the 2/2-weave mats, two of the 3/3-weave mats, and three mats of unidentified weave (Figure 46.58b, c, e, f). Because the outer edge of an intricate selvage is a 90° self-selvage, some of the smaller mat fragments with a 90° selvage finish could also be the remains of intricate selvages.

Most of the Primary mats from Salmon are deteriorated and missing their selvages. However, there is the suggestion that mats with intricate selvages were also in use during the Primary occupation. Late Primary burial 33W012, the so-called bow priest, was found wrapped with a long narrow plaited band that excavators identified as a strap (FS 80,026 and 80,027, Figure 46.58d). The construction of this band resembles that of an intricate selvage and it could easily be a selvage from one of the associated mats. A row of holes along one edge suggests the former presence of twining elements. However, Keith Adams (personal communication 2003), who excavated the burial, remembers this as a separate strap rather than as part

of the mat. Another Primary mat (FS 80,392) from a Primary trash deposit in Room 97W includes a fragment of a 90° self-selvage with a slight curvature; this object could also be part of an intricate selvage. Many of the Secondary plaited mats exhibit intricate selvages, and there is little doubt that this was the most common form of selvage finish at Salmon during the Secondary occupation.

As noted by Adovasio (1977:117), a thorough analysis of intricate selvages can be time consuming because the range of variation can be quite high. The pace of my analysis did not permit me to record all of the variability in the intricate selvages from Salmon. (See Adovasio and Gunn 1986 for an example of a detailed analysis.) This would be a worthwhile endeavor in the future, however, given the potential of this attribute to reveal low-visibility differences in technological style.

Regional Comparisons. As at Salmon, most of the matting from Pueblo Bonito and Chetro Ketl is woven in 2/2 plaiting (Judd 1954:50; Vivian 1931: Photos I, III). However, 3/3 plaiting is also known from Chaco (Judd 1954:50; Kent and Loehr 1974:25, 26). Although Morris (1919) did not publish weave structure information for his Aztec collections, my recent survey of the collection at the American Museum of Natural History recorded extensive quantities of both 2/2- and 3/3-twill plaited mats (Webster 2004). Many of the mats from Chaco, Aztec, Mesa Verde, and Antelope House are decorated with intricate selvages with twining (Adovasio 1977:148–153; Nordenskiöld 1893: Plate XLVIII; Rohn 1971:233, Figure 46.272), suggesting that this was a common Pueblo style on the Colorado Plateau between AD 1100 and 1300, if not earlier. Based on published descriptions, it appears that some of the intricate selvages from Chaco Canyon (Kent 1974:25, Figures 3d, 5; Vivian 1931: Photo VI) are twined with four rows of 2-strand twining, rather than the single row of 2-strand twining found at Salmon and Aztec.

Threaded or Sewn Willow Mat

The remains of a "wood slat curtain" (recorded as SA 43W027) was found to the west of burial 43W 019, a richly furnished Secondary female (?) burial (Figure 46.16, upper, and Table 46.33). Excavators recorded the curtain as part of the burial, but had some question about its association, noting that it might have been associated with the burned roof stratum (F-2-07) instead.

Excavators described the curtain as consisting of about 40 partially burned willow slats that had been shaped, drilled with small holes, and threaded together with yucca cordage. The field dimensions

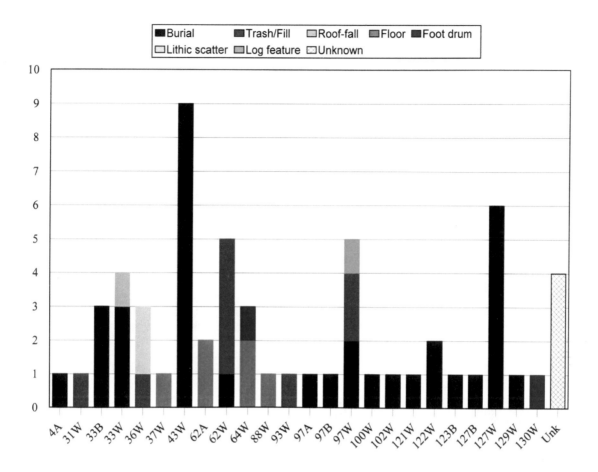

Figure 46.56. Distribution of plaited mats.

were reported as 22 cm wide x 36 cm long. These 40 slats were treated with preservatives in the field and reportedly collected. The only fragments I encountered of this object during analysis were one small drilled piece of willow (FS 80,120.2) and about two dozen fragments of 2s-Z yucca cordage (FS 80,116). Perhaps additional pieces of this object will be found when the wooden artifact assemblage is examined.

Regional Comparisons. Threaded or sewn willow mats have been reported from several Chacoan great houses and other sites in the Southwest, where their use appears to have been related to mortuary contexts, great house ceiling construction, and ritual settings. At Pueblo Bonito several were associated with multiple-interment burials and ritual contexts (Judd 1954:50, 51, 326, 330, Plate 10a, b; Pepper 1909: 197, 236). At Pueblo del Arroyo, one was found beneath the broken ceiling of a storeroom (Judd 1959:9, 131, Plate 7b). Similar mats covered the ceiling poles and door drops at Chetro Ketl (Tschopik 1939:95, fn. 8). One is also reported from BC 51, a small house

site at Chaco (Tschopik 1939:94). Numerous examples are known from the West Ruin at Aztec, where Morris (1919:55–56, Figure 34, 1924:167, 1928:354, 373–382) found them in association with at least six ceilings, two floors, and two burials. They have also been reported from kivas and burials at Mesa Verde (Rohn 1971:231–232, Figures 270–271).

Twined Reed Mats, Including a Possible Reed Quiver

One definite twined reed object and two other possible examples were found at Salmon Pueblo (Table 46.33). The definite example was found unlabelled in an exhibit case in the Salmon Ruins Museum; it was assigned a new catalog number, FS 80,489 (Figure 46.59). This unburned and relatively well preserved object consists of a large section of a reed blind or mat constructed of pairs of *Phragmites* elements, each approximately 78 cm long and 1 cm in diameter, twined together with six spaced rows of 2(2z-S)Z yucca cordage. The first, second, and fifth rows of twining are single rows of 2-strand twining,

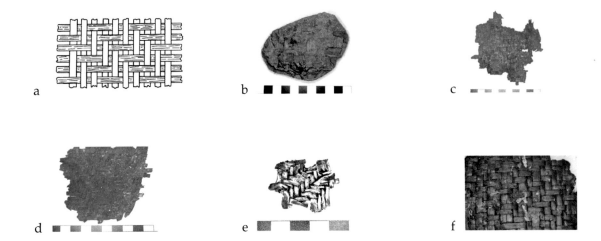

Figure 46.57. Body weaves of plaited mats. (a) Schematic diagram of 2/2 twill plaiting structure. (b) FS 80,419 (SA 121W039), impression of coarse 2/2-twill plaited mat with Burial 121W033. (c) FS 80,340 (Feature 64W041), coarse 2/2-twill plaited mat, Room 64W (Tower Kiva). (d) FS 80,141 (SA 43W070), fine 3/3-twill plaited mat, Burial 43W057 (lower mat). (e) FS 80,036 (no field number), fine 3/3-twill plaited mat consolidated with a preservative, Room 33W roof-fall. (f) FS 80,117.2 (SA 43W028), coarsely woven patterned mat with 2/2 and 3/3 plaiting intervals, Burial 43W019.

whereas the third, fourth, and sixth rows are paired rows of 2-strand twining. The distance between the twining rows ranges from 7 to 17 cm. In its present condition, the object measures about 78 cm long (complete length) and 24 cm wide (incomplete width). Both side selvages are missing. Loose ends of twining cords extending beyond the reeds suggest that the mat was originally at least 12 cm greater in width. Thus, the object originally measured 78 cm long and at least 36 cm wide, and probably wider.

FS 80,489 could be one of the two reed bundles or blinds reported in the field notes but not located during analysis, or it could be neither of these objects. The first was associated with late Primary burial 33W012, the "bow priest" burial. This twined object, identified in the field as SA 33W022, was described on the significant artifact form as a rolled-up "reed Venetian blind" that possibly contained seeds. From the field sketch, the object appears to have been about 50 cm long and 10 cm wide in its rolled condition (see Figure 46.10).

Although an in situ photograph of this reed object has not been found, an in situ photograph of some of the wooden objects with this burial shows them to be relatively well preserved (Figure 46.9). Thus, it is possible that FS 80,489 could be the "reed blind" from this burial. However, the significant artifact form states that only 5 percent of this object was collected. Moreover, the worked fiber artifacts I analyzed from this burial are now quite deteriorated. (The wooden artifacts from this burial, which I did not examine, might have been colored with pig-

ments, which would account for their better preservation.) Furthermore, if the field map is accurate, the reed mat cataloged as FS 80,489 is almost 30 cm longer than the reed blind reported from burial 33W012.

Rather than a reed blind or mat, it is possible that the object associated with burial 33W012 might have been a reed quiver or some other kind of container. Cylinder-like objects made of twined reeds have been reported from several Chacoan sites, including "Chacoan" rooms 72 and 1222 at the West Ruin at Aztec (Webster 2004) and a cache known as the "Cacique's Sanctum" from a road ramp near Chetro Ketl (Mathien 2004: Figure 8f). The two twined-reed objects from the Cacique's Sanctum were identified as quivers (Mathien 2004:92, Figure 8f). Morris also identified one of his reed-stem containers (AMNH 29.0/5335) as a quiver in his field catalog. He further suggested that these twined reed objects might have served as protective sheaths for feathers (Morris 1919:59). The dimensions of these objects range from 58 long x 8 wide cm and 32 long x 5.2 wide cm for the reed cylinders from Aztec (AMNH 29.0/8488 and 29.0/5335; additional examples are known) to 71.1 long and 35.6 long cm (width not provided) for the two quivers from the Cacique's Sanctum.

FS 80,489 could also be Significant Artifact 81W 341, a reed bundle reported from Room 81W, adjacent to the Tower Kiva. No object with this SA number was found during analysis. However, this object could be stored with the wooden artifact assemblage, which I did not analyze. (A quick survey

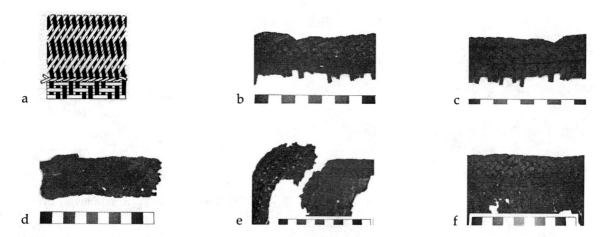

Figure 46.58. Intricate selvages from plaited mats. (a) Schematic diagram of intricate selvage with S-twist twining; from Adovasio and Gunn 1986: Figure 161. (b) FS 80,485.1 (SA 43W059 and 43W060), upper face of intricate selvage with S-twist twining on 2/2-twill plaited mat, probably from Burial 43W057. (c) FS 80,485.1 (SA 43W059 and SA 43W060), lower face of intricate selvage with S-twist twining on 2/2-twill plaited mat, probably from Burial 43W057. (d) FS 80,026 (SA 33W021), plaited "strap" found with Burial 33W012, possibly an intricate selvage from a mat. Row of holes suggests former presence of twining elements. (e) FS 80,131 (SA 43W0059 and 43W060), intricate selvage fragments with curved outline from fine 3/3-twill plaited mat, Burial 43W057 (upper mat). (f) FS 80,137 (SA 43W070), intricate selvage on fine 3/3-twill plaited mat, Burial 43W057 (lower mat).

of the wooden artifacts failed to turn up this item.) Described on the significant artifact form and field notes as a horsetail reed bundle found oriented east-west near the floor of the northwest corner of Room 81W, this object was reportedly associated with a large quantity of unusually well preserved plant remains. The field notes do not provide the dimensions of the object. The only photograph found of this object is a blurry Polaroid black-and-white field photograph showing the bundle in situ. In that photo, the object appears to be in very poor condition and does not resemble FS 80,489.

Regardless of whether FS 80,489 is the reed blind from burial 33W012, the reed bundle from Room 81W, or some other unidentified object from the site, this object most likely dates to the Primary occupation and was associated with a special-use context. Late Primary burial 33W3012 was the richest burial at Salmon—clearly that of a very important person. Likewise, Room 81W, adjacent to the Tower Kiva, was a special-use room that saw its most intensive use during the Primary occupation. It was in this room that the raised platform and weaving tools were found. If FS 80,489 was associated with burial 33W012, it might have been a reed quiver. If it was from Room 81W, it might have served as a covering for the floor or platform. Either way, twined reed objects and threaded willow mats were rare at Salmon and appear to have occurred only in special rooms or mortuary contexts. A similar pattern of use

is found at Chaco Canyon, Aztec, and Mesa Verde.

Regional Comparisons. Reeds or other objects twined together with cordage were relatively common at Chaco and Aztec, where they occurred in mortuary or special-use contexts. At Pueblo Bonito, several were found in association with multiple-interment burials (Judd 1954:50, 327–330). Twined mats have also been found with burials at small site BC 51 (Tschopik 1939:94–95) and with burials, roofs, and floors at nearby Tseh So (Brand et al 1937:99). As discussed above, reed objects having the same construction but in a cylindrical shape were found by Morris in the West Ruin of Aztec and at the "Cacique's Sanctum" near Chetro Ketl. Morris (1928:357) also found a twined reed mat in Room 112 at Aztec.

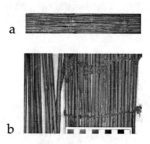

Figure 46.59. Twined reed object from unknown provenience. (a) FS 80,489, overall view. (b) FS 80,489, detail showing rows of twining.

Table 46.33. Threaded willow and twined reed blinds or mats.

Fea./Artifact (SA) Number	New FS Cat No.	Room & Context	Occup.	Twined	Threaded	Structure	Comments
SA 33W022	N/a	33W, burial 33W012	Pri	?	–	Unknown	Not found; SA form says only 5% recovered. Possibly a reed quiver? Could be FS 80,489?
SA 43W027	80,116, 80,120.2	43W, burial 43W019	Sec	–	X	Elements drilled & threaded w/ 2s-Z yucca cordage	Wood slat curtain or blind; at least 40 slats recorded in the field; analyzed specimen consists only of one fragment of cordage and a drilled willow stick.
SA 81W341	N/a	81W, roof-fall	Pri	?	–	Unknown	No item found with this SA number. Object described in field notes as a reed bundle made of horsetail reed, associated with large quantity of plant materials.
Unknown	80,489	Unknown	Unkn	X		2-strand twining (S)	*Phragmites* elements twined together with yucca cords. Object found unlabelled in exhibit case. Could be SA 33W022?

Similar reed mats are also reported from Mug House at Mesa Verde (Rohn 1971: Figure 273) and Antelope House in Canyon del Muerto (Adovasio and Gunn 1986:314, Figure 118).

Baskets

Thirty-four baskets were identified in the Salmon assemblage—8 plaited and 26 coiled. All baskets from Primary occupation contexts are plaited baskets, and all baskets from mortuary contexts are coiled; the latter occurred with six Secondary burials. Eight baskets came from roof-fall, 14 were found in the trash or fill (two from the interstitial fill of the Tower Kiva), and five were found on floors. Another is from an unknown context (Figure 46.60).

Plaited Ring Baskets

Eight plaited ring baskets were identified (Table 46.34 and Figures 46.11, 24, 61, 62). Some of the unidentified plaited fragments in Table 46.32 might also be the remains of plaited baskets. Several of the ring baskets are quite large. The rim fragments from one incomplete example, FS 80,183 (Feature 62A004, Figure 46.62b), have a circumference of 44 cm. The most common plaiting structure is 2/2 diagonal twill (five baskets, 62.5%), followed by 3/3 twill (two baskets, 25%), and diamond twill (one basket, 12.5%; Figures 46.57a, 62). All ring baskets appear to be constructed of narrow yucca elements, either whole leaves of narrowleaf yucca (*Yucca angustissima*) or cut strips of *Yucca baccata*. Weave density is relatively standardized, with element width ranging from 0.25 to 0.4 cm, and element density ranging from 2–3 per cm in the coarsest baskets to 3–4 per cm in the finest ones.

All ring baskets have 180° self-selvages, constructed by folding the plaiting elements over one or more willow (?) rods and securing them with a row of 2-strand twining worked in yucca strips (Figure 46.63a). Five baskets are twined S-wise, two are twined Z-wise, and one selvage is missing. All of the ring baskets have a single rod at the rim (e.g., Figures 46.62c-d, 63b) except for the basket recorded as Features 61A012 and 61A013 (FS 80,179/80,180.1), which has two stacked rods (Figure 46.63c, d). In this latter example, some of the yucca elements wrap all the way around the rods, producing a partial 360° coiled selvage. No examples of ornamental braided rims like those found on Pueblo III ring baskets from the Mesa Verde area and Antelope House (Adovasio and Gunn 1986: Figure 195; Morris and Burgh 1941: 23, Figure 8) were identified in Salmon's assemblage.

Three ring baskets are attributed to the Primary occupation, one to the mixed deposit in Room 62W, and four to Secondary contexts (Table 46.34). Like the plaited mats, all plaited baskets from known Primary contexts are woven in 2/2 twill. Two Primary baskets were recovered from the interstices of the Tower Kiva (Room 61A), where they may have been nested together and formed part of a ritual deposit (Figures 46.24, 63b-d). The other Primary basket came from a Primary structured trash deposit in Room 62W; it is colored red with hematite (Figure 46.62a). (See discussion of colored artifacts at the end

Table 46.34. Plaited ring baskets.

Feature or Artifact (SA) No.	New FS No.	Room and Context	Occ	Number Baskets Repres.	Weave Structure					Selvage Finish			Number Rods at Rim	Comments
					2/2 Twill	3/3 Twill	Diamond Twill	Elements per cm	Avg. Elem. Width cm	180° Self-selvage Twine S	180° Self-selvage Twine Z	Missing		
Feature 31W008	80,013	31W, pit fill	Sec	1	–	X	–	2.0-3.0	0.3-0.4	X	–	–	1	Includes part of rod; rim circumference at least 24.0 cm
SA 36W044 Bot samp 36W4018	80,045	36W, trash above roof	Sec	1	X	–	–	3.5?	0.4	–	X	–	1	Includes part of rod; rim circumference at least 10.0 cm
SA 36W049 SA 36W056 Bot samp 36W4142	80,047, 80,048, 80,052	36W, burned roof	Sec	1	–	–	X	2.0-3.0	0.3-0.4	–	X	–	1	Includes part of rod; concentric diamond design has 1-, 3-, and 5-span floats; rim circumference at least 30.0 cm
Features 61A012, 61A013	80,179, 80,180.1	61A, interstitial space	Pri	1	X	–	–	2.5-3.0	0.3-0.4	X	–	–	2	Some 3-span floats near rim; stitches wrap 360° around the two rods, producing a coiled selvage; rim circumference at least 24.0 cm
Feature 61A013	80,180.2	61A, interstitial space	Pri	1	X	–	–	2.5	0.3-0.4	X	–	–	1	Probably a different basket from 80,180.1; rim circumference at least 20.0 cm
Feature 62A004	80,183	62A, trash	Sec	1	X	–	–	2.5	0.3-0.4	X	–	–	1	Some 3/3 shifts; rim circumference at least 44.0 cm
–	80,232	62W, trash	Mix	1	–	X	–	3.0-4.0	0.25-0.3	X	–	–	1	rim circumference at least 9.0 cm
–	80,325	62W, trash	Pri	1	X	–	–	3.0-4.0	0.25-0.3	–	–	–	1?	Includes possible rod fragment (disarticulated); small fragments. Basket is colored red.

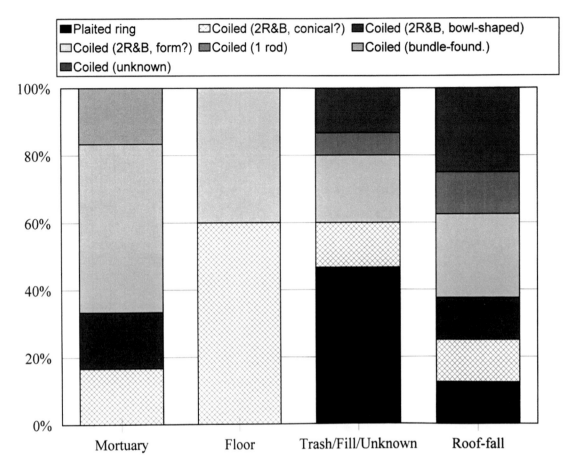

Figure 46.60. Distribution of plaited and coiled baskets by vessel form and basket structure.

of the chapter.) Thus, all Primary examples of ring baskets at Salmon came from midden deposits in the ritual core of the pueblo. Secondary ring baskets are woven in 2/2, 3/3, and diamond-twill weaves, and came from trash and roof deposits in Rooms 62A and 62W and the northwest quadrant of the pueblo.

Regional Comparisons. Plaited ring baskets have been noted at sites throughout the Colorado Plateau, including Chaco, Aztec, Mesa Verde, and Antelope House. Judd (1954:160, Pls. 40, 41a) reported four plaited baskets from Pueblo Bonito, all woven in 3/3 twill. Three of these are ring baskets; the fourth, a square basket, lacks a rod at the rim. Plaited baskets were also found at Chetro Ketl, but no weave structure information is available. The ring baskets from the West Ruin at Aztec are woven in 2/2, 3/3, and diamond-twill weaves. One ring basket from "Chacoan" Room 49 at Aztec has paired rods at the rim, like the Salmon example (Webster 2004). One of the ring baskets from Pueblo Bonito and one from Aztec have ornamental rim braids, similar to those found at Mesa Verde and Antelope House (Adovasio and

Gunn 1986: Figure 195; Morris and Burgh 1941: Figure 8c, d). As noted, this feature was not identified in the ring basket assemblage from Salmon.

Coiled Baskets

The assemblage contains the remains of 26 coiled baskets (Table 46.35 and Figure 46.64). Nineteen (73.1%) are close coiled with two-rod-and-bundle, bunched foundations and noninterlocking stitches (Figures 46.4–6, 16, 21, 22, 31, 39, 40, 65, 66). Two of these, FS 80,016 (Figure 46.65b) and 80,324.1, might have stacked foundations. However, I believe their present appearance is more likely due to their crushed and flattened condition. Two baskets (7.7%) have a one-rod foundation and spaced interlocking stitches (Figure 46.67a-c). Another (3.8%) appears to have a grass-bundle foundation and noninterlocking stitches (Figure 46.67e). The structures of four coiled baskets (15.4%) are unknown (not collected, not located, or too fragmentary to analyze).

Eight of the 26 baskets (30.8%) have circular normal centers (e.g., Figure 46.65d, e). The centers of the

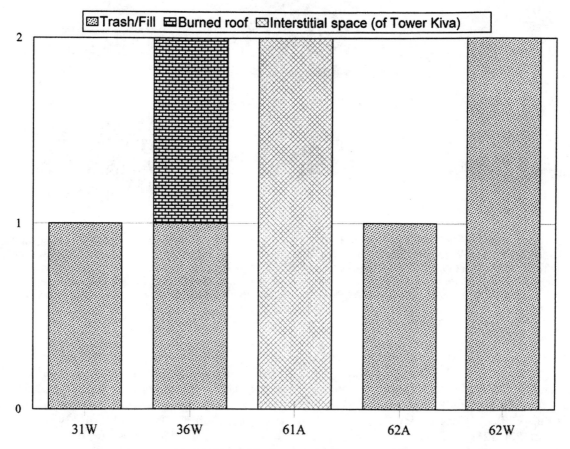

Figure 46.61. Distribution of plaited ring baskets.

other baskets are missing or unknown. There are no examples of oval centers. None of the baskets have intact rim finishes. The direction of coiling in all baskets is consistently right to left. One basket, FS 80,349 (Feature 64W011), exhibits a native repair on the base, worked in a stitch-and-wrap technique (Figure 46.66e). All baskets in the assemblage are degraded and most are carbonized; it is impossible to ascertain if any were originally decorated.

The raw materials used to make the two-rod-and-bundle and one-rod foundation baskets appear to have been sumac (*Rhus trilobata*) for the rods and stitches, and narrowleaf yucca for the bundles. The remains of leaf epidermis on some of the bundles suggest that these were originally yucca leaf strips (welts) that have since broken down into fiber. The grass used to make the bundle-foundation basket is unidentified.

The most finely woven baskets in the assemblage are the two with one-rod foundations: FS 80,408 (SA 101W003) with 5 stitches and 5 rows per cm, and FS 80,192.2 with 3 stitches and 3 rows per cm. Both have spaced stitches. Most of the two-rod-and-bundle bas-

kets from Salmon are relatively coarse in appearance. The finest example is FS 80,324.1 with 8 stitches and 2.5 rows per cm. The two coarsest examples are FS 80,005/80,010 with 4–5 stitches and 2 rows per cm, and FS 80,112-80,114 (SA 43W025, Figure 46.65c) with 4–4.5 stitches and 1.9 rows per cm.

The temporal association of the coiled basket assemblage is highly skewed. Only one coiled basket (SA 129W005, apparently not collected) is attributed to the Primary occupation. Three other baskets are from temporally mixed contexts in Room 62W, and it is possible that some of these could also date to the Primary occupation. Given that coiled baskets are known from contemporaneous contexts at Chaco and other sites (e.g., Judd 1954:162–170), the scarcity of identified Primary coiled baskets at Salmon more likely represents a problem of preservation or interpretation rather than the absence of coiled basketry during this period. All other coiled baskets in the assemblage are attributed to the Secondary occupation except for two miniature baskets (not found) identified by excavators as Secondary/Intermediate from Room 36W trash.

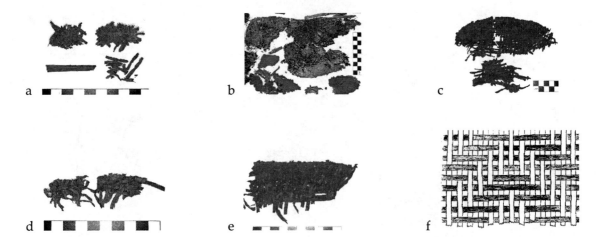

Figure 46.62. Plaited ring baskets. (a) FS 80,325 (no field number), body and possible rod fragments from red-stained 2/2-twill plaited basket, Room 62W trash. (b) FS 80,183 (Feature 62A004), remains of large 2/2-twill plaited basket, Room 62A trash. Rim selvage at top of photo. (c) FS 80,013 (Feature 31W008), rim and body fragments of 3/3-twill plaited basket, Room 31W pit fill. (d) FS 80,232 (no field number), rim fragments of 3/3-twill plaited basket, Room 62W trash. (e) FS 80,047 (SA 36W049), rim fragment of basket with diamond-twill weave, Room 36W roof-fall. For in situ view, see Figure 46.11. (f) FS 80,047, schematic diagram of diamond-twill weave.

Of the 26 coiled baskets in the sample, seven were recovered from roof-fall (where they may have been lying on the roofs or floors of the rooms above), seven came from trash deposits, six were found with or near burials (33B001, 43W005, 43W019, 43W057, 127W106, and 127W126), five were found on floors, and one is from an unknown context (Table 46.35 and Figure 46.64). In my opinion, all of the baskets found on floors are the remains of either conical baskets, flat plaques, or small steep-sided baskets. All baskets from floor contexts came from the Tower Kiva (Room 64W) or surrounding rooms (37W, 58W, 62A).

Although most of these baskets are now fragmentary, basket form can be established from field photographs for some examples and hypothesized for others. Three baskets were nearly intact when found. FS 80,479 (SA 31W011?, Figure 46.6), found in a pit dug into trash on the roof of Room 31W, was a large, steep-sided, bowl-shaped basket with a flat base approximately 25–30 cm in diameter and gently flaring sides about 10 cm deep. FS 80,128 (SA 43W055, Figures 46.21, 22, 65d), found near burial 43W057, was a shallow bowl-shaped basket with a concave base and a rim diameter of approximately 16 cm. FS 80,224 (Figures 46.31, 66b), from Room 62W trash, was a deep conical basket of unrecorded size, probably about 15 cm in diameter.

Four or perhaps six other two-rod-and-bundle-foundation baskets may be the remains of additional conical baskets like the one from Mesa Verde illustrated in Figure 46.66f. All of these examples are coarsely woven and incomplete, and contain fragments of either steep-sided walls, flat bases 15–16 cm in diameter, or both. These include FS 80,005/80,010 (Figures 46.4, 5) from Room 30W roof-fall, fused to burnt corn; FS 80,112-80,114 (SA 43W025, Figures 46.16, lower, 65c) found near burial 43W019; FS 80,161 (SA 58W019, Figure 46.65e) from the floor of Room 58W; FS 80,184 and 80,185 (SA 62A042, Figures 46.28, 66a) from the floor of Room 62A, associated with burnt corn and feather down; FS 80,230 (Figure 46.66c) from Room 62W trash; and FS 80,349 (Feature 64W011, Figures 46.40, 66d, e) from the floor of Room 64W. This latter basket exhibits the stitch-and-wrap repairs. Examples consisting only of flat bases (see Table 46.35) could be the remains of flat plaques rather than the bases of steep-sided containers. However, their size is roughly equivalent to the bases of other known conical baskets (e.g., Figure 46.66f; Morris and Burgh 1941: Figure 29a, c).

If FS 80,224 and the other coarsely woven basket fragments with steep-sided walls or bases roughly 16 cm in diameter are the remains of conical baskets, then the use of this basket form appears to have been confined to the ritual core of Salmon and the northwest quadrant (Table 46.36). Given this distribution, and the fact that at least two of these baskets were associated with corn and one with feathers, it is likely that these baskets played a ritual role at Salmon and served to hold corn, other foodstuffs, or other ritual paraphernalia during ceremonial events. Based on examples illustrated by Morris and Burgh (1941: Figure 29a, c; see Figure 46.66f) from Mesa Verde,

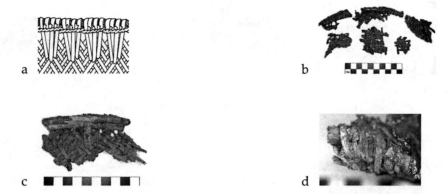

Figure 46.63. Rim selvages on plaited ring baskets. (a) Schematic diagram of 180° self selvage secured with row of S-twist twining. The Salmon baskets are twined with yucca strips instead of cordage; adapted from Adovasio 1977: Figure 137. (b) FS 80,180.2 (Feature 61A013), rim and body fragments from 2/2-twill plaited basket with single rod at rim, Room 61A, interstitial fill of Tower Kiva. For in situ view, see Figure 46.24. (c) FS 80,179 (Features 61A012 and 61A013), rim fragment from 2/2-twill plaited basket with paired rods at rim, Room 61A, interstitial fill of Tower Kiva. For in situ view, see Figure 46.24. (d) FS 80,180.1 (Features 61A012 and 61A013), close-up of rim fragment showing paired rods and coiled yucca elements, Room 61A, interstitial fill of Tower Kiva. For in situ view, see Figure 46.24.

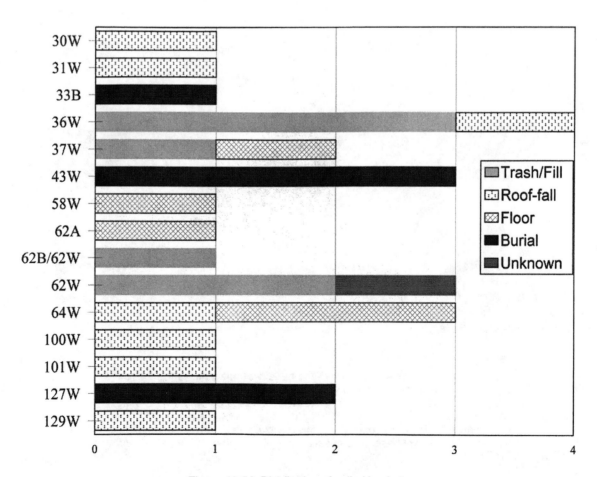

Figure 46.64. Distribution of coiled baskets.

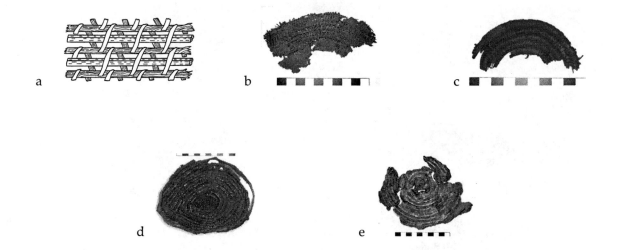

Figure 46.65. Coiled baskets with two-rod-and-bundle foundations. (a) Schematic diagram of two-rod-and-bundle, bunched, foundation with simple, non-interlocking stitches; adapted from Kidder and Guernsey 1919: Figure 80. (b) FS 80,016 (no field number), flattened fragment with stacked or bunched foundation, Burial 33B001. (c) FS 80,114 (SA 43W015), fragment of coarse base, probably from conical basket or flat plaque, found near Burial 43W019. For in situ view, see Figure 46.16. (d) FS 80,128 (SA 43W055), nearly complete bowl-shaped basket with normal center, found near Burial 43W057. For in situ view, see Figures 21 and 22. (e) FS 80,161 (SA 58W019), basket base with normal center, possibly from conical basket, Room 58W floor.

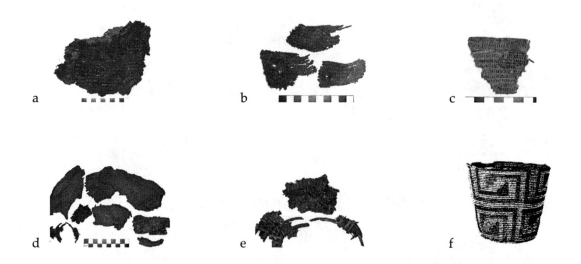

Figure 46.66. Possible conical coiled baskets with two-rod-and-bundle foundations. (a) FS 80,184 (SA62A042), fragment of basket wall fused to corn, Room 62A, floor. For in situ view, see Figure 46.28. (b) FS 80,224 (Botanical Sample 62W5053), basket base and wall fragments, Room 62W trash. For in situ view, see Figure 46.31. (c) FS 80,230 (no field number), fragment of basket wall, Room 62W trash. (d) FS 80,349 (Feature 64W011), base and wall fragments probably from conical or bowl-shaped basket, Room 64W (Tower Kiva) floor. For in situ view, see Figure 46.40. (e) FS 80,349 (Feature 64W011), detail of stitch-and-wrap repairs on basket base. (f) Conical basket with colored design from Mesa Verde, adapted from Morris and Burgh 1941: Figure 29a.

Table 46.35. Coiled baskets.

Feature or Artifact (SA) No.	New FS No.	Room and Context	Occ	Number Baskets Repres.	2 rod and bundle	1 rod	bundle	Unknown	No. Rows/cm	No. Stitches per cm	Normal Center	Center Missing	Rim Missing	Comments
–	80,005, 80,010	30W, occ fill	Sec	1	X	–	–	–	2.0	4.0-5.0	X	–	X	Base only, at least 19.0 cm diameter; roof-fall assoc with burnt corn. 80,010 is impression on sandstone slab. Poss. base of conical basket?
SA 31W011?	80,479	31W, pit on roof	Sec?	1	X	–	–	–	2.0	6.0	–	X	X	Large steep-sided basket bowl? Field dimensions 30 x 37 cm wide, 10 cm high
–	80,016	33B, burial 33B001, multiple burial	Sec	1	X	–	–	–	2.0	3.0-5.0	–	X	X	Large fragment. Foundation probably bunched but could be stacked (is flattened)
SA 36W058	80,049	36W, roof-fall	Sec	1	X	–	–	–	–	4.0-5.0?	–	X	X	Disarticulated fragments; probably 2 rod and bundle but could be 1 rod and bundle
Bot samp 36W2039	80,050	36W, trash	Sec	1	X	–	–	–	2.0	7.0-8.0	–	X	X	Small fragments
–	80,066	36W, trash	Sec/Int	1	–	–	–	X	–	–	–	–	–	Miniature; not found. 1977 analysis describes as "woody tissue spiraled to form oval measuring 1.0 x 1.8 cm"
–	80,067	36W, trash	Sec/Int	1	–	–	–	X	–	–	–	–	–	Miniature; not found. 1977 analysis describes as small basket of flexible material, 0.7 cm high
SA 37W081	80,069	37W, floor	Sec	1	X?	–	–	–	–	6.0-7.0	X	–	X	Base only; very degraded
–	80,073.3	37W, trash	Sec	1	X	–	–	–	2.5	6.0	–	X	X	Small fragments
SA 43W012	80,107	43W, burial 43W005	Sec	1	–	–	X?	–	–	8.0	X	–	X	Either a grass bundle foundation or a rod and bundle foundation with a disarticulated rod. Only one row of coiling present. Field dimensions 8.0 cm diameter x 0.5 cm high. Now 1.4 cm diameter, consisting of the basket start only. Normal center has large opening, 0.5-0.6 cm diameter. Basket paho?
SA 43W025	80,112, 80,113, 80,114	43W, near burial 43W019	Sec	1	X	–	–	–	1.9	4.0-4.5	X?	–	X	Base and wall fragments; relatively coarse weave; field dimensions 15.0 cm diameter. Possibly from conical basket?
SA 43W055	80,128	43W, near burial 43W057	Sec	1	X	–	–	–	2.0	7.0	X	–	X	Nearly intact bowl-shaped basket, 14.0 cm diameter x 5.0 cm high. Bone awl imbedded in weave when found

Table 46.35 (continued)

Feature or Artifact (SA) No.	New FS No.	Room and Context	Occ	Number Baskets Repres.	2 rod and bundle	1 rod	bundle	Un-known	No. Rows/cm	No. Stitches per cm	Normal Center	Center Missing	Rim Missing	Comments
SA 58W019	80,161	58W, floor	Sec	1	X	-	-	-	2.0	-	X	-	X	Base only, suggests steep-sided conical basket. Base 16.0 cm diameter
SA 62A042 Bot samp 62A1034?	80,184, 80,185	62A, floor	Sec	1	X	-	-	-	2.0	6.0	-	X	X	Conical basket? Large fragment 17.0 cm long x 20.5 cm high. Thick coils. Fused to corn; assoc with feather down?
—	80,192.2	62B/62W trash	Mix	1	-	X	-	-	3.0	3.0	-	X	X	One fragment only. Spaced stitches encircle rather than pierce the foundation
Bot samp 62W5053	80,224	62W, trash	Mix	1	X	-	-	-	2.0	8.0	-	X	X	Conical basket
—	80,230	62W, trash	Mix	1	X	-	-	-	2.0	5.0	-	X	X	Basket wall suggests a steep-sided conical basket
—	80,324.1	62W, unknown	Unkn	1	X	-	-	-	2.5	8.0	-	X	X	Basket wall fragments. Foundation probably bunched but could be stacked (is flattened)
SA 64W096	80,346	64W, floor	Sec	1	X	-	-	-	2.0	6.0	X	-	X	Small base or flat plaque, 6.5 cm diameter
Feature 64W011	80,349	64W, floor	Sec	1	X	-	-	-	2.0	5.6	X	-	X	Steep-sized conical basket or poss. bowl-shaped. Mouth opening diam estimated at 17.0 cm. At least 7.0 cm high. Stitch+wrap repairs on base
—	80,352, 80,354	64W, roof-fall	Sec	1	X	-	-	-	1.5-2.0	5.0-6.0	-	X	X	Small fragments. Both field samples probably from same basket
—	80,397	100W, roof-fall	Sec	1	-	-	-	X	-	-	-	X	X	Disarticulated rods, stitches, one possible bundle
SA 101W003	80,408	101W, trash in roof-fall	Sec	1	-	X	-	-	5.0	5.0	-	X	X	Small fragment; fine coiling
SA 127W121	80,435	127W, burial 127W106	Sec	1	X?	-	-	-	-	-	-	-	X	Small deteriorated fragments
SA 127W137	N/A	127W, burial 127W126	Sec	1	X?	-	-	-	-	-	-	-	X	Not found. Looks like a 2-rod-and-bundle foundation in field photo
SA 129W005	N/A	129W, roof-fall	Pri?	1	-	-	-	X	-	-	-	-	X	Not collected? Described on SA form as coiled basket

Table 46.36. Distribution of possible conical baskets.

New FS Cat. No.	Room	Context	Intrasite Location
80,005 and 80,010	30W	Roof-fall; associated with burnt corn	Northwest quadrant
80,112 through 80,114	43W	Found near Burial 43W019 and wood-slat curtain	Northwest quadrant
80,161 Kiva	58W	Floor	Room adjoining Tower
80,184 and 80,185 Kiva	62A	Floor; associated with burnt corn and feather down	Room adjoining Tower
80,224 Kiva	62W	Trash deposit	Room adjoining Tower
80,230 Kiva	62W	Trash deposit	Room adjoining Tower
80,349	64W	Floor; fallen from kiva bench	Tower Kiva

and others displayed at the Edge of the Cedars Museum in Blanding, Utah, it is very likely that these baskets were decorated.

The most intriguing coiled basket in the assemblage is the small basket that appears to have been made with a bundle foundation, FS 80,017 (SA 43W 012, Figure 46.67e), found with burial 43W005. Reportedly 8 cm in diameter and 0.5 cm high when found in the field, the basket is now only 1.4 cm in diameter and consists only of the initial center coil. The SA form describes it as "essentially unrecoverable" and states that only the bottom was found.

In its present condition, this basket appears to have a bundle foundation. However, the inclusion of one small disarticulated rod of sumac with the sample raises the possibility that it might have had a rod-and-bundle foundation. Given the fact that excavators described the basket as having a "grass reed construction" and that the raw material of the bundle looks more like grass than yucca leaf (which is the usual bundle material in rod-and-bundle baskets), bundle-foundation coiling is likely.

Aside from its unusual foundation construction (bundle-foundation coiling was relatively rare on the Colorado Plateau until Pueblo IV), what makes this basket even more interesting is the large, 0.5–0.6 cm opening at the center (Figure 46.67e). This could have been a small basket "paho," similar to undated examples reported by Walter Hough (1914:123, Plate 24, Figure 317) from Bear Creek Cave on the Blue River near the Upper Gila (Figure 46.67f; see regional comparisons). Unfortunately, the Salmon example is incomplete and no field photos have been found, so its original form may never be known.

Two other miniature baskets are reported from Room 36W at Salmon, but neither was found during my analysis. The student analysts who examined these baskets in 1977 described FS 80,066 as a minia-

ture oval basket 1 x 1.8 cm in size, made of woody tissue spiraled to form an oval, and FS 80,067 as a miniature basket 0.7 cm high of an unidentified, flexible material. No photographs of these objects have been located. These sketchy descriptions also suggest small baskets with grass-bundle foundations. If so, then this basket type is known to occur at Salmon only in the northwest quadrant.

Regional Comparisons. Baskets with one-rod foundations and interlocking stitches have been reported in small quantities from Salmon, Aztec (Webster 2004), Pueblo Bonito (Judd 1954:163, Plate 42b), Pueblo del Arroyo (Judd 1959:128), and numerous other sites in the Southwest (Morris and Burgh 1941). However, the vast majority of close-coiled baskets at Chaco, Aztec, and other Puebloan sites on the Colorado Plateau are made with two-rod-and-bundle, bunched foundations. This was the most common foundation structure in the region from Basketmaker II to Pueblo III (Morris and Burgh 1941). Many of the cylindrical, elliptical, and bifurcated baskets from Pueblo Bonito were made using this technique (Judd 1954:165–170, 307–320, Plates 44, 45, 85, 87). Baskets with three-rod bunched foundation are known from Pueblo Bonito (Judd 1954:166–170; Pepper 1920:107) and Aztec Ruins (Webster 2004), but were not identified in the Salmon assemblage. The three-rod technique is also associated with some specialized basket forms, including a cylindrical basket from Pueblo Bonito (Judd 1954:168) and a large basketry shield from Aztec (Morris 1924:187, Figure 18).

Steep-sided conical (also called truncated) coiled baskets are known from Salmon, the West Ruin at Aztec (Morris 1919:56), Mesa Verde (Morris and Burgh 1941: Figure 29a, b), Antelope House (Adovasio and Gunn 1986: Figure 134), and a cave cache from southeastern Utah housed at The Edge of the

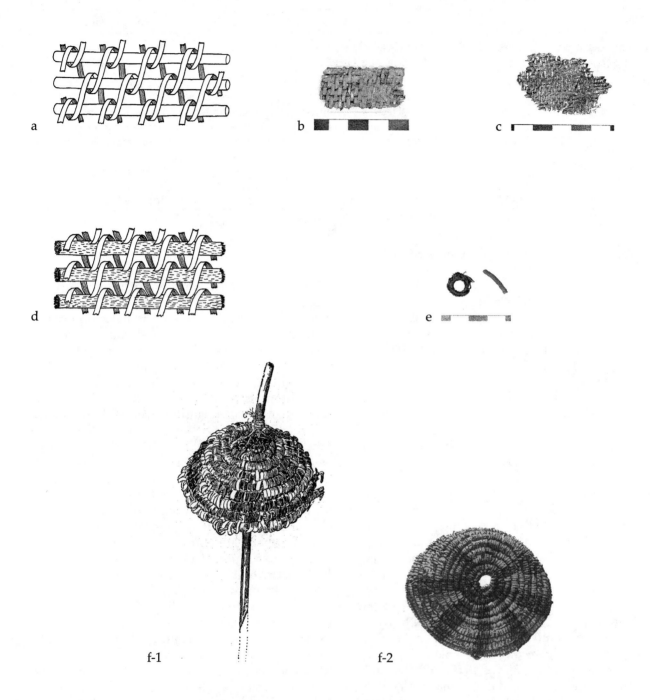

Figure 46.67. Coiled baskets with one-rod and grass-bundle foundations. (a) Schematic diagram of one-rod foundation with interlocking stitches; adapted from Morris and Burgh 1941: Figure 3a. (b) FS 80,192.2 (no field number), fragment of basket wall with one-rod foundation, Room 62B/62W trash. (c) FS 80,408 (SA 101W003), fragment of basket wall with one-rod foundation; Room 101 roof-fall. (d) Schematic diagram of bundle foundation with non-interlocking stitches; adapted from Morris and Burgh 1941: Figure 3e. (e) FS 80,107 (SA 43W012), initial coil of a possible bundle-foundation basket with 0.5 cm opening at center, Burial 43W005. (f) Basket pahos from Bear Creek Cave, southeastern Arizona; from Hough 1914: Figure Pl. 24 and Figure 317.

Cedars Museum. Baskets of this form appear to date to the AD 1200s. These baskets have not been reported from Chaco Canyon. In contrast to the Chaco cylindrical baskets, which have vertical walls like the cylinder jars, the walls of steep-sided conical baskets are gently sloped (compare Judd 1954: Plate 45 with Morris and Burgh 1941: Figure 29a, b). Many of these baskets highly decorated and may have served a ritual function.

Miniature baskets with bundle-foundations are known from Chaco (Judd 1954:163–164), Aztec (burial 25 in Room 111, adjacent to early Chacoan Kiva L; Webster 2004), Hawikuh (NMAI 12/4700, unknown provenience, Webster 2003), and probably Antelope House (Kiva B, Adovasio and Gunn 1986:315, 317, Table 137). Another possible example comes from Poncho House (Peabody Museum's Web site, PM 23-7-10/A5669; object not examined). Examples from Salmon, Pueblo Bonito, Hawikuh, and Poncho House appear to have a small intentionally made hole at the center; they might have been mounted on sticks like the basket "pahos" reported by Hough (1914:122–123, Figure 317, Plate 24) from Bear Creek Cave in the Upper Gila (Figure 46.67e). At this point there appears to be a strong correlation between miniature baskets with bundle foundations (and perhaps miniature baskets in general) and mortuary, kiva, and ritual contexts.

Plaited Pouches

The plaited pouch is another object that seems to have played a ritual role at Salmon. The assemblage contains three examples—one from the bench of the Tower Kiva (Room 64W) and two from burials 43W 003 and 43W005, two richly furnished burials in Room 43W (Figures 46.42, 46.68). All pouches are attributed to the Secondary occupation (Table 46.37).

The pouches are finely woven in 2/2 twill with what appear to be narrow rush (*Scirpus* sp.) elements averaging 0.3–0.4 cm in width. Element density ranges from 2.5–3 elements per cm. Two pouches have the remains of mouth openings at one end, produced by folding the plaiting elements over a 2s-Z or 2(2z-S)Z yucca cord to make a 180° self-selvage (Figure 46.68b, e). Neither example has intact twining cords, but faint vestiges of cordage on the mouth of SA 43W041 (FS 80,159.3) suggest that the mouth opening was twined (Figure 46.68b). The tapered mouth opening of Feature 64W013 (FS 80,336) was produced by overlapping pairs of adjacent elements and plaiting them as one (Figure 46.68f).

When complete, all of these pouches were elliptically shaped and relatively large in size. The largest example was SA 43W041 (FS 80,084 and 80,085, Figure 46.68a), described on the significant artifact form as originally 47 cm long x 17 cm wide and now 30 cm long x 21 cm wide. The original field dimensions of SA 43W006 (FS 80,092 and 80,093, Figure 46.68c) are not provided, but the two largest fragments measure approximately 9 x 12 and 8 x 11 cm. The most complete example, Feature 64W013 (FS 80,338, Figures 46.42, 46.68d), originally measured 22 x 15 x 9 cm in the field and is now 20.5 x 14.5 x 4 cm. For comparison, Morris (1919:54, Figure 32) described a

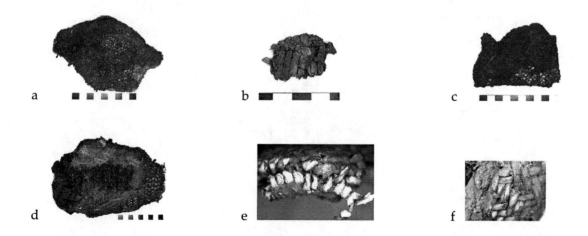

Figure 46.68. Plaited pouches. (a) FS 80,084 (SA 43W041), large fragment of pouch, Burial 43W003. (b) FS 80,159.3 (SA 43W041), detail of mouth opening showing vestiges of twining cords, Burial 43W003. (c) FS 80,093 (SA 43W006), large fragment of pouch, Burial 43W005. (d) FS 80,336 (Feature 64W013), nearly complete pouch with tapered mouth opening, Room 64W (Tower Kiva) bench. Note plant materials inside. For in situ view, see Figure 46.42. (e) FS 80,336 (Feature 64W013), detail showing overlapping elements at tapered mouth opening. (f) FS 80,336 (64W013), plaited pouch.

Table 46.37. Plaited pouches.

Feature or Artifact (SA) No.	New FS Cat. No.	Room and Context	Occ	Number pouches repres.	2/2 twill plaiting	No. elements per cm	Avg. element width (cm)	180° self-selvage folded over cord	Selvage (mouth opening) missing	Comments
SA 43W041	80,084, 80,159.3	43W, burial 43W003	Sec	1	X	3.0	0.3-0.4	X	–	Filled with plant materials
SA 43W006	80,092, 80,093	43W, burial 43W005	Sec	1	X	3.0	0.3-0.4	–	X	Filled with plant materials
Fea. 064W013	80,336	64W, bench 64W004	Sec	1	X	2.5	0.4	X	–	Tapered mouth opening; filled with plant materials

complete example from Aztec about 32 x 12.5 cm, and larger unpublished examples are present in the collection (Webster 2004).

All three of the Salmon pouches contained plant materials when found. Excavators described the fill of SA 43W041 as unburned yucca scraps, and the fill of SA 43W006 as corn tassels, carbonized juniper twigs, the calyx of a grassy plant, and unidentified seeds. Feature 64W013 also appears to contain corn tassels and a variety of reeds, sticks, and grasses. (As noted in the introduction to this chapter, I do not have Vorsila Bohrer's ethnobotanical identifications for these materials.) The well-preserved example published by Morris (1919:54) from Aztec, and other examples I have seen in the Aztec collections (Webster 2004), are also filled with corn tassels. In several of the unburned Aztec pouches, the long, unworked ends of the plaiting elements have been folded inside the bag, and I suspect that the unburned "yucca" reported inside SA 43W041 represents the deteriorated remains of similar plaiting elements.

As noted, the vegetal-stuffed pouches with burials 43W003 and 43W005 at Salmon were found in the vicinity of the head, leading excavators to suggest they might have served as pillows. However, the discovery of one on the bench of the Tower Kiva at Salmon suggests a ritual use for these objects.

Regional Comparisons. Plaited yucca pouches filled with plant materials have been found at Chaco, Aztec, and Salmon, and several other sites in the northern Southwest. In all cases, the principal stuffing was corn tassels. Judd (1954:161, Plate 41b) reported one example, which he interpreted as a possible pillow, from beneath the head of burial 5 in Room 326 at Pueblo Bonito. My casual inspection of Pepper's Pueblo Bonito collections located two other examples from Rooms 24 and 160 (Webster 2004). At the West Ruin of Aztec, Morris (1919:54, Figure 32; 1924:173; 1928:309, 350, 358, 387) recovered at least eight plaited pouches from Chacoan and Mesa Verdean contexts, including Mesa Verde burial 34 in Room 1352, and several from rooms situated near Kiva L, the early Chacoan kiva. The wear on one bag led Morris (1919:54) to identify that object as a pad or pillow. Additional examples of plaited pouches are known from Antelope House (Adovasio and Gunn 1986: Figure 153) and Grand Gulch (personal observation, American Museum of Natural History).

Although Morris (1919:54) and others have suggested that these objects might have been pillows, their strong association with corn tassels raises the possibility that they might have served as ritual paraphernalia for a particular ceremony or society.

This is supported by the interpretation of two similar plaited baskets from a rock shelter in the Galisteo Basin (Fenn 2004:88–95). The baskets, which produced a radiocarbon date of AD 1480 ± 25, are tapered at both ends and of a slightly different construction than the Salmon and Aztec baskets. Ethnobotanists Mollie Toll and Pamela McBride have identified the assemblage as the working pharmacopoeia of a healer. Although these baskets contained mostly wild plants and no corn tassels, they suggest a similar interpretation for the Pueblo III bags from Chaco, Salmon, and Aztec.

Pot Rests or Coils of Basketry Raw Materials

The assemblage contains 33 cylindrical objects that could have served as pot rests, coils of basketry raw materials, or both (Tables 46.38 and 46.39). These objects were recovered from roof-fall, trash deposits, and directly on floors (Figure 46.69). Three Primary examples, all coiled, came from the interstices of the Tower Kiva (Room 61A, Figures 46.26, 27, 70d). The vast trash deposit in Room 62W produced another 10 coiled examples, including one from a Primary trash midden (Figure 46.70f) and nine from mixed Primary-Secondary trash (Figure 46.70a-c, e). The Secondary floor of the Tower Kiva (Room 64W) produced four examples, three plaited and one coiled (but see comments below regarding the coiled pot rest; Figures 46.33–37). The Secondary floor of Room 62A produced another plaited pot rest. Coiled rings appear to have been characteristic of the Primary occupation. Only one possible Primary example of a twill-plaited ring was found, and its temporal attribution is questionable. Both coiled and plaited examples came from Secondary contexts.

Coiled Pot Rests or Raw Materials

The assemblage contains 23 coiled objects that could be coiled pot rests or coils of basketry raw materials (Table 46.38 and Figures 46.13, 26, 27, 32, 37, 69, 70). The coils appear to consist of sumac twigs, yucca leaves, willow twigs, juniper bark, and pine needles. Many of the coils are wrapped crosswise with yucca ties, and some are tied with square knots. The ties used to wrap FS 80,068.1 (SA 37W075) and FS 80,330.1 are colored red.

Exterior diameters of these objects range from 2.7 cm for a tiny coil of sumac or willow twigs (Figure 46.70c, right) to 22.5 cm for a large coil of what appear to be pine needles (Figure 46.70a). Most of the juniper bark coils were or still are closely bound with yucca cordage or ties (Figure 46.70d-f). In my opinion, these juniper bark coils probably served as

Table 46.38. Coiled pot rests or coils of rawmaterials.

Feature or Artifact (SA)	New FS Cat. No.	Room & Context	Occ	No. of Objects Repres.	Raw Material	Max Diam.*	Comments
SA 37W075	80,068.1	37W, post-occ fill	Pri?	1	Sumac twigs?	F 19.0	Tied with yucca square knot; tie stained red
SA 37W077	N/A	37W, trash	Sec?	1	Unk twigs	F 8.0	Not found; 50% recovered?
SA 43W017	N/A	43W, post-occ fill	Pri?	1	Unk twigs	Unk	Not collected
SA 43W018	80,145	43W, post-occ fill	Pri	1	Yucca leaves	F 17.0	No evidence of wrapping
SA 43W022	N/A	43W, burial 43W019 or roof-fall	Sec	1	Willow twigs?	F 27.0	Not found; 1% reportedly recovered as botanical sample
–	80,178	60B, roof	Sec	1	Juniper bark	L 16.0	Unburned, ties missing
Fea. 61A014	N/A	61A, interstitial sp	Pri	1	Unknown	F 15.0	Not found; no description provided on form
SA 61A025	80,181	61A, interstitial sp	Pri	1	Juniper bark	L 15.0	Wrapped with fine and coarse yucca cordage
Fea. 61A017	N/A	61A, interstitial sp	Pri	1	Sumac or yucca?	F 15.0	Not found; have in-situ photo
Bot sample 62W5055	80,225	62W, occ fill	Pri	1	Pine needles	L 22.5	Wrapped crosswise with yucca leaves
–	80,227.4	62W, trash	Mixed	1	Sumac or willow	L 8.0	Basketry splints
–	80,237.2	62W, trash	Mixed	1	Sumac or willow	L 2.7	Basketry splints
–	80,287	62W, trash	Mixed	1	Sumac or willow	L 4.5	Small bundle of twigs (coiled zigzag)
–	80,316.1	62W, trash	Mixed	1	Juniper bark	L 19.0	Now just a mass of juniper bark; remains of yucca ties
–	80,317	62W, trash	Mixed	1	Juniper bark	L 13.5	Wrapped crosswise with juniper bark (?)
–	80,318	62W, trash	Mixed	1	Juniper bark?	L 15.0	Wrapped crosswise with yucca ties
–	80,326	62W, trash	Mixed	1	Juniper bark	L 16.0	Fragment of yucca stuck to surface; remnants of tie?
–	80,330.1	62W, trash	Mixed	1	Juniper bark	L 18.0	Remnants of yucca tie with square knot; tie stained red
–	80,331	62W, trash	Mixed	1	Sumac?	L 17.0	Remnants of yucca ties fused to surface
–	80,332	62W, trash	Pri	1	Juniper bark	L 15.0	Remnants of yucca ties
Fea. 64W012	80,350	64W, floor	Sec	1	Yucca leaves	F 19.0	No evidence of wrapping; possibly the interior coil of a plaited pot rest?
–	N/A	81W, roof-fall	Pri	1	Juniper bark?	F 15.0	Not collected; described in notes as circle of bark
SA 100W002	80,484	100W, roof-fall	Sec?	1	Yucca leaves	F 14.0	No evidence of wrapping

Max ext. diameter (in cm); F = field, L = lab.

Table 46.39. Plaited pot rests.

Feature or Artifact (SA) No.	New FS Cat. No.	Room and Context	Occ	Number pot rests repres.	2/2 twill plaiting	Other or Unknown	No. elements per cm	Avg. element width cm	Max ext diam*	90° self-selvage	Comments
SA 36W048	80,046	36W, burned roof	Sec	1	X	–	5.0	0.2	F 11.0	X	Truncated form; nearly complete
Bot samp 36W4182	80,053	36W, roof-fall	Sec	1	X	–	4.0	0.2–0.3	L 8.0	–	Fragmentary
–	80,072	37W, trash	Sec	1	X	–	3.0	0.3	L 9.0	–	Continuous radial plaiting; 25% complete
SA 43W013	80,111, 80,144	43W, trash/ roof-fall; assoc w/ 43W003?	Sec	1	X	–	3.0–4.0	0.25–0.3	L 11.5	–	Truncated form, beveled lip, Intentional 2/3/2 and 2/1/2 shifts
SA 62A053	80,188	62A, floor	Sec	1	X?	–	2.5	0.4	F 8.0?	–	Only a few interacting elements; 1/3 complete
Feature 64W035	80,337	64W, floor	Sec	1	X	–	3.3	0.3	F 14.0	X	Described on feature form as doughnut shaped; now disarticulated
SA 64W089	80,344	64W, floor	Sec	1	X	–	3.0	0.4	L 13.0	X	Truncated form?; relatively complete
SA 64W090	80,345	64W, floor	Sec	1	X	–	3.0–3.5	0.3	L 13.0	X	Doughnut or truncated form
–	80,412	101W, trash	Pri?	1	–	X	––	0.3	L 3.0	–	Jumbled elements; looks like twill plaiting with 2 or 3 span floats
SA 119W046	80,416	119W, roof-fall	Sec	1	X	–	3.0	0.3	L 12.8	X	Probably doughnut form

*Max ext diameter (cm); F = field, L = lab.

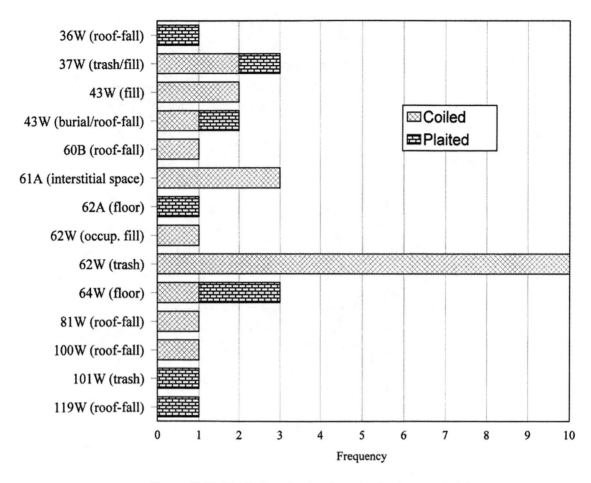

Figure 46.69. Distribution of pot rests and coils of raw materials.

pot rests, whereas most, if not all of the sumac, willow, and pine needle coils (e.g., Figures 46.13, 26, 70a-c) may have been bundles of raw materials for craft production—for instance, sumac is used for the stitches and foundations of coiled baskets. Most of these coiled twig and pine needle objects were recovered from known Primary contexts or mixed Primary/Secondary trash, and it is conceivable that many if not most of them could date to the Primary occupation. The distribution of most of these objects in rooms surrounding the Tower Kiva (Rooms 37W, 61A, 62W, 81W) suggests that this central area may have served as a locus for storing basketry raw materials and perhaps also for making baskets.

The yucca coils could represent something else entirely. Although some may have served as raw materials, the fact that none of these coils show evidence of crosswise wrapping suggests to me that some or all could be the deteriorated cores of plaited yucca pot rests, now lacking their exterior layer of plaiting. Significant Artifact 64W012 (FS 80,350, Figure 46.37), found on the floor of the Tower Kiva

with three plaited pot rests, seems a particularly good candidate for this.

Plaited Pot Rests

Ten plaited pot rests were identified in the assemblage (Table 46.39 and Figures 46.23, 33–36, 69, 71). Some of the unidentified plaited objects in Table 46.32 might also be the remains of plaited pot rests, as could some or all of the three yucca coils discussed in the preceding section. Except for one example for which the weave could not be identified, all plaited pot rests in the assemblage are woven in continuous 2/2 radial plaiting with narrow yucca elements (see Advasio and Gunn 1986:348–349). One well-preserved example, FS 80,111 and 80,144 (SA 43W013, Figure 46.71c) exhibits 2/3/2 and 2/1/2 shifts. All intact selvages are 90° self-selvages. In some cases, the long unworked ends of the elements were tucked back into the pot rest to provide additional support.

Two main forms of plaited pot rests are represented. Two examples have a simple doughnut form

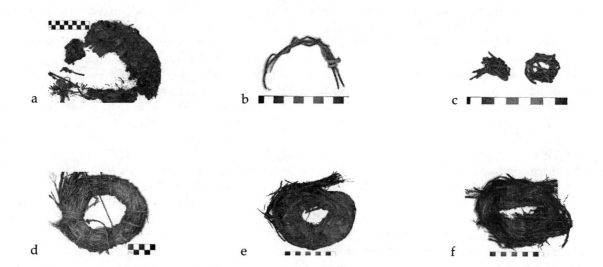

Figure 46.70. Coiled pot rests and coils of raw materials. (a) FS 80,225 (Botanical Sample 62W5055), coil of pine needles wrapped crosswise with yucca ties, Room 62W Primary occupational fill. (b) FS 80,227.4 (no field number), small bundle of sumac or willow splints, Room 62W trash. (c) FS 80,237.2 (no field number), small bundle and coil of sumac or willow splints, Room 62W trash. (d) FS 80,181 (SA 61A025), coil of juniper bark wrapped with yucca cordage, Room 61A, interstitial fill of Tower Kiva. For in situ view, see Figure 46.27. (e) FS 80,330.1 (no field number), coil of juniper bark wrapped with red-stained yucca-leaf tie, Room 62W trash. For in situ view, see Figure 46.32. (f) FS 80,332 (no field number), coil of juniper bark with remnants of yucca-leaf ties, Room 62W Primary trash.

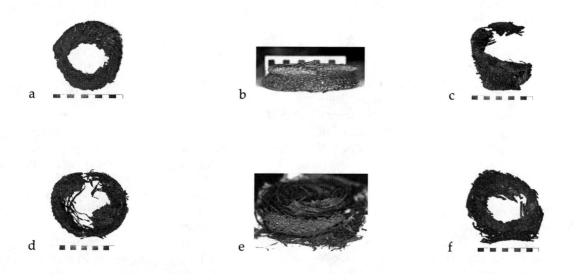

Figure 46.71. Plaited pot rests. (a) FS 80,046 (SA 36W048), plan view of truncated pot rest, Room 36W roof-fall. (b) FS 80,046 (SA 36W048), side view of truncated pot rest. (c) FS 80,144 (SA 43W013), side view of truncated pot rest, Room 43W roof-fall. For in situ view, see Figure 46.23. (d) FS 80,344 (SA 64W089), plan view of truncated pot rest, Room 64W (Tower Kiva) floor. For in situ view, see Figures 46.34 and 46.35. (e) FS 80,345 (SA 64W090), side view of truncated or doughnut-shaped pot rest, Room 64W (Tower Kiva) floor. For in situ view, see Figures 34 and 36. (f) FS 80,416 (SA 119W046), plan view of doughnut (?)-shaped pot rest, Room 119W roof-fall.

(Figure 46.71f; cf. Adovasio and Gunn 1986: Figures 156–157) and three are truncated with a beveled lip (Figure 46.71a-d; cf. Adovasio and Gunn 1986: Figures 158–159). Another had either a doughnut or truncated form (Figure 46.71e). The remaining examples are too incomplete to identify.

Element density ranges from 2.5 to 5 elements per cm, and element width from 0.2 to 0.4 cm. The most finely woven example is FS 80,046 (SA 36W048, Figure 46.71a, b), a nearly complete truncated pot rest with 5 elements per cm. Exterior diameters of the best-preserved examples range from 11 to 13 cm, and interior diameters from 6 to 8 cm. The thickness ranges from 2.5 to 4 cm.

With one exception, all of the plaited pot rests are attributed to the Secondary occupation. The exception is in jumbled condition and only tentatively identified as Primary. Based on this small sample, plaited pot rests appear to have been absent or extremely uncommon at Salmon during the Primary occupation and were the prevailing form of pot rest during the Secondary occupation.

Regional Comparisons. Plaited and coiled pot rests have been found at all sites in the region (e.g., Magers 1986; Osborne 1980; Rohn 1971). Pot rests made of plaited yucca, feather-wrapped cord, and coiled juniper bark have been reported from Pueblo Bonito (Judd 1954:173, Plate 46; Pepper 1920:96), and an example of coiled juniper bark is illustrated from Pueblo del Arroyo (Judd 1959:131, Plate 38h). Gallo Cliff Dwelling in Chaco Canyon produced several plaited yucca pot rests, including one plaited around a feather-cord core (Kent and Loehr 1974:16, Figures 28–30). Morris (1928:183, 308, 367) collected large numbers of these items from the West Ruin at Aztec, including plaited pot rests of yucca and coils of cedar bark, cornhusks, grass, and twigs. All of the twig coils from Aztec came from rooms that Morris identified as Chacoan, suggesting a similar stockpiling of basketry raw materials at Aztec during early occupation as I have proposed for Salmon.

Cotton Cloth

The Salmon assemblage contains 10 examples of cotton cloth attributed by excavators to the Primary, Intermediate (?), and Secondary occupations (Table 46.40). Five were associated with mortuary contexts (33W012, 43W005, 43W057, 62W122, and 123B005). Additional examples came from roof-fall, trash deposits, and the Secondary floor of the Tower Kiva (Room 64W, Figure 46.72). Most of the cotton cloth found at Salmon survived only as small deteriorated or carbonized fragments (e.g., Figures 46.8, 74a, b),

but two small, unburned examples were found in the well-preserved, mixed-occupation trash in Room 62W (Figure 46.73d, e), and two relatively large cotton fabrics were associated with Secondary burial 43W005 and the Primary roof-fall of Room 127W (Figures 46.50, 73a-c, 74d-f). Given the highly perishable nature of cotton fiber, it is likely that cotton cloth saw much greater use at Salmon than the evidence suggests, in burial contexts and elsewhere.

Eight examples in the assemblage are woven in 1/1 plain weave (Figures 46.73, 74a, b). Another is woven in 2/1 twill (Figures 46.50, 74c-f). The cloth from infant burial 62W122 was not located and may not have been collected. A well preserved piece from Room 62W, analyzed by Gayle Potter in 1979 and formerly on exhibit in the Salmon Museum, also was not found. All eight examples I analyzed are made with single-ply, z-spun warp and weft yarns. The diameter of the warp elements ranges from 0.03 to 0.06 cm, and the diameter of the weft elements ranges from 0.08 to 0.12 cm. Thread counts for the plain-weave fabrics range from 22 warps and 9 wefts in the finest fabric (FS 80,348) to 8 warps and 7 wefts in the coarsest example (FS 80,199.1). This latter fabric, tied in a square knot (Figure 46.73e), is frayed and the weave density has undoubtedly loosened. The mode fabric density for the plain weave fabrics is 11–12 warps and 9–10 wefts per cm. The more densely woven 2/1 twill fabric has 10 warps and 30 wefts per cm.

Intact selvages are present on two examples. SA 43W007 (see table for catalog numbers) contains both warp and weft selvages, and FS 80,019 has an intact section of warp selvage (Figure 46.73d). The weft selvage of SA 43W007 is worked in 2-strand twining (S), and both warp selvages are worked in 2-strand twining (Z). The edges of twill-weave fabric FS 80,441 (SA 127053) are rolled and hemmed (Figure 46.74d); the original selvage finish is unknown.

The largest and best-preserved plain-weave fabric from Salmon is SA 43W007 (see table for catalog numbers), which served as the innermost burial wrapping for adolescent burial 43W005 Although the original size of the blanket is unknown, one large mass of the cloth measures 35 x 13 cm (Figure 46.73a). Carbonized and consolidated, this blanket consists of at least 60 fragments in addition to the large mass. Thread counts for the fabric are 11 warps and 10 wefts per cm, with a warp diameter of 0.03 cm and a weft diameter of 0.10 cm. This combination of finely spun warps and barely spun wefts gives a slight diagonal twill appearance to this plain-weave fabric. The intact warp and weft selvages are worked

Table 46.40. Cotton fabrics.

Feature or Artifact (SA) No.	New FS Cat. No.	Room and Context	Occ	Number Fabrics Repres.	1/1 Plain Weave	2/1 Twill	Un-known	No. warps per cm	No. Wefts per cm	Warp selvage 2-strand twining Z	Warp selvage 2-strand twining S	Edges Rolled and Hemmed	Comments
–	80,023.3 80,030.3	33W, burial, 33W012	Late Pri	1	X?	–	–	–	–	–	–	–	Traces only; looks like plain weave
SA 43W007, Bot samp 43W2062	80,090.3, 80,091.2, 80,094, 80,095, 80,096, 80,097.1	43W, burial 43W005	Sec	1	X	–	–	11	10	X	X	–	Large carbonized textile; size of mass is 35 x 13 cm; small holes could be weft-wrap openwork or the work of insects. Selvage cords are 3z-S
–	80,139	43W, burial 43W057	Sec	1	X	–	–	14	9	X	–	–	Two tiny fragments
–	80,151	43W, roof-fall	Sec	1	X	–	–	12	10	–	–	–	Two tiny carbonized fragments; related to Burial 43W057?
SA 62W113	N/A	62W, infant burial 62W122	Unkn	1	–	–	X	–	–	–	–	–	Not found; no additional info
–	80,199.1	62W, trash	Mix	1	X	–	–	8	7	–	–	–	Strip of unburned cloth tied in square knot
–	80,209	62W, trash	Mix	1	X	–	–	–	16	–	–	–	Not found; unburned and finely woven; weft count from Potter's analysis
–	80,348	64W, floor	Sec	1	X	–	–	22	9	–	–	–	One tiny carbonized fragment; cotton string also reportedly found
Feature 123B004	80,424.2	123B, burial 123B005	Int/Sec	1	X	–	–	11	10	–	–	–	Degraded; preserved as small chunks; one piece has 2s-Z cotton yarn running through it
SA 127W053	80,441	127W, roof-fall	Pri/Int or Sec	1	–	X	–	10	30	–	–	X	Large carbonized textile; was 35 x 10 cm in-situ, in several layers; probably originally decorated with weft stripes; edges of two fragments hemmed

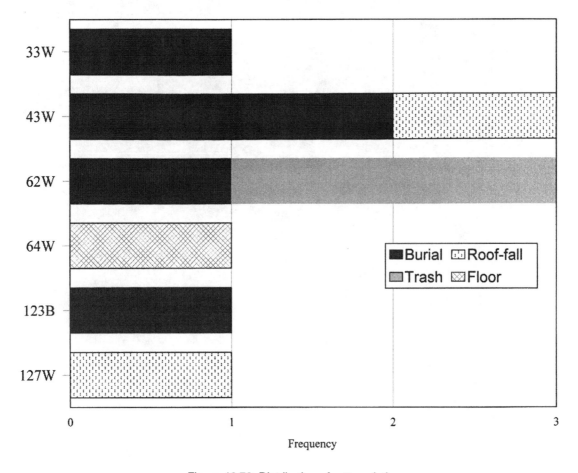

Figure 46.72. Distribution of cotton cloth.

in 2-strand twining with 3z-S yarns. The corner tassels are missing.

A few areas of the textile exhibit clusters of holes that might have been produced by weft-wrap openwork (Figure 46.73b), which is a weaving technique in which small decorative holes are produced by wrapping weft yarns around selected groups of warps (Kent 1983:143–148). Excavators noted the presence of these holes on the significant artifact form, and suggested that they were stitch holes. Unfortunately, the carbonized condition of SA 43W007 makes it difficult to discern the individual yarns, thus complicating the analysis. In some areas of this fabric, the warp and weft elements appear to deviate from their original alignments, suggesting intentional manipulation by the weaver. In other places, the holes appear to run through two or more layers of fabric, suggesting the work of insects. After examining this fabric several times under 30x magnification,

I am not convinced that this is weft-wrap openwork. However, I think there is enough of a possibility to warrant mentioning it here. Were I forced to weigh in on one side of the question, I would say that the holes were most likely caused by insects.

If these holes were, in fact, produced by weft-wrapping, then they resemble the simple weft-wrapping technique illustrated by Kent (1983: Figure 77) for fabrics from Bear Creek Cave in the Upper Gila and Snaketown in the Middle Gila. They definitely do not resemble the more intricate weft wrapping structures found in later Hohokam, Salado, and Sinagua textiles. Unlike the Bear Creek Cave and Snaketown examples, the Salmon fabric appears to have double- and triple-width holes separated by single warp elements (Figure 46.73c), a technique not illustrated by Kent. Weft-wrap openwork was not practiced to any extent on the Colorado Plateau (Kent 1983; Teague 1998), and then not until relative-

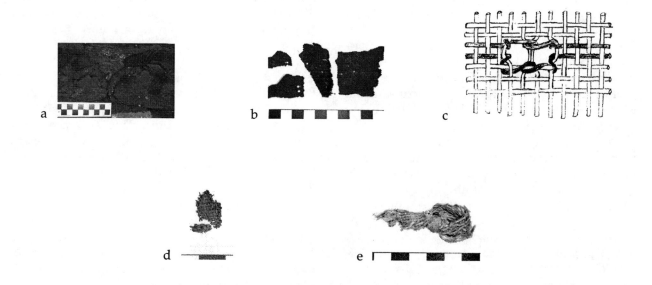

Figure 46.73. Cotton plain-weave and possible weft-wrap openwork fabrics. (a) FS 80,091 (SA 43W007), mass of carbonized plain-weave cloth, Burial 43W005. (b) FS 80,097 (SA 43W007), small holes in fabric, intentional weft-wrap openwork or insect holes, Burial 43W005. (c) FS 80,097 (SA 43W007), sketch of possible weave structure of paired holes. (d) FS 80,139 (no field number), unburned scrap of plain-weave cloth, Burial 43W057. Smaller fragment is remains of an intact warp selvage worked in Z-twist 2-strand twining. (e) FS 80,199.1 (no field number), unburned strip of plain-weave cloth tied in square knot, Room 62W trash.

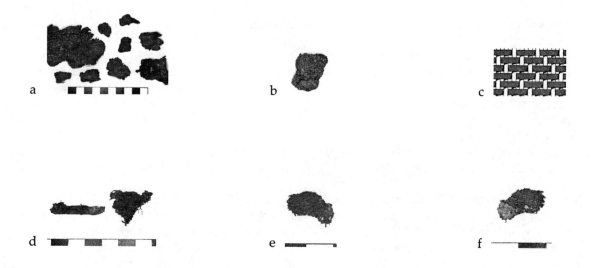

Figure 46.74. Cotton plain-weave and twill-weave fabrics. (a) FS 80,424.2 (Feature 123B004), degraded chunks of plain-weave cloth, Burial 123B005. (b) FS 80,424.2 (Feature 123B004), detail of one chunk showing plain-weave structure. (c) Schematic diagram of 2/1-twill weave structure; adapted from Kent 1983: Figure 90a. (d) FS 80,441 (SA 127W053), two fragments of 2/1-twill weave cloth with hemmed edges, Room 127W roof-fall. For in situ view of large piece of fabric, see Figure 46.50. (e) FS 80,441 (SA 127W053), one face of 2/1 weave structure, showing 2-span floats. (f) FS 80,441 (SA 127W053), reverse face of 2/1 weave structure, showing 1-span floats.

ly late (AD 1200s), so if this fabric was decorated by weft wrapping, it could have been traded in from somewhere south of the Mogollon Rim.

I might have dismissed this weft-wrap openwork identification entirely if not for the presence of another tentatively identified artifact in the same burial assemblage—the previously described small basket worked in possible bundle-foundation coiling (SA 43W012=FS 80,107). Weft-wrap openwork and bundle-foundation coiling are both southern constructions, and if my tentative identifications are correct, they would provide evidence of two southern artifact types in the same burial. I must emphasize that my identifications of both of these artifacts are tentative, given their poor and carbonized condition.

The other large cotton fabric, FS 80,441 (SA 127W053, Figure 46.50), came from the burnt roof-fall of Room 127W. Ceramics from this F-1-4 stratum include large quantities of both Primary and Secondary sherds, and the blanket could date to either occupation; excavators identified the stratum as Secondary. Unlike the other cotton fabrics in the Salmon assemblage, which are woven in plain weave, this textile is woven in 2/1 diagonal twill (Figure 46.74c, e, f). The original size of the fabric is unknown, but it covered a 35 x 10 cm area when exposed in the field, and this represented more than one layer of cloth. The warp and weft elements are 0.03 cm in diameter, and the fabric has a thread count of 10 warps and 30 wefts per cm. Two fragments have rolled and hemmed edges (Figure 46.74d). The original selvages appear to be missing.

Although this fabric is carbonized and completely black, it likely was originally patterned with some combination of red, brown, and white stripes. Undecorated diagonal-twill cloth is rare in the Southwest. Rather, this is probably the remains of what Kent (1983:160–161; Figures 93, 94) has referred to as "Anasazi striped twill," the most common type of decorated cotton cloth on the Colorado Plateau during Pueblo III.

Regional Comparisons. Cotton fabrics are found throughout the northern Southwest in Pueblo II and Pueblo III settings (Kent 1957, 1983; Teague 1998). Cotton plain-weave cloth has been recovered from various sites in Chaco Canyon, including Chetro Ketl (Kent 1957:662; Reiter 1933:23), Pueblo Bonito (Judd 1954:69; Pepper 1920:107), Pueblo del Arroyo (Judd 1959:11, 108, 123), Gallo Cliff Dwelling (Kent and Loehr 1974: Chart 1), BC 51 (Tsochopik in Kluckhohn and Reiter 1939:36, 96, 97), and the Cacique's Sanctum (Mathien 2004: Table 1). Some of this cloth has been colored by painting, dyeing, or staining (Kent and Loehr 1974:21–23, Chart 1; Pepper 1920:68–69;

Reiter 1933:23). Morris (1928:306, 317, 319, 329, 350, 358, 360, 367, 378–381, etc.) also recovered numerous fragments of cotton cloth from the West Ruin at Aztec.

Examples of striped twill weaves are known from Aztec Ruins (Webster 2004) and Chaco Canyon (Kent 1957:662; Pepper 1902:107, Figure 39) and are especially common in the Kayenta region (Kent 1983; Magers 1986). Chaco and Aztec also produced diamond-twill, herringbone-twill, or twill-tapestry weaves (Pepper 1920:107, Figure 39; Webster 2004). These latter structures were not identified in the Salmon assemblage.

I am presently aware of only one weft-wrap openwork fabric from the San Juan Basin—an unpublished fragment from Chetro Ketl housed at the Maxwell Museum. That fabric could easily be a trade item from the Hohokam region. In his discussion of cotton fabrics from Pueblo Bonito, Judd (1954:69) reported "one tiny bit of openwork stuff," which may turn out to be another example. Otherwise, weft-wrap openwork was confined to the Hohokam, Sinagua, and Upper Gila regions until sometime in the AD 1200s, when it appeared, and was probably made to a limited extent, in the Kayenta region.

Twined Fur and Feather Blankets or Robes

The assemblage contains the remains of 15 twined rabbit-fur and turkey-feather robes (Table 46.41). Four are tentatively attributed to the Primary occupation and one to the Intermediate/Secondary (i.e., early Secondary) period, and the remaining 10 are probably Secondary. All except two, from trash and roof-fall deposits, occurred as mortuary wrappings (Figure 46.75). Although all of these robes are now completely disarticulated into small bits, many were still intact when uncovered in the field, albeit missing their fur or feathers (e.g., SA 43W026 and 43W040 from burial 43W019, SA 43W069 from burial 43W057, and Feature 123B004 from burial 123B005, Figures 46.15, 17, 45).

Examples of both fur and feather blankets were found at Salmon. A fur blanket, dated to the Intermediate/Secondary (i.e., early Secondary) occupation, was associated with burial 123B005 (Figures 46.45, 77d). The cordage from the robe found with Primary (?) burial 127W147 also bears the suggestion of fur wrapping. The probable remains of feather blankets were associated with at least six Secondary burials (43W003, 43W005, 43W019, 127W055, 127W 099, 127W115). The one from burial 43W005 still bears the remains of matted feathers (Figure 46.76a). The remaining seven examples are highly deteriorated and could be the remains of either fur or feath-

Table 46.41. Twined fur and feather robes.

Feature or Artifact (SA) No.	New FS Cat. No.	Room and Context	Occ	Number Objects Repres.	2-strand twining	No interfac. elements	Warp selvage	Weft selvage	Selvages missing	Fur	Feather	Fur or Feather	Comments
SA 33W023; Bot samples 33W2020, 33W2021	80,023.2, 80,028, 80,029, 80,030.2, 80,031 80,033.2, 80,034	33W, burial 33W012	Late Pri?	1	–	X	–	–	X	–	–	X	Mostly loose elements; some perpendicular strands fused to mat FS 80,023.1.
SA 43W039	80,086	43W, burial 43W003	Sec	1	–	X	X	–	–	–	X ?	–	Loose cordage; includes section of 3(2z-S)Z header cord; matted feathers fused to mat FS 80,085
SA 43W008 SA 43W010 (robe) SA 43W015 (header cord)	80,089.2, 80,090.1, 80,091.3, 80,091.4, 80,097.2, 80,098, 80,099, 80,100, 80,101, 80,102, 80,103, 80,104.1, 80,105, 80,106, 80,108	43W, burial 43W005	Sec	1	X	–	X	X	–	–	X	–	Includes section of 3 (2z-S)Z header cord (excavators identified it as an "ornament")
SA 43W026, SA 43W040	80,115, 80,117.1, 80,118, 80,123, 80,124, 80,125	43W, burial 43W019	Sec	1	X	–	X	X	–	–	X	–	Includes section of 3(2z-S)Z header cord. Warp reenters weave every third weft turn
SA 43W069	80,136, 80,137.1, 80,138, 80,140.1, 80,143	43W, burial 43W057	Sec	1	X	–	–	X	–	–	–	X	Yarns twist up sides then separate for twining

Table 46.41 (continued)

Feature or Artifact (SA) No.	New FS Cat. No.	Room and Context	Occ	Number Objects Repres.	2-strand twining	No interfac. elements	Warp selvage	Weft selvage	Selvages missing	Fur	Feather	Fur or Feather / Feather	Comments
—	80,368.1, 80,369.1,	84W, trash	Pri?	1	X	–	X	–	–	–	–	X	Warp selvage worked in plain weave
—	80,387.2	97W, burial 97W1006	Sec?	1	–	X	–	–	X	–	–	X	Loose cordage from robe
—	80,388.2, 80,389.2	97W, burial 97W1007	Sec?	1	X?	–	–	–	X	–	–	X	Parallel and perpendicular strands fused to mat
Feature 123B004	80,423, 80,424.1	123B, burial 123B005	Int/Sec	1	X	–	–	–	X	X	–	–	Well preserved hide wrapping
SA 127W091	80,432	127W, burial 127W055	Sec	1	X	–	–	–	X	–	X?	–	Very deteriorated; warp elements heavily coated with burned debris (feathers?)
SA 127W100	80,433.2	127W, burial 127W099	Sec	1	–	X	–	–	X	–	X?	–	Loose cordage from robe
—	N/A	127W, burial 127W106	Sec	1	–	X	–	–	X	–	–	X	Not collected; traces visible in field photo
Bot samp 127W3032	80,436, 80,437.1, 80,438	127W, burial 127W115	Sec	1	–	X	–	–	X	–	X	–	Loose cordage from robe
SA 127W154, Bot samp 127W4036	80,439	127W, burial 127W147	Pri?	1	–	X	–	–	X	?	–	–	Loose cordage from robe; faint suggestion of fur wrapping
—	80,460.1	129W, roof-fall	Pri?	1	X?	–	–	–	X	–	–	X	Loose cordage from robe

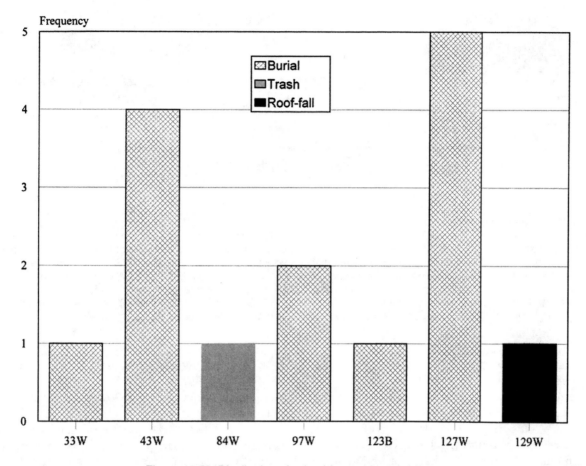

Figure 46.75. Distribution of twined fur and feather blankets.

er robes. Generally speaking, feather blankets appear to have been more common than fur ones at Salmon, with fur ones more typical of the earlier occupation and feather blankets of the Secondary occupation. This corresponds with the faunal data from Salmon, which shows increased quantities of turkey bones through time (see Durand and Durand, Chapter 50).

The warp and weft elements of these twined blankets are spun from yucca fiber. Some appear to be 2s-Z cords, others 2(2z-S)Z. As noted in the earlier discussion of cordage, these two structures are essentially the same, except that in the former case the constituent plies are single, and in the latter, they are plied. Given the difficulty of discerning the individual plies in these carbonized yarns, it is possible that all of these elements originally shared the same construction. The warp elements of these blankets were wrapped with fur or feather strips, whereas the weft elements were not. The remains of hide or quill wrapping are still present on several carbonized examples (Figures 46.76b, 77d). The warp diameter ranges from 0.2 cm for cords lacking the fur or feath-

er wrapping to 0.4 cm for cords with evidence of wrapping. The weft diameter ranges from 0.2 to 0.6 cm. Thick yucca cords found with several of the specimens are believed to be the remains of header cords.

Eight examples still contain interacting foundation elements, all worked in open simple two-strand weft twining (Figure 46.77a). Weft spacing ranges from 2 to 5 cm, with a mode of 2–3 cm, and warp spacing ranges from 0.6–1.2 cm, with a mode of 1 cm. In examples containing contiguous rows of twining (those from burials 43W005, 43W019, 43W057, 123B 005, and 127W055), the direction of twining alternates every row—one row twined S-wise, the next twined Z (Figure 46.77a).

Fragments of intact weft (side) selvages occur with three examples. Those from burials 43W005 (FS 80,100) and 43W019 (FS 80,118) are simple 180° self-selvages (cf. Adovasio 1977:37, Figure 43); the latter is represented by the folded selvage of the header cord (Figure 46.76f). In FS 80,138 from burial 43W 057, the weft elements twist around each other sev-

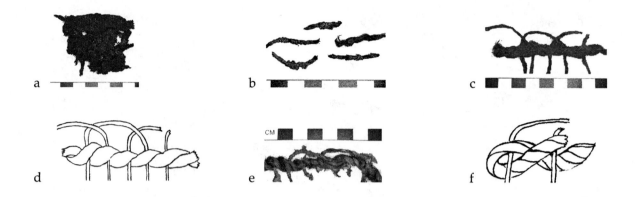

Figure 46.76. Twined fur and feather blankets. (a) FS 80,104 (SA 43W008 and 43W010), fragment of carbonized twined robe with matted feathers, Burial 43W005. (b) FS 80,099 (SA 43W008 and 43W010), carbonized warp elements with remnants of quill wrapping, Burial 43W005. (c) FS 80,100 (SA 43W008 and 43W010), section of warp selvage showing header cords worked in S-twist 2-strand twining. Warp reenters weave every third weft turn. Burial 43W005. (d) FS 80,100 (SA 43W008 and 43W010), schematic diagram of warp selvage. (e) FS 80,124 (SA 43W026 and 43W040), section of warp selvage showing header cords worked in Z-twist 2-strand twining. Warp reenters weave every third weft turn. Burial 43W019. For field sketch of twining framework, see Figure 46.15. (f) FS 80,118 (SA 43W026 and 43W040), schematic diagram of warp selvage showing S-twist twined header cords making 180° turn at weft (side) selvage, Burial 43W019.

eral times before separating for the next row of twining (cf. Adovasio 1977: Figure 44d).

Fragments of the warp (end) selvage occur with five examples. Four of these, from burials 33W012, 43W003, 43W005, 43W019, consist of warp loops twined together with thick header cords or containing fragments of header cords. Each cord has a 3(2z-S)Z structure, and their diameter ranges from 0.4 to 0.6 cm. The best-preserved warp selvages, those from burials 43W005 and 43W019, are worked in two-strand twining (Figure 46.76c-f). In each case the warp re-enters the fabric between every third twist of the header cord (Figures 46.76c-e; cf. Figure 46.77e1 and f). The cords from burial 43W005 are twined S-wise (Figure 46.76c, d), whereas some of the header cords from burial 43W019 are twined S (Figure 46.76f) and others are twined Z (Figure 46.76e). The latter may represent cords from different ends of the blanket.

The header cords and warp turns from burials 33W012 and 43W003 are no longer intact. However, an in situ field photograph of late Primary burial 33W012 shows what appears to be a section of the header cord twined S-wise, suggesting that this blanket had the same type of header cord arrangement as the Secondary examples.

A completely different warp selvage is found on a robe from a Primary (?) trash deposit in Room 84W (FS 80,368.1 and 80,369.1, Figure 46.77b, c). Instead of a twined header cord, this selvage has two strands of weft that interlace with the warps in an over-one, under-one weave. These fragments are believed to represent the lower warp selvage of a twined blanket. Samuel Guernsey (1931: Plate 54c) has illustrated an identical structure for the lower warp selvage of a Pueblo I feather blanket from Tsegi Canyon.

Regional Comparisons. The Salmon twined blankets are most similar to twined blankets from Mesa Verde and northeastern Arizona. Although twined blankets have been found at Chaco and Aztec (Judd 1954:72–73; Morris 1919:47–48), their construction details are still unpublished. Nordenskiöld (1893: Figure 67) has illustrated a twined feather blanket from Step House at Mesa Verde that exhibits almost the same construction features as the Salmon blankets, except that all wefts in that blanket are twined S-wise (Figure 46.77f). In contrast, several other feather blankets from Adobe Cave, Mug House, and Long House at Mesa Verde alternate the direction of twining each row (Osborne 1980: Figure 413; Rohn 1971: Figures 133, 134). A twined blanket from Antelope House in Canyon del Muerto also alternates the direction of twining (Magers 1986: Figure 75, lower left), as does an unpublished example at The Edge of the Cedars Museum.

Twined feather blankets from Tsegi Canyon (Guernsey 1931: Plate 54c), Antelope House (Magers 1986: Figure 75, lower left), northeastern Arizona (Kent 1983: Figure 56d), Long House at Mesa Verde (Osborne 1980: Figure 413), and southeastern Utah (The Edge of the Cedars Museum) all exhibit the same general foundation structure as the Salmon examples, including a twined upper selvage and a plain-weave lower selvage (compare Figures 46.76c-

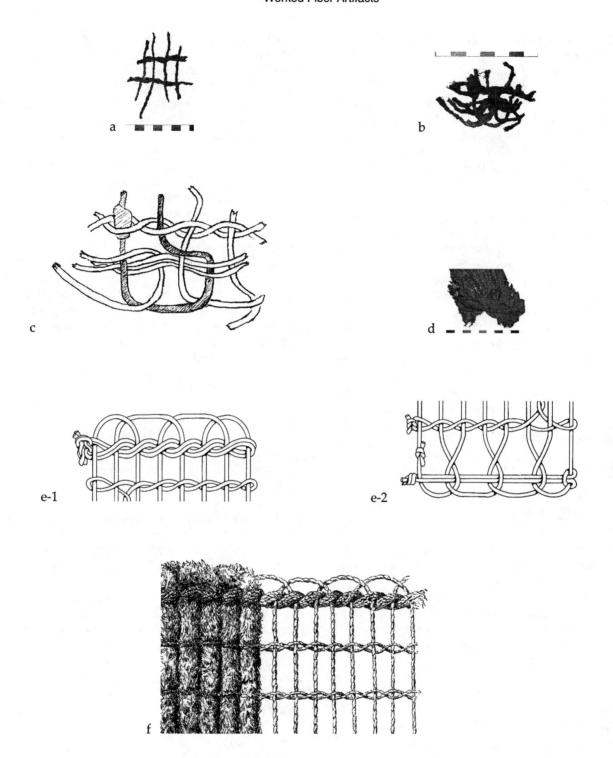

Figure 46.77. Twined fur and feather blankets. (a) FS 80,140 (SA 43W069), intact section of 2-strand twining framework, upper row twined S-wise, lower row twined Z-wise, Burial 43W057. For in situ view, see Figure 46.17. (b) FS 80,368.1 (no field number), section of lower warp selvage showing upper row of S-twist 2-strand twining and lower row of 1/1 plain weave, Room 84W trash. (c) FS 80,368.1, schematic drawing of lower warp selvage. (d) FS 80,424.1 (Feature 123B004), fragment of carbonized fur robe and binding cords from Burial 123B005. For in situ view, see Figure 46.45. (e) Schematic diagram of common upper (1) and lower (2) selvage finishes on twined robes from northeastern Arizona; adapted from Kent 1983: Figure 56d. (f) Schematic diagram of twined feather robe from Step House at Mesa Verde; adapted from Nordenskiöld 1893: Figure 67.

f, 77b, c with Figure 46.77e, f). In contrast, a Pueblo I fur blanket from the Tsegi region (Guernsey 1931: Figure 54a), an early fur blanket from Mule Creek Cave in the Upper Gila (Cosgrove 1947: Figure 23a), and an undated fur blanket from Ventana Cave in southern Arizona (Haury 1950: Figure 101) exhibit very different structures (Kent 1983: Figure 56). Until technical data for the Chaco and Aztec twined blankets become available, all that can be said is that the Salmon blankets conform to the general Four Corners pattern of twined blanket construction.

Although some kind of frame or suspension system was probably used to construct these twined blankets, examples of these frames have yet to be identified in Southwestern sites. Their arrangement remains conjecture (see Kent 1983: Figure 56e for several possible methods). Guernsey (1931:92) suggested that the twined blankets from Tsegi Canyon were made by suspending the warp loops from a bar and allowing the other end of the warp to hang free. Given that the Salmon blankets exhibit virtually the same warp selvages as some of the Tsegi blankets, and assuming that the Salmon blankets were actually made at the site, blanket weavers at Salmon may have used a similar arrangement (e.g., Kent 1983: Figure 56e, no. 5).

Sandals

Twined Sandals (Including Fragments of Sandals or Tumpbands)

Two basic types of footwear were worn at Salmon Pueblo: twined sandals and plaited sandals. Of the 13 possible twined sandals in the assemblage (Table 46.42), 10 are almost certainly finely woven sandals, one is a coarsely woven sandal, and two are the remains of either finely woven sandals or tumpbands. Although these objects came from a variety of contexts, none were associated with burials (Figure 46.78).

All 10 of the finely woven twined sandals exhibit S-twist 2-strand twining (Figures 46.79, 80). At least six have raised geometric designs on the underside of the sole, produced by alternating rows of plain weave, twining, and/or weft-wrap (Hays-Gilpin et al. 1998:56, Figure 5.8a; see Figures 46.79f, 80c). All are made with a coarsely processed 3z-S yucca warp and a highly processed 2z-S yucca weft. Warp diameter range is 0.8–2 mm, and weft diameter is 0.5–1.3 mm. Warp counts are 3–5 per cm, and weft counts are 8–50 per cm. The wide range of the weft counts is due to the fact that the weave has loosened up on some of the more deteriorated examples. Weft counts of 25–50 per cm are the norm. Five of these

sandals have intact sections of side selvages; all are 180° self-selvages. One, with a cupped heel, has an intact heel selvage decoratively worked in countered warp-wrap (Figure 46.80b, d). Another has the remains of either a pointed toe or toe notch (Figure 46.79c, left). One (FS 80,182, Figure 46.80) has the remains of a toe loop and heel strap, and another (FS 80,210) has the remains of side loops. Most of the sandals are carbonized black. None of the unburned examples show evidence of colored designs.

Most of these finely woven sandals are extremely deteriorated, consisting only of small fragments (Figure 46.79). However, one unburned, nearly complete twined sandal (FS 80,182, Figures 46.25, 80) was recovered from the Primary fill of the interstitial space of the Tower Kiva (Room 61A). This well-preserved sandal, 20.7 cm long and 7.8 cm wide, has a rounded toe and a decorative cupped heel. The back of the heel is finely woven in a countered 1/1 warp-wrap structure, which produces a two-faced weave (Figure 46.80d). Warp-wrapping is structurally equivalent to weft-wrapping (see Emery 1966: 215, Figures 323, 324), except that the warp is the active element. A remnant of a 2(2z-S)Z toe loop is present at the toe end, and remnants of a 3(2z-S)Z heel tie protrude from the side of the heel. The underside of the sandal is patterned with a raised geometric design of stepped motifs, which cover at least two-thirds of the sole. There is a large hole at the heel.

The sandal is now a faded wine-red color; the red colorant was identified as iron, or hematite, by X-ray fluorescence spectrometry. The weaving elements appear to have been stained red prior to weaving.

Two other finely twined objects in the assemblage could be the remains of twined sandals or tumpbands. The warp configuration of these objects differs from that of the other sandals. FS 80,014 consists only of a tiny fragment and some disassociated weft yarns. Although only one warp strand is present, it appears to be a 2z-S yarn instead of a 3z-S one. Given the miniscule size of the specimen, no further identification is possible. The other object, FS 80,443 (Figure 46.81c), is almost certainly something other than a twined sandal. The weft elements in this object make two full 360° turns at the side selvage instead of a single 180° turn, and the warp configuration is 3s-Z instead of 3z-S. The wefts are 2z-S. In my opinion, this could be the remains of a twined tumpband.

The temporal association of these 12 finely woven twined objects is unclear. Earl Morris (1928:412), writing of twined sandals at Aztec Ruins, expressed

Table 46.42. Twined sandals or possible tumpbands.

Feature or Artifact (SA) No.	New FS Cat. No.	Room and Context	Occ	Number objects repres.	Weave Structure				Side Selvage		Comments
					2-strand twining (S)	3-strand twining (S)	No. wraps per cm	No. wefts per cm	180° self-selvage	360° self-selvage	
—	80,014	31W, roof-fall	Pri/Int?	1	X	–	5.0	9.0	X	–	Sandal or tumpband; 1 tiny fragment; unusual 2z-S warp?
SA 43W050	80,127	43W, lithic scatter 43W042	Primary	1	X	–	3.0	8.0	X	–	2 small fragments; includes section of pointed toe or toe notch
Feature 61A023	80,182	61A, interstitial space	Primary	1	X	–	4.0	26.0	–	–	Nearly complete; colored red; raised design on underside; rounded toe with toe loop; cupped heel worked in countered warp-wrap technique
—	80,210	62W, trash	Mix	1	X	–	5.0	15.0	X	–	12 fragments from midsole; raised design on underside; remnants of side loop
—	80,212.1	62W, trash	Mix	1	X	–	4.0	28.0	X	–	5 small fragments
Bot samp 62W2066	80,223	62W, trash	Mix	1	X	–	N/a	N/a	–	–	Tiny fragments only; remains of raised design on underside
—	80,262	62W, backfill	Unk	1	X	–	N/a	N/a	–	–	2 tiny fragments, carbonized
—	80,272	62W, trash	Mix	1	X	–	4.0	32.0	–	–	Small fragment from midsole or heel; raised design on underside
—	80,294	62W, trash	Mix	1	X	–	4.0	50.0	X	–	5 fragments; raised design on underside
SA 101W002	80,406, 80,407	101W, trash on roof	Sec	1	–	X	2.0	9.0	–	X	Thick, heavy sandal; 2/1 weave; about 60 percent complete
—	80,411	101W, occ fill	Primary	1	X	–	5.0	30.0	X	–	Rounded toe; toe finish missing; about 10 percent of sandal
SA 127W051	80,442	127W, roof-fall	Pri/Int?	1	X	–	3.3	48.0	–	–	4 fragments of midsole and heel; raised design on underside
—	80,443	127W, roof-fall	Pri/Int?	1	X	–	3.5	48.0	–	X	Sandal or tumpband; large fragment; unusual 3s-Z warps; wefts make two 360° turns at side selvage

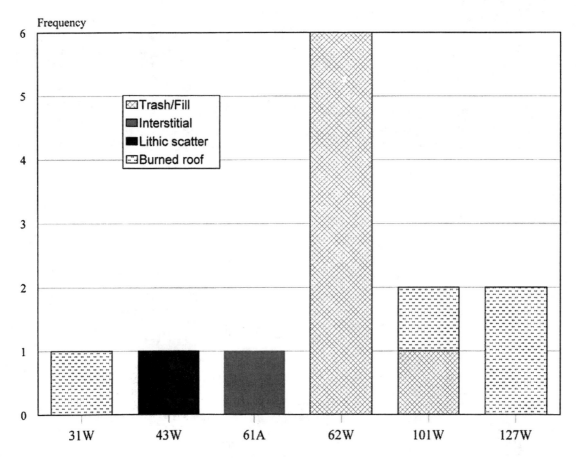

Figure 46.78. Distribution of twined sandals.

the opinion that twined sandals ceased to be made before the "Mesa Verde" period. The Salmon data seem to support his observation. Three of the Salmon twined sandals came from strong Primary contexts: FS 80,182 from the Primary interstitial fill of the Tower Kiva, FS 80,127 from a Primary lithic scatter in Room 43W, and FS 80,411 from Primary occupational fill in Room 101W. Two other twined objects (including the possible tumpband) came from roof stratum F-1-4 of Room 127W, which contained nearly 30 percent Mancos Black-on-white sherds. I have thus tentatively reclassified the twined objects from this stratum as Primary. Nearly half of the sherds from roof stratum F-1-06 of Room 31W, where the other twined sandal or tumpband was found, also date to the Primary and early Secondary occupations. I have also reclassified this artifact. The other six sandals came from the culturally mixed trash deposit in Room 62W, which contained both early and late materials. Given that the production of these sandals is known to have extended into the McElmo phase at Aztec, and based on the available

ceramic data, I consider it likely that all of these finely twined objects at Salmon date to the Primary or early Secondary occupations.

The final twined object in the assemblage differs considerably from all the others. FS 80,406 and 80,407 (SA 101W002, Figure 46.81b) are fragments of a thick, coarsely woven twined sandal, about 60 percent complete. When reassembled, the dozen or so fragments produce an object 11.5 cm wide (complete width), 16.5 cm long (incomplete length), and about 1.1 cm thick. The warp and weft have a woody appearance, and could have been made of yucca or some other coarse plant material. The sandal is woven in S-twist 3-strand twining with a 2/1 weave (Emery 1966: Figures 315–316; see Figure 46.81a). The warp elements are coarsely spun 2(2s-Z)S, about 5 mm in diameter, and the weft elements are more finely spun 2z-S, 2 mm in diameter. There are 2 warps and 9 wefts per cm. At the side selvages, the weft elements make a full 360° turn around the outside warps and reenter the weave. The warp selvages are missing.

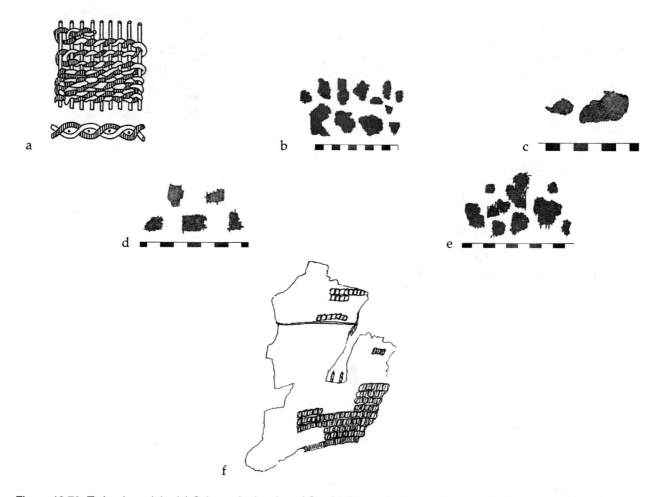

Figure 46.79. Twined sandals. (a) Schematic drawing of S-twist 2-strand twining structure. (b) FS 80,210 (no field number), fragments from midsole, Room 62W trash. (c) FS 80,127 (SA 43W050), fragments from toe region, Feature 43W042 lithic scatter. Fragment at left is portion of a pointed toe or toe jog. (d) FS 80,294 (no field number), fragments from midsole or heel, Room 62W trash. Raised knots are visible on three lower fragments. (e) FS 80,411 (no field number), fragments from toe and midsole regions, Room 101W occupational fill. Note curvature of upper fragment, probably part of rounded toe. (f) FS 80,442 (SA 127W051), schematic drawing of visible areas of raised knots on underside of midsole and heel. Some areas obscured by consolidated soil, Room 127W roof-fall.

The function of this object is unclear. Although it could have been worn as a sandal, it would not have been comfortable due to its rigid construction. There is no clear evidence of sandal ties. Morris found several almost identical objects at Aztec Ruins (Webster 2004), at least one of which had a hole at the heel, suggesting it might have been worn. An alternative hypothesis, discussed further in the following section, is that these items could have served as sandal effigies. Excavators attributed the Salmon artifact to the Secondary occupation, and at this point there is nothing to suggest an earlier date. Two other coarsely woven objects from Salmon, both from Secondary contexts, could be additional examples of these sandals or part of a related tradition (see Miscellaneous Worked Fiber Artifacts).

Regional Comparisons. The finely woven twined sandals from Salmon represent the continuation of a highly specialized textile tradition that developed in the Four Corners region during late Basketmaker II and early Basketmaker III. The later Pueblo II examples are characterized by rounded to pointed toes, sometimes a jog or notch at the outer edge at the little toe, shaping for the right or left foot, sometimes colored geometric designs on the upper surface and/or raised geometric designs on the underside, and often cupped heels. Hays-Gilpin et al. (1998:47–48) referred to this as the "shaped toe-cupped heel style." In addition to Salmon, Pueblo-period examples are known from Pueblo Bonito (Judd 1954:74–80, Figures 10, 11, Plate 17; Pepper 1920:93–95, Figure 34), Chetro Ketl (Reiter 1933:41, Plate XII; Vivian

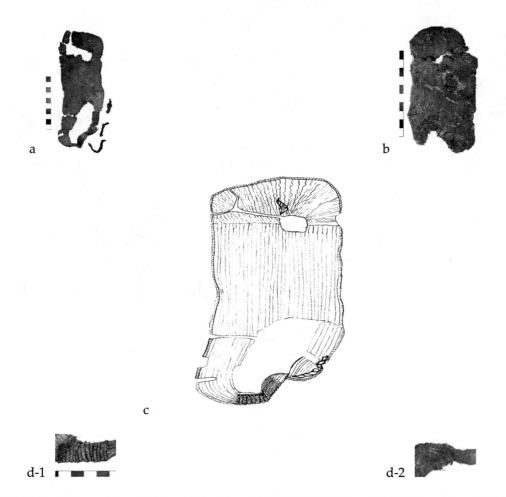

Figure 46.80. Nearly complete, red-stained twined sandal FS 80,182 (Feature 61A023) from Room 61A, interstitial space of the Tower Kiva. (a) Overall view. For in situ view, see Figure 46.25. (b) Underside of toe and midsole regions showing geometric pattern of raised knots. (c) Schematic drawing showing heel finish and remnants of heel loop. Toe fragments fitted together. (d) Close-up of (1) inner surface and (2) outer surface of cupped heel showing two-faced weave worked in countered warp-wrapping.

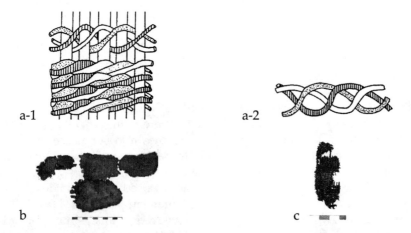

Figure 46.81. Unidentified twined objects. (a) Schematic diagram of S-twist 3-strand twining structure. (b) FS 80,406 and 80,407 (SA 101W002), reassembled fragments of coarsely woven twined object (sandal?), Room 101W trash. (c) FS 80,443 (no field number), finely-woven twined object (tumpband?) worked in S-twist 2-strand twining with 3s-Z warps, Room 127W roof-fall.

1931:23–27, Photo IVa, Figure 8), Pueblo del Arroyo (Judd 1959:124), Aztec Ruins (Morris 1919:50–52), Antelope House (Magers 1986:257–259), Ruin 1 in Monument Valley (Kidder and Guernsey 1919:103–106, Pueblo type IIb, Plate 39b, c), Village of the Great Kivas at Zuni (Roberts 1932:104; NMNH 351830), Wupatki (Stanislawski 1963: Figure 55d-f, fragments misidentified), Cottonwood Wash in southeastern Utah (Kankainen 1995:67), and Long House at Mesa Verde (Osborne 1980:328). To my knowledge, the only places where Pueblo period twined sandals occur in substantial quantities are Chaco Canyon, Salmon, Aztec, and Antelope House.

As noted, Morris (1928:412) speculated that twined sandals were no longer being produced by the time of the Mesa Verde occupation. Of the 41 examples found by Morris at Aztec Ruins, 35 came from Chaco trash, 5 from undated deposits, and only 1 from a known Mesa Verde context. Given that most of the twined sandals from Salmon and the above-mentioned sites also appear to come from contexts contemporaneous with the Late Bonito or McElmo phase, Morris's argument seems to be supported. However, more work remains to be done on this question.

At Chaco, Salmon, and Aztec, these sandals appear to be closely associated with Chacoan deposits or ritual settings, suggesting a connection between this sandal style and the Chacoan regional system. Given their complicated, labor-intensive construction, it is possible that by Chacoan times (if not earlier), these sandals served a specialized purpose, perhaps as ritual or dance paraphernalia, rather than everyday footwear. Both the West Ruin at Aztec (Morris 1928:381) and Chetro Ketl (Reiter 1933:23, 41, Plate VII) produced an example with cotton wefts, an entirely impractical fiber for daily use. Because the production of these sandals was highly standardized and required considerable specialized knowledge and skill, the technical information required to make these objects may have been passed down through certain kin groups or sodalities, perhaps ones with ancestral ties to particular Basketmaker groups.

Twined tumpbands are known from a number of Southwestern sites, with considerable apparent variability in their construction. I have discussed one possible example from Salmon with a 3s-Z warp. Guernsey (1931:99, Plate 10c, h, I) described a Pueblo I carrying band or tumpline from northeastern Arizona with a 3-ply warp and other examples with a 2-ply warp, but did not provide the direction of twist. Magers (1986:240) described twined tumplines from Antelope House made with 2z-S and 3s-Z yucca ele-

ments, but did not differentiate the warp and weft. Rohn (1971:235–237) described several tumpbands from Mug House with 2s-Z and 2z-S warps, and Judd (1954:171–172) and Morris (1919:52) have described tumpbands from Pueblo Bonito and Aztec, respectively, but did not provide the warp structure.

As for the thick twined sandals, the only other examples I know of come from the West Ruin at Aztec, where Morris (1924:167; 1928:357, 361) found at least 12 of these heavy sandals or sandal-like objects in a Mesa Verde burial and in refuse. I have examined only one of the Aztec examples (AMNH 29.0/8789), which has the same 3-strand twining (S) and 2/1 weave structure as the Salmon example. Although these items could have functioned as some kind of winter sandal, their rigid structure would have made them uncomfortable to wear. An alternative hypothesis is that they served some kind of ritual purpose at Salmon and Aztec, either as ritual footwear or as sandal effigies. Perhaps they are related to the wood and stone sandal effigy forms found at Chaco, Aztec, and other Pueblo II and Pueblo III sites whose symbolic meaning has yet to be deciphered.

Plaited Sandals

The Salmon assemblage contains 20 plaited objects that are probably the remains of plaited sandals (Table 46.43 and Figures 46.82–84). The assemblage also contains a carbonized shoe sock with a plaited sandal sole (Figure 46.85a); this object is discussed separately below. Most of these plaited sandals came from trash deposits, roof-fall, or specialized features (Figure 46.82). None occurred in mortuary contexts.

All plaited sandals in the assemblage were woven in 2/2 twill (Figure 46.57a). All but one have narrow yucca-leaf elements 0.2–0.3 cm in width and a weave density of 3–5 elements per cm. A more coarsely woven sandal from Room 100W (FS 80,396, Figure 46.83h) has slightly wider elements, 0.3–0.4 cm in width. The selvage of this object is curvilinear, suggesting that it is the remains of a sandal and not a mat. Two sandals (FS 80,271.2 and 80,291, Figures 46.83c, e) from Room 62W trash are stained red.

Like the twined sandals, most of the plaited sandals from Salmon are extremely fragmentary. However, FS 80,200 (SAW082) from Room 62W is nearly complete (Figures 46.30, 84c). This elaborate, finely worked sandal was made for the left foot, and measures 10.5 cm wide and 24 cm long. It has a rounded toe (the tip of the toe is missing) and a toe jog along one side. The sandal has a decorative border that was produced by transposing (crossing) elements at regular intervals (Figure 46.84d, e). It also has a

Table 46.43. Plaited sandals and shoe-sock.

Feature or Artifact (SA) No.	New FS Cat. No.	Room and Context	Occ	Number Objects Repres.	2/2 Twill	Intentional Shifts	Un-ident.	No. elements per cm	Avg. element width cm	90° self-selvage	180° self-selvage	Comments
–	80,007	30W, trash	Sec/Int	1	X	–	–	3.0-4.0	0.2-0.3	X	–	Plaited sandal? 4 small fragments
–	80,021	33B, roof-fall	Sec	1	X	–	–	3.0	0.3	X	–	Heel end of finely plaited sandal; flat heel
–	80,041, 80,042	33W, trash	Pri	1	X	–	–	4.0	0.2	X	–	Fine weave; several fragments; one with curved edge suggests heel
–	80,071	37W, trash, roof-fall	Sec	1	X	–	–	4.0	0.2-0.3	X	–	Two fragments; probably a sandal
–	80,073.2	37W, trash	Sec	1	X	–	–	4.0	0.2	–	–	Plaited sandal?; fine weave
SA 43W071	80,126	43W, lithic scatter 43W042	Pri	1	X	–	–	5.0	0.2	–	–	Fine weave; fragmentary; very deteriorated
–	80,147	43W, roof-fall	Sec	1	X	–	–	3.0	0.3	X	X	Heel portion, square, slightly cupped; 90° side selvage; 180° end selvage; end selvage a double selvage
–	80,152	43W, roof-fall	Sec	1	X	X	–	5.0	0.2	–	–	Fine weave; 2 fragments, both exhibiting intentional 2/4 shifts; shifts create diagonal design
SA 62A030	N/A	62A, floor	Sec	1	–	–	X	N/a	N/a	–	–	Not found; described as a fine sandal or possibly a mat; fragment 10.0 x 14.0 cm
–	80,192.1	62B-62W, trash	Mix	1	X	–	–	3.0-4.0	0.2-0.3	X	–	2 small fragments; probably from sandal
SA 62W082	80,200	62W, trash	Mix	1	X	X	–	3.0-4.0	0.2-0.3	X	X	Nearly complete; jogged toe; transposed elements along edge; remnants of toe and side loops

Table 46.43 (continued)

Feature or Artifact (SA) No.	New FS Cat. No.	Room and Context	Occ	Number Objects Repres.	2/2 Twill	Intentional Shifts	Un-ident.	No. elements per cm	Avg. element width cm	90° self-selvage	180° self-selvage	Comments
–	80,212.2	62W, trash	Mix	1	X	–	–	4.0	0.2-0.3	–	–	Small fragment; probably a sandal; fine weave; found with twined sandal
–	80,217	62W, trash	Mix	1	X	–	–	3.0	0.3	?	–	Deteriorated fragments; curved outline
–	80,267.1	62W, trash	Mix	1	X	–	–	4.0	0.2-0.3	X	–	Probable remains of sandal; fine weave
–	80,271.2	62W, trash	Mix	1 ?	X	–	–	3.3	0.3	X	–	3 fragments; 1 stained red; fine weave; elements frayed on underside
–	80,291	62W, trash	Mix	1	X	–	–	4.0	0.2-0.3	X	–	3 fragments; elements stained brick red
–	80,310	62W, trash	Mix	1	X	–	–	3.3	0.3	X	–	2 fragments; about 20% of sandal
–	80,321	62W, trash	Mix	1	X	–	–	3.2	0.3	X	–	8 deteriorated fragments; about 10% of sandal
Bot samp 97W2017	80,385	97W, log feature 97W2007	Pri	1	X	–	–	4.0	0.2	X	–	Small fragment from flotation sample
–	80,396	100W, roof-fall	Sec	1	X	–	–	3.0	0.3-0.4	X	–	3 fragments; 1 fragment tapers at end—could be curvature of toe?; 20% of sandal
–	80,476	129W, roof-fall	Pri?	1	X	–	–	3.0-4.0	0.2-0.3	X	–	Carbonized shoe-sock with looped turkey-feather upper attached to plaited sole

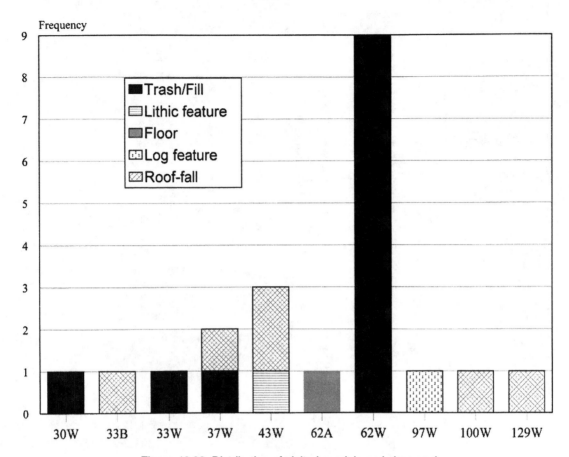

Figure 46.82. Distribution of plaited sandals and shoe-sock.

slightly cupped heel that was made by folding the plaiting elements over an added yucca-leaf foundation, then clipping them off. The presence of a few yucca-leaf knots along the edge indicates the former location of a toe loop and side loops (Figure 46.84d).

Two other examples (FS 80,021 and FS 80,147) contain intact heels—the former a flat heel and the latter slightly cupped (Figure 46.46.83a, d). The cupped heel of FS 80,147 was produced by placing a pair of yucca strips along the edge of the heel, then wrapping the plaiting elements over the strips on the upper surface of the heel and around adjacent elements on the underside of the heel, resulting in a double selvage (Figure 46.83d).

One other example (FS 80,152, Figure 46.84a) exhibits intentional shifts. In this case, rows of 2/2 weave alternate with rows of 2/4 weave to produce a diagonal design (Figure 46.84b). The fineness of the elements suggests that this is the remains of a sandal, rather than a mat.

Finally, two of the plaited sandals are stained red (FS 80,271.2 and 80,291, Figure 46.83c, e). The former is a pinkish red color, the latter a brick red. Only one of the three fragments of FS 80,271.2 is red, whereas the entire sample of FS 80,291 is red. The red colorant of FS 80,291 was identified as iron using X-ray fluorescence spectrometry. The fact that the color is still bright beneath the cross-woven elements suggests that the elements were stained prior to weaving.

Excavators attributed three of the plaited sandals to the Primary occupation (Primary trash in Room 33W, a Primary lithic scatter in Room 43W, and a Primary log feature in Room 97W), one to an Intermediate/Secondary context (Room 30W, trash), and the rest to Secondary strata. However, some of the same uncertainties that characterize the dating of the twined sandals also apply to these objects. Plaited sandal fragment FS 80,212.1 was extracted from the same batch of fragments as twined sandal FS 80,212.2, suggesting that the two were closely associated in the Room 62W trash. I have already suggested that this twined sandal dates to the Primary (or early Secondary?) occupation. The presence of

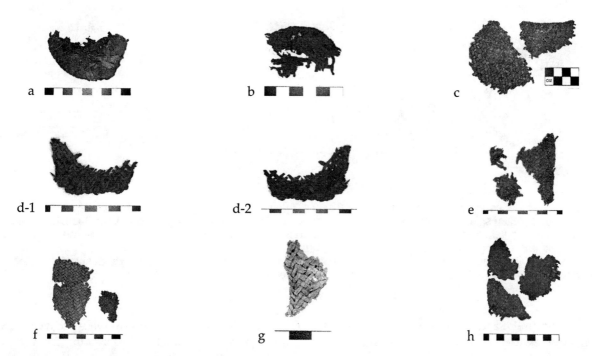

Figure 46.83. Plaited sandals. (a) FS 80,021 (no field number), heel fragment, Room 33B roof-fall. (b) FS 80,042 (no field number), possible heel fragment, Room 33W trash. (c) FS 80,271.2 (no field number), side selvage and body weave fragments, Room 62W trash. (d) FS 80,147 (no field number), (1) lower and (2) upper views of square heel, Room 43W roof-fall. (e) FS 80,291 (no field number), side selvage and body weave fragments, stained red, Room 62W trash. (f) FS 80,310 (no field number), side selvage and body weave fragments, Room 62W trash. (g) FS 80,385 (Botanical Sample 97W2017), side selvage fragment, Room 97W, Primary log feature 97W2007. (h) FS 80,396 (no field number), side selvage and body weave fragments. Fragment at upper left may reflect curvature of toe, Room 100W roof-fall.

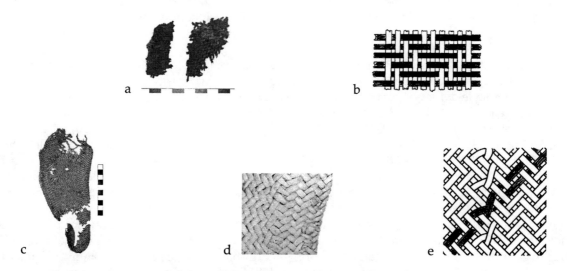

Figure 46.84. Plaited sandals with intentional shifts. (a) FS 80,152 (no field number), body weave fragments with intentional 2/4 shifts in alternate rows, Room 43W roof-fall. (b) FS 80,152, schematic diagram showing rows of staggered 2/4 shifts alternating with rows of 2/2 weave. (c) FS 80,200 (SA 62W082), nearly complete sandal with decorative border, Room 62W trash. For in situ view, see Figure 46.30. (d) FS 80,200 (SA 62W082), detail of decorative border showing transposed elements. Knots indicate former presence of side loops. (e) FS 80,200 (SA 62W082), schematic diagram of transposed elements; adapted from Adovasio 1977: Figure 133.

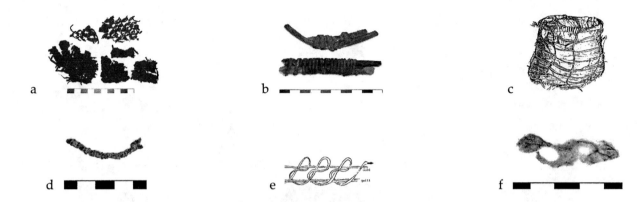

Figure 46.85. Miscellaneous worked fiber artifacts. (a) FS 80,476 (no field number), fragments of carbonized shoe-sock with looped upper and plaited sole, Room 129W roof-fall. (b) Wooden artifacts with wrapped elements from Room 62W trash. Upper, FS 80,306 (no field number), possible hoop fragment from an openwork basket; lower, FS 80,274 (no field number), possible handle fragment. (c) Openwork basket from West Ruin at Aztec; from Morris 1919: Figure 35. (d) FS 80,245.2 (no field number), cordage-wrapped feather artifact, Room 62W trash. (e) FS 80,245.2, schematic diagram showing method of wrapping cordage. (f) FS 80,358 (no field number), modern silk fabric, Room 67W roof-fall.

both a plaited sandal and a twined sandal in Primary lithic scatter Feature 43W042 confirms that both styles were contemporaneous at Salmon. Given that many of the red-stained artifacts from Salmon are also from well-supported Primary contexts, I think that the two red-stained plaited sandals from the culturally mixed Room 62W trash deposit could also date to the Primary (or early Secondary?) occupation. Several other plaited sandals from Room 62W (the nearly complete sandal FS 80,200, for instance) could date to this early period as well. Because finely woven plaited sandals appear to have been made and used well into the Pueblo III period at Mesa Verde and other areas, it is not possible to further refine the dating of the Salmon plaited sandals.

Regional Comparisons. Finely plaited sandals worked in 2/2 twill are found throughout the region and were a popular style of footwear during Pueblo II and Pueblo III (e.g., Judd 1954:73, Plate 16; 1959:9, Figure 3; Kidder and Guernsey 1919:101–102; Magers 1986:255–257, Figure 83; Mathien 2004: Table 1; Morris 1919:49–50, Figure 29; Nordenskiöld 1893: Plate XLVI, nos. 2, 3, 5; Osborne 1980:325–330, Figures 392–399; Pepper 1920:93, 162, Figure 34a; Rohn 1971: 111–112, Figure 130; Vivian 1931: Photo III). Elaborate plaited sandals with raised longitudinal designs on the soles have been reported from Pueblo Bonito and Aztec (e.g., Judd 1954:73, Plate 16c and c1; AM NH 29.0/8932 from Room 95 at Aztec) but were not identified in the Salmon assemblage.

Looped Shoe-Sock with Plaited Sole

The fragmentary and carbonized remains of a shoe-sock with a plaited sole and looped turkey-feather-cord upper (FS 80,476) were recovered from the roof-fall stratum F-1-8 of Room 129W (Figure 46.85a). Although excavators classified the F-1-8 stratum as Secondary, I suggested in my discussion of Room 129W that many of the artifacts from this stratum date to the Primary occupation. I have tentatively reclassified this shoe-sock as Primary.

The sole of this shoe-sock is a 2/2-plaited yucca sandal with elements 0.2–0.3 cm wide. The sandal has a weave density of 3–4 elements per cm and a 90° self-selvage, and resembles other plaited sandals in the Salmon assemblage. The sock portion is worked in a simple looping stitch with 2s-Z yucca cords that are 0.2 cm in diameter. The cords bear the carbonized remains of wrapped turkey-feather quills, indicating the former presence of a feather pile. The fabric has two loops per cm, with each loop 0.5 cm wide and 1 cm high. The upper surface of the sandal is covered with the carbonized remains of feathers, suggesting that the looped fabric was a complete sock attached to a sandal sole. The sock was attached by inserting the looping yarn down through the sole, around a plaiting element, then back up again. In one fragment, the yarns appear to be twined around a plaiting element.

Regional Comparisons. Looped socks are known from a number of sites, including Aztec, Mesa Verde, and Chaco Canyon. At Pueblo Bonito, Pepper (1920: 107) found two feather-cord stockings in the refuse of Room 25. A pair of looped socks made of yucca cordage and animal hair were also associated with "Cacique's Sanctum" near Chetro Ketl (Mathien 2004:93, Figures 10–12). These were characterized by their student excavator as "high top ceremonial slippers." One of these socks had a reinforced plaited sole like the Salmon example; the other did not. The deposit in which they were found is believed to date to the early 1100s. Morris (1928:184, 367) found five looped socks at Aztec, three with the burial of three children (burial 54 in Room 1532) and the rest from trash deposits. The Aztec examples appear to date to the later Mesa Verde occupation. It is not known if any of these have plaited soles. Kent (1983:50–51, Figure 17) illustrated similar shoe-socks with plaited soles from Nitsie Canyon in the Kayenta area. Rohn (1971:112, Figures 131, 132) also illustrated an example without a plaited sole from Mug House at Mesa Verde.

Miscellaneous Worked Fiber Artifacts

Several unique objects, some of unknown function, were recovered at Salmon Pueblo. These are listed in Table 46.32 (unknown plaited objects) and Table 46.44.

Objects of Wrapped Wood or Twigs

Twig bundle. A small twig bundle (FS 80,032.2) was part of the mortuary assemblage with the "bow priest" burial, 33W012. The bundle was found tied around the neck of the individual and on top of the lower matting. Measured from the color field photograph (not illustrated), the tie was about 20 cm from the back of the neck to the tip of the bundle. The twigs, 0.15 cm in diameter, appear to be unpeeled willow or sumac. The bundle was made by wrapping the twigs together and tying the bundle with one of the twigs. The type of knot is unidentified.

Wooden handles. Two objects probably served as handles for axes or other types of implements. A small stick, spirally wrapped with a long narrow strip of yucca (FS 80,077), was found in the Secondary roof-fall of Room 37W. This unburned object is 4.7 cm long and 1.1 cm in diameter. The mixed trash deposit in Room 62W produced another unburned object of wrapped wood (FS 80,274, Figure 46.85b, lower), consisting of a pair of wooden (willow?) sticks spirally wrapped with split-twig elements (sumac?). One of the wooden elements appears to have been peeled, the other is not, and the wrapping elements are unpeeled. The object is 9.9 cm long, 1.5 cm wide, and 0.9 cm thick, and it has 3.5 wraps per cm. It resembles the handles for hafted axes illustrated by Nordenskiöld (1893: Plate XXXVI, nos. 4 and 6) from Mesa Verde.

Hoop from an openwork basket? The wrapped object FS 80,306 (Figure 46.85b, upper) is an unburned fragment of a wooden hoop that is spirally wrapped with a yucca leaf or flattened twig. The fragment measures 9.3 x 1.3 x 0.8 cm. The hoop consists of two unpeeled willow (?) sticks, 0.4 and 0.6 cm in diameter, and the wrapping elements are 0.5 cm wide. The spacing of the wrapping is irregular, averaging 1.25 wraps per cm. This could be the remains of a cornhusk-lined openwork basket like the ones found at the West Ruin at Aztec (Morris 1919:57, Figure 35; see Figure 46.85c) and probably also Pueblo Bonito. During my brief survey (Webster 2004), I saw at least a dozen examples of these baskets from Aztec, some perfectly preserved, including five from Room 1222, seven from Room 48, 15 from Room 72, and 2 from Room 78—all rooms rich in Chacoan materials. I also recorded four likely examples from Room 160 at Pueblo Bonito. Other examples are reported from Antelope House (Adovasio and Gunn 1986: Figures 202, 203). If not a basket, FS 80,306 could be part of a snowshoe frame (cf. Morris 1919: Figure 36; Nordenskiöld 1893: Plate XLVIII2) or some other latticework object.

Objects of Wrapped Cordage

Feather tie or ornament. A fragment of a small feather object, consisting of a length of wrapped yucca (?) cordage enclosing a feather quill (FS 80,245.2, Figure 46.85d), was recovered from the culturally mixed trash deposit in Room 62W. The cord was constructed by wrapping parallel elements of 3z-S yucca cordage and a feather quill together in a figure-eight fashion with fine 2z-S yucca (?) cordage (Figure 46.85e). The diameter of the 3z-S yarn is 1 cm and the 2z-S yarn, 0.8 cm. No feathers remain on the quill. The fragment is 4.5 cm long x 0.4 cm wide, and the cord has 10 wraps per cm. This object probably served as some kind of feather ornament or tie.

Possible altar tassel. Two fragments of a yellow wrapped cord (FS 80,403, Figure 46.86a) were recovered from the roof-fall and trash of Room 100W. Together, the two pieces form a strand about 4.3 cm long and 0.3 cm in diameter. The interior cord is 2s-Z yucca cordage, 0.15 cm in diameter. This cord is closely wrapped in a spiral fashion with a finer 2 or 3z-S yucca cord, is 0.10 cm in diameter, and has 9 wraps per cm. In places where the interior of the cord is exposed, the yarns appear a bright mustard-yellow color. This wrapped cord closely resembles some of the wrapped strands from Pueblo Bonito that Judd (1954:274, Plate 83a) identified as probable altar tassels (Figure 46.86h). Although excavators identified the N-1-03 stratum where FS 80,403 was found as Secondary, its resemblance to a ritual item from Pueblo Bonito suggests a possible Primary attribution.

Table 46.44. Miscellaneous worked-fiber objects.

Feature or Artifact No.	New FS Cat No.	Room and Context	Occ	No. of Objects Repres.	Object Type	Comments
Bot sample 33W2024	80,032.2	33W, burial 33W012	Pri – late?	1	Twig bundle	Reportedly tied around individual's neck
–	80,077	37W, roof-fall/ trash	Sec	1	Stick wrapped with yucca leaf	Spirally wrapped
–	N/A	43W, burial 43W007	Sec	1	Unidentified twined (?) object	Not collected; visible in field photo
Bot sample TX/61A-1	N/A	61A, interstitial space	Sec?	1	Textile of unknown type	Not located; recovered from "above end of vega" [sic]
–	80,205.2	62W, trash	Mixed	1	Selvage of sandal or basket?	V-shaped wrapped selvage; no plaited elements present
–	80,245.2	62W, trash	Mixed	1	Feather ornament	Weft-wrapped; yucca warp and weft
–	80,274	62W, trash	Mixed	1	Wood handle for hafted axe?	Spirally wrapped
–	80,306	62W, trash	Mixed	1	Hoop from openwork basket?	Willow spirally wrapped with yucca(?)
–	80,329.2	62W, trash	Mixed	1	4 sets of yucca chains	2 with 3 links, 1 with 4 links, 1 with 5 links; links tied with overhand knots and 1 square knot
SA 64W086	80,343	64W, foot drum 64W118	Sec	1	Yucca pad?	Unknown function; semi-circular form; 1/1 plain weave; weft faced?
–	80,358	67W, roof-fall	Modern/ historic	1	Silk cloth (ribbon?)	3/1 (?) satin weave
–	80,403	100W, roof-fall/trash	Pri?	1	Cordage artifact (altar tassel?)	Mustard yellow color; core is 2s-Z; wrapping is 2z-S or 3z-S; spirally wrapped

Yucca-Leaf Objects

Selvage from an Unknown Object. A well preserved V-shaped fragment of an unidentified yucca object (FS 80,205.2, Figure 46.86b) was recovered from mixed trash in Room 62W. The object, about 5 cm long and 4 cm wide, consists of a bundle of narrow yucca-leaf strips formed into a V-shape and wrapped with narrow yucca leaves. The object was constructed by passing each narrow (0.2 cm wide) strip around the bundle and back around itself, then inserting the end of the strip into the bundle, to be wrapped by successive strips (Figure 46.86c). This object could represent the selvage from a plaited sandal or a plaited basket lacking a rod at the rim, or it could be some sort of novelty item or doodle.

Yucca chains. The Room 62W trash deposit produced four yucca-leaf chains (FS 80,329.2, Figure 46.86e). Each was made with a series of overhand knots, and one has a square knot at the end. Two of the chains have three links, one has four links, and the other has five. These items were probably used to bind or hang bundles of plant materials.

Unidentified 1/1 plaited object. A fragment (3 x 9.5 cm) of a plaited object of unknown form and function (FS 80,459, Figure 46.86f) was recovered from Primary trash in Room 129W (Table 46.32). FS 80,469, a smaller fragment of 1/1 plaiting from the same room, is believed to be another piece of this object. This could be the remains of a plaited mat or band, or possibly a sandal. The object was woven in simple 1/1 plaiting of narrow yucca leaves and has a squared off corner with 90° self-selvages. Its structure is relatively flimsy, making it unlikely that this object served as a sandal.

The 1/1 plaiting structure is relatively uncommon in basketry from the Colorado Plateau. Of the 466 pieces of plaited basketry studied by Adovasio

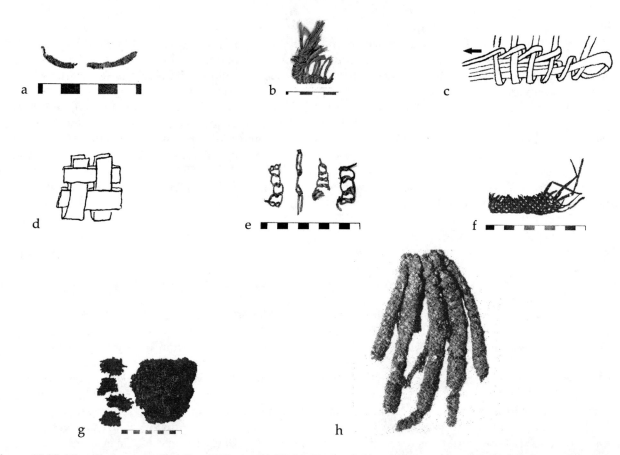

Figure 46.86. Miscellaneous worked fiber artifacts. (a) FS 80,403 (no field number), two fragments of a possible altar tassel with yellow cordage core; Room 100W roof-fall. (b) FS 80,205.2 (no field number), yucca selvage from an unknown object, Room 62W trash. (c) FS 80,205.2, schematic drawing of selvage construction. (d) FS 80,228 (no field number), sketch of small 1/1 plaited square, Room 62W trash. (e) FS 80,329.2 (no field number), yucca chains, Room 62W trash. (f) FS 80,459 (no field number), fragment of 1/1 plaited object with intact selvage, possibly from a mat or band, Room 129W Primary trash. (g) FS 80,343 (SA 64W086), coarsely woven plain-weave pad or sandal (?), Room 64W (Tower Kiva) footdrum Feature 64W118. (h) Altar tassel from Pueblo Bonito; from Judd 1954: Pl. 83a.

and Gunn (1986:329–342, Type XX, Figures 141–147) from Antelope House in Canyon del Muerto, only 60 fragments were woven using this technique. Adovasio and Gunn identified these fragments as the remains of mats or bands. I also recorded two narrow yucca-leaf bands worked in 1/1 plaiting from the West Ruin at Aztec (AMNH 29.0/5290 and 29.0/5291 from Room 1222; Webster 2004). In Chaco Canyon, plaited sandals worked in 1/1 plaiting are known from Pueblo Bonito and Chetro Ketl (Judd 1954: Figure 8; Reiter 1933:41, Plate XI3), and two possible 1/1-plaited mats are described from the small site of Tseh So (Brand et al. 1937:99, 109).

Square 1/1 plaited object. A small square object worked in 1/1 plaiting (FS 80,228, Figure 46.86d), perhaps a small charm or game piece, was found in the mixed trash deposit in Room 62W (Table 46.32). Measuring only 2 cm square and 0.6 cm thick, FS 80,228 is a woven square made of yucca leaf ele-

ments folded 180° at each end to produce an object two elements wide and four layers thick. The function of this object is unknown. It could be some kind of charm or gaming piece, or just a casual doodle.

Woven Objects

Unidentified plain-weave object. A carbonized, rigid, semi-circular fragment of a yucca object woven in weft-faced plain weave (FS 80,343, Figure 46.86g) was recovered from the vicinity of the foot drum of the Tower Kiva (Room 64W, Feature 64W118). The largest of the five fragments measures 10.3 cm wide (complete width) and 11 cm long (incomplete length). Both side selvages are present; they are 180° self-selvages. The weft is 3s-Z yucca, 0.3–0.4 cm in diameter, and the warp is 2s-Z yucca, 0.4 cm in diameter. The warp is overlain by what appears to be a strip of narrowleaf yucca (?), now shredded, or a bundle of yucca fiber. The object is coarsely woven with one warp and three wefts per cm.

This object might have served as a pad, or it could be another example of a thick sandal-like object similar to FS 80,406/80,407 (Figure 46.81b), discussed above. Its construction differs considerably from that sandal, in terms of both the warp and weft configuration (the elements in FS 80,406/80,407 are plied z-S, whereas those in FS 80,343 are plied s-Z) and the side-selvage finish (FS 80,406/80,407 has a 360° selvage, FS 80,343 a 180° selvage). I suspect these were two different kinds of objects. Morris found a number of thick sandal-like objects at Aztec, including one that might have been a pad (AMNH 29.1/8316; Webster 2004). After the Aztec assemblage is analyzed and the variability of these objects is assessed, we will be in a better position to interpret their function. In the meantime, it seems likely that FS 80,343, with its coarse warp and rigid texture, is related in some way to this thick sandal tradition. The association of FS 80,343 with the floor drum of the Tower Kiva suggests a ritual use for this object.

Unidentified twined (?) object. A probable twined object (no SA or catalog number) was found near the feet of Secondary burial 43W057. This item is not mentioned in the burial report, and evidently it was not collected. In the color field photographs it looks like an unburned, tan-colored, weft-faced object made with coarse, rigid warps and finer wefts (Figure 46.20). The raw material appears to be yucca, and the weave structure looks like weft-faced twining or plain weave. The object is incomplete. From the field photographs, the sizes of the two pieces are estimated to be about 6 cm wide and 7 cm long for one fragment and 6 cm wide and 10 cm long for the other. It is unclear whether any selvages are present.

These fragments might represent a coarsely twined bag or sandal; in the photographs they bear their closest resemblance to a twined bag. However, no other examples of twined bags are known from Salmon Pueblo, and Kent (1983:110) has stated that they did not occur at Puebloan sites after Basketmaker III. The object definitely is not a finely woven twined sandal, nor does it have an obvious sandal form. It also does not appear to be as rigid or thick as the thick, twined sandals from Salmon and Aztec, but given the fact that thick sandals are known to occur in a burial context at Aztec, this is one possible identification. Morris found two thick, twined sandals with burial 25 at Aztec West, one of the most important burials at the site. The inclusion of such an object with one of the most richly furnished burials in Room 43W would not be altogether surprising.

Unknown textile. The field records report a "textile" from a Secondary deposit in the interstices of the Tower Kiva. This object evidently was not collected and nothing further is known.

Modern silk cloth. As noted, the assemblage contains one piece of modern cloth, FS 80,358 (Figure 46.85f), recovered from the roof-fall of Room 67W. This well-preserved, albeit fragmentary scrap of tan silk fabric is woven in a 3/1 (?) satin weave. The fragment, 4.8 cm long and 1.5 cm wide, could be the remains of a commercial ribbon or perhaps a scarf. It is woven from unspun silk warp and wefts that are 0.03 cm in diameter, and has 36 elements per cm.

Coarse Matting or Roofing Material

Excavators collected numerous samples of plant materials that they identified in the field as matting (Table 46.45). Although I initially assigned them new catalog numbers, I was unable to find any evidence of weave structure. In my opinion, most of this material probably represents roof thatching or other closing material. The exception is FS 80,421, which is a collection of wood fragments (sticks), possibly related to burial 122-1.

Table 46.45. Coarse matting or roofing material with no identifiable weave structure.

Feature or Artifact (SA) No	New FS Cat. No.	Room and Context	Occupation
–	80,006	30W, occ fill	Secondary
–	80,012	31A, mixed	Unknown
	80,063	36W, structured trash	Sec/Intermediate
–	80,064	36W, trash	Secondary
–	80,074.1	37W, trash	Secondary
Feature 059W001	80,162–80,172	59W, trash and contact between strata	Secondary
Feature 059W007	80,173	59W, contact between strata	Secondary
–	80,175	59W, trash	Secondary
–	80,363	82W, roof-fall	Secondary
–	80,421	122A, Feature fill (collection of sticks with Burial 122-1?)	Secondary

PATTERNS IN USE AND PRODUCTION OF FIBER ARTIFACTS

The Use of Color Pigments

Several red, yellow, and blue artifacts were identified in the Salmon assemblage or mentioned in the field records (Table 46.46). Red artifacts include a twined sandal, two plaited sandals, two plaited mats, a plaited ring basket, fragments of three plaited mats, baskets, or sandals, and numerous yucca ties or knots. Some of the yucca ties and knots have an orange appearance; they could have been colored either red or yellow or not been colored at all. Most of the red objects are a purplish-red color. The colorant used to stain three of the artifacts (FS 80,182, FS 80,291, and FS 80,325, see Figures 46.62a, 80, 83e) was identified as iron, or hematite, by nondestructive X-ray fluorescence spectrographic analysis conducted by Dr. Nancy Odegaard, conservator at the Arizona State Museum, and Dr. David Smith, professor in the Department of Chemistry, University of Arizona. The elements in these artifacts appear to have been stained red prior to weaving.

Yellow artifacts include a possible altar tassel, two samples of cordage, and several yucca leaf knots. The yellow colorant is assumed to be a mineral pigment, but the color has not been tested. One example of blue cordage was reportedly found with the yellow cordage in a Secondary (?) infant burial in Room 100W. Evidently the cordage from this burial was not collected.

The highest concentration of colored artifacts came from Rooms 61A, 62W, and 100W. The significance of this distribution is unclear, given that Rooms 61A and 62W also contained the greatest number of unburned fiber artifacts at the site. Many of the Salmon fiber artifacts are carbonized black, and some may have been stained with color originally as well. Most colored artifacts in the present sample either date to the Primary occupation or come from the culturally mixed sample from Room 62W and could date to the Primary occupation as well.

A recent survey of the Pueblo Bonito and Aztec assemblages (Webster 2004) revealed several examples of red-stained artifacts. Most are the same purplish-red color as the Salmon objects. Red-stained artifacts from Pueblo Bonito include a plaited sandal from Room 2 and cordage from Room 25. Red-stained objects from the West Ruin at Aztec include a finely twined sandal from Room 54, a sandal from Room 72, and a thick, heavy twined sandal from Room 1252. The sandals from Rooms 54 and 72 were

associated with Chaco trash, whereas the heavy sandal from Room 1252 might date later. All of these rooms contained substantial quantities of ritual materials.

A Possible Ritual Cache of Fiber Artifacts

The interstices (Room 61A) of the Tower Kiva produced a perishable assemblage containing two plaited ring baskets, three pot rests or coils of basketry materials, and a nearly complete, red-colored twined sandal (Table 46.13 and Figures 46.24–27). This could be a ritual offering placed there during construction of the Tower Kiva, ca. AD 1088–1089.

A similar pattern has been reported from two sites in Chaco Canyon. The road ramp above Chetro Ketl (the "Cacique's Sanctum") produced a cache of mostly perishable ritual materials that Mathien (2004:98) has suggested might have been deposited as an offering during road construction. That assemblage included two reed cylinders bound together with yucca cordage, fragments of rush matting, two yucca sandals, two reeds shaped like arrows, a wooden arrow point, several pieces of cotton cloth, yucca string, and two well-preserved shoe-socks.

Judd (1954:323) also found "sacrificial deposits" in several house walls and at least three kivas at Pueblo Bonito. Although most of these deposits consist of nonperishable materials (this could be a problem of preservation), the extensive deposit from Kiva Q yielded the remains of a twined sandal (?) and some shredded juniper and rush materials, in addition to a large quantity of bone, stone, clay, shell artifacts, and seeds. Morris also found offerings beneath the pilasters of several kivas at Aztec, but none included preserved fiber artifacts. Ritual deposits of perishables and other artifacts were also found in some kivas at Antelope House (Morris 1986:281–284).

Mortuary Patterns

Twenty-nine (41%) of the 71 inhumations found at Salmon contained evidence of perishables. Because the preservation of organic materials is highly dependent on the nature of the burial environment, many of the burials interred in less favorable conditions could have originally contained burial wrappings as well. Table 46.47 shows the types of worked fiber artifacts associated with the 29 burials. Nearly 90 percent of these burials were wrapped in plaited mats (several in multiple mats), almost 45 percent in twined fur or feather robes, and about 17 percent in cotton cloth. In most cases, the cotton cloth was poorly preserved and limited to a few tiny fragments; other burials may have contained cotton cloth

Table 46.46. Colored artifacts.

Fea. or Artifact (SA) No.	New FS Cat. No.	Room and Context	Occup	Object Type	Red	Yellow	Blue	Hema-tite?*
SA 37W075	80,068.1	37W, post-occ fill	Primary?	Yucca-leaf tie used to bind coil of sumac (?) twigs	X	–	–	–
Fea. 61A023	80,182	61A, interstitial sp	Primary	Twined sandal	X	–	–	X
–	80,194	62W, trash	Mixed	Yucca-leaf square knot	X	X	–	–
–	80,203.2	62W, trash	Mixed	Yucca cordage	–	X	–	–
–	80,204.1	62W, trash	Mixed	Yucca-leaf square knots	X	–	–	–
–	80,214	62W, trash	Mixed	Yucca-leaf square knots	X	–	–	–
Bot sample 62W2024	80,220	62W, trash	Mixed	Plaited basket or mat	X	–	–	–
–	80,260	62W, trash	Mixed	Yucca ties	X	–	–	–
–	80,263	62W, trash	Mixed	Yucca-leaf square knot	X	–	–	–
–	80,271.2	62W, trash	Mixed	Plaited sandal	X	–		
–	80,291	62W, trash	Mixed	Plaited sandal	X	–	–	X
–	80,296	62W, trash	Mixed	Yucca-leaf square knot	X	X	–	–
–	80,298	62W, trash	Mixed	Yucca-leaf square knot	X	–	–	–
–	80,301	62W, trash	Mixed	Yucca-leaf square knots	X	X	–	–
–	80,305	62W, trash	Mixed	Yucca-leaf square knots	X	X	–	–
–	80,307	62W, trash	Mixed	Yucca-leaf square knot	X	X	–	–
–	80,309	62W, trash	Mixed	Yucca-leaf square knots	X	–	–	–
–	80,312	62W, trash	Mixed	Plaited sandal, basket, or mat	X	–	–	–
–	80,323	62W, trash	Primary	Yucca cordage	X	–	–	–
–	80,324.2	62W, unknown	Unassigned	Yucca-leaf square knot	X	–	–	–
–	80,325	62W, trash	Primary	Plaited ring basket	X	–	–	X
–	80,330.1	62W,trash	Mixed	Yucca-leaf tie used to bind coil of juniper-bark pot rest	X	–	–	–
–	80,334	62W, trash	Mixed	Yucca-leaf square knot	X	X	–	–
–	80,372	90W, trash	Secondary	Yucca-leaf knot (partial)	X	X	–	–
–	80,392	97W, trash	Primary	Plaited mat	X	–	–	–
–	80,403	100W, roof-fall or trash	Primary?	Yucca cordage artifact (altar tassel?)	–	X	–	–
–	N/A	100W, burial 100W302	Primary	Plaited mat	X	–	–	–
–	N/A	100W, infant burial, no no.	Secondary?	Cordage (not collected?)	–	X	X	–
–	80,472	129W, trash	Primary?	Plaited sandal, basket, or mat	X	–	–	–

*Pigment identified as hematite.

Table 46.47. Distribution of worked fiber artifacts with 29 Salmon burials..

Burial No.	Plaited Mat	Twined Robe	Cotton Cloth	Coiled Basket	Plaited Pouch	Sewn/ Twined Mat	Cordage	Knots	Other
4A002, Secondary	X	–	–	–	–	–	X	X	–
33B001, Secondary	X	–	–	X	–	–	X (bowstring)	–	–
33B002, Secondary	X	–	–	–	–	–	–	–	–
33W012, Lt Primary	X	X	X	–	–	X	–	X	Twig bundle
36W003, Secondary	–	–	–	–	–	–	X	–	–
43W003, Secondary	X	X	–	–	X	–	–	–	–
43W005, Secondary	X	X	X	X	X	–	–	X	–
43W019, Secondary	X	X	–	X	–	X	–	–	–
43W057, Secondary	X	X	X	X?	–	–	–	X	Unidentified twined object
62W122, Primary?	X	–	X	–	–	–	–	–	Braid of hair (or yucca?)
97A1001, Secondary	X	–	–	–	–	–	–	X	–
97B002, Secondary	X	–	–	–	–	–	–	–	–
97W1006, Secondary?	X	X	–	–	–	–	–	–	–
97W1007, Secondary?	X	X	–	–	–	–	–	–	–
100W, no number, Sec?	–	–	–	–	–	–	X (blue & yellow)	–	–
100W302, Primary	X	–	–	–	–	–	–	–	–
102W001, Secondary	X	–	–	–	–	–	–	–	–
121W033, Secondary	X	–	–	–	–	–	–	–	–
122-11, Secondary?	X	–	–	–	–	–	–	–	–
123B005, Inter/Sec	X	X	X	–	–	–	X	–	–
127B001, Secondary	X	–	–	–	–	–	–	–	–
127W055, Secondary	X	X	–	–	–	–	–	–	–
127W099, Secondary	X	X	–	–	–	–	–	–	–
127W106, Secondary	X	X	–	X	–	–	–	–	–
127W107, Secondary	X	–	–	–	–	–	–	–	–
127W115, Secondary	X	X	–	–	–	–	–	X	–
127W126, Secondary	–	–	–	X	–	–	–	–	–
127W147, Primary?	X	X	–	–	–	–	–	–	–
129W007, Secondary	X	–	–	–	–	–	–	–	–
% burials with item	89.7%	44.8%	17.2%	20.7%	6.9%	6.9%	17.2%	20.7%	6.9%

that did not survive. (It should be noted that excavators failed to observe many of the cotton fragments that I found intermixed with pieces of twined robes and mats in the sample, and easily could have overlooked other instances of its presence.) Twelve of the 29 burials (41%) were wrapped only in matting, nine (31%) in both mats and twined robes, and four (14%) in all three kinds of wrappings. Baskets, all coiled, accompanied six (21%) of these burials. Two burials (7%) contained plaited pouches filled with plant materials, and two others (7%) were associated with twined reed or sewn willow mats. Cordage and knots, some used as binding cords to hold the wrap-

pings in place, were found with roughly 20 percent of the burials. With the possible exception of the unidentified object with burial 43W057l, no sandals occurred in mortuary contexts.

Irwin-Williams (Chapter 16) attributed only three burials to the Primary occupation. One was a child found in Room 129 without artifacts. The second was an adult female in Room 4W. The third, 100W302, was an unflexed adult found face-down on the floor of Room 100W near a Primary trash heap. As noted, Irwin-Williams (1980:174) suggested that this person's death might have led to the abandonment of this room in Chaco times. According to the field notes, the skull of this individual was covered with red pigment and the imprint of plaited matting. In my opinion, the mat, which did not survive, was probably colored red (see previous discussion of red-stained artifacts). Unlike the other Type 1 rooms at Salmon, Room 100W was never modified or reused during the Secondary occupation, except for trash disposal (Adams and Reed, Chapter 7).

In addition to the two Primary burials in Rooms 100W and 129W, I view two other burials with perishables as possible Primary burials: burial 62W122, an infant interred in Primary occupational fill in Room 62W, associated with a mat, cotton cloth, and braided hair (these items were not located); and burial 127W147, an infant interred in a small pit in a Primary floor in Room 127W, associated with a plaited mat, twined robe, and red ocher.

The only definite Primary burial to produce a diverse burial assemblage was 33W012. This elderly male was accompanied by a wide range of perishable objects, some clearly ceremonial in nature—a bow, nine cane arrows, a prayer stick, layers of matting worked in fine and coarse weave, a twined fur or feather robe, cotton cloth, a small twig bundle, and a reed blind or perhaps a quiver (see discussion of Room 33W for catalog and figure numbers). Irwin-Williams (Chapter 16) identified these as the kinds of accoutrements one might find with a Puebloan Bow Priest, and suggested that this individual might have been a survival from the Chacoan occupation who remained in the pueblo after most of the population had gone.

Several interesting similarities exist between this "bow priest" burial and several burials clustered nearby, attributed to the Secondary occupation; these include burial 33B001 from Room 33B, a later remodel of the same room where the "bow priest" was found, and burials 43W003, 43W005, 43W019, and 43W057 from Room 43W, adjoining Room 33 to the northwest. One individual in burial 33B001, a multiple burial of three individuals, was accompanied by two bows and arrows. This burial also contained matting, a coiled basket, and a White Mountain Red Ware (?) bowl.

The four burials from Room 43W were especially rich in perishable artifacts (see discussion of Room 43W for catalog and figure numbers). 43W003, an adolescent female, was wrapped in a twined robe and matting and accompanied by an elliptically shaped plaited pillow or pouch filled with plant materials. No pottery was found with this burial. Burial 43W005, a child less than 12 years old, was one of the richest burials at Salmon. Wrapped in cotton cloth, a twined robe, and plaited matting, this individual

was accompanied by a small bundle-foundation (?) basket, several small twigs identified as possible miniature arrows, and, like 43W003, a plaited pouch containing a large quantity of plant materials, including corn tassels. Like 43W003, no pottery was found with 43W005. Burial 43W019, an adult female, was wrapped in a twined robe and at least two plaited mats, one with a decorative weave, and associated with at least two coiled baskets, two Mesa Verde Black-on-white bowls, and possibly the remains of a sewn willow mat. 43W057, also an adult female, was wrapped in cotton cloth, a twined robe, and two beautifully worked mats. Burial accompaniments included a Mesa Verde Black-on-white mug and possibly a basket.

To summarize, burials 33B001 and 43W005 both contained bow or arrow paraphernalia, like the late Primary "bow priest" burial 33W012. Also like burial 33W012, burial 43W019 may have contained a specialized mat or blind. Burials 43W003 and 43W005 both contained plaited pouches filled with plant materials. Two burials, 33B001 with a White Mountain Red Ware bowl, and 43W005 with a southern basket form and possibly an imported cotton textile from the south, contained southern-style artifacts.

Potter (1981), who considered only the "Mesa Verde" burials in her thesis, argued for status differentiation between the Secondary burials of Room 43W and all other Secondary burials at Salmon. She noted that no other burials at the site exhibited as great a diversity of burial offerings, especially in regards to perishable artifacts. Although preservation factors might account for this difference, this seems unlikely, given that many other rooms at the site (Room 127W, for instance) also burned, preserving organic materials with several burials. None of these are as richly furnished as the burials in the northwest cluster.

Based on the rich assemblages of fiber artifacts with the burials in Room 43, Potter suggested that these individuals might have been fiber specialists. What I suggest instead is that certain rooms in the northwest part of the pueblo were used as burial chambers by multiple generations of a particular kin group or sodality, perhaps individuals who identified themselves in some way with the founding population of Salmon Pueblo. If a certain social group was associated with this part of the pueblo during the Chacoan occupation, its descendents might have maintained a relationship with this part of the pueblo during the Secondary occupation. Or perhaps a connection was established to this part of the pueblo by real or fictive kin as part of a cultural revitalization movement like that discussed by Bruce

Bradley for Aztec, Salmon, and Wallace Ruin (1996: 246, 251). Indeed, many of the same kinds of objects associated with the burials in Rooms 33 and 43 at Salmon were also found in "Chacoan" mortuary and ritual contexts at Pueblo Bonito and Aztec West. Although the perishable burial accompaniments are not as rich, a similar clustering of burials occurs in several other rooms at Salmon, including Rooms 97 and 127. This use of rooms as burial vaults seems to find its closest parallels in the multiple-interment burial rooms in the western section of Pueblo Bonito (Judd 1954:325–342).

Unlike most rooms at Salmon, Room 43W was never modified by the Secondary occupants, but was set aside for burials and other purposes. A similar situation is seen in Room 100, the site of the other adult Primary burial, which was also never remodeled. The fact that these rooms were maintained for special use during the Secondary occupation suggests that the people who occupied the pueblo during this period possessed intimate knowledge about the earlier significance of certain rooms at the site. These mortuary patterns, and similarities among the worked fiber mortuary assemblages, suggest a strong degree of cultural continuity between the Primary and Secondary occupations at Salmon, more than one would expect if one group of people completely abandoned a pueblo and a second unrelated group later moved in.

EVIDENCE FOR TEXTILE AND BASKETRY PRODUCTION

Evidence for loom weaving at Salmon is currently limited to a single Primary context. In Room 81W, a ceremonial room adjacent to the Tower Kiva, excavators found a concentration of four wooden weaving tools and a small ceramic bowl on a roof-like platform or rack (Table 46.48 and Figures 46.43, 44). Although the field notes indicate that four wooden tools were found, only three appear to have been assigned significant artifact numbers and collected. Two are small battens for backstrap looms, only one of which was located (SA 81W253=W080-23, Figure 46.87a). SA 81W253 measures 4 cm wide and 22.4 cm long, and is highly polished at the ends. SA 81W251, not located, is described on the SA form as a possible weaving stick 25 cm in length, very thin, and smoothed at both ends. Another object, SA 81W354, also not located, is described on the significant artifact form as a flat and smoothed piece of wood with a smoothed square edge and one broken end. Its size and function are unknown. Field sketches of these latter two objects are shown in Figure 46.87b and c.

A small, smooth-sided bowl (SA 81W252) was found 45 cm from batten SA 81W253 (Figure 46.43). Excavators considered the two objects to be associated. On the significant artifact form and in the field notes, the bowl is described as round-bottomed, decorated with black paint, with two small mending holes on one side. Its presence among the wooden objects is intriguing because small bowls were used both prehistorically and historically in Mexico and historically in the Rio Grande to support the spindle shaft during spinning. To my knowledge, the use of a bowl is not characteristic of historic Hopi spinning.

This inferred use of backstrap looms at Salmon corresponds with other evidence for the weaving of cotton textiles at Chaco, Aztec, and Mesa Verde. All of the loom parts I have seen from these sites (including loom bars from Pueblo Bonito and a complete loom from Aztec) correlate with the use of the backstrap loom. The association of the Salmon weaving assemblage with a room adjacent to the Tower Kiva also fits the regional pattern recorded thus far for Chaco and Aztec. (My study of weaving at Chaco and Aztec is still in the preliminary stage, and these conclusions are liable to change.) At the West Ruin of Aztec, a complete backstrap loom, including both

Table 46.48. Weaving tools.

Object's Field ID	New FS Cat. No.	Room and Context	Occup	No. of Objects	Object Type	Comments
SA 081W251	N/A	81W, roof-fall	Primary	1	Wooden batten	Described on SA form as "possible weaving stick"; smoothed and shaped on ends
SA 081W252	N/A	81W, roof-fall	Primary	1	Small ceramic bowl with rounded base	Used to support base of spindle?
SA 081W253	W080-000023	81W, roof-fall	Primary	1	Wooden batten	Described on SA form as "loom tool" with rounded end
SA 081W354	N/A	81W, roof-fall	Primary	1	Unknown	Described on SA form as "wood tool"; found with other weaving tools

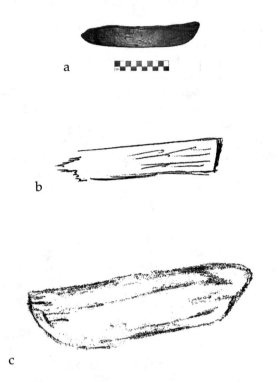

Figure 46.87. Weaving tools from Room 81W. (a) W080-23 (SA 81W253), batten for backstrap loom. For in situ view, see Figures 43 and 44. (c) SA 81W251, field sketch from significant artifact form. (b) SA 81W354, field sketch from significant artifact form.

end bars and a batten, and two wooden spindle whorls were recovered from Room 115, adjoining Chacoan Kiva L, analogous to the Tower Kiva at Salmon. Other weaving-related artifacts (possible loom bars, yucca needles threaded with cotton yarn, possible cotton seeds) came from Chaco trash in Rooms 48 and 1222 (Webster 2004).

At Pueblo Bonito, all published examples of backstrap loom bars are also associated with ceremonial rooms (Kiva D, Room 32, and the burial chamber in Room 320). All but one of the possible spindle whorls were found in rooms (226, 266, and 327) adjacent to kivas. Two possible loom anchors for waist (backstrap) looms came from storeroom 296, and a squash-rind spindle whorl came from Room 2, both located in the oldest part of the pueblo (Judd 1954:153–155, Figure 42a, b, Plates 38k, n, o, 39b, c, 72h, i; Pepper 1920:38, 157, Figure 64f). These distributions suggest that the weaving and spinning of cotton at Chaco, Salmon, and Aztec was already a

ritually focused activity by ca. 1100 AD, just as it was at the time of European contact (Webster 1997, 2000).

In another possible reference to loom weaving at Salmon, R. Adams and P. Reed (Chapter 7) have described the occurrence of small post or loom holes in the Secondary floors of several single-story Type 1 plaza-facing rooms. I have not seen the feature maps for these rooms and cannot verify this information. However, present evidence from Chaco, Aztec, and Mesa Verde suggests that loom holes were not common floor features at these sites, so at this point I am skeptical that wide upright looms were in use at Salmon. Future study of the Secondary floor features at Salmon may help resolve this question.

Citing the absence of cotton seeds, bolls, and other cotton plant parts at Salmon, Bohrer and Doebley (Chapter 35) have argued that cotton was not grown at the site. If it had been a significant crop, macrobotanical evidence should have survived in the burned rooms or in the extensive unburned trash deposit in Room 62W. Bohrer believed that cotton cordage and woven goods were imported into Salmon during both the Primary and Secondary occupations. Based on the presence of weaving tools in Room 81W, I think that some weaving of cotton textiles did occur at the site, using, in all likelihood, imported cotton fiber. However, given the limited evidence for weaving at Salmon, it is likely that cotton textiles were also traded into the site to meet the needs of the community.

Instead of cotton fabrics, it was the manufacture of baskets, sandals, mats, and turkey-feather blankets that probably dominated production of perishables at the site, perhaps rivaling the production of pottery. Presently, the only evidence for these craft activities at Salmon are the coils of plant raw materials—sumac, yucca, willow—that I have tentatively interpreted as bundles of prepared raw materials for craft production from Room 62W and several other rooms. Other indirect evidence includes an increase in quantities of turkey bones at Salmon (see Durand and Durand, Chapter 50), which appears to correspond with the increased use of twined turkey-feather blankets during the Secondary occupation. Exactly where the production of these craft items was occurring is still to be resolved. Information about the distribution of bone awls and of stone tools related to yucca processing (Bohrer and Adams, Chapter 38) could shed additional light on the loci of perishables production at Salmon.

Chapter 47

LITHIC ASSEMBLAGE FROM SALMON RUINS

by Phillip H. Shelley

Archaeological work at Salmon Pueblo produced an assemblage of more than 120,000 lithic items, including projectile points, other flaked tools, ornaments, debitage, and ground stone. Lithic research is one of the topics that received no new attention during the Salmon Research Initiative. Some references have been updated in this chapter but most of what is presented here was taken (with editing) from the 1980 Salmon final report, from earlier lithic studies on Salmon, and from Phil Shelley's 1983 dissertation.

SALMON LITHICS LABORATORY PERSONNEL, METHODOLOGY, AND SAMPLING

When the Salmon Project was initiated in the early 1970s, lithic studies were not considered critical to understanding Puebloan adaptations. The Salmon lithic laboratory was thus one of the first for such a large-scale endeavor. It was organized and in operation during the summer of 1972 (Irwin-Williams and Bronstein 1972), but because of personnel changes, it went through several transformations over the course of the project. The various laboratory directors were Nancy Bronstein, Lonnie Pippin, Rex Adams, Eugene Hattori, Tim McCormack, Robert Lawrence, and, ultimately, Phil Shelley (from 1977 through 1980). More than 15 students worked in the lithics laboratory, and two of these individuals completed master's theses on Salmon materials at Eastern New Mexico University (Roger Moore in 1981 and Jimmy McNeil in 1986). Phil Shelley completed his doctoral dissertation on Salmon lithics at Washington State University in 1983 (Shelley 1983). With his permission, much of Shelley's dissertation is included here, as it adds substantially to our understanding of lithic use at Salmon.

The initial lithic analysis for Salmon used a "shotgun" approach to search for patterned variation of attributes (Irwin-Williams 1973; Shelley 1983:47). Many attributes were recorded for debitage, tools, and cores, but there was no clear connection between the collected data and specific research questions. Furthermore, the attribute analysis was very time consuming. Except for a test case (R. Adams 1980b), such analysis was rarely used for other projects and never for the Salmon assemblage. Instead, Tim McCormick developed a rough-sort analysis designed to collect basic data for a high percentage of all lithic artifacts from the site (McCormick and Cameron 1974). Whereas the attribute analysis called for the collection of too much data without clear justification, the rough-sort approach perhaps erred on the other side. Only five attributes were recorded: raw material type, gross artifact class (e.g., debitage, projectile point, metate), artifact condition, provenience, and count. The gross artifact categories did not discriminate general classes into usable, traditional morphological types (e.g., slab, trough, or basin metate) or identify presence or absence of cortex on debitage. Thus, the scantiness of the data collected significantly limited the usefulness of the analysis. These shortcomings were apparent to Shelley when he assumed direction of the lithics laboratory in 1977. Still, with roughly 40,000 items analyzed to that point, Shelley wanted to maintain consistency in approach. As he acknowledged in retrospect, however, data were collected for more than 70,000 lithic artifacts during his tenure, and revising the rough sort would have been a prudent course of action. Nevertheless, roughly 112,000 items were analyzed using the rough-sort system. Of these, 52,600 could be confidently assigned to an unmixed temporal period (Table 47.1).

Concurrently with the rough-sort analysis, attribute analyses were undertaken on morphologically defined tool classes. These analyses were designed to answer questions concerning variation within and between recognized tool classes. Studies of this type for Salmon include Moore's (1981) projectile point thesis and McNeil's (1986) examination of ornaments. Because tools were selected on the basis of morphology only, the resulting samples were generally not appropriate for addressing spatial and functional questions in conjunction with ceramic, ethnobotanic, and faunal data.

Table 47.1. Frequency of Salmon lithic artifacts by strata type (T, F, C, etc.) and cultural component (n = 52,660).

	T	F	C	G	H	I	L	Other	Total
Primary	731	2377	4509	4919	957	193	627	2473	16,786
	4.4%	14.2%	26.9%	29.3%	5.7%	1.1%	3.7%	14.7%	100.0%
Secondary	0	6025	20,053	1097	956	1031	837	5875	35,874
	0.0%	16.8%	55.9%	3.1%	2.7%	2.9%	2.3%	16.4%	100.0%

T: construction debris, G: occupational fill, L: pit/feature fill, F: roof/roof fall, H: floor surface, C: structured (stratified) trash, I: structural floor, Other: predominantly postoccupational fill and unstructured trash.

Consequently, Shelley developed attribute-level analyses for all other types of lithic artifacts (Shelley, Chapter 47). This analysis was undertaken on a sample of lithic items from various living surfaces; this work was completed by Shelley for his dissertation and is reproduced here. Because the finely tuned attribute studies were developed late in the project, and because of the number and complexity of variables examined, only 794 items were analyzed using this system.

The field methodology for treatment of lithic materials was determined largely by the overall field approach for the Salmon Project. Specialized procedures for lithic materials consisted of (1) extra protection of lithic materials by individual wrapping and bagging; (2) preservation of adhering material on certain artifacts with potential for residue studies via a "no-washing" policy; and (3) collection of soil matrix samples. While minimizing archaeologically introduced edge damage (Muto 1979; Schutt 1978), separate bagging also minimized the potential for matching and refitting artifacts (Cahen et al. 1979). In retrospect, the best solution to this problem might have been to include all material from a single provenience in one bag, after individually wrapping each item. In this way, the artifacts would have been protected and the analysts would have been able to view the larger sample from the provenience, perhaps representing a discrete prehistoric activity.

Washing lithic artifacts, whether or not visible materials can be seen adhering, is standard procedure in most Southwest archaeology laboratories, but the practice can result in loss of much information about tool use (Briuer 1976; Clouse 1977; Holloway and Shafer 1978). In depositional situations where there is a high probability that deposition was rapid and that the material adhering to the tool is the result of use, it is best to avoid washing items until artifacts are examined in the laboratory. To confidently utilize observations on the presence or absence of exogenous materials on a tool, it is necessary to compare materials from a control sample to

the tool to be certain that the adhering material is in fact culturally and not environmentally derived. From the 1978 Salmon field season forward, tools were not washed and soil matrix samples from identified depositional situations were collected as control samples. Though none of these samples have been analyzed, and no residue studies were conducted on the original Salmon Project, the materials are available for future investigation.

LOCAL AND REGIONAL RAW MATERIALS

To evaluate the availability of the local rocks used to make tools, raw material transects were conducted on the Pleistocene terraces adjacent to the site (Shelley, Chapter 47). Information from these transects allowed qualitative and quantitative comparisons between the local resources and the raw materials found at the site.

Regional studies of raw materials were conducted after a review of the geological literature and consultations with geologists. Any nonlocal material present in the assemblage was identified in the nearest primary or secondary deposits, and comparative samples were collected. In some instances (e.g., Narbona Pass chert), it was possible to establish the origin of nonlocal materials, whereas in others (e.g., baked shale) it was possible only to establish probable source areas. When possible, raw materials were assigned labels according to the classification of northwestern New Mexico material types developed by geologist Helene Warren and reported in Harris et al. (1967). Warren developed her typology by examining lithic materials at their source areas. Although it depends on macroscopic characters and hence cannot be considered completely diagnostic, it has proved to be useful and is widely used within the San Juan Basin and adjacent areas.

The San Juan, Animas, and La Plata River terraces were sampled by transects to assess variation in local lithic resources. "Local" is here considered synonymous with "catchment area" (Vita-Finzi and Higgs 1970:5–7). Chisholm (1968) concluded that the area routinely exploited by agriculturalists is usually within a 4 km radius of the settlement. This figure was used to delimit an area around Salmon Pueblo to be sampled for local lithic materials; La Plata River gravels, although 12 km from Salmon, were also considered local and so were sampled (Figure 47.1). Like the San Juan and Animas River gravels, they are an easily accessible, concentrated lithic source. More than 1000 rocks were examined per drainage. A statistical comparison (the Wilcoxon signed ranked test; Conover 1971) of the lithology of these various alluvial gravels shows that the San Juan and Animas terraces are not significantly different at the 0.001 significance level. These results were anticipated because of differences in the bedrock geology of the streams' respective headwaters, as well as in patterns of glacial erosion at the headwaters during the Pleistocene (Atwood and Mather 1932; Baker 1968; Bandoian 1968; Silver 1951).

The principal difference in lithologies between the drainages is the frequent inclusion, in La Plata River terraces, of granodiorite, sandstone, and cryptocrystalline silicate rocks. Such materials are relatively scarce on the San Juan and Animas Rivers. In addition, certain variants within previously published raw material type descriptions (Warren in Harris et al. 1967:120–125) occur in relatively high frequencies in La Plata terraces. These include a white to light tan (Munsell 2.5Y 9/2 to 2.5 and 8.5/6) chert with dark inclusions, and the distinctive Brushy Basin chert, which resembles Warren's Type 1040 (reported in Harris et al. 1967:120–121). This Brushy Basin chert is a micro to cryptocrystalline, pale green (Munsell 5G 8/2), silicified sediment that exhibits no relict sedimentary structure and has occasional quartz inclusions.

The increased frequency of granodioritic and sandstone rocks in La Plata River terraces is not particularly important to an interpretation of the availability of local lithic raw material, but the presence of Warren's Type 1040 is. Brushy Basin chert was frequently used for flaked stone tool production in the San Juan Basin, and was thought to have been imported to Salmon (Harris et al. 1967:120–121). However, its presence in La Plata River gravels suggests that it was locally available to the Salmon inhabitants. The relative frequencies of lithic raw materials observed in these transects are shown in Table 47.2.

Other raw materials that occur locally but that are uncommon in terrace gravels include silicified woods and chalcedony as lag from the pediment surface on the south and north sides of the San Juan River, and sandstones (Ojo Alamo, Nacimiento, and San Jose) from bedrock exposures north and south of the San Juan River. These local rock types, plus those from the terrace gravels, were the most important in both the Chacoan and Secondary lithic production systems at Salmon Pueblo.

An additional local lithic source that must be considered for the Secondary occupation is within the site itself. Materials lost or discarded during the Chacoan occupation were available for use by the Secondary occupants. For example, parts of ground stone tools produced during the Chacoan occupation (e.g., trough metates) were used as building elements in Secondary architectural contexts.

Production specialization is related to the presence of distribution systems, so archaeological evidence on the distribution and use of nonlocal raw material may provide an additional means for identifying the degree of lithic specialization. Identifying the source areas for these raw materials may also provide a basis for determining the extent of the distribution system by which specialists acquired these materials.

Even though the sources of imported raw materials cannot be evaluated quantitatively, in some instances it is possible to delimit zones of origin for nonlocal lithic materials. The degree of certainty with which areas of origin can be determined is dependent upon the degree of internal homogeneity of specific rock types (Ayers 1978; Aspinall and Feather 1972; Jack 1976). A metamorphosed sedimentary rock such as Brushy Basin chert varies greatly in composition, and is therefore quite difficult to characterize, by any technique. Other materials, such as the homogeneous and distinctive Narbona (Washington) Pass chert, a hydrothermal chalcedony, can be characterized by many techniques.

Trace element determination techniques (such as neutron activation or x-ray fluorescence) were not applied to the Salmon lithic materials. Instead, lithic materials were assigned to rock classes using published geological and archaeological type descriptions. The assignments were based on physical and mineralogical characteristics. Therefore, in most instances only general statements regarding probable source area can be made.

CONTEXT OF THE LITHIC SAMPLES

Lithic analyses were conducted at the same time as other analyses during the Salmon Project. Materials were analyzed as they were received in the laboratory, regardless of their context. This resulted in a basic level of analysis of tool and raw material types for more than 112,000 lithic items.

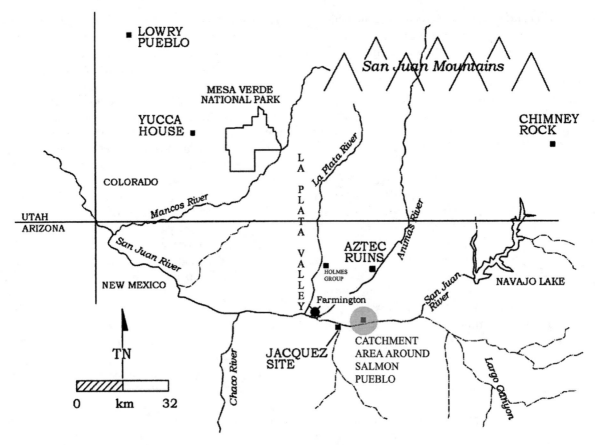

Figure 47.1. Map of region around Salmon showing catchment area sampled for lithic raw materials.

During the course of analysis, Salmon Project personnel became concerned about substantial differences between the stratigraphic associations of the Chacoan and Secondary occupations. The majority of the Chacoan assemblage occurred in G (occupational fill) strata, whereas most of the Secondary occupation materials occurred in C (structured trash) strata (see Table 47.1). Field personnel suggested that this difference might be more apparent than real. They had observed that where trash was lying on floors, it was extremely difficult to observe a physical separation between the upper portion of the G strata and lower C deposits. In these instances, the G designation was assigned to material in contact with or just above assumed living surfaces. Because identification of activity areas was planned, it became important to determine whether G strata actually resulted from occupation of the room floors. Several studies have addressed such concerns. For example, Priesnitz (1979) made an attempt to reconstruct pottery vessels from four Chacoan occupation rooms where trash (C strata) rested directly on top of floor fill (G strata). A minimum number of identifiable vessels was determined for each room, and sherds from

both types of strata in the four rooms were matched (Priesnitz 1979:87–113). In all cases, Priesnitz found that sherds from the same vessel had been assigned to both the floor fill and the overlying trash. In the four rooms studied, the percentages of vessels that were stratigraphically mixed were 80, 62, 25, and 2 percent (Priesnitz 1979:123–124).

Similarly, in 8 of 16 cases, chi-square tests showed no significant difference at the 0.05 level between the relative frequencies of ceramic types in combined G, H, and I strata (all floor associated) and the C strata immediately overlying them (Franklin 1980:303–311). These results indicate that where Chacoan floors are directly overlain by trash deposits (as they are in 14 of 21 cases in the lithic sample), there is a 50 percent probability that the floor fill material is part of the postoccupational trash. As Franklin (1980:320–321) noted, however, there is also the possibility that the distinction between G and C strata was valid, but that the same types and frequencies of material were deposited in both.

Lithics from Chacoan floor-associated deposits were compared with those from overlying strata using relative frequencies of tool types and artifact

Table 47.2. Raw material types in the San Juan, Animas, and La Plata river drainages.

Raw Material	San Juan n = 1000	Animas n = 1000	La Plata n = 1000
Quartzite coarse grained (F,G)	36.1	40.2	8.1
Quartzite fine grained (F,G)	14.1	14.7	11.5
Andesite (F,G)	10.4	2.6	1.2
Granite (F,G)	9.4	18.1	47.4
Sandstone (G)	7.7	7.0	20.1
Basalt coarse grained (F,G)	6.2	3.6	0.8
Basalt fine grained (F,G)	5.4	1.6	0.7
Metamorphic other (F,G)	3.9	3.1	2.6
Schist (G)	2.3	3.2	–
Orthoquartzite-nacimiento (F,G)	2.2	0.2	–
Chert other (F)	1.2	0.4	2.1
Igneous other (F,G)	0.5	0.2	2.0
Limestone other (G)	0.3	0.2	–
Gneiss (G)	0.2	0.5	–
Felsite (F,G)	0.2	1.7	1.0
Mudstone-siltstone* (F)	–	–	2.0
Sedimentary other (G)	–	0.2	–
Slate (G)	–	0.1	–
Greenstone (G)	–	1.5	0.2
Quartz massive (F,G)	–	0.1	–
Indeterminate	–	0.2	0.5

*Warren's Lithic Type No. 1040 (Harris et al. 1967:120–121).
F = suitable for making flaked stone tools; G = suitable for making ground stone tools.

raw material classes. In small samples, some variables were combined (e.g., both retouched and non-retouched flake tools were grouped as flake tools). In the 14 cases where trash deposits lay on the floor, tests indicated no significant difference at the 0.05 level between materials from the floor-associated G stratum and the superimposed C stratum. In the remaining five cases, where other types of deposits overlay the floor-associated material, the overlying deposits were significantly different in only one case. In this instance, the assemblages were significantly different in artifact lithology frequencies but not in tool type frequencies (Table 47.3); however, the combinations made because of small sample size may have decreased the sensitivity of these tests.

Another factor that may have affected the stratigraphic associations of Chacoan and Secondary assemblages is a single enigmatic lithic feature (Feature 42, Room 43W). More than 88 percent of the 2761 lithic items are unground sandstone fragments and unmodified quartzite cobbles. I can offer no behavioral interpretation of this feature, but it is a unique kind of secondary trash deposit. If the lithic assemblage from this feature were subtracted from the G stratum sample (see Table 47.3) and added to

the C stratum sample, Chacoan occupation C materials would equal 43.3 percent and G materials 12.9 percent of the total. These proportions of post-occupational trash to floor-associated materials may be more representative of the true relationship than are the unaltered frequencies.

These comparisons and discussions do not unequivocally demonstrate that the substantial differences in the stratigraphic associations of Chacoan and Secondary lithic materials are more apparent than real. They do, however, support such an interpretation. In any case, the comparisons show that the assemblages from the two contexts are quite similar.

The information on debitage and core attributes presented here is based on intensive analysis of a sample of assemblages from living surfaces (Table 47.4); the sample contains 794 items (252 Chacoan and 542 Secondary). The proveniences from which the materials came were selected judgmentally. The purpose of the sampling was to obtain as wide a range of information as possible from a set of living surfaces, so the activities that took place on these surfaces could be inferred. Plant remains were expected to provide useful information, yet they were not always well preserved, so the first criterion in

Table 47.3. Chi-square comparisons of artifact lithologies for Chacoan occupation floor units and immediately overlying strata.

Room	Floor Unit	Overlying Strata Type	Degrees of Freedom (K-1)	Chi-square Statistic	Significant at 0.05 Level ?
1W	G-5-53	roof	17	8.45	no
1W	G-6-57	roof	19	16.37	no
3W	G-1-04	roof	15	10.66	no
6W	G-1-10	trash	21	22.42	no
33W	G-1.5-14.5	trash	19	9.03	no
43W	G-1-10	trash	23	19.65	no
62W	G-1-40	trash	17	8.97	no
62W	G-2-47.5	trash	13	13.29	no
82A	G-1-23	trash	15	10.86	no
82W	G-1.5-23.5	trash	15	15.39	no
84W	G-1-06	trash	17	8.94	no
93W*	H-4-28	roof	13	11.72	no
93W*	H-6-36	artificial fill	11	5.38	no
98W	G-1-07	trash	15	19.07	no
101W	G-1-08	trash	9	13.37	no
124W	G-2-08	kiva floor	13	30.82	yes
128A	G-1-06	artificial fill	9	12.3	no
129W	G-1-92.1	trash	11	6.34	no
193W	G-1-93	trash	13	9.97	no
129W	G-2-136.8	trash	13	3.88	no

*This room excavated to these levels before institution of G strata designation.

sample selection was the degree of preservation of plant macrofossils from the flotation samples. Twenty-two Chacoan floors and two Chacoan roofs were classed as having samples with "best" or "moderate" botanical preservation (Bohrer 1980:167–168). From these, seven floors and one roof were selected so as to provide a wide distribution of locations in the pueblo. This resulted in selection of one floor from the West Wing, two floors from the west arm, one floor and a roof adjacent to the centrally located Tower Kiva, two floors from the east arm, and one floor from the East Wing. Secondary occupation floors or roofs, which had similar conditions of preservation, were then selected from the same or adjacent rooms (Figure 47.2). From this group of proveniences, all lithic, ceramic, botanical, and faunal materials were analyzed intensively. The results of these analyses were to be used to address questions about spatial and functional patterns and associations. Unfortunately, these analyses were never completed.

This admittedly small sample comprises 1.9 percent of the lithics from Chacoan occupation floor and trash strata and 1.8 percent of the lithics from Secondary occupation floor and trash strata. Because this sample is small and was not randomly selected, inferences derived from the analyses are tentative.

However, these samples provide the only information to date on some of the aspects of flaked stone technology that may relate to specialization.

In contrast, the attribute information on projectile points and tchamahias (stone digging stick tips) comes from analysis of all artifacts of these classes in the Salmon assemblage. Because they are based on a complete sample, inferences from these analyses are much firmer than the core and debitage attribute data.

LITHIC RESOURCE EXPLOITATION PATTERNS

Given the predominance of locally available lithic materials in both Chacoan and Secondary occupation assemblages, the reuse of materials and surfaces, and the relative insensitivity of rough-sort analysis, a quantitative evaluation using lithic data of the hypothesis concerning "increased effective control over the environment" (Irwin-Williams 1977:73) must be delayed until the data generated through attribute analysis can be more fully reduced and manipulated. Even so, some quantitative data can be brought to bear on the hypothesis.

Data presented here show that the "total range of raw material employed in everyday life" (Irwin-Williams 1977:73) was greater in the Secondary occupation than in the Chacoan occupation. This is

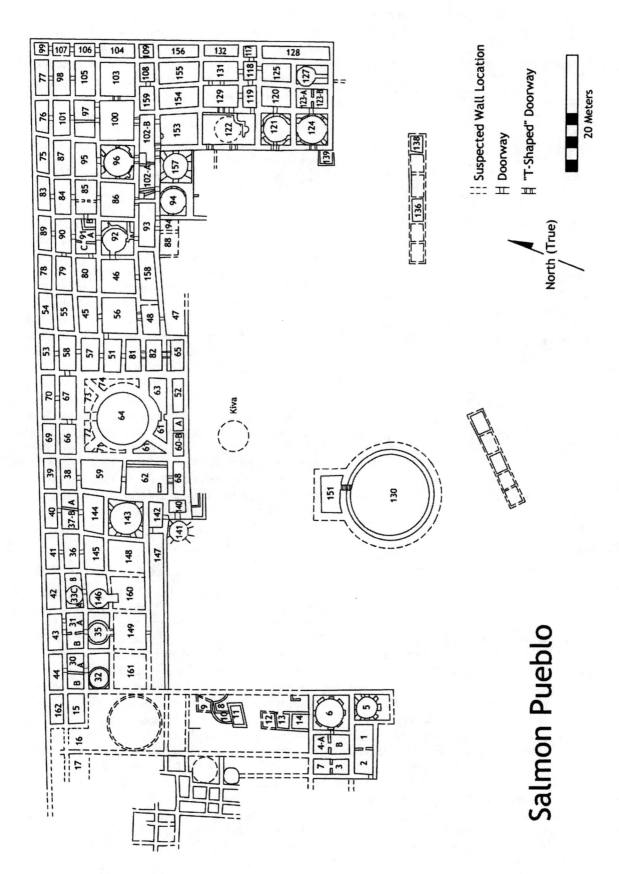

Salmon Pueblo

Suspected Wall Location
Doorway
"T-Shaped" Doorway

20 Meters

North (True)

Figure 47.2. Map showing rooms sampled for intensive lithic study at Salmon.

Table 47.4. Proveniences from which all lithic materials were analyzed at an attribute level.

Room	Stratum	Cultural Affiliation	Frequency
6A	H-1-05.2	S	101
6A	L-1-05.3	S	16
6W	L-1-10	C	4
6W	G-1-01	C	25
6W	O-1-03	C	12
8A	H-1-07	S	30
30W	H-2-12	C	17
30W	I-2-13	C	3
56W	H-1-05	C	15
56W	I-1-06	C	10
57W	H-1-08	S?	21
58W	H-1-08	S	58
58W	H-2-11	S	43
62W	G-1-40	C	31
81W	F-2-13	C	10
82W	H-1-26	C	11
82W	G-1-23	C	12
82W	G-1.5-23.5	C	8
84W	H-1-08	C	17
93W	H-1-14	R	2
93W	H-2-22	S	48
93W	I-5-34	C	22
101W	H-1-09	C	17
124A	G-1-05	S	115
124A	L-9-0.5	S	19
124A	I-1-07	S	23
124A	H-1-06	S	31
124A	F-1-07	S	16
124W	H-2-09	I?/S	21
129W	G-2-136.9	C	36
Total (30 rooms)			794

C = Chacoan; S = Secondary; I = Intermediate; R = Redeposited (uncertain); ? = assignment uncertain.

contrary to the expected results derived from the model proposed by Irwin-Williams, but reuse factors may account for this pattern to a large degree.

It seems reasonable to suggest that the aspect of the model that led to these expected test results should be reexamined and possibly modified. For example, should one expect that decreasing social complexity (as extant during Secondary times) would necessarily lead to less selectivity and more random variation in lithic exploitation patterns of raw materials to produce tools for day-to-day jobs at Salmon when one considers lithomechanical constraints and local raw material availability? It seems not. Instead, perhaps lithic specialization suggests increasing social complexity.

Tables 47.5 and 47.6 contrast the distributions of raw materials among flaked stone lithic and tool classes for the Salmon Chacoan and Secondary occupations, respectively. These tables describe all flaked stone artifacts assigned to the Chacoan and Secondary occupations of Salmon Ruins, including ornaments; both locally and regionally available materials are included. When the small samples (less than 50 items) of raw material are disregarded, few substantial differences between occupations are apparent in the raw materials used for the various classes of tools.

Coarse and fine-grained quartzites appear to have been preferred for unifacial and bifacial core chopping tools during both occupations. However, the Secondary occupants also selected substantial amounts of basalts and andesites for these tools. As indicated by transect studies, these materials are readily available, and they are quite knappable.

Local cherts, chalcedonies, and petrified woods were favored in both occupations for flake tool and projectile point production. Of these cryptocrystalline silicates, chert was the most favored (see Tables 47.5 and 47.6). In the Chacoan occupation sample, which is one third the size of the Secondary occupation sample, there are substantially more tested and untested nodules of chert, chalcedony, and petrified wood (352 in Chacoan context and 244 in Secondary context). This suggests that the Chacoan artisans more commonly warehoused these raw materials for use in projectile point and flake tool production, as would be expected if they were more specialized than the Secondary occupation flintworkers.

Primary (Chacoan) Occupation

The importation of lithic raw material through a regional exchange system during the Chacoan occupation seems to be supported by patterned variation in the frequency and spatial distribution of Narbona (Washington) Pass chert at Salmon. Minimal manipulation of attribute data also suggests that this material was entering Salmon as reduced cores, as indicated by the complete absence of Chacoan decortication flakes and the total lack of cortex on discarded cores. This may reflect an attempt to minimize transportation costs and waste, or differentiation-specialization in procurement. A future comparison of other Narbona Pass core attributes (e.g., size, systematics, and directionality) with those derived from some Chaco Canyon sites (e.g., Pueblo Alto) may facilitate an expanded explanation of the occurrence of Narbona Pass chert in the Salmon Chacoan assemblage.

Table 47.5. Primary component flaked stone rough sort percentages for all strata.

Lithic Class	Obsidian Other (1) n=16	Basalt Fine (5) n=432	Basalt Coarse (6) n=773	Andesite (9) n=722	Igneous Other (18) n=286	Limestone Other (21) n=85	Mudstone/ Siltstone (23) n=17	Ortho-quartzite Nacimiento (29) n=17	Ortho-quartzite Other (30) n=15
Modified stone (5) n=605	0.0	2.3	2.3	10.9	18.5	4.7	11.8	5.9	0.0
Unmodified stone (6) n=733	0.0	0.9	0.3	10.2	12.6	2.4	5.9	11.8	0.0
Hammerstone (29) n=246	0.0	0.5	0.8	1.9	2.4	10.6	5.9	0.0	20.0
Chopper-uniface (30) n=99	0.0	1.2	0.6	1.0	0.3	0.0	0.0	0.0	0.0
Chopper-biface (31) n=108	0.0	1.4	1.7	2.2	0.0	2.4	0.0	0.0	0.0
Core-chopper (53) n=62	0.0	1.9	0.8	0.6	0.0	0.0	0.0	0.0	0.0
Core-pounder (54) n=82	0.0	1.2	0.5	0.0	0.7	0.0	0.0	11.8	0.0
Core-chop-pounder (55) n=66	0.0	1.2	0.4	0.6	0.3	1.2	0.0	0.0	0.0
Chopper-pounder (56) n=358	0.0	4.2	2.3	3.2	1.7	4.7	0.0	0.0	0.0
Pounder-abrader (57) n=155	0.0	1.9	1.2	2.5	3.8	0.0	5.9	11.8	0.0
Chopper-abrader (58) n=122	0.0	5.3	0.9	1.7	2.4	0.0	0.0	0.0	0.0
Chop-pound-abrad (61) n=188	0.0	6.3	1.6	4.6	2.1	0.0	0.0	5.9	0.0
Core-abrader (62) n=31	0.0	0.9	0.6	0.3	0.3	1.2	0.0	0.0	0.0
Composite-other (66) n=27	0.0	0.7	0.4	0.3	0.7	0.0	0.0	0.0	0.0
Core rejuven. flk. (63) n=8	0.0	0.0	0.0	0.3	0.0	0.0	5.9	0.0	0.0
Core-other (69) n=128	0.0	2.1	0.1	1.1	0.3	4.7	11.8	0.0	0.0
Flake tools ret w/out proj (76) n=35	6.3	0.0	0.4	0.1	0.0	0.0	0.0	0.0	0.0
Flake tls non-ret w/proj (77) n=45	6.3	0.0	0.0	0.1	0.0	0.0	0.0	0.0	0.0
Flake tls non-ret w/proj (78) n=637	37.5	3.5	4.5	3.2	0.7	4.7	5.9	5.9	0.0
Projectile point (84) n=54	12.5	0.0	0.0	0.0	0.0	0.0	0.0	0.0	20.0
Debitage (93) n=9167	37.5	64.8	80.6	55.3	52.8	63.5	47.1	47.1	40.0

Table 47.5 (continued)

Lithic Class	Quartzite Fine (37) n = 1584	Quartzite Coarse (38) n = 5101	Metamorphic Other (45) n = 406	Chalcedony/Agate (48) n = 658	Petrified Wood (50) n = 429	Jasper (51) n = 44	Chert Other (52) n = 2061	Chert Narbona Pass (55) n = 19	Quartz Massive (56) n = 10
Modified stone (5) n = 605	4.0	4.5	14.0	0.5	1.7	6.8	3.4	0.3	21.1
Unmodified stone (6) n = 733	3.1	4.7	8.4	1.2	0.7	20.5	12.4	0.3	57.9
Hammerstone (29) n = 246	0.8	2.9	2.2	0.3	0.5	0.0	1.5	0.0	0.0
Chopper-uniface (30) n = 99	0.6	1.2	1.7	0.0	0.2	0.0	0.0	0.0	0.0
Chopper-biface (31) n = 108	0.4	1.2	0.7	0.0	0.0	0.0	0.0	0.0	0.0
Core-chopper (53) n = 62	0.7	0.6	0.0	0.0	0.2	0.0	0.1	0.0	0.0
Core-pounder (54) n = 82	0.6	0.9	0.7	0.0	0.0	0.0	0.5	0.0	5.3
Core-chop-pounder (55) n = 66	0.4	0.6	1.0	0.0	0.2	0.0	0.5	0.0	0.0
Chopper-pounder (56) n = 358	0.8	4.9	4.7	0.0	0.0	0.0	0.3	0.0	0.0
Pounder-abrader (57) n = 155	0.8	1.6	2.7	0.0	0.0	0.0	0.0	0.0	0.0
Chopper-abrader (58) n = 122	0.3	1.0	3.9	0.0	0.2	0.0	0.0	0.0	0.0
Chop-pound-abrad (61) n = 188	1.2	1.4	4.4	0.0	0.0	0.0	0.0	0.0	0.0
Core-abrader (62) n = 31	0.1	0.3	0.7	0.0	0.0	0.0	0.0	0.0	0.0
Composite-other (66) n = 27	0.1	0.2	0.5	0.3	0.2	2.3	0.0	0.0	0.0
Core rejuven. flk. (63) n = 8	0.1	0.0	0.0	0.0	0.0	0.0	0.1	0.5	0.0
Core-other (69) n = 128	2.3	0.6	0.2	3.2	5.4	2.3	3.4	2.3	0.0
Flake tools ret w/out proj (76) n = 35	0.3	0.1	0.0	0.9	0.7	0.0	0.3	1.6	0.0
Flake tls non-ret w/ proj (77) n = 45	0.2	0.1	0.0	1.5	1.2	0.0	0.4	2.6	0.0
Flake tls non-ret w/ proj (78) n = 637	3.9	2.1	1.5	13.2	15.1	2.3	7.0	19.2	5.3
Projectile point (84) n = 54	0.3	0.0	0.0	2.9	1.2	4.5	0.9	0.0	0.0
Debitage (93) n = 9167	79.0	71.1	52.5	76.0	72.4	61.4	69.0	73.3	10.5

Categories (raw material or tool class) with at least 0.1% are shown. Lithic rough sort category codes are indicated in parentheses in column and row headings.

Table 47.6. Secondary component flaked stone rough sort percentages for all strata.

Lithic Class	Obsidian Other (1) n = 115	Basalt Fine (5) n = 1647	Basalt Coarse (6) n = 2113	Andesite (9) n = 2202	Igneous Other (18) n = 404	Limestone Other (21) n = 279	Mudstone/ Siltstone (23) n = 41	Ortho-quartzite Nacimiento (29) n = 22	Ortho-quartzite Other (30) n = 331	Quartzite Fine (37) n = 4432
Modified stone (5) n=391	0.0	0.7	1.7	1.5	9.4	2.5	2.4	4.5	0.3	0.9
Unmodified stone (6) n=568	0.0	0.2	0.9	1.6	11.4	2.5	12.2	0.0	0.3	1.1
Hammerstone (29) n=297	0.0	1.0	0.5	1.4	1.7	0.0	0.0	0.0	0.6	0.7
Chopper/uniface (30) n=169	0.0	0.9	1.2	1.3	1.0	0.0	0.0	0.0	0.0	0.2
Chopper-biface (31) n=171	0.0	0.7	0.9	1.0	2.0	0.0	0.0	0.0	0.0	0.2
Core/chopper (53) n=89	0.0	0.9	0.4	0.5	0.7	0.7	0.0	4.5	0.0	0.4
Core/pounder (54) n=81	0.0	0.7	0.3	0.1	0.0	0.0	0.0	0.0	0.3	0.5
Core/chopper/pounder (55) n=104	0.0	0.9	0.2	0.5	0.0	0.0	0.0	0.0	0.6	0.3
Core-other (69) n=530	0.0	1.9	0.9	1.5	1.5	2.2	2.4	4.5	3.0	2.4
Chopper/pounder (56) n=307	0.0	1.5	2.0	2.0	1.5	0.4	2.4	4.5	0.3	0.4
Pounder/abrader (57) n=103	0.0	0.4	0.5	0.7	1.0	0.4	0.0	0.0	0.0	0.2
Chopper/abrader (58) n=91	0.0	0.4	0.8	0.7	0.7	0.0	0.0	0.0	0.0	0.1
Chopper/pounder/abrader (61) n=65	0.0	0.3	0.5	0.3	0.2	0.0	0.0	0.0	0.0	0.1
Core/abrader (62) n=32	0.0	0.2	0.2	0.2	0.0	0.0	0.0	0.0	0.0	0.2
Composite-other (66) n=118	0.0	0.8	0.7	1.1	1.5	0.0	0.0	0.0	0.6	0.3
Core rejuven. flake (63) n=12	0.0	0.0	0.0	0.0	0.0	0.0	0.0	0.0	0.0	0.1
Flake tools ret w/out proj (76) n=165	0.9	0.5	0.2	0.2	0.0	0.0	0.0	0.0	0.6	0.5
Flake tls non-ret w/proj (77) n=198	1.7	0.4	0.3	0.1	0.0	0.4	0.0	0.0	0.0	0.3
Flake tls non-ret w/proj (78) n=2306	17.4	4.9	3.1	5.1	3.5	3.9	7.3	13.6	3.6	7.1
Projectile point (84) n=228	7.0	0.0	0.0	0.0	0.0	0.0	0.0	0.0	4.5	0.6
Debitage (93) n=24,331	73.0	82.8	84.6	80.2	63.9	87.1	73.2	68.2	85.2	83.5

Table 47.6 (continued)

Lithic Class	Quartzite Coarse (38) n = 5640	Metamorphic Other (45) n = 941	Chalcedony/Agate (48) n = 2645	Petrified Palm (49) n = 63	Petrified Wood (50) n = 63	Jasper (51) n = 176	Chert Other (52) n = 6736	Chert Narbona Pass (55) n = 179	Quartz Massive (56) n = 29
Modified stone (5) n=391	2.6	2.3	0.3	0.0	0.3	1.1	0.6	0.0	3.4
Unmodified stone (6) n=568	3.1	2.1	1.4	0.0	1.0	7.4	1.9	0.0	34.5
Hammerstone (29) n=297	2.9	2.4	0.0	0.0	0.1	0.6	0.2	0.0	0.0
Chopper/uniface (30) n=169	1.3	1.2	0.0	0.0	0.0	0.0	0.0	0.0	0.0
Chopper-biface (31) n=171	1.6	0.7	0.0	0.0	0.0	0.0	0.0	0.0	0.0
Core/chopper (53) n=89	0.4	0.3	0.1	0.0	0.0	0.0	0.0	0.0	0.0
Core/pounder (54) n=81	0.5	0.4	0.0	0.0	0.1	0.0	0.1	0.0	0.0
Core/chopper/pounder (55) n=104	0.4	0.9	0.0	1.6	0.3	0.0	0.2	0.0	0.0
Core-other (69) n=530	0.8	1.9	1.8	3.2	2.8	1.1	2.0	1.1	0.0
Chopper/pounder (56) n=307	2.6	2.0	0.0	0.0	0.1	0.0	0.1	0.0	0.0
Pounder/abrader (57) n=103	0.7	1.6	0.0	0.0	0.0	0.0	0.0	0.0	0.0
Chopper/abrader (58) n=91	0.6	1.4	0.0	0.0	0.0	0.0	0.0	0.0	0.0
Chopper/pounder/abrader (61) n=65	0.3	2.1	0.0	0.0	0.0	0.0	0.0	0.0	0.0
Core/abrader (62) n=32	0.1	0.3	0.0	0.0	0.0	0.0	0.0	0.0	0.0
Composite-other (66) n=118	0.5	0.7	0.0	0.0	0.0	0.0	0.2	0.0	0.0
Core rejuven. flake (63) n=12	0.0	0.0	0.0	0.0	0.0	0.0	0.1	0.0	0.0
Flake tools ret w/out proj (76) n=165	0.1	0.0	1.1	1.6	0.8	1.7	1.0	1.1	0.0
Flake tls non-ret w/proj (77) n=198	0.1	0.0	1.9	1.6	1.1	1.7	1.1	2.8	0.0
Flake tls non-ret w/proj (78) n=2306	2.8	1.0	12.6	12.7	14.6	11.9	11.1	24.6	0.0
Projectile point (84) n=228	0.0	0.0	2.2	0.0	0.6	8.5	1.3	2.2	0.0
Debitage (93) n=24,331	78.4	78.5	78.5	79.4	78.1	65.9	80.3	68.2	62.1

Categories (raw material or tool class) with at least 0.1% are shown. Lithic rough sort category codes are indicated in parentheses in column and row headings.

During the Chacoan occupation the most frequently occurring imported lithic material was Narbona Pass chert, Warren's Type 1080 (Harris et al. 1967:121). Field reconnaissance during this project and others has indicated that this material has a very limited natural distribution; it is limited to the Narbona Pass volcanic field in the Chuska Mountains of northwestern New Mexico (Harris et al. 1967:122). Project personnel have found cobbles of this material in the alluvial gravels of semiperennial water courses that drain the Narbona Pass area, but even in these cases the material has been transported only 1–3 km downslope from primary deposits. This source area lies southwest of Salmon more than 100 km, across an extremely xeric landscape.

This material was likely reaching Salmon by way of an "indirect acquisition system" (Ericson 1977: 119–120), as suggested by the distance involved, its frequency in the assemblage, the availability of local cryptocrystalline silicates, and the possible existence of an extensive Chacoan trade system (Altschul 1978; Grebinger 1973; Irwin-Williams 1977; Judge 1979; Lightfoot 1979; Martin and Plog 1973). Some exchange system models use the spatial patterning of artifacts to elucidate whether past exchange systems were redistributive or reciprocal in nature (Clark 1979; Dalton 1975; Hodder and Orton 1976; Renfrew 1977). The expected pattern for goods exchanged within a reciprocal system is one of decreasing frequency with increasing distance from the center of the production or resource area (i.e., a distance-decay model; Hodder 1974; Hodder and Orton 1976; Irwin-William 1977; Renfrew 1975). However, a redistributive system would likely produce a pattern of secondary high-frequency areas ("peaks") at various locations distant from the production or source area (Hodder and Orton 1976:153; Renfrew 1977:85–86). A sample of material collected through survey and testing of archaeological sites on the San Juan River was rough sorted by the Salmon lithics laboratory in an effort to define the nature of this exchange system.

The relative frequency data from these survey sites indicate a concentration of Narbona Pass chert at Chacoan outliers and local sites near the outliers. There is no linear fall-off pattern from west to east as would be expected if the exchange system had been reciprocal. This redistributive pattern is further supported to some degree by the relative frequency data on imported ceramics from these sites (Whalley 1980). The relative frequency of Chacoan occupation imported cryptocrystalline silicates is shown in Table 47.7. These imports occur in such low frequencies that little can be said concerning them. Yet, it should

be noted that the six pieces of Brushy Basin chert debitage have in all probability intruded into Chacoan deposits (see Secondary Occupation below). A comparison of the stages represented by the imported materials with those of the local cryptocrystallines (Table 47.8) indicates that in most cases the imported materials were used for a much more limited range of morphological tool class, which may indicate a set of specific limited functions for these exotics. It is interesting that the site areas with high concentrations of Narbona Pass chert correspond to a large degree with the areas of high imported ceramic frequencies (Franklin, Chapter 28).

The total Secondary assemblage is much larger than the Chacoan, but most of the Narbona Pass chert (68.3%) occurs in the assemblage of the latter occupation. This nonlocal material is believed to have reached Salmon Pueblo primarily via the Chacoan distribution network, although it also occurs in substantial amounts in Secondary deposits. This occurrence probably reflects some reuse of surfaces and consequent mixing of materials, but the Secondary inhabitants of Salmon also might have reused Narbona Pass chert items obtained from Chacoan deposits. To investigate this possibility, we compared changes in the frequency of this material in all Chacoan and Secondary occupation contexts. During the Chacoan occupation, the highest frequency of Narbona Pass chert (61%) was in structured trash (C strata) and on floors (27%). In contrast, the highest frequency of Narbona Pass chert during the Secondary occupation was on roofs (47%) that were structurally above the Chacoan occupation Narbona Pass trash and floor concentrations. This pattern suggests that during Chacoan times, second-story floors were incompletely cleaned, with the debris being dumped into first-story rooms immediately below. Reuse of the second-story floors by Secondary folks resulted in the mixing of later materials with Chacoan de facto refuse (Schiffer 1976). A similar pattern of activity location and trash discard for the Chacoan occupation has also been inferred from site-wide depositional patterns (R. Adams 1980a:273–284).

In a further attempt to understand the distribution of Narbona Pass chert, Chacoan and Secondary situations were sought where reuse of surfaces was not evident; one such situation, with a relatively large sample size, was the structured trash deposits in the stratified mounds in Room 100W. If the strata in this room are arranged only by the Salmon ceramic chronology, then the highest frequency of Narbona Pass chert is in intermediate occupation strata (Figure 47.3), which brings into question the assignment of these strata to the intermediate occupation.

Table 47.7. Percentage of imported raw material types by lithic class, Chacoan occupation. Due to inclusion here of all tool classes and materials regardless of size, percentages and sample sizes (n) may differ slightly from those in other tables.

Tool Class	Narbona Pass chert (n = 386)	cf. Jemez Obsidian (n = 2)	Indeter. Obsidian (n = 16)	Brushy Basin chert (n = 6)
Core material*	0.6	–	–	–
Cores	2.3	–	–	–
Core rejuvenation flake	0.5	–	–	–
Unretouched flake tools	21.8	50.0	43.7	–
Retouched flake tools	1.6	50.0	6.3	–
Projectile points	–	–	12.5	–
Debitage**	73.2	–	37.5	100.0
Primary flakes	–	–	–	–
Secondary flakes	–	–	50.0	–
Tertiary flakes	100.0	–	50.0	–

*Tested or untested raw material nodule.
**Flake percentages based on debitage total.

Table 47.8. Percentage of local raw material types by lithic class, Chacoan occupation.

Tool Class	Chalcedony (n = 660)	Petrified Palm (n = 7)	Petrified Wood (n = 429)	Jasper (n = 44)	Chert (n = 2079)
Core material	0.6	–	2.4	27.3	–
Hammer/chop/peck stone*	1	–	0.5	–	–
Early stage chop/peckstone**	0.2	14.3	1	2.3	–
Cores	3.1	–	5.4	2.3	–
Unretouched flake tools	14.6	14.3	16.4	2.3	–
Retouched flake tools	0.7	–	0.7	–	–
Projectile points	2.9	–	1.2	4.5	–
Knife	–	–	–	–	–
Drills	0.2	–	–	–	–
Biface (other)	0.2	–	–	–	–
Debitage	75.2	71.4	72.4	61.3	69
Primary flakes	11.2	–	–	–	9.8
Secondary flakes	44.4	–	28.6	–	17
Tertiary flakes	44.4	–	71.4	–	73.2

*Extensively battered.
**Moderately battered.

This affiliation was defined exclusively by an increase in McElmo Black-on-white pottery (Franklin 1980:69–78), which was present throughout the entire occupation of Salmon. The ceramic ordering contradicts the relative stratigraphic position of units C-9-14 and C-13-18. Both occurred on the Chacoan floor (H-1-19) as lower trash units in two separate mounds; the ceramic seriation, however, placed them in separate occupations. If these strata are contemporaneous, and they probably are, then the highest frequency of Narbona Pass chert in each mound is in the same relative position. Narbona Pass chert was therefore likely discarded in Room 100W primarily during the Chacoan occupation. The frequency of imported Chacoan occupation ceramics such as Chaco Black-on-white exhibits a similar stratigraphic distribution (Franklin 1980:69–78).

For Chacoan contexts, 49 rooms contained 386 pieces of Narbona Pass chert, but only 2 rooms contained more than 18 pieces (Table 47.9). These two rooms, however, yielded more than 46 percent of the total. Room 31W contained 135 pieces of Narbona Pass chert, and Room 43W contained 44 pieces. These two rooms are adjacent to each other and both yielded unusually high frequencies of imported ceramics (Franklin 1980:342). This concentration of Narbona Pass chert and imported ceramics within a small area of the site probably indicates a restricted

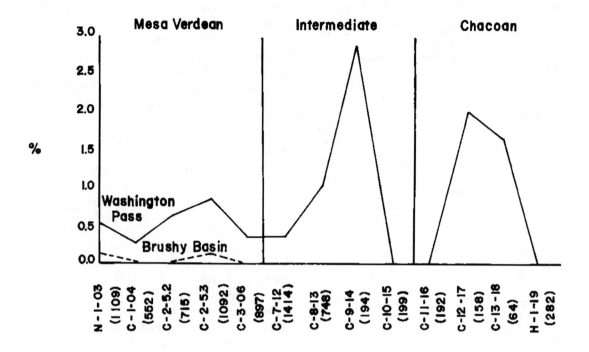

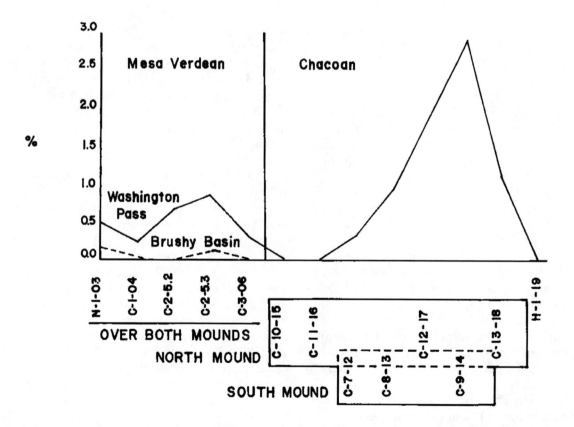

Figure 47.3. Stratigraphic frequency of Narbona Pass chert and Brushy Basin chert in Room 100W. Top graph shows strata arranged in ceramic sequence; lithic count in parentheses. Bottom graph has strata in relative stratigraphic order.

Table 47.9. Mean frequency of Narbona Pass artifacts in select Chacoan rooms or strata.

Room	Strata	Mean Number of NP Artifacts/Stratum
31W*	C-2-06.5	27.6
	C-3-08	
	C-4-09	
	G-1-10	
	H-2-11	
43W*	G-1-10	14
	G-1.2-10.2	
	C-2-12	
81W*	F-2-13	7
91W	C-9-23	6
	C-13-27	
	C-14-28	
30W	C-2-08	5.3
	C-3-09	
	F-2-11	
82W*	G-1-23	5
129W*	F-2-86	3
100W	C-12-17	3
	C-13-18	

* Indicates rooms with relatively high intrusive ceramic contents.

distribution for the discard—and by inference, for the use—of imported resources in the Chacoan occupation. This pattern is as expected if this material was not equally available to all households in the settlement. This does not demonstrate, of course, that Narbona Pass chert tools were made by specialists. The occurrence of both tools and debitage in these contexts does suggest, however, that production as well as use was involved.

Tools made of local cryptocrystalline materials seem to have been cycled laterally to a much greater extent than those made from imports. For example, local chalcedony, petrified wood, and chert all appear to have initially entered the site in core material (nodular) form. Flakes derived through reduction were used without modification or were modified into flake tools and morphologically defined tools (i.e., projectile points). Obviously, many flakes were discarded or lost prior to use. At some stage in their reduction, the cores were cycled into the ground stone tool manufacturing and maintenance system, as indicated by the morphological similarity between experimentally produced pecking

stones from this and other projects (Figure 47.4). This is not surprising because the results of several experiments in lithic technology indicate that cryptocrystalline cores make the best pecking stones (Crabtree personal communication; Holmes 1919; Pond 1930).

Local noncryptocrystalline materials (igneous and metamorphic) appear to have entered the site in cobble form and were cycled through the system in much the same manner as the cryptocrystalline materials. One major point of difference is a higher frequency of used core tools; this may reflect an additional use of these materials in plant food preparation (Dodd 1979). This inference is based on the observation that even though two distinct activity sets—ground stone manufacturing-maintenance and plant food processing using an anvil—produce similar observable tool damage, the detachment of cryptocrystalline flakes during processing would be a deterrent to plant food processing with such materials. In all probability, this difference in cycling reflects a quantitative variation in the availability of raw materials and tasks performed. For example, the high frequency of these relatively coarse grained materials in T strata indicate that these materials were selected for activities associated with wall building. Experiments conducted by Salmon personnel to investigate building block manufacture and modification using local materials highlighted several considerations: these raw materials were readily available and abundant; these activities expended tools at a relatively rapid rate; squared and rounded tool edges resulting from this activity were a hindrance to resharpening; sandstone scoring was accomplished more easily with a relatively coarse material; and the heavier the core (within limits), the easier the job, due to the fact that less acceleration is needed to achieve the same force. Given these considerations, coarse-grained materials would seem to have had a shorter use-life and would have entered the archaeological record at a higher frequency than other, finer-grained materials.

Table 47.10 presents data for Chacoan occupation ground stone raw material and tool class combinations. (Secondary occupation ground stone data are presented later.) Few substantial differences are apparent when the tool classes unique to a single occupation (i.e., stone hoes or tchamahias) and the small samples (less than 50 items) are excluded from consideration. The major difference in these samples is the selection of sandstone for manos during Secondary times and metamorphic cobbles in the Chacoan occupation. I believe this variation is a function of overall changes in milling technology, but discussion of this relationship is deferred until

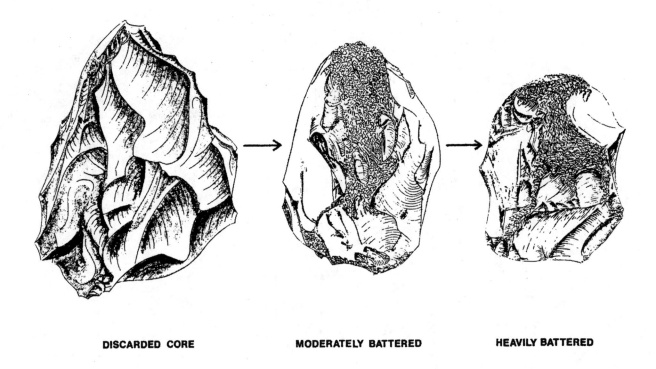

DISCARDED CORE   **MODERATELY BATTERED**   **HEAVILY BATTERED**

Figure 47.4. Drawing showing formation of a cryptocrystalline hammerstone through use of discarded core.

ground stone technology is discussed later in this chapter.

The other major local lithic resource is sandstone. If one were to consider the amount of sandstone used in the construction of the Pueblo, this material would be the most heavily exploited of all local lithic materials. Even without considering material used in construction activities, sandstone is the second most frequent lithic material in the Chacoan occupation assemblage (see Table 47.5). It is also extensively represented in terms of tool types (Figure 47.5). Based on field observation of sandstone extraction areas (see Nials, Chapter 3), little modification of sandstone occurred at the extraction sites. This inference is further supported by the relatively frequent occurrence of T strata (construction debris) material at the site; most of the building blocks were probably manufactured at the site. Given the multifunctional nature of sandstone (building blocks, metates, and grist trough parts) and its reduction byproducts (e.g., chinking, abraders, and wall core fill), this exploitation pattern represents an efficient and economic expenditure of energy.

Other materials, such as those used for ornaments and pigmentation—which, though made of stone, are outside the more general lithic system—are relatively sparse in the Chacoan occupation

assemblage (see Table 47.5). These materials were probably highly prized, and items made from them were carefully curated (Schiffer 1976), making them unlikely finds in the archaeological record. Additionally, reuse probably accounts for some of this sparsity. It is also possible that since no ornament material exists within the Salmon catchment area that is not also available within Chaco Canyon proper, the exploitation of these materials by Chacoan occupation Salmon inhabitants was minimal. Though distributional studies of exotic materials used for ornaments and pigments might provide insights into the Chacoan ideological subsystem at Salmon (Irwin-William 1977:94–95), the small sample size of these materials precludes any such studies.

Secondary Occupation

Table 47.6 presents the Secondary Occupation lithic assemblage according to raw material type and strata category; it includes all raw materials processed through the Salmon lithic laboratory, including those used for ornaments. Percentages of exotic and local raw material types from the Secondary occupation sample are shown in Tables 47.11 and 47.12. The data show a clear increase in the use of obsidian during the Secondary occupation. The validity of macroscopic identification of these obsidians to

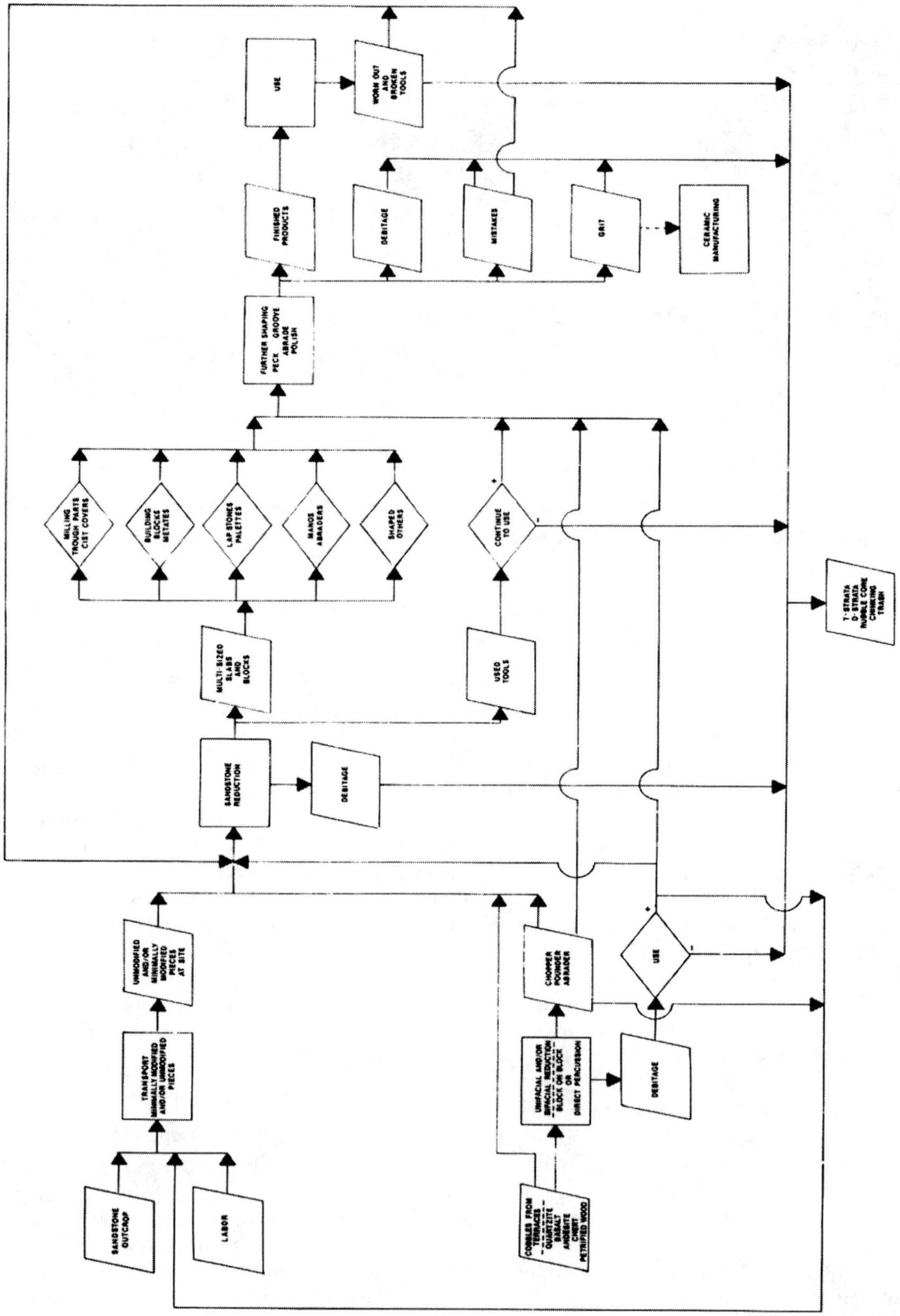

Figure 47.5. Projectile points from the Chacoan occupation at Salmon.

Table 47.10. Ground stone rough sort percentages for all strata, Primary component. Categories (raw material or tool class) with at least 0.1% are shown. Lithic rough sort category codes are indicated in parentheses in column and row headings.

Lithic Class	Granite (11) n = 55	Sandstone (24) n = 2069	Conglomerate/ Breccia (25) n = 2	Sedimentary Other (32) n = 5	Schist (34) n = 22
Milling bin wall (3) n = 4	0.0	0.2	0.0	0.0	0.0
Shaped stone slab (4) n = 249	0.0	12.0	0.0	0.0	0.0
Metate (14) n = 51	1.8	2.4	0.0	0.0	0.0
Lapstone/palette (16) n = 38	0.0	1.5	0.0	0.0	0.0
Anvil stone (17) n = 12	0.0	0.0	0.0	0.0	0.0
Mano (24) n = 123	9.1	4.7	0.0	0.0	0.0
Abrader, ungrooved (27) n = 87	1.8	3.0	0.0	0.0	0.0
Polishing stone (28) n = 55	1.8	0.1	0.0	0.0	22.7
Grinding stone (35) n = 296	9.1	1.6	0.0	0.0	13.6
Polished stone (44) n = 10	3.6	0.0	0.0	0.0	4.5
Ground stone other (51) n = 78	3.6	1.5	0.0	0.0	4.5
Ground stone indet. (52) n = 788	1.8	22.5	100.0	0.0	4.5
Debitage (93) n = 6222	67.3	50.3	0.0	100.0	50.0

Table 47.10 (continued)

Lithic Class	Gneiss (35) n = 8	Quartzite Fine (37) n = 1302	Quartzite Coarse (38) n = 4178	Green Stone (39) n = 303	Metamorphic Other (45) n = 303
Milling bin wall (3) n = 4	0.0	0.0	0.0	0.0	0.0
Shaped stone slab (4) n = 249	0.0	0.0	0.0	0.0	0.0
Metate (14) n = 51	0.0	0.0	0.0	0.0	0.0
Lapstone/palette (16) n = 38	0.0	0.1	0.1	0.0	0.0
Anvil stone (17) n = 12	0.0	0.0	0.3	0.0	0.0
Mano (24) n = 123	0.0	0.3	0.4	0.0	0.3
Abrader, ungrooved (27) n = 87	12.5	0.0	0.4	0.0	1.7
Polishing stone (28) n = 55	0.0	0.3	0.5	7.2	5.0
Grinding stone (35) n = 296	25.0	1.2	4.8	0.0	11.6
Polished stone (44) n = 10	12.5	0.2	0.0	1.4	0.0
Ground stone other (51) n = 78	0.0	0.3	0.6	5.8	2.6
Ground stone indet. (52) n = 788	25.0	1.4	6.0	34.8	8.6
Debitage (93) n = 6222	25.0	96.2	86.8	50.7	70.3

source area is questionable, given the variation observed in the field within these flows. XRF study of 10 Secondary age samples of obsidian revealed that all were from the Valle Grande source in the Jemez Mountains (Shackley 2005). It seems reasonable to conclude that most (if not all) of the Salmon obsidian came from Jemez. Regardless of specific source areas, these imported materials show a higher frequency of use for projectile point manufacturing than do any other silicate materials. Additionally, no obsidian cores were recovered from unquestionably Secondary or Chacoan occupation contexts. Whether these materials entered Salmon in nodular or re-

duced form remains unknown without data on the frequency of cortex. But based on the "site entry pose" of Brushy Basin chert (Shelley, Chapter 48), the only other imported tool stone material not represented in core form, the probability exists that obsidian reached Salmon in other than nodular form.   Narbona (Washington) Pass chert was the most frequent import in Secondary contexts; it is concentrated within Secondary occupation roof (F) strata. As stated earlier, these situations were heavily affected by the mixing of Chacoan and Secondary de facto refuse. We believe that these items represent reuse of surfaces and materials by Secondary occu-

Table 47.11. Percentage of imported raw material types by lithic class, Secondary occupation. Due to inclusion here of all tool classes and materials regardless of size, percentages and sample sizes (n) may differ slightly from those in other tables.

Tool Class	Narbona Pass chert (n = 181)	cf. Jemez Obsidian (n = 11)	cf. Grants Obsidian (n = 2)	cf. San Francisco Mtn. Obsidian (n = 2)	Indeter. Obsidian (n = 115)	Brushy Basin chert (n = 41)
Core material*	–	–	–	–	–	–
Cores	1	–	–	–	–	–
Unretouched flake tools	27.4	27.3	–	–	19.1	26.5
Retouched flake tools	1	18.2	–	–	0.9	–
Projectile points	2.2	27.3	–	–	7	–
Biface (other)	0.6	9.1	–	–	–	–
Debitage**	67.8	18.1	100	100	73	73.5
Primary flakes	–	–	–	–	28.6	–
Secondary flakes	–	–	–	–	57.1	–
Tertiary flakes	100	–	–	–	14.3	100

*Tested or untested raw material nodule.
**Flake percentages based on debitage total.

Table 47.12. Percentage of local raw material types by lithic class, Secondary occupation.

Tool Class	Chalcedony (n = 2655)	Petrified Palm (n = 61)	Petrified Wood (n = 2236)	Jasper (n = 179)	Chert (n = 6760)
Core material	1.7	–	1.3	8.5	2.4
Hammer/chop/peck stone[1]	–	–	0.1	–	0.1
Early stage chop/peck stone[2]	0.1	1.6	0.4	–	0.6
Cores	1.8	3.2	2.8	1.2	2
Core rejuvenation flake	–	–	Tr	–	Tr
Unretouched flake tools	14.5	14.3	15.7	13.6	12
Retouched flake tools	1	1.6	0.8	1.6	0.9
Projectile points	2.1	–	0.6	8.4	1.2
Knife	Tr	–	–	0.7	Tr
Drills	–	–	0.1	–	Tr
Biface (other)	0.2	–	0.2	1.3	0.5
Debitage[3]	78.5	79.1	78	64.7	80
Primary flakes	14.3	–	–	–	23.8
Secondary flakes	28.6	–	–	–	23.8
Tertiary flakes	57.1	–	–	–	53.4

[1]Extensively battered.
[2]Moderately battered
[3]Flake percentages based on debitage total.
Tr = present, but less than 0.1%.

pants. This interpretation is further supported by the fact that not only were these artifacts concentrated in Secondary occupation roof contexts, but they were also concentrated largely on roofs in the same Chacoan rooms that have high concentrations of Narbona Pass chert. For example, 182 pieces of Narbona Pass chert occurred in 52 Secondary occupation rooms or stratigraphic units. In 75 percent of these cases, however, it occurred with a frequency of only one or two pieces. Rooms or stratigraphic units with more than two pieces per stratum are listed in Table 47.13.

Brushy Basin chert was imported to Salmon from a location at least 100 km distant, from the Four Corners area, probably in the form of finished or nearly finished tools or possibly as traded craft products. This is the only lithic raw material that is unique to the Secondary occupation assemblage (see Shelley, Chapter 48).

Table 47.14 shows the distribution of Secondary occupation ground stone items by type and raw material. Many types and materials overlap considerably with those of the Chacoan occupation. The

Table 47.13. Mean frequency of Narbona Pass artifacts in select Secondary rooms/strata.

Room	Strata	Mean Number of NP Artifacts/Stratum
31W*	F-1-06	60
37W	C-2-08	
	C-3-09	12.5
37B	C-1-03	12
100W	C-2-05	
	C-3-06	8
100W*	N-1-03	5
43W*	F-1.5-6	4
30A&B*	F-1-3	3

*Denotes Secondary roofs that overlie Chacoan concentrations of Narbona (Washington) Pass chert.

tchamahias of Brushy Basin chert from the Secondary occupation, as discussed, are an exception to this general pattern of similarity.

LITHIC RESOURCE SPECIALIZATION

Prior studies of specialization have examined raw materials with the expectation that a specialist's products would exhibit more selectivity in raw material (e.g., Appel 1979; Evans 1973, 1978; Hantman et al. 1979; Rattray 1979; Rice 1981; Spence and Kimberlin 1979; Stone 1979). The ability to recognize subtle variations in mechanical properties of the raw material, and to recognize and acquire relatively high quality lithic materials—in other words to be more selective—likely increases with experience. Thus we assume certain relationships between specialization, distribution systems, and the increased expertise of specialists.

Resource selectivity is measured by the range of applicable tool classes and reduction stages found within a given category of raw material. For example, the presence of a siliceous rock, such as Narbona Pass chert, in the form of projectile points and debitage but not as knives and scrapers, constitutes evidence for selectivity. But a lack of metates made from Narbona Pass chert does not indicate selectivity, because cherts are not suitable material for producing metates.

Because these kinds of determinations can only be made comparatively, it was first necessary to establish the total range of mechanically equivalent raw material types available to the occupants at Salmon. In addition, it was necessary to demonstrate that inferences of increased selectivity were not a result of the frequency of occurrence of raw materials within the site's catchment area. Thus a high proportion of projectile points made of petrified wood does not imply selectivity if petrified wood was the only flakable stone in the site catchment. After determining the distribution of raw materials in the area around Salmon, it was then possible to compare variation in patterns of raw material exploitation. These patterns were then compared to the variation expected if resource selectivity was occurring at Salmon Pueblo.

EXPERTISE AND STANDARDIZATION IN FLAKED STONE
Debitage and Cores

If the Chacoan occupation flintworkers were more specialized than their Secondary counterparts, their work should exhibit more expertise. Sheets (1974) suggested that one measure of expertise in lithic production is the frequency of artisan error, with the underlying assumption that specialists make fewer "critical mistakes" (Sheets 1974:371). Sheets defined critical mistakes as hinge and step flake terminations. Mechanical models do indicate that hinge and/or step terminations are caused by misapplication of force (Faulkner 1972:123–124), but it could be argued that such terminations constitute critical mistakes only if they preclude recovery, or if the core trajectory must be redirected to accomplish recovery. This definition makes it possible to use various kinds of mistakes to define various levels of expertise; such an approach is taken here.

A comparison of artisan error as measured by the number of hinge and/or step terminations observed on cores is shown in Table 47.15; all cryptocrystalline and vitreous silicates are combined. This could be questioned if these materials were not mechanically equivalent, but such is not the case. Experimentation with local and imported siliceous materials indicates that they all possess similar "desirable properties" for flaked tool production (Crabtree 1972:18).

The data shown in Table 47.15 indicate a significantly higher error rate in Secondary core reduction. As measured by the frequency of hinge and step terminations on discarded cores, Chacoan occupation flintworkers erred less frequently. This relative expertise in flake production suggests that Chacoan flintworkers had better control in maintaining core morphology and in the application of force.

A comparison of errors in flake production, as indicated by flake terminations, also shows that

Table 47.14. Ground stone rough sort percentages for all strata, Secondary component. Categories (raw material or tool class) with at least 0.1% are shown. Lithic rough sort category codes are indicated in parentheses in column and row headings.

Lithic Class	Basalt Fine (5) n = 1496	Basalt Coarse (6) n = 2013	Andesite (9) n = 2085	Granite (11) n = 36	Igneous Other (18) n = 370	Sandstone (24) n = 2828	Conglomerate/ Breccia (25) n = 5	Brushy Basin Chert (28) n = 28
Milling bin wall (30) n = 63	0.1	0.0	0.0	0.0	0.0	2.1	0.0	0.0
Shaped stone slab (4) n = 598	0.1	0.0	0.0	0.0	0.0	20.9	0.0	0.0
Metate (14) n = 146	0.0	0.0	0.0	5.6	0.0	5.0	0.0	0.0
Lapstone, palette (16) n = 61	0.0	0.0	0.0	2.8	0.0	1.7	20.0	0.0
Anvil stone (17) n = 15	0.0	0.0	0.0	0.0	0.0	0.2	0.0	0.0
Mano (24) n = 416	0.1	0.0	0.2	11.1	0.0	13.2	0.0	0.0
Abrader, ungrooved (27) n = 21	0.0	0.0	0.1	0.0	0.0	0.5	0.0	3.6
Polishing stone (28) n = 27	0.9	0.1	0.8	0.0	1.1	0.2	20.0	0.0
Axe, grooved (32) n = 27	0.1	0.1	0.4	0.0	0.0	0.0	0.0	0.0
Axe, notched (33) n = 59	0.2	0.3	0.5	0.0	1.6	0.2	0.0	0.0
Grinding stone (35) n = 365	0.7	0.7	2.7	8.3	7.0	2.6	20.0	0.0
Tchamahia (42) n = 18	0.0	0.0	0.0	0.0	0.0	0.0	0.0	64.3
Polished stone (44) n = 53	0.4	0.2	0.1	0.0	1.9	0.1	0.0	14.3
Ground stone other (51) n = 554	1.2	1.6	3.5	8.3	8.4	4.7	0.0	0.0
Ground stone indet. (52) n = 1085	5.1	7.4	6.7	11.1	10.3	8.6	40.0	0.0
Axe/maul, grooved (59) n = 15	0.1	0.1	0.1	0.0	0.0	0.0	0.0	0.0
Axe/maul/notched (60) n = 17	0.0	0.2	0.1	2.8	0.0	0.0	0.0	0.0
Debitage (93) n = 15, 523	91.2	88.8	84.7	50.0	69.7	40.0	0.0	17.9

Table 47.14 (continued)

Lithic Class	Sediment Other (32) n = 12	Schist (34) n = 24	Gneiss (35) n = 30	Quartzite Fine (38) n = 3875	Quartzite Coarse (38) n = 5001	Greenstone (39) Gn = 444	Metamorphic Other (45) n = 919
Milling bin wall (30) n = 63	0.0	0.0	0.0	0.0	0.0	0.0	0.0
Shaped stone slab (4) n = 598	0.0	0.0	0.0	0.1	0.0	0.0	0.0
Metate (14) n = 146	0.0	0.0	0.0	0.0	0.0	0.0	0.0
Lapstone, palette (16) n = 61	0.0	0.0	0.0	0.1	0.1	0.0	0.0
Anvil stone (17) n = 15	0.0	0.0	0.0	0.0	0.2	0.0	0.1
Mano (24) n = 416	0.0	0.0	0.0	0.1	0.5	0.2	0.2
Abrader, ungrooved (27) n = 21	0.0	0.0	0.0	0.0	0.1	0.0	0.1
Polishing stone (28) n = 27	16.7	0.0	13.3	0.6	0.3	4.5	2.6
Axe, grooved (32) n = 27	0.0	4.2	3.3	0.1	0.1	0.5	0.5
Axe, notched (33) n = 59	0.0	8.3	0.0	0.1	0.2	1.6	0.7
Grinding stone (35) n = 365	0.0	4.2	3.3	0.9	2.2	2.0	2.4
Tchamahia (42) n = 18	0.0	0.0	0.0	0.0	0.0	0.0	0.0
Polished stone (44) n = 53	8.3	0.0	0.0	0.2	0.1	2.7	0.5
Ground stone other (51) n = 554	0.0	4.2	0.0	0.7	3.4	6.3	3.6
Ground stone indet. (52) n = 1085	25.0	16.7	10.0	1.6	4.4	14.6	8.4
Axe/maul, grooved (59) n = 15	0.0	4.2	0.0	0.0	0.0	1.1	0.0
Axe, maul/notched (60) n = 17	0.0	0.0	0.0	0.0	0.0	0.7	0.4
Debitage (93) n = 15, 523	50.0	58.3	60.0	95.5	88.4	65.8	80.4

Chacoan occupation flintworkers made fewer errors (Table 47.16), with a relative frequency of 5.2 percent of determinable flake terminations compared to 23 percent in the Secondary sample. The Chacoan occupation error rate is similar to the 4.2 percent error frequency found in a Mayan sample (Sheets 1974: Table 1). Likewise, the 23 percent frequency of hinge and step termination errors on Secondary flakes is essentially equivalent to the 22.1 percent error frequency found by Sheets in a Secondary Anasazi sample (Sheets 1974: Table 1). If the underlying assumption that specialists are better knappers is correct, then the measures presented above suggest that Chacoan occupation flintworkers were more specialized.

As stated, the frequency of cores redirected during manufacturing can provide support for measures of expertise in a highly structured reduction system (i.e., one with specific identifiable stages, such as Levallois, Folsom projectile point, or Mesoamerican polyhedral blade/blade core technologies). However, distinguishing redirected cores is a difficult and subjective exercise if the reduction system is not highly structured. The prehistoric Puebloan lithic technologies at Salmon Pueblo do not appear to have been structured in this sense; therefore, redirected cores could not be identified clearly.

The degree of systematics or method (Crabtree 1972:2) should be correlated with the degree of specialization in the two reduction systems. "Systematics" are defined here as the amount of variation in platform or platform remnant establishment and preparation, in core technological or morphological class, and in the dorsal surface morphology of flakes. The more variation, the less specialized a sample is. The underlying assumption is that specialists have better control of manufacturing techniques than do nonspecialists.

If specialists strive to consistently produce tools that conform to culturally recognized parameters, then cultural concepts also impose restrictions. As previously discussed, Chacoan and Secondary flintworking technology at Salmon Pueblo was generally similar. During both occupations, reduction of cryptocrystalline and vitreous silicates was oriented toward producing flakes for use and for making projectile points (see below). Therefore, cultural limits on these Puebloan lithic technologies were probably similar.

Table 47.17 presents a comparison of proximal core and flake attributes in the two samples. Not only is there a quantitative difference in the amount of variation within the two samples, but there is also a qualitative difference. Chacoan occupation debi-

tage shows a consistent mode of platform establishment via single flake detachment, whereas the Secondary sample shows more variability in platform establishment (see Table 47.17). There also appears to be a consistent method of platform preparation by flaking and then abrasion in the Chacoan sample, whereas the Secondary sample exhibits relatively little platform preparation of any kind. This probably indicates that Secondary occupation flintworkers were less familiar with basic techniques of producing flaked stone tools. This lack of familiarity, when combined with the greater variation in proximal core and flake attributes, suggests that the Secondary flintworkers were less skilled, and hence less specialized than their Chacoan counterparts.

Projectile Points

Projectile points were the largest class of bifacial tools recovered from Salmon Pueblo. Most of the 282 whole and partial points were made on flake blanks (83% of the Chacoan occupation population and 71% of the Secondary occupation population). If Chacoan projectile points were produced by specialists they should be relatively more standardized in size, shape, and method of manufacture. Statistical analyses were therefore conducted to objectively identify the degree of standardization and expertise in projectile point manufacturing. Discriminant function analysis was used to isolate and define variations that differentiate the Chacoan and Secondary projectile points. Only attributes from whole points were used in these analyses.

It was assumed that the fewer the number of variables needed to successfully discriminate a given sample, the more technology standardized the sample. In addition, when the variables, which substantially contributed to the quantitative isolation of groups, had been identified, their technological significance could be evaluated qualitatively.

Discriminant function analysis is a statistical procedure for separating subpopulations based upon multivariate data (Sokal and Rholf 1969:488–492). A classification function is calculated that discriminates between groups using all or a reduced set of the variables at hand. The two major methods of discriminant function analysis are direct and stepwise. "In the direct method, all variables input are used to create a discriminant function, but the stepwise method selects only those variables that contribute significantly to discrimination" (Matson and Lipe 1977:57).

Discriminant analysis assumes "that discriminating variables have a multivariate normal distribution and that they have equal variance-covariance

Table 47.15. Frequency of flaked stone production errors on discarded cores, Chacoan and Secondary occupation attribute data. Includes only cores exhibiting no postmanufacturing use.

	Chacoan	Secondary
Number of cores	18	23
Core errors, hinge/step scars	15	93
Mean error per core	0.83	4.04
Successful removals, feather scars	85	52
Mean feather per core	4.67	2.26

Table 47.16. Frequency of flaked stone production errors as indicated by hinge and step flake terminations, Chacoan and Secondary occupation. Includes only whole flakes and distal flake fragments.

	Chacoan	Secondary
Number of flakes	71	80
Hinge terminations	2	11
Step terminations	1	3
Feather terminations	55	47
Indeterminate terminations	13	19
Error of determinable terminations	5.17	22.95

Table 47.17. Relative frequencies of variation in core platform and flake platform remnant establishment and preparation, Chacoan and Secondary occupations. Flake data limited to whole flakes and proximal flake fragments; core data limited to unused cores.

	Platform/Platform Remnant Establishment			Platform/Core Front/Dorsal Face Juncture Preparation			
	Cortex	One Flake Scar	Multiple Scars	Flaked	Abraded/ Rubbed	Flaked & Abraded	None
Chacoan Occupation							
Flakes (n = 59)	13.6	86.4	–	22.0	–	88.0	–
Cores (n = 18)	–	81.4	18.6	18.6	–	81.4	–
Secondary Occupation							
Flakes (n = 71)	18.3	42.3	39.4	12.7	14.1	7.0	66.2
Cores (n = 23)	8.7	26.1	65.2	17.4	13.0	8.7	60.9

Table 47.18. Depositional context of Salmon Pueblo whole projectile points.

Strata Type	Chacoan Occupation (n = 33)	Secondary Occupation (n = 161)
Stratified trash (C strata)	44.3	50.4
Unstructured trash (B, M, and N strata)	19.3	15.2
Feature fill (L strata)	1.9	1.6
Floors (G, H, and I strata)	17.2	9.6
Roofs (F and E strata)	15.4	22.8
Other (T, D, J, K, and W strata)	1.9	0.4
Total	100.0	100.0

matrices within each group" (Klecka 1975:435). Although these assumptions cannot be made for the Salmon data, "in practice the technique is very robust, and these assumptions need not be strongly adhered to" (Klecka 1975:435).

As a result of the number of variables used and the amount of time available, an optimal solution was sought using a stepwise method (Klecka 1975: 448). Initially, three stepwise methods available in SPSS (Nie and Hull 1979) were tried (Wilks Lambda, Mahalonobis Distance, and Minimum Residual; Klecka 1975:447–449). The best classification results were obtained with Wilks Lambda.

As with other lithic materials, projectile points were assigned to periods by stratigraphic association; there were 33 points from Chacoan proveniences and 161 from Secondary (Table 47.18). In the initial series of tests, cases with missing values were eliminated and continuous and discrete data were treated separately. More variables were available than the computing system could manipulate, so subsets of variables were selected. One set of variables was selected subjectively, and the other was chosen randomly. Subjective selection was based upon experience gained through observation of the projectile points. These observations led to selection of the following discrete attributes:

Blade tip shape
Blade shape
Notch shape
Raw material
Cortex

Additional discrete attributes were selected randomly from the remaining group of variables:

Condition
Biface type
Blade edge condition
Shoulder type
Nature of stem/base juncture
Luster

In this analysis the stepwise solution discarded about 85 percent of the randomly selected variables and about 10 percent of the subjectively selected variables. The results of this discriminant function analysis are shown in Table 47.19. These results were encouraging, but not strongly so, due to the low frequency of correctly classified cases.

A similarly structured analysis was conducted, using a subjectively and randomly selected group of continuous variables. The subjectively selected variables used were as follows:

Blade width
Blade tip angle
Number of flakes on blade
Number of flakes on stem
Notch width
Blade edge length

The randomly selected variables included the following:

Total length
Weight
Notch depth
Thickness

The results of this analysis of continuous variables were similar to those obtained with discrete variables. The similarity occurred both in correctness of classification and in the ratio of subjective to randomly selected variables discarded. Twenty-six subsequent analyses used permutations and combinations of the most sensitive continuous and discrete variables, as indicated by preceding analyses. Finally, the most sensitive continuous and discrete variables were combined (after converting the continuous into discrete variables) in a single analysis. The following variables were used in this analysis:

Number of flakes on blade
Number of flakes on base
Notch depth
Blade length
Base shape
Type of hafting
Raw material
Luster
Translucence
Hue

The results of this combined analysis are shown in Table 47.20. An examination of the variates that discriminated between projectile points indicated that the first function, which accounted for 68.2 percent of the variance, consisted of variables relating to the degree of flake blank modification. These variables' standardized discriminant function coefficients and the relative frequency of variable states in the populations (Table 47.21) showed that Chacoan occupation projectile points generally underwent less flake blank modification than Secondary projectile points. This was indicated by the relatively low number of flake scars on the blade and base. Low scores for these two variables alone were enough to separate most of the Chacoan projectile points from the whole sample. This finding was further supported by visual inspection, which revealed that Chacoan projectile points were frequently only bi-marginally or uni-marginally modified

Table 47.19. Classification results from discriminant function analysis of Salmon projectile point data.

| Actual Group Membership | No. of Cases | Predicted Group | |
		Chacoan	Secondary
Chacoan	33	20 60.60%	13 39.40%
Secondary	161	63 39.10%	98 60.90%
Percent of grouped cases classified correctly: 60.80			

Table 47.20. Classification results from additional discriminant function analysis of Salmon projectile point data.

| Actual Group Membership | No. of Cases | Predicted Group | |
		Chacoan	Secondary
Chacoan	33	26 78.80%	7 21.20%
Secondary	161	31 19.30%	130 80.70%
Percent of grouped cases classified correctly: 79.89			

Table 47.21. Descriptive statistics of variables contributing substantially to the discrimination of Chacoan and Secondary occupation whole projectile points.

	Chacoan (n = 33)	Secondary (n = 161)
Number of flakes on edge/face:		
Minimum	4	6
Maximum	8	20
Mean	5.9	10.4
Number of flakes on base/face:		
Minimum	2	5
Maximum	6	12
Mean	3.4	6.1
Notch depth (mm):		
Minimum	1	3
Maximum	2.8	6
Mean	2	4.1
Blade length (mm):		
Minimum	8.5	7.5
Maximum	25.5	51
Mean	20.5	25.5
Hafting type:		
Notched	99%	92%
Stemmed	1%	8%
Base shape:		
Straight	50%	40%
Convex	45%	30.90%
Concave	5%	29.10%

flakes (Figure 47.6). In contrast, most of the Secondary projectile points are bifacially modified (Figure 47.7). The Chacoan occupation flintworkers were thus able to produce flakes of a desired size and shape for subsequent projectile point manufacturing. The inference that Chacoan flake blanks were minimally modified is further supported by the relatively shallow notches on Chacoan projectile points (see Table 47.21).

The second discriminant function, which accounted for 26.3 percent of the variance, consisted of variables having to do with base shape. Comparison of variable states indicated that not only had Secondary occupation projectile points undergone more modification, but they also exhibited a wider range of variation in basal finishing (see Table 47.21). Secondary occupation projectile points may be notched or stemmed, and if they are notched, they may have either straight, concave, or convex bases. In contrast, Chacoan occupation projectile points are almost all notched, with predominantly straight and convex bases. Secondary projectile points are also identified through discriminant analysis as having a relatively wider range of luster and translucency. This variation may reflect the slight changes in material selection already discussed.

To assess the possibility that some of the patterns presented might reflect a disproportionate frequency of repair in the samples, whole projectile points were examined for reworking. In the Chacoan occupation sample, 15 percent of the projectile points were reworked, compared to 18.2 percent of the Secondary sample. This difference in the frequency of reworking has probably not substantially affected the patterns presented here.

Because of the relatively small size of the Chacoan sample, it might be argued that they showed less variability because of sampling error. That is, there might have been equal interhousehold variability in projectile point form, but only a few households were represented in the Chacoan sample versus many in the Secondary sample. This would make it appear that the Chacoan points were less variable, particularly if a large number of Chacoan points had come from a single cache. Despite the previously mentioned hazards of working with distributional data from Salmon Pueblo, gross differences of this sort would likely be detected. Evidence discussed in the following paragraphs indicates, however, that the distributions of the Chacoan and Secondary samples were similar.

In his study of the projectile points from Salmon Pueblo, Moore found that 41.9 percent of the rooms with Chacoan occupation materials also had projec-

Figure 47.6. Projectile points from the Chacoan occupation at Salmon.

Figure 47.7. Projectile points from the Secondary (San Juan) occupation at Salmon.

tile points (Moore 1981:70). In contrast, 71.4 percent of the rooms that contained Secondary occupation artifacts also contained projectile points. The average number of points per room in the Chacoan occupation sample was 2.8, and in the Secondary sample the average was 5.3 (Moore 1981:70–74). The distribution of points among provenience types is rather similar to that for lithic artifacts in general, indicating that points were probably affected by the same or similar processes that governed the distribution of the lithic sample in general.

An examination of horizontal spatial distribution of the projectile points showed that 86.1 percent of the Chacoan sample came from 15 assumed living and storage rooms, and the remaining 13.9 percent of the Chacoan points came from three assumed ceremonial or special function rooms. In the Secondary occupation, 63.3 percent of the projectile points came from 28 assumed living and storage rooms, 21 percent came from 11 assumed ceremonial or special function rooms, and 25.7 percent were from the plaza. Chacoan trash deposits were very poorly preserved in the plaza, if in fact they had ever existed there. In contrast, virtually all areas sampled in the plaza had extensive Secondary occupation trash.

Inferences on room type were based on architecture (i.e., kivas were inferred to be ceremonial or special function rooms), proximity or connectivity to kivas (special function or ceremonial), and position within the pueblo and presence or absence of features such as hearths (habitation and storage). Using these criteria, there are 22 possible Secondary occupation ceremonial or special function rooms (11 of which yielded 21 percent of the Secondary points) and 7 such possible Chacoan occupation (three of which yielded 13.9 percent of the Chacoan points).

The spatial patterning of the projectile points in this analysis is generally proportional to the distribution of Chacoan and Secondary occupation materials. It should be noted, however, that 8 (about 24%) of the whole Chacoan occupation projectile points came from two caches, whereas 26 (about 16%) of the Secondary occupation projectile points came from seven caches. This difference is probably not great enough to have had substantial impact on the patterns of variability discussed previously.

In conclusion, the ability to produce flakes of a desirable size and shape for projectile points, so as to necessitate only minimal postdetachment modification, suggests above-average expertise. This reductive control and relatively standardized method of manufacturing supports inferences of greater Chacoan occupation specialization, as does the consistency in patterns of basal finishing.

A "tabletop" typological analysis of stylistic variation in part of the Salmon sample, by Moore, also indicated relatively little stylistic variation in the Salmon Chacoan sample (1981:96). Moore identified two stylistic types of projectile points in the Chacoan sample and six or seven in the Secondary sample

(1981:98). A major stylistic difference was in the basal finishing of the projectile points. Moore observed the same trends in notching and base shape as presented here, but regional comparisons led him to assign temporal significance to some of the Secondary variances (Moore 1981:116). The relative briefness of the Salmon Pueblo Secondary occupation casts some doubt on this interpretation, but in any case, the small degree of stylistic variation Moore observed in the Chacoan sample agrees with our statistical results and further supports the inference of production specialization during this occupation.

Comparison of Salmon Pueblo to Other Sites

After discriminant analysis on an intrasite level, projectile point attribute data collected by Moore (1981) on a sample of projectile points (from sites at Aztec Ruins, Chaco Canyon, Mesa Verde National Park, and the San Juan Valley Archaeological Project–La Plata River survey) were submitted to a similar discriminant analysis in conjunction with Salmon data. The points from Chaco Canyon and Mesa Verde were from sites ranging from late Pueblo I through Pueblo III. La Plata survey sites were basically Pueblo II to Pueblo III, and the Aztec Ruins points were from both the initial Chacoan occupation and the later San Juan–Mesa Verde reoccupation of that site.

The expected outcome of this manipulation was that if the major source of temporal-cultural variation had been isolated, then points from these localities would be classified by time (i.e., points from various geographical localities would be classified together into temporally discrete groups). This analysis used the classification functions derived from Salmon data and included all Salmon projectile point data along with the data from Chaco Canyon and Mesa Verde. The assumption was, as previously stated, that these data would be classified such that the site of derivation would be inconsequential in terms of group membership.

The output of this analysis was not as expected. The functions instead classified (grouped) these data according to their respective culture area (i.e., Chaco Canyon, Salmon, Mesa Verde), with 80 percent of grouped cases correctly classified. At this point the lack of extendability indicated by the selection operation with Salmon data was acknowledged. Also, because temporal variation seemed to be less significant than spatial variation, more cases (sites) and more variables (metric and nonmetric) needed to be added to the analysis. Data from Aztec Ruins and the San Juan Valley's La Plata River survey sites

were added and all metric and nonmetric variables were included. By "stepping backwards" (Nie and Hull 1979:186) through the variables when comparing the Salmon Chacoan occupation to all others, discriminant analysis selected 45 nonmetric and 6 metric variables to culture area in 100 percent of the cases. Tables 47.22 and 47.23 show the Eigenvalue, the percent of accountable variance of the canonical discriminant functions, and the classification results.

The analysis was rerun with this selection procedure. Selected cases were correctly classified 100 percent of the time, but nonselected cases could only be correctly classified with 78 percent success. No distinct pattern of misclassification was present.

When the Secondary occupation was compared to all others, discriminant analysis selected 45 nometric and 14 metric variables to derive four functions that correctly classified grouped cases with 95 percent success. Tables 47.24 and 47.25 show the Eigenvalue and percent of accountable variance of discriminant functions and the classification results.

There is some patterning to the misclassification in this analysis, with the most consistent cross-over occurring between the Salmon Secondary occupation and the Mesa Verde (National Park) samples. This analysis was also rerun with the selection procedure; the results showed that selected cases could be correctly classified with 100 percent success, but nonselected cases could be correctly classified only 84 percent of the time.

Implications of Statistical Analysis

The major source of variation between the Salmon Chacoan and Secondary occupation projectile points is technological rather than stylistic. When this information is combined with the results of classifying samples from other sites or cultural areas, it is apparent that the principal difference between Salmon (Chacoan or Secondary occupations) and these other areas is stylistic. This suggests that the variation in projectile points represents variation introduced through subregional stylization.

There are two possible explanations for this subregional constancy in style: (1) limited information flow and interaction was occurring, which resulted in somewhat isolated and concomitantly limited variation in subpopulations; and (2) projectile points were being manufactured for nonhousehold consumption in a recognized style either idiosyncratically or through some socially determined factors, or both.

Information on other settlement and technological subsystem characteristics suggests that both of these possible explanations may account for this

1042 Phillip H. Shelley

Table 47.22. Classification results from discriminant function analysis of projectile metric and nonmetric variables.*

| Actual Group | No. of Cases | Predicted Group Membership | | | | |
		Salmon Primary	Aztec	Mesa Verde	Chaco	La Plata
Salmon Primary	31	31 100.0	0 0.0	0 0.0	0 0.0	0 0.0
Aztec	47	0 0.0	47 100.0	0 0.0	0 0.0	0 0.0
Mesa Verde	21	0 0.0	0 0.0	21 100.0	0 0.0	0 0.0
Chaco	27	0 0.0	0 0.0	0 0.0	27 100.0	0 0.0
La Plata	20	0 0.0	0 0.0	0 0.0	0 0.0	20 100.0
Salmon Unclassified	297	155 52.2	12 4.0	86 29.0	44 14.8	0 0.0

Percent of grouped cases correctly classified = 100.0

*Discrimination used all metric and nonmetric variables, stepping backwards, using cases from Salmon Primary Component, Aztec Ruins, Mesa Verde National Park, Chaco Canyon National Monument, San Juan Valley Archaeological Project La Plata River survey sites, and Salmon Unclassified samples.

Table 47.23. Evaluative scores for discriminant functions derived from and used to classify cases in Table 47.22.

Function	Eigenvalue	Percent of Variance	Comulative Percent	Canonical Correlation
1	28.39544	61.26	61.26	0.9828434
2	12.87213	27.77	89.03	0.9632824
3	2.96887	6.4	95.43	0.8648924
4	2.11715	4.57	100.00	0.8241323

Table 47.24. Classification results from discriminant function analysis of projectile point data from Salmon Secondary component and other Anasazi sites.*

| Actual Group | No. of Cases | Predicted Group Membership | | | | |
		Salmon Secondary	Aztec	Mesa Verde	Chaco	La Plata
Salmon Secondary	156	148 94.9	1 0.6	5 3.2	1 0.6	1 0.6
Aztec	47	1 2.1	46 97.9	0 0.0	0 0.0	0 0.0
Mesa Verde	21	2 9.5	0 0.0	19 90.5	0 0.0	0 0.0
Chaco	27	3 11.1	0 0.0	0 0.0	24 88.9	0 0.0
La Plata	23	0 0.0	0 0.0	0 0.0	0 0.0	23 100.0
Salmon Unclassified	191	146 76.4	12 6.3	22 11.5	11 5.8	0 0.0

Percent of grouped cases correctly classified = 94.89.

*Discrimination using all metric and nonmetric variables, stepping backwards, using cases from Salmon Secondary Component, Aztec Ruins, Mesa Verde National Park, Chaco Canyon National Monument, San Juan Valley Archaeological Project La Plata River survey sites, and Salmon Unclassified samples.

Table 47.25. Evaluative scores for discriminant functions derived from and used to classify cases in Table 47.24.

Function	Eigenvalue	Percent of Variance	Comulative Percent	Canonical Correlation
1	18.44831	56.24	56.24	0.9739516
2	11.15304	34.00	90.24	0.957975
3	2.27307	6.93	97.17	0.8333525
4	0.92873	2.83	100.0	0.6939199

subregional stylization. For example, the San Juan Valley Archaeological Project survey data from the La Plata River shows relatively little interaction when compared to sites from the San Juan, as measured in terms of intrusive ceramics from outside areas during the AD 1050–1180s (Whalley 1980:78–88). Projectile points from the La Plata River form the most distinct group in discriminant analysis, and throughout various runs of discriminant analysis, they were 100 percent correctly classified to area.

In addition, if one considers the relatively well defined division of labor on an intrasite level at Salmon, as indicated by the concentration of plant food processing areas and metate manufacturing or maintenance activities during the Chacoan occupation in conjunction with the intersite specialization indicated by the Secondary occupation tchamahia data, then production or work for nonhousehold consumption seems to be a viable explanation.

Summary

The minimal flake blank modification that is a basic characteristic of Salmon Chacoan occupation projectile points suggests a much better control of core reduction technology than that expressed by the Secondary occupation projectile points. This situation is also reflected in core and flake attribute data. In addition, fewer variables/variable states were necessary to assign group membership to Chacoan points than were required for Secondary points. These statistical results, qualitative analysis of the discriminant variables, and Moore's (1981) typological analysis together suggest that the Chacoan occupation points were much more standardized than the Secondary projectile points. The Chacoan occupation projectile point makers were therefore the more specialized.

PRODUCTION AND USE OF GROUND STONE

Milling technology differs substantially between the assemblages of Secondary and Chacoan occupations of Salmon Pueblo. During the Secondary occupation, milling bins surrounding slab metates (Figure 47.7) served as containers or confiners for both the grain being milled and the resultant meal; this

inference is based upon the similarities between the Salmon Pueblo bins and ethnographically documented Puebloan milling technology (Bartlett 1933:14–15; Morgan 1881:150; Kennard 1979:561).

According to ethnographic studies in the Southwest, it is likely that the grinding facilities at Salmon Pueblo were used mainly to produce corn meal. However, as noted by Bunzel (1929), the additional use of metates to grind clay and tempers for pottery production cannot be ruled out.

The kind of fixed milling feature used by the Chacoans (Figure 47.8) is what Morris termed a "milling trough" (1928:235). To avoid confusion with milling bins (Figure 47.9), the term "grist trough" is used here for these features. Ethnographers have not observed such features among Puebloans. According to the archaeological record, grist troughs were used with trough metates, and consist of a number of slabs that served as grist basins set into a living surface or floor. In most instances, vertical dividers were set at intervals along the length of the grist basin. Unlike those of bins, these dividers did not extend along the sides of the metate when it was set in a grinding position, and there was no rear confining slab. Presumably, the grain being milled was contained by the trough of the metate surface. Grist troughs have been identified at Aztec Ruins (Morris 1928), at Pueblo Alto in Chaco Canyon (William Gillespie, personal communication), and at Salmon Pueblo, and they are associated with the original or Chacoan occupation at both Salmon and Aztec Ruins. Firm dates are not yet available for these features at Pueblo Alto.

The shift from grist troughs to milling bins was accompanied by a change in mano form from a predominantly cobble or cobble-like "grinding stone," for use with trough metates, to a shaped, rectilinear sandstone mano for use with slab metates. Similar trends in types of metates and milling features have been documented for other Chacoan outliers (Table 47.26).

Chaco Canyon sites (Table 47.27) show that trough metate forms predominated in their early or original occupations. Slab metates have been noted at Chaco Canyon sites, but they are usually associ-

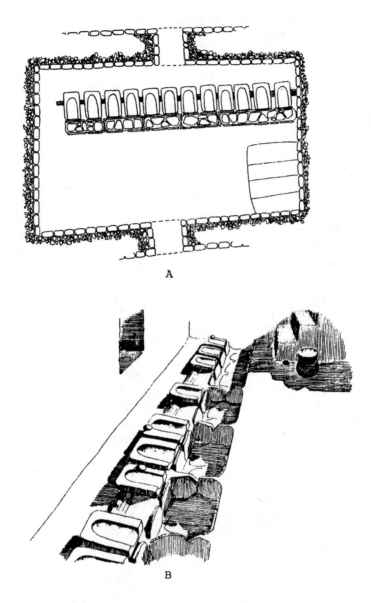

Figure 47.8. Chacoan milling bin (grist trough) in Room 97W (floor H-6-36). Metates removed in ancient times; reconstruction based on adobe impressions: (a) plan view, (b) oblique view.

ated with later occupations (see notes for Table 47.27). In ceramic and architectural traits, these later occupations of Chaco Canyon sites appear to be Mesa Verde–San Juan related.

Information from the Mesa Verde area (Table 47.28) indicates that the change in metate form occurred there sometime between AD 1100 and 1150 (compare the frequencies at Big Juniper House with those from site 499). Shortly thereafter, people began to move off of Mesa Verde, and by the mid-1200s the mesa-top was all but abandoned (Cordell 1975). These changes in milling technology were a pan-

Anasazi Pueblo III innovation, and do not appear to have been related throughout the region to specialization in ground stone tool manufacture or use. However, at Salmon Pueblo, these changes may have been associated with changes in the degree of specialization in metate manufacturing, maintenance, and use.

At Salmon Pueblo, specialization in ground stone tool production during the Chacoan occupation is indicated by the presence of what appears to be a centralized area for metate manufacturing and/or maintenance. The Chacoan period produced

43 classifiable metates in 12 room strata units with an average of 3.6 per unit (standard deviation 4.9). One Chacoan occupation stratum in Room 84W (H-1-8) contained 17 metates (39.5% of the total) in various stages of manufacturing and refurbishing. One of these metates (Artifact 4015) is an open-end trough metate that has been broken transversely in the process of refurbishing. That it was broken in maintenance is indicated by the presence of a freshly pecked and roughened surface on the shorter section up to the break, whereas the longer portion on the other side of the break exhibits a used/ground surface.

In addition to the metate in Room 84W (H-1-8) are numerous siliceous battered cores thought to have been used for metate manufacture and maintenance. Modern experiments have demonstrated the superiority of siliceous hammerstones for ground stone tool production using pecking and grinding techniques (Pond 1930:27–73). There are 212 battered siliceous cores from 82 room stratigraphic units in the Chacoan occupation sample, with an average frequency of 2.6 per stratum (standard deviation 4.1). Room 84W (H-1-8) produced 43 (20%) of these tools.

The lithic assemblage from Room 84W (H-1-8), when compared with those from similar deposits in other Chacoan contexts at Salmon Pueblo, indicates that this area was a workshop for metate manufacturing and/or maintenance. This segment of the lithic system was apparently in the hands of specialists. No similar concentrations of ground stone tool manufacturing equipment or manufacturing byproducts were identifiable in Secondary occupation contexts. For example, the most concentrated occurrence of whole and partial metates in a Secondary context was five, or 10.4 percent, in Room 129W (C-76-83). Likewise, the largest concentration of battered chert cores was 53 (5.8%) in Room 100W (stratum N-1-3).

I proposed earlier that if stone tools were used by other specialists, they should be spatially concentrated. At Salmon, during both occupations, metates were emplaced and used in substantial immobile architectural features. Because they were much less subject to displacement than artifacts were, the distribution of these milling features is the most reliable indicator of the spatial organization of milling tool use at Salmon Pueblo.

A comparison of fixed milling locations in Chacoan and Secondary contexts is made in Table 47.29. The number of metates per location and the number of locations per occupation (Figures 47.10 and 47.11) indicate that milling areas were considerably more localized during the Chacoan than during the Sec-

ondary occupation of Salmon Pueblo. At a given milling location, the arrangement of milling features also allowed more individuals to participate in these activities at the same time; this conclusion is based on the inferred number of metates used in these locations, as well as upon the size of the milling areas. Ethnographic information on the organization of milling bins does not indicate this level of concentration in historic Pueblos. For example, in a study of 50 Hopi milling bins, Bartlett found that "every Hopi house has at least two mealing bins" (1933:14); in Bartlett's terminology, this is two slab metates in bins. In addition, "the greatest number of bins seen in any one house [room] was … six in a row" (Bartlett 1933:14). Both Bartlett (1933:3–4) and Connelly (1979:561–562) have reported that among the Hopi, milling equipment is household property and milling is a household activity. There are no ethnographically reported occasions of communal use of milling facilities among Puebloans. Similarly, no non-Chacoan archaeological occurrences of such large concentrations of milling features have been reported from the Anasazi region. This concentration of milling features does not necessarily indicate that milling was done by specialists, although it probably implies a more complex socioeconomic organization at Salmon Pueblo than was typical for non-Chacoan villages.

A change in the size of metate grinding surfaces provides an indication of the relative intensiveness of Chacoan occupation milling activities. Chacoan occupation trough metates have an average grinding surface area of 1187 sq cm. In contrast, Secondary occupation slab metates have grinding surfaces that average 935.5 sq cm. This suggests that Chacoan milling was more efficient, which gives some support to the notion that the Chacoan millers were more specialized than the Secondary ones.

Despite the poor preservation of Chacoan occupation floor features, there are more than twice as many Chacoan compared to Secondary milling features (see Table 47.29). This finding suggests greater specialization at Salmon Pueblo within the larger Chacoan system.

RESULTS AND IMPLICATIONS OF THE SPECIALIZATION STUDY

An examination of the evidence concerning degree of selectivity of raw materials as an indication of specialization revealed less specialization than had been anticipated, perhaps because local raw materials are so abundant. For example, the Pleistocene terraces and sandstone outcrops flanking the San Juan River provided both the Chacoan and

Table 47.26. Relative frequencies of metate form, Salmon Pueblo and other Chacoan outliers.

Site	Dates	Trough Metates	Slab Metates	Unknown Metates[a]	Comments
Salmon Pueblo					
Chacoan	AD 1088–1116	75%	22%	3% (n = 43)[b]	
Intermediate		22%	78%	— (n = 9)[b]	
Secondary	AD 1185–1263	21%	77%	2% (n = 48)[b]	
Aztec Ruins					
Chacoan	AD 1110–1120 (Robinson et al. 1974:60)	Present	Present	77 (n = 7)	No relative frequencies could be calculated from the published descriptions of Aztec Ruins.
Secondary	Mid-1200s (Robinson et al. 1974:60)				Some insights into metate distribution can be gained from the following statements: "a mealing bin with two slab metates associated with Mesa Verde ceramics was found in Room 27" (Morris 1928:291). "I have never seen a trough metate enclosed in a bin" (Morris 1928:236).
Guadalupe Ruin					
Chacoan	AD 918–1125 (Pippin 1979: 78, 87)	76%	14%	77 (n = 7)	Most trough metate fragments were used as secondary building elements, and Pippin associated the trough metates with his Chaco occupation (1979:815).

[a] At Salmon Pueblo these are large rocks that have been used as nether grinding stones; from other sites, they are unclassifiable fragments.
[b] Whole and classifiable fragments only.

Table 47.27. Relative frequencies of metate form, Chaco Canyon sites. All relative frequencies were calculated by Shelley from the numbers presented in the respective reports.

Site	Dates	Trough Metates	Slab Metates	Unknown Metates[a]	Comments[b]
Pueblo Bonito	AD 1030–1130 (Vivian 1973:109)	100%	–	(n = 7)	"There is no record of a metate with overall (slab)."
BC-50 (Tseh So)	AD 1040 (Vivian 1973:109)	100%	–	(n = 84)	Brand et al. 1937:90
Leyit Kin	AD 1011–1045 (Dutton 1938:91)	88%	10%	2% (n = 53)	(Dutton 1938:68); Vivian stated that all slabs are from Dutton's Unit III, which dates to the mid-12th century (Vivian 1973:92).
BC-51	AD 1040+ (Vivian1973:109)	86%	14%	(n = 22)	Woodbury 1939:58
Kim Kietso	AD 1050–1124+ (Vivian 1973:109)	73%	3%	22% (n = 32)[c]	Vivian 1973:91
Pueblo Del Arroyo	AD 1052–1117 (Judd 1939:7)	56%	2%	42% (n = 43)	Judd 1959:135
BC-362	AD 1088–1109 (Bannister 1973:136)	99%	1%	(n = 89)	Voll 1984:4, 5, 10, 12, 53 as quoted by Vivian 1973:92
BC-236	Unknown	17%	83%	(n = 18)	Vivian (1973:92) quoted Bradley (1959) as saying that slab metates come only from upper levels that date to the 13th century.

[a] Unclassifiable fragments.
[b] Citations in the comments section relate to the frequency data.
[c] Vivian presented these as "probably fragments," and they are considered here to be unknown.

Table 47.28. Relative frequencies of metate form, Mesa Verde sites. All relative frequencies were calculated by Shelley from the numbers presented in the respective reports.

Site	Dates	Trough Metates	Slab Metates	Unknown Metates[a]	Comments[b]
875	AD 950–1075 (Lister 1965:109)	61%	29%	(n = 17)	(Lister 1965:90–91)
866	AD 1000–1075 (Lister 1966:61)	80%	20%	(n = 10)	(Lister 1966:42–43)
Big Juniper House	AD 1080–1130 (Swannack 1969:179)	72%	28%	(n = 40)	(Swannack 1969:112)
Badger House	AD 1075–1128 (Hayes & Lancaster 1975:184)	87%	13%	(n = 220)	(Hayes & Lancaster 1975:151–152)
499	AD 1100–1150 (Lister & Lister 1964:88)	6%	94%	(n = 16	(Lister & Lister 1964:65–66)
Mug House	AD 1200–1300 (Rohn 1971:25)	–	100%	(n = 105)	(Rohn 1971:201–202)

[a]Unclassifiable fragments.
[b]Citations in the comments section relate to the frequency data.

Secondary inhabitants of Salmon Pueblo with most of their lithic raw materials, which were directly acquired in cobble and block forms and used for both flaked and ground stone tool production. However, the relatively high frequency of tested and untested nodules of local cryptocrystalline silicates in Chacoan contexts might represent warehousing by specialists. A few additions to this rich local supply of raw material were made by importing tools or pieces of "foreign" stone.

Flaked and ground stone tools and tool materials discarded or lost during the Chacoan occupation were apparently recycled to some degree by the Secondary occupants; this essentially increased the local lithic resource area of the Secondary occupants to include not only local natural deposits but cultural deposits as well. The most commonly imported lithic material during the Chacoan occupation was Narbona Pass chert from the Chuska Mountains, which apparently reached Salmon Pueblo by way of the Chacoan exchange system. The concentration of this material in two rooms may indicate restricted access to this material by specialists. Brushy Basin chert was imported only during the Secondary occupation, apparently in the form of finished tools.

For the most part, evidence for differential intra-site distribution of tools and byproducts indicating lithic specialization is poor at Salmon Pueblo. The concentration of Narbona Pass chert tools and debitage has already been described. One possible specialist work area is indicated by the concentration in

Table 47.29. Fixed milling locations at Salmon Pueblo.

Location	Number of Metates
Chacoan Occupation Grist Troughs	
129W (H-2-94)[a]	6 (if single row)
	12 (if double row)
97W (H-2-14)	12+
93W (H-6-36)	6
82W (H-2-24)[b]	3–4
Total min = 27	
Total max = 34	
Average min = 6.75	
Average max = 8.50	
Mesa Verdean Occupation Milling Bins	
31A (H-1-05)	3
119W (H-6-14)	3
93W (H-2-22)	3
93W (H-1-14 & H-2-22)	1
6A (H-1-05.2)[b]	1
30A (H-1-04)	1
91A (I-1-07)	1
86W (H-1-05)	1
123A (H-1-05)	1
Total = 14	
Average = 1.55	

* Reconstructed on the basis of imprints in adobe.
[a]Only southern half of room excavated to this level; milling trough extends into northern half for some unknown distance.
[b]May be ceremonial in nature as inferred from architecture and location (i.e., Room 6A is a kiva, and Room 82W is adjacent to a large kiva).

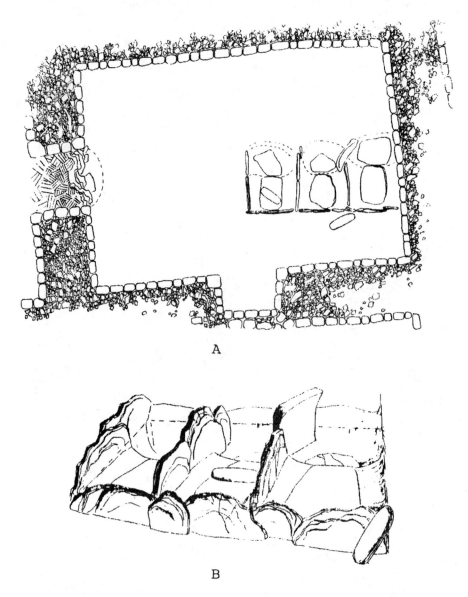

Figure 47.9. Secondary occupation milling bin in Room 119W (floor H-6-15); (a) plan view, (b) oblique view.

a single Chacoan room (Room 84W) of metates in various stages of manufacture and maintenance, along with manufacturing byproducts. This type of distribution is not found in the Secondary assemblage. Metate production and refurbishing was therefore likely done by one or more specialists during the Chacoan occupation of Salmon Pueblo. In general, however, the tidiness of the Chacoan occupants (e.g., cleaning floor surfaces prior to resurfacing) and the changes brought about by the Mesa Verdean reoccupation have made it difficult to identify the locations where particular kinds of stone tools were made or used. This limits the reliability of most studies of spatial patterning, at least of small, portable artifacts.

We thought that the more specialized an occupation, the more standardized the products would be. In addition, it was expected that specialists' work would exhibit a higher degree of expertise as indicated by good-quality workmanship and a relatively low frequency of manufacturing errors. Flaked stone technology provided evidence regarding these patterns.

Comparison of Chacoan and Secondary projectile point attribute data indicate more standardization and control in Chacoan occupation projectile

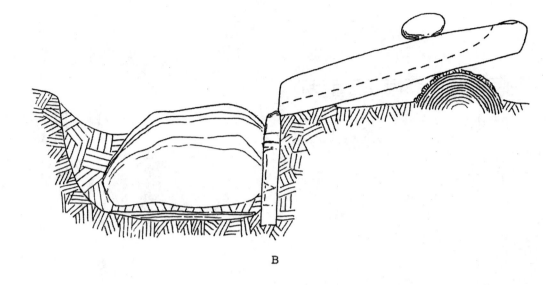

B

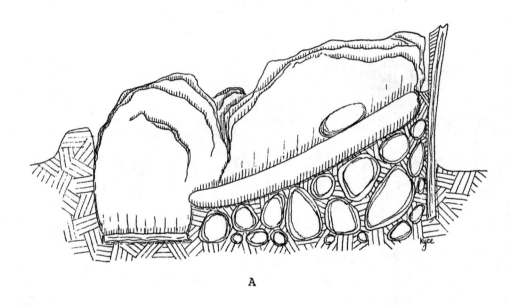

A

Figure 47.10. Side views of (a) Secondary (San Juan) milling bin and (b) Chacoan grist trough.

point production, as measured by the number and types of variables that distinguished Chacoan points. Not only were fewer variables required to distinguish Chacoan projectile points, but the technological attributes indicated a more standardized and expert approach to projectile point flake blank production and subsequent tool manufacturing. These results were as expected if Chacoan artisans were more specialized.

Further indications of Chacoan flintworking expertise were found in debitage and core data.

Variation in debitage and core technological attributes was interpreted as indicating greater control, fewer mistakes, and more systematic flaked stone production by Chacoan occupation flintworkers than by Secondary knappers. However, due to sampling procedures and sample sizes, these results should be accepted cautiously.

Another aspect of specialization, the organization of tool-using groups, was also explored. A comparison of the distribution of fixed milling locations in equivalent Chacoan and Secondary excavation

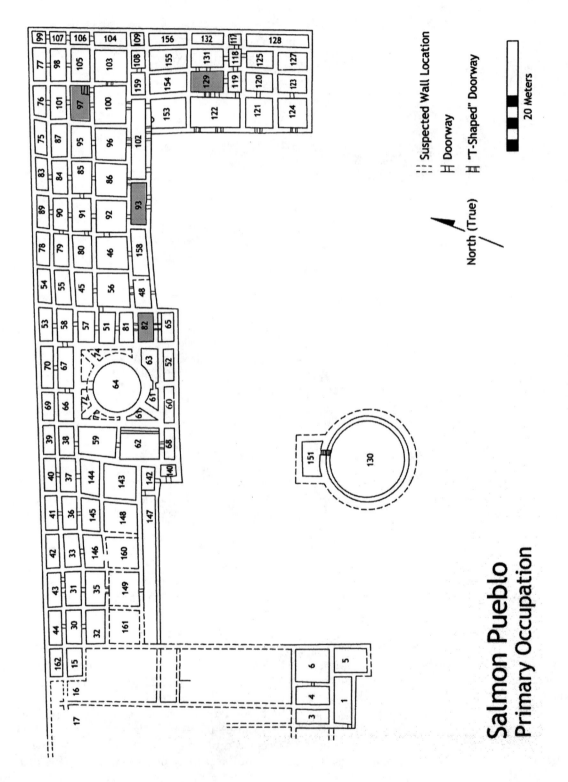

Salmon Pueblo
Primary Occupation

Figure 47.11. Location of Chacoan grist troughs (with multiple milling stations).

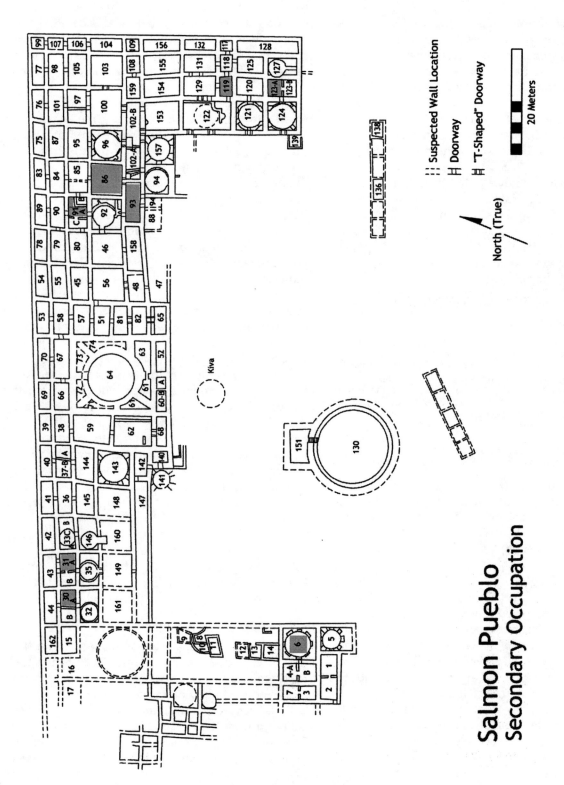

Salmon Pueblo
Secondary Occupation

Figure 47.12. Location of Secondary (San Juan) milling bins.

contexts indicates a greater concentration of milling equipment at a few loci and a greater number of milling features—both overall and per locus—in the Chacoan occupation, which apparently reflects different degrees of specialization in the way that maize grinding was organized and accomplished.

The data from Salmon show however that specialization within lithic systems was not always greater in the Chacoan occupation. During the Secondary occupation, the characteristics and frequencies of Brushy Basin tchamahias and Brushy Basin debitage indicate importation of specialists' products.

These analyses indicate that overall, the extent and intensity of specialization in the lithic systems were greater during the Chacoan occupation than during the Secondary occupation of Salmon Pueblo. It now seems appropriate to evaluate the implications of these interpretations with regard to general models of the Chacoan system.

TREE CUTTING DURING THE CHACOAN ERA

As noted by Judd (1954:239):

> It is a curious paradox that in Chaco Canyon, where literally thousands of pines were felled for building purposes, few stone axes have been recovered. Pepper lists but eight from his four seasons at Pueblo Bonito. The National Geographic Society's explorations in the same ruin disclosed only four (pl. 70, middle) with fragments of three others, and one of these latter, a grooved sandstone pebble (U.S.N.M. No. 335866) half again as large as a man's thumb, doubtless met some youngster's plea for an ax like father's. *All are from Late Bonitian rooms or rubbish.* (Emphasis added)

Similarly, Breternitz stated that as of December 1976, for all of Chaco Canyon (including Pueblo Bonito), there were "80 axes … from 18 sites ranging in time from late Basketmaker III through the Classic Bonito Phase townsites, averaging 4.4 axes per site" (1976:15).

Based on rough-sort data, 276 axes were recovered from Salmon Ruin. Of this total, 207 (75%) can be confidently assigned a temporal-cultural affiliation. Of these, 202 (98%) are associated with the Secondary occupation of Salmon Pueblo. Of the remaining 2 percent that were originally assigned to the Chacoan occupation, the results of attribute analysis indicate that three (60%) should have been classified as mauls. Even though these three each exhibit a minimal section of discontinuous edge, this edge has been formed via flake removals, probably as a result of flakes detached through use; they exhibit no indications of a bit ever having been established through grinding. Other attributes such as attachments for hafting are finished, and the flake removals truncate this modification in some in-

stances indicating that these are, in fact, finished tools. The other two Chacoan axes recorded during rough sort are actually no more than medial sections of grooved ground stone tools, and accurate distinction between axes and mauls at this level is impossible. It therefore seems that no axes are clearly associated with the Chacoan occupation at Salmon Pueblo (though four hafted mauls are present.)

Given this information and in an effort to understand how the Chacoans might have felled their trees, contextual information was sought that might indicate whether trees were chopped, burned, or sawed down. Though no systematic observations on the nature of building timber ends was made in the field, a post facto examination of photographs and timbers still in situ indicated that in all instances where conditions of preservation were such that confident observations could be made, Chacoan context building beam ends were relatively flat. This may indicate sawing because axed ends would probably be cone shaped (Iverson 1956). Flat ends were noted in instances where neither aesthetics nor engineering dictated such flatness (i.e., where vigas extend into wall core). No consistent observations on the presence or absence of charring could be made post facto.

To explore the possibility of sawing, possible technological similarities were sought within the Chacoan litho-technological system as indicated by the Salmon sample. Other sawing (i.e., bidirectional cutting) situations were thought to exist within T strata contexts. Analysis and experimentation had shown that building block manufacturing was most commonly and most expediently accomplished by first deeply scoring (sawing) rough blocks with a large flake tool or a bifacially flaked core tool prior to breaking. Given the job at hand, flake tools seemed to be the best candidates for the job. In an effort to establish the utility of these kinds of tools for this kind of work, a series of experiments were initiated by Salmon lithics laboratory personnel.

Experimental Procedures and Results

Two major attempts to saw conifers with flake tools were undertaken. In both attempts the tools used were large (10+ cm working edge length) primary and secondary decortication flakes of quartzite and andesite. The raw materials for these tools were collected from the Pleistocene gravels along the San Juan River. This material was selected due to its predominance in Salmon Primary T strata tool assemblages as well as others' experimental work with wood sawing (Crabtree, personal communication). The trees selected for felling were as close as possible to the average age, size, and species of those found in Salmon Chacoan contexts (K. Adams, Chapter 40).

The first tree was a ponderosa pine located on Bureau of Land Management land northeast of Aztec, New Mexico. Permission to carry out this experiment was obtained through the Public Broadcasting Association's Odyssey Series filming. The actual experimentation was carried out by P. Shelley and R. Adams. A large unmodified primary decortication flake was used to remove the bark from the tree 20 cm up from the base and around the tree for a width of some 20 cm; this girdling was done to keep from skinning one's knuckles on the bark because the tools were unhafted. Girdling was accomplished via sawing, grooving, and prying for approximately 20 minutes. From that point on the task became more difficult. This experiment was conducted during the late spring or early summer, and the sap was running. The accumulation of sap on the tool effectively dulled it in a matter of minutes and necessitated resharpening via direct bifacial flaking prior to actual attrition of the edge. Additionally, as the incision was deepened, more of the flake face came into contact with the margins of the incision and the frictional coefficient of the work increased greatly, resulting in an exponential relationship between energy expended and the deepness of the incision.

In 2 hours we managed to saw a groove totally around the tree's circumference to a depth of only 2.5 cm; it would have taken 14–20 hours to complete the task. Time was limited, so the experiment was arrested at this point and the tree was felled by using a metal wire saw and then pushing the tree over.

Conclusions based upon the results of this attempt were that (1) sawing trees with stone tools while sap is running is something only a neophyte to tree-felling would try; (2) girdling is easily and efficiently accomplished with flake tools while sap is running; and (3) regardless of how it is sawn (i.e., with stone or metal tools), if a tree is severed not completely but nearly so, and then pushed over, a pulled pitch center will be observable.

These conclusions led to the search for a standing dead tree. The only standing dead conifer readily available was an ornamental pine in a citizen's front yard; it had been killed by frost the year before. Permission was acquired for the experiment, which was carried out by R. Adams. Girdling was conducted in the same manner, except that a wider section of the trunk was debarked. Then three rather than one circumcisions were made within the debarked zone. In this manner the three incisions could be deepened alternately and then splints of wood could be pried or chiseled out toward the central incision, avoiding the problem of the increased fric-

tion observed in the first attempt. Girdling was more difficult due to the lack of pliability and increased denseness of the dead bark, and it took about twice as long. This experiment proceeded well until similar problems with sap were encountered at a depth of 3–3.5 cm.

A third experiment is currently underway; a ponderosa pine on private property has been girdled and will be allowed to stand dead for at least 2 years. At that time the method developed by R. Adams will be tried again.

Archaeological Implications of Experimental Results

Though the results of these experiments are inconclusive, they do support the feasibility of stone saw tree-felling. Furthermore, they indicate that girdling of conifers with simple flake tools is an easy task, taking less than 20 minutes on average for a live tree with a 15–20 cm diameter at the cut line. If a technique of girdling and then felling was practiced by the Chacoans, then a large number of trees showing the same cut date would be available for harvest from a standing lumber yard. This could explain the large clustering of cut dates from numerous Chaco sites (Bannister 1964), including Salmon Ruins. If tools similar to those of these experiments were used prehistorically, they probably would not have been manufactured at the exploitation areas, but would have been discarded in these areas when they were considered to be expended. If this was the case, the resultant discarded material would have a low archaeological visibility.

The pulled pitch center noted experimentally with the conifer that was pushed over after near complete severance appears identical to those illustrated in Morris's report on Aztec Ruins (1919:43–45). Morris believed that chopped ends were removed by way of circumcision, wedging, and grinding after the tree had been felled (1919:44). If this is so, it seems difficult to explain the appearance of the centers of the beams in his illustrations. If this explanation were extended to Salmon beams, it would be difficult to explain this added energy expenditure as indicated by the presence of flat ends of vigas that extend into wall cores.

There are many axed beam ends in Chaco Canyon sites, which date to the Chacoan occupation of the canyon (J. Dean and W. Robinson, personal communications). Yet whether or not these are in Chacoan construction context is unclear, as no systematic study of this has been undertaken. At Salmon there are axed ends on building timbers, but they are in Secondary building contexts (e.g., a deflector upright in Room 6A). If Chacoan occupation building timber was reused in this fashion, then there would be building materials with axed ends that date to the Chacoan occupation.

Alternatively, if the division of labor was such in the Chacoan system that there were groups of loggers, then the shortage of axes associated with Chacoan sites may reflect sample error. There is also a possibility that the loggers were not an internal part of the Chacoan system but were part of the hinterland population that provided the Chacoans with building timbers through trade.

CHACOAN MODELS

Recent models of the Chacoan phenomenon (Irwin-Williams 1977; Judge 1979) have proposed that distribution of goods among communities within the region (presumably through exchange) was important to the operation of the prehistoric Chacoan system. These authors disagree to some extent on what goods were likely to have been moved around the region, and what mechanisms might have accomplished this. Reciprocal exchange, centralized redistribution, and marketplaces have been suggested as mechanisms. Except for data from ceramic clay and temper analyses, there is little evidence of what goods were being distributed and even less as to the mechanisms involved. Nevertheless, if one accepts the relationship between specialization and exchange, as suggested by Bates and Lee (1977), then all of these models predict or imply the presence of some degree of specialization. Consequently, the identification of relatively greater specialization within the Chacoan occupation of the lithic sample from Salmon Pueblo has not provided support for any one regional exchange model over another, but only for this general class of models.

The results presented here generally conform to Irwin-Williams's (Chapter 2) modeled expectations for Salmon Pueblo. The degree and kinds of specialization documented within the Chacoan occupation suggest some ways in which the Salmon Pueblo community might have functioned in the past Chacoan interaction system. These suggestions are based on the assumption that the kinds of production specialization observed at Salmon Pueblo belong to larger organizational patterns that include the exchange or transfers of goods, at either the intra- or intercommunity level.

THE ROLE OF SALMON PUEBLO IN THE CHACOAN SYSTEM

Salmon Pueblo lithic artifacts functioned within two major realms of specialization: (1) metate manufacturing, maintenance, and use (through ethnographic analogy, primarily cornmeal production) and (2) flaked stone tool production. The spatial concentration of metate manufacturing and maintenance likely indicates intracommunity specialization, although it could also indicate that metates were made for export. Ethnographic studies outside the Southwest have documented specialization in metate manufacturing for nonlocal consumption (Cook 1967). It seems unlikely here, however, because the sandstone used for metates at Salmon is generally similar to raw materials widely available and widely used elsewhere in the San Juan area. The Salmon Pueblo specialization therefore appears to have been one of labor and skill, rather than acquisition of a scarce raw material.

The concentration of milling activities indicated by the distribution of milling features suggests that cornmeal was produced for consumption outside the producer's residence. With only the data used here, however, such nonhousehold consumption is not clearly assignable to either an intra- or intercommunity level.

Judge (1979) has suggested that the large backrow, ground-floor rooms in many of the Chaco Canyon towns were used as storerooms or granaries. Furthermore, in modeling the development and operation of the past Chacoan system, various authors have stressed the conflict between Chaco Canyon's limited agricultural productivity and its apparently dense population. In this light, the movement of cornmeal from Salmon to Chaco Canyon seems plausible. This is presented and further developed below as a hypothesis, though one that cannot be tested by this study, which is confined to the manufacture and use of stone tools at Salmon Pueblo.

Puebloan maize appears to have been most commonly stored on the cob, as noted in the Secondary occupation remains of Salmon Pueblo (K. Adams 1980:318) and ethnographically at recent pueblos (Kennard 1979:557; Ortiz 1979:289). However, if maize was intended to be consumed away from the site, then milling prior to redistribution could have reduced transportation costs by eliminating the nonedible portion of the maize and reducing the bulk of transported goods.

To the extent that specialization occurred at the individual, household, village, or regional level, economic interdependence would have been promoted, along with the development of surpluses that could be exchanged for other goods or services. Cornmeal could have been one such product.

Flintworking is the second inferred major realm of specialization. In a comparative analysis of projectile point samples from Salmon Pueblo and other

Anasazi sites, Moore (1981) suggested that local styles were maintained through time, and that stylistic differences between localities were greater than changes within localities or in the region as a whole (Moore 1981:52–83). According to Moore's interpretation, Salmon's tools were likely manufactured for local consumption.

As shown in the spatial relationships between Chacoan outliers and adjacent sites (Marshall et al. 1979), and according to the preceding discussion, I think that Salmon Pueblo was a provider of goods for its own population and perhaps for other settlements in its locality. These goods probably included projectile points and metates. Such a role for Salmon is also suggested by the manufacture of Chacoan style ceramics, presumably for local consumption, with local materials during the initial occupation of Salmon Pueblo (Franklin 1980:437). In addition, the Chacoan community at Salmon Pueblo may have provided subsistence goods, including cornmeal, to other members of the larger Chacoan interaction group. This role is compatible with the concept of an urban center under conditions of economic expansion (Trigger 1972). If Salmon Pueblo was a Chaco Canyon urban outpost, settling populations at Salmon Pueblo could have generated energy for the larger Chaco Canyon system.

The production of surplus cornmeal seems feasible also in light of Salmon Ruin's physiographic situation. Both Irwin-Williams (personal communication) and Nials (personal communication) have suggested that the Salmon area's agricultural potential was well suited for intensive farming production, watered by runoff from slopes. A similar function for other Chacoan satellite communities, located in agriculturally productive areas, has been suggested by Marshall et al. (1979:338–339). Similarly, the site's association with the contemporaneous Bonito phase road network (Marshall et al. 1979) may indicate that the Salmon community was involved with the intraregional movement of relatively large quantities of goods or people.

ARCHAEOLOGICAL INVESTIGATIONS OF LITHIC SPECIALIZATION

Archaeologists attempting to elucidate specialization must first consider site-specific formation and transformation processes. For example, at Salmon Pueblo, studies of portable artifact distribution were generally nonproductive, partially due to the "cleanliness" of the Chacoan occupants and their orderly abandonment of the site. Thus, few lithic items entered the archaeological record at their location of manufacture or use. In addition, one massive transformation effected by the thirteenth-century reoccupation and renovation of the site further decreased the reliability of most distributional studies. This does not mean that distributional studies of the archaeological deposits cannot provide evidence for identifying specialization, but for this to be possible, specific conditions such as use-related deposition without redeposition must have prevailed so that use-context associations would be preserved (Schiffer 1976).

Similarly, catchment area characteristics must be considered if specialization is to be inferred from limited access to raw materials. The factors limiting raw material availability include not only its spatial distribution, but also its state of occurrence. For example, chalcedony on a pediment surface is quite accessible, but chalcedony in veins in a subsurface rock stratum is relatively inaccessible, even though the stratum may be widespread. In the latter example, accessibility may be limited not by a restricted distribution for the material, but by the need for labor or technology to extract it. When the natural occurrence of raw materials is relatively unlimited, as is the case with most of the Salmon Chacoan lithic raw materials, then by extension, accessibility is unlimited. Consequently, analytic methods must be devised to identify subtle, qualitative variations in raw materials that may indicate increased selectivity by specialists.

The most effective means of investigating specialization at Salmon Pueblo proved to be the study of artifactual evidence that was least affected by depositional transformations. The two most productive approaches were examination of technological standardization and determination of the level of manufacturing expertise. These types of data are certainly related both analytically and theoretically. They are the recognizable differences that make, for example, Marshalltown trowels distinguishable from Stanley trowels, regardless of style.

Chapter 48

SITE ENTRY POSE OF BRUSHY BASIN TCHAMAHIAS AND IMPLICATIONS FOR CRAFT SPECIALIZATION AT SALMON RUINS

by Phillip H. Shelley

Tchamahia is a Keres word given to the tool form by the Hopi (Parsons 1936:555). Ethnographic documentation reveals that the Hopis use tchamahias as altar equipment during the Snake Ceremony (Parsons 1936:596, 673). Parsons has pointed out that the traditional association of the tchamahia with the Snake Ceremony may stem from the Snake Clan's origination amongst the Keres of Acoma and Laguna (Parsons 1936:714), where "each clan owns a tsamahiya … which may be symbolically fed … and … rocked … like a baby" (Ellis 1959: 330). Ellis (1959:330) described these tchamahias as a "smooth unworked stone about a foot or more in length, one-half to three-quarters of an inch in thickness and tapered at one or both ends." Ellis (1967) later presented data indicating that ethnographically and archaeologically known tchamahias may not always be the same kinds of objects, and this variation may relate to differences in tool function. The only use-detached bit flake recovered from Salmon that might be considered a primary-context artifact or de facto refuse (Schiffer 1976:33) was found in plaza excavations adjacent to a kiva. White (1942:196) has noted, based on ethnography, the communal cultivation of a ceremonial corn plot in back of the Santa Ana Pueblo church. As noted by Woodbury (1954:166) and Hayes (1976:83), the use of tchamahias in exclusively ceremonial contexts may be a relatively recent phenomenon. Contextual information and microwear analysis of Salmon tchamahias (Table 48.1), as well as inclusion of a hafted tchamahia in a cache of agricultural tools from Chaco Canyon (Hayes 1976:75), indicate that the Brushy Basin tchamahias were apparently used to cultivate agricultural plots (Figure 48.1).

Since the 1930s (Morris 1939; Woodbury 1954), archaeologists working in the Four Corners area have recognized that the distinctive Brushy Basin chert (often referred to as hornstone) was selected for the manufacture of a certain morphological class of tools called tchamahias. Morris (1939:139) considered these tools to be a San Juan Mesa Verde trait. Although no precise exploited source area has been reported, archaeologists have used a statement by Morris (based on information related to him by a Navajo man) to infer that this raw material was located "in the Four Corners area" (Morris 1939:140).

BRUSHY BASIN CHERT

Brushy Basin chert is a member of the Morrison Formation, a massive sedimentary rock unit with outcrops in New Mexico, Arizona, Utah, and Colorado. This chert (Warren's Type 2552; Harris et al. 1967:220–221) shows tremendous variation in degree of crystallinity, silica content, color, and "banding." It is a microcyptocrystalline silicified siltstone or limestone that retains relict sedimentary structure (laminations); it ranges from a light

Table 48.1. Use and wear observations for Salmon Ruin tchamahias. Sample includes all whole, partial, and fragmentary tools where bit observations could be made (n = 13).

Edge Angle
  Mean = 64°
  S = 12°
  Range 48–84°

Stria Direction on Face at Bit
  Present on 100% of tools
  62% parallel to long axis
  31% oblique to long axis
  7% perpendicular to long axis

Location of Use-Polish on Bit Micro-Flake Scars
  Present on 54% of tools
  98% Low and high point polish
  2% Low point polish only

Micro-Flake Direction Definition*
  71% unidirectional
  29% bidirectional
  43% salient
  57% diffuse

*Less than 3 mm maximum dimension.

Figure 48.1. Photograph of Brushy Basin chert quarry along the San Juan River.

yellow (Munsell 2.5Y 8.5/6) to a moderate yellow-ish brown (10YR 5/4). The laminations are highly variable in thickness and color, but are typically 0.5 cm thick and brilliant greenish yellow (7.5Y 8.5/8) to yellowish gray (10Y 8.5/2) in color. Also, many samples contain fossilized seeds or insects.

This material, which is limited to the Second-ary assemblage at Salmon, exhibits a unique site entry pose. The concept of "site entry pose" is adapted from Gearing's (1958) "structural pose," which he used to characterize seasonal variation amongst the eighteenth-century Cherokee. This concept provides a viable framework for discussing the lithic acquisition patterns (direct and indirect) of an assemblage that contains multiple local and imported lithic materials. Variations in the acquisi-

Figure 48.2. Ground surface of Brushy Basin chert quarry showing lithic debitage.

tion patterns are likely related to the state of occurrence of the raw material in the site's natural and cultural catchment area, the transport distance, the utility of material (or tools made from it) in any particular state, and the utility of debitage produced by further reduction. Determining the means of a raw material's entry into a site's lithic system can allow differentiation between generalized trade in lithic raw materials and trade in craft products. The identification of such a difference, when possible, has implications regarding variation in regional adaptive systems and quantitative patterning in the archaeological record.

As part of the regional raw material study conducted in conjunction with the Salmon Ruin research project, an area was located that showed aboriginal exploitation of a localized, high-quality variant of the Brushy Basin member approximately 108 km downstream from Salmon on the San Juan River (Figure 48.2). Although work on the Salmon project has identified a closer Brushy Basin geologic unit, no evidence was found of aboriginal exploitation.

The lithic procurement area is located on an erosional spur of a mesa on the southeast side of Todaskoni Wash, near the confluence of this drainage with the San Juan River. The surface of this

spur is literally paved with debitage; there are more than 500 pieces of debitage per square meter (Figure 48.3). The reduction debris, based on the prominence of bulbar attributes of flakes and bulbar scars of cores, indicates that mainly hard-hammer initial reduction occurred at the outcrop. The aborted cores among the lithic debris indicate that the intended objective of the reduction activity was a Stage 1 "edged" biface (Callahan 1976:131) or tchamahia blank. It also appears that at some location other than the outcrop, these Stage 1 bifaces were further reduced by soft-hammer techniques to Stage 2 bifaces (Figure 48.4). This inference is based on the preservation of manufacturing-related, expanded-diffuse bulbar scar remnants on ground and polished tchamahias and a general flattening in the tool's cross-section that appears to have occurred prior to finishing. After the desired cross-section, outline, and lamination pattern were obtained, the Stage 2 bifaces were ground and polished into final form. Replicative experimentation indicates that effective grinding of cryptocrystalline silicate material requires a slurry of water and grit between the active and the passive abraders (Pond 1930). Because of the need for slurry, this stage in the reduction sequence was likely conducted along the banks of the San Juan River.

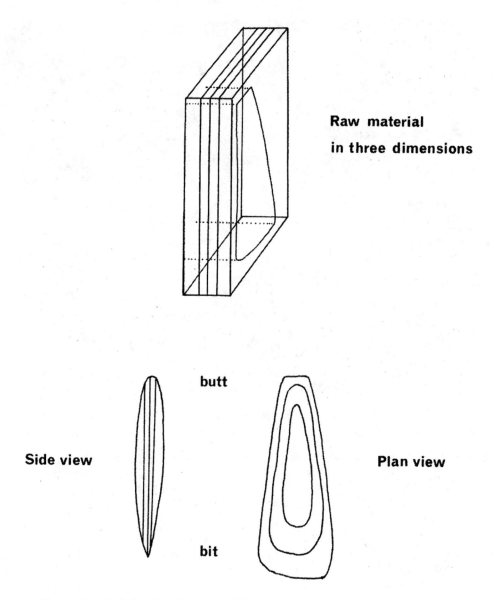

**Raw material
in three dimensions**

butt

Side view

bit

Plan view

Figure 48.3. Relationship of raw material lamination pattern to finished tool form.

The variation in surface texture of the hafting area shows that some tchamahias were "lapped" to a finer degree than others prior to hafting. When grinding was deemed sufficient, the tool was hafted via binding and mastic, as indicated by postmanufacturing surface area microphenomena. It appears that prehistoric tchamahia craftsmen deliberately bisected the natural laminations of the Brushy Basin chert in such a manner that the laminations describe a series of relatively continuous concentric lines that internally circumscribe the finished tool's outline in plan view (see Figure 48.3). This outline pattern was observed on 95 percent of the Brushy Basin tchamahias from Salmon. Variation in the degree of flake scar obliteration by

way of grinding may be explained by deliberate attempts to achieve this pattern. For example, if the tchamahia from Salmon were ground to such an extent that all of the manufacturing-related flake scars were removed, then much, if not all, of the laminae pattern would also have been eradicated. Attempts to achieve this patterning can be seen in the discarded bifaces in the quarry refuse (see Figure 48.4).

BRUSHY BASIN TCHAMAHIAS

The unhafted portions of the Salmon tchamahias became damaged and further polished by use in fine-grained sediments and by an occasional encounter with a rock. Sometimes through use (or

Figure 48.4. Representative sample of aborted bifaces from quarry site. Numbers identify individual tools; (o) is obverse view.

misuse) tchamahias were broken transversely, as indicated by a majority of transverse fractures on Salmon tools that truncate the polished surfaces. Many tchamahias show evidence of refurbishing by percussion and pecking techniques. It is interesting that the only evidence of pecking on tchamahias occurs as transverse fractures. There is no indication of refurbishing (grinding of flaked or pecked surfaces) by Salmon inhabitants.

In some instances, Salmon knappers apparently made attempts, via percussion, to reestablish

quality working bits on tchamahias by removing 90-degree angles created by use-generated transverse fractures. All such known attempts were futile. The technology employed to notch, stem, edge, or otherwise refurbish the hafting (butt) or cutting (bit) ends was more appropriate for working the much coarser grained igneous or metamorphic rocks used for other ground and pecked tools at Salmon. Such techniques were not successfully employed on the finer Brushy Basin tchamahias. Brushy Basin chert is a cryptocrystalline silicate

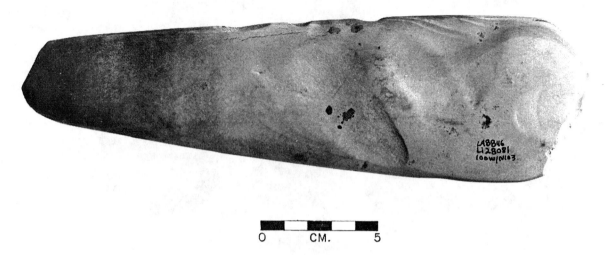

Figure 48.5. Tchamahia from Room 100W at Salmon.

that does not respond well to pecking techniques. This misapplication of a lithic technique seems to indicate a lack of familiarity on the part of the Salmon knappers with the mechanical properties of Brushy Basin chert.

DEBITAGE

Simple flake tools are the most frequent tool type in the Secondary lithic assemblage at Salmon; they account for 45 percent of the tools. In the Salmon assemblage, 88 percent of the Brushy Basin debitage consists of flakes generated by refurbishing, as indicated by the presence of ground and polished dorsal surfaces or platform remnants. These refurbishing flakes were often used as simple flake tools for cutting and scraping different types of materials (e.g., animal parts, plant parts), as well as for sawing soft materials (as indicated by microwear analysis). Brushy Basin refurbishing flakes show a higher incidence (more than 50%) of postdetachment use than any other similarly used cryptocrystalline material. Brushy Basin chert therefore appears to have been a preferred flake tool material. Had the Salmonites acquired this material directly, they would have transported it in a form that would have allowed them to take advantage of flakes generated by further reduction.

SUMMARY AND CONCLUSIONS

In the Salmon assemblage, more than 60 percent of the formal tools made from Brushy Basin chert are "finished" tools, 37 percent are refurbished tools, and at least 80 percent of the debitage is indicative of refurbishing activities (Figure 48.5).

Brushy Basin chert thus arrived at Salmon Pueblo as finished or nearly finished tools.

Imported obsidian and Narbona (Washington) Pass chert both occur in the Salmon Secondary assemblage as cores, as used and unused debitage, and as formal tools (projectile points). A possible synonymous pose may be that of turquoise, but because of turquoise working processes (incising, crumbling, and abrading) and the low archaeological visibility of the byproducts of these processes, combined with the small sample size of turquoise in the Salmon assemblage (34 pieces), the site entry pose of this material remains unknown.

The on-site misapplication of lithomechanical techniques and the high frequency of postdetachment use of refurbishing debitage (Table 48.2) suggest that the Secondary occupants of Salmon were obtaining Brushy Basin tchamahias by way of

Table 48.2. Frequency of postdetachment use of cryptocrystalline debitage from Secondary assemblage at Salmon.

Raw Material	Frequency (n)	% Used
Chalcedony	2402	16.69
Silicified palmwood	50	20.00
Silicified wood	2160	19.21
Jasper	126	23.01
Chert, other	5972	14.63
Chert, fossil	13	30.76
Narbona (Washington) Pass chert	166	31.92
Brushy Basin chert	22	54.55

indirect acquisition (trade). This also seems a likely possibility at other sites where the occurrence of Brushy Basin tchamahias has been reported. There is no indication from any site in the published reports of these tools appearing in a less than finished stage of manufacture.

Furthermore, the remarkable degree of homogeneity in metric and morphological attributes, which were not affected by the variability introduced through use-refurbish-reuse processes, suggests that Brushy Basin tchamahias were standardized. This standardization may indicate that relatively few individuals were involved in Brushy Basin tchamahia production. The low frequency of occurrence, which is typical for these tools, may also support the inference that relatively few individuals were involved in their production. For example, at Awatovi, there were eight Brushy Basin tchamahias in an assemblage of more than 8300 lithic artifacts (Woodbury 1954:23, 165–166). In the Secondary component at Salmon, a minimum of 28 and a maximum of 51 Brushy Basin tchamahias were recovered, in an assemblage of more than 75,000 items. This suggests that perhaps full-time (and at least part-time) specialists were producing these tools, which were then traded into Salmon and other sites.

Tchamahias provide the only known example of specialization within the Secondary occupation lithic system. When compared with Primary component indications of specialization within the lithic system, the Secondary occupation at the Salmon Site appears to have shifted its relationship to regional adaptational strategies. At this time, Salmon became a consumer of specialized lithic tools, in contrast with the earlier role of producing specialized tools.

Chapter 49

PRELIMINARY ANALYSIS OF FAUNAL MATERIAL FROM SALMON RUINS

by Arthur H. Harris

Faunal materials from Salmon Ruins were received by the Laboratory for Environmental Biology (LEB) for identification over a period of several years. One portion of the materials was identified under contract; the remainder served as a practical exercise in a graduate-level course, Bioarchaeology. All identification was done under my supervision. For analysis and interpretation I used the data from contract and class research, along with some information available from earlier reports by personnel at the Arizona State Museum (Kelley et al. 1974; Beezley 1975).

METHODOLOGY

Identifications were accomplished by standard techniques, using the literature and, in particular, synoptic comparative material in the resource collections at the LEB. Other data recorded in addition to identifications included the element or portion of element involved, the side of the animal represented, the sex and age (at death) when determinable, presence of cuts, whether worked by man, presence of obvious pathologies, and comments on the condition of the bone (particularly whether burned or not). I depended primarily upon the work sheets of the original identifiers.

Most fish and bird elements were separated for later submission to experts in those groups; however, lack of available funds ultimately prevented obtaining low-level taxonomic identifications.

Because of different levels of competency, particularly between the contract personnel and some class members in Bioarchaeology, all data are not equally trustworthy. I have interpreted all data conservatively to prevent acceptance of unjustified identifications or other biased data; because of the conservatism, there has been some loss of informational content. This is most serious in the determination of the minimum number of individuals (MNI) necessary to account for the presence of the identified elements, because in some cases it was unclear whether two or more fragments could have come from the same element and thus from the same individual.

Analysis was primarily based on MNI; gross bone fragment counts and bone weight techniques are believed to be much more biased than MNI (see Heller 1976). The MNI is calculated by counting the most common element (treating different sides as different elements); also taken into account are obvious features of size, age, and sex. More elaborate techniques, such as described by Chapin (1971), were not used.

The use of MNI as a basis for calculating relative proportions of taxa making up the archaeological fauna is not without bias (Harris 1968; Heller 1976). Two points are of particular importance: the site unit used to calculate MNI and the assumption that the MNI is equally easy to determine for all taxa.

The available data leave the stratum-room unit as the logical unit upon which to base MNI. Thus all recovered and identified faunal elements from a particular stratum in a particular room were used to determine the minimum number of individuals required to supply those elements. The other alternative was to use the occupation-site unit—that is, all available elements from a given occupation for the entire site. The logistics of a unit of that size are far beyond the resources available at this time. The MNI figures used in comparison with units other than the stratum-room unit (e.g., occupation-site) are based on manipulations of MNI from the stratum-room units.

Taxa differ in their ease of recognition. For example, even small fragments of bones are often easily identifiable as jackrabbit (*Lepus* sp.). However, even entire limb elements may not allow separation of *Cynomys gunnisoni* from *Spermophilus variegates* at the generic level because of extensive similarities in size and configuration. Likewise, medium-sized artiodactyls such as deer, pronghorn, and mountain sheep may be unrecognizable even to family because of similarity of limb elements combined with the cultural fragmentation of limbs of large mammals.

"Cf." (*confer* = compare) indicates identifications that are probable but not certain, and "?" indicates what is essentially an informed guess. Individual species accounts should also be consulted for information on the likelihood of correct specific identifications.

Table 49.1 gives a complete list of taxa identified from the site (LEB plus Arizona State Museum). The identifications and MNI for analyzed units are given in Tables 49.2 through 49.16. A list of taxa with MNI by occupation level is presented in Table 49.17.

DESCRIPTIONS OF SPECIES

Osteichthyes (Bony Fish)

The only specific identification of fish available is that of the Colorado squawfish (*Ptychocheilus lucius*), identified by Kelley et al. (1974). This species is recorded historically from the San Juan drainage. Its relatively large size could make it a favored fish for eating. A number of other species are possible.

Most of the material was such that MNI estimates were rendered useless. In practice, the presence of fish elements translated to an MNI of 1 in each stratum-room unit in which fish elements were found.

Bufo sp. (Common Toads)

Kelley et al. (1974) recorded the presence of this genus. Natural occurrence would be expected rather than human use. I have speculated elsewhere (Harris 1963a) that ruins may even be attractants to toads for hibernation sites.

Cnemidophorus sp. (Whiptailed Lizards)

Kelley et al. (1974) recorded the presence of whiptailed lizards. At least three species occur now in the area and members of the genus would be expected to use the site for shelter.

Crotalus sp. (Rattlesnakes)

This genus of rattlesnake was recorded by Kelley et al. (1974). The prairie rattlesnake (*C. viridis*) is not uncommon today in the region and could be present either naturally or with the connivance of humans.

Branta canadensis (Canadian Goose)

The Canadian goose was reported by Kelley et al. (1974) and by Beezley (1975). We identified goose in one room, but could not assign it to genus. Migrating geese would be expected along the San Juan.

Cf. Aythya affinis (Lesser Scaup)

This duck is common in migration throughout the waterways of the state (Ligon 1961). It was tentatively reported by Beezley (1975).

Cf. Anas platyrhynchos (Mallard)

Mallards both breed and winter in New Mexico (Ligon 1961). It is expectable along the San Juan River.

Cf. Mergus (Mergansers)

The fish-eating ducks are common winter visitors to the area, apparently nesting only seldomly in New Mexico, at higher elevations than Salmon Ruins (Ligon 1961).

Aquila chrysaetos (Golden Eagle)

Kelley et al. (1974) and Beezley (1975) recorded the presence of golden eagles. Eagles are widespread in archaeological faunas, and judging from ethnographic accounts, were probably used ceremonially.

Meleagris gallopavo (Turkey)

Turkey was one of the most common animals at Salmon Ruins. According to Ligon (1961:103), Merriam's turkey (the subspecies native to northwestern New Mexico) "was confined to the conifer-oak mountain forests of the Southwest." Presumably, all the archaeological remains are of domestic birds; the plentitude and casual discard indicates their use for food (see Reed 1951). Eggshell was present, at least during the Secondary occupation, and the general size and thickness of the fragments are consistent with this species.

Grus canadensis (Sandhill Crane)

Sandhill cranes are known from archaeological sites in the Cochiti area, in the Rio Grande drainage; Harris (1968) suggested their use as food in that region, although pointing out that procurement for feathers could not be ruled out.

These large birds may occur along the San Juan River during migration. Spring migration generally occurs from February to early March and fall migration during September and October (Ligon 1961).

Cf. Fulica americana (American Coot)

Remains of probably one individual are similar to the American coot, but differ sufficiently to throw identification into some doubt. In any case, a water bird appears to be represented, probably used for food and/or feathers.

Zenaida macroura (Mourning Dove)

Beezley (1975) reported one bone of mourning dove. This is currently a common game bird in the area during the warmer seasons.

Table 49.1. Taxa identified from Salmon Ruins. Only the most specific identifications available are recorded here; in some genera, other unrecognized species are almost certainly present.

Ptychocheilus lucius	Colorado squawfish
Bufo sp.	Common toad
Cnemidophorus sp.	Whiptailed lizard
Crotalus sp.	Rattlesnake
Branta canadensis	Canadian goose
Anas platyrhynchos	Mallard
Aythya affinis	Lesser scaup
Mergus sp.	Merganser
Aquila chrysaetos	Golden eagle
Meleagris gallopavo	Turkey
Grus canadensis	Sandhill crane
Fulica americana	American coot
Zenaida macroura	Mourning dove
Ara macao	Scarlet macaw
Ara militaris	Military macaw
Picidae	Woodpeckers
Pica pica	Black-billed magpie
Corvus corax	Common raven
Lanius ludovicianus	Loggerhead shrike
Icteridae	Blackbird family
Sylvilagus auduboni	Desert cottontail
Lepus californicus	Black-tailed jackrabbit
Eutamias sp.	Chipmunk
Ammospermophilus leucurus	White-tailed antelope squirrel
Spermophilus spilosoma	Spotted ground squirrel
Spermophilus variegates	Rock squirrel
Cynomys gunnisoni	Gunnison's prairie dog
Sciurus aberti	Abert's squirrel
Thomomys bottae	Botta's pocket gopher
Perognathus sp.	Pocket mouse
Dipodomys ordi	Ord's kangaroo rat
Dipodomys spectabilis	Banner-tailed kangaroo rat
Castor canadensis	Beaver
Peromyscus sp.	White-footed mouse
Onychomys leucogaster	Northern grasshopper mouse
Neotoma cf. *albigula*	White-throated wood rat
Microtus sp.	Vole
Erethizon dorsatum	Porcupine
Canis familiaris	Domestic dog
Urocyon cinereoargenteus	Gray fox
Procyon lotor	Raccoon
Mustela frenata	Long-tailed weasel
Taxidea taxus	Badger
Lynx rufus	Bobcat
Ursus americanus	Black bear
Cervus elaphus	Elk
Odocoileus hemionus	Mule deer
Antilocapra americana	Pronghorn
Ovis canadensis	Mountain sheep

Table 49.2. Minimum number of individuals by stratum, Room 1W.

	Stratum				
Taxon	A	B	C	D	E
Fish	–	–	1	1	–
Meleagris gallopavo	1	1	–	–	–
Sylvilagus cf. *auduboni*	–	–	–	–	–
Sylvilagus sp.	2	1	1	–	–
Lepus californicus	1	–	–	–	–
Cynomys gunnisoni	1	–	1	–	–
Cf. *Thomomys*	1*	–	1*	–	–
Peromyscus sp.	–	–	1	–	–
Onychomys leucogaster	1	–	–	–	–
Odocoileus hemionus	1	1	1	–	1
Antilocapra/Ovis	1	–	–	1	–

*Same individual,

Table 49.3. Minimum number of individuals by depths,* Room 2W.

Taxon	Depth 1.55–1.65	Depth TT, 5.40–5.50
Anatidae	1	–
Sylvilagus sp.	2	–
Lepus californicus	1	–
Thomomys bottae	1	–
Peromyscus/Onychomys	1	–
?Vulpes	1	–
Artiodactyla	1	1

*No strata designations assigned.

Table 49.4. Minimum number of individuals by stratum, Room 4B.

	Stratum		
Taxon	A-1-01	B-1-02	H-1-03 & I-1-04
Fish	–	1	–
Meleagris gallopavo	1	1	1
Sylvilgus auduboni	1	2	–
Sylvilagus sp.	–	2	2
Lepus californicus	–	1	1
Thomomys bottae	–	2	–
Spermophilus ?spilosoma	–	1	–
Cf. *Spermophilus variegatus*	–	1	–
Cf. *Sciurus aberti*	–	1	–
Castor canadensis	–	1	–
Peromyscus sp.	–	5	1
Onychomys leucogaster	–	–	1
Neotoma sp.	–	1	–
Cf. *Procyon lotor*	–	1	–
Odocoileus hemionus	–	1 (cf.)	1
Antilocapra americana	–	1	–

Table 49.5. Minimum number of individuals by stratum, Room 4W.

Taxon	Stratum				
	B-2-05	F-1-06	G-2-07	H-2-08	H-3-11, H-3-12
Fish	–	–	1	–	–
Meleagris gallopavo	1	–	1	–	1
Bird	1	1	–	–	–
Sylvilagus auduboni	1	–	1	–	–
Sylvilagus sp.	–	1	1	–	1
Lepus californicus	1	–	1	–	1
Cynomys/S. variegatus	1	1	–	–	–
Dipodomys	1	–	–	–	–
Cf. *Castor canadensis*	1	–	–	–	–
Peromyscus sp.	1	–	1	–	–
Felidae	–	–	–	1	–
Cervus elaphus	–	–	1	–	–
Odocoileus hemionus	1	1	1	1	–
Antilocapra americana	–	1	–	–	–

Table 49.6. Minimum number of individuals by stratum, Room 5A.

Taxon	Stratum				
	A-1-01	B-1-02	C-1-03	G-1-04	H-1-05, I-1-06
Bird	–	–	1	–	–
Meleagris gallopavo	1	1	–	1	–
Homo sapiens	–	1	–	–	–
Sylvilagus sp.	1	2	1	2	1
Lepus californicus	1	1	1	2	–
Spermophilus spilosoma	–	1	–	–	–
Thomomys bottae	–	–	–	1	1
Peromyscus sp.	–	–	–	1	–
Neotoma sp.	1	–	–	–	–
Canidae	–	–	1	–	–
Odocoileus hemionus	–	–	1	1	1
Large mammal	1	1	–	–	–

Ara macao and *Ara militaris* (Scarlet Macaw and Military Macaw)

Macaw identification was based on data from Hargrave (1970), but some findings are unfortunately inconsistent with the information in Hargrave's report. Thus, we cannot place as much confidence in the identifications as would be ideal. The identification of scarlet macaw appears reasonably acceptable; that of military macaw is less certain.

The present geographic ranges of macaws reach north to central Sonora in the case of the military macaw and to southern Tamaulipas and Oaxaca for the scarlet macaw. Macaws obviously were trade items at Salmon Ruins, as they were elsewhere in the Southwest (Hargrave 1970).

Picidae (Woodpeckers)

Kelley et al. (1974) tentatively identified one bone as picid. Flickers (*Colaptes auratus*) in particular seem to have been widely valued for their decorative feathers; possibly this is the case here. A number of species of woodpeckers occur in the area today.

Corvus corax (Common Raven)

Common ravens occur now in the San Juan valley. They have been known to be used in a ceremo-

Table 49.7. Minimum number of individuals by stratum, Room 5W.

Taxon	Stratum		
	G-2-06, H-2-07	B-2-09	H-2-07
Meleagris gallopavo	1	–	–
Sylvilagus sp.	–	–	1
Odocoileus hemionus	–	1	1
Cf. *Antilocapra americana*	–	1	–

nial manner. For example, associated wing elements have been reported in circumstances suggesting a wing fan (Hargrave 1939).

Lanius ludovicianus (Loggerhead Shrike)

Kelley et al. (1974) identified two bones to this species. Although edible, use of the plumage seems more likely than procurement for food.

Icteridae (Blackbirds)

Two bones were assigned to this family by Kelley et al. (1974). Although some species have striking plumage that might warrant hunting, it should be noted that several kinds of blackbirds are potentially destructive to crops, possibly requiring protective measures.

Sylvilagus auduboni (Desert Cottontail)

The desert cottontail is the most common species near the site today, occurring in virtually all major terrestrial habitats. Nuttall's cottontail (*Sylvilagus nuttalli*) occurs only a short distance to the north, in heavy piñon-juniper woodland, mesic drainages, and higher vegetational zones (Harris 1963b). These two cottontails can often be distinguished by their lower jaws or third lower premolars (Findley et al. 1975). All specifically identifiable cottontails were *S. auduboni*.

Lepus californicus (Black-tailed Jackrabbit)

Only the black-tailed jackrabbit now occurs near the site area, and all jackrabbit elements are probably this species. Two other species—the white-tailed jackrabbit *L. townsendi* and the snowshoe hare *L. americanus*—occur in the higher mountains to the north. Of these, the former is not distinguishable from *L. californicus* by most elements recoverable from archaeological sites; thus *L. towsendi* cannot be ruled out on a morphological basis. The site's jackrabbits are assigned on the basis of current distribution and the lack of credible evidence for use of *L. towsendi* habitat by the Puebloans.

Cf. *Eutamias* (Chipmunks)

Kelley et al. (1974) listed two bones as cf. *Eutamias*. The Colorado chipmunk (*E. quadrivittatus*) is currently found in rock outcrops along the San Juan valley (Harris 1963b).

Cf. *Ammospermophilus leucurus* (White-tailed Antelope Squirrel)

Kelley et al. (1974) also listed two bones as *Citellus* cf. *leucurus*. This species, now generally placed in the genus *Ammospermophilus*, occurs throughout the immediate region except probably in the more developed riparian habitats (Harris 1963b).

Spermophilus spilosoma (Spotted Ground Squirrel)

This small ground squirrel was noted in an earlier study to occur "only in relatively flat grasslands south of the San Juan River" (Harris 1963b). Its presence at the site might suggest use of those grasslands for small game, but little information is available from the region on rangeland degradation by domestic livestock and its effect on the distribution of grassland mammals. The squirrel may have occurred nearby in aboriginal times.

Spermophilus variegates (Rock Squirrel)

Rock squirrels are almost always associated with rocky outcrops, occasionally with steep-sided arroyos, and at times in well-developed riparian habitats (Harris 1963b). It likely occurs now along the breaks of the San Juan, although the nearest known records are at Flora Vista and near the present Navajo Reservoir (Findley et al. 1975). It may have occurred naturally at the site.

Cynomys gunnisoni (Gunnison's Prairie Dog)

Although much of the *Cynomys* material is identifiable morphologically only to the generic level, all remains were referred to *C. gunnisoni* as the only expectable species.

Prairie dogs generally avoid areas with high water tables or heavy shrub or arboreal vegetation. Thus their presence at the site most likely was through the agency of humans; possibly the prairie dogs invaded cleared, unused croplands. Open grasslands and uncultivated croplands are the preferred habitat today in the area (Harris 1963b). Bailey (1932) reported the historic use of Gunnison's prairie dog by Navajos in New Mexico.

Sciurus aberti (Abert's Squirrel)

One dentary was identified tentatively as *S. aberti*. Although complete dentaries generally are identifiable with confidence in the absence of other expectable species of *Sciurus*, partial dentaries can be confused with those of rock squirrels (*Spermophilus variegatus*). Abert's squirrel is rather strictly limited to ponderosa pine forest; however, the single tentative identification cannot be taken as indicative of the use of such habitat by site inhabitants.

Thomomys bottae (Botta's Pocket Gopher)

The only pocket gopher occurring in the study area is *T. bottae*, although the northern pocket gopher (*T. talpoides*) occurs in the high mountains. Most of the archaeological gopher material is not assignable to species on a morphological basis, but rather is assumed to be of this species because of geographic and ecologic considerations.

Because of their fossorial nature, Botta's pocket gophers often occur naturally in archaeological sites, but they are also known to be eaten in modern times in Mexico (Leopold 1959) and in the past by Puebloans at Arroyo Honda. There is no evidence of their use at Salmon Ruins.

Perognathus sp. (Pocket Mice)

Only one individual was identified. Both the silky pocket mouse (*P. falvus*) and the plains pocket mouse (*P. flacescens*) occur in the area. The first, in particular, would be apt to occur naturally at the site. Utilization is unlikely.

Dipodomys ordi (Ord's Kangaroo Rat)

This rodent occurs commonly from the site area southward, particularly in areas of friable substratum. A burrower, it is apt to be a natural component of the recovered fauna.

Dipodomys spectabilis (Bannertailed Kangaroo Rat)

This is a considerably larger animal than *D. ordi* and it tends to inhabit somewhat grassier, heavier soils. Its large, complex den mounds are easily recognized and could invite excavation for the animal itself or for stored seed. Whether this actually occurred is unknown; its occurrence could be natural.

Castor canadensis (Beaver)

Beavers occur now along the San Juan River. Their occurrence at the site almost certainly records usage for food or fur, or most likely both.

Peromyscus sp. (White-footed Mice)

Mice of the genus *Peromyscus* are ubiquitous in the Southwest. Several species occur in the vicinity of Salmon Ruins; their presence at the site would be expected both during and after human occupancy. No evidence suggests utilization.

Onychomys leucogaster (Northern Grasshopper Mouse)

This mouse is widespread in the sagebrush and grassland areas of the San Juan Basin. It shares the general comments on behavior recorded above for *Peromyscus*.

Neotoma sp. (Wood Rats)

One or another species of wood rats inhabits almost every part of the Southwest. In the San Juan region of New Mexico, four species occur (Harris 1963b), with three possible near the site. Beezley (1975) recorded *Neotoma* cf. *albiqula*; our material was specifically unidentifiable. Wood rats are good eating and are utilized for food by various peoples (Bailey 1932; Leopold 1959); unfortunately, their habit of building dens in abandoned structures, fallen walls, and the like makes it difficult to tell if they were utilized at a particular site. There seems to be no concrete evidence for use at Salmon Ruins.

Microtus sp. (Voles)

A relict population of the eastern meadow vole (*M. pennsylvanicus*) occurs now along the San Juan River; the few vole remains are likely of this species. This vole is limited now to well-developed sedge beds near permanent water. Occurrence at the site may record the nearby presence of such habitat, use by humans, or the past defecations or regurgitations of bone-containing materials by predators at the site.

Erethizon dorsatum (Porcupine)

Porcupines are expectable in the site area; Kelley et al. (1974) identified one element and tentatively identified a second. Although probably indicating utilization, it is not impossible that fallen debris was used by porcupines for denning.

Canis sp. (Dogs)

Canis remains are surprisingly scant in our material, but Kelley et al. (1974) indicated 53 bones as probably representing domestic dog (*Canis familiaris*) and one bone definitely domestic dog; less specifically identified canids were also present. Our own material could have represented domestic dog or coyote (*C. latrans*), or both. Both species are expectable.

Vulpes spp. and *Urocyon cinereoargenteus* (Foxes)

Red fox (*Vulpes vulpes*), kit fox (*V. macrotis*), and gray fox (*Urocyon cinereoargenteus*) occur in the site area today. Of these, only the gray fox was positively identified (Beezley 1975). All of these foxes likely were used for ceremonial purposes.

Table 49.8. Minimum number of individuals by stratum, Room 6A.

Taxon	Stratum					
	A-1-01	B-1-02, B-2-03	C-1-04	C-2-05	C-3-5.5, N-1-5.1	H-1-5.2
Unidentified fish	–	–	1	–	–	–
Bird	–	–	–	–	1	–
Meleagris gallopavo	–	–	1	1	1	–
Syvilagus cf. *auduboni*	–	–	1	–	6	–
Sylvilagus sp.	1	1	1	4	1	1
Lepus californicus	–	–	1	1	1	–
Spermophilus spilosoma	–	–	–	–	1	–
Cynomys gunnisoni	–	–	1	2	1	–
Cynomys/S. variegatus	–	1	–	–	–	–
Thomomys bottae	–	–	–	1	–	–
Peromyscus sp.	–	–	–	1	–	–
Peromyscus/Onychomys	–	–	–	–	1	–
Lynx	–	–	–	–	1	–
Odocoileus hemionus	1(?)	–	1	–	1	1
Antilocapra americana	–	–	–	–	1	–
Artiodactyla	–	–	–	1	–	–
Large mammal	–	1	–	–	–	–

Cf. *Procyon lotor* (Raccoon)

These animals are potentially destructive of crops (Bailey 1932) and probably would be hunted in the immediate vicinity of the site for this reason, if not for flesh and fur. Bailey (1932) suggested that raccoons were relatively scarce in the San Juan valley; the few bones tentatively identified as those of raccoons suggest a similar situation in the past.

Mustela frenata (Long-tailed Weasel)

Long-tailed weasels occur throughout the San Juan valley of New Mexico. Beezley (1975) recorded one bone assignable to this species. The fur, sometimes with included skull portions, may have been used ceremonially (Seme 1980).

Taxidea taxus (Badger)

Badgers occur throughout the area in a variety of habitats. As with the other carnivores, presence is probably linked to use by humans. Badgers burrow extensively, however, and their occurrence could be intrusive, altahough the limited number of bones argues otherwise.

Ursus americanus (Black Bear)

Four bones were recorded by Kelley et al. (1974) as being those of this species of bear. Although now commonly limited to the rougher, higher elevations, bears should have occurred along the San Juan valley in the past.

Cervus elaphus (Elk)

The possible presence of elk is based solely on one bone of very uncertain identification. Today, elk live predominantly to the north, from well-developed woodland growth into the forested mountain habitats.

Odocoileus hemionus (Mule Deer)

Mule deer is the only expected species of *Odocoileus* in the San Juan Basin. Its distribution is limited primarily by the availability of cover and browse. It would have occurred along the valley proper and in rougher country in the surrounding areas.

Table 49.9. Minimum number of individuals by stratum, Room 6W.

Taxon	Stratum		
	G-1-01	C-1-02	L-1-10
Bird	–	1	–
Large bird	–	–	1
Sylvilagus sp.	1	–	1
Lepus californicus	–	–	1
Cynomys/S. variegatus	–	1	–
Medium-large mammal	–	1	–
Large mammal	1	–	1

Antilocapra americana (Pronghorn)

Pronghorns (frequently miscalled antelope) have been mostly extirpated from the San Juan region, though they were once common (Bailey 1932). The grasslands supported the largest numbers, but sightings have occurred in recent years in sagebrush flats surrounded by open woodland (Harris 1963b). Animals would not be expected in riparian situations, but should have been available above the breaks of the San Juan.

Ovis canadensis (Mountain Sheep)

Historically these sheep have been limited in northern New Mexico and southern Colorado to high mountain situations (Bailey 1932). There are few historical data regarding occurrences at lower elevations in the area. Widespread occurrence of remains in archaeological sites, however, strongly suggests occurrence in at least the more rugged areas below the forested zone as well as in the high mountain meadows and above timberline.

DISCUSSION

Today, the Salmon Ruins area is dominated by riparian growth in the San Juan valley and by arid grasslands and sagebrush-grasslands outside the valley proper. Woodland plants occur in the valley breaks and are increasingly common to the north at higher elevations. Ponderosa pine and Douglas fir appear south of the New Mexico–Colorado state line and become major components north of the line, giving way to spruce-fir forest at higher elevations, and eventually to above-timberline habitat less than 50 miles from the site (see Harris 1963b and Harris et al. 1967 for a general description of the region).

From a bioarchaeological point of view, one of the most remarkable features is the provincialism—the reliance upon animals found close to the site to the near or absolute exclusion of forms from more distant habitats. Except for the macaws—obvious imports—only elk (based on a single queried identification) and Abert's squirrel (a single uncertain identification) would not be expected within a few miles of the site, and argument could be advanced for possible presence of elk within that distance.

The evidence does not absolutely exclude use of the more distant habitats, but does allow several statements. For one, hunting of small game, at least, probably was not carried out as far north as well-developed piñon-juniper woodland or ponderosa

pine forest. If this was the case, Nuttall's cottontail and clear evidence of Abert's squirrel would be present. Also, elk tend to inhabit the higher mountains in summer, descending to lower elevations in winter. Winter hunting into the upper woodland and lower forest region would be expected to produce elk; thus these habitats were likely not utilized for big game procurement, at least during the colder parts of the year.

Relatively low percentages of pronghorn and mountain sheep (Table 49.17) suggest the absence of hunting in prime habitat, with only those animals venturing close to the site being taken.

Of the major groups known to have been used, the artiodactyls are by far the more important as a source of animal protein. One measure of the importance of a given taxon is the amount of edible meat obtainable per individual and the frequency of members of that taxon. By such measure, the artiodactyls from the Secondary occupation produced approximately 12 times the amount of edible meat as did the cottontail rabbits and jackrabbits taken together, and about eight times the amount of edible meat represented by turkey remains. Other occupation categories give similar results. The greater supply of meat produced by the artiodactyls must be balanced against the likely higher constancy of supply represented by the domestic birds and the easily hunted and abundant lagomorphs.

Table 49.17 allows comparisons between the different occupations at Salmon Ruins. Once again, the site appears conservative in that, in my opinion, there was no significant change in the use of animal resources during the times represented. This may be seen most clearly when several selected groups are abstracted from the table and presented separately (Table 49.18). The groups chosen are those least likely to be affected by the "noise" of noncultural presence or impulse hunting—that is, those basic to the economy and which would be expected to change with differences in cultural emphasis or resource perturbations. Considering the very considerable sources of potential bias (Harris 1963a), significant variation between occupation categories must be considered nil.

In brief, then, the Salmon Ruins site appears to have been inhabited by people using mostly or entirely local animal resources (except, of course, the exotic macaws) and, furthermore, the data show little change in resource exploitation through time.

Table 49.10. Minimum number of individuals by stratum, Room 7A.

| Taxon | Stratum | | | |
	A-1-01	F-1-02	B-1-03	I-1-04
Fish	–	1	–	–
Meleagris gallopavo	1	–	1	–
Lagomorpha	1	–	–	–
Sylvilagus auduboni	5	–	1	–
Sylvilagus sp.	–	2	4	1
Lepus californicus	1	1	–	–
Cynomys gunnisoni	1	–	1	–
Cynomys/S. variegatus	–	1	–	–
Thomomys bottae	1	1	1	–
Dipodomys ordi	–	1	1	–
Peromyscus sp.	1	–	1	–
Neotoma sp.	1	–	1(?)	–
Artiodactyla	1	–	–	–
Large mammal	–	1	–	–

Table 49.11. Minimum number of individuals by stratum, Room 7W.

| Taxon | Stratum | | | |
	B-1-01	N-1-02, F-1-03	F-1-03, G-1-04	I-1-05, K-1-07
Meleagris gallopavo	1	1	–	–
Sylvilagus cf. *auduboni*	2	–	–	–
Sylvilagus sp.	1	1	–	1
Lepus californicus	1	1	1	–
Cynomys/S. variegatus	1	–	–	1
Peromyscus/Onychomys	1	–	–	1
Odocoileus hemionus	–	–	1	–
Artiodactyla	1	–	–	1
Medium mammal	–	–	–	1
Large mammal	–	1	–	–

Table 49.12. Minimum number of individuals in several strata and rooms.

Stratum and Room	Taxa	Min. Number of Individuals
Room 33W, Stratum L-2-17.1	*Ara* sp.	1
	Cf. *Spermophilus variegatus*	1
Room 86W, Stratum H-3-14	Cf. *Ara*	1
Room 91W, Stratum C-6-20	*Meleagris gallopavo*	1
	Ara macao	1
	Cf. *Lepus*	1
Rooms 97A, 97B, or 97W, Stratum B-1-02	*Meleagris gallopavo*	1
	Sylvilagus sp.	1
	Lepus californicus	1
	Cynomys gunnisoni	1
Room 124, Stratum B-1-02	*Meleagris gallopavo*	1

Table 49.13. Minimum number of individuals by stratum, Rooms 97A and 97B.

Taxon	Stratum			
	B-1-02	C-1-03	H-1-04	I-1-05
Fish	–	1	–	–
Meleagris gallopavo	–	5	–	–
Bird	1	1	1	–
Sylvilagus auduboni	–	2	–	–
Sylvilagus sp.	–	2	–	1
Lepus californicus	1	2	–	1
Spermophilus variegatus	–	–	1	1
Cynomys gunnisoni	–	3	–	–
Cynomys/S. variegatus	–	–	1	1
Thomomys bottae	–	1	–	–
Castor canadensis	–	–	–	1
Peromyscus sp.	–	2	1	–
Peromyscus/Onychomys	–	–	1	–
Neotoma sp.	–	–	–	1
Canis sp.	1	1(cf.)	–	–
Lynx rufus	–	1	–	–
Odocoileus hemionus	–	1	–	1
Cf. *Antilocapra americana*	–	–	–	1
Artiodactyla	–	1	–	–

Table 49.14. Minimum number of individuals by stratum, Room 97W.

Taxon	Stratum				
	B-1-02	C-2-05	C-1-04	N-1-03	G-1-05
Meleagris gallopavo	1	–	2	2	1
Sylvilagus auduboni	–	–	–	2	2
Sylvilagus sp.	1	–	2	1	–
Lepus californicus	–	–	1	1	1
Cynomys gunnisoni	1	–	–	–	1
Cynomys/S. variegatus	–	–	1	1	1
Thomomys bottae	–	–	1	–	–
Peromyscus sp.	–	1	–	1	1
Onychomys leucogaster	–	–	–	1	–
Neotoma sp.	–	–	–	1	–
Odocoileus hemionus	–	–	1	1(cf.)	–
Medium mammal	–	1	–	–	–

Table 49.15. Minimum number of individuals by stratum, Room 100W.

Taxon	Stratum				
	C-1-04	C-1-4.1	C-2-05	C-2-5.1	C-2-5.3
Fish	1	–	1	–	1
Cf. *Mergus*	–	–	–	–	1
Anatidae (duck)	1	–	–	–	–
Meleagris gallopavo	4	1	3	1	3
Grus canadensis	1	–	–	–	–
Pica pica	1	1 (cf.)	1	–	–
Small passeriformes	1	–	–	–	–
Small bird	–	–	1	–	1
Sylvilagus auduboni	1	–	–	–	–
Sylvilagus sp.	6	1	3	1	2
Lepus californicus	4	–	1	1 (?)	1
Spermophilus sp.	–	–	–	1	1(?)
Cynomys gunnisoni	6	–	1	2	2
Thomomys bottae	2	–	1	–	–
Dipodomys ordi	2	–	–	–	–
Castor canadensis	1	–	–	–	–
Peromyscus sp.	2	–	1	–	–
Neotoma sp.	1	–	–	1	–
Microtus sp.	–	1	–	–	–
Small cricetidae	–	–	–	–	1
Cf. *Canis*	–	–	–	–	1
Cf. Fox	1	–	–	–	–
Lynx rufus	1	–	–	–	–
Medium carnivore	–	–	–	–	1
Odocoileus heminous	1	–	–	1	2
Antilocapra americana	2	–	1	1	–
Ovis canadensis	2	–	–	1	–
Artiodactyla	–	1	–	–	–

Table 49.15 (continued)

Taxon	Stratum				
	C-3-06	C-7-12	C-7-12.1	C-8-13	C-9-14
Fish	1	–	–	1	1
Cf. *Mergus*	–	1	–	1	–
Cf. *Anas platyrhynchos*	–	1	–	–	–
Anatidae (duck)	1	–	–	–	–
Anatidae (goose)	1	–	–	–	–
Cf. *Fulica americana*	1	–	–	–	–
Meleagris gallopavo	4	4	2	3	3
Grus canadensis	–	–	–	–	1
Small bird	1	–	–	–	–
Sylvilagus sp.	12	2	1	1	3
Lepus californicus	4	1	1	1	2
Lagomorpha	–	–	–	1	–
Spermophilus sp.	–	–	–	–	1

Table 49.15 (continued)

Taxon (continued)	Stratum				
	C-3-06	C-7-12	C-7-12.1	C-8-13	C-9-14
Cynomys gunnisoni	3	2	–	1	–
Thomomys bottae	2	–	–	–	–
Perognathus sp.	–	–	–	–	1
Dipodomys spectabilis	1	–	–	–	–
Castor canadensis	1	–	–	–	–
Peromyscus sp.	1	2	–	1	1
Neotoma sp.	1	–	–	–	–
Cf. *Microtus*	–	1	–	–	1
Fox	–	1	–	–	–
Canidae	–	–	–	1	–
Taxidea taxus	–	–	–	–	1
Lynx rufus	1	–	–	–	1
Odocoileus heminous	1	2	1	1	1
Antilocapra americana	1	–	–	1	1
Ovis canadensis	–	–	–	1	–

Table 49.15 (continued)

Taxon	Stratum				
	C-11-16	C-12-17	C-13-18	N-1-03	C-2-05.2, C-2-05.5, C-7-12.7
Fish	1	1	–	1	–
Snake	–	–	–	–	1
Anatidae (duck)	–	–	–	1	–
Meleagris gallopavo	2	–	–	2	3
Ara sp.	–	–	–	–	1
Bird	1	–	–	–	–
Sylvilagus sp.	4	–	1	4	1
Lepus californicus	1	–	–	1	–
Cynomys gunnisoni	–	–	–	1	1
Thomomys bottae	–	–	–	–	1
Castor canadensis	1	–	–	–	–
Peromyscus sp.	–	–	–	–	1
Canis	–	–	–	1	–
Cf. *Taxidea taxus*	1	–	–	–	–
Odocoileus heminous	1	–	–	2	1
Antilocapra americana	1	–	–	–	–
Ovis canadensis	1	–	–	–	–
Small mammal	–	1	–	–	–
Large mammal	–	1	1	–	–

Table 49.16. Minimum number of individuals from mixed Primary strata and from unevaluated strata, Room 129W.

Taxon	Mixed Primary Strata C-54–61, C-59–66, C-60–67	Unevaluated Strata C-22.5–30.5 mixed with U-2–78.5
Unidentified fish	1	–
Meleagris gallopavo	3	–
Ara cf. macao	–	1
Ara militaris	1	–
Large bird	1	–
Sylvilagaus sp.	3	–
Lepus californicus	2	–
Artiodactyla	1	–

Table 49.17. Minimum number of individuals or number of occurrences (fish, bird egg shell) for each occupational category, based on stratum-room units. (Percentages of the total fauna recovered from each occupation category are given in parentheses for each taxon.)

Taxon	Primary?	Primary	Inter-mediate?	Inter-mediate	Secondary?	Secondary	Post-Secondary
Fish	3(13)	3(6)	2(3)	–	–	9(3)	
Cf. Anas platyrhynchos	–	–	1(2)	–	–	–	–
Cf. Merges	–	–	1(2)	–	–	–	–
Anatidae	–	–	–	–	–	2(1)	–
Duck	–	–	–	–	–	1(.3)	–
Goose	–	–	–	–	–	1(.3)	–
Cf. Fulica americana	–	–	–	–	–	1(.3)	–
Meleagris gallopavo	2(9)	6(12)	12(23)	3(12)	5(19)	34(12)	4(12)
Grus canadensis	–	–	1(2)	–	–	2(1)	–
Ara spp.	–	2(3)	–	1(3)	–	1(.3)	–
Pica pica	–	–	–	–	–	3(1)	–
Small Passeriformes	–	–	–	–	–	1(.3)	–
Small bird	–	–	–	–	–	3(1)	–
Large bird	–	2(3)	–	–	–	–	–
Bird	1(3)	1(2)	–	2(8)	–	4(1)	1(3)
All Bird	6(26)	15(29)	17(33)	6(24)	5(19)	65(22)	5(15)
Sylvilagus auduboni	–	1(2)	–	3(12)	4(15)	19(6)	5(15)
Sylvilagus sp.	5(22)	10(20)	7(13)	2(8)	3(12)	56(19)	5(15)
All Sylvilagus	5(22)	11(22)	7(13)	5(20)	7(27)	75(26)	10(30)
Lepus californicus	1(3)	6(12)	5(10)	3(12)	3(12)	25(9)	4(12)
Lagomorpha	–	–	1(2)	–	–	–	1(3)
All Lagomorpha	6(26)	17(33)	13(25)	8(32)	10(38)	100(34)	15(45)
Spermophilus spilosoma	–	–	–	–	–	3(1)	–
Spermophilus variegatus	–	1(2)	–	–	–	2(1)	–
Spermophilus sp.	–	–	–	–	–	2(1)	–
Cynomys gunnisoni	1(3)	–	3(6)	–	1(3)	23(8)	3(9)
Cynomys/S. variegatus	–	2(3)	–	3(12)	3(12)	3(1)	1(3)

Table 49.17 (continued)

Taxon	Primary?	Primary	Inter-mediate?	Inter-mediate	Secondary?	Secondary	Post-Secondary
Cf. *Sciurus aberti*	–	–	–	–	–	1(.3)	–
Thomomys bottae	1(3)	–	–	–	1(3)	13(3)	1(3)
Perognathus sp.	–	–	1(2)	–	–	–	–
Dipodomys ordi	–	–	–	–	–	4(1)	–
Dipodomys spectabilis	–	–	–	–	–	1(.3)	–
Dipodomys sp.	–	–	–	1(3)	–	–	–
Castor canadensis	1(3)	–	–	1(3)	–	4(1)	–
Peromyscus sp.	1(3)	1(2)	4(8)	1(3)	2(8)	17(6)	1(3)
Onychomys leucogaster	–	–	–	–	1(3)	1(.3)	–
Peromyscus-Onychomys	–	1(2)	–	1(3)	–	2(1)	–
Neotoma sp.	–	–	–	–	1(3)	6(2)	2(6)
Microtus sp.	–	–	2(3)	–	–	1(.3)	–
Small Cricetidae	–	–	–	–	–	1(.3)	–
Canis sp.	–	–	–	–	–	3(1)	1(3)
Cf. Fox	–	–	1(2)	–	–	1(.3)	–
Canidae	–	–	1(2)	–	–	1(.3)	–
Cf. *Procyon lotor*	–	–	–	–	–	1(.3)	–
Taxidea taxus	1(3)	–	1(2)	–	–	–	–
Felidae	–	1(2)	–	–	–	–	–
Lynx rufus	–	–	1(2)	–	–	4(1)	–
Medium carnivore	–	–	–	–	–	1(.3)	–
Cervus elaphus	–	1(2)	–	–	–	–	–
Odocoileus hemionus	3(13)	5(10)	5(10)	2(8)	2(8)	17(6)	1(3)
Antilocapra americana	1(3)	1(2)	2(3)	1(3)	–	8(3)	–
Ovis canadensis	1(3)	–	1(2)	–	–	3(1)	–
Antilocapra/Ovis	1(3)	–	–	–	–	–	–
Artiodactyla	–	2(3)	–	1(3)	–	3(1)	1(3)
All Artiodactyla	6(26)	9(18)	8(15)	4(16)	2(8)	31(11)	2(6)
Medium mammal	–	2(3)	–	–	–	1(.3)	–
Large mammal	–	2(3)	–	–	–	2(1)	2(6)
Total	23	51	52	25	26	294	33

Table 49.18. Percentage of selected taxa in the various occupational categories.

Taxon	Primary?	Primary	Inter-mediate?	Inter-mediate	Secondary?	Secondary	Post-Secondary
Meleagris gallopavo	9%	12%	23%	12%	19%	12%	12%
Sylvilagus sp.	22%	22%	13%	20%	27%	26%	30%
Lepus californicus	4%	12%	10%	12%	12%	9%	12%
Artiodactyla	26%	18%	15%	16%	8%	11%	6%

Chapter 50

VARIATION IN ECONOMIC AND RITUAL FAUNA AT SALMON RUINS

by Kathy Roler Durand and Stephen R. Durand

Salmon Ruins is one of the largest great house structures outside of Chaco Canyon, and it was the focus of the largest field project conducted at any Chacoan outlier (Irwin-Williams and Shelley 1980b). The scale of this multiyear project and the size of the site itself generated a huge quantity of artifacts and data. The faunal remains recovered from Salmon were one of the least studied sets of artifacts; beyond the notable presence of macaw burials, little is known about Salmon's fauna. Fortunately, zooarchaeology has come a long way in 30 years, giving us new perspectives and techniques to apply to the study of Salmon's animal bones.

The work reported here was undertaken in conjunction with the Center for Desert Archaeology's new Salmon Research Initiative, through partnership with the Salmon Ruins Museum (P. Reed 2002; see Reed, Chapter 1). As detailed below, we have learned much from this research about the dietary and ritual practices of the inhabitants of Salmon Ruins and how they changed over time.

BACKGROUND

We have chosen to reanalyze a sample of the faunal remains from Salmon Ruins for several reasons. First, in the original faunal analysis, Harris (Chapter 49) reported MNI (minimum number of individuals) values and did not report any raw bone counts (NISP or number of identified specimens). Although this was common practice in the 1970s, it is now clear that MNI values have serious problems (Grayson 1984; Ringrose 1993) and should generally be used in conjunction with NISP, or raw count data. In addition, the sample Harris analyzed included many problematic strata for which context and dating were unclear, making changes through time difficult to discern. Furthermore, his data were collected by numerous individuals—some inexperienced students—using different collections in different labs (Harris, Chapter 49). We have tried to avoid these problems in our analysis by using samples from the clearest contexts (selected in consultation with Phillip Shel-

ley) and by using a single analyst (Kathy Durand). Perhaps the most important reason for reanalyzing the Salmon fauna is improvement in the sophistication of faunal analysis since Harris's time. There are currently many excellent studies of Chacoan fauna that can be compared to the results from Salmon, notably due to the work of Nancy Akins (1985, 1987) and others associated with the Chaco Project (e.g. Gillespie 1991; Windes 1987d). This chapter focuses largely on the analysis of the Salmon fauna; we provide a comparison of the patterns at Salmon with those found at other Chacoan sites in a separate paper (Durand and Durand 2005).

Most of the analyses that follow are based on NISP measures (Tables 50.1 and 50.2). NISP allows us to calculate comparative indices and will allow others to use these data in their own research. The MNI values (also provided in the tables) were calculated using the most common element (e.g., left proximal humerus) for each species, while also taking mature and immature elements into account. The problem with MNI can readily be seen by comparing the values in Tables 50.1 and 50.3. For example, if calculated by period for the whole site, the MNI value for cottontails is 8 for the Primary and 8 for the Secondary period, for a total of 16 animals. If these same values are calculated room by room, however, we have 25 cottontails, based on the same assemblage! Thus, except where specifically indicated (for example, in the discussion of the macaw burials), the following analysis is based entirely on NISP values (raw counts).

The bones analyzed herein were recovered from structured trash deposits, features, roofs, and floors (including samples from B, C, D, E, F, G, H, and L strata; see Adams and Reed, Chapter 7). To ensure the contextual integrity of the sample, strata defined as unstructured fill, backfill, present ground surface, alluvial deposits, bioturbated deposits, or unknown were not included in this analysis. To date, 3874 bones and bone fragments from Salmon Ruins have been analyzed. Table 50.4 lists the strata and field

Table 50.1. Salmon Ruins NISP and MNI values by period of occupation.

Common Name	Scientific Name	Primary		Secondary		Total NISP
		NISP	MNI	NISP	MNI	
Very small mammal	—	15	–	10	–	25
Small mammal	—	187	–	118	–	305
Medium mammal	—	10	–	29	–	39
Large mammal	—	196	–	65	–	261
Small-medium mammal	—	31	–	101	–	132
Medium-large mammal	—	9	–	8	–	17
Cottontail	*Sylvilagus* sp.	265	8	245	8	510
Jack rabbit	*Lepus* sp.	54	4	118	5	172
Black-tailed prairie dog	*Cynomys ludovicianus*	1	1	0	0	1
Prairie dog	*Cynomys* sp.	73	7	11	2	84
Pocket gopher	*Thomomys* sp.	12	2	1	1	13
Kangaroo rat	*Dipodomys* sp.	0	0	1	1	1
Beaver	*Castor canadenisis*	1	1	3	1	4
Mouse	*Peromyscus* sp.	5	1	15	2	20
Grasshopper mouse	*Onychomys* sp.	0	0	1	1	1
Woodrat	*Neotoma* sp.	9	1	0	0	9
Canid	*Canis* sp.	2	1	1	1	3
Red fox	*Vulpes fulva*	1	1	0	0	1
Fox	*Vulpes* sp.	4	1	0	0	4
Bobcat	*Felis rufus*	1	1	0	0	1
Small carnivore	—	1	–	0	–	1
Medium carnivore	—	1	–	0	–	1
Elk	*Cervis elaphus*	0	0	1	1	1
Mule deer	*Odocoileus hemionus*	5	1	0	0	5
Deer	*Odocoileus* sp.	12	2	0	0	12
Pronghorn	*Antilocapra americana*	9	1	0	0	9
Deer/pronghorn	*Odocoileus/Antilocapra*	2	–	0	–	2
Bighorn sheep	*Ovis canadensis*	12	1	12	1	24
Deer/sheep	*Odocoileus/Ovis*	2	–	0	–	2
Medium artiodactyl	—	224	–	16	–	240
Large artiodactyl	—	17	–	0	–	17
Small bird	—	3	–	1	–	4
Medium bird	—	3	–	3	–	6
Large bird	—	40	–	262	–	302
Turkey	*Meleagris gallopavo*	10	2	46	3	56
Crane	*Grus* sp.	1	1	0	0	1
Stellar's jay	*Cyanocitta stelleri*	1	1	0	0	1
Flicker, raven, etc.	Order Passeriformes	1	–	0	–	1
Macaw*	*Ara* sp.	2	1	0	0	2
Rattlesnake	*Crotalus* sp.	0	0	1	1	1
Fish	—	5	–	2	–	7
Sucker family	Catostomidae	0	0	2	1	2
Minnow family	Cyprinidae	1	1	1	1	2
Sucker/minnow	Catostomidae/Cyprinidae	5	–	5	–	10
Unidentifable	—	521	–	1041	–	1562
Total NISP	—	1754		2120		3874

*These values represent 2 macaw elements in Room 33W. There are parts of 7 other macaw skeletons at the site, but the rooms in which they occur were not analyzed for this portion of the study.

Table 50.2. Salmon Ruins NISP values by room.

Common Name	Scientific Name	33	36	43	62	63	81	130	Total NISP
Very small mammal	—	2	5	0	7	0	10	1	25
Small mammal	—	70	73	15	41	1	100	5	305
Medium mammal	—	5	14	0	3	0	3	14	39
Large mammal	—	33	33	53	9	8	96	29	261
Small-medium mammal	—	22	86	1	5	0	7	11	132
Medium-large mammal	—	6	6	0	4	0	0	1	17
cottontail	*Sylvilagus* sp.	68	191	8	63	2	173	5	510
Jack Rabbit	*Lepus* sp.	29	108	4	11	0	19	1	172
Black-tailed prairie dog	*Cynomys ludovicianus*	0	0	0	0	0	1	0	1
Prairie dog	*Cynomys* sp.	22	3	3	8	0	47	1	84
Pocket gopher	*Thomomys* sp.	4	0	3	1	0	5	0	13
Kangaroo rat	*Dipodomys* sp.	0	0	0	1	0	0	0	1
Beaver	*Castor canadenisis*	0	2	0	1	0	1	0	4
Mouse	*Peromyscus* sp.	1	12	0	3	0	4	0	20
Grasshopper mouse	*Onychomys* sp.	0	0	0	1	0	0	0	1
Woodrat	*Neotoma* sp.	1	0	0	2	0	6	0	9
Canid	*Canis* sp.	0	1	0	0	0	2	0	3
Red fox	*Vulpes fulva*	1	0	0	0	0	0	0	1
Fox	*Vulpes* sp.	0	0	1	0	0	3	0	4
Bobcat	*Felis rufus*	0	0	0	0	1	0	0	1
Small carnivore	—	0	0	0	0	0	1	0	1
Medium carnivore	—	0	0	0	0	0	1	0	1
Elk	*Cervis elaphus*	0	0	0	0	0	0	1	1
Mule deer	*Odocoileus hemionus*	0	0	0	1	0	4	0	5
Deer	*Odocoileus* sp.	2	0	2	1	1	6	0	12
Pronghorn	*Antilocapra americana*	0	0	5	2	0	2	0	9
Deer/pronghorn	*Odocoileus/Antilocapra*	0	0	2	0	0	0	0	2
Bighorn sheep	*Ovis canadensis*	8	1	3	0	0	1	11	24
Deer/sheep	*Odocoileus/Ovis*	0	0	0	0	2	0	0	2
Medium artiodactyl	—	17	6	50	15	121	27	4	240
Large artiodactyl	—	2	0	11	0	2	2	0	17
Small bird	—	0	1	2	0	0	1	0	4
Medium bird	—	1	2	2	1	0	0	0	6
Large bird	—	7	220	30	19	1	1	24	302
Turkey	*Meleagris gallopavo*	0	30	7	16	0	1	2	56
Crane	*Grus* sp.	1	0	0	0	0	0	0	1
Stellar's jay	*Cyanocitta stelleri*	0	0	0	0	0	1	0	1
Flicker, raven, etc.	Order Passeriformes	0	0	1	0	0	0	0	1
Macaw	*Ara* sp.	2	0	0	0	0	0	0	2
Rattlesnake	*Crotalus* sp.	0	0	0	1	0	0	0	1
Fish	—	0	0	1	3	0	3	0	7
Sucker family	Catostomidae	0	2	0	0	0	0	0	2
Minnow family	Cyprinidae	1	1	0	0	0	0	0	2
Sucker/minnow	Catostomidae/Cyprinidae	5	5	0	0	0	0	0	10
Unidentifable	—	77	581	124	327	10	262	181	1562
Total NISP	—	387	1383	328	546	149	790	291	3874

Table 50.3. Salmon Ruins MNI values by room for selected species.

Common Name	Scientific Name	Room Number						
		33	36	43	62	63	81	130
Cottontail	*Sylvilagus* sp.	4	7	1	4	1	7	1
Jack rabbit	*Lepus* sp.	3	5	2	2	–	2	–
Beaver	*Castor canadenisis*	–	1	–	–	–	1	–
Mule deer	*Odocoileus hemionus*	–	–	–	1	–	1	–
Deer	*Odocoileus* sp.	1	–	–	1	1	1	–
Pronghorn	*Antilocapra americana*	–	–	1	1	–	1	–
Bighorn sheep	*Ovis canadensis*	1	–	–	–	–	–	–
Large bird (prob. turkey)	—	1	5	2	1	1	1	1
Turkey	*Meleagris gallopavo*	–	3	2	2	–	1	1

Table 50.4. Samples strata and field specimens number by room.

Room	Strata*	Field Specimen Numbers
33	C - Structured trash	1049, 1380, 1945, 2261, 2263, 2264, 2267, 2270, 2273, 2275, 2276, 2278, 2279, 2281, 2288, 2292, 2293, 2299, 2301, 2305, 2306, 2307, 2309, 2310, 2311, 2319, 3292, 3346, 3354, 3359, 3362, 3366, 3369, 3370, 3378, 3426, 3427, 3428, 3430, 3433, 3439
36	C - Structured trash	1031, 1035, 1037, 1038, 1039, 1041, 1042, 1044, 1045, 1046, 1049, 1051, 1052, 1053, 1054, 1055, 1056, 1057, 1059, 1061, 1062, 1063, 1064, 1065
43	B - Postoccupational fill	1936, 2148
	C - Structured trash	2128
	G - Occupational fill	1745, 1751, 3210, 3211, 3212, 3213, 3214, 3215, 3216, 3217, 3218, 3219, 3220, 3222, 3223, 3225, 3227, 3228, 3229, 3230, 3231, 3232, 3233, 3237
62	C - Structured trash	1075, 1129, 1131, 1134, 1137, 1139, 1141, 1937
	G - Occupational fill	1079, 1082, 1136, 3234, 3235, 3236, 3238
	H - Floor surface	3239
	L - Feature fill	1084, 1085
	O - Zonal floor	1072, 1093
63	B - Postoccupational fill	3249
	E - Roof surface	3245, 3247
	F - Roof/roof-fall	3241, 3243, 3246, 3248, 3250, 3251
	G - Occupational fill	3242, 3244
81	F - Roof/roof-fall	3143, 3144, 3145, 3147, 3148, 3149, 3150, 3153, 3155, 3156, 3157, 3158, 3159, 3160, 3161, 3162, 3163, 3164, 3165, 3166, 3167, 3168, 3169, 3170, 3171, 3172, 3173, 3174, 3175, 3176, 3177, 3178, 3179, 3180, 3181, 3182, 3694
130	B - Postoccupational fill	4205
	H - Floor surface	4198
	L - Feature fill	1408, 1644, 1681, 3380, 3381, 3382, 3383, 3384, 3385
	F - Roof/roof-fall	4192, 4193, 4194, 4195, 4196, 4197, 4199, 4200, 4202, 4204, 4206, 4207, 4209, 4210, 4211, 4231, 5055, 5056, 5059

*Stratigraphic definitions can be found in McClellan (1980).

specimen numbers of the samples from each room. Almost 3900 bones were examined for this study, but we consider this a work in progress. To date, we have samples from Rooms 33, 36, 43, 62, 63, 81, and 130 (the Great Kiva; Figure 50.1). Sampled materials from Rooms 33, 43, 63, and 81 date to the Primary, or Chacoan occupation at Salmon, whereas those from Rooms 36 and 130 date to the Secondary, or post-Chacoan occupation. Room 62 contained material from both periods. Several rooms that we intended to include here (Rooms 31, 61A, 64, and 127) either did not contain bones, had very few bones, or had bones in unclear strata. Large samples from Rooms 100 and 129, as well as a larger sample from Room 62, are currently being studied and will be included in a future volume of work at Salmon Ruins.

ECONOMIC FAUNA AT SALMON RUINS

Dietary fauna in the Southwest typically include artiodactyls (bighorn sheep, deer, elk, and prong-horn), lagomorphs (cottontails and jack rabbits), and sometimes turkeys and fish. Other species were eaten on occasion, but these groups provided the vast majority of the meat in prehistoric Southwestern diets. For Salmon Ruins, there are interesting patterns in most of these categories. Faunal changes through time at Salmon point to changes in the local environment and an increasing reliance on domestic fauna for protein.

Table 50.2 lists the NISP values for each species by room. These same data are grouped by Primary and Secondary occupation periods in Table 50.1 (note that Room 62 contained bones from each period). Only the two loose macaw bones recovered from Room 33 are included in these tables because most of the macaw remains at Salmon were intact burials, thus inflating their raw counts. The macaw remains, along with the other ritual fauna, are discussed in detail below. Turkeys are discussed in both the economic and ritual sections of this report, as they appear to have been important for both purposes. At least two turkey burials were found at Salmon, including one that was adjacent to a macaw burial in Room 100. This turkey burial, which was recognized during excavation and well documented, helps to demonstrate the ritual importance of the species, as does the large number of turkey feather blankets among the perishable artifacts (Webster, Chapter 46). The sheer frequency of turkeys, coupled with their typical deposition with other food debris, demonstrates their role in the diet of Salmon's inhabitants.

Artiodactyls

Artiodactyls made up a much larger percentage of the overall assemblage in the Primary period (23%) than they did in the Secondary period (3%). This rises to 39 percent and 9 percent of total NISP, respectively, when large mammals (likely all artio-dactyls) are added. Table 50.5 shows the distribution of artiodactyls and large mammal remains by room and time period. It is apparent that the artiodactyl remains are more numerous and diverse from the Primary period regardless of sample size, as both periods are represented by large samples of similar size. In fact, the largest total sample, from Secondary period remains in Room 36, contains the fewest artiodactyl bones, whereas the two smallest samples, from Primary levels in Rooms 43 and 63, contain high proportions of artiodactyl bones.

The frequencies of artiodactyls in different samples and assemblages are often compared using Szuter and Bayham's (1989) Artiodactyl Index:

$$AI = \frac{artiodactyls}{(artiodactyls + lagomorphs)}$$

This index was designed to allow archaeologists to compare assemblages with different sample sizes. The denominator includes lagomorphs due to their abundance in assemblages across the Southwest. Note that the lagomorph NISP, as a percent of total NISP, is relatively high for both the Primary (26% of total NISP) and Secondary (34% of total NISP) periods.

Applying this comparative index at Salmon, the Artiodactyl Index for the Primary period is 0.47, whereas for the Secondary period it drops to 0.07 (Table 50.6). As noted above, this large difference does not appear to be due to sample size. Furthermore, both periods contain elements from all portions of the skeleton (Tables 50.7 and 50.8), suggesting that the decline in the Secondary period is not just a reflection of the schlepp effect.[1] Such conclusions must remain conjectural until larger Secondary samples are obtained, as the small number of elements in the Secondary sample prohibits statistical

---

[1]The schlepp effect, which was formally defined by Perkins and Daly (1968), is the idea that large, heavy species may be partially processed at the kill site. Thus, most of the bones would be left at the kill site and all portions of the skeleton would not be present at the associated habitation site. Bones useful for tool making (especially metapodials) or those which are more difficult to extract from the meat (such as ribs) are more likely to be carried back to the habitation site. Large game or those obtained at greater distances from the habitation site are most likely to be processed in this way.

Table 50.5. Salmon Ruins artiodactyl and large mammal NISP by room and period of occupation.

Common Name	Scientific Name	Room Number 33	36	43	62	63	81	130	Total NISP
Primary Occupation									
Large mammal	—	33	–	53	6	8	96	–	196
Mule deer	*Odocoileus hemionus*	0	–	0	1	0	4	–	5
Deer	*Odocoileus* sp.	2	–	2	1	1	6	–	12
Pronghorn	*Antilocapra americana*	0	–	5	2	0	2	–	9
Deer/pronghorn	*Odocoileus/Antilocapra*	0	–	2	0	0	0	–	2
Bighorn sheep	*Ovis canadensis*	8	–	3	0	0	1	–	12
Deer/sheep	*Odocoileus/Ovis*	0	–	0	0	2	0	–	2
Medium artiodactyl	—	17	–	50	9	121	27	–	224
Large artiodactyl	—	2	–	11	0	2	2	–	17
Total Primary NISP	—	62	–	126	19	134	138	–	479
Secondary Occupation									
Large mammal	—	–	33	–	3	–	–	29	65
Elk	*Cervis elaphus*	–	0	–	0	–	–	1	1
Bighorn sheep	*Ovis canadensis*	–	1	–	0	–	–	11	12
Medium artiodactyl	—	–	6	–	6	–	–	4	16
Total Secondary NISP	—	–	40	–	9	–	–	45	94

Table 50.6. Lagomorph, artiodactyl, and turkey indices for Salmon Ruins by period of occupation.

	Primary	Secondary	Combined
Cottontail NISP (A)	265	245	510
Jack rabbit NISP (B)	54	118	172
Lagomorph NISP, cottontails + jack rabbits (C)	319	363	682
Lagomorph index (A/C)	0.83	0.67	0.75
Artiodactyl NISP (D)	283	29	312
Artiodactyls + lagomorphs (E)	602	392	994
Artiodactyl index (D/E)	0.47	0.07	0.31
Turkey NISP	10	46	56
Large bird NISP	40	262	302
Turkeys + large birds (F)	50	308	358
Turkeys + large birds + lagomorphs (G)	369	671	1040
Turkey index (F/G)	0.14	0.46	0.34

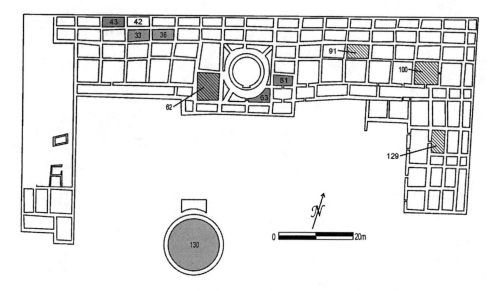

Figure 50.1. Generalized Chacoan ground plan of Salmon Ruins showing rooms sampled for this analysis (shaded); analysis is ongoing for the rooms that are hatched.

evaluation of the schlepp effect. However, two unusual Primary deposits must be recognized as contributing to the magnitude of the difference in the AI between periods. Room 63, a triangular room next to the Tower Kiva, produced only 139 identified bones; 126 are artiodactyl, with another 8 classified as large mammal. All portions of the artiodactyl skeleton are represented in the assemblage, but by far the most common elements are shaft fragments. A similarly remarkable set of artiodactyl bones was found in Room 43, associated with a large lithic scatter (Feature 043W042 in stratum G-1-10). This set contains 13 broken ribs and at least 25 spiral-fractured long bone fragments, suggesting that the bones were being processed for marrow extraction. It is interesting that Room 43 also contains the richest burials at the site, leading Webster (Chapter 46) to conclude that this section of Salmon may have been used by those with the highest social status at the site.

It seems apparent that artiodactyls were very important to the diet of Salmon's Primary inhabitants, but much less so to its later inhabitants. The decreasing reliance on artiodactyls over time at Salmon is contrary to the pattern found by Speth and Scott (1989) for other prehistoric Puebloan and Hohokam sites, at which the comparative frequency of artiodactyls increased over time. They have argued that the increase in the AI over time is actually due to the depletion of game in the vicinity of the site. As game are depleted over time around a permanent village, hunters are forced to go greater distances to

obtain animals. This, in turn, leads to an increasing focus on large game because they provide more meat for the effort as hunters must go increasingly greater distances from the settlement for game. However, Speth and Scott (1989:78) also noted that at some as yet unknown threshold of resource depletion, brought about by reduced community mobility or by increased horticultural activity, it may be necessary to adopt other strategies to obtain protein. At this point, artiodactyls would be expected to decline, not rise, in an assemblage. These strategies may include growing more crops with higher protein yields, increasing reliance on domestic animals or fish, exchanging for meat with neighboring groups, or increasing group mobility. We believe that this threshold of resource depletion was crossed during the Secondary period and that the inhabitants of Salmon increased their reliance on domestic animals (turkeys) to compensate.

Turkeys

There is considerable evidence that turkeys suddenly represent a large percentage of the faunal remains at Pueblo III sites in the Mesa Verde and Sand Canyon regions (Munro 1994). At Salmon, the Turkey Index

$$TI = \frac{(turkey + large\ bird)}{(turkey + large\ bird + lagomorphs)}$$

is inversely related to the Artiodactyl Index, increasing from 0.14 in the Primary period to 0.46 in the Secondary—a threefold increase (see Table 50.6).

Table 50.7. Salmon Ruin artiodactyl and large mammal NISP by element class and occupation period. The chi-square computations show observed and expected values (in parentheses). Chi-square = 14.08, p = 0.050, df = 7.

Common Name	Scientific Name	Skull	Horn/ Antler	Torso	Front Limb	Front Feet	Hind Limb	Hind Feet	Limb	Indet.	Total
Primary Occupation											
Large mammal		16	0	30	1	0	1	0	0	148	196
Mule deer	Odocoileus hemionus	0	0	0	1	0	1	3	0	0	5
Deer	Odocoileus sp.	2	0	1	3	2	0	3	1	0	12
Pronghorn	Antilocapra americana	2	3	0	1	0	0	2	1	0	9
Deer/pronghorn	Odocoileus/Antilocapra	0	0	0	0	0	0	0	2	0	2
Bighorn sheep	Ovis canadensis	3	0	0	2	2	0	1	4	0	12
Deer/sheep	Odocoileus/Ovis	0	0	0	1	0	1	0	0	0	2
Medium artiodactyl		6	25	19	7	8	22	8	13	116	224
Large artiodactyl		5	0	6	3	1	0	0	2	0	17
Total Primary NISP		34	28	56	19	13	25	17	23	264	479
Total Primary NISP percents*		16%	13%	26%	9%	6%	12%	8%	11%		
Secondary Occupation											
Large mammal		14	0	17	1	0	1	0	1	31	65
Elk	Cervis elaphus	1	0	0	0	0	0	0	0	0	1
Bighorn sheep	Ovis canadensis	0	1	2	2	1	3	3	0	0	12
Medium artiodactyl		2	0	4	3	0	1	1	5	0	16
Total Secondary NISP		17	1	23	6	1	5	4	6	31	94
Total Secondary NISP Percents*		27%	2%	37%	10%	2%	8%	6%	10%		
Chi-Square Computations											
Total Primary NISP		34 (39)	28 (22)	56 (61)	19 (19)	13 (11)	25 (23)	17 (16)	23 (22)		215
Total Secondary NISP		17 (12)	1 (7)	23 (18)	6 (6)	1 (3)	5 (7)	4 (5)	6 (7)		63
Total		51	29	79	25	14	30	21	29		278

*The indeterminate category is not used in the percentages computations.

Table 50.8. Salmon Ruins artiodactyl and large mammal NISP by element class, occupation period, and room.

	Room	Horn/ Skull	Front Antler	Front Torso	Hind Limb	Hind Feet	Limb	Feet	Limb	Indet.	Total
Primary Occupation	33	3	0	10	4	7	2	2	12	22	62
	43	15	24	25	5	1	5	6	5	40	126
	62	8	1	7	0	0	2	0	0	1	19
	63	1	0	2	4	2	6	0	1	118	134
	81	7	3	12	6	3	10	9	5	83	138
Total NISP		34	28	56	19	13	25	17	23	264	479
Secondary Occupation	36	11	0	15	2	0	1	0	2	9	40
	62	2	0	3	0	0	1	1	2	0	9
	130	4	1	5	4	1	3	3	2	22	45
Total NISP		17	1	23	6	1	5	4	6	31	94

This increase can also be illustrated by comparing the frequencies with the total NISP for each period. Turkeys and large birds are only a small component of the identified Primary assemblage (4.1%), whereas they make up almost one-third of the identified assemblage in the Secondary period (28.5%).

The frequency of immature birds as shown in the assemblage also increased dramatically through time at Salmon, going from 7 percent of the turkey and large bird elements in the Primary period to 30 percent in the Secondary. As seen in Table 50.9, this is a statistically significant difference ($2 = 7.01$, $p = 0.008$, df = 1), lending strong support to the idea that turkeys were being raised during the Secondary period. Another source of supporting evidence that turkeys were raised at Salmon in the Secondary period (though possibly earlier elsewhere, cf. Windes 1987d) comes from the presence of two healed long bone fractures (Figure 50.2) that occurred on a right ulna and a left humerus from two different turkeys found in Room 100 (a room not included in this report, but currently being studied). Three fractured turkey elements were also found in a room at Eleanor Ruin (a right and left tibiotarsus and a right scapula; Durand and Durand 2002), and two broken bones were reported by Gillespie (1991:292) from 29SJ633 in Chaco Canyon (a right ulna and a left tibiotarsus). In the case of Eleanor and Salmon Ruins these were complete breaks (in which the bone fractured into two separate pieces) that had fully healed, although they were poorly aligned. It seems unlikely that the birds would have survived such injuries in the wild, which supports the argument that turkeys were being raised at the sites. Further evidence that turkeys were being raised at the site includes the increase over time in the number of strata containing eggshell fragments. In the Primary period, 11 percent

of the strata (101 of 941 strata) contained eggshell, compared to 16 percent (212 of 1364) of the strata in the Secondary period. In addition, three likely turkey pens were identified at the site (Rooms 62B, 127E, and 128A-B; Reed, Chapter 8).

All parts of the turkey skeleton are represented in the remains from both periods at Salmon (Table 50.10) but there are very few legs in the Primary period assemblage. This seems all the more unusual as they represent more than a third (36%) of the elements from the Secondary period. A chi-square test (see Table 50.10) indicates that the difference in element frequencies between these two periods is statistically significant ($2= 24.78$, $p < 0.001$, df = 5). Furthermore, the difference in observed versus expected values for legs was the biggest contributor to the difference between assemblages. Although 15 leg bones were expected for the Primary period, only 3 were present, whereas for the Secondary period 89 were expected but 101 were present. Wing bones were slightly overrepresented in the Primary period (13 observed, but 10 expected) and one could imagine a scenario in which turkeys were hunted in this period and consumed at the hunting location, with the wings brought back for their feathers while the legs and other bones were left behind. However, the skull bones were found in the same frequency as they were in the Secondary period, and the necks were actually overrepresented in the Primary period, so they clearly were not bringing only the wings back to the site. It is possible that some of the "missing" leg bones will be found in the bone tool assemblage from the Primary period, which is currently being studied.

Regardless of what caused the paucity of leg bones in the Primary period assemblage, it is clear that turkeys were utilized much more extensively in

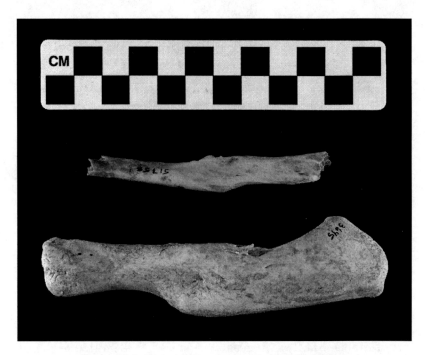

Figure 50.2. Broken turkey bones from Room 100W.

the Secondary period. As discussed above, this change likely was tied to a decreased reliance on artiodactyls in the Secondary period.

One source of protein that remained fairly stable over time at Salmon was the lagomorphs. As a group, these animals make up a high percentage of the overall fauna in the Salmon assemblage, although they do show a slight increase in the Secondary period (from 26% in the Primary period to 34% in the Secondary period).

Lagomorphs

Lagomorphs include cottontails (*Sylvilagus* sp.) and jack rabbits (*Lepus* sp.). Both genera are ubiquitous across the Southwest and were an important component of the prehistoric diet. These genera differ in a few important ways, however, allowing us to derive meaning from changes in their relative frequencies over time. First, cottontails prefer bushy, nondisturbed habitats, and jack rabbits prefer more open terrain (Szuter and Bayham 1989) and can more easily coexist with human settlements. Second, jack rabbits can be hunted by groups using nets so that larger numbers of them can be obtained at one time in comparison to cottontails (Beaglehole 1936; Gnabasik 1981; Szuter and Bayham 1989). This means that long-term settlement of an area often leads to an increase in the frequency of jack rabbits in comparison to cottontails.

As seen in Table 50.6, the Lagomorph Index decreased over time in the Salmon Ruins assemblage, beginning at 0.83 in the Primary period and dropping to 0.67 in the Secondary period. The proportion of jack rabbits increased over time from 17 percent to 33 percent of all lagomorph bones at the site (although cottontails remained the most numerous lagomorph from both periods). This suggests either a decline in the local environment (with native plants gradually disappearing in the area around the site) or a change in hunting practices (with more communal hunting of jack rabbits being adopted). As the proportion of jack rabbits nearly doubled at the site, we believe that both of these changes may have occurred. Communal hunting of jack rabbits in the Secondary period, together with raising turkeys, could have helped make up for the decrease in artiodactyl meat in the diet.

Fish

Of the four dietary groups listed above, fish seem to have had a low, constant presence at Salmon. Detailed identification of many of the fish elements was completed by Virginia Butler at Portland State University (Table 50.11). There is little difference between periods for these remains. The majority of the bones are vertebrae and cannot be identified to the species or genus level. At least two different species of fish were present in the Second-

Table 50.9. Chi-square table of turkey and large bird NISP comparing maturity and period of occupation. Expected values in parentheses, chi-square = 7.01, p = 0.008, df = 1.

Occupation	Immature	Mature	Total
Primary	2 (8)	28 (22)	30
Secondary	62 (56)	148 (154)	210
Total	64	176	240

ary period (one from the *Catostomidae*, or sucker, family and one from the *Cyprinidae*, or minnow, family), and at least one species was present in the Primary period (either a *Catostomidae* or a *Cyprinidae*). Based on the size of one of the vertebra, there was one very large fish (longer than half a meter) in the Secondary assemblage (specimen 1063.219). Harris (Chapter 49) reports that one species of fish—*Ptychocheilus lucius*, or the Colorado squawfish—has been ruled out as a match for the elements identified by Butler (see Table 50.11). Thus, at least three species of local fish appear to have been consumed at Salmon.

It is likely that fish were more important to the Salmon diet than their frequencies suggest. Many fish bones would have fallen through the 1/4-inch screens used during the excavation of Salmon, as numerous studies have demonstrated (Cameron 1995:90; Shaffer 1992). Of course, this also likely affected the frequencies of lagomorphs and rodents in the assemblage. The nearby San Juan River would have provided a steady source of protein for Salmon's inhabitants during both occupation periods.

BURNING

Some evidence of burning was found on all categories of economic fauna, except fish, from both occupation periods (Table 50.12). The lack of burning on fish remains may be due to the extremely poor survival rate of cooked fish bone (Nicholson 1992, 1996). In addition, some rodent remains from the Primary period (prairie dogs and wood rats) showed evidence of burning damage and may have thus been a small component of the diet. Approximately 4

percent of the artiodactyl elements from the Primary strata show evidence of burning (see Table 50.12), whereas about 14 percent of the Secondary artiodactyl elements exhibit burning damage. It is possible that the fire that swept through the pueblo at abandonment caused burning damage on some of the Secondary deposits. Catastrophic fires would affect roofs, site furniture, and other wooden structural elements and may have also affected the top levels of the stratified deposits (Bennett 1999).

In the Primary period assemblage, approximately 5 percent of the unidentifiable fragments and 7 percent of the miscellaneous mammals show some burning damage versus 13 percent and 20 percent, respectively, for the Secondary period. In contrast to this pattern, however, the lagomorphs and turkey/large bird groups from the Secondary period show much less burning damage than from the Primary (about 10% for the Primary period lagomorphs vs. 6% for the Secondary and 6% for the Primary turkeys vs. about 2% for the Secondary). Thus, the increase in burning damage for the Secondary period artiodactyls may not have been due to the catastrophic fire event. They may have been utilizing these animals more thoroughly due to their scarcity in the Secondary period diet. Increased processing may also have been the cause of the greater burn damage on unidentifiable bone fragments and miscellaneous mammal categories from the Secondary period.

BONE TOOLS

A formal study of the bone tools has never been undertaken for the Salmon collection. Nevertheless, we do have some preliminary data regarding these artifacts. More than 320 bone tools and worked bone items have been identified in the faunal assemblage. Table 50.13 lists the counts for five categories of tools and worked bone for most of the rooms included in this study. No tools were recovered from Rooms 63 and 130. By far the most common tool type found in both occupation periods was the awl; in fact, this was the only formal tool type identified in the Primary period tools studied so far. From the Secondary period, nine bone tubes and a large mammal rib

Table 50.10. Chi-square table of turkey and large bird NISP comparing element class and period of occupation. Expected values are in parentheses, chi-square = 24.78, p < 0.001, df = 5.

Occupation	Skull	Neck	Body	Wing	Pelvis	Leg	Total
Primary	7 (6.1)	13 (5.8)	9 (9.4)	13 (10.3)	3 (1.4)	3 (15.0)	48
Secondary	35 (35.9)	27 (34.2)	56 (55.6)	58 (60.7)	7 (8.6)	101 (89.0)	284
Total	42	40	65	71	10	104	332

Table 50.11. Fish remains from Salmon Ruins (identified by Virginia Butler, Portland State University).

Cat. No.	Taxon	Element	Comments
Primary			
1049.9	Cyprinidae/Catostomidae	Caudal vertebra	
2267.6	Cyprinidae/Catostomidae	Caudal vertebra	
2275.15	Cyprinidae/Catostomidae	Abdominal vertebra	
2281.11	Cyprinidae/Catostomidae	Caudal vertebra	
3354.15	Cyprinidae/Catostomidae	Abdominal vertebra	
3354.41	Cyprinidae	Basioccipital	
Secondary			
1045.2	Cyprinidae/Catostomidae	Caudal vertebra	
1051.3	Cyprinidae/Catostomidae	Abdominal vertebra	
1055.15	Cyprinidae/Catostomidae	Abdominal vertebra	
1061.72	Catostomidae	Basioccipital	
1063.216	Catostomidae	Cleithrum, right	Does not match *Xyrauchen texanus*
1063.217	Cyprinidae	Pharyngeal, right	Cf. *Gila cypha*
1063.218	Cyprinidae/Catostomidae	Abdominal vertebra	
1063.219	Cyprinidae/Catostomidae	Abdominal vertebra	Diameter 12.05 mm*
1323.18	Cyprinidae/Catostomidae	Caudal vertebra	
1323.31	Cyprinidae/Catostomidae	Caudal vertebra	

*Diameter = width, see Casteel (1976). This is a large vertebra. By comparison, a vertebra from an Owens Valley sucker, *Catostomus fumeiventris*, that is 418 mm long has a vertebra diameter of 8.00 mm. This vertebra is probably from a fish more than half a meter long.

Table 50.12. Salmon Ruins burned bone NISP by occupation period and animal class. Chi-square = 117.08, p < 0.001, df = 4. Chi-square expected values are in parentheses.

Occupation/Animal	Calcined	Possibly Charred	Browned	Burned	Unburned	Total
Primary						
Miscellaneous mammals	6	1	10	16	219	252
Lagomorphs	1	10	20	32	256	319
Artiodactyls	6	7	1	4	461	479
Rodents	0	0	7	6	88	101
Carnivores	0	0	3	1	6	10
Turkey/large bird	0	2	1	3	44	50
Other birds	0	0	1	0	8	9
Fish	0	0	0	0	5	5
Unidentified fragments	3	13	7	2	496	521
Total Primary NISP	16	33	50	64	1583	1746
Secondary						
Miscellaneous mammals	40	8	5	8	205	266
Lagomorphs	9	4	9	1	340	363
Artiodactyls	7	4	2	0	81	94
Rodents	0	0	1	0	31	32
Carnivores	0	0	0	0	1	1
Turkey/large bird	1	3	2	1	301	308
Other birds	1	0	0	0	3	4
Reptiles	0	1	0	0	0	1
Fish	0	0	0	0	2	2
Unidentified fragments	78	59	3	27	874	1041
Total Secondary NISP	136	79	22	37	1838	2112
Chi-square Computations						
Primary total	16 (69)	33 (51)	50 (33)	64 (46)	1583 (1548)	1746
Secondary total	136 (83)	79 (61)	22 (39)	37 (55)	1838 (1873)	2112
Total Primary + Secondary	152	112	72	101	3421	3858

Table 50.13. Salmon Ruins bone tool counts by room and occupation period.

	Room							
	33	36	43	62	63	81	130	Total
Primary Occupation								
Awl	13	–	2	2	0	2	–	19
Tube	0	–	0	0	0	0	–	0
Preform	0	–	0	0	0	0	–	0
Worked	2	–	1	0	0	1	–	4
Other	0	–	0	0	0	0	–	0
Total Primary	15	–	3	2	0	3	–	23
Secondary Occupation								
Awl	–	19	–	10	–	–	0	29
Tube	–	9	–	0	–	–	0	9
Preform	–	1	–	1	–	–	0	2
Worked	–	3	–	2	–	–	0	5
Other*	–	0	–	1	–	–	0	1
Total Secondary	–	32	–	14	–	–	0	46
Total Primary + Secondary	15	32	3	16	0	3	0	69

* This is a large mammal rib with one serrated edge.

that was serrated on one edge were also recovered. To date, almost twice as many tools have been identified in the Secondary period assemblage (46) as in the Primary (23).

GENERAL TRENDS

The economic fauna at Salmon Ruins changed in several significant ways through time. The frequency of artiodactyls, as reflected in the Artiodactyl Index, decreased substantially from the Primary to the Secondary periods. Turkey remains, on the other hand, significantly increased through time. The dramatic increase in turkey remains, plus other evidence such as the significantly higher number of immature elements and the healed fractures, suggests that they were being raised during the Secondary period. Also, the evidence shows that the utilization of lagomorphs increased over time at Salmon Ruins, as did the proportion of jack rabbits to cottontails, supporting the overall picture of turkey and small game replacing artiodactyl meat in the diet of Salmon's Secondary inhabitants.

RITUAL FAUNA AT SALMON RUINS

Ritual fauna are distinguished from economic fauna because their primary use was not economic in nature. This means that in the ancient Southwest these species were hunted (or raised) not for their meat, but for their feathers or fur. Ritual fauna can be identified, in part, by their relative rarity in an assemblage, the context in which they are recovered,

and/or the apparent purpose for which they were used. Sometimes, members of the same species or even parts of the same animal can be used for both economic and ritual purposes, so information about depositional context is crucial to the interpretation of remains. At Salmon, the unusual deposition of several species is taken to indicate their ritual importance to the community. Examples include the burial of several complete macaws and turkeys and the placement of the horn from a bighorn sheep under a foot drum in the Great Kiva. Other ritually important species are likely several small, colorful birds that would have provided little meat but whose feathers have been used extensively in modern and historic Puebloan ritual practices (K. Durand 2003). It is interesting that not a single bone from any species of hawk has been found at Salmon, although hawks are considered one of the most common classes of ritual birds at many Chacoan sites (Akins 1985:323).

Macaws

Parts of nine macaws have been recovered at Salmon—both scarlet and military macaws—that may date to the Primary occupation (Table 50.14; see discussion below). Five of these were formal burials; three contained the tracheal rings that Hargrave (1970:59) considered a clear sign of the interment of complete bodies. This is a large number of macaws for one site, and it is more macaws than have been recovered at any other Chacoan site except Pueblo Bonito, which had 31 macaws (Hargrave 1970:52). In

Table 47.14. Ground stone rough sort percentages for all strata, Secondary component. Categories (raw material or tool class) with at least 0.1% are shown. Lithic rough sort category codes are indicated in parentheses in column and row headings.

Lithic Class	Basalt Fine (5) n = 1496	Basalt Coarse (6) n = 2013	Andesite (9) n = 2085	Granite (11) n = 36	Igneous Other (18) n = 370	Sandstone (24) n = 2828	Conglomerate/ Breccia (25) n = 5	Brushy Basin Chert (28) n = 28
Milling bin wall (30) n = 63	0.1	0.0	0.0	0.0	0.0	2.1	0.0	0.0
Shaped stone slab (4) n = 598	0.1	0.0	0.0	0.0	0.0	20.9	0.0	0.0
Metate (14) n = 146	0.0	0.0	0.0	5.6	0.0	5.0	0.0	0.0
Lapstone, palette (16) n = 61	0.0	0.0	0.0	2.8	0.0	1.7	20.0	0.0
Anvil stone (17) n = 15	0.0	0.0	0.0	0.0	0.0	0.2	0.0	0.0
Mano (24) n = 416	0.1	0.0	0.2	11.1	0.0	13.2	0.0	0.0
Abrader, ungrooved (27) n = 21	0.0	0.0	0.1	0.0	0.0	0.5	0.0	3.6
Polishing stone (28) n = 27	0.9	0.1	0.8	0.0	1.1	0.2	20.0	0.0
Axe, grooved (32) n = 27	0.1	0.1	0.4	0.0	0.0	0.0	0.0	0.0
Axe, notched (33) n = 59	0.2	0.3	0.5	0.0	1.6	0.2	0.0	0.0
Grinding stone (35) n = 365	0.7	0.7	2.7	8.3	7.0	2.6	20.0	0.0
Tchamahia (42) n = 18	0.0	0.0	0.0	0.0	0.0	0.0	0.0	64.3
Polished stone (44) n = 53	0.4	0.2	0.1	0.0	1.9	0.1	0.0	14.3
Ground stone other (51) n = 554	1.2	1.6	3.5	8.3	8.4	4.7	0.0	0.0
Ground stone indet. (52) n = 1085	5.1	7.4	6.7	11.1	10.3	8.6	40.0	0.0
Axe/maul, grooved (59) n = 15	0.1	0.1	0.1	0.0	0.0	0.0	0.0	0.0
Axe, maul/notched (60) n = 17	0.0	0.2	0.1	2.8	0.0	0.0	0.0	0.0
Debitage (93) n = 15, 523	91.2	88.8	84.7	50.0	69.7	40.0	0.0	17.9

Table 47.14 (continued)

Lithic Class	Sediment Other (32) n = 12	Schist (34) n = 24	Gneiss (35) n = 30	Quartzite Fine (38) n = 3875	Quartzite Coarse (38) n = 5001	Greenstone (39) Gn = 444	Metamorphic Other (45) n = 919
Milling bin wall (30) n = 63	0.0	0.0	0.0	0.0	0.0	0.0	0.0
Shaped stone slab (4) n = 598	0.0	0.0	0.0	0.1	0.0	0.0	0.0
Metate (14) n = 146	0.0	0.0	0.0	0.0	0.0	0.0	0.0
Lapstone, palette (16) n = 61	0.0	0.0	0.0	0.1	0.1	0.0	0.0
Anvil stone (17) n = 15	0.0	0.0	0.0	0.0	0.2	0.0	0.1
Mano (24) n = 416	0.0	0.0	0.0	0.1	0.5	0.2	0.2
Abrader, ungrooved (27) n = 21	0.0	0.0	0.0	0.0	0.1	0.0	0.1
Polishing stone (28) n = 27	16.7	0.0	13.3	0.6	0.3	4.5	2.6
Axe, grooved (32) n = 27	0.0	4.2	3.3	0.1	0.1	0.5	0.5
Axe, notched (33) n = 59	0.0	8.3	0.0	0.1	0.2	1.6	0.7
Grinding stone (35) n = 365	0.0	4.2	3.3	0.9	2.2	2.0	2.4
Tchamahia (42) n = 18	0.0	0.0	0.0	0.0	0.0	0.0	0.0
Polished stone (44) n = 53	8.3	0.0	0.0	0.2	0.1	2.7	0.5
Ground stone other (51) n = 554	0.0	4.2	0.0	0.7	3.4	6.3	3.6
Ground stone indet. (52) n = 1085	25.0	16.7	10.0	1.6	4.4	14.6	8.4
Axe/maul, grooved (59) n = 15	0.0	4.2	0.0	0.0	0.0	1.1	0.0
Axe, maul/notched (60) n = 17	0.0	0.0	0.0	0.0	0.0	0.7	0.4
Debitage (93) n = 15, 523	50.0	58.3	60.0	95.5	88.4	65.8	80.4

fact, only a few sites in the entire Southwest have produced more macaws (Hargrave 1970:52)—these include Wupatki (41), Point of Pines Ruin (27), Turkey Creek (12), and Grasshopper Ruin (20; Olsen 1990:60). In the only written report about the macaw burials at Salmon, Shelley (Chapter 47) noted that they represent the northernmost occurrence of these birds. Furthermore, he noted that Salmon is one of only two sites (the other being Galaz Ruin in the Mimbres region) at which *Ara militaris*, or the military macaw, has been found. Species identifications of these remains were originally made by Arthur Harris and Brett Russell (Shelley, Chapter 47) and have been confirmed here using Hargrave's (1970: 10–14) diagnostic criteria.

A partial macaw skeleton was recovered from a hearth in the Primary strata of Room 33 (Shelley, Chapter 47). Although no photos have been found from the excavation of this macaw, field notes indicate that it was originally an articulated skeleton, found at the eastern edge of a cobble-lined hearth (Feature 43) under a layer of ash with a large cobble placed on top of the burial. The pelvis of this macaw was not completely fused, and the tendinal bridges on the tibiotarsus bones were incomplete, suggesting that it was immature. Based on Hargrave's (1970:5) descriptions, it was new-fledged and approximately 11–12 months in age. Due to the incomplete nature of the skeleton, no species determination was made.

Two loose macaw elements, a left coracoid and right tibiotarsus, were recovered from structured trash deposits in units adjacent to the hearth. These remains also date to the Primary period. The porous nature of this tibiotarsus bone and the fact that its tendinal bridge had not begun to form suggest that this macaw would have been slightly younger than the other macaws found at Salmon (between 4 and 11 months of age, likely closer to 4 months, based on Hargrave 1970:4–5).

A macaw's beak, or premaxilla, along with two other cranial bones (a jugal and palatine bone) and one small bone from the wing (scapholunar) were recovered from within the floor stratum (I-3-17) in Room 86W. No other elements were recognized during excavation of this individual. If these were the only elements of this bird present, they likely were part of a skin or bag when they were placed into the floor. With so few elements, no species identification could be made. This macaw was originally thought to date to the Secondary occupation (R. Adams 1980a; Shelley, Chapter 47), but a re-analysis of the ceramics from this unit suggests the Primary period instead (Paul Reed, personal communication 2005).

A nearly complete scarlet macaw skeleton was recovered from structured trash deposits in the northwest corner of Room 91W (stratum C-6-20). The bird was 1–3 years old, and the skeleton shows some evidence of pathology in the wings. The left carpometacarpus had excessive bony growth on its proximal end, and the first and second phalanges in the right wing were fused together at their common joint, possibly after a break in the second (distal) phalanx. The dating of this skeleton is more problematic, as it was in a structured trash deposit that contained ceramics from all occupation periods.

Room 100W contained two macaw skeletons, one adjacent to a turkey burial and another located on the doorsill between Rooms 97W and 100W. The latter skeleton is currently missing, although excellent photos of it do exist. From the photos, it appears to have been complete with intact tracheal rings; it was buried either on the doorsill with two large cobbles placed on top or under the doorsill as an offering (Figures 50.3 and 50.4). The other macaw skeleton, found adjacent to the turkey burial (which was described as a "crane-like bird" in the original field notes and summary), was not recognized as an articulated skeleton until the turkey burial was discovered. By that point, only the skull and beak of the macaw remained in situ; however, the bags from this excavation level contain most of the other elements from the macaw's skeleton (see Table 50.14). Both burials, plus a second turkey burial that was also not recognized during excavation, were located in stratified trash (stratum C-2-05.5) above the room's Primary floor (stratum H-1-19).

A reexamination of the pottery from this stratum (Paul Reed, personal communication 2005) and the contextual information in the original field notes indicate that this macaw dates to the Primary period. The burials were placed near the southeast corner of the room, next to the foundation cobbles of the south wall. The turkey was on its side with its head to the southwest, and the macaw appears to have been positioned near the turkey's tail and legs (to the north of the turkey). This macaw was reported by Harris and Brett (Shelley, Chapter 47) to be *A. militaris*, and based on Hargrave's (1970:10–14) criteria, we concur. However, several features of the skeleton better match *A. macao*, particularly on the premaxilla or upper beak, so we consider this a tentative classification. This macaw was 1–3 years old, likely closer to 1 year as the tendinal bridge is not fully formed. Some evidence of pathology was present. The left ulna had roughening on the shaft similar to that shown by Hargrave (1970:35, Figure 17b), and the right ulna had a large knob of bone on its shaft.

Figure 50.3. Setting of macaw burial in doorsill of Rooms 97W and 100W.

The clearest example of a miltary macaw skeleton came from Room 129W. Harris and Russell considered this bird to be *A. militaris*, and based on the morphology of the basitemporal plate and the proximal humerus, we concur. As mentioned above, this particular species was extremely rare in the Southwest, making this a unique find. This skeleton is less complete than most of the other macaw skeletons but still exhibits 13 tracheal rings. There are no leg bones with the skeleton, but any remaining leg bones may have been removed by Peter Bullock in 1996 for DNA analysis. The other regions of the body—the skull, trunk, and wings—are all represented. No pathologies were noted. This macaw is estimated to have been an adolescent, 1–3 years old, based on the degree of closure of the fenestrae at the base of the skull. The bird was buried in stratified trash (stratum C-22.5-30.5) with ceramics dating to all periods of occupation; thus the dating of this skeleton is unclear.

In the summer of 2005, the remains of two additional macaws were collected from an area of rodent disturbance in Room 42. This room is immediately north of Room 33, where one macaw burial and two elements from another macaw were recovered (described above). The rodent dug a tunnel and made a burrow in Room 42 and threw the disturbed materials, including the macaw bones, into Room 33 (Larry Baker, personal communication 2005). The ceramics from this material have not been analyzed but appear to be from the Secondary period (Larry Baker, personal communication 2005). Of course, we do not know whether the ceramics were associated with the macaws due to the meandering nature of the disturbed area. Although we cannot be certain that the macaw bones are from intact burials, this seems likely due to the representation of all portions of the skeleton (head, wings, torso, and legs) for each bird (see Table 50.14). At least one of these macaws had been covered in red ochre prior to burial (Figures 50.5 and 50.6). Although there are two right and two left femora in this set of bones, the maximum length of one of the left femora is more than 2 mm larger (at 61.1 mm) than the other three (58.8, 58.5, and 58.8 mm), so it is possible that three macaws are represented.

A minimum of nine macaws have been recovered at Salmon, five of which clearly date to the Primary period (in Rooms 33, 86, and 100). These five include the skeleton from the Room 97/100 doorsill, which has not been located yet but was found in strata that date to the Primary period (R. Adams 1980a). The other two macaws were recovered from more mixed strata (Rooms 91 and 129). Based on the

Figure 50.4. Close-up view of macaw burial from doorsill of Rooms 97W and 100W.

location of the latter two macaws at the bottoms of these strata, we believe they may date to the late Primary period, but this is a tentative conclusion at present. The date for the macaws from Room 42 also is currently unknown.

Turkeys

Turkeys likely played a role in both the ritual and economic life at Salmon Ruins. We see evidence of their economic role in their sheer numbers during the Secondary period, plus the deposition of most turkey elements in layers of trash along with the other food debris. There are several clues, however, that also point to their role in ritual activity. The first clue is the presence of two turkey burials in Room 100W, one of which was adjacent to a macaw burial. A second clue is found in the large number of turkey feather objects among the perishables, especially turkey feather blankets which were apparently more common than fur blankets at Salmon (Webster,

Chapter 46). The final clue comes from the ethnographic record. In a review of the importance of birds in Puebloan ritual, Tyler (1991:71) discussed the importance of turkey feathers in Puebloan ritual belief and practice, arguing that the turkey was equal to the eagle in "its importance in ceremony and myth."

The turkey burial beside the macaw in Room 100W was a nearly complete skeleton in excellent condition (Figure 50.7). Numerous unfused bones, including the pelvis, radius, ulna, carpometacarpus, tibiotarsus, and tarsometatarsus, indicate that this bird was a juvenile. The left humerus shaft had been broken in two and healed, although poorly aligned (see Figure 50.2). The sternum was misshapen, which may have been related to the fractured wing. Many large and small mammal bones were in the bags with the turkey (including cottontail, pocket gopher, mouse, and artiodactyl elements), suggesting that they were found in the fill surrounding its burial.

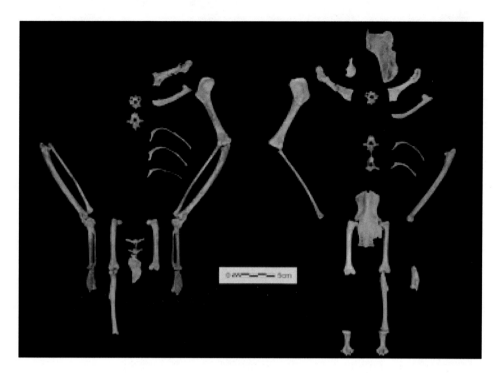

Figure 50.5. Macaw skeletons from Room 42.

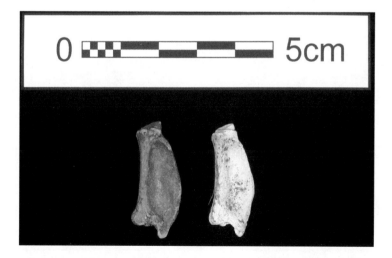

Figure 50.6. Macaw phalanges from Room 42. Thick red ochre can be seen adhering to the wing bone from one macaw (left), but none occurs on the other macaw wing bone (right).

Kathy Roler Durand and Stephen R. Durand

Figure 50.7. Turkey burial near macaw burial in southeast corner of Room 100W.

Figure 50.8. Second turkey burial in Room 100W.

The second turkey burial recovered from Room 100W was a nearly complete, fully mature bird (Figure 50.8). Some unique cultural inclusions in the fill surrounding these burials included two turquoise frog beads, a projectile point, and a piece of tabular sandstone with ochre on it.

Other Ritual Fauna

The other clear example of the ritual use of fauna at Salmon was a bighorn sheep horn core that was found inside the west foot drum/floor vault in the Great Kiva (Room 130). It is interesting that Morris found the horn core from a bighorn sheep in a kiva wall niche in the Aztec Ruin Annex (Morris 1924:247, cited in Richert 1964:22). In Salmon's Great Kiva, the west floor drum also contained a quartzite bird effigy (possibly an owl), a quartz crystal, turquoise, and a turquoise inlay artifact. The east foot drum contained offerings too, including turquoise, a turquoise bead, and several calcite beads (R. Adams 1980a).

Several other of the rarer species recovered at Salmon likely were used for ritual rather than economic purposes. These include the red fox, bobcat, crane, and Stellar's jay. Fur and feathers from these species are common in modern Puebloan ritual practices, and coupled with their relative scarcity and lack of butchering marks, this suggests that they played a similar role in prehistory (K. Durand 2003). Nevertheless, in comparing the Salmon assemblage to that from Guadalupe Ruin, a Chacoan outlier to the south of Chaco Canyon with a faunal assemblage of similar size, there are significantly more likely ritual species at Guadalupe Ruin than were found at Salmon. This is particularly true for birds, which were extremely abundant at Guadalupe Ruin, with 31 species (excluding turkeys) represented in the post-Chacoan assemblage and four species in the much smaller Chacoan assemblage (K. Durand 2003; Pippin 1987; Roler 1999). In comparison, only three species of birds (excluding turkeys) were recovered in the Chacoan or Primary assemblage at Salmon and none in the post-Chacoan or Secondary period. The macaws are the notable exception—without them, the Salmon faunal assemblage is remarkable in its near lack of ritual fauna.

SUMMARY

Clearly, macaws were an important aspect of ritual practice at Salmon Ruins. Great effort and expense would have been required to obtain these birds in trade from lands to the south. Macaws today are extremely important to Puebloan ritual practice; they represent the sun and the south or southeast directions at most pueblos (Tyler 1991). The brilliant

red plumage of the macaw makes it unique in the animal kingdom and irreplaceable for rituals requiring red feathers.

There is another interesting pattern among other red artifacts that we believe would have related to the singular importance of macaws at Salmon. Webster (Chapter 46) found an aspect of the perishable artifacts from the Primary period at Salmon that is unique—the weaving elements, such as twine or reeds, were dyed red prior to construction. Thus, the finished product was entirely red in color. All of these objects were found in Primary strata in rooms in the eastern half of the ruin or adjacent to the Tower Kiva (Room 64; Webster, Chapter 46).

Phil Shelley (personal communication 2004) also noticed an interesting pattern among the imported lithic raw materials at Salmon. During the Primary period, most of the Narbona Pass chert, which is reddish in color, was found in the eastern half of the ruin, whereas the obsidian came from the western half. Given these patterns, one might expect the macaws to be restricted to the eastern half of the pueblo as well. This type of patterning for macaws has been noted at Pueblo Bonito (Creel and McKusick 1994; K. Durand 2003; Pepper 1996 [1920]) as well as at Cameron Creek, Galaz, and Old Town in the Mimbres area (Creel and McKusick 1994:519). This was not the case at Salmon Ruins, however, where the known macaws are almost evenly divided between the two halves of the site (four in the eastern half and five in the western half). Nevertheless, the patterning among other red artifacts at Salmon Ruins and the large number of macaw burials found at the site demonstrate that macaws and red were important symbols at the pueblo.

CONCLUSIONS

Many kinds of animals played an important role in community life at Salmon Ruins. The inhabitants of Salmon ate the meat from a variety of species to obtain protein in their diet, created useful tools from the animals' bones, and used feathers, fur, and horns from a few special animals for ceremonial purposes. It is apparent from the data collected for this study that some aspects of faunal utilization changed over time at Salmon, notably the species used in the diet.

Large game decreased significantly over time at Salmon, with a corresponding increase in the frequency of turkeys. This involved a shift in the basic way that meat was obtained, from hunting to a reliance on animal husbandry. A slight increase in small game was also seen, as lagomorphs increased from 26 percent to 34 percent of the total NISP. These changes were accompanied by a corresponding change in farming practices (Adams 2005; Chapter 43, this report), in which there was a decreased reliance on maize and an increased reliance on beans and gathering wild plant foods through time.

Any number of factors might explain the shift away from artiodactyls. Resource depletion from over-hunting, decreased access to prime hunting areas due to population increase (packing; Munro 1994), centralization or restriction of large game hunting (Driver 1996; Muir 1999), and/or environmental change may explain the apparent increase in turkey at Salmon Ruins and in other places in the greater Southwest (Akins 1987; Driver 1996; Gillespie 1991; Munro 1994; Muir 1999; Windes 1987d) during the twelfth and thirteenth centuries.

Spielmann and Angstadt-Leto (1996) have argued persuasively that significant amounts of protein are required to maximize nutrition in a maize-based diet. Thus, selection would favor people who incorporated protein into their diet. We have shown that the farmers at Salmon Ruins obtained protein from large mammals in the early years of occupation and switched to turkey through time.

Most researchers would agree that the origins and development of an agricultural subsistence strategy is a process rather than an event; that process did not remain static after the introduction of maize, beans, and squash into the Southwestern diet. We believe the evidence suggests that by the end of the occupation of Salmon, turkeys were domesticated and were an important part of the food production strategys. What may have begun as a commensal relationship between humans and turkeys (as a feather source and occasional food source) developed over time into keeping and raising these birds as a protein source. According to K. Adams (2005; Chapter 43, this report), there was increased usage of beans and wild plants in the Salmon diet through time. If we are correct and Adams is correct, there was a switch to a more protein-rich diet through time that would have conferred a selective advantage on the later inhabitants of Salmon. Rather than viewing the Secondary occupation as having declined from the majesty of the Chacoan occupation, it may be that this later occupation was a more successful adaptation to the exigencies of the Southwestern landscape, an adaptation that included a more balanced and dependable diet.

In regard to nondietary fauna, at least five macaws were present at Salmon in the Primary period, likely representing a very important aspect of ritual at the site. This is supported by patterning among other red-hued artifacts (perishables and lithics) during this period, in addition to the macaw

burials or offerings. So far, surprisingly few other kinds of ritual fauna have been identified at Salmon, particularly in comparison to other great houses such as Pueblo Alto (Akins 1985, 1987) or Guadalupe Ruin (K. Durand 2003; Pippin 1987; Roler 1999), both of which had incredibly diverse avian assemblages from the Secondary, or post-Chacoan, period. Instead, there seems to have been a focus on macaws for ritual at Salmon that is not evident in the remains of most other Chacoan great houses. This includes nearby Aztec Ruin, where macaw remains have been identified but "the evidence is meager" (Gary Brown, personal communication 2005), with possibly only two macaws present (Lekson 1999:100).

The role of animals in the life of Salmon's inhabitants has become clearer through this study, yet there is much work to be done. Among other things, a larger sample will help clarify whether there were really few ritual fauna, aside from macaws, at Salmon. Secondary period samples from additional rooms will also help confirm the low frequency of artiodactyl remains from this period. Two things are clear from the present study: First, there were fairly dramatic changes in the meat eaten at Salmon through time, moving from large game to small game and raising of turkeys. Second, macaws represent an important aspect of the ceremonial life at Salmon, at least during the Primary period. Although larger faunal samples may alter our future understanding of some aspects of Salmon prehistory, this incredible group of macaws will remain as markers of the ritual life of this ancient pueblo.

Acknowledgments

We thank Paul Reed and Larry Baker for inviting us to study Salmon's faunal remains. Paul Reed and Nancy Espinosa have been extremely helpful in tracking down the relevant field notes and photos for the macaws. Phil Shelley has been an invaluable colleague, sharing his wealth of knowledge about all things Salmon. We are extremely grateful to Nancy Akins for sharing with us her unpublished, revised Artiodactyl and Lagomorph Indices for various sites in Chaco Canyon. Virginia Butler provided invaluable expertise by analyzing the fish remains for us on short notice. Last but not least, we thank the numerous students at Eastern New Mexico University who helped clean and label the bones, including Beau DeBoer, Robin Gillespie, Noel Lanci, and Thomas Lloyd. Noel Lanci also organized the bone tools and collected the data regarding bone tool frequencies in the sampled rooms. This paper is dedicated to the memory of Noel Lanci, an incredible spirit who left the world much too soon.

Chapter 51

KIVA WALL PAINTINGS AT SALMON RUINS

by Howard N. Smith, Jr.

Excavations during the 1972 and 1973 field seasons at Salmon Ruin revealed the remains of wall paintings in four kivas (Figure 51.1).* The kiva art was recorded by the author in 1973 as an ancillary project to a rock art survey of the San Juan Basin (H. Smith 1974); this chapter describes the kiva paintings of Salmon Ruin and places them into a cultural perspective.

The prehistory of the San Juan Basin in northwestern New Mexico is long and complex and is thus generally beyond the scope of this paper. However, two specific developments are of primary significance: the intrusions of the Chacoan and Mesa Verdean cultures into the region. These two cultural influences had a profound effect on the indigenous people of the area and are an integral part of the history and development of the Salmon Pueblo, and thus of the kiva paintings.

The Salmon Pueblo, as originally constructed in the late eleventh century AD (Irwin-Williams 1972), reflects the intrusion of Chacoan culture into the San Juan Basin. This Chacoan influence is especially manifested in the architecture of the pueblo. The original community was built in the form of a large C with a great kiva in the central plaza. The structure stood three stories at the highest point and contained several hundred rooms; the original construction of the pueblo mirrors traditional Chacoan building techniques. One unusual feature of the pueblo is the Tower Kiva, a relatively large Chacoan kiva built on the second floor of the structure. Despite the complexity and development of Chacoan society, however, the Salmon Pueblo was abandoned less than 100 years after its construction.

The Salmon pueblo was reoccupied and rebuilt in the late twelfth century. This restructuring of the settlement does not reflect Chacoan culture; rather it appears to embody Mesa Verdean culture. The evidence of Mesa Verdean influence is exemplified in the ceramics and in a change in architecture and building techniques. The new occupants constructed rooms within the original structure, and a large number of kivas were built within what have been identified as Chacoan rooms. The Salmon Pueblo was abandoned for the last time in the latter half of the thirteenth century.

The significance of the Salmon kiva paintings, and Anasazi wall paintings in general, lies in the fact that they represent an important and beautiful aspect of a little known and even less understood prehistoric art form. Archaeological investigations in a number of Anasazi settlements have revealed evidence of kiva wall paintings, but the amount of evidence that has withstood the weathering of time and neglect is relatively meager. In 1978 and 1979 Constance Silver conducted a study that documented about 600 mural paintings in kivas, of which only about 60 have been preserved, most in poor condition (Silver 1980:2–6). The art forms of the Salmon kivas thus represent a significant contribution to this slowly accumulating data set.

In an extensive analysis of Anasazi wall painting, Watson Smith (1952) concluded that the practice of painting murals on the walls of kivas began in the eleventh century, during the later part of the Pueblo II period. The center of origin appears to have been in the eastern San Juan drainage basin of southeast Utah and southwest Colorado. Within 200 years (Pueblo III), the art form had spread throughout the San Juan region and to the Little Colorado and Rio Grande drainage areas. Although the practice of painting spread geographically, Watson Smith stated that "it failed to develop very much in technical or artistic features in its imagery" (1952:67) during this period. Kiva art during the Pueblo II–III periods consisted of simple geometric forms with the occasional depiction of zoomorphic figures and the even rarer portrayal of anthropomorphs (W. Smith 1952:55–68).

---

* This paper originally appeared in *Collected Papers in Honor of John W. Runyan*, Archaeological Society of New Mexico No. 7, 1982. It is reprinted here with permission, with minor editing. Note that Smith's discussion of Salmon's chronology is dated and does not reflect the latest revisions (see Reed, Chapter 12).

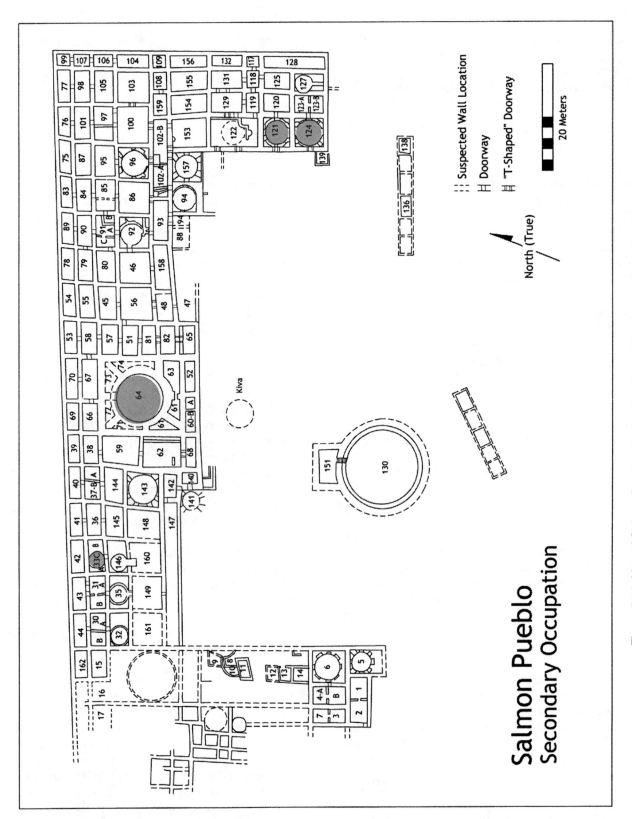

Salmon Pueblo
Secondary Occupation

Figure 51.1. Map of Salmon Pueblo showing locations of four kivas with wall paintings.

Figure 51.2. Wall painting from Kiva 33C showing anthropomorphic figures.

The developmental period is the focus here; however, it is important to note that sometime near the beginning of the Pueblo IV period in Anasazi prehistory the art of kiva wall decoration took on a new vigor in several regions. From the fourteenth to seventeenth centuries, kiva wall painting became an almost flamboyant art form. The probable origin of this change and its sociocultural implications are presented by Polly Schaafsma (1980) in her discussion of the origin of the Pueblo Kachina Cult. The most beautiful and significant examples are found at the Pottery Mound (Hibben 1975), Kuaua (Dutton 1963), and Awatovi (W. Smith 1952) pueblos.

The practice of painting wall murals in kivas has continued at most pueblos into historic and modern times, as reported by many researchers. As an art form, the vigor of the paintings has diminished. However, the ceremonial significance of the art has continued, representing the development and maintenance of a thousand-year-old tradition of which the paintings at Salmon Pueblo are a part.

As stated previously, evidence of wall painting was found in four of the kivas at the Salmon site. These kivas are denoted by the room numbers 33, 64 (Tower Kiva), 121 (Painted Kiva), and 124, as shown on the map in Figure 51.1. The first example of kiva painting at Salmon comes from Room 33, a small kiva located in the northern part of the pueblo. The painting is a portrayal of two anthropomorphic figures (Figure 51.2). The figures are small—approximately 20 cm in height. They were painted in white on the adobe-plastered western wall of the kiva. The wall on which these paintings were found collapsed in 1973 and the art was destroyed.

In the Tower Kiva, fragments of wall plaster—baked when the kiva was destroyed by fire—were found lying on the floor surface of the room (Figure 51.3). The Tower Kiva wall art included the depiction of what appears to be a bird (Figure 51.4) and a geometric pattern: a triangle shape with a border of small dots. The figures were painted in red on a white background. The original location of some of the paintings on the kiva wall is not known due to the effects of the fire.

The third example of kiva painting at Salmon was found in Room 121, which has come to be known as the Painted Kiva (Figure 51.5). The paintings in this kiva were the best preserved at the site and also contain the largest number of elements. The Painted Kiva mural consists of a dark red dado, 60 cm in height. Its upper edge is embellished with sets of triangle shapes in pairs or threes, with intervening sets of four small "hook" figures (Figure 51.6). Each of these hook figures has a stepped design on the left side of its base. The apices of the figures are oriented upward. The upper portion of the wall was painted white with small round red dots around each of the triangles; the dots appear to have been painted with fingertips. It should be noted that the triangle figure with bordering dots was also a feature of the Tower Kiva paintings.

Another figure in the Painted Kiva mural is an anthropomorph—a human figure with a humped back and apparently holding a bow (Figure 51.7). It is located on the western wall of the kiva and is approximately 25 cm in height. It was painted in red on a white background above the dado. The figure appears to be contemporaneous with the rest of the exposed painting in the kiva. An interesting feature of this human figure is the depiction of movement (i.e., running). There is also evidence of painting on the underlying levels of plaster in the Painted Kiva; however, an investigation of such evidence has not yet been undertaken.

The kiva next to the Painted Kiva revealed the fourth example of wall painting at Salmon. The painting in this kiva (Room 124) consists of a series of round white dots painted on a tan plastered wall surface (Figure 51.8). The dots are located on the northeastern wall of the kiva near the floor surface. They appear to have been painted with fingertips and are located so as to encircle a small wall niche. The painting in this kiva does not show the same quality of technique as seen in the other examples.

Of central importance to the analysis of Salmon's kiva paintings are the kivas themselves. Three of the kivas (rooms 33, 121, and 124) were built within what have been identified as Chacoan rooms in the

Figure 51.3. View of wall of Tower Kiva showing intact plaster and painted design.

Figure 51.4. Close-up photograph of bird depicted on wall of Tower Kiva.

Figure 51.5. Photograph of large wall mural in Kiva 121A.

Figure 51.6. Close-up view of hook figures on wall of Kiva 121A.

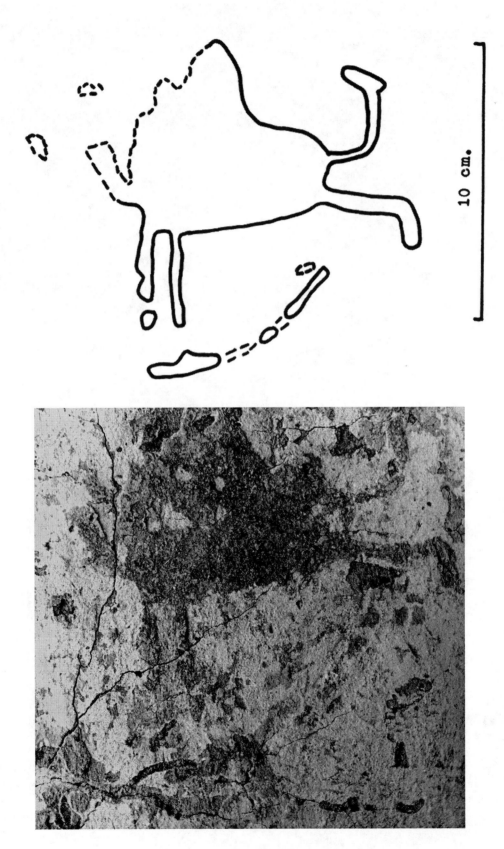

Figure 51.7. Photograph and drawing (by Barbara Smith) of human figure on Kiva 121A wall.

Figure 51.8. Photograph of wall painting in Kiva 124A.

original structure. Although the Tower Kiva (Room 64) has been identified as a Chacoan feature, its paintings appear to be a manifestation of the second occupation of the pueblo. The kiva burned late in the settlement's occupation (circa 1250 AD), and the wall painting fragments appear to be on the most recent layer of wall plastering. Such evidence suggests that the wall paintings are indeed a feature of the later, post-Chacoan-influenced occupation of the site.

Additional evidence suggesting that the concept of kiva wall art at Salmon was not a result of Chacoan cultural intrusion comes from Chaco Canyon, where kiva art does not appear to have been a significant feature of ceremonialism. The examples of kiva wall art at Chaco Canyon sites are very few, and Watson Smith (1952:64) concluded that the art form was introduced to the Chaco area at a relatively late date.

Thus a Chacoan origin for wall painting in the San Juan Basin and at Salmon Pueblo specifically can probably be eliminated. But was kiva painting an indigenous development or was the art form inspired by yet another outside cultural influence? The evidence, although not substantial, is consistent, and seems to suggest that kiva art, as practiced at Salmon, was a Mesa Verdean feature and not a local development. The primary evidence for such a conclusion is the distribution of a specific mural design element: dados embellished with repeated

series of triangles bordered with dots such as those found in Salmon rooms 64 and 121. This particular design element is found in the kivas of several Mesa Verdean sites, such as Painted Kiva House, Cliff Palace, Spruce Tree House, and New Fire House (Nordenskiold 1893; W. Smith 1952; Schaafsma 1980). Additional examples of this design motif are found at Three Turkey House (W. Smith 1952) and Canyon de Chelley (Mindeleff 1897) in Arizona. It seems significant that the same design motif was also painted in three kivas at Aztec Ruin, a pueblo with a history identical to that of Salmon and located only 10 miles away.

The portrayal of anthropomorphic figures and a hump-backed hunter in the Salmon kiva paintings is also of importance to this analysis. Two hump-backed and phallic hunters are depicted in a painted mural at New Fire House at Mesa Verde in association with triangles bordered in dots (W. Smith 1952: 62; Schaafsma 1980:141–142). The significance of this occurrence is obviously limited and inconclusive. However, in conjunction with the evidence of the distribution of other kiva mural elements and the relative dates of the Salmon kivas exhibiting wall painting, it is apparent that by the mid-thirteenth century not only was Anasazi kiva painting geographically widespread, but its symbolism was (or at least was becoming) homogeneous. Such evidence would also seem to suggest that the ceremonial practices and beliefs of the Anasazi were likewise coalescing.

In summary, excavations at the Salmon site have brought to light wall paintings in four kivas that were a feature of the late occupation of the pueblo (most probably thirteenth century) and were the result of Mesa Verdean cultural influences of the period. The Salmon kiva paintings represent the Pueblo III expansion of an art form and, most likely, the spread of new or innovative cultural concepts.

Without a doubt, a great deal more research is needed to more fully understand the development of kiva wall painting. Such research can and should explore several areas. It is essential that we increase our understanding of the origin and cultural development of this art form. Kiva painting was and is a highly specialized art form and thus would hardly have been a casual or sporadic cultural feature. It is most possible that kiva painting, even in its earliest stages of development, was an important if not essential feature of Anasazi ceremonialism. In the case of Salmon, the ultimate question concerns the cultural significance of the elements in the paintings.

Kiva art, much like rock art, has long been considered to be an interesting facet of Southwestern archaeology. It was beautiful to behold, but was peripheral to the goals of research. However, this situation seems to be changing and increasing attention to the subject cannot help but shed a new light on the understanding of the dynamics of Anasazi culture and the origins of contemporary pueblo religious practices.

Chapter 52

DIFFERENTIAL STRUCTURAL WOOD USE AT SALMON RUINS

by Thomas C. Windes and Eileen Bacha

During the AD 800s in the northern San Juan region, large villages were founded along the Dolores River valley and most of the tributaries flowing south into the San Juan River. These villages became regional centers and the focus for developing social systems that mirrored the later rise of Chaco great house communities throughout the San Juan Basin in the following centuries (Varien et al. 2000; Wilshusen and Blinman 1992; Wilshusen and Ortman 1999; Wilshusen and Van Dyke 2006; Wilshusen and Wilson 1995; Windes 2006; Windes and Ford 1996). By the late AD 800s a shift in environmental conditions had forced many of these communities out of the higher elevations into lower terrain south of the San Juan River (see Kohler et al. 2005). This event corresponded with the arrival of the first stone-masonry structures in the San Juan Basin, including those in Chaco Canyon, which formed the large cultural "bumps" (Lekson 1991, 1999) on the landscape to the delight of archaeologists in the twentieth and twenty-first centuries. The growth of these very large masonry structures became the focus for much recent research, particularly in Chaco Canyon, but many others that have generally escaped close scrutiny were located far and wide across the landscape. By the late AD 1000s, during the heyday of the unparalleled labor efforts in Chaco Canyon devoted to building new great houses and remodeling older ones, a number of great houses were also built north of the San Juan River in what traditionally has been regarded as the San Juan–Mesa Verdean cultural region, a region distinct from the Chacoan society to the south (but see Cameron 2005). Understanding the perceived differences between these two societies that occupied Salmon was one of the primary goals of the Salmon Project (Irwin-Williams, Chapter 2).

From a long-term perspective, which dovetails with general historical origins and migration accounts of Puebloans, the Chacoan move north might be seen as a return of people to homelands left two centuries or more earlier when poor environmental conditions uprooted many Puebloan groups (Van

Dyke 2004). Two of the largest great houses built in the north, representing only a few that have seen the research spade—Salmon and Aztec Ruins—have become symbols of the enigmas that drive archaeological inquiry toward an understanding of the development, spread, and demise of Chacoan culture.

Aztec Ruin consists of three clustered great houses (Aztec North, Aztec West, and Aztec East) that were built between about the mid-AD 1000s and the AD 1200s (Brown et al. 2005; McKenna and Toll 1992:137–138; Windes and McKenna 2001). Two of these were partly excavated in the early days of Southwest archaeology (Morris 1928; Richert 1964) and correspondingly suffer from a lack of detailed notes necessary to answer many of the questions regarding the Chacoan and subsequent occupations. Aztec North remains unexcavated. The Aztec ruins have provided much structural wood that dates harvest and construction episodes through time and other facets of behavior useful in understanding the society that created the spectacular structures. Our understanding of the use of structural wood at Aztec provides an important model for comparing wood data from Salmon.

THE SALMON PROJECT

Between 1972 and 1978, a large-scale excavation project at Salmon Ruin investigated the first large Chacoan great house in the northern San Juan region since Earl Morris's work in the 1910s and 1920s at nearby Aztec Ruins. This project, by Cynthia Irwin-Williams and Eastern New Mexico University, sought to explore the nature of Chacoan great house outliers and the difference between the initial Chacoan society and the subsequent occupations that occurred afterwards, which produced much San Juan–Mesa Verdean cultural material and remodeling within the same bounded architectural space initially constructed in the Chacoan-style (Irwin-Williams, Chapter 16).

Salmon saw extensive use, with massive construction in the late AD 1000s and continued use, perhaps intermittent at times, through the late-AD 1200s. The poorly known intermediary occupation provided cultural continuity between the initial Chacoan occupation and the later San Juan–Mesa Verdean one (see Cameron 2005 for a discussion of Chacoan and Mesa Verdean "cultures"), although we are unsure of the relationship of the intermediary occupation to the others (see Brown et al. 2005 for a similar situation at Aztec). The many changes in architecture through remodeling, renovation, and urban renewal, with massive deposits of refuse and architectural remains marking the site during its final use, created a cultural treasure-trove for research. This long-used site, however, was beset by complex fill stratigraphies and problems related to excavation logistics, staff turnover, a very large somewhat inexperienced work force, and the lack of staff continuity within many room and kiva excavations—not an unusual scenario for multiyear work in the 1970s at any large site.

A final, detailed Salmon excavation report was not produced, although a final report to funding agencies was finished in 1980 (Irwin-Williams and Shelley 1980). The Center for Desert Archaeology's Salmon Reinvestment Program, begun in 2001, which has jump-started research at Salmon, provides grant funding (through the New Mexico Historic Preservation Division) for the new tree-ring dates obtained during this study. The current three-volume report on 35 years of archaeology at Salmon Ruins is the primary contribution of the Center–Salmon Ruins research partnership.

The Salmon synthetic volume (Reed 2005a) helps to explore the Chacoan presence north of the San Juan River in the Middle San Juan or Totah area (McKenna and Toll 1992), which incorporates most of the San Juan River valley in northern New Mexico and its lower northern tributaries. The core area borders the San Juan River between the modern towns of Shiprock and Bloomfield, New Mexico, where broad stretches of terrain bordering the river provide low terraces and a number of side drainages that are optimal places to practice horticulture. The south side of the river is littered with small houses and occasionally larger ones that probably served as community centers (Wheelbarger 2005). The north side, too, probably once provided acreage for housing and farming, but the spread of modern towns has made an accurate assessment of this habitation difficult (Toll 2005). Puebloan movement into the Middle San Juan probably occurred in the AD 900s or AD 1000s, coincidental with the spread of Chacoan-like communities throughout the San Juan Basin. It was during the mid-1000s that the first

indication of planning and construction took place at Salmon Pueblo (see Baker 2005).

Salmon is one of several Chaco-style great house sites in the northern San Juan that have been tested or excavated: Aztec East (Richert 1964), Aztec West (Morris 1928), Bluff (Cameron et al. 1997), Chimney Rock (Eddy 1977, 2004), Escalante (Reed et al. 1979), Lowry (Martin 1936), Sterling (Bice 1983; Franklin and McKenna 2004), and Wallace Ruin (Bradley 1988, 2004). All reflect architectural characteristics that have prompted researchers to label these structures as Chacoan outliers (see Van Dyke 1999; Powers et al. 1983). In a region dominated by a San Juan–Mesa Verdean occupation, the Chacoan sites are unusual additions to the material culture and, most notably, the architectural tradition of the region. Few of these Chacoan houses (except for Aztec East and West and Salmon Ruin) have yielded enough structural wood to look closely at harvest and construction behavior. Of the excavated northern great houses, only Lowry Ruin reveals coeval construction with Salmon Ruin (White and Breternitz 1976); both must be considered some of the earliest great houses built north of the San Juan River. In Chaco, Peñasco Blanco and Kin Klizhin reflected some construction and remodeling at about AD 1088, when Salmon was being constructed, which prompted Wilcox (1993) to propose that a common stockpile of beams was used to build Salmon and Peñasco Blanco. This notion can however be dismissed given the discrepancy in species use and probable source areas from which the trees were gathered.

RESEARCH FOCUS

Despite a century of research, Chaco Canyon, home to one of the most enigmatic societies in North America, remains a puzzling settlement. Its most prominent symbol is the massive architectural great house, with the largest concentration of such buildings located in arid, resource-deficient Chaco Canyon. The proliferation of these edifices to the north also has drawn much attention and speculation as to why they appeared and who built them. Much debate has centered on Salmon and Aztec Ruins concerning their roles in the Chacoan world. Both, as well as the vast majority of northern outliers, were built near the end of the massive era of great house construction and cultural florescence in Chaco Canyon in the AD 1000s. For this reason, many have seen Salmon and Aztec as built and inhabited by migrants from Chaco Canyon, as the canyon suffered from environmental and corresponding subsistence failure in the AD 1080s and 1090s (see Dean and

Funkhouser 2002: Figure 3.5b). A wave of displaced migrants or budding daughter communities from Chaco may have founded Salmon (Irwin-Williams, Chapter 2; Judge et al. 1981:88; Vivian 1990:483–484), although productive downturns in Chaco would have created the opportunity for northern leaders to seize the initiative to build their own bases of power and to establish patron-client relationships locally (Sebastian 1992:135–136), turning the San Juan region into a competing district with Chaco (Powers et al. 1983:345). Bradley (2004) has suggested that some outliers were founded as missions as part of Chacoan expansion. Salmon might instead have simply been part of a pan-Southwest Puebloan tradition (Mobley-Tanaka 1993:41) or been built by local groups emulating the large structures in Chaco to participate in the larger regional system (e.g., Roney 2004). Because Salmon Ruin and Chaco Canyon are nearly connected by the Great North Road, Salmon was well placed as a center to provide tribute to Chaco in Wilcox's (1993, 2004) scheme of northern conquest from Chaco Canyon. Thus, Wilcox would have Salmon founded as a Chacoan military outpost to conquer the northern region. The consensus for the founding of Salmon Ruin rests primarily upon two possibilities: Salmon was founded by a group or groups from Chaco Canyon, or it was locally inspired by events in Chaco and created as a competing or allied seat of power.

The harvesting and use of structural wood provides one avenue to address the basic question: Was Salmon founded by a migration of Chacoans from Chaco Canyon, as an outpost of direct Chacoan control of a local population, or as a result of a local populace imitating the Chacoan societal fabric as a means to concentrate power and to participate in a broad regional network? Resolution of this problem does not automatically mean that all northern great houses derived from the same origins, but at least it does provide clues as to why some of the northern great houses evolved.

The founding of Aztec West shortly after the construction of Salmon poses similar possibilities for determining its origins. Reed (2002) has argued that social disintegration at Salmon led residents north to construct Aztec East, after Aztec North and West were built (see McKenna and Toll 1992). What can the wood structural remains tell us in regards to these possibilities of great house origins and construction dynamics?

STRUCTURAL WOOD FOR DATING

From the earliest beginnings of dendrochronology in the late 1910s and into the 1980s, structural wood was considered primarily for its temporal value. Little thought was given to structural wood for its role in understanding human behavior. Thus, large quantities of wood, much like the mounds of masonry and mortar that normally comprised the fill of deteriorated great houses, escaped collection or were discarded. In addition, local historic inhabitants often plundered the sites (e.g., Morris 1919:9), a problem that probably affected any standing architecture at Salmon Ruins.

Large-diameter elements have always provided the grist for collected samples. These large timbers, primarily roofing vigas, were sought in part because of collection strategies that harkened back to the beginnings of tree-ring dating in the 1920s. In the early days of dendrochronology, only certain species of trees—primarily ponderosa and piñon pines and Douglas fir—provided datable ring-growth patterns (Ahlstrom 1985; Nash 1999). Wood from other species, typically *Populus* and *Juniperus*, was generally discarded. The growth of *Populus* sp. along gullies, washes, rivers, and valleys (cottonwood), or in the wetter higher elevations (aspen), ensures steady tree growth but with complacent and relatively few rings that are unsuitable for dating. Juniper, which grows in the most xeric conditions of any conifer, is highly sensitive to environmental conditions and typically suffers from erratic growth, which often includes missing, compressed, and double rings, making it difficult to date. It was not until the 1960s that juniper began to provide dating success at the Laboratory of Tree-Ring Research (Richard Warren, personal communication 2005).

The selection of large-diameter tree species also had a practical side rooted in the early tree-ring collection philosophy (see Nash 1999; Stokes and Smiley 1968). Normally, a sawn section of timber provides the complete record of ring growth. When such samples were taken from intact structures, particularly those held in the public trust such as in national parks, there was discontent about the visual impact from sampling and the destruction of a public resource. Sawn timbers in situ were still taken in national parks as late as 1961 (e.g., Hobler and Hobler 1978). An alternative method of collection was the use of hand augers to extract 1-inch diameter cores. As can be imagined, this laborious process did not facilitate large numbers of samples, limiting collection to the most obvious large-diameter pine and Douglas fir elements—generally roof vigas that stood the best chance of dating success. It was not until the mid 1960s that portable electric drills came onto the market, allowing many more samples to be extracted at far less effort. The favored size tool for sampling by this time was the half-inch diameter hollow drill bit. But few organizations outside of the Laboratory of Tree-Ring Research in Tucson possessed drilling equipment, so most samples were collected as fragments or sawed segments.

NORMATIVE PUEBLOAN TREE-HARVESTING STRATEGIES

Understanding Puebloan behavior in regards to normal wood harvesting efforts for house construction provides a base for understanding the construction norm at Chaco great houses. Several avenues provide insights into expectations of prehistoric tree harvesting behavior. Knowledge about which physiological constraints affect different tree species, and familiarity with the nature of the local environment, can help produce reasonable expectations of ancient tree stands, if any, in the Salmon area. Local tree resources in the vicinities of both Salmon and Aztec Ruins are similar today, and they may have provided the architects and designers of the two great houses with similar material and procurement choices. The perceived similarity of tree resources for the two centers is important in light of the findings of the actual species selected for construction at the two great houses. An understanding of the use of wood among small-house populations is critical to "reading" local tree availability. Finally, historic and modern tree stands provide information about local conditions and change, if any, over time.

Among populations on the Colorado Plateau, local trees provided the wood used for construction. Innumerable sites yielding structural wood (e.g., Ahlstrom 1985; Robinson 1967: Table 4) almost always yielded species immediately available today. Extensive wood research by the senior author in the cliff ruins in Mesa Verde, Natural Bridges, Walnut Canyon, Canyon del Chelly, and Sonora, Mexico, indicates that groups selected tree species for construction that can still be seen today from the fronts of the dwellings. Excavated open sites also traditionally yield structural wood found closest to the site.

Inhabitants living in small houses utilized local tree resources. Harvesting and dressing trees was done by a limited labor supply of small or extended families, who did not have the manpower to go great distances to procure numerous quality but heavy logs. It was far easier to build near the resource than to obtain it by laborious travel and hauling. For the most part on the Colorado Plateau, small domestic groups required wood that was generally in the near vicinity of marginal forested lands among cottonwoods, piñons, and junipers. The high-altitude coni-

fers (firs and spruces) and aspens did not grow in areas favorable for farming except in small isolated groves along north-facing canyons and mesas.

We can model the effects on the local environment as people used the local resources and were forced to go farther for wood as it was depleted. Building needs are periodic events that may allow trees time to recover, but the relentless need for firepit fuel and other domestic uses can also deplete an area of wood (see Betancourt and Van Devender 1981; Kohler and Matthews 1988). A case example is the Pueblo I community at Grass Mesa along the Dolores River nestled in a valley area surrounded by piñon, juniper, ponderosa pine, Douglas fir, oak, and cottonwood trees that were locally plentiful (Kohler et al. 1984: Table 19). Eventually, about 145 pithouses and 725 surface structures were built and a maximum 300 residents lived at the site. Juniper was favored for construction at first, followed by increased amounts of ponderosa pine and Douglas fir, and then cottonwood and piñon. Nevertheless, all the major tree species found in the immediate vicinity today are represented in the archaeological record.

Construction of the Pueblo I great kiva at Grass Mesa demanded far greater labor and village cooperation than the domestic structures. Lightfoot (1988: Table 5) has estimated that approximately 9000 hours were required to build the great kiva. Juniper was used exclusively for the many upright roof posts, but unfortunately roofing remains were absent. Given the length of straight beams needed for the roof construction, only ponderosa pine and Douglas fir, both locally available (Lightfoot 1988: 258), would have satisfied structural requirements. We cannot be sure whether special efforts were made during construction to satisfy symbolic needs by wood procurement of firs and spruce far beyond the local resources. But the site record reveals that almost entirely local wood resources were used to satisfy practical construction requirements (Kohler et al. 1984) without resorting to distant species that may have fulfilled ritual or other nonpractical needs.

On the other hand, our knowledge of structural wood resources from sites located in wood-deficient areas is poor, and we generally lack understanding of acceptable labor costs for settlements in areas that today lack tree resources. That is, we are unsure if inhabitants required tree resources to be locally available as one requisite for settlement or if they were willing to expend much labor in order to satisfy the needed construction requirements. How far were groups willing to go for adequate structural wood? In Chaco Canyon, wood was routinely brought from at least 80 km away (English et al. 2001; Reynolds et al. 2004) during the AD 1000s and early AD 1100s for the construction of great houses, although local trees were used mostly in small-house construction.

Other important criteria for choosing an area must have been the availability of drinking water and, for farmers, water resources adequate for crop production. The amount of wood needed for pit structure and storage room roofs, not to mention for firewood and other ancillary domestic and ritual uses, required trees nearby. In many places where wood resources today are sparse or absent, so too are archaeological house structural wood remains. The amount of recycling in forest-poor areas was probably high, which was certainly true in Chaco Canyon and the interior of the San Juan Basin among the small-house populations where structural wood is seldom recovered.

We do not know for sure whether some communities faced wood scarcity but overcame it by increasing their efforts to obtain wood some distance from their home settlements. Given the sparse wood cover across the San Juan Basin interior today, however, we must expect that obtaining adequate wood resources for construction and other purposes must always have been a problem, exacerbated by the long-term use of the land. Most habitation sites within the basin, however, are located along drainages where water concerns could best be resolved and which must have had some cottonwood stands before the stone axe denuded the region. We expect that much of the ebb and flow of inhabitants in and out of the interior San Juan Basin was correlated not only with environmental and social disruptions but also with the availability of wood resources.

RECONSTRUCTING THE TREE RESOURCES IN THE SALMON REGION

Knowledge of the past and present tree resources in the general vicinity of Salmon Ruin is germane to understanding the potential wood available to the builders of the multistoried Salmon great house. To understand the potential for wood resources in the region, we must know the general parameters for the growth of various species of trees that typically contribute to construction material stocks. There is no single, existing reference that shows current locations of tree species that were used in the Salmon construction. However, Karen Adams's work during the original Salmon Project in the 1970s (and more recently) has resulted in much data (Adams 1979; Chapter 40). Environmental conditions, which provide limitations to the growth extent of different species of trees, have changed little over the past several thousand years (Adams

and Bowyer 2002:41; Betancourt 1984; Gillespie 1985:36). New advances in science in recent years have provided more accurate determinations of tree resources (Durand et al. 1999; English et al. 2001; Reynolds et al. 2004).

Studies using the new techniques would greatly advance our understanding of construction behavior at Salmon Ruin, but they have not yet been done. In lieu of the new sourcing techniques, three areas of research were used here to determine the probable areas of timber procurement available to the builders of Salmon Ruin, based on the premise that the most desirable trees were those located in the closest source areas. Information derived from excavated small-house structural timbers, historical accounts, and the current locations of trees helps to model the prehistoric woodland setting. Large conifers were typically scarce in the Salmon and Aztec areas even before Anglo settlement took place. Accounts by explorers in the mid-1800s and more recent observations, supported by historic and prehistoric site investigations, suggest that local tree resources were little different during the construction at Salmon and Aztec ruins.

Some of the earliest insights into tree growth in the region were documented by the Dominguez-Escalante expedition of 1776–1777 (Miller 1976) and the Macomb expedition of 1859, which crossed from the mouth of Largo Canyon, 23 km east of Salmon Ruin, up the Los Piños River valley, and across the terraces to the Animas River valley and the Aztec Ruins, and then continued north to the upper La Plata River valley. These expeditions have provided information on regional tree resources that may also apply to the conditions and resources when Salmon and Aztec were built. Although it is not clear what resources were available to the builders of great houses, the 1859 expedition documented conditions before the arrival of Europeans and their devastation of forests in their quest for grazing, fuel, and building materials for housing, mines, and railroads. In 1859, Newberry (1876:79–81, 103, 110) described terraces covered with piñon, juniper, and sage, bordering river valleys with thickets of buffalo-berry (squaw-berry), alder, and willow, along with groups and occasional stands of cottonwood trees marking the river courses adjacent to saltbush-covered bottomlands. In the Los Piños River valley, now flooded by Navajo Dam, Newberry described these typical bottomlands along with scattered yellow (ponderosa) pines marking the river's course through the open sage-covered country. Near the head of the La Plata River valley, in the Hesperus, Colorado area where the expedition camped, Newberry (1876:81) reported "gigantic pines" scattered about singly and in groups within the gramma grass–covered valley, a report similar to the shift from piñon, juniper, and sage to tall pines, oak, aspen, and cottonwood noted there by the Dominquez-Escalante expedition (Miller 1976:48–49). Little has changed today, except that many of the ponderosa pines and other large conifers have been eradicated from their lower boundaries except along steep, relatively inaccessible slopes.

O'Sullivan photographed the area immediately around Salmon Ruin in 1874 (see Reed, Chapter 4; 2002), revealing conditions similar to Newberry's accounts. Morris (1919:7) described a similar landscape around Aztec Ruins: a desolate river valley with narrow fringes of willows, skunk brush, squaw or buffalo berries, and stands of cottonwoods skirting the river banks (Morris 1919:7). The expanses between the watercourses and terraces were clad in intermittent growth of sage and chico (rabbit) brush. Scattered piñon and juniper trees across the terraces, however, provided a "plentiful supply of timber for fuel and construction" (Morris 1919:7).

The arrival of settlers in the Animas and San Juan River valleys may have had a severe impact on the great houses in the same vicinities. Morris (1919: 9) described looters who cut and carried away many timbers from the Aztec ruins, including the loss of ceiling timbers and doorway lintels. Undoubtedly, many of these ancient pieces ended up in houses throughout the area.[1] Early photos of Salmon Ruin reveal little standing architecture, although we assume that any exposed building timbers would have been the target of early looting.

According to the current landscape, only native species of juniper, piñon, willow, and cottonwood would have been locally suitable for prehistoric building construction. It is not surprising that juniper, willow, and cottonwood are represented in the wood inventories from both Salmon and Aztec ruins. Piñon is seldom found in pueblo great house construction because of its crooked growth, its lack of long straight stems, and its value for piñon nuts, pine gum, and fuel (e.g., Hovezak 1992; Miller and Albert 1993). The lack of willow beams is also not surprising, given its unsuitable stem growth for the main structural elements. But willow was commonly used to make mats and closing elements in some Aztec West roofs (Morris 1919:55–56, 365–366). Most

likely willow (*Salis* sp.) was labeled as "nonconiferous" during tree-ring analyses (Richard Warren, personal communication 2005); much nonconiferous wood was found during the Salmon excavations that was used for roof closing material.

Piñon is rare in the area today, becoming somewhat common only about 8 km or more from Salmon (K. Adams 1979:161; see Chapter 40). Piñon (*Pinus edulis*, Colorado piñon) requires abundant summer rainfall for establishment, whereas Utah juniper (*J. osteosperma*) flourishes in a winter-wet/summer-dry climate (Neilson 1987:95, 97). If local availability had been much higher prehistorically, then we should expect that piñon would have been common at Salmon. Although piñon nuts were common to both occupations, few piñon-tree parts were found at the site, suggesting that in prehistoric times it was also rare (Adams, Chapter 40). On the other hand, juniper parts were common throughout the occupation for construction timbers, fuel, and many other needs (K. Adams 1979; Lentz, Chapter 41), indicating that it was locally plentiful.

A substantial amount of firewood is needed each year for a large habitation site, with between 400 and 500 cords of wood consumed annually for a 200-room pueblo (Fish 1996: Table 1)—making a serious impact on any local tree stands. If old-growth piñon stands had been present near Salmon, the amount of dead wood available for fuel (Floyd et al. 2003) would have made it a highly desired product. At Zuni Pueblo, at least, piñon firewood traditionally was gathered only from dead wood, but there was enough present in 1992 to provide an estimated 9200 cords of firewood (Miller and Albert 1993:75). Now the Zuni collect wood from both dead and living trees (Peter McKenna, personal communication, 2005), impacting the health of their forests.

If piñon had been abundant locally, the Salmon inhabitants would have exploited the other resources that are common to piñon woodlands and important to Puebloan activities. Birds are an essential part of Puebloan ritual, with about 100 species being important, even for such mundane tasks as building a room, dedicating a new building, or planting a new field (Tyler 1991:ix–xii). Stands of piñon are home to piñon jays and Clark's nutcracker (San Miguel and Colyer 2003:91–93), birds that may have been prized for their feathers (Miller and Albert 1993:76), but none were found at Salmon. Among the Zuni, piñon jays are an important source for feathers dedicated to the western direction symbol of blue, for prayer sticks dedicated to war and hunting, and as symbolic killers of ghosts (Tyler 1991). Turkeys and macaws were found at Salmon, but the relative lack of small

---

[1]The Masonic Temple, San Juan Lodge No. 25, in Aztec contains the Master's Chair built for three people that is inscribed as being made from wood taken from the Aztec Ruins. The chair was built by C. R. Beers and others in 1914. It was observed by the senior author in 2003, and the inscriptions were confirmed in June 2005.

birds (Durand and Durand 2005; see Chapter 50) compared to the great houses in Chaco Canyon might suggest that the diversity of local small birds was low because of the lack of piñon trees. The lack of small colorful birds at Salmon may also indicate that ritual and ceremony associated with the use of small birds was of less importance than in Chaco, or that the plumage of macaws was used instead. The small sample of faunal material analyzed by Durand and Durand (Chapter 50) also failed to yield any porcupine bones, an animal common to piñon forests because of its preference for edible piñon bark and treetops.

A Survey of Ponderosa Pine and Douglas Fir in the Vicinity of Salmon Ruin

Wood use within prehistoric sites along the San Juan River and local tributaries within the Salmon area (Figure 52.1) should reflect which local tree resources were available for construction at the time of occupation. A number of drainages and highlands provide potential source areas for the wood that was gathered for construction at Salmon. The primary drainages along the San Juan River above and below Salmon are potential areas that might yield excavation information germane to our understanding of prehistoric tree sources (Tables 52.1–52.2). The distance of each drainage from Salmon provides information about the level of difficulty in transporting distant trees from potential source areas (Table 52.3). The maximum distance between the primary side drainages above and below Salmon that may have contributed wood is 94 km (from the mouth of the La Plata River east to the mouth of the Los Piños and Francis Rivers).

Juniper and piñon dominate the mesa country along the various drainages flowing into the San Juan River in the Navajo Reservoir district (e.g., see Hefner 1985:8). Along the deep canyon tributaries draining into the San Juan River, ponderosa pines and Douglas firs favor the north-facing slopes where there is adequate moisture (snow) to maintain them (see Hall 1944:6). We do know that extensive cutting has eradicated the more peripheral stands of ponderosa pines and Douglas firs in regions where railroads, mines, and heavy settlement occurred in historic times, but the drainages of the San Juan River studied here appear to have been little affected by these historic impacts. It is important to note that many of the drainages that have scattered stands of ponderosa pines and Douglas fir appear not to have experienced extensive settlement immediately prior to the founding of the Salmon settlement. The sites that provide much of the prehistoric wood informa-

tion mainly date from the Basketmaker and Pueblo I periods along the upper San Juan River past Navajo Dam, and along Gobernador and Largo-Gallina Canyons. The closest sources today are found 34 km (21 miles) from Salmon in Gobernador Canyon (Douglas fir) and 59 km (35 miles) from Salmon in Largo Canyon (Douglas fir and ponderosa pine) with large stands of Douglas fir and ponderosa pine and the first stands of aspen appearing 77–90 km (48–57 miles) from Salmon in the Largo area.

If early populations had impacted the local tree resources, there were several centuries during which new trees could have been reestablished; however, large straight conifers were probably never plentiful in these areas. Ponderosa pines and Douglas firs do not occur in large enough numbers to satisfy the demands for thousands of roofing timbers of an even girth and straightness. Surely, some of these were harvested by the builders of great houses, but the volume needed for the massive buildings demanded harvests within true forests.

Small-House Wood Use in the Salmon Area

Settlement in the greater Salmon area was common before the great house was constructed (see Hogan and Sebastian 1991; Toll 2005; Wheelbarger 2005), although the size of the local population and its impact on the local ecology both remain unknown. Nevertheless, current tree stands suggest that local resources may have been adequate for great house construction, although it would have denuded the local area of trees (see Kohler and Matthews 1988; Samuels and Betancourt 1982). Otherwise, cottonwoods and junipers compose the primary tree cover in the valley along the San Juan River.

House excavations in the general Salmon region have yielded a paucity of structural wood, a testament in part to scavenging and the scarcity of adequate timber for construction. Some wood has been recovered to indicate what local trees were available. Wood from the La Plata Project along the lower La Plata River, northwest of Salmon Ruin, and in and around the Bolack Ranch along the south side of the San Juan River not far from Salmon has shown a preference for juniper. As a structural material, juniper provides more durable qualities than pine, but if local pine were prevalent, this would certainly be reflected in the archaeological deposits (e.g., Adams and Bowyer 2002:141).

Some unusual core-and-veneer masonry at the Sterling site (Bice 1983) has earned this structure the label of a Chacoan great house, although it fails to match the size of the nearby Salmon Ruin (Franklin

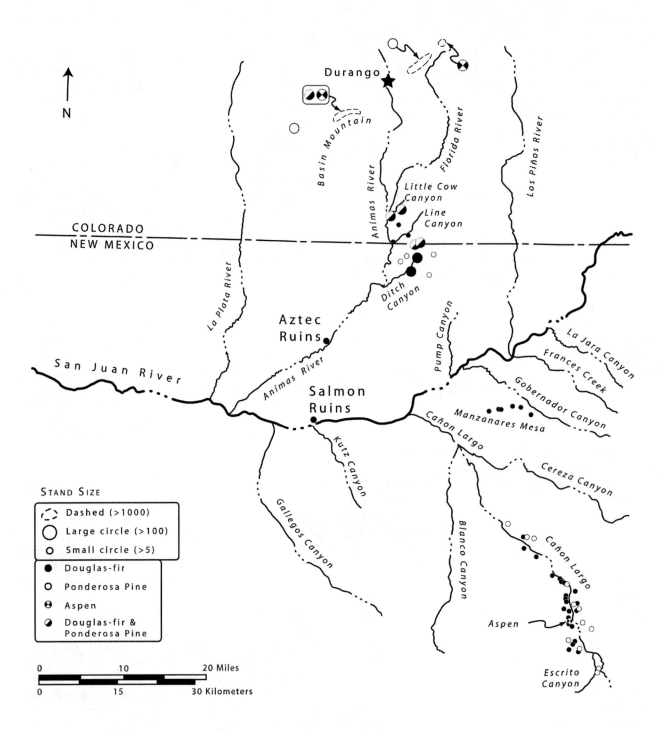

Figure 52.1. The region around Salmon Ruin showing drainages with the closest known sources of nonlocal conifers (Douglas fir and ponderosa pine) and aspen. (Map by Chris Millington.)

Table 52.1. Construction wood recovered from prehistoric small sites in the Salmon region, AD 600s–1500s.

Location	Juniper		Piñon		Ponderosa Pine		Douglas Fir/Spruce/Fir		Populus sp.		Artemisia Non-Conif		Totals	
	No.	%	No.	%	No.	%	No.	%	No.	%	No.	%	No.	%
Local Area														
San Juan River/Bolack Ranch[a]	5	100	–	–	–	–	–	–	–	–	–	–	5	100
San Juan River, Box B site[b]	common	–	–	–	–	–	–	–	common	–	–	–	common	100
Sterling Site[c]	9±	56	–	–	4	25	–	–	3	19	–	–	16	100
Far Local Area														
La Plata River valley below CO line, NM170[d]	124	96	5	4	–	–	–	–	–	–	–	–	129	100
Mouth of Largo[e]	67	87	8	10	–	–	–	–	–	–	2nc	3	77	100
Largo & Salt Creek[f]	121	97	4	3	–	–	–	–	–	–	–	–	125	100
Gobernador[g]	830+	91+	83+	9	–	–	–	–	–	–	–	–	913	101
Non-Local Area														
San Juan & lower La Jara & Pine R[h]	58	87	7	10	1	2	–	–	–	–	1	2	67	100
Upper San Juan River[h]	154	67	18	8	49	21	–	–	–	–	8	4	229	100
Upper Bancos R., NM/CO line[h]	107	58	7	4	68	37	–	–	4	2	–	–	186	101
Upper Piedra & San Juan Rivers, CO[h]	42	38	4	4	65	58	–	–	1	1	–	–	112	101
Mesa Mountains[i]	15	15	88	85	–	–	–	–	–	–	–	–	103	100
Ridges Basin to Animas R.[k]	94	13	16	2	591	83	9	1	–	–	6	1	716	100
Totals	1626	61	240	9	778	29	9	Tr.	8	Tr.	17	1	2678	100

[a] Wheelburger, personal communication 2004.
[b] After Hogan and Sebastian (1991).
[c] Laboratory of Tree-Ring Research records.
[d] Toll, personal communication (2004, in press) and collections from Morris 41.
[e] After Bussey et al. 1973: Chronology, p. 1. LA 8662, LA 8665.
[f] Great Kiva roofing dated in the AD 800s excavated by Hibben and Dick (1944). Counts from the tree-ring laboratory.
[g] From Hall (1944).
[h] From Dittert et al. (1961) and Eddy (1966).
[i] Cave sites in the mesa country between the Animas and Los Piños Rivers (Cueva Grande, n = 13, Grotto Cave, 14, Mesa Mt. Cave, 5, Simon Canyon Cave, 4], and Site H, 38). Excavations by Temple Cornelius and Mr. Hoofnagle, Durango Public Museum Project (Daniels 1940; Flora and Daniels 1940–1941). Counts from the tree-ring laboratory. Dates in the 900s–1200s, with eight in the 1400s and 1500s from Grotto Cave.
[k] From tree-ring records of 8 Zeke Flora sites and about 24 Ridges Basin (ALP) Project sites (Yoder and Potter 2005).

Table 52.2. Construction wood recovered from historic sites in the Salmon region.

Species	Juniper No.	Juniper %	Piñon No.	Piñon %	Ponderosa Pine No.	Ponderosa Pine %	Douglas Fir No.	Douglas Fir %	Spruce or Fir No.	Spruce or Fir %	Populus sp. No.	Populus sp. %	Oak No.	Oak %	Artemisa No.	Artemisa %	Totals No.	Totals %
Dinetah Area[a]	412	36	650	57	32	3	39	3	–	–	17	2	–	–	–	–	1150	79
San Juan River & lower Pine & La Jara[b]	161	71	42	–	14	18	3	1	–	–	–	–	1	T	7	3	228	16
Upper Bancos; NM/CO line[b]	61	100	–	–	–	–	–	–	–	–	–	–	–	–	–	–	61	4
Upper San Juan & Piedra in CO[b]	5	25	1	5	14	20	–	–	–	–	–	–	–	–	–	–	20	1
Totals	639	–	693	–	60	–	42	–	–	–	17	–	1	–	7	–	1459	100

a From Towner (2003). Includes Blanco, Largo, Gobernador, Frances, La Jara, and Los Pinos Canyons.
b From Dittert et al. 1961. Includes historic and historic/prehistoric mixed.

Table 52.3. Distances from Salmon Ruins to the nearest side drainages along the San Juan River and to potential distant tree sources.

Mouth of the La Plata Valley: 26.8 km west of Salmon (and another 30 km upstream to the CO border)
Mouth of the Animas River: 22 km west (and another 27.4 km upstream to Aztec Ruins and 27.6 km more to the CO border)
Mouth of Gallegos Canyon: 10.0 km west
Mouth of Kutz Canyon: 0 km south (directly across the San Juan River from Salmon Ruins)
Mouth of Largo Canyon: 23.3 km east
Mouth of Gobernador Canyon: 43.2 km east
Mouth of Francis Canyon: 67 km east
Los Piños Canyon: 67 km east (and another 25 km upstream to the CO border)
Salmon to the head of Ditch Canyon: 50 km (to Aztec Ruins overland: 16.7 km)
Aztec to the head of Ditch Canyon: 33.3 km

Distances to the nearest non-local forested source areas:
Salmon to the nearest Douglas fir stands in Gobernador Canyon: 35.2 km
Salmon to the nearest Douglas fir and ponderosa pine stands in Largo Canyon: 52.1 km
Salmon to the nearest aspen stands in Largo Canyon: 79.8 km
Salmon to the nearest Douglas fir stands in Ditch Canyon: 58.5 km
Salmon to the nearest Douglas fir and ponderosa pine stands north of Ditch Canyon: 62 km

and McKenna 2004). It yielded 16 tree-ring samples, with only the four ponderosa pine yielding dates, in the mid AD 1000s. Of interest here is the use at Sterling of nonlocal pine along with local species of juniper and *Populus*. The presence of ponderosa pine in the small sample suggests unusual efforts by the builders to obtain nonlocal wood for construction at Sterling, which marks Chacoan interaction at the site.

Historic and Prehistoric Tree Resources Northeast, East, and Southeast of Salmon Ruin

To the east-southeast of Salmon, Hall (1944:6) reported that in the Gobernador Canyon, juniper and piñon grew everywhere except in the valley bottoms, where occasional cottonwoods grew along the edges of the washes (see also Hefner 1987:11). On the highest mesa tops and in some side canyons, ponderosa pines and Douglas firs were reported. Prehistorically, around the village of Gobernador, about 90 percent of nearly 830 samples recovered from burned roofing in sites dating to the AD 700s and 800s (Hall 1944:17–18, Appendix F) were juniper, with the remainder piñon. Although ponderosa pine and Douglas fir may have grown in the vicinity, it was probably not useful for building because it was still too distant, occurred in too few numbers, and was not of usable size or shape. Today, isolated small stands observed by the author consist of large old trees that may have begun growth during a rare favorable climatic period. In the mature stands seen today, most trees would have been too small or too large for house construction.

Towner (2003) inventoried numerous early Navajo sites in the same region, recovering 1150 dendrochronological samples from 62 sites. These samples provide another picture of the wood resources used for construction in early historic times in the Navajo Reservoir district and to the southeast of Salmon. The overwhelming wood used was piñon (56.5%) and juniper (35.8%), which covers the vast majority of trees in the region. Although cottonwoods are relatively common along the banks of many drainages, they were seldom used in construction (1.5%). But the use of some ponderosa pine (2.8%) and Douglas fir (3.4%) appears to substantiate the presence of small stands of these trees, similar to their low numbers observed today and those reported from prehistoric sites by Hall (1944). Most ponderosa pine and Douglas fir (58%) in the sample came from three Navajo sites located far apart in Francis Canyon, at the head of San Rafael Canyon off Gobernador Canyon (in 3-Corn Ruin), and in Largo Canyon (in Tapacito Ruin). Either these inhabitants made the extra effort to secure the rare trees or their site locations placed them close to or within isolated stands of the large trees. Ron Towner (personal communication, 2005) of the tree-ring laboratory believes that all three sites had large conifers within a kilometer or so. Finally, the Laboratory of Tree-Ring Research has noted small ponderosa pine stands on Burnt Mesa about 20 km up and east of the Los Piños River from Navajo Dam, (Ron Towner, personal communication 2005).

Historic and Prehistoric Trees West, North, and Northwest of Salmon Ruin

There are no stands of ponderosa pine or Douglas fir immediately north of Salmon along the Animas River until well past the Aztec ruins. Near the upper drainages of Ditch Canyon, which drains into the Animas River at Cedar Hill, New Mexico, about 20 km north of Aztec along the Colorado border, are extensive stands of ponderosa pine and Douglas fir, which almost certainly provided materials for the Aztec constructions. The large conifers found in the Ditch Canyon area are illustrative of the potential prehistoric tree resources in the mesa and canyon country along the Colorado border. The few sampled by the Laboratory of Tree-Ring Research were nearly a half millennium in age.

The first isolated groves of Douglas fir are found in the southern side canyons along the upper Ditch Canyon about 10 km from the confluence with the Animas River. At least five pockets of Douglas fir are located at the heads of these north-facing side canyons, with between about 10 and 80 trees each. On the mesa tops north of the main canyon 3 km from these are scattered individual ponderosa pines, then groups of ponderosa pine, and then within the low drainage areas on the mesa tops are stands of hundreds of Douglas fir and ponderosa pine in a forest dominated by juniper and piñon. The latter stands are about 6.5 km north of Ditch Canyon near the state border. The large stands yield a mixture of mature and immature trees, precisely the range of tree sizes needed for great house construction. This source is the closest to Aztec Ruins, about 37 km away and an additional 18 km walk from Salmon Ruins. Other canyons just to the north, such as Line and Little Cow Canyons, also yield clusters of Douglas fir and scattered ponderosa pine. Despite the large numbers of suitable Douglas fir trees found in the canyons, however, these were not sought for the majority of structural elements. True forests of ponderosa pine and aspen are found north of Ditch Canyon, in Colorado, near the head of the Florida River about 37 km (for ponderosa pine) and 69 km (for aspen) from Cedar Hill, where timbers fitting the construction needs at Salmon and Aztec were found in great numbers. Other large groves of ponderosa pine and Douglas fir may be found along the higher mesas of the Southern Ute Reservation near Ridges Basin to the west of the Animas River, but these remain unmapped.

The lower La Plata River valley, south of the Colorado border, failed to yield these large conifers historically or in prehistoric sites. Excavations yielded almost exclusively juniper and piñon among the roofing and fuel remains at sites dating to the AD 600s and 1000s from the La Plata Roads Project (Wolky Toll, personal communication 2005). In the La Plata and Animas River valleys today, isolated stands of Douglas fir and ponderosa pine are found only far up the side canyons along the higher mesas close to the Colorado border and farther north at a distance greater than that to Ditch Canyon.

In general, the local tree resources in the vicinities of both Salmon and Aztec ruins are similar, and thus would probably have provided the architects and designers of the two great houses with similar material and similar procurement choices. The perceived similarity of tree resources for the two centers is important in light of the findings of the actual species selected for construction at the two great houses.

LOGISTICAL STRATEGIES FOR THE TRANSPORTATION OF TREES

For sites located within areas devoid of suitable trees, long-distance hauling was not always the answer. At Homol'ovi, it was expedient to simply collect driftwood from the banks of the Little Colorado River (Adams and Hedberg 2002). Some advocate the San Juan River as the transportation mode for bringing timbers to Salmon and Aztec during construction (K. Adams 1979:130; Hatch 1994:135; Kane 1993:51, 2004). Seasonal flows were used in historic times to float logs down southwestern rivers (see Stone 2003:34 for a picturesque example in the early 1900s on the Embudo Creek, a tributary of the Rio Grande), and spring runoff coincides with the time when most of the timbers for Salmon were probably cut. Although the idea of river transport is intriguing, it poses logistical problems of retrieval during periods of deep, fast-moving waters, the most opportune time to achieve success. More important, the bruising and scarring incurred by the practice would have left evidence on the product. During dry years, when there is minimal runoff, a log-floating strategy would have been difficult if not impossible to implement. Wood harvests for Salmon occurred during the AD 1080s when precipitation was 3.3 standard deviations below normal for the Durango, Colorado, area (Dean and Robinson 1977), which would have affected the nearby snowpack and runoff into the San Juan River from the Los Piños and Animas rivers. There are few whole pieces at Salmon left to inspect for surface damage, but no timbers in the large Aztec West ruin sample exhibit this damage. Given the high standards of Chacoan craftsmanship in almost every endeavor, it seems unlikely that the Chacoans would have allowed disfiguration of the timbers. Damage of any kind, including that which would be caused from bark removal, is never seen on eleventh-century Chacoan great house elements, whereas for example in Mesa Verde, such damage was observed on 13 percent of a wood sample (Graham 1965:172–173). Many juniper beams cut in the AD 1200s for Aztec East exhibit considerable exterior damage, which is attributed to beam-diameter reduction and limb knob removal to produce an element of more uniform size. We might expect driftwood to be entering the construction record but there is no evidence for this. Thus, although river transportation was feasible, the tradition of carrying beams from great distances for construction (Ahlstrom et al. 1978:13; Jones 1931:37; Nabokov and Easton 1989:403, Parsons 1936:1178; Stevenson 1904:349) was arguably the primary practice during the Chacoan Salmon construction.

THE SALMON SAMPLE

There is little documentation of the structural wood collection at Salmon Ruin. Since primary emphasis was on the depositional histories across the site—an important goal for sure—features and architectural units received less attention. Making detailed plan views and cross sections of features was not routine, nor were detailed notes taken on the context and attributes of the many pieces of wood recovered in the fill during excavations. Thus, much information about the use of wood, such as roofing and lintels in doorways, niches, and ventilators, was not collected. The lack of data on Salmon's in situ wood inhibits comparison of its architectural wood with other Chacoan great house samples in recent years.

The long use of the architectural space—over a period of two centuries—and the extensive remodeling that took place hampered the separation of the initial construction wood from later materials recovered during excavation. Most rooms from which structural wood was recovered, including reused roofing, provided a variety of species that may have derived from several construction episodes. Most important, the identification of specific pieces of wood to the various functions was only coarsely noted, so that with few exceptions the sample cannot be separated into its many component architectural uses.

Nevertheless, the Salmon Project staff was interested in the local environment. Lentz (1984; Chapter 41) studied the region around Salmon to understand the nearby resource base, while Karen Adams (1979; Chapter 40) and Vorsila Bohrer (Chapters 34, 35) studied the ethnobotanical materials recovered from the excavations as well as the modern plants found in the area. To the north, Peter McKenna later investigated the distribution of conifers in the Animas River valley to assess the tree resources in the greater vicinity of Aztec Ruins.

Field records housed at the Salmon museum include notes, daily logs, lists of specimens, drawings, feature forms, and Polaroid photographs, compiled in thick three-ring binders by room and kiva. Some rooms are detailed in up to nine binders. To reconstruct the entire excavation history and sample identification is a formidable task and was not possible for this report (see Reed, Chapter 8, for a summary). For the most part, structural elements were left in situ and not sampled (Larry Baker, personal communication 2005), probably to preserve them and the architecture for future tourist viewing and to reduce stabilization efforts. Most of the in situ elements visible during the documentation of 2002 and 2003 had not been sampled, confirming Baker's knowledge of sampling at the site, although field notes indicate that at least a few door, niche, and ventilator lintels were sampled during excavation. Numerous vigas and latillas that had been burned off at the walls were not sampled, but presumably they were represented among the collapsed roofs exposed during the room excavations. The majority of these still-visible prehistoric stubs were sampled during the recent work; thus some redundancy in dates and species with the excavated sample is to be expected.

Roofing undoubtedly accounts for the vast majority of samples recovered from the site. Intact or partly intact Chacoan roofs were recovered from Rooms 37W, 58W, 60A, 118W, 119W, and 129W. The suffixes to room numbers indicate their cultural-temporal origins: rooms with a W added to the number are original Chacoan rooms, whereas generally those with A, B, C, etc., reflect Secondary room divisions when new walls divided the Chacoan rooms into smaller spaces that were often reroofed with early Chacoan timbers. But the lack of recording control over the fragmented burned elements that occurred throughout the site must have mixed Primary and Secondary construction elements within the room fills. In addition, the later inhabitants of Salmon reused much of the site so thoroughly that many Chacoan deposits were disturbed and mixed with later materials.

Stabilization Wood at Salmon

Great houses need constant stabilization once they are excavated and left open for visitation and interpretation. At Salmon, most of the repairs were made by Navajo workers led by Larry Baker, now the museum's director, after the initial National Park Service stabilization took place in 1973. For the most part, replacement wood contrasts with prehistoric in situ wood in species, color, weathering, the presence of bark, steel-axe cut limb trim, and uneven spacing, although the difference is not always apparent (Table 52.4). Potential replacements were also suspected in areas where cement and steel rebar had been placed within or around any wall aperture.

Luckily, stabilization crews used local cottonwood and tamarisk trees, which were not heavily favored during prehistoric construction. Replacement wood is particularly evident in doorways and ventilators, where the small-diameter lintels were subject to rapid deterioration and new ones were necessary to prevent wall collapse. In the deep northeastern rooms of the site, the replacement viga stubs of cottonwood are also noticeably different from the prehistoric selection of juniper vigas; they are the only cottonwood vigas at the site.

Stabilization crews also used local cottonwood for repairs at Aztec and in Chaco Canyon. Unfortunately, the widespread use of prehistoric *Populus* sp. in these structures makes it difficult to separate historic from prehistoric elements unless limb trim or the beam end treatments are visible. The stabilization of the masonry around the replaced elements and the arrangement of the elements often provides additional clues of historic repairs. Rare expeditions by stabilization crews to the mountains to obtain high-altitude conifers introduced modern elements into the architectural record that cannot always be separated from prehistoric elements. But the worst strategy employed at some ruins was the undocumented reuse of prehistoric elements from other sites (Windes and McKenna 2001). Happily, this practice was not employed at Salmon (Larry Baker, personal communication 2005).

Judging from documentation at Salmon in 2002 and 2003, small structural elements, especially those found as door and ventilator lintels that were the grist of the samples from Aztec Ruins and many other great houses, were ignored for potential sampling. Some of these lintels were salvaged and curated during later stabilization work at the site. It is suspected that many, like those features repaired in Chaco Canyon great houses, were rotted and fragmentary and were simply ignored or discarded, especially if they were *Populus* (cottonwood or aspen), a species useless for tree-ring dating. Rooms left open for tourist viewing revealed doors and ventilators that still displayed their original wooden lintels or that had been replaced with modern species (e.g., *Tamarix* sp. and Russian olive, *Elaeagnus*

angustifolia). About 25 percent of the wood in Aztec West has been replaced by modern wooden elements or suffers from modern reuse of prehistoric pieces, but at Salmon only a few historic elements (about 5% overall, n ≥ 85) have replaced prehistoric ones. Not all historic elements were documented during the recent work, however, particularly in walls that did not include prehistoric elements.

The Prehistoric Sample

Nearly 1800 prehistoric wooden elements have been documented from Salmon; of these, 1667 were submitted for dendrochronological analysis, including 225 recently gathered from the ruin and the Salmon Museum collections by Salmon staff, the authors, and volunteers. Another 61 samples, thought to be *Populus* sp., were sent to the University of Minnesota Plant Pathology Laboratory for species identification (e.g., Tennessen et al. 2002); these were not submitted for dating but are listed in Table 52.5. Approximately 71 percent of the tree-ring samples were burned or were charcoal fragments created by the massive fires that swept the site, and another 11 percent were rotted. Of the total sample, 562 yielded tree-ring dates.

In comparison, the sample from Aztec West (n = 3988, as of October 2005) yielded almost no burned samples, although admittedly a large number of burned samples were discarded by Earl Morris during his early excavations. The Aztec East and West ruins reveal little signs of widespread burning. The degree of preservation among the various great houses is surprisingly different and may relate to different cultural practices that affect the final state of a site after the inhabitants have decided to leave and not return (see Schlanger and Wilshusen 1993). Salmon was burned extensively in the early AD 1100s, perhaps multiple times throughout the remaining AD 1100s, and then finally when the last occupants left in the late AD 1200s (Reed, Chapter 8). Aztec West suffered from some extensive fires, but these were less widespread than at Salmon. An archaeomagnetic date from one burned kiva at Aztec West indicates that protohistoric groups were responsible for burning some Aztec structures after temporary reuse.

All wood from Salmon was analyzed by Karen Adams for species identification and for possible use in tree-ring dating (see K. Adams 1979). Although ethnobotanical materials recovered during the excavations were thoroughly covered by a handbook on recovery and preservation methods (Bohrer and Adams 1977), pollen and flotation and macrobotanical specimens were given preferential treat-

Table 52.4. Historic architectural wood from Salmon Ruin documented in 2002 and 2003.

Function 6 / Species 9	Primary		Secondary		Door Lintels		Vent / Niche Lintels		Intramural		Other		Totals	
	No.	%	No.	%	No.	%	No.	%	No.	%	No.	%	No.	%
Populus sp.														
Cottonwood	–	–	–	–	–	–	–	–	–	–	–	–	–	–
Aspen	1	5	–	–	–	–	–	–	–	–	–	–	1	2
Unknown	17	81	1	100	1	33	–	–	–	–	1	100	20	49
Pinus sp.														
Piñon	–	–	–	–	–	–	–	–	–	–	–	–	–	–
Ponderosa	1	5	–	–	–	–	–	–	–	–	–	–	1	2
Other														
PSF[a]	–	–	10	–	–	–	–	–	–	–	–	–	10	24
Douglas fir	–	–	–	–	–	–	–	–	–	–	–	–	–	–
Juniper	2	10	–	–	–	–	–	–	1	100	–	–	3	7
Tamarisk/Russian olive	–	–	–	–	2	67	4	100	–	–	–	–	6	15
Totals	21	101	11	100	3	100	4	100	1	100	1	100	41	99
Unknown	4	–	36	–	–	–	–	–	–	–	–	–	40	–

[a]PSF = Ponderosa pine, Douglas fir, spruce, or fir.

Table 52.5. Prehistoric Chacoan architectural wood from Salmon Ruin documented in 2002 and 2003.

Function 6 / Species 9	Primary		Secondary		Door Lintels		Vent/ Niche Lintels		Intramural[a]		Tie Beams		Other		Totals	
	No.	%	No.	%	No.	%	No.	%	No.	%	No.	%	No.	%	No.	%
Populus sp.																
Cottonwood	–	–	–	–	3	5	–	–	1	17	1	2	–	–	5	2
Aspen	–	–	–	–	1	2	–	–	–	–	–	–	–	–	1	T
Unknown	1[b]	2	–	–	25	44	10	28	2	33	5	9	2	5	45	18
Pinus sp.																
Piñon	–	–	2	11	–	–	–	–	–	–	1	2	–	–	3	1
Ponderosa	9	19	4	21	21	37	25	69	2	33	13	25	7	19	81	32
Other																
Douglas fir	1	2	–	–	–	–	–	–	–	–	1	2	–	–	2	1
Spruce/Fir	–	–	2	11	4	7	1	3	1	17	2	4	7	19	17	7
D/P/SF[c]	–	–	–	–	–	–	–	–	–	–	1	2	2	5	3	1
Juniper	37	77	11	58	3	5	–	–	–	–	29	55	19	51	99	39
Totals	48	100	19	101	57	100	36	100	6	100	53	101	37	99	256	101

[a] Six juniper pilaster posts from Kiva 121A are excluded because of thirteenth-century origins.
[b] This is likely a historic replacement.
[c] Douglas fir/ponderosa pine/spruce-fir. Field identifications.

ment (Bohrer, Chapter 34). Structural wood, on the other hand, was primarily desired for its dating potential and the use of selected species. Because of the lack of coring tools and the nature of the work, cross-sections were desired from the larger elements (see Bohrer and Adams 1977: Plate 1), although such sections made up only a small number of the overall sample.

The number of dendrochronological samples retrieved from Salmon excavations is impressive, but caution must be exercised in light of the various conditions that hampered their retrieval. Unlike the wood resources at Aztec, where thousands of wood elements are still in their original contexts, Salmon suffered from devastating fires that left much of the roofing in fragments mixed with other materials in the room fills. Many roof deposits were not mapped or piece-plotted, so it is difficult to trim the inevitable redundancy of the sample created by the many fragments left of the burned roofing. The number of years to complete excavation units and the changing field personnel may also have contributed to collection of multiple samples from the same roofing elements. Rex Adams (personal communication, 2005) believes that over the course of excavations, some roofing elements in the fill may have been sampled multiple times. The size of the Salmon excavation sample prohibited matching the recent samples with the excavation ones, contributing an unknown amount of redundancy to the sample.

In few cases did the tree-ring laboratory provide matches of pieces from the same tree stem (3% from the 1972 sample of 420 specimens, the only list so annotated), but the true numbers from the site must be much lower than the raw sample count. It was the practice of the tree-ring laboratory in the 1970s to discard samples that had very short ring series of little scientific value and that would only take up precious storage space. These were not assigned laboratory numbers, so large numbers of Salmon samples may have gone unanalyzed in this fashion.

At neighboring Aztec Ruins, Morris collected most of his samples by drilling the large vigas in selected rooms. The vast remainder was ignored for sampling, and many of these were later used for his house construction, now the Visitor's Center. Deric O'Bryan sampled wood in parks throughout the Southwest in 1941, including Aztec and Salmon, for a new tree-ring laboratory founded by Harold Gladwin at Gila Pueblo. Others were taken from Salmon and Aztec during the 1920s or early 1930s during the tree-ring laboratory's Beam Expeditions (see Nash 1999). Luckily, thousands of wood elements at Aztec are still in situ, and these provide a massive database

with which to compare the samples derived from Salmon. Aztec West had yielded 4388 documented elements as of September 2005 (3971 were sampled), and Aztec East had generated another 948 as of November 2004. Perhaps another thousand prehistoric elements have been reused in the Visitor's Center or stored in the wood pile at the East ruin.

The dated sample is an unusual one in the very high numbers of pith and cutting dates (Table 52.6). The preservation of structural wood was unusually good (Rex Adams, personal communication 2005), but it is hard to reconcile the large number of burned rooms at the site with the relatively high numbers of cutting dates (378 of 503, or 75%). The hot, destructive fires evident at Salmon typically result in fragmented roofing elements, leaving numerous pieces from the same element without the original outer surfaces. These poorer pieces may have been culled from the sample. By contrast, our recent sample of 214 specimens yielded a more typical cutting date rate of 28 percent. Good preservation would not be expected from burned rooms, where the structural elements are highly oxidized, fragmented, and mixed together. Although the mixture of elements suggests that the sample is representative, there is suspicion of a skewed sample given the lack of a large number of expected noncutting dates.[2]

The sparse number of *Populus* sp. samples is also suspicious. *Populus* sp. is unsuitable for tree-ring dating, so they may simply have been tossed out. The 1972 field season collection is revealing in that large numbers of samples were returned from the tree-ring laboratory without being analyzed, probably because they were duplicates or had too few rings to be useful for dating. These included 354 *Populus* sp. specimens and another 16 sacks full of *Populus* sp. (Table 52.7) fragments that are not part of this review. An additional 59 sacks of specimens were not identified by species. Subsequent laboratory reports in the later years failed to mention any returned samples, as if they had been culled before shipment to the laboratory. About 100 boxes of charcoal samples and wood are housed at the Salmon Ruins Museum, and these may include the

_____

[2]The discrepancy in the unexpected success of above-average numbers of samples with pith and outside rings may be explained by notes taken by field hand Debra Autry on June 26, 1974. Her page 1 notes on Room 90 provide this noteworthy paragraph: "wood, carbonized or not, is not retained unless it is over 1" in diameter—preferably about 3" [7.5 cm] in diameter—and has been excellently preserved, with outside and inside rings intact, for dendrochronology and identification analysis." This means that many samples were discarded without being analyzed because they were not "excellently preserved."

Table 52.6. List of pith and cutting dates from the Salmon tree-ring analysis.

Date Symbol 1	Total	Date Symbol 2	Juniper	All Others	Total	Date Symbol 1	Date Symbol 2	Total	Date Symbol 1	Date Symbol 2	Total
+	2	++B	1	–	1	+	vv	1	fp	++B	1
±	4	++v	1	–	1	+	rB	1	fp	++vv	1
±p	1	++vv	6	3	9	±	B	1	fp	+L	1
+fp	3	+B	1	–	1	±	+B	1	fp	+r	7
±fp	4	+C	–	4	4	±	rB	1	fp	+rB	2
-p	48	+CB	–	1	1	±	b	1	fp	+v	2
±p	17	+cLB	1	–	1	±	L	1	fp	+vv	3
fp	94	+L	–	1	1	±	–	–	fp	L	2
np	3	+r	21	61	82	±p	vv	1	fp	r	23
P	349	+rB	6	–	6	–	–	–	fp	rB	2
		+rL	2	–	2	+fp	vv	4	fp	rL	1
		+rLB	3	–	3	+fp	+rLB	1	fp	v	5
	525	+v	4	5	9	+fp	rB	2	fp	vv	44
		+vv	10	4	14	–	–	–	–	–	–
		B	11	–	11	-p	+r	3	np	none	3
		C	–	6	6	-p	+rB	1	–	–	–
		cL	1	–	1	-p	+rLB	2	P	++vv	4
		cLB	2	–	2	-p	+vv	11	P	+c	4
		L	2	2	4	-p	L	1	P	+cB	1
		r	61	149	210	-p	r	15	P	+cLB	1
		rB	24	–	24	-p	rB	7	P	+r	60
		rL	2	1	3	-p	v	8	P	+rB	3
		v	23	22	45	–	–	–	P	+rL	2
		vv	63	56	119	±p	B	5	P	+v	7
						±p	r	3	P	+vv	5
			245	315	560	±p	vv	1	P	B	4
						±p	++vv	4	P	C	6
						±p	+r	2	P	cL	1
						±p	rB	2	P	cLB	2
								80	P	r	158
									P	rB	8
									P	rL	2
									P	v	30
									P	vv	51
											446

Table 52.7. Dendrochronological samples not analyzed from the Salmon excavations of 1972.[a]

Species:	Individual Specimens		Sacks[b]	
	No.	%	No.	%
Ponderosa pine	354	26	16	10
Spruce/fir	61	4	6	4
Populus sp.	354	26	16	10
Juniperus sp.	227	17	33	20
Non-coniferous	363	27	35	21
Mixed	–	–	59	36
Totals	1359	100	165	101

[a] Samples returned to Salmon Ruins from the Laboratory of Tree-Ring Research (noted on laboratory work sheets).
[b] The term "sacks" presumably indicates large paper (or cloth) sacks from Salmon full of burned roofing and other wooden elements that were sent to the tree-ring laboratory for analysis. These specimens were separated by species but not dated. These were returned to the Salmon ethnobotanical laboratory and either reintegrated into the collection or discarded. A preliminary search of the Salmon collection in 2005 failed to relocate the 1972 samples.

1972 materials as well as the work of subsequent years that has not been analyzed.

Species

Aside from the unknown quantities of wood materials not analyzed, the large tree-ring sample provides an accounting of the tree species selected for construction at Salmon. Of these, 1563 were identified to species by the tree-ring laboratory, the University of Minnesota, and by the author. The Salmon sample is dominated by two species of tree wood: nonlocal ponderosa pine (37%) and local juniper (38%). There also is a large amount of spruce and fir (14%) along with lesser amounts of Douglas fir (2%) and *Populus* sp. (cottonwood and aspen, 7%). Almost no piñon was used for structural wood (Figure 52.2)—a meager nine pieces were recovered (0.6%). The relative use of these different species of trees in construction is probably accurate except for *Populus*. The large amount of wood used for layering across the latillas is not considered construction wood for this report but represents a considerable use of additional wood resources. At Salmon, this material was probably a thick mat of juniper splints or nonconiferous woods, such as willows (*Salix* sp.). The closing material allows the thick adobe flooring/roofing to rest over the supporting roofing framework without falling through to the floor below.

The analyzed sample does not include small fragmented specimens or species not useful for tree-ring dating. If the wood returned from the tree-ring laboratory in 1972 is any indication (see Table 52.7), it is clear that *Populus* sp., in particular, was more prevalent than suggested from the tree-ring analyses. *Populus* sp. represented 26 percent of the returned individual specimens, and 10 percent of the sacks of returned specimens. Much of the in situ *Populus* sp. recently documented at the site was used as lintels, so the true impact of *Populus* sp. at the site is undoubtedly too low. The unsystematic sampling of wall apertures (doors, ventilators, and niches) probably skewed the presence of *Populus* sp. as being poorly representative at the site. The number of returned *Populus* sp. pieces in 1972 also suggests that much of the roofing was probably *Populus* sp. latillas, but unfortunately we do not know how many may have been nonlocal aspen. Nonconiferous material was common among the returned materials (27% of the returned samples and another 35 unanalyzed sacks), and it probably came from the mass of closing materials that covered the roof latillas. From our recent sampling, we know that both *Populus* sp. and ponderosa pine were favored for lintels.

At Aztec West, aperture lintels were a mix of high-altitude conifers and aspen in the core unit, but juniper and *Populus* sp. dominated the elements in the subsequent construction periods. Juniper vigas began to be used during the later Aztec building periods, whereas ponderosa pine and an occasional spruce-fir or Douglas fir were used exclusively during the core construction. Construction at Salmon followed similar patterns but was far less reliant on the harvesting of nonlocal trees.

Element Function

The vast majority of sample elements from Salmon do not have assigned functions. Many of the roofing elements were labeled vigas or latillas in the initial field notes, terms used interchangeably by Salmon diggers. In some cases, the closing material consisted of branches that were occasionally saved as tree-ring samples, presumably if they were big enough. Thus, we are left with three avenues to tease out the potential use of each sample: diameter, species, and age. From our small recent in situ sample, restricted mostly to the central back rooms, the vast majority of vigas were juniper, whereas latillas and lintels were rarely juniper (see Table 52.5).

Diameter

Juniper stems pose problems when using diameters to select for function because of their sharp stem taper from tree base to trunk top. In our sample, the majority of the viga stubs remained in only one wall.

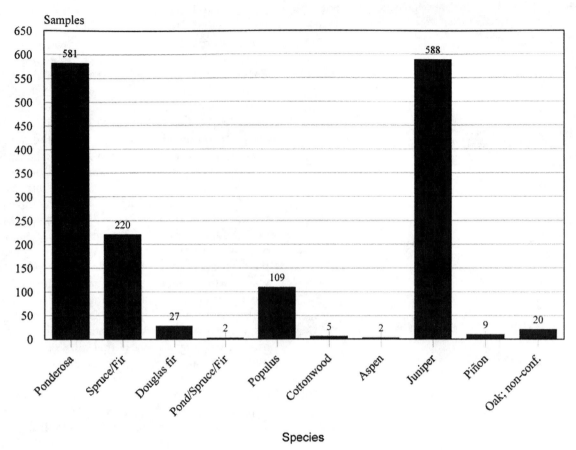

Figure 52.2. Tree species used in the Chacoan construction of Salmon Ruin derived from the tree-ring sample.

Viga positions were commonly alternated so that the large base end of one viga was set next to a small (top) end of another—the strongest positioning for the beam roof supports (Figure 52.3). But many times it is not clear whether the sole viga end-piece is the small or the large end unless it survives in the walls with others in the set where there is a clear distinction in size between stem tops and bottoms. When the recent viga sample is separated arbitrarily at 10 cm in diameter, then the lower mean diameter (5.4 cm, sd = 2.0, n = 60) is similar to latillas and lintels, whereas the larger sizes are typical of vigas (16.1 cm diameter, sd = 4.9, n = 49). Of course, with so many charred, unmeasured fragments recovered during the Salmon excavations, sizes provide little help in resolving function calls.

Our data from the Aztec ruins provide comparative sizes of different element types and their species. At Aztec West, juniper primaries were a maximum average diameter of 19.1 cm (sd 5.8, n = 84) but were significantly smaller than other conifer vigas (23.9 cm diameter, sd = 4.2, n = 116, t = 6.78, Δ = 0.001);

however, the different species used for latillas (*Populus* sp., mostly aspen, and ponderosa pine) were the same maximum diameter (6.9 cm, sd = 2.0, n = 173 versus 6.9 cm, sd = 1.7, n = 674, respectively). Thus, size differences between vigas and latillas are obvious. Aztec East, which used almost all juniper for the vigas and latillas, also demonstrated the large differences in diameters. Vigas averaged 16.5 cm in diameter (n = 181, sd = 5.1) but were generally found in smaller rooms than in Aztec West; latillas were 7.5 cm in maximum diameter (n = 506, sd = 1.6).

Species

Tree species can help determine element function. Our recent work revealed that the majority of Salmon room vigas were juniper. Vigas consisted of slow-growing junipers that had long ring series and were likely to produce a date. Latillas have a poor record of dating because they are smaller, have shorter ring series, and were less likely to be juniper. Too few latillas now survive in situ to predict the species most commonly used, if any, although the

Figure 52.3. Room 79, north wall showing the burned-off ends of the roof vigas and the butt-ends for the Room 78 vigas. (Photograph by Tom Windes, March 2005.)

returned 1972 samples suggest that *Populus* sp. latillas were common. Our recent sample includes juniper and pine used for latillas (n = 6). Batches of samples within a room at Salmon with similar short-ring series and of ponderosa pine or spruce-fir probably represent fast-growing saplings gathered for latillas from the higher elevations some distance from the site. Unlike at Aztec, it is difficult to assign a latilla function based on species because a variety of species at Salmon may have been used.

Many of the excavated juniper samples failed to produce a date and must have been from charred latilla fragments, although many of these may have been from Secondary roof remodeling. At Aztec West more than 1000 aspen were used for latillas, except in the initial core area where ponderosa pine predominated. Only one latilla in the large Aztec West sample was of juniper. The later-built Aztec East, however, used almost all juniper vigas and

latillas, indicating the change in species preference from mostly nonlocal to local trees by the mid to late AD 1100s.

Recent work at Salmon has confirmed that juniper was a preferred species for most room vigas, and that 6–9 vigas were needed per room. Room samples often show a species dichotomy, with a few older juniper elements (interpreted as the vigas, Figure 52.4) mixed with large numbers of ponderosa pine, spruce, and/or firs of much younger age (the latillas). With this guide in hand, we can now understand some of the planning logistics employed for the construction.

Age

Before dense local habitation, local juniper ages should have been highly variable unless there had been unusual environmental events that encouraged widespread succession of young new junipers. In the

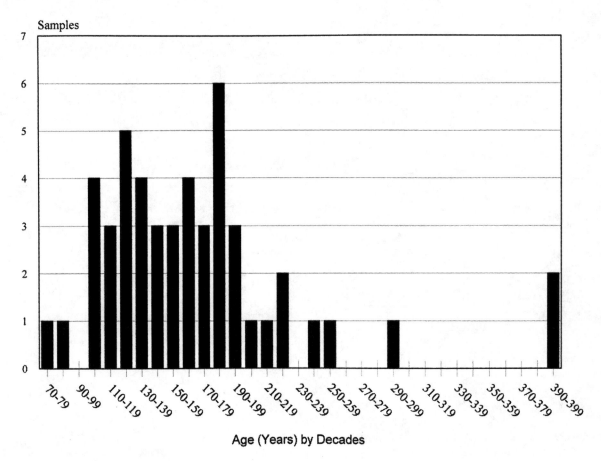

Figure 52.4. Ages of juniper beams cut between AD 1088 and 1090. The old ages suggest that the dated samples were predominantly vigas.

higher elevations, where ponderosa pine, Douglas fir, and spruce-fir are found, we might expect scattered park conditions with a range of tree ages. But fire or other unusual events might have produced tree-succession growth of replacement species, resulting in large groves of young saplings. Dense thickets of young trees of similar age were commonly harvested for latillas during the construction of the Chaco Canyon great houses. The age variability was thought to be much higher in the Salmon latillas (Windes 1987a: Figure 7.13) than at Chaco, but the earlier study erroneously combined both viga and latilla data. Overall, the latilla selection is similar in age to the harvests observed at the Chaco Canyon great houses.

The room-by-room samples provide a curious dichotomy of ages for the elements. Among the larger samples, a few specimens are aged over a century or more, whereas the great majority are much younger, generally less than 60 years. If similar growing conditions prevail for the harvested trees of the same species, then a general hypotheses of age can be predicted: larger diameter trees are older than smaller diameter trees. We know, of course, that the largest elements were employed as vigas in structural roofs, and the latillas that overlie them are much smaller (Figures 52.5a, b, and 52.6). Lintels for doorways and ventilators are even smaller, although these latter elements do not seem to have provided much to the present sample. The dichotomy in ages can be explained by the sampling of both primary (vigas) and secondary (latillas) roof-support beams, which would be expected from the samples taken from the many burned room roofs. Among room samples of the same species, the age dichotomy is significantly different, which supports the distinction made here between vigas and latillas.

Samples from Rooms 51, 61A-B, 62, and 129 were used to test this hypothesis (Table 52.8). In Room 129, all the dated elements were ponderosa

Figure 52.5. (a, left) Room 60A, showing a series of latillas overlying mostly hidden vigas. Note burned viga in foreground. (b, right) Room 60A with latillas removed, exposing the underlying vigas. Note strip of adobe flooring left intact along the wall. (Photographs by Peter George.)

Table 52.8. Statistics for viga and latilla ages from Rooms 51W, 61A-B, 62W, 62A, and 129W.

	Age	Mean Age	Stand. Dev.	Range	CV %
Room 129W					
N = 8	AD 1088	68.76	16.41	49 (37–86)	23.87%
N = 31	AD 1089–1090	29.81	7.27	28 (18–41)	24.39%
T–test	0.0001				
Room 51W					
N = 8	under 100 yrs	39.39	14.75	43 (26/68)	37.45%
N = 2	over 100 yrs	139.00	41.01	26 (126/152)	29.53%
Room 61 A, B					
N = 11	under 100 yrs	53.66	20.67	68 (24–92)	38.52%
N = 3	over 100 yrs	143.37	14.00	28 (130–158)	9.76%
Room 62 W, A					
N = 11	under 100 yrs	64.56	19.72	54 (37–99)	30.55%
N = 4	over 100 yrs	126.00	12.62	27 (112–139)	10.02%

Figure 52.6. Photograph of Room 118, showing an unusually complex, collapsed roofing. Note the small poles packed together and layer of twigs and branches and then adobe. Underlying beam is a latilla, which was supported by vigas not visible. (Photographs by Peter George.)

those exceeding a century in age and those much younger was significant ($\Delta = 0.0000$).

At Aztec Ruins, where we have a large sample of juniper vigas and latillas, the age differences between the vigas and latillas is dramatic. At Aztec East, the difference between the two sets is remarkable even though the vigas are much smaller than those at Salmon because of the difference in room sizes: large at Salmon and small at Aztec East. To compensate for the difference, the large-room juniper vigas from Aztec West, which did not have juniper latillas (mean age 167 years, sd = 63, n = 73), were compared to the juniper latillas from Aztec East (mean age 88 years, sd = 30, n = 76) to approximate the juniper sample from Salmon. The significant difference between the two sets (t = 9.98, df = 147, Δ < 0.0001) supports the interpretation at Salmon that the oldest trees in the juniper sample were vigas. The few samples from Salmon that were identified as juniper vigas support the hypothesis above: all were cut from trees exceeding a century's growth.

Unfortunately, in the room notes only a few samples are labeled as to the type of structural element. The only sample of small juniper poles of known function in the recent Salmon sample, the unusual 61 tie-poles from Room 62, are smaller than latillas (Δ = 5.6 cm diameter, sd = 1.4) but revealed considerable overlap in ages with vigas and latillas. They would be difficult to separate from vigas and latillas on the basis of species and age alone.

Beam Preparation and End Treatment

Chacoan great house construction typically reveals extraordinary efforts to flatten the beam ends (Windes and McKenna 2001: Table 52.2). Shelley (Chapter 47) reported that an unsystematic survey at Salmon revealed that all Chacoan construction timbers were flat on the ends, which was attributed to sawing. The only sample noted with axe-cut ends was in a Mesa Verdean deflector (Shelley, Chapter 47), although this cannot be considered a representative sample for either early or late tree-harvest practices. Several exceptions noted in the tree-ring laboratory notes and in photographs provide evidence that many beam ends were not end-flattened. In at least one case, timbers with the forked ends were left for roofing without end modification, a style that is not a normal Chacoan beam practice (Figure 52.7) and which suggests wood from a Secondary construction. Another photograph shows a beam end that appears to have been nibbled down but with the beaver-tail cut still protruding, while others reveal round ends cut with a stone axe (Figure 52.8). In 1976 the tree-ring laboratory noted stone

pine; they yielded two groups of ages, averaging 69 and 30 years and cut in the same year. Room notes indicate that 138 samples were collected from the intact roof, but only 70 are listed in the tree-ring laboratory results; perhaps the others were duplicates and were thus discarded. A sketch map indicates probably four vigas in the room, which approximates in number the three samples with the oldest ages, suggesting that the oldest samples were vigas.

In Room 51W the oldest two samples averaged 139 years old, whereas the remaining samples averaged a mere 39 years old. Again, the difference is suspected to have been between two vigas and the more numerous latillas. The difference in overall samples from Rooms 51, 61A-B, and 62 between

Figure 52.7. Room 119, forked juniper roofing (?) elements against the wall. Not a Chacoan-style arrangement of beams. (Photograph by Peter George.)

axe–cut ends on 12 of the samples, but the lab did not report them from other years. Nine of these were simply noted as having been cut with a stone axe, probably for expedient axe-cut beam ends. In addition, three (a fir, a pine, and a juniper) were erroneously noted as "abraded flat," reflecting the laboriously attained nicked-flat ends common to Chacoan end treatment. Our recent field sample revealed a mixture of end treatments dominated by expedient cuts without the excessive labor dedicated to nibbling the ragged axe-cut ends flat (Figure 52.9) that is common in other great houses. Most of the recent sample of end treatments came from Room 62, where an abundance of small tie-pole ends were evident. These were cut between AD 1116 and 1118, long after the initial room construction and, thus, may not be representative of early workmanship. Although the end-treatment sample is spotty, it does indicate that the Chacoan pattern of removing all vestiges of the stone axe cuts on the beam ends was practiced at Salmon.

The Salmon staff recognized the different end treatments of the stems used for structural purposes at the site and took steps to understand specific harvesting techniques from them. In particular, it was thought that the trees might have been cut down using small flake tools rather than the more commonly accepted practice of felling trees with a stone axe (Shelley, Chapter 47). Because it would have been quite difficult to flush the beam ends with an ax, some other means must have been employed to yield ends described in this paper as nibbled flat. Experiments by the Salmon staff using the small flakes that are found by the thousands at Salmon to cut down modern ponderosa pines proved to be an excruciatingly slow and painful process. Subsequent investigation of this end treatment at Chaco indicated that the flattened ends were produced not during harvesting but as a secondary process using flake tools to remove the ragged pointed projection typically left by simple axe cutting (Windes and McKenna 2001: Figure 4). Our recent Salmon work found a variety of end treatments, from the most expedient cuts (beaver tail, irregular, angular) to the most laborious workmanship (nibbled flat). Although the sample was small and mostly of juniper, nibbled flat ends were dominant (7 of 11).

We have little information about other facets of beam preparation at Salmon. The presence of bark, however, does suggest some preparation differences between Salmon and Aztec. Whereas bark is almost never found on Chacoan elements at Aztec West or in Chaco Canyon great houses, the Chacoan sample at Salmon yielded bark on almost every juniper sample that dated (98%, or 49 of 50). This suggests less careful beam preparation (lack of bark removal)

Figure 52.8. Room 61B, showing roofing timbers and tie logs extending from the surrounding rooms into an interstitial space. (Photograph by Peter George.)

at Salmon than at the other great houses. But the removal of bark from the depressions around limbs in juniper trees is often missed during bark removal, so we cannot be sure how much bark may have been left on the samples analyzed by the tree-ring laboratory except to note that the laboratory would routinely avoid limb areas for a section to analyze.

Total Structural Elements Used at Salmon

Estimating the number of elements and the potential number of trees required for construction at Salmon is fraught with difficulties, but it does provide general base-line figures that help to determine the magnitude of the tree-harvesting effort. Although the number of rooms for much of Salmon was determined through excavation and wall clearing (see Reed, Chapter 8; Reed 2002), the West Wing was a difficult area that experienced much remodeling and reconstruction from the mid-1100s through the 1200s. Thus, Chacoan room counts must

be extrapolated from the patterns known for the rest of the site. Beam sockets (Figures 52.10–52.11) and general Chacoan building practices help to provide reasonable estimates for the different types of structural elements required for the building (Table 52.9; see Windes and McKenna 2001). We estimate that the initial Chacoan building required between 7500 and 9500 trees to provide the 15,000 to 17,000 elements needed primarily for roofing and wall apertures. The San Juan occupation during the McElmo and Mesa Verde phases, which resulted in many small kivas and subdivided rooms required far less timber, suggesting that much of the structural wood was recycled Chacoan wood. Without dates for most of this Secondary wood use, however, it is not clear how much new tree cutting took place. If all new wood was required for the Secondary constructions, then about 2900–5600 more trees, mostly juniper, would have been cut for the needed elements after about AD 1120.

The short stems of juniper trees would have provided a maximum of a single viga or latilla each, but the tall, straight conifers growing in the higher, more moist environments probably furnished two or three elements per stem (see also Wilcox and Shenk 1977:85). One tree could have provided an estimated four or more lintels. At Aztec, about 8–10 lintels were used per door, and 10–14 lintels were used in ventilators, with the highest numbers employed in the thick outer walls of the structure. Based on estimates from Pueblo del Arroyo (Windes et al. 1994) in Chaco Canyon, approximately 400–1000 juniper trees were needed for roof closing material at Salmon if only juniper splints were employed. We know that in at least some instances an additional layer of tightly packed small poles covered the latillas, which in turn was covered by a layer of branches and twigs before the final application of a thick layer of adobe (see Figure 52.6). Few if any of these small poles would be expected to produce a tree-ring date. The amount of nonconiferous wood returned to the Salmon staff in 1972 indicates that much of the closing material might have been willow or other brush material, reducing the devastation to the local juniper stands but perhaps eradicating any willows along the nearby San Juan River. If the 38 percent presence of juniper indicated by the tree-ring sample is relatively accurate, and if much of the closing material was juniper, then the impact to the local ecology would have been severe, with the potential removal of thousands of local trees. But the continued use of the site and the need for firewood and other uses of tree wood would have impacted the local forest cover to an alarming degree (see Kohler et al. 1984;

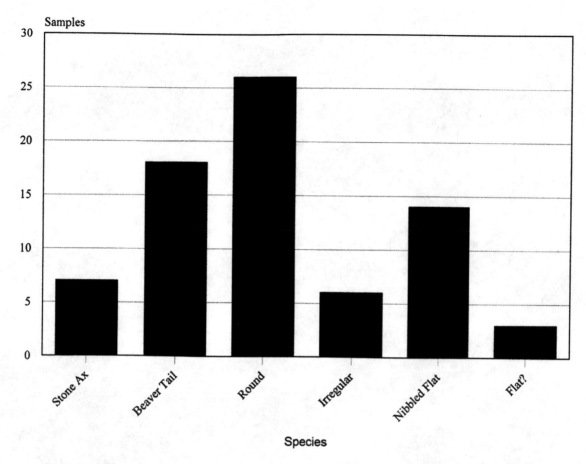

Figure 52.9. Beam ends recorded during recent field work at Salmon (most samples from Room 62).

Kohler and Matthews 1988; Samuels and Betancourt 1982).

During the Secondary occupation, builders scavenged logs from the Chacoan structures when rooms were subdivided and smaller rooms were built inside the large Chacoan rooms. Because so little juniper from the Secondary occupation produced a date, it is difficult to assess how much new wood was procured as an alternative to reusable timbers without correlating the excavation data with the wood samples. The high number of juniper elements associated with the Secondary constructions, however, suggests that many late roofs were made from freshly cut local trees but that long-distance procurement was generally ignored.

It is interesting to note that stone axes were plentiful in the late deposits, where more than 200 were recorded, but axes were absent in the Chacoan deposits (Shelley, Chapter 47). The lack of Chacoan axes might be expected if most of the harvesting and beam preparation took place at some distance from the pueblo, although it is difficult to fathom their total absence at the site. The situation is similar in Chaco Canyon (Breternitz 1997:992–993; Windes 1987c:294). On the other hand, if local or scavenging strategies within Salmon were routinely practiced then axes might be expected to be common, frequently worn out at the site and abandoned there. Axes might be particularly common among later deposits if considerable recutting was done to old beams to refit them into new structural contexts. It might also be that the difference can be attributed to cultural values: axes were prized by Chacoans, who, when living in Chaco, either traveled considerable distances to obtain the raw materials or traded for them. Late occupants, familiar with the plentiful quantities of nearby river and terrace cobbles from which to make axes, simply assigned them little value and left them behind when they departed.

Various roof styles (Windes and McKenna 2001:120, Figure 1) produce different numbers of latillas, although not necessarily different numbers of cut trees. Wall elevation maps and beam sockets in currently open rooms at Salmon suggest that roofs

Figure 52.10. Room 79, showing the south wall viga sockets. Note the blocked ventilator in lower right corner with rotted wood lintels. (Photograph by Tom Windes, March 2005.)

may have employed paired sets of latillas (Roof Style B), although some sketch maps of wall sockets suggest that the placement was somewhat haphazard with single, double, and triple element sets used within the same roof. Photographs typically show long latillas (see Figures 52.5a, b, and 52.6), which suggests that Style A was most common, with whole overlapped saplings set in the roofs and opposing sets anchored in the walls at each end of the room. Thus, when there are 14 and 16 latilla sockets in the two room ends, respectively, then a total of 30 whole saplings were used. In the Type B roof style, short latillas spanned only the nearest supports, but several latillas could have been cut from a single tree. Based on limited information, the predominant roofing style at Salmon appears to have been Style A, which requires less effort to build than Style B.

THE DATED SAMPLE FROM SALMON

The success rate for dating wooden elements from Salmon Ruin is 34 percent (n = 559), generally on par with other sites in the Southwest. But this figure is misleading in that different species provide vastly different rates of dating success. Notably, *Populus* sp., spruce-fir, and one-seed juniper provide few, if any, datable samples. On the other hand, Douglas fir, piñon, and other species of juniper provide high rates of dating success. Ponderosa pine, commonly favored for construction in Chacoan great houses, provides only moderate dating success overall and is particularly undatable among small-diameter elements such as lintels. At most sites, the location of the construction to specific local resources as well as the correlation to specific environmental regimes can be a large factor in the success or failure of the tree-ring dating. Some periods were marked by erratic climatic conditions, which provide desirable ring-growth patterns for an analyst that are easily recognizable, and they assist in dating success. Otherwise, long periods of stability, whether wet or dry, lower the success rate, particularly for specimens with short ring series (i.e., young trees favored

Figure 52.11. Room 80, showing the roof viga sockets in the north wall. Note the ventilator and central doorway. (Photograph by Tom Windes, March 2005.)

for latillas and lintels). Sites in the interior San Juan Basin or along its margins (e.g., Salmon) would be expected to generally provide poor tree-ring dating success because of their proximity to species of cottonwood and one-seed juniper, which almost never produce dates.

Reed (Chapter 12) has covered in detail the relationship of the tree-ring dated sample to construction events at the site. Based on architectural information and associated tree-ring dates, he has defined six separate building episodes that created the overall final design of the great house. All six episodes yielded tree-ring specimens (Table 52.10). In addition, numerous remodeling that is not documented in the tree-ring record took place during the Secondary occupation at Salmon. A brief overview of these tree-ring results is germane to this chapter (Tables 52.11–52.12). Only a few cutting dates prior to the massive harvesting in AD 1088 were obtained from the sample, and these were at first dismissed as reused pieces gathered from earlier small-house

structures in the area (R. Adams 1980a: 215). Six early cutting or near-cutting dates clustered in the site's East Wing were of ponderosa pine and Douglas fir, ranging in age between AD 1068 and 1072, which suggests a singular episode of construction using nonlocal wood.

Baker (2005) has argued that these samples and their associated rooms represent an early, perhaps initial roomblock at the site before the overall main complex was built. Small, initial roomblocks incorporated within the larger later great house format are not unusual and have been noted in several of the early great houses in and around Chaco Canyon (Lekson 1984; Windes 2006; Windes and Ford 1996). The placement of this potential early block of rooms in and around Room 122 at Salmon, however, is unusual in its location within the East Wing, rather than within the central core of the great house, where it exists in all other known cases.

It is also unusual that the East Wing location would require the initial roomblock to be oriented

Table 52.9. Construction elements and total trees needed for the great house and Secondary constructions at Salmon Ruin.

No. per unit:	Rm No.[c]	Vigas 6–8	Latillas 26–50	Door lintels[a] 8–10	Vent lintels[a] 10–14	Posts 0–4	Misc.	Splints[b] (Jun. trees)	Element Totals
CHACOAN	–	–	–	–	–	–	–	–	–
Rooms (type)									
Large, sq. (1)	19	152	950	152–190	380–532	48[d]	–	–	1682–1872
Long, narrow (2)	162	972	4860	1296–1620	3240–4536	?	?	–	10368–11988
Large rect. (3)	6	36	180	48–60	0	?	?	–	264–276
Gallery (4)[e]	6	46	360	48–60±	0	?	?	–	454–466
Misc., small (5, 14)[f]	52	104	520	216–270	0	?	100[g]	–	940–994
Kivas									
Large, cribbed[b]	2	500±	40±	0	0	–	40[i]	(9–25)	540
Great kiva[h]	1	30	643	40	0	–	–	(14–35)	713
Total elements[j]	–	1810	7553	1800–2240	3620–5068	48	140	–	14961–16849
Adjusted 2[j]	–	1249	5212	–	–	–	–	–	–
Adjusted 3[j]	–	1062	4431	–	–	–	–	–	–
Adjusted 4[j]	–			450–560	905–1267				
Total trees	–	1062–1249	4431–5212	450–560	905–1267	48	140	388–998	7424–9474
SAN JUAN									
Rooms[k]									
Subdivided rooms	35	35–70	525–2100	?	0	0	?	(57–146)	617–2316
Kivas[k]									
Small, non-cribbed	8	16–48	120–240	0	0	0	?	(5–13)	141–301
Medium, cribbed[k]	12	1200–1800	180–360	0	0	6	?	(16–41)	1402–2207
Great kiva[h]	1	30	643	40	0	0?	?	(14–35)	713
Total trees	–	1281–1948	1468–3343	40	0	6	?	21–55	2873–5537

[a] Calculated for a door per room.

[b] Total room roof area × 5 cm fw .236 – .606 m³ = number of splints. Total room roof area × 5 cm fw .236 – .606 m³ = number of juniper trees (after Windes et al. 1994). Based on work at Pueblo del Arroyo (Windes et al. 1994), a single one-seed juniper tree yields between .236 and .606 m³ of splints. Other species of juniper might yield more. Salmon roof areas based on 4426 m² for Chacoan rooms, 58 m² each for elevated kiva and unnumbered kiva in NW corner, 165 m² for great kiva, 691 m² for San Juan rooms, and 259 m² for San Juan kivas (included 2 unnumbered in west wing).

[c] Includes estimated second and third stories.

[d] Posts are difficult to estimate without detailed notes. I assume that large square living rooms had roof support posts based on notes from Room 56 (4 per room, not counting post steps).

[e] Gallery-like rooms (93, 102, 128, 142, 147, and 158).

[f] Small miscellaneous rooms and irregularly shaped-interstitial spaces estimated for an average of 2 vigas each and 10 latillas per room.

[g] This number approximates only those small poles photographed for Room 181 (see Figure 5). There may be far more rooms similar to this one.

[h] Estimate from Morris's (1921) field notes and his rebuilt great kiva (Room 64) walls.

[i] Later support beams set in recess around elevated kiva (Room 64) walls.

[j] Adjusted for 2 and 3 non-juniper vigas and latillas cut from a single tree. Assume one viga or latilla per juniper tree. Four lintels are calculated for each tree cut. Assume one viga or latilla per juniper tree.

[k] Based on number of crib logs recorded at Spruce Tree House, 6-pilaster Kivas C and D (102 and 126 logs, respectively) and at 42SA6651, Kiva A (4 pilasters: 100 crib logs, 32 flat roof-top logs) in Natural Bridges. Street (2001:156) estimates 200 logs for flat-roof Kiva I (non-cribbed), with 4 large recesses, at Long House. For this exercise, assume 15–30 roof-top logs ("latillas") for small San Juan rooms and tops of kivas and 100 crib logs for a small kiva (4 pilasters) and 150 crib logs for a medium-size 6-pilaster kiva. Crib logs are listed under the viga column. Small non-cribbed kivas yield 2–6 vigas.

Table 52.10. List of tree elements by species recovered from different rooms at Salmon Ruin.

Room	Aspen	Cotton-wood	Conifer	Doug Fir	Fir	Juni-per	Non Conifer	Popu-lus	Piñon Pine	Ponde-rosa Pine	Spruce/ Fir	White Fir	Quercus	Ponde-rosa Pine?	Ponderosa/ Spruce-Fir Doug Fir	Total
Roomblock 1																
61	—	—	—	—	—	—	—	—	—	2	—	—	—	1	—	3
63	—	—	—	—	—	1	—	—	—	22	1	—	—	—	—	24
64	—	—	—	—	25	5	—	—	—	2	—	—	—	—	—	32
71	—	—	—	—	—	—	—	—	—	1	—	—	—	—	—	1
72	—	—	—	—	—	—	—	—	—	—	—	—	—	—	—	0
73	—	—	—	—	—	—	—	—	—	—	—	—	—	—	—	0
74	—	—	—	—	—	—	—	—	—	—	—	—	—	—	—	0
Roomblock 2																
38	—	—	—	—	—	—	—	—	—	—	—	—	—	—	—	0
39	—	—	—	—	—	—	—	—	—	—	—	—	—	—	—	0
59	—	—	—	—	17	4	—	—	—	3	—	—	—	—	—	24
62	—	1	1	2	8	57	3	6	2	38	9	4	—	—	1	132
66	—	—	—	—	—	—	—	—	—	—	—	—	—	—	—	0
69	—	—	—	—	—	4	—	—	—	—	—	—	—	—	—	4
Roomblock 3																
51	—	—	—	—	3	3	—	—	—	16	—	—	1	—	—	23
53	—	—	—	—	—	18	—	—	—	11	—	—	—	—	—	29
57	—	—	—	1	4	3	—	—	—	13	—	—	—	—	—	21
58	—	—	—	—	—	2	—	—	—	2	—	—	—	—	—	4
67	—	—	—	—	5	16	—	—	—	32	—	—	—	—	—	53
70	—	—	—	—	—	4	—	—	—	—	—	—	—	—	—	4
81	—	—	—	—	4	—	—	—	—	2	—	—	—	—	—	6
82	—	—	—	—	15	5	—	2	—	13	—	—	—	—	—	35
Roomblock 4																
45	—	—	—	—	—	2	—	1	—	1	—	—	—	—	—	4
54	—	—	—	—	—	3	—	—	—	—	—	—	—	—	—	3
55	—	—	—	3	—	—	—	—	—	—	—	—	—	—	—	3
56	—	—	—	—	—	—	—	—	—	2	—	—	—	—	—	2
75	—	—	—	1	3	2	—	—	—	2	—	—	—	—	—	8
76	—	—	—	—	—	2	—	—	—	—	—	—	—	—	—	2
77	—	—	—	—	—	2	—	—	—	—	—	—	—	—	—	2
78	—	—	—	—	1	4	—	—	—	—	—	—	—	—	—	5
79	—	—	—	—	—	—	—	—	—	—	—	—	—	—	—	0
80	—	—	—	—	—	—	—	—	—	—	—	—	—	—	—	0
83	—	—	—	—	—	11	—	—	—	—	—	—	—	—	—	11
84	—	—	—	1	19	13	—	1	—	59	—	—	—	—	—	93
85	—	—	—	—	—	—	—	—	—	—	—	—	—	—	—	0
86	—	—	—	—	—	3	—	1	—	—	—	—	—	—	—	4
87	—	—	—	—	—	—	—	—	—	—	—	—	—	—	—	0
89	—	—	—	2	—	5	—	2	—	9	—	—	—	—	—	18

Table 52.10 (continued)

Room	Aspen	Cotton-wood	Conifer	Doug Fir	Fir	Juni-per	Non Conifer	Popu-lus	Piñon Pine	Ponde-rosa Pine	Spruce/ Fir	White Fir	Quercus	Ponde-rosa Pine?	Ponderosa/ Spruce-Fir Doug Fir	Total
90	—	—	—	3	7	39	—	1	—	34	1	—	—	1	—	86
91	—	—	—	—	—	26	—	7	—	—	—	—	—	—	—	33
92	—	—	—	—	1	5	—	—	—	1	—	—	—	—	—	7
95	—	—	—	—	—	—	—	—	—	—	—	—	—	—	—	0
96	—	—	—	—	2	8	—	—	—	1	—	—	—	—	—	11
97	—	—	—	—	1	9	—	3	—	—	—	—	—	—	—	13
98	—	—	—	—	—	8	—	—	—	2	2	1	—	—	—	13
100	—	—	—	—	1	—	—	—	—	13	—	—	—	—	—	14
101	1	3	—	—	—	10	—	11	—	5	1	—	—	—	—	31
103	—	—	—	—	—	—	—	—	—	—	—	—	—	—	—	0
105	—	—	—	—	—	5	—	—	—	—	—	—	—	—	—	5
Roomblock 5																
30	—	—	—	—	5	7	—	—	—	2	—	—	—	—	—	14
31	—	—	—	—	—	11	1	1	—	4	—	—	—	—	—	17
32	—	—	—	—	—	2	—	—	—	1	—	—	—	—	—	3
33	—	—	—	—	2	4	—	4	—	21	—	—	—	—	—	31
35	—	—	—	—	—	—	—	—	—	—	—	—	—	—	—	0
36	—	—	—	—	2	26	—	4	1	31	2	—	—	2	—	68
37	—	—	—	—	1	9	—	9	1	34	2	—	—	—	—	56
40	—	—	—	—	—	2	—	—	—	—	—	—	—	—	—	2
41	—	—	—	—	—	—	—	—	—	2	—	—	—	—	—	2
42	—	—	—	—	11	17	—	1	1	13	7	5	—	—	—	55
43	—	—	—	—	—	—	—	—	—	—	—	—	—	—	—	0
44	—	—	—	—	—	—	—	—	—	—	—	—	—	—	—	0
143	—	—	—	—	—	1	—	—	—	—	—	—	—	—	—	1
144	—	—	—	—	—	—	—	—	—	—	—	—	—	—	—	0
145	—	—	—	—	—	—	—	—	—	—	—	—	—	—	—	0
146	—	—	—	—	—	—	—	—	—	—	—	—	—	—	—	0
148	—	—	—	—	—	—	—	—	—	—	—	—	—	—	—	0
149	—	—	—	—	—	—	—	—	—	—	—	—	—	—	—	0
160	—	—	—	—	—	—	—	—	—	—	—	—	—	—	—	0
161	—	—	—	—	—	—	—	—	—	—	—	—	—	—	—	0
Roomblock 6																
47	—	—	—	—	—	—	—	—	—	—	—	—	—	—	—	0
48	—	—	—	—	—	1	—	—	—	—	—	—	—	—	—	1
52	—	—	—	—	—	—	—	—	—	—	—	—	—	—	—	0
60	—	1	—	—	1	2	—	2	—	1	—	3	—	—	—	10
65	—	—	—	—	—	—	—	—	—	—	—	—	—	—	—	0
68	—	—	—	—	—	1	—	—	—	—	—	—	—	—	—	1
88	—	—	—	—	—	—	—	—	—	—	—	—	—	—	—	0
93	—	—	—	—	—	1	—	—	—	4	—	—	—	—	—	5
94	—	—	—	—	—	—	—	3	—	2	—	—	—	—	—	5

Table 52. 10 (continued)

Room	Aspen	Cotton-wood	Conifer	Doug Fir	Fir	Juni-per	Non Conifer	Popu-lus	Piñon Pine	Ponde-rosa Pine	Spruce/ Fir	White Fir	Quercus	Ponde-rosa Pine?	Ponderosa/ Spruce-Fir Doug Fir	Total
102	—	—	—	—	—	1	—	—	—	1	—	1	—	—	—	3
108	—	—	—	—	—	6	—	—	—	—	—	—	—	—	—	6
129	—	—	—	—	1	7	—	—	—	58	—	—	—	—	—	66
131	—	—	—	—	—	—	—	—	—	—	—	—	—	—	—	0
134	—	—	—	—	—	—	—	—	—	—	—	—	—	—	—	0
140	—	—	—	—	—	—	—	—	—	—	—	—	—	—	—	0
141	—	—	—	—	—	—	—	—	—	—	—	—	—	—	—	0
142	—	—	—	—	—	—	—	—	—	—	—	—	—	—	—	0
147	—	—	—	—	—	—	—	—	—	—	—	—	—	—	—	0
158	—	—	—	—	—	—	—	—	—	—	—	—	—	—	—	0
159	—	—	—	—	—	—	—	—	—	—	—	—	—	—	—	0
Roomblock 7																
19P	—	—	—	—	—	2	—	—	—	1	—	—	—	—	—	3
94	—	—	—	—	—	1	—	3	—	2	—	—	—	—	—	5
99	—	—	—	—	—	1	—	—	—	—	—	—	—	—	—	1
104	—	—	—	—	—	—	—	—	—	—	—	—	—	—	—	0
106	—	—	—	—	—	1	—	—	—	1	—	—	—	—	—	1
107	—	—	—	—	—	—	—	—	—	1	—	—	—	—	—	1
109	—	—	—	—	—	—	—	—	—	—	—	—	—	—	—	0
117	—	—	—	—	—	—	—	—	—	—	—	—	—	—	—	0
118	—	—	—	—	3	13	—	11	—	3	—	—	—	—	—	30
119	—	—	—	—	1	8	—	2	1	7	—	—	—	—	—	19
122	—	—	—	—	1	10	—	—	—	21	—	—	—	—	—	32
132	—	—	—	—	—	2	—	—	—	—	—	—	—	—	—	2
153	—	—	—	—	—	—	—	—	—	—	—	—	—	—	—	1
156	—	—	—	—	—	—	—	—	—	—	—	—	—	—	—	1
157	—	—	—	—	—	—	—	—	—	—	—	—	—	—	—	—
Roomblock 8																
10	—	—	—	—	—	—	—	—	—	—	—	—	—	—	—	0
11	—	—	—	—	—	—	—	—	—	—	—	—	—	—	—	0
13	—	—	—	—	—	—	—	—	—	—	—	—	—	—	—	0
14	—	—	—	—	—	—	—	—	1	—	—	—	—	—	—	1
15	—	—	—	—	—	1	—	—	—	—	—	—	—	—	—	1
17	—	—	—	—	—	2	—	—	—	—	—	—	—	—	—	2
18	—	—	—	—	—	—	—	—	—	—	—	—	—	—	—	0
162	—	—	—	—	—	—	—	—	—	—	—	—	—	—	—	1
Roomblock 9																
1	—	—	—	—	—	—	1	1	—	3	—	—	—	—	—	5
2	—	—	—	—	—	—	1	—	—	—	—	—	—	—	—	1
3	—	—	—	—	—	3	—	—	—	—	—	—	—	—	—	3
4	—	—	—	—	—	2	—	2	—	3	—	—	1	—	—	8
7	—	—	—	—	—	3	—	—	—	—	—	—	—	—	—	3
8	—	—	—	—	—	—	—	—	—	2	—	—	—	—	—	2

Table 52. 10 (continued)

Room	Aspen	Cotton-wood	Conifer	Doug Fir	Fir	Juni-per	Non Conifer	Popu-lus	Piñon Pine	Ponde-rosa Pine	Spruce/ Fir	White Fir	Quercus	Ponde-rosa Pine?	Ponderosa/ Spruce-Fir Doug Fir	Total
Roomblock 10																
120	–	–	–	–	–	–	–	–	–	–	–	–	–	–	–	0
125	–	–	–	–	–	–	–	–	–	–	–	–	–	–	–	0
128	–	–	–	–	–	–	–	–	–	2	–	–	–	–	–	2
Roomblock 11																
5	–	–	–	–	–	4	–	–	–	–	–	–	–	–	–	4
6	–	–	–	–	1	–	–	–	–	2	–	–	–	–	–	3
121	–	–	–	4	2	21	–	–	–	4	–	–	–	–	–	31
123	–	–	–	–	–	1	–	–	–	–	–	–	–	–	–	1
124	–	–	–	–	–	23	2	2	–	2	–	–	–	–	–	29
127	–	–	–	–	–	4	2	3	–	11	–	–	–	–	–	20
Roomblock 12																
130	–	–	–	–	–	–	–	–	–	–	–	–	–	–	–	1
151	–	–	–	–	–	2	–	–	–	–	–	–	–	–	–	2
021P	–	–	–	–	–	3	–	–	–	–	–	–	–	–	–	3
Search Area 3	–	–	–	–	–	4	–	–	–	2	–	–	–	–	–	6
08BW	–	–	–	–	–	–	–	1	–	2	–	–	–	–	–	3
151W	–	–	–	–	–	2	–	–	–	–	–	–	–	–	–	2
General Site	–	–	–	–	–	12	–	1	2	15	–	–	–	–	–	30
PL-5	–	–	–	–	–	1	–	–	–	–	–	–	–	–	–	1
TM-4	–	–	–	–	–	1	–	–	–	–	–	–	–	–	–	1

Table 52. 11. List of dated tree-ring samples recovered from Salmon Ruins 1930s to 2003. TRL = Tree-Ring Laboratory.

Record No.	TRL No.	Inside Date	Inside Date Sym.	Out-side Date	Outside Date Sym.	Code	Age (yrs)	Terminal Ring	TRL Species ID
004W	SAL-202	970	fp	1052	v v	2	83.10	I	Jun
008BW	SAL-1106	1043	p	1088	r	1	46.00	C	PP
008BW	SAL-1105	1052	p	1088	c	1	37.00	C	PP
030B	SAL-246	1018	fp	1063	v v	2	46.10	I	Jun
030W	SAL-1332	939	p	1078	vv	2	140.00		Jun
030B	SAL-1	1054	p	1092	r	1	39.00		DF
030B	SAL-263	1062		1092	vv	2	31.10	I	DF
030B	SAL-2	1051		1094	r	1	44.00		DF
030B	SAL-238	1077	p	1094	r	1	18.00	C	DF
030B	SAL-240	1037	p	1094	+r	18	58.00	I	DF
030B	SAL-241	1030	p	1094	+r	18	65.00	I	Jun
030B	SAL-249	1071	p	1094	r	1	24.00	I	Jun
030B	SAL-261	1078	p	1094	r	1	17.00	I	DF
030W	SAL-376	1082	fp	1105	v	1	24.00	C	PP
031A	SAL-471	985	fp	1017	v v	2	33.10	I	Jun
031A	SAL-469	970	fp	1023	v v	2	54.10	I	Jun
031W	SAL-1335	870	p	1027	vv	2	158.00		Jun
031B	SAL-474	959	fp	1029	v v	2	70.10	I	Jun
031W	SAL-1333	875±		1030	vv	2	156.10		Jun
031W	SAL-1334	939		1030	vv	2	92.00		Jun
031W	SAL-1439	891	±p	1089	vv	2	289.00	I	Jun
031B	SAL-475	1014	fp	1092	+r	18	79.10		Jun
031A	SAL-15	1027	p	1093	r	1	67.00		Jun
031W	SAL-472	1026	1093	+r	18	1	68.10	C	Jun
031A-W	SAL-468	994	±p	1094	r	1	101.00	C	Jun
031W	SAL-473	976	±fp	1094	rB	1	121.10	C	Jun
033W	SAL-1222	876	fp	1043	v v	2	168.00	I	Jun
033C	SAL-463	956	p	1060	vv	2	105.00	I	PP
033C	SAL-22	973	fp	1087	v v	2	115.10		PP
033C	SAL-464	1047		1087	v v	2	41.10	I	PP
033W	SAL-901	1006	p	1089	v	1	84.00	I	PP
033W	SAL-902	1063	p	1089	r	1	27.00	I	PP
004W	SAL-1477	811		1016	v v	2	206.00		Jun
084W	SAL-1229	830	+p	1084	+vv	18	255.00	I	Jun
084	SAL-951	1051	p	1087	+r	18	37.00	C	PP
084	SAL-971	1045	p	1087	+r	18	43.00	C	PP
084	SAL-979	1007	p	1087	++vv	29	81.00	I	PP
084	SAL-980	1050	p	1087	r	1	38.00	I	PP
084W	SAL-1479	857	±p	1087	++vv	18	231.00		Jun
084	SAL-970	1055	p	1088	v v	2	34.00	I	PP
084	SAL-978	1063	p	1088	r	1	26.00	I	PP
084	SAL-984	1057	p	1088	r	1	32.00	I	PP
084	SAL-946	1052	p	1089	r	1	38.00	I	PP
084	SAL-949	1053	p	1089	r	1	37.00	I	PP
084	SAL-952	1054	p	1089	+r	18	36.00	C	PP
084	SAL-955	1058	p	1089	r	1	32.00	I	PP
084	SAL-956	1063	p	1089	r	1	27.00	I	PP
084	SAL-957	1040	p	1089	+r	18	50.00	C	PP
084	SAL-960	1059	p	1089	r	1	31.00	I	PP
084	SAL-965	1061	p	1089	r	1	29.00	I	PP
084	SAL-966	1041	p	1089	+r	18	49.00	C	PP
084	SAL-967	1066	p	1089	v v	2	24.00	I	PP
084	SAL-968	1051	p	1089	+r	18	39.00	C	PP
084	SAL-972	1057	p	1089	+r	18	33.00	C	PP
084	SAL-973	1040	p	1089	+r	18	50.00	C	PP
084	SAL-974	1051	p	1089	+r	18	39.00	C	PP
084	SAL-977	1037	p	1089	+r	18	53.00	C	PP
084	SAL-981	968	p	1089	+v	18	122.00	C	Jun
084	SAL-983	1028	p	1089	+r	18	62.00	C	PP
084W	SAL-1225	1062	p	1089	r	1	28.00	C	PP
084W	SAL-1227	1066	p	1089	r	1	24.00	C	PP
084W	SAL-1481	910	p	1089	v	1	180.00	I	Jun
084	SAL-953	1055	p	1092	+CB	18	38.00	C	PP
084	SAL-948	1056	p	1094	+r	18	39.00	I	PP
084	SAL-954	1060	p	1094	r	1	35.00	I	fir
084	SAL-958	1054	p	1094	r	1	41.00	I	fir
084	SAL-961	1066	p	1094	r	1	29.00	I	PP
084	SAL-962	1065	p	1094	r	1	30.00	C	PP

Table 52.11 (continued)

Record No.	TRL No.	Inside Date	Inside Date Sym.	Outside Date	Outside Date Sym.	Code	Age (yrs)	Terminal Ring	TRL Species ID
033W	SAL-903	1054		1089	+r	18	36.00	C	PP
033W	SAL-1220	1057	p	1089	r	1	33.00	I	PP
033W	SAL-1221	1049	p	1089	r	1	41.00	I	PP
033W	SAL-1223	1050	p	1089	v	1	50.00	I	PP
033C	SAL-24	1038	p	1094	v	1	57.00	PP/Pop	PP/Pop
033A	SAL-34	988	fp	1100	v	1	113.10		PP
033C	SAL-17	966	fp	1100	v	1	135.10	C	PP
033W	SAL-461	1084	fp	1103	r	1	20.00	C	PP
036W	SAL-1137	925	fp	1046	v v	2	122.00	I	Jun
036W	SAL-1151	926	fp	1074	v v	2	149.10	I	Jun
036W	SAL-1158	902	fp	1074	v v	2	173.10	I	Jun
036W	SAL-1159	932	fp	1083	v v	2	152.10	I	Jun
036W	SAL-1136	1016	p	1089	r	1	74.00	I	PP
036W	SAL-1138	1052	p	1089	r	1	38.00	I	PP
036W	SAL-1139	917	p	1089	v	1	173.00	C	Jun
036W	SAL-1143	1056	p	1089	r	1	34.00	I	PP
036W	SAL-1144	1050	p	1089	r	1	40.00	I	PP
036W	SAL-1145	1053	p	1089	v	1	37.00	I	PP
036W	SAL-1146	1066	p	1089	r	1	24.00	I	PP
036W	SAL-1147	1050	p	1089	r	1	40.00	I	PP
036W	SAL-1150	1055	p	1089	r	1	35.00	I	PP
036W	SAL-1153	1055	p	1089	r	1	35.00	I	PP
036W	SAL-1347	943	p	1089	v v	2	147.00		Jun
036W	SAL-1140	974	fp	1093	+rB	18	120.10	C	Jun
036W	SAL-1080	1060	p	1094	r	1	35.00	C	Jun
036W	SAL-1141	1051	p	1094	r	1	44.00	I	Jun
036W	SAL-1148	1036	p	1094	r	1	59.00	I	Jun
036	SAL-1152	1035	+p	1094	r	1	60.00	I	Jun
036	SAL-1154	1039	p	1094	r	1	56.00	I	Jun
036	SAL-1155	1057	p	1094	r	1	38.00	I	Jun
036	SAL-1157	1053	fp	1094	r	1	42.00	I?	Jun
036	SAL-1077	1069	fp	1105	r	1	37.10	I	PP
036W	SAL-1078	1058	fp	1105	r	1	48.10	I	PP
036W	SAL-1079	1058	fp	1105	r	1	48.10	C	PP
036W	SAL-1084	1069	fp	1105	r	1	36.10	I	PP
084	SAL-963	1071	p	1094	r	1	24.00	I	PP
084	SAL-964	1074	p	1094	r	1	21.00	I	fir
084	SAL-975	888	p	1095	v v	2	208.00	I	Jun
086W	SAL-908	948	fp	1021	v v	2	74.10	I	Jun
089W	SAL-1189	970	p	1082	v v	2	113.00	I	Jun
089W	SAL-1178	1046	p	1086	v	1	41.00	C	DF
089W	SAL-1188	1041	p	1086	+r	18	46.00	I	PP
089W	SAL-1179	1054	p	1089	v	1	36.00	I	PP
089W	SAL-1183	1072	p	1089	v v	2	18.00	I	PP
089W	SAL-1186	1053	p	1089	c	1	37.00	I	PP
089W	SAL-1187	1068	p	1089	r	1	22.00	I	PP
089W	SAL-1175	917	p	1092	+rB	18	176.00	C	Jun
089W	SAL-1190	1078	p	1093	+r	18	16.00	C	PP
089W	SAL-1181	1060	p	1094	r	1	35.00	I?	PP
089W	SAL-1185	1074	p	1094	r	1	21.00	I	DF
090W	SAL-399	934	fp	996	v v	2	63.10	I	PP
090W	SAL-512	820	+p	1058	v v	2	239.10	I	Jun
090W	SAL-511	927p	p	1065	v v	2	139.10	I	Jun
090W	SAL-385	920		1079	++v	19	160.10	I	Jun
090W	SAL-508	1001	p	1080	v v	2	80.10	I	Jun
090W	SAL-133	953	fp	1082	++B	19	130.00	C	Jun
090W	SAL-888	1015	fp	1087	v v	2	73.00	I	PP
090W	SAL-130	1051		1088	r	1	38.00	C	DF/Pop
090W	SAL-132	1052	p	1088	r	1	37.00	C	PP
090W	SAL-388	994	fp	1088	+r	18	95.10	I	Jun
090	SAL-939	1062	p	1089	r	1	28.00	I	PP
090	SAL-942	1051	p	1089	r	1	39.00	I	PP
090	SAL-943	1028	p	1089	r	1	62.00	I	PP
090	SAL-944	1075	p	1089	r	1	15.00	I	PP
090	SAL-945	1064	p	1089	+r	18	26.00	I	PP
090W	SAL-136	1047	p	1089	r	1	43.00	C?	PP
090W	SAL-513	969	+p	1089	v	1	121.00	I(?)	Jun
090W	SAL-516	888	+p	1089	v	1	102.00	I(?)	Jun

Table 52. 11 (continued)

Record No.	TRL No.	Inside Date	Inside Date Sym.	Outside Date	Outside Date Sym.	Code	Age (yrs)	Terminal Ring	TRL Species ID
037W	SAL-1377	865	±p	983	++vv	18	119.00		Jun
037W	SAL-1375	854		999	vv	2	146.00		Jun
037W	SAL-1378	905	p	1061	++vv	18	157.00		Jun
037W	SAL-1376	956	p	1079	+vv	18	124.00		Jun
037W	SAL-868	1051	p	1088	v v	2	38.00	I	PP
037W	SAL-1374	942	p	1088	+vv	18	147.00		Jun
037W	SAL-570	1060	p	1089	r	1	30.00	I	PP
037W	SAL-870	937	fp	1089	v	1	153.10	I	Jun
037W	SAL-1095	1062	p	1089	r	1	28.00	I	PP
037W	SAL-1096	1046	p	1089	r	1	44.00	I	PP
037W	SAL-1231	1063	p	1089	r	1	27.00	I	PP
042W	SAL-1122	936	p	1089	rL	1	154.00	I	Jun
042W	SAL-1123	946	p	1089	+rL	18	144.00	C	Jun
043W	SAL-1051	928	fp	1028	v v	2	101.10	I	Jun
043W	SAL-1048	890	fp	1048	vv	2	159.10	I	Jun
043W	SAL-1050	888	fp	1057	+vv	18	170.10	I	Jun
043W	SAL-1055	893	fp	1077	v v	2	185.10	I	Jun
043W	SAL-1447	1034	p	1082	vv	2	49.00		SF
043W	SAL-1127	1065	p	1089	r	1	25.00	I	PP
043W	SAL-1049	1060	p	1091	r	1	32.00	C	PP
043W	SAL-890	1065	p	1093	r	1	29.00	C	PP
043W	SAL-894	1053	p	1093	rB	1	41.00	I	Jun
043	SAL-1450	1004	p	1094	rB	1	91.00		Jun
043W	SAL-1052	1066	p	1094	r	1	29.00	I	fir
043W	SAL-1054	1054	p	1094	r	1	41.00	I	fir
043W	SAL-1056	1051	p	1094	r	1	44.00	I	fir
043W	SAL-1128	1057	p	1094	cL	1	38.00	C	Jun
043W	SAL-1129	1028	p	1094	r	1	67.00	C	Jun
043W	SAL-1132	1005	p	1094	rL	1	90.00	C	Jun
043W	SAL-1134	1053	p	1094	r	1	42.00	C	Jun
043W	SAL-1135	993	p	1094	cLB	1	102.00	C	Jun
043W	SAL-1443	1022	p	1094	v	1	73.00		Pnn
043W	SAL-1444	1021	p	1094	r	1	74.00	C	Jun
090W	SAL-517	889	+p	1089	r	1	101.00	C	Jun
090W	SAL-887	907	+	1089	rB	1	183.00	I	Jun
090W	SAL-396	1064	fp	1093	r	1	30.00	C	Jun
090W	SAL-886	1073	p	1093	c	1	21.00	C	PP
090W	SAL-413	1050	fp	1094	r	1	45.00	C	DF
090W	SAL-937	1065	p	1094	r	1	30.00	I	fir
090W	SAL-405	1148	fp	1207	vv	2	60.10	I	Jun
090W	SAL-389	1195	fp	1248	vv	2	54.10	I	DF
090W	SAL-885	1197	p	1261	r	1	65.00	I	Jun
091A	SAL-293	858	±fp	964	vv	2	107.10	I	Jun
091W	SAL-430	838	±fp	1015	vv	2	178.10	I	Jun
091W	SAL-1483	959		1054	vv	2	96.00	I	Jun
091A	SAL-292	956	fp	1076	vv	2	121.10	I	Jun
091W	SAL-1482	974		1082	+vv	18	109.00	I	Jun
091C	SAL-1059	1037	p	1085	++vv	29	49.00		PP
091A	SAL-519	1053	p	1088	+c	18	135.00	I	PP
091A	SAL-291	901	±p	1089	+r	18	189.00	I	Jun
091A	SAL-429	908	fp	1089	rB	1	182.00	I	Jun
091C	SAL-1058	1060	p	1089	v v	2	30.00	I	PP
091D	SAL-1063	1051	p	1089	+r	18	39.00	I	PP
091D	SAL-521	957	p	1090	+r	18	134.00	C	Jun
091D	SAL-1064	1057		1090	+r	18	34.00	I	PP
091D	SAL-1060	1060	p	1091	+r	18	32.00	I	PP
091A	SAL-428	1063	fp	1092	vv	2	30.10	I	PP
091D	SAL-1061	1051	p	1094	r	1	44.00	I	fir
092W	SAL-230	974	fp	1020	vv	2	46.10	I	PP
092B	SAL-300	971	p	1086	+v	18	116.00	I	PP
092B	SAL-302	1056	p	1087	vv	2	32.00	I	PP
092B	SAL-303	1045	fp	1091	+vv	18	47.10	i	PP
093W	SAL-297	1002	fp	1057	vv	2	56.10		PP
093W	SAL-141	1054	fp	1090	+v	18	37.10	I	PP
093W	SAL-142	1051	p	1090	+r	18	40.00	I	PP
097B/W	SAL-1219	1019		1074	v v	2	56.00	I	fir

Table 52. 11 (continued)

Record No.	TRL No.	Inside Date	Inside Date Sym.	Outside Date	Outside Date Sym.	Code	Age (yrs)	Terminal Ring	TRL Species ID
043W	SAL-1452	984	p	1094	r	1	111.00	C	Jun
043W	SAL-1460	1053	p	1094	r	1	42.00	C	Jun
043W	SAL-899	1070	p	1106	v	1	37.00	I	PP
048W	SAL-1256	881	±p	1049	v v	2	169.00	I	Jun
051W	SAL-572	1059	p	1089	v	1	31.00	I	PP
051W	SAL-573	1055	p	1089	r	1	35.00	I	PP
051W	SAL-574	1065	p	1089	r	1	25.00	I	PP
051W	SAL-579	964	p	1089	v	1	126.00	I(?)	PP
051W	SAL-580	1038	p	1089	v	1	152.00	I(?)	PP
051W	SAL-586	1047	p	1089	v v	2	43.10	I	PP
051W	SAL-588	1037	p	1089	v	1	53.00	I	PP
051W	SAL-589	1056	p	1089	r	1	34.00	I	PP
051W	SAL-590	1064	p	1089	v	1	26.00	I	PP
051W	SAL-913	1022	p	1089	+r	18	68.00	C	PP
051W	SAL-575	932	fp	1090	r	1	159.10	I	Jun
053W	SAL-1015	794	+	1007	v v	2	214.00	I	Jun
053W	SAL-1022	960	p	1087	v v	2	128.00	I	Jun
053W	SAL-1025	1052	+p	1088	+r	18	37.00	C	PP
053W	SAL-1013	892	fp	1089	+r	18	198.00	C	Jun
053W	SAL-1019	917	fp	1089	+r	18	173.00	C	Jun
053W	SAL-1023	1065	p	1089	r	1	25.00	C	PP
053W	SAL-1024	1052	p	1089	+r	18	38.00	C	PP
053W	SAL-1027	944	fp	1089	+rB	18	146.10	C	Jun
053W	SAL-1029	1079	p	1089	r	1	11.00	I	PP
053W	SAL-1030	1076	p	1089	r	1	14.00	I	PP
053W	SAL-1032	1056	p	1089	r	1	34.00	I	PP
053W	SAL-1033	1059	p	1089	+r	18	31.00	C	PP
053W	SAL-1034	900	+p	1089	r	1	190.00	I	Jun
054W	SAL-1107	920	+p	1088	v v	2	169.00	I	Jun
054W	SAL-1109	849	p	1088	v v	2	240.00	I	Jun
055W	SAL-481	1044	p	1090	+r	18	47.10	I	DF
055W	SAL-482	1023	p	1090	+r	18	68.10	I	DF
097B/W	SAL-1512	973	p	1089	v	1	117.00	I	Jun
097B-W	SAL-662	927	p	1089	r	1	163.00	I	Jun
097W	SAL-527	974	p	1068	+r	18	95.00	I	Jun
097W	SAL-526	909	p	1089	+r	18	181.00	C	Jun
097W	SAL-528	952	p	1089	+r	18	138.00	I	Jun
097W	SAL-663	860	+p	1089	v	1	221.00	I	Jun
098W	SAL-537	848	+p	1051	v v	2	204.00	I	Jun
098W	SAL-533	845	p	1062	+vv	18	218.10	I	Jun
098W	SAL-1509	870	±p	1063	++vv	18	194.00	I	Jun
098W	SAL-535	796	+p	1088	+rLB	18	293.00	C	Jun
098W	SAL-534	937	p	1089	+v	18	153.10	I	Jun
098W	SAL-536	970	p	1089	+cLB	18	120.00	C	Jun
100W	SAL-875	1027	p	1089	+c	18	63.00	I	PP
100W	SAL-1103	1048	p	1090	+r	18	43.00	I	PP
100W	SAL-1104	1065	p	1100	v v	2	36.00	I	PP
100W	SAL-876	1070	p	1106	r	1	37.00	I	PP
101W	SAL-1265	952	p	1052	v v	2	101.00	I	Jun
101W	SAL-673	885	+p	1089	+rB	18	205.00	C	Jun
101W	SAL-674	976	p	1089	+rB	18	114.00	C	Jun
101W	SAL-675	982	p	1089	v	1	108.00	C	SF
101W	SAL-1484	1048	p	1089	+v	18	42.00	C	Jun
101W	SAL-1267	878	±p	1090	r	1	213.00	I	Jun
102B	SAL-912	1040	p	1076	v v	2	37.00	I	WF
102B	SAL-314	1018	fp	1088	v v	2	71.10	I	PP
105W	SAL-1262	846	p	989	v v	2	144.00	I	Jun
105W	SAL-1514	882	p	1001	+vv	18	120.00	I	Jun
106W	SAL-1314	945	p	1066	v v	2	122.00	I	Jun
108W	SAL-1318	898	fp	1025	v v	2	128.10	I	Jun
108W	SAL-1315	865		1063	+vv	18	199.00	I	Jun
108W	SAL-1317	855	fp	1203	v v	2	349.10	I	Jun

Table 52. 11 (continued)

Record No.	TRL No.	Inside Date	Inside Date Sym.	Outside Date	Outside Date Sym.	Code	Age (yrs)	Terminal Ring	TRL Species ID
055W	SAL-483	1047	p	1095	v	1	49.00	I	DF
056W	SAL-594	1065	p	1089	r	1	25.00	I	PP
056W	SAL-595	1069	p	1090	r	1	22.00	I	PP
057W	SAL-927	888	+fp	987	v v	2	100.10	I	Jun
057W	SAL-926	935	fp	1038	v v	2	104.10	I	Jun
057W	SAL-1073	1048	p	1088	r	1	41.00	C	PP
057W	SAL-596	1057	p	1089	r	1	33.00	I	PP
057W	SAL-924	911	p	1089	+rB	18	179.00	C	Jun
057W	SAL-921	1043	p	1090	+r	18	48.00	I	fir
057W	SAL-1072	1060	p	1090	+r	18	31.00	I	DF
058W	SAL-597	1050	p	1089	r	1	50.00	I	PP
059W	SAL-1092	1028	p	1104	+v	18	77.00	C	PP
059W	SAL-1094	950	+fp	1106	v v	2	157.10	I	PP
060A	SAL-54	1053	p	1090	r	1	38.00		WF/Pop
060A	SAL-144a	1053	p	1090	r	1	38.00	I	WF
060A	SAL-55	1021	p	1093	+C	1	73.00		DF/Pop
061A	SAL-120	1050	p	1088	v v	2	39.00		Pop/Pop
061A	SAL-122	1037	fp	1088	rL	1	52.00		Pop/Pop
061A	SAL-124	1027	p	1088	v v	2	62.00		PP
061A	SAL-128	931	p	1088	r	1	158.00		PP
061A	SAL-143	1047	fp	1088	r	1	142.00	C	PP
061A	SAL-144b	1022	fp	1088	v v	2	67.10	I	PP
061A	SAL-287	1022	p	1088	r	1	67.00	C	PP
061A	SAL-290	1037	fp	1088	r	1	52.00	C	PP
061A	SAL-118	1065	p	1089	C	1	25.00		PP
061A	SAL-289	998	fp	1089	r	1	92.00	I	PP
061B	SAL-373	1050	fp	1089	v v	2	40.10	I	PP
061B	SAL-542	960	fp	1089	+L	18	130.10	C	PP
061B	SAL-545	1014	+p	1089	L	1	76.00	I	Jun
061B	SAL-549	1011	fp	1089	L	1	79.10	I	PP/Pop

Record No.	TRL No.	Inside Date	Inside Date Sym.	Outside Date	Outside Date Sym.	Code	Age (yrs)	Terminal Ring	TRL Species ID
118W	SAL-1209	1062	p	1089	r	1	28.00	C	fir
118W	SAL-1211	1066	p	1105	r	1	40.00	C	PP
119W	SAL-1065	1028	p	1070	r	1	43.00	C	PP
119W	SAL-1067	1024	p	1070	r	1	47.00	C	PP
121A	SAL-425	963	p	1008	v v	2	46.10	I	Jun
121A-W	SAL-456	1038	fp	1071	v v	2	34.10	I	DF or fir
121A	SAL-157	1013	p	1072	r	1	60.00	I	DF
121A	SAL-422	1025	p	1072	r	1	48.00	I	DF
122W	SAL-185	986	fp	1086	+v	18	101.10	O	Jun
121A-W	SAL-160	1066	fp	1092	v v	2	27.10	I	DF
121B	SAL-146	1066		1094	r	1	29.00	C	PP
121A	SAL-159	1060	fp	1105	r	1	46.00	C	PP
121A-W	SAL-455	1073	fp	1105	v	1	33.10	C	PP
122W	SAL-218	1017	p	1068	r	1	52.00	C	PP
122W	SAL-217	1021	fp	1069	v v	2	49.10	I	PP
122W	SAL-220	1037		1070	r	1	34.00	I	PP
122W	SAL-219	1061	fp	1091	v v	2	31.10	I	PP
122W	SAL-179	1059	fp	1097	v v	2	39.10	I	PP
122W	SAL-177	1057	fp	1105	r	1	49.00	C	PP
122W	SAL-164	1053		1106	r	1	54.00	I	PP
123B	SAL-283	1003	fp	1047	v v	2	45.10	I	PP
124A	SAL-351	1012	p	1072	v	1	61.00	I	DF
127W	SAL-861	1004	fp	1052	v v	2	49.00	I	PP
127W	SAL-694	1057	p	1105	c	1	49.00	C	PP
127W	SAL-866	1069	p	1105	r	1	37.00	I	PP
127W	SAL-691	1064	p	1106	r	1	43.00	I	PP
127W	SAL-863	1079	p	1106	r	1	28.00	I	PP

Table 52. 11 (continued)

Record No.	TRL No.	Inside Date	Inside Date Sym.	Out-side Date	Outside Date Sym.	Code	Age (yrs)	Termi-nal Ring	TRL Species ID
061B	SAL-550	1030	fp	1089	L	1	70.10	I	PP
061A	SAL-119	1067	p	1090	+r	1	24.00		PP
062W	SAL-1385	939		1029	v v	2	91.00		PP
062A	SAL-322	986	fp	1064	v v	2	79.10	I	PP
062A	SAL-71	954	p	1066	v v	2	112.00		PP
062A-W	SAL-319	1038	fp	1074	v v	2	37.10	I	PP
062A	SAL-73	949	fp	1087	+r	1	139.00		PP
062W	SAL-1163	1034	p	1088	r	1	55.00	I	PP
062A	SAL-76	1013	p	1089	r	1	77.00		WF
062W	SAL-1162	1050	p	1089	r	1	50.00	I	PP
062W	SAL-1164	956	p	1089	r	1	134.00	C	PP
062W	SAL-1165	1040	p	1089	r	1	50.00	I?	PP
062W	SAL-1166	1025	p	1089	r	1	65.00	C	PP
062W	SAL-1167	1026	p	1089	v	1	64.00	I?	PP
062W	SAL-1168	1038	p	1089	r	1	52.00	C?	PP
062W	SAL-1169	999	p	1089	r	1	91.00	C	PP
062W	SAL-1383	1004	p	1089	+vv	18	86.00		PP
062W	SAL-1384	871		1089	+vv	18	119.00		PP
062W	SAL-1427	1045	p	1089	+r	18	45.00	C	SF
062A	SAL-66	1017	p	1090	C	1	74.00		WF
062A	SAL-1391	997	p	1099	++vv	18	103.00		Jun
062W	SAL-1388	1047	p	1102	vv	2	56.00		Jun
062W	SAL-323	990	fp	1107	r	1	118.00	I	fir
062A	SAL-1389	1019	±p	1110	++vv	18	92.00		Jun
062	SAL-1387	1025	p	1112	vv	2	88.00		Jun
062W	SAL-1392	1058	±p	1116	B	1	59.00	C	Jun
062	SAL-1160	988	p	1116	cLB	1	128.00	C	Jun
062W	SAL-1170	1059	p	1116	r	1	58.00	C	Pnn
062W	SAL-1393	1058	±p	1116	B	1	59.00	C	Jun
062W	SAL-1394	1043	±p	1116	B	1	74.00	C	Jun
062W	SAL-1395	1014	±p	1116	B	1	103.00	C	Jun
062W	SAL-1396	1008	±p	1116	B	1	109.00	C	Jun
062W	SAL-1397	1057	p	1116	r	1	60.00	C	Pnn
062W	SAL-1398	1062	p	1116	rB	1	55.00	C	Jun
062W	SAL-1399	1058	±p	1116	r	1	59.00	C	Jun
129W	SAL-744	1043	p	1079	v v	2	37.10	I	PP
129W	SAL-700	1014	p	1088	v	1	75.00	C	PP
129W	SAL-703	1031		1088	r	1	58.00	C	PP
129W	SAL-704	1008	p	1088	r	1	81.00	C	PP
129W	SAL-712	1019	p	1088	r	1	70.00	C	PP
129W	SAL-747	1003	p	1088	r	1	86.00	C	PP
129W	SAL-748	1006	p	1088	v	1	83.00	C	PP
129W	SAL-751	1029	p	1088	r	1	60.00	C	PP
129W	SAL-702	1058	p	1089	+r	18	32.00	C	PP
129W	SAL-706	1071	p	1089	+r	18	19.00	C	PP
129W	SAL-713	1053	p	1089	+r	18	37.00	C	PP
129W	SAL-716	1052	p	1089	+r	18	38.00	C	PP
129W	SAL-720	1064	p	1089	+r	18	26.00	C	PP
129W	SAL-732	1050	p	1089	+r	18	40.00	C	PP
129W	SAL-733	1046	p	1089	+r	18	44.00	C	PP
129W	SAL-1207	1072	p	1089	r	1	18.00		PP
129W	SAL-705	1061	p	1090	+r	18	30.00	I	PP
129W	SAL-707	1060	p	1090	+r	18	31.00	I	PP
129W	SAL-708	1061	p	1090	+c	18	30.00	I	PP
129W	SAL-714	1057	p	1090	+r	18	34.00	I	PP
129W	SAL-715	1064	p	1090	+r	18	27.00	I	PP
129W	SAL-717	1070	p	1090	+r	18	21.00	I	PP
129W	SAL-718	1054	p	1090	+r	18	37.00	I	PP
129W	SAL-719	1060	p	1090	+r	18	31.00	I	PP
129W	SAL-721	1056	p	1090	+r	18	35.00	I	PP
129W	SAL-722	1053	p	1090	+r	18	38.00	I	PP
129W	SAL-724	1064		1090	+r	18	27.00	I	PP
129W	SAL-727	1065		1090	+r	18	26.00	I	PP
129W	SAL-728	1072		1090	+r	18	19.00	I	PP
129W	SAL-731	1059	p	1090	+r	18	32.00	I	PP
129W	SAL-734	1062	p	1090	+r	18	29.00	I	PP
129W	SAL-735	1068	p	1090	+r	18	23.00	I	PP
129W	SAL-737	1066	p	1090	+r	18	25.00	I	PP
129W	SAL-738	1045	p	1090	+r	18	46.00	I	PP
129W	SAL-739	1060	p	1090	+r	18	31.00	I	PP
129W	SAL-740	1062	p	1090	+r	18	29.00	I	PP

Table 52.11 (continued)

Record No.	TRL No.	Inside Date	Inside Date Sym.	Outside Date	Outside Date Sym.	Code	Age (yrs)	Terminal Ring	TRL Species ID
062W	SAL-1400	1061	p	1116	r	1	56.00	C	Jun
062W	SAL-1401	1012	p	1116	rB	1	105.00	C	Jun
062W	SAL-1403	1024	p	1116	B	1	93.00	C	Jun
062W	SAL-1404	1001	p	1116	B	1	116.00	C	Jun
062W	SAL-1405	1004		1116	B	1	113.00		Jun
062W	SAL-1418	1007	±p	1116	B	1	110.00		Jun
062W	SAL-1419	1062	p	1116	v	1	55.00		Jun
062W	SAL-1420	1043	p	1116	v	1	64.00		Jun
062W	SAL-1421	1005	±p	1116	L	1	112.00	C	Jun
062W	SAL-1423	1033	p	1116	B	1	84.00	C	Jun
062W	SAL-1424	1063	p	1116	v	1	54.00	C	Jun
062W	SAL-1425	1063	p	1116	B	1	54.00	C	Jun
062W	SAL-1426	1048	p	1116	v	1	69.00		Jun
062W	SAL-1406	1055	t	1118	v	1	64.00		Jun
062A	SAL-68	1102	p	1257	r	1	156.00		DF
063W	SAL-113	947	p	1025	vv	2	79.00	I	PP
063W	SAL-342	985	fp	1059	++vv	29	75.10		PP
063W	SAL-117	970	p	1084	vv	2	115.00		PP
063W	SAL-112	982	p	1088	r	1	107.00		PP
063W	SAL-340	1042	fp	1088	r	1	47.00	C	PP
063W	SAL-341	932		1088	r	1	157.00		PP
063W	SAL-344	1003	fp	1088	r	1	86.00	C	PP
063W	SAL-345	1002	fp	1088	r	1	87.00	C	PP
063W	SAL-346	1060	p	1088	r	1	29.00	C	PP
063W	SAL-116	1063	p	1089	r	1	27.00		PP
064W	SAL-633	972	p	1066	vv	2	95.10	I	fir
064W	SAL-1125	895	+p	1079	vv	2	185.00	I	Jun
064W	SAL-619	1008	p	1088	r	1	81.00		fir
064W	SAL-632	1008	p	1088	r	1	81.00	I	fir
064W	SAL-624	1024	p	1090	r	1	67.00	I	fir
064W	SAL-625	1034	p	1090	r	1	57.00	I	fir
067	SAL-991	859	fp	1074	vv	2	116.10	I	Jun
129W	SAL-741	1068	p	1090	+r	18	23.00	I	PP
129W	SAL-745	1065	p	1090	+r	18	26.00	I	PP
129W	SAL-1201	1071	p	1090	+r	18	20.00	I	PP
129W	SAL-743	1071	p	1106	r	1	36.00	I	PP
130W	SAL-760	1122	p	1186	vv	2	65.00	I	fir
130W	SAL-852	1157	p	1209	vv	2	53.00	I	DF
130W	SAL-841	1125	p	1231	vv	2	107.00	I	fir
130W	SAL-847	1190	p	1232	vv	2	43.00	I	fir
130W	SAL-761	1123	p	1236	vv	2	114.00	I	fir
130W	SAL-758	1165	p	1242	vv	2	78.00	I	DF
130W	SAL-855	1210	fp	1242	vv	2	33.10	I	DF
130W	SAL-756	1128	p	1244	vv	2	117.00	I	Jun
130W	SAL-806	1168	fp	1244	r	1	77.10	I	DF
130W	SAL-814	1163	fp	1244	v	1	82.00	I	Jun
130W	SAL-827	1199	p	1255	vv	2	57.00	I	DF
130W	SAL-799	1183	fp	1257	vv	2	75.10	I (?)	Jun
130W	SAL-846	1212	p	1258	vv	2	47.00	I	DF
130W	SAL-816	1118	+p	1259	vv	2	142.00	I	Jun
130W	SAL-854	1196	p	1259	vv	2	64.00	I	fir
130W	SAL-823	1121	p	1260	vv	2	140.00	I	Jun
130W	SAL-802	1215	p	1261	vv	2	47.00	I (?)	Jun
130W	SAL-767	1180	fp	1262	+r	18	83.00	I	Jun
130W	SAL-801	1197	fp	1262	+r	18	66.10	I (?)	Jun
130W	SAL-812	1140	+p	1262	v	1	123.00	I (?)	Jun
130W	SAL-822	1195	p	1262	r	1	68.00	C	Jun
130W	SAL-836	1184p	p	1262	vv	2	79.00	I	Jun
130W	SAL-839	1168	±p	1262	+r	18	95.00	I	Jun
130W	SAL-842	1166	p	1262	+v	18	97.00	I	DF
130W	SAL-849	1178	p	1262	vv	2	85.00	I	fir
130W	SAL-853	1199	p	1262	vv	2	64.00	I	fir
130W	SAL-752	1194	p	1263	v	1	70.00	I	Jun
130W	SAL-753	1141		1263	r	1	123.00	C	Jun
130W	SAL-754	1130	+p	1263	r	1	34.00	I	Jun
130W	SAL-759	1175	+p	1263	rB	1	89.00	C	Jun

Table 52. 11 (continued)

Record No.	TRL No.	Inside Date	Inside Date Sym.	Out-side Date	Outside Date Sym.	Code	Age (yrs)	Termi-nal Ring	TRL Species ID
067	SAL-989	912	fp	1080	v v	2	169.10	I	Jun
067	SAL-986	994	fp	1089	+r	18	96.10	I	Jun
067	SAL-987	1064	p	1089	r	1	26.00	I	PP
067	SAL-988	857	fp	1089	v v	2	233.10	I	Jun
067	SAL-990	1062	p	1089	r	1	28.00	I	PP
067	SAL-993	1063	p	1089	r	1	27.00	I	PP
067	SAL-994	882	+p	1089	r	1	208.00	I	Jun
067	SAL-995	869		1089	+r	18	34.00	C	Jun
067	SAL-996	1056	p	1089	v v	2	34.00	I	PP
067	SAL-997	1066	p	1089	r	1	24.00	C	PP
067	SAL-998	965	+p	1089	+r	18	125.00	C	Jun
067	SAL-999	1066	p	1089	r	1	24.00	I	PP
067	SAL-1000	1071		1089	r	1	19.00	I	PP
067W	SAL-1503	931		1037	+vv		107.00		Jun
067W	SAL-1002	857	+p	1038	v v	2	182.00		Jun
067W	SAL-1001	1063	p	1089	r	1	27.00	I	PP
067W	SAL-1003	1063	p	1089	r	1	27.00	I	PP
067W	SAL-1005	955		1089	+r	18	135.00	C	Jun
067W	SAL-1006	1060	p	1089	r	1	30.00	I	PP
067W	SAL-1007	1064	p	1089	r	1	26.00	I	PP
067W	SAL-1008	951	p	1089	r	1	139.00	I	Jun
067W	SAL-1011	926	p	1089	+r	18	164.00	C	Jun
067W	SAL-1012	912	p	1089	+rL	18	178.00	C	Jun
067W	SAL-1212	1063	p	1089	r	1	27.00	I	PP
067W	SAL-1214	1061	p	1089	r	1	29.00	I	PP
067W	SAL-1215	1046	p	1089	r	1	44.00	I	PP
067W	SAL-1216	899	p	1089	r	1	191.00	I	Jun
067W	SAL-1504	924	±	1089	+B	1	166.00	C	Jun
067W	SAL-1213	1063	p	1094	r	1	32.00	C	PP
069W	SAL-1113	930	+fp	1089	+rLB	18	160.10	C	Jun
069W	SAL-1115	875	+p	1089	+r	18	115.00	C	Jun
070W	SAL-1118	687	+p	958	v v	2	272.00	I	Jun
075W	SAL-307	1047	fp	1106	r	1	60.10		PP

Record No.	TRL No.	Inside Date	Inside Date Sym.	Out-side Date	Outside Date Sym.	Code	Age (yrs)	Termi-nal Ring	TRL Species ID
130W	SAL-762	1177		1263	r	1	87.00	I	Jun
130W	SAL-763	1119	+p	1263	r	1	145.00	C	Jun
130W	SAL-764	1180		1263	r	1	84.00	C	Jun
130W	SAL-765	1152		1263	v	1	112.00	I	Jun
130W	SAL-766	1114		1263	rB	1	150.00	C	Jun
130W	SAL-768	1188		1263	r	1	76.00	C	Jun
130W	SAL-769	1180	+p	1263	r	1	84.00	C	Jun
130W	SAL-770	1191	p	1263	r	1	73.00	C	Jun
130W	SAL-771	1190	+p	1263	r	1	74.00	C	Jun
130W	SAL-773	1192	p	1263	r	1	72.00	I (?)	Jun
130W	SAL-775	1192	p	1263	r	1	72.00	I (?)	Jun
130W	SAL-776	1141	+p	1263	rB	1	123.00	C	Jun
130W	SAL-778	1175	fp	1263	rB	1	89.10	C	Jun
130W	SAL-779	1179	p	1263	r	1	85.00	C	Jun
130W	SAL-780	1170	p	1263	r	1	94.00	C	Jun
130W	SAL-781	1180	+p	1263	v	1	84.00	I (?)	Jun
130W	SAL-782	1164	+p	1263	r	1	100.00	C	Jun
130W	SAL-784	1188	p	1263	r	1	76.00	I (?)	Jun
130W	SAL-785	1191	p	1263	r	1	73.00	I	Jun
130W	SAL-787	1219	p	1263	r	1	44.00	I	Jun
130W	SAL-788	1175	p	1263	r	1	89.00	C	Jun
130W	SAL-789	1153	+p	1263	v	1	111.00	I	Jun
130W	SAL-790	1140	+p	1263	v	1	124.00	I	Jun
130W	SAL-791	1142	+p	1263	r	1	122.00	I (?)	Jun
130W	SAL-792	1192	p	1263	r	1	72.00	I (?)	Jun
130W	SAL-793	1153	p	1263	r	1	111.00	I	Jun
130W	SAL-794	1162	+p	1263	r	1	102.00	C	Jun
130W	SAL-795	1190	p	1263	r	1	74.00	C	Jun
130W	SAL-796	1140	+p	1263	r	1	124.00	I	Jun
130W	SAL-798	1150	+p	1263	r	1	114.00	I (?)	Jun
130W	SAL-800	1160	+p	1263	rB	1	104.00	C	Jun
130W	SAL-803	1140	+p	1263	rB	1	124.00		Jun
130W	SAL-804	1173	p	1263	rB	1	91.00		Jun
130W	SAL-805	1140	+p	1263	rB	1	124.00	I	Jun
130W	SAL-807	1164	p	1263	v	1	100.00	I	Jun
130W	SAL-808	1189	p	1263	rB	1	74.00	C	Jun

Table 52.12. List of tree-ring symbols and abbreviations. Symbols after Ahlstrom (1985) and Windes and McKenna (2001).

Species: DF = Douglas fir
              Jun = juniper
              Pnn = piñon
              PP = ponderosa pine
              SF = spruce or fir
              Pop = *Populus* sp. (aspen or cottonwood)
              non-conf = non-coniferous wood

Ring Condition:

Complacent = Little patterning is evident in the sample so that dating is difficult if not impossible. Common among trees with a plentiful precipitation supply (e.g., cottonwood and high-altitude conifers).

Compressed = Outer rings are so narrow that distinguishing patterning or the absence of rings is not possible. In dated samples, a "++" symbol would be used.

Erratic = Ring growth is erratic and difficult to match patterning for dating purposes. Common for juniper growth and may include partial, double, or missing rings.

Missing rings = Two or more growth rings are absent, which can be attributed to erratic growth and/or to drought conditions.

Short = The number of rings is too few to adequately date and cross reference. Usually less than 30-50 rings.

Terminal Ring:

I = Incomplete outer ring (tree died during growing season). Growing season varies by species and area.

C = Complete outer ring (tree died during dormant season). Dormant season varies by species and area.

Date symbols for the inside date: Field observation by author noted in a subscript.

p = pith present

np = near actual pith (old usage).

fp = far from actual pith (old usage).

±p = pith ring is present but because of the difficult nature of the specimen, an exact date cannot be assigned to it (common among juniper specimens).

± = the innermost ring is not the pith ring, and an absolute date cannot be assigned to it. A ring count is involved.

Date symbols for the outside date: Field observation by author noted in a subscript.

+ = Cannot be dated with certainty because one to five outer rings may be missing.

++ = The outermost rings of a sample cannot be dated. Typically, the rings are uniformly small, making it impossible to recognize patterning in ring widths or to identify missing rings. This pattern reflects very slow growth and is the mark of a dying tree. Dates with this symbol are considered derived from deadwood.

vv = Definite evidence for a cutting/death date is absent, and it is unknown how many outer rings have been lost.

v = A subjective judgment that the outer ring is at or within 1–5 years of the actual tree death date. Typically considered a death or near death date, but weakest in confidence.

r = Less than a full section is present, but the outermost ring is continuous around the available circumference. Considered a death date, but more confident than above.

c = The outermost ring is continuous around the entire circumference. Considered a death date but more confident than above.

L = A characteristic surface patination and smoothness, which develops just under the bark, is present. Considered a confident death date.

G = Beetle galleries are present on the surface of the specimen. Considered a death date of greater confidence than above.

B = Bark is present. Considered the strongest affirmation of the actual death date, unless a "+" or "++" is also present for this symbol or those above.

east, given that nearly all Puebloan domiciles are set to face somewhere along an arc of east to south, to take advantage of the sun. The eastern orientation, of course, is predicated on the initial use of the early building for habitation. The later expansion of the East Wing and its incorporation within the larger structure oriented it to face *west* into the interior plaza. More likely, this small early block of architecture may have been razed and the timbers salvaged after construction at Salmon was begun. A similar small, early roomblock was razed when Pueblo Alto was built (Windes 1987a, 1987b); this small roomblock at Alto was built with thick, massive walls similar to the great house that overlaid it.

For the most part, Salmon timbers were cut for the first and second stories between AD 1088 and 1090 (Figure 52.12) to roof the basic room plan of the Chacoan great house. Small clusters of dates between AD 1092 and 1094 mark a second round of harvesting that may mark new additions. These samples are mixed with AD 1088–1089 samples in some rooms. Plotting the newer dates by rooms reveals a curious clustering along a single row of rooms on either side of the elevated kiva, one tier of rooms in from the back rooms. The later samples are found in a string of rooms (30-31-33-36) west of the elevated kiva and in an equivalent set (55-79-90-84) to the east, except that Room 79 failed to produce any dated samples. In addition, one room along the back tier above each row in the same relative position produced dates between AD 1092 and 1094 (in Rooms 43 and 78; Figure 52.13). These late dates probably reflect the construction of two blocks of third-story rooms to either side of the elevated kiva (see Reed, Chapter 12).

It is possible that the context of the late dates is misleading. If a single tier of third-story rooms was built along the very back of the pueblo, it is possible that these collapsed first after abandonment and fell into the rooms directly in front. However, O'Sullivan's photographs of Salmon from 1874 clearly show third-story sections of the pueblo along the second or third row of rooms from the back wall. Thus, the dates may also be the result of sampling biases, perhaps marking a larger block of three-story rooms than may have existed along the back tiers of the central roomblock. Reed (Chapter 12) has argued that the third-story additions covered most of the central roomblock, three rooms deep from the back wall, but the dendrochronological evidence for this is limited. AD 1092–1094 dates were also recovered from beams in Room 121 in the southeast roomblock and in front of the elevated kiva in Room 60A, marking other architectural modifications, although these

samples were probably elements reused for minor repairs.

Rooms

All rooms could not be discussed in detail, but the sample spotlights the trends observed in the use of wood for construction throughout the roomblocks. The Primary great house construction centered on the elevated kiva and then extended east and west from there. The core unit is of interest due to its central placement and its importance to the overall plan of the structure. How wood was selected and treated for use in construction in this block of rooms may reveal conformance or not to a generalized Chacoan model of great house construction. Certainly there are units within the core that reflect maximum efforts in tree selection and harvesting, such as the elevated kiva (see below), but as a unit the effort appears to have been variable, with the use of both local and far-distant trees. Overall, the three blocks composing the core unit—the elevated kiva and its attendant rooms (Construction Unit 1) and the rooms around and below the elevated kiva (Units 2 and 3)—are dominated by nonlocal ponderosa pine elements followed by local juniper and nonlocal fir (Table 52.13). Much of the juniper, however, came from the large set of tie poles added to a new support wall in Room 62 in AD 1118. With this juniper sample removed from the totals, the emphasis upon nonlocal roofing elements is more pronounced. We can only quickly examine rooms with the largest tree-ring samples in order to assess the complicated timber history. Many rooms had too few dated samples to address wood use here.

In contrast to the core unit at Salmon, almost no nonlocal wood was used during the initial constructions at Aztec West; wood was first harvested there at about AD 1098 or shortly thereafter while Salmon was barely in its tenth year of existence. The large elevated kiva (Kiva L) and a few attendant rooms were built first while the overall footprint of the great house was prepared, and foundations were poured over the next decade (Brown et al. 2005). The large sample from the Aztec West core unit (n = 1066 samples) reveals that nonlocal conifers of ponderosa pine, spruce-fir, and Douglas fir made up 72 percent of the wood materials (roofing and lintels), with another 25 percent being *Populus* sp. (see Table 52.13). Given the widespread presence of cottonwood along the nearby Animas River, it could be erroneously assumed that the Aztec *Populus* sp. was almost all cottonwood. Chaco builders chose instead to carry thousands of high-altitude, nonlocal aspen

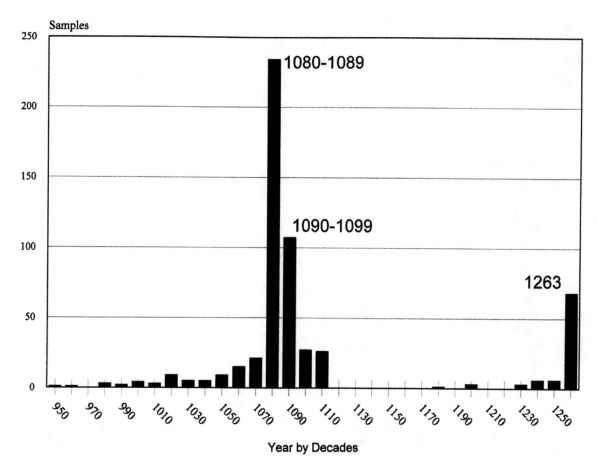

Figure 52.12. Tree-ring dates (cutting and noncutting) from Salmon Ruins.

trees to the site. Eighty-three percent of the core unit *Populus* sp. was aspen (n = 198). Nearly 800 *Populus* sp. specimens from the site were examined for subspecies (see Tennessen et al. 2002), confirming the overwhelming preference for aspen rather than cottonwood in the construction (mostly as roof latillas). Salmon yielded few samples that could be classified between the two species (most were too rotted), but cottonwood was favored over aspen, although the sample is too small to be meaningful. Many more *Populus* sp. samples are curated, however, and have not been analyzed.

The deep rooms adjacent to the Salmon elevated kiva differ from the others in the main roomblocks. Especially notable is Room 62, one of the largest in the site (43.5 m²), which yielded hundreds of textiles during excavations (Webster, Chapter 46) and 194 tree-ring samples (82 from recent work). In addition, sacks of juniper (2), *Populus* sp. (2), nonconiferous (2), and mixed species (15) fragments were returned unanalyzed from the 1972 laboratory work along

with individual fragments of ponderosa pine (6), *Populus* sp. (1), juniper (3), and fir (2). The room architecture underwent a number of modifications that may have related to efforts to shore up the great mass of stone in the elevated kiva that towered above it on the east side. Two retaining walls, one covering the other, shored up the initial east masonry wall (Figure 52.14). The first retaining wall, 50 cm wide, reached the height of the roof vigas that dated at AD 1089, and the second, outer one was about 150 cm shorter and 30–40 cm wide. Two large vertical posts were embedded in the second retaining wall to help support the three vigas at the north end of the room (Figure 52.15). The second, outer retaining wall formed a flat shelf between the north wall and the upright posts, and arrayed along the top of the shelf was a tight layer of juniper tie poles (n = 37, 5.9 cm diameter, sd = 1.2) reaching back through the initial retaining wall. These tie poles had been cut with stone axes more or less flush with the outer facing of the second retaining wall but left exposed along the

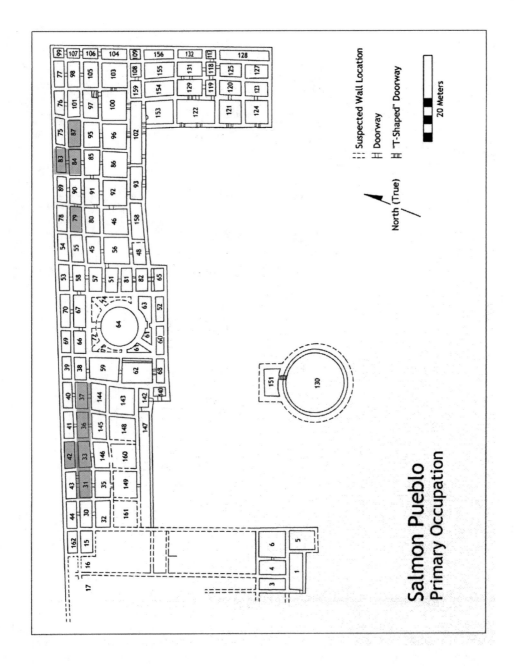

Salmon Pueblo
Primary Occupation

Figure 52.13. Probable third-story additions to Salmon Ruins in AD 1094–1095, based on tree-ring dates. Other evidence suggests more massive third-story additions along the central roomblocks. (Map revised by Eileen Bacha.)

Table 52.13. Wood use in the architectural core units at Salmon and Aztec West Ruins.

Core Units	Non-local Woodlands High Altitude Conifers						Mixed Local and Non-local High & Low Altitude Populus sp.					Local Woodlands Low Altitude Conifers				Total	%
	PP[a]	SF	DF	PSF[b]	All	%	Pop[c]	Cot	Aspen	All	%	Jun	Pnn	All	%		
Salmon																	
Kiva & suite	47	25	–	–	72	88	–	–	–	–	–	10	–	10	12	82	18
East suites	44	33	2	2	81	42	15	1	–	16	8	94	2	96	50	193	43
West suites	88	31	1	–	120	70	2	–	–	2	1	51	–	51	29	173	39
Totals	179	89	3	2	273	61	17	1	–	18	4	155	2	157	35	448	100
Aztec West																	
Kiva & suite	207	21	9	12	249	66	9	15	101	125	33	1	2	3	1	377	34
East suites	101	39	29	75	244	72	27	10	34	71	21	22	1	23	7	338	30
West suites	168	35	27	66	296	75	33	9	29	71	18	25	3	28	7	395	36
Totals	476	95	65	153	789	71	69	34	164	267	24	48	6	54	5	1110	100
Totals w/o lintels[d]	117	41	15	43	216	65	18	2	97	117	35	1	–	1	T	334	–

[a] COT = cottonwood, DF = Douglas fir, Jun = juniper, Pnn = piñon, PP = ponderosa pine, Pop = *Populus* sp., PSF = ponderosa pine / spruce / fir, SF = spruce or fir.
[b] Field calls; did not distinguish between ponderosa pine, Douglas fir, and spruce / fir.
[c] Not identified as to aspen or cottonwood.
[d] Aztec lintels removed from totals because majority of Salmon samples presumably do not include lintels.

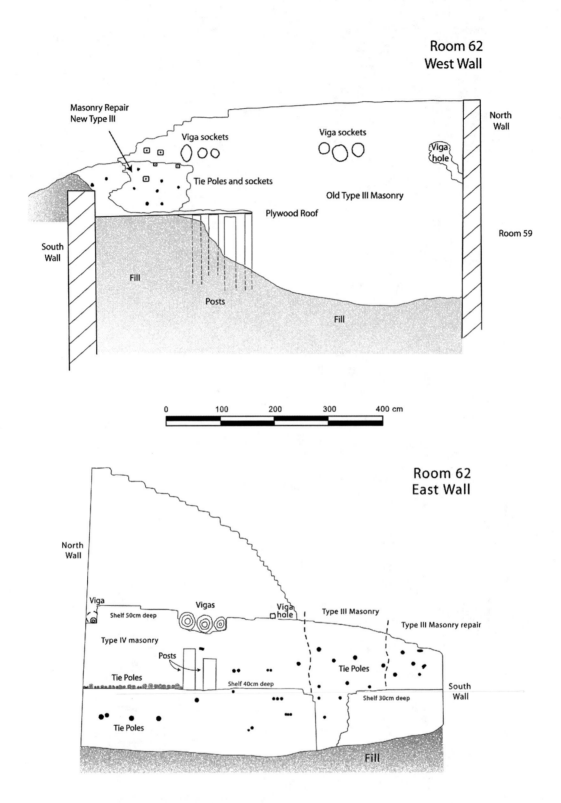

Figure 52.14. Room 62 east and west wall elevations showing the roof vigas and their supporting posts and the two retaining walls that buttress the east wall. Note the numerous tie poles, which indicate additions made in AD 1118. (Original maps by J. Schubert, G. Jordan, and E. Bacha, 9 June and 21 July 2002. Digitally redrafted by Chris Millington.)

Figure 52.15. Room 62, upright posts set in the smaller, east retaining wall built ca. AD 1118. Posts support the roof vigas directly above. Note the numerous small tie-poles anchoring the two additions. (Photograph by Tom Windes, March 2005.)

top of the shelf. The addition contained numerous small poles of different species set randomly and horizontally through the retaining walls to tie the walls into the original Type IV-style masonry wall. Six of these had been saw cut, evidently during the room excavations, but the remainder had not been sampled until recently. Two of the excavated samples must be SAL-4074 and -4075, which were juniper that dated at AD 1116. Other previous juniper samples within the same excavation field number sequence that failed to date probably contained two more tie poles. But three of the saw-cut tie poles were field identified as pine, and all of the field samples from the same group as the dated juniper poles above were pine samples that dated at AD 1088 and 1089. A single tie pole dated at AD 1118, which indicates that the entire reinforcing was added at or shortly after AD 1118. The mixture of species seems at first to indicate both local and nonlocal procurement. Only the recently sampled juniper tie poles produced a date, leaving the procurement period uncertain for the remaining species of tie poles. The juniper is probably local wood, cut primarily during the AD 1116 dormant season, whereas the ponderosa pine, fir, Douglas fir, and *Populus* sp. may have come from recycled elements.

There is support for this interpretation among the series of small tie poles used to patch the original masonry veneer in the west Type III masonry wall. None of the tie poles were juniper but one spruce-fir dated at AD 1089+r, indicating a reused pole. Be-

neath the patched masonry in the west wall is a tight cluster of large upright posts (6?) that must have supported the roof vigas at the south end of the room. All the large posts in the room dated between AD 1088 and 1089, but they must be former vigas that were obtained elsewhere on the site, as it was unlikely that they were needed at the time of room construction. All the posts and room vigas left in situ are ponderosa pine. Most vigas in the general area, however, were juniper. We suspect that the pine posts came from rooms within the general core area, where ponderosa pine was favored during the initial construction. But juniper stems would not have been capable of spanning the large living rooms, and perhaps the reused timbers used as posts in Room 62 came from living rooms that had been vacated.

In summary, Room 62 must have suffered from structural failure caused by the weight of the elevated kiva after its initial construction in AD 1089. Repairs were initiated in the fall or winter of AD 1116 but not completed until AD 1118 or later, at which time the room may have been used for refuse deposits to help alleviate the structural forces imposed by the elevated kiva architectural mass. The deliberate in-filling of rooms to help distribute the weight of adjacent architecture was also noted at Aztec West (Brown et al. 2005). The reuse of small poles and probable vigas suggests that part of the great house roofing elsewhere in the site was dismantled by AD 1118. A single date of AD 1257r marks some later use of the room. If this Douglas fir specimen came from one of the posts in the room, it would mark efforts to shore up the room much later than interpreted above, at about the time the Great Kiva was being considered for rebuilding.

Room 62 yields the latest dendrochronological evidence for construction at Salmon until the mid AD 1200s, but many other lines of archaeological evidence indicate that remodeling and new construction was ongoing throughout the AD 1100s, similar to the efforts at Aztec Ruins (Brown et al. 2005), although these later events did not match the intensity and short timing of the initial great house construction. Although dendrochronological evidence from Salmon is absent for most of the AD 1100s and early 1200s, there was widespread scavenging and reuse of the initial Chacoan timbers as well as local tree harvesting for continued building episodes. The latter wood, however, failed to produce any dates because of the nature of the erratic tree growth, the local species (juniper and *Populus* sp.) selected for building, and the probable widespread use of small poles that had few rings.

The suite of door-connected rooms adjacent to the elevated kiva on the east side (Rooms 51, 57, 81, 82) yielded 84 analyzed tree-ring samples dominated by ponderosa pine (51%), spruce-fir (31%), and juniper (13%), along with a small handful of Douglas fir (1) and *Populus* sp. (2), and a rare oak specimen. Few samples dated (25%), but all were between AD 1088 and 1090, indicating that room construction was completed by AD 1090 or slightly later. Otherwise, there is little to add to the wood use in this series of rooms, which are similar to others along the main central roomblock.

Central Roomblock, West Section

West of the elevated kiva (Room 64) are many deep, two-story rooms and several with a third story. The complex depositional histories in these rooms makes it difficult to separate the probable different story roof elements recovered from them. Room 30 was later subdivided into two rooms, 30A and 30B, during the Secondary occupation. No wood was analyzed from Room 30A, although nonconiferous (1), *Populus* sp. (24), and juniper (8) samples were returned. Much of the roof for Room 30B was recovered, but the elements from the overall room space illustrate the problems with the room wood histories. Sixty-nine samples from the room complex were processed through the tree-ring laboratory but only 10 produced dates. Eight dated at 1092 or 1094; these were mostly Douglas fir that may have been third-story elements but were later used for roofing Room 30B. A single cutting date at 1105 may mark

some minor remodeling or feature construction at the site, as a scatter of dates from the 1105–1106 period is found in a number of rooms. The vast majority of samples came from Room 30B (n = 60), on juniper (67%) that failed to date (83%). The dominant juniper samples suggest either newly cut elements for roofing the small room or the reuse of Chacoan latillas. Other species of trees in the nondated sample probably indicate at least some reuse of Chacoan wood in the last roofing, which is confirmed by the 1092 and 1094 dated samples. Finally, much wood was returned unanalyzed from the 1972 collections, including 194 *Populus* sp. samples that must mark a set of roof latillas, and 8 sacks of mixed species, including juniper and nonconiferous wood that might have been closing material. This room, along with many others in the associated rooms, was burned.

Room 31 experienced a history similar to Rooms 30 and 36. It was also probably three stories, and it was subdivided into two rooms (Rooms 31A and B) during the Secondary occupation. A mere three samples produced dates (AD 1093–1094), from the 37 processed. Room 31A provided 17 samples, dominated by juniper elements (n = 14), of which none dated. Again, newly cut beams are possible along with reused Chacoan beams for the Room 31A roof. Unanalyzed wood fragments returned from the laboratory yielded sacks of juniper (1), ponderosa pine (1), and nonconiferous wood (4) along with 19 juniper specimens, 2 *Populus* sp., and 1 ponderosa pine.

Instead of being subdivided, Room 33 was used as a kiva (Room 33C) during the Secondary occupation. The overall complex yielded 55 ponderosa pine samples and one juniper; 14 produced dates. The dichotomy in ages (over 113 and under 84) from the dated samples suggests that both vigas and latillas were present. Cutting dates clustered at AD 1089 (all associated with Chacoan deposits and probably all latillas based on age), but there was also one at 1094 (latilla?) and three between 1100 (2 vigas) and 1103 (a latilla?). The 20–23 samples associated with the kiva indicate the reuse of Chacoan wood in terms of dates (AD 1060vv–1100v) and species (only 4–5 were juniper). The latest date (1103, on a very young specimen, 20 years old, probably a small element from room furniture or a small feature) came from the Chacoan deposits. The returned unanalyzed materials, however, yielded a mixture of species: sacks of mixed woods (7) and juniper (5), plus individual specimens of ponderosa pine (2), juniper (10), *Populus* sp. (3), and a nonconiferous piece.

A large sample (n = 68) also came from Room 36W along the back tier of multistory rooms. This room had burned during the Chacoan occupation and then filled with deposits that were later covered over during a Secondary flooring. Later a kiva was built above the flooring (Room 36C) together with two interstitial spaces (Rooms 36A-B). Many new samples (n = 23) were collected in 2002 or were found in the collections, but only a viga dated. None of the samples were attributed to the Secondary kiva constructions. Field notes indicate that multiple duplicate samples were collected from the roofing, which was not intact. An upright beam was found in one corner, but whether this was a post or a roof beam is unknown. Tree-ring dates indicate wood from three cutting episodes—AD 1089, 1094, and 1105—but field notes do not help to distinguish these various sets from one another. The AD 1089 dates probably mark the initial first- and second-story roofing construction. Species and specimen ages indicate that the initial roofing consisted of juniper vigas and ponderosa pine latillas. The wood cut in AD 1094 was all young juniper, suggesting some sort of Secondary construction unit built of small poles. Above, we argued that the 1094 dates represent the probable third-story roofing of the room or the one behind it (Room 41). The 1105 cluster is of young ponderosa pine trees, indicating small poles from some feature.

Room 37 is instructive because 25 samples recently collected from door and ventilator lintels provide insights into species selection for wall aperture construction. None of these produced dates, but they reveal that fir and ponderosa pine were used exclusively for lintels in this room. The east ventilator in the south wall had been plugged with masonry, but the Mesa Verde B/w sherd used for chinking dates the modification to the AD 1200s. A juniper pole sampled in the fill behind the south door that led into Room 144 (SAL-1381) was only 9.5 cm in diameter but was 182 years old and dated at AD 1089+v. This element represents collapsed roofing in Room 144 and probably is the small end of a viga. The vast majority of the undated specimens collected from the room during excavation (24 of 27) were not juniper but ponderosa pine and fir that must have been small diameter, young latillas. Otherwise, the excavated samples yielded six cutting dates from the growing season of AD 1089 and no later dates. All the dated juniper samples were very old specimens—all over 124 years—that probably came from collapsed vigas cut in AD 1089.

Room 37 had been subdivided late in its use into two smaller rooms, 37A and 37B. Little roofing was directly associated with the two smaller rooms, which presumably had been roofed with reused

Chacoan timbers. Figure 52.16 illustrates the Secondary viga sockets placed in the west wall of the room for Room 37B above the first-story latilla sockets for the initial Chacoan roofing, which had been burned and covered over by fill prior to the placement of Room 37B.

Room 43 was in the back tier of rooms and most probably was three stories high. Secondary architecture was not evident, so the entire sample was assigned to the Chacoan architectural history. Fifty-seven samples were processed, including 13 new ones obtained from the Salmon Museum collections, 5 of which dated. Dates at 1094 dominated the dated sample (13 of 23), which revealed dated and undated elements of juniper, fir, and a *Populus* sp. and a piñon element. The recent samples were small elements that ranged in diameter between 4.2 and 7.1 cm but came from a range of old and very young trees (18–111 years). It is an odd collection of elements that may represent parts of the upper story latillas, but strangely none of our recent samples could duplicate the earlier excavated room samples because the oldest aged group of complete cross-sectioned samples that we obtained was much younger than the fragmented older specimens from the initial collection.

Central Roomblock, East Section

In the eastern section, Room 84 provided the largest tree-ring sample (95 pieces), with Room 91 contributing 52 samples and Room 101 contributing 31 samples. After that, the numbers of samples are greatly reduced, with only 20 from Room 98, etc. This area of the main roomblock was widely burned. Room 84 revealed a large number of dated samples (39), helping to define the roofing from the room. Two tree harvest events are apparent from the dates: AD 1088–1089 and AD 1094–1095. The early dates must mark the lower story roofing, and the later dates mark the probable upper third story. Species and age of the dated specimens suggest a roof dichotomy of six old juniper vigas—between 122 and 255 years, 5 from the early roof(s)—and ponderosa pine and fir latillas (31 of 33 less than 50 years old). Most of the undated samples were juniper (18), but they cannot be assigned an architectural function based on the dendrochronological information. Their large number suggests latillas, but it is unlikely that pine and juniper would be mixed together as secondary poles in the same roof.

Room 90 also produced groups of cutting dates indicating that the initial roof construction took place just after trees were cut in AD 1088 and in the fall of 1089, with a second effort in the spring of 1094 to

Figure 52.16. Room 37 showing the burned west wall and two large viga sockets placed when the Chacoan room was partitioned into two smaller rooms (37A and 37B). Note the latilla sockets below the viga holes for the initial Chacoan roof. (Photograph by Peter George.)

roof a possible third-story room. Many undated samples were juniper (26) and ponderosa pine (14), which may have been latillas for various roofs, but without ages or diameters, their function cannot be determined. Many samples (136) are documented for the room, 50 of them from recent work. Most of the latter, however, were modern first-story viga and latilla replacements (46). Material returned unanalyzed from the laboratory (not part of the 136 samples) was prolific: sacks of juniper (4), fir (1), non-coniferous (1), and mixed woods (9) along with individual specimens of ponderosa pine (5), *Populus* sp. (1), juniper (3), and fir (5). There was a conspicuous absence of *Populus* sp. samples.

Paired ventilators and central doorways were evident in the north and south walls, with most of the exposed lintels replaced during stabilization (Figure 52.17). The east vent in the south wall, however, yielded three rotted prehistoric *Populus* sp. lintels, which could not be identified to the subspecies. Between each trio of vigas in the north and south walls is a single square stone protruding from the masonry that appears to be a roof support but that Larry Baker (personal communication, 2003) says was introduced during stabilization by the National Park Service in 1973. Except for the Great Kiva, Room 90 produced the most AD 1200s dates (3) from the site. Two were noncutting dates (AD 1207vv and

1248vv), but the third was cut in AD 1261 during the growing season. These elements must mark a late modification of the room that took place at about the same time that the Great Kiva was being rebuilt.

Room 91 saw extensive remodeling into three separate units (A–C) during later occupations, but the overall dating is similar to Room 84 with timbers cut during the similar two episodes: AD 1089–1091 and 1094. There is no tree-ring evidence to mark the remodeled units, so either the wood for them was removed from the room, Chacoan wood was recycled for the new roof, and/or the Secondary construction only yielded wood that failed to date. The dated sample is small (n = 16) but suggests that the harvest took place in an area with conditions slightly different than Room 84's because of the missing terminal rings during the years from 1088 through 1090, which were not evident in the Room 84 sample. Most of the juniper (22 of 30, or 73%) failed to produce dates, leaving their function indeterminate. The dated juniper samples were all old trees (96 to 189 years), suggesting use as vigas; the number of dated juniper samples approximates the number of vigas expected to support a roof. The dated ponderosa pine and fir samples were from young trees (< 50 years) except for one 135-year-old specimen that must have been a viga or post. The sample appears skewed, however, in that there were no undated

Room 90

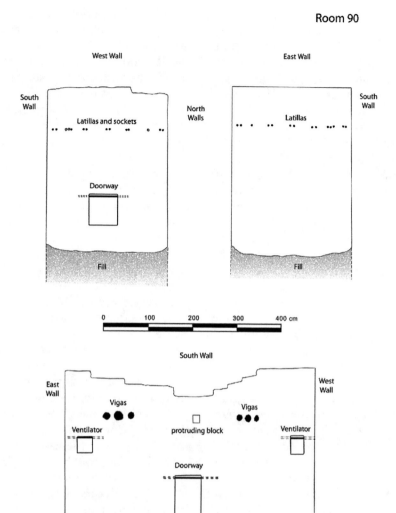

Figure 52.17. Room 90 east, west, and south wall elevations. Views show the typical placement of roof beam sockets and doorway and ventilator apertures in a Chacoan greathouse. (Original maps by J. Schubert and E. Bacha, 15 June 2003. Digitally redrafted by Chris Millington.)

pines and only one fir. If the roofs had been covered with numerous latilla poles of nonjuniper, then multitudes of undated nonjuniper specimens should have been present. In this case, the large number of undated juniper samples might represent small elements cut for the later remodeling. A small number of *Populus* sp. samples (4) failed to produce dates, and these might be interpreted as either latillas or lintels from the room. However, the unanalyzed specimens present a slightly different picture, with *Populus* sp. (3 sacks), fir (3 sacks), juniper (3 sacks), and mixed materials (6 sacks) more common than in the analyzed sample. Another seven *Populus* sp.

samples were returned in 1972, and three more, along with four of juniper, went unanalyzed from Room 90A. Thus, one or more roofs were probably represented in the sample with vigas cut from juniper trees and the smaller latillas cut from cottonwood or aspen trees. The sample of undated juniper pieces may have come from remodeling episodes that used locally cut trees.

Room 98 just east of Room 101 was also reinvestigated recently, revealing a south wall with eight viga stubs, some of them historic replacements (two of *Populus* sp., but one of these was aspen). Two of the recently dated vigas revealed old juniper trees that were similar in age, species, and dates to the other old junipers from the excavations with cutting dates between AD 1088 and 1089. Two latillas left in the west wall that did not produce dates were from spruce or fir trees, while an original viga left in the south wall was an old juniper (205 years) that dated at AD 1088+B. The south door was blocked by room fill and by the collapsed roof from the room directly south (Room 105). Two 14 cm diameter juniper vigas that had fallen across the door opening were cored for samples. Only one dated, at AD 1001+vv, but field observation indicates that it was a near-cutting date, which suggests a reused beam procured from some earlier structure in the vicinity.

Few samples were originally analyzed from Room 101 (n = 17), but recent efforts documented 49 elements still visible. Many of these were viga stubs. Six of the burned juniper stubs were sampled; they await analysis. The five in the south wall are historic replacements; two are cottonwood. The 18 latilla stubs in the west wall also appear to be historic and were not sampled. The first-story door centered in the north wall had been stabilized and three lintels were replaced with modern tamarisk or Russian olive branches, but the remainder were original Populus sp. as were the lintels in the door opposite in the south wall. Sixteen of these lintel samples were submitted to the University of Minnesota for species identification, which revealed that three were cottonwood and one was aspen. The others were too rotted to identify, but the results indicate that both local and nonlocal species of Populus sp. were harvested for construction elements. The few cutting dates obtained from the room were between AD 1089 and 1090 and consisted of five old juniper specimens (101–213 years of age), presumably vigas, and one young 42-year-old spruce or fir that might have been a roof latilla. No ventilators were evident for this room.

East Wing

Room 122 may be the most important room in the hypothesized early block of rooms built in the AD 1070s, but it was only partly excavated. Nevertheless, the amount of wood recovered from it is impressive and probably represents roofing. Thirty-three samples from the room were analyzed; they were ponderosa pine (21), juniper (10), and fir (1), and one without a species identification. Of the eight dated samples, the seven youngest specimens (< 55 years) were pine and possible latillas, whereas the 101+ year juniper may have been a primary. Dates suggest at least three harvest episodes. Two cutting dates—at AD 1068 and 1072—cluster with a few

others of the period in the adjacent rooms. A near-cutting date at AD 1086 may relate to a common episode of construction marked by cutting dates in nearby rooms between AD 1088 and 1089 that established the basic plan of Salmon. Two cutting dates at AD 1105 and 1106 coincide with others from nearby Rooms 118, 121, 127, and 129, marking a common construction episode, perhaps the addition of a second story. In all cases, the 10 AD 1105–1106 dates were cutting dates from young (< 55 years) ponderosa pine trees.

Room 121 also yielded numerous other samples that were not analyzed by the laboratory. Among the 13 sacks of returned samples were fir (1), juniper (1), nonconiferous (9), and unidentified species (2). A scattering of other species present among the analyzed samples were also returned along with 15 Populus sp. Finally, Room 121A also yielded sacks of juniper (1) and mixed species (1) along with 7 juniper, 3 ponderosa pine, and 1 fir samples. Overall, the variety of wood species recovered from the room suggests either that roofs were built of different species or that they represent different construction episodes that relied primarily on a single species or two. Presumably, the Populus sp. and young ponderosa pine elements represent roof latillas, perhaps from at least two different roofs.

Room 129 in the East Wing produced the largest wood sample from Salmon. Field notes indicate that 138 dendrochronological samples were collected during the 2 years of excavation in 1974 and 1975 but that only 64 samples were eventually analyzed (or the remainder was discarded at the tree-ring laboratory as having too few rings). The room burned early in the site occupation and then was used for trash deposits. The room was unique at the site for its large number of small Chacoan and later San Juan refuse piles. Tree-ring dates indicate that tree cutting for a burned roof took place between AD 1088 and 1090 or 1091; it is the only roof at the site composed strictly of ponderosa pine. A single date at AD 1106 indicates some later activity, which may not be roof related. The room's location in the middle of the East Wing and its association with the earliest site construction suggest its special place within the overall site, reflected in part by the selection of only pine for its roofing. Although many textiles were recovered from the roof, they have been assigned to both Primary and Secondary occupations (Webster 2005; see Chapter 46). Perhaps the refuse piled in the room was placed specifically in this room rather than in more secular contexts. An equinox alignment passing through the room and the elevated kiva (Baker and Mantonya 2002) may have had some significance for the use of the room and for the later deposition of cultural materials.

Living Rooms

The largest rectangular rooms at the pueblo were used for habitation by the Chacoans. A series of contiguous living rooms was built to the east and west of the elevated kiva, but only those primarily along the eastern row were excavated. Others were located in the East and West Wings. These rooms yielded few roofing specimens despite the fact that presumably large quantities of wood were necessary to roof them, including larger than normal vigas to span the 5.6 x 5.6 m rooms along the central roomblock. Large conifers about 6 m long would have been needed to span such rooms, but it is unlikely that juniper trees could have fulfilled that need. Sufficiently long timbers could only have been obtained from trees at some distance from the pueblo.

The field notes from Room 56 indicate that a collapsed, "articulated" burned roof rested nearly at the initial floor level. Only a handful of roofing samples were collected, however. Why were so few samples taken from a nearly intact roof? We believe that the preservation of these large living rooms may have differed from the rooms along the back of the roomblock and along the wings. The roofs of the single-story large living rooms were either removed and recycled elsewhere (e.g., used as posts in Room 62?) or if they collapsed deep into the room, as in Room 56, then they were below the surrounding terrain and near the adobe/clay floor, where moisture would have been trapped. This would ensure fluctuating wet conditions and the rapid decomposition of any wood unless the wood had been carbonized by fire. Unfortunately a quick reading of the notes failed to yield any clues as to the condition of the wood. The multiple stories behind the living rooms were more likely to have had better preservation because of the presence of multiple roofs and the fact that the upper roofs would have fallen upon substantially higher deposits above the subsurface where moisture would have been a problem.

Three of the large living rooms had later kivas built in them, a pattern similar to Pueblo Alto in Chaco (Windes 1987a) where three of the five living rooms were remodeled into kivas. At Salmon, these room kivas failed to yield much wood. We are unsure if the initial living room roofs were left on when the kivas were built inside the rooms or if they were dismantled, which seems more likely. The Room 92 kiva yielded only three dates, which were on pine initially cut for the Chacoan construction. Overall,

only 6 of the 33 specimens analyzed from the excavated eight large living rooms produced a date.

A large square habitation area, Room 86, yielded at least seven postholes that probably served as post steps and roof supports. Field notes from habitation Room 56 indicate that at least six posts or postholes were found in the Chacoan flooring. Two postholes located under doorways must have served to support post steps, which were relatively common in the early great houses at Chaco (e.g., Judd 1964: Plate 14; Windes 1987b: Figures 2.15, 2.17, 2.19, and 2.28) to assist travel over the elevated door sills. Four posts or postholes were found on the floor that were "reinforced" with adobe, presumably the style of thick adobe collars seen in the large (nonhabitation) rooms at Pueblo Bonito (Windes 1987b: Plate 10.3). These built-up roof supports are unusual, but they were also found near Bennett's Peak in the surface storage rooms of a Pueblo I house dating to the early AD 800s (Morris 1959:170, Figures 2–3) and AD 1000s houses on Chimney Rock (Truell 1972:30, Figure 13), and thus have considerable style longevity for roof support architecture. A four-post square pattern is suggested for the room (Reed, Chapter 8). Other large habitation rooms at Salmon may also have had roof supports, but the notes from them are unclear. None of the dated samples could be correlated to room posts.

Roofing in early large great house rooms at Pueblo Bonito, Una Vida, and Pueblo Alto was unusual in that the posthole patterns were offset along one side of the room (Figure 52.18; Windes 1987a). An unpublished Judd photograph shows vigas that failed to span one of the large Pueblo Bonito rooms, which accounts for the offset posthole patterns. Could a similar roofing scheme have been utilized for the large Salmon living rooms that would have permitted the use of smaller, shorter beams? Two of the room posts noted above were sampled but cannot be connected with the laboratory results. Room 56 revealed 13 "latilla" holes in the north wall below the door sill level that may have contained the poles for a room-wide bench (Lekson 1984:46–48, Figure 3.3) or some other type of room furniture. Detailed notes on this feature are lacking. The foundations for a possible elevated kiva, similar to Room 64, were also found under Room 56.

Kivas

Room 64 (Tower Kiva)

The architectural core of the site is dominated by the elevated kiva, Room 64, and its attendant rooms. This area may not have been part of the initial construction at the site (see Baker 2005), but certainly it

Figure 52.18. Pueblo Bonito, Room 308, showing the use of short vigas to span only part of the room. This technique was probably also used in the larger greathouse rooms where post support holes are offset along one side of the room. (Courtesy of the National Museum of Natural History; photograph by Neil Judd.)

was planned in the final layout as seen today. Although the Tower Kiva (Room 64) in the center of the Salmon great house was the focal point of the site, a possible second large elevated kiva offset to the east (see Room 56 above) was either never completed (only foundations were found) or razed. This may have been the initial elevated central kiva, or it was to be the paired twin to Room 64. The few timbers from Room 64 that produced dates indicate that primary harvesting for the roof took place between AD 1088 and 1090, suggesting that preparations and construction took several years. Of all the wood samples from great houses, that from Room 64 is the most unique in its overwhelming use of spruce and/or fir for construction.

But the Tower Kiva provides a complicated structural history similar to many other rooms at the site. The burned dated elements mark a single construction unit. A number of paired logs arrayed in a crib fashion in the burned fill indicated that a cribbed roof was built to span the low Chacoan-style

pilasters. These pilasters contained short logs at the base that were burned before the last roofing burned (see Reed, Chapter 8). The mass of fir indicates Chacoan roofing, which yielded some dates, but could it have been recycled? There is the nagging occurrence of the undated juniper (5 of 6 pieces), which may be associated with Secondary roof construction, although the lone dated piece suggests that it is part of the AD 1088/1090 harvests.

Given its size, elevated position, and massive construction effort, Room 64 was probably the most important enclosed space at the site, followed by the Great Kiva. Aside from its massive masonry foundation and buttressing, which allowed the large, circular structure to be elevated to a second-story level, the roof was built entirely of rare wood materials seldom seen in great house construction. Nowhere else do we have evidence of a single architectural unit employing timbers mostly of high-altitude spruce and fir. Even Chimney Rock Pueblo and its attendant small houses, built at 2439 m (8000 ft) elevation in the heart of spruce-fir country to the north in the Colorado mountains, failed to yield complete architectural units of this wood species, where fir comprised only 10 percent of the total from the great house and none from the small houses (Eddy 1977: Table 29, 2004; Truell 1972: Tables 23, 26, and 27).

It is not just the architecture that sets this area apart from the surrounding roomblocks. The kiva is known for the large number of human bodies found in it, many of them burned (Akins 2005), and a lot of other materials, including nearly 30 pottery vessels and much corn. The contents of the adjacent rooms, full of textiles and bird bones (Durand and Durand 2005; Webster, Chapter 46), signify the cultural significance of the center core. Even without the unusual artifacts and faunal remains, the construction elements alone make this area especially distinct and elaborately planned.

Rooms 130 and 151 (Great Kiva and Antechamber)

The Great Kiva offers a number of insights into behavior at Salmon. Although it was built as part of the overall Chacoan construction effort in the late AD 1000s, substantial roofing remains that were preserved by fire revealed that the structure had been rebuilt or reroofed at about AD 1263. The species used in the kiva bore the unmistakable imprint of the later occupants, who relied heavily on juniper trees. Although suitable juniper probably was locally available (see above), a number of aspects about the kiva sample suggest that it was procured from some distance at higher elevations. An unusually high number of junipers in the sample produced dates (77 of 127, or 61% success) compared to the rest of the site (179 of 590, or 30%), representing a mixture of Chacoan and probable late construction elements. We suspect that the rate would be higher except for an unexplained group of 20 juniper samples from the Great Kiva that were analyzed after 1975 without producing a single date (see Table 52.11). Given that this group of samples came from the same population of roofing timbers, it is at variance with the remaining sample. It is improbable that the excavators by chance alone removed a complete set of undatable roof timbers given the very high dating success (72%) obtained from the first samples gathered from the roof. Richard Warren (personal communication, 2004) of the tree-ring laboratory attributes the lack of dating to the usual nuances of juniper growth: short, erratic, and compressed rings. If laboratory analyses were consistent, then the alternative to the groups of undated samples may lay in the harvesting. If trees

for the Great Kiva roof were harvested in different areas and kept separate from one another during the building process, then we might expect the various batches to reveal different dating (and age) characteristics. Although keeping batches separate from one another seems an unlikely process, it may have happened if gangs of workers, associated by kinship, neighborhood, or other ties, harvested and built sections of the structure independently from one another.

Despite the high numbers of juniper elements suffering from erratic growth (compressed, missing, and double rings), which is common to the species, 46 percent produced dates. The juniper elements were old (mean age 95 years, sd = 25, n = 60; Figure 52.19) and were unlikely to have been procured locally given the extensive human use of the area over the preceding 175 years and the one to three centuries needed for forest reestablishment (West and Van Pelt 1987: Figure 1). Douglas fir and ponderosa pine provide the length, straightness, and strength (Forest Products Laboratory 1974: Table 8) that would have been needed as the initial load-bearing beams for the Great Kiva roof; local species (cottonwood, juniper, and piñon) would have been unsuitable. The scattering of Douglas fir, spruce, and fir in the roofing remains probably reflects mostly fragments of the large primaries on which the weight of the roofing rested. The many juniper elements recovered must have come from the numerous roofing secondaries and leaner poles needed to complete the roof.

The small number of spruce-fir (n = 13) and Douglas fir (n = 11) samples, cut in the same early AD 1200s period that were associated with the juniper roofing elements, suggests that a common harvest area was utilized in the higher elevations where north-facing slopes contained a mixture of juniper, spruce-fir, and Douglas fir. The area most suitable for this combination of growth is in the Navajo Reservoir district, about 42 km (26 miles) east of Salmon, following the San Juan or Los Piños Rivers upstream to Colorado. The closest source for a few Douglas fir trees would have been 35 km away along the north-facing slopes in Gobernador Canyon.

Other single late construction events cannot be distinguished in the excavation record without, perhaps, time-consuming recourse to the extensive field notes. Given the paucity of juniper dates from elsewhere in the site, it is presumed that juniper for room and small kiva construction was obtained from a different, most likely local environment than during the Chacoan construction. For instance, juniper (n = 79) was the majority species in six of the nine,

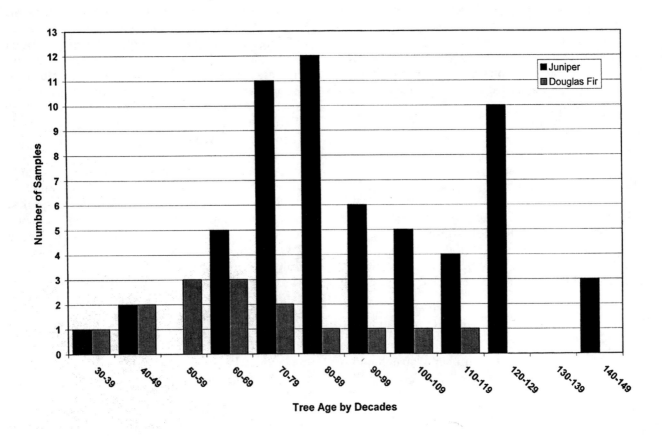

Figure 52.19. Tree ages for Salmon beams of juniper and Douglas fir from the Great Kiva.

late small Mesa Verde-style kivas, yet only a single sample (1%) dated. Juniper samples procured from kivas on Mesa Verde, on the other hand, have an extremely high dating success rate where growing conditions for the same species of juniper were more favorable. Besides the Great Kiva, only a handful of AD 1200s samples, from three rooms, produced dates, but these reveal that juniper and Douglas fir were harvested together, also suggesting at least some long-range procurement in the AD 1200s.

It is unfortunate that we do not have functional information for the roofing elements from the Great Kiva or for the majority of site samples. Presumably, the burned Great Kiva roofing yielded a mixture of primaries and secondaries of juniper, giving equal chance to the dating success of both. The age structure of the sample does reveal a bimodal pattern that suggests a correlate between older trees used as primaries (e.g., larger diameter trees) and younger, smaller-diameter trees as secondaries. The special place of the Great Kiva within the site and community may have demanded an increased labor effort to procure the "better" trees from afar, although the

large beams necessary for construction of the huge structure may simply have not been locally available, which forced a return to areas previously harvested by Chacoan builders.

The initial Great Kiva at Salmon was burned (R. Adams 1980a:241); fire may have left little wood to be recycled when it was rebuilt in the AD 1200s. The frequency of burned great kivas in the Southwest suggests that it was common practice to burn them as part of a standardized ritual terminating their final use. The timing of Salmon's Great Kiva's first decommissioned status would be informative regarding the possible end of Chacoan political involvement in the area. When the Great Kiva was rebuilt in the AD 1200s, there was probably plenty of available old Chacoan wood still available at the site that could have been reused but was not used in the new construction. Perhaps house wood was owned by the last residents living at the site and was not available for recycling. Or maybe the use of new sanctified timbers was required for a structure of this importance, which was not to be contaminated by older recycled wood.

Other Kivas

The remaining kivas at Salmon were small and built late. Most were constructed into existing rectangular rooms, while others were built as part of new additions to the south ends of the wings, and some were built in the plaza, probably as units associated with late habitation suites nearby. Given the preference for juniper elements in structures built in the AD 1200s at Salmon and Aztec, assemblages dominated by juniper are probably late-cut wood, although few of these elements produced dates. Overall, most kivas yielded a mixture of species and tree-ring dates that indicate the reuse of Chacoan timbers, but very few pieces of wood suspected of being cut in the AD 1100s and 1200s produced dates.

The late kiva in Room 124 was dominated by juniper elements (23 of 30 samples), none of which dated. The lone dated sample, at AD 1072, was a Douglas fir that must have been salvaged from some initial construction in the East Wing. Most of the nonjuniper in the sample may have been recycled wood. Unanalyzed samples from 1972 revealed that much *Populus* sp. (7 sacks) and nonconiferous wood (3 sacks) was present; these may have come from roof latillas and closing materials.

The Room 124 kiva was architecturally similar to the one in Room 121, where juniper was also dominant (26 of 42 samples), but only one dated, at AD 1008vv. Six large juniper posts embedded into the Room 121 kiva pilasters (Figure 52.20) also failed to produce dates. Presumably these posts were cut in the AD 1100s or 1200s. Room 96's kiva also yielded mostly juniper (8 of 11 samples), but none dated. The lack of dating success for juniper among the kivas suggests that it was procured from local trees suffering from the effects of a dry local environment.

WOOD HARVESTS

The large number of cutting dates from the Salmon excavations provides an excellent data set for determining when trees were harvested for the construction of the great house (Tables 52.14–52.15). Determining the period of cutting for an individual tree is dependent on the completeness of the outermost growth ring. An incomplete ring indicates that the tree was cut during the growing season (Ahlstrom 1985; Robinson 1967), which varies by tree species as well as by environmental zone (Windes and McKenna 2001: Figure 2). Basically, the higher the elevation, the shorter the growing season. A complete outer growth ring indicates that the tree was dormant and no longer growing when cut. For the datable species found in the Salmon construction, trees cut during the growing season were harvested in the late spring, summer, or early fall, whereas dormant trees were harvested in the fall, winter, or early spring. The growth cycle does not

Figure 52.20. Room 121, looking east at the posts embedded into the kiva pilasters. (Photograph by Tom Windes, March 2005.)

Table 52.14. Tree harvest periods by species and selected years.

Year	Frequency	DF	Fir	Jun	Pop	Pnn	PP	SF	WF
1087	9	–	–	2	–	–	7	–	–
1088	38	1	2	3	–	–	32	–	–
1089	163	–	1	49	–	–	110	2	1
1090	42	3	3	3	–	–	30	–	3
1091	2	–	–	–	–	–	2	–	–
1092	5	2	–	2	–	–	1	–	–
1093	9	1	–	5	–	–	3	–	–
1094	44	6	8	21	–	1	8	–	–
1105	10	–	–	–	–	–	10	–	–
1106	8	–	–	–	–	–	8	–	–
1116	23	–	–	21	–	2	–	–	–
1262	6	1	–	5	–	–	–	–	–
1263	56	1	–	55	–	–	–	–	–

I = incomplete outer ring, tree cut during growing season; C = complete outer ring, tree cut during dormant season.
SAL-160, 219, 302, 303, 306, 314, 428, 477, 836, 849, 853, 888, 967, 1022, 1058, 1107, 1109, 1119, and 1183
were removed from analysis because of uncertainty regarding the end tree-ring date (vv).

coincide with the calendar year. Unfortunately, ponderosa pine, juniper, and piñon have long growing seasons that span the entire period mentioned above. Luckily, Douglas fir (not a true fir), spruces, and firs have very short spring growing seasons, providing a short possible harvest period for a set of construction materials if cut during the growing season.

The majority of timbers procured for the Salmon construction were cut during the growing season. But the mix of tree species cut during both the growing and dormant seasons helps pinpoint the harvest strategies employed by the construction crews. Based on the many buildings that have produced tree-ring dates, small-house construction normally required a single harvesting year to procure timbers for construction. These harvests may have included dead wood if the sites were located in dense forested areas. But large construction efforts required considerable planning, organization, and logistics to procure the necessary building materials, which may have taken several years.

As a group, the Salmon cutting dates do not indicate the same intensity of harvesting seen at Aztec West, built two decades later. Instead, the Salmon dates suggest a minimal harvest collection that reached its maximum in a mere year, AD 1089, and then declined. Of course, the data base contains many undated samples, which might present a different interpretation if all had dated.

The assessment of outer-ring growth for the dated ponderosa pine samples can provide two interpretations. Those with incomplete outer rings were obviously cut during the growing season in the year dated. But it is those that were cut during the dormant season that provide the swing interpretation from fall to spring. Of course these may have been cut during the winter separate from other harvests, but the combination of both incomplete and complete outer rings in the same year suggests fall or spring harvesting when both types of outer ring growth occur together. It could be argued that harvesting took place each fall when both incomplete and complete outer rings occurr in the same year, or alternatively, harvesting could have taken place in the spring of each following year, when dates with complete outer rings of the previous year are matched with incomplete rings of the next year (see Table 52.15). This would mean that the largest groups dated between AD 1088 and 1090, with major harvesting in the spring of each year. For instance, the 1089 dates could all have been cut in the fall of 1089 or the 19 complete outer-ring samples from 1088 could have been harvested with the 79 incomplete outer-ring samples of 1089 during a spring 1089 cutting. There is no way to ascertain which possibility is correct, but other great house samples suggest that spring is the likely harvest period (Windes and McKenna 2001). It is clear, however, that major tree harvesting for Salmon was over by the spring or summer of AD 1090.

The juniper harvests present a different picture, as juniper's growing season probably begins somewhat earlier than ponderosa pine if we consider juniper to be local and growing in warmer climes than

Table 52.15. Completeness of outer tree rings in Salmon wood assemblage.

Year	Outer Ring	Douglas Fir	Fir	Juniper	Populus	Piñon	Ponderosa Pine	SF	WF	Calendar Date	Procurement Area
1087	I	–	–	–	–	–	3	–	–	spr/sum/fall 1087	non-local
	C	–	–	–	–	–	2	–	–	fall 1087-spr 1088	
1088	I	–	1	1	–	–	7	–	–	spr/sum/fall 1088	non-local
	C	1	–	1	–	–	19	–	–	fall 1088-spr 1089	
1089	I	–	–	22	–	–	74	–	–	spr/sum/fall 1089	local, non-local
	C	–	1	22	–	–	29	2	–	fall 1089-spr 1090	
1090	I	3	3	3	–	–	27	–	1	spr/sum/fall 1090	non-local
	C	–	–	–	–	–	1	–	–	fall 1090-spr 1091	
1091	I	–	–	–	–	–	1	–	–	spr/sum/fall 1091	?
	C	–	–	–	–	–	1	–	–	fall 1091-spr 1092	
1092	I	1	–	1	–	–	1	–	–	spr/sum/fall 1092	far local
	C	–	–	1	–	–	1	–	–	fall 1092-spr 1093	
1093	I	–	–	1	–	–	–	–	–	spr/sum/fall 1093	local, far local
	C	–	–	3	3	–	–	–	–	fall 1093-spr 1094	
1094	I	3	8	8	–	–	4	–	–	spr/sum/fall 1094	far local
	C	2	–	12	–	–	3	–	–	fall 1094-spr 1095	
1105	I	–	–	–	–	–	4	–	–	spr/sum/fall 1105	non-local?
	C	–	–	–	–	–	6	–	–	fall 1105-spr 1106	
1106	I	–	–	–	–	–	7	–	–	spr/sum/fall 1106	non-local?
	C	–	–	–	–	–	–	–	–	fall 1106-spr 1107	
1116	I	–	–	–	–	–	–	–	–	spr/sum/fall 1116	local
	C	–	–	16	–	2	–	–	–	fall 1116-spr 1117	
1262	I	1	–	4	–	–	–	–	–	spr/sum/fall 1262	local
	C	–	–	1	–	–	–	–	–	fall 1262-spr 1263	
1263	I	1	–	24	–	–	–	–	–	spr/sum/fall 1263	local
	C	–	–	28	–	–	–	–	–	fall 1263-spr 1264	

I = incomplete outer ring, tree cut during growing season; C = complete outer ring, tree cut during dormant season. SAL-160, 219, 302, 303, 306, 314, 428, 477, 836, 849, 853, 888, 967, 1022, 1058, 1107, 1109, 1119, and 1183 were removed from analysis because of uncertainty regarding the end tree-ring date (vv).

ponderosa. The equal number of 1089 dated junipers with incomplete and complete outer rings suggests a single harvest episode when juniper had almost finished growth in the fall. In the Salmon area, that might be in September, depending on the year. If juniper was cut at the same time as the ponderosa pine in the spring, then the delayed growth of ponderosa pine would likely yield greater numbers of trees still in the dormant stage. Considering either alternative discussed above, the great majority of pines were cut during the growing season—the opposite expectation when compared to juniper. Thus, two separate harvest sessions are suggested for the 1089 collection of these two tree species: one local in the fall (juniper) and one nonlocal in the spring (pine). The larger junipers destined for primary roof supports may have needed time for curing that was unnecessary for the smaller elements (Lange 1959:146; Syngg and Windes 1998; Windes and McKenna 2001:125).

Several rooms at Salmon provided large samples from which to assess harvest strategies. Room 129 yielded 40 tree-ring samples, presumably from mostly different roofing elements given its intact roof when found. This overall sample is unusual in the exclusive use of ponderosa pine and the outer ring conditions that mark the group as a nearly unique set. Most of the sample elements had very small outer rings—which is common for the years AD 1090 and 1091 when they were harvested (Ron Towner, personal communication 2005)—indicating dry years. These are difficult to read, resulting in the laboratory notation "1090 [ring] may be absent." No other grouping in the sample provides a block of samples with this potential missing ring, which suggests that the trees were cut as a single group that grew together and suffered the same effects of a dry year. Thus, the room sample was probably cut selectively just for Room 129. If it was reroofed and remodeled from earlier times, the exclusive use of pine sets it apart from all others.

Local versus Nonlocal Procurement

The information gathered from prehistoric and historic sites in the area (see Tables 52.1–52.2) and the general knowledge of current tree species locations indicates that juniper and cottonwood would have been locally available to the builders of Salmon, whereas piñon and isolated stands of ponderosa pine and Douglas fir were found farther away (far local—within a day's journey). But large numbers of young ponderosa pines, aspens, firs, and spruces are found only in the higher, cooler elevations along the northern drainages and mesa tops near the Colorado

border or beyond (nonlocal). The latter locations of course provide different logistical requirements for travel and effort in acquiring these trees.

Two species of trees provided the bulk of the structural wood requirements for the Salmon builders: local juniper and nonlocal ponderosa pine. Three construction phases show selection of one species dominant over the others: the elevated central kiva and its adjoining interstitial rooms, the Great Kiva, and the southeast roomblock (construction unit 11). The special significance of the Tower Kiva probably accounts for the use of nonlocal wood that could only be obtained from the greatest distance of any species in our sample.

Extra efforts were also made to procure wood at great distances for construction of the Chaco Canyon great houses (Dean and Warren 1983; English et al. 2001; Windes and Ford 1996; Windes and McKenna 2001), but the scarcity of suitable trees for great house construction at Chaco accounts for the dominant use of nonlocal resources. Salmon and Aztec Ruins are located among more plentiful resources where the bulk of the needed wood could have been procured locally. Both were situated in similar locales of wood species (juniper and cottonwood) that were used in the great house constructions. Plans by the builders to select specific species for structural timbers provide insights into the background and experiences of the building supervisors. For the Aztec West ruins, builders of the central core rooms took the most expensive route for procuring wood. Ponderosa pine, spruce-fir, and aspen were widely used in this construction (see Table 52.13), but as construction extended out from the core units, a switch to local resources occurred with the increased use of juniper (Brown et al. 2005). Special preparation of the structural elements and the use of nonlocal species indicates that the builders knew from prior experience the techniques and rules employed in construction at Chaco Canyon. Unfortunately, wood treatment observations for the Salmon sample are mostly lacking, but species use helps to compare the trends between the two great houses.

The central core units at Salmon also reveal special treatment noted by the extensive use of nonlocal woods in construction (see Table 52.13), although only about 61–65 percent was nonlocal, compared to 96 percent in the Aztec West core unit. How various species of wood were utilized in great house construction and the special treatment of the individual elements would not have been common knowledge to outsiders and would have been limited to those allowed access to the great house interior. The end treatment of many elements (see

Windes and McKenna 2001: Figure 4) would be hidden once placed in the walls, so these techniques required specialized knowledge likely limited to the builders and their supervisors.

Central core units at Salmon and Aztec West reflect high labor efforts in their selection of structural wood, and we know that this extra effort was expanded to the treatment of the individual elements at Aztec West. In both cases, specialists with the required construction knowledge appear to have directed the projects. These specialists must have received their training and experience in great house building projects in Chaco Canyon in slightly earlier structures because the techniques and use of wood replicates those of Chaco. The massive building efforts in Chaco (Lekson 1984: Figures 5.1 and 5.2) in the late AD 1000s would have required the most laborers and building supervisors of any period, but they would have become available for new construction projects just as planning for Salmon was under way. We expect that these experts would have moved on to other projects, much like the master builder groups that moved from project to project during the massive public building projects (mainly cathedrals) in medieval Europe (James 1982:49–63, 133–138; Rodwell 1981:127–127). Despite the site similarities between Salmon and Aztec West, the selection of tree species differs, which suggests that different leaders followed the accepted model of Chacoan great house construction but also incorporated personalized choices.

Symbolic Use of Wood

Species identifications determine potential harvest sources for much of the wood procured for construction at Salmon and many other great houses, and they provide detailed cultural preferences as indicated by the different groups involved in the many varied aspects of great house construction. Van Dyke (2004) has argued that during the construction of McElmo-style Chacoan great houses, which were built slightly later than Salmon, the horizontal dimensions and verticality within the cosmology of the Puebloan six sacred directions and the center place was reflected in the architectural design of the buildings in Chaco Canyon (see also Rapoport 1969:76). The rebirth and reformatting of Chacoan cosmology, according to Van Dyke (2004:426), was an effort to reestablish power and legitimacy among leaders and to connect with the glories of the past. At Salmon this may have been reflected in the duality of the centrally located, large elevated kiva (Tower Kiva, Room 64) along a north-south alignment with the lower great kiva (Room 130) in the plaza. Aside

from the positioning at the site, the use of specific wood species in the construction may also have enhanced the tie to the sacred and the profane. The unique use of fir from the cool, wet, and high locations for the elevated kiva roofing reflects the symbolism of the north, of the mountains, and of life-giving water. We do not know what wood species was used for the Chacoan-era great kiva superstructure—ponderosa pine is suspected—but its later reconstruction using Douglas fir and juniper provides the symbolic duality of timbers from the warm, dry, lower elevations which symbolize the mesa-and-plain country to the south. A spruce bark scale recovered from the Chacoan-era foot drum in the Great Kiva (K. Adams 1979:123, 157) may also reflect the symbolism of the use of high-altitude trees in the pantheon of rituals and cosmology connected with the kiva activities.

A similar architectural plan was devised at Aztec West, where a centrally located elevated kiva (Kiva L) with pilaster logs of ponderosa pine and a great kiva in the lower plaza were built slightly off a north-south alignment. The use of ponderosa pine for pilaster logs was unusual, although not unique, because juniper was usually favored for the practical purposes of rot resistance and strength density necessary to support the great weight of a cribbed roof as in Kiva L. We know nothing of the roofing element species employed in Kiva L and the great kiva at Aztec West because the burned materials were not saved. But the importance given to the kiva alignments at both sites is evident because they do not align within the overall symmetry of the building plan, which had followed the cardinal directions.

In historic Puebloan society, woods of ponderosa pine, pine, juniper, oak, spruce, and fir play important roles in dance and ceremony; participants may travel considerable distances to obtain these tree materials (Jones 1931:41; Robins et al. 1916:42–43; Whiting 1966:63). Spruce is tied to prayer sticks during rain ceremonies (White 1962:309) and is commonly used on masks, altars, and dancers (White 1962:253, Figure 35). Certain mountains and species of trees are important in representing the cardinal directions (Stevenson 1894:28, 124; White 1962:110–111). Ponderosa pine trees are cut at Zuni for use in kiva ceremonies (Stevenson 1904:516), whereas spruce or juniper trees were used in several shrines in the Jemez Mountain region (Douglass 1917:345–346, 358, 362–365). Douglas fir was the last to grow up through the various underworlds in the emergence myth at Santa Ana (Tyler 1991), imparting it with special significance, at least to one pueblo. Perhaps the choice of Douglas fir instead of ponderosa pine as the primary structural supports for the Secondary Great Kiva was a conscious effort to symbolize this connection between the underworld and their present world. Or the selection could have simply been based on convenience and the logistics of harvesting the closest stands of Douglas fir trees.

Fire Ecology

Although local resources could have provided some of the necessary timbers for construction, much of the wood must have come from higher elevations at some distance from the site. This premise is based on the suitable environments specific for the growth of different species encountered at the site and the extent of trees of different species observed within the region today. If high-altitude forest resources were indeed part of the harvesting strategy, then manipulation of this resource must be considered as a distinct possibility.

Fire is an important natural factor in the propagation of ponderosa pine (and aspen; Barnes 1975), a species that comprises a major component of the Salmon and Aztec structural wood. With fire comes an increased number of trees (Swetnam 1990; Touchan et al. 1996), which would be a desired commodity for great house builders. The forests used by the Salmon builders were likely in pristine condition because there were few residents in the area in the several centuries leading up to the construction at Salmon and other area great houses. They probably had access to a mixed-age forest that contained the narrow size ranges desired for roofing timber. These old stands should have had high variability in the ages among timbers cut of similar sizes.

Fire encourages rapid growth of thick stands of "dog-hair" saplings (Biswell et al. 1973), which would have been most optimum for harvesting large numbers of timbers from a very small area, resulting in a considerable savings in labor investment. We know that wildfire has been used by Native American groups (Arno 1985; Gruell 1985; Fish 1996:126–129; Savage and Swetnam 1990; Swetnam and Baisan 1996:29). Such fires may not have burned over large areas, however, and were "very site and time specific and not ubiquitous" (Swetnam and Baisan 1996:29). At this point, it would not be possible to distinguish natural fires from manmade ones, but given the organizational capabilities of great house builders, the potential strategy must be considered.

Lightning is the most common natural cause of fires in ponderosa forests, especially in the Southwest (Bahre 1991:124; Fish 1996:127; Swetnam and Baisan 1996:29). In this region, ponderosa pine, which is slow to regenerate (see Pearson 1950; Wright et al. 1973), relies on periodic fires to set the conditions for propagation. Before historic fire-suppression became standard, fires occurred within ponderosa pine forests every 5–20 years, setting the stage for seed crops to regenerate (Swetnam 1990; Zwolinski 1996; Weaver 1951). "An accurate picture of the presettlement ponderosa pine forest would most likely describe a mosaic of large, yellow-bark ponderosa pine, but also with a few dense patches and stringers of small, blackjack pines (young ponderosa pine)" (Dahns and Geils 1997:28). In spruce-fir forests that are relatively immune to the frequent fires common to ponderosa pine forests because of their growth at higher, wetter altitude, there may have been 100 years or more between large fires (Veblen et al. 1994). When they occurred, however, species regime change was common because of the fire's intense destruction.

DISCUSSION

Although all great house construction in Chaco Canyon and at Aztec and Salmon consumed large numbers of trees, the magnitude of the timber harvests provides relative scales for the respective labor requirements and organizational capabilities. The construction at Pueblo Bonito, which consumed about 25,000–50,000 trees (Windes and McKenna 2001:123), seems to have been the most demanding of the great house projects, but its construction was spread over many decades; Salmon's harvesting took place in a mere 3 years. The effort at Pueblo Bonito required harvesting efforts three to six times greater than at Salmon. Pueblo del Arroyo, with an equivalent number of rooms (approximately 239 rooms and three large kivas; Lekson 1984: Figure 66) to Salmon, although it is a smaller structure in terms of the basic plan, required between 6300 and 18,800 trees for its construction (Windes et al. 1994). Although the estimates are approximate, both Salmon and Pueblo del Arroyo required about the same numbers of trees. The higher number estimated at Pueblo del Arroyo results from the many door and ventilator lintels, which were not as numerous at Salmon. In the general plan, Salmon is similar to Aztec West (and Hungo Pavi in Chaco) and probably required about the same number of trees, although Salmon's harvests were dwarfed by the requirements needed for the three main Aztec great houses.

It is not difficult to understand the difference in strategies between the Chacoan and the later San Juan construction episodes: one was highly organized, and one was not. There was also an apparent shift in labor expertise at Salmon (and Aztec) after the initial core units were built. The core units appear to have been initially planned and constructed by skilled Chacoan crews who then turned to local builders for the remaining work. The differences in labor effort may rest upon the labor demands on the local populace and the size of the available workforce, although we cannot be sure that small experienced work crews could have been adequate to carry out the Chacoan construction demands (Lekson 1984; Windes and McKenna 2001). It is the nature of the initial great house construction, however, that merits closer scrutiny as to how the labor force was employed and how technical its capabilities were. The effort to obtain quantities of nonlocal wood implies the importance of certain tree species for construction, so the subsequent treatment of the wood during finishing was probably also highly technical and labor intensive. Although we know little of the actual wood finishing treatment at Salmon, this behavior is well documented in other great house constructions (Windes and McKenna 2001). Observations of the Salmon wood by Shelley (Chapter 47), the tree-ring laboratory, and the authors suggest that similar detailed and laborious work was conducted during the initial Salmon construction, although its magnitude is unknown.

It is more difficult to understand what happened to the structural wood at Salmon after its initial placement in the great house between the AD 1080s and AD 1095. Considerable scavenging for timbers was most likely conducted some time by or after about AD 1116, but the absence of tree-ring dates and the lack of detailed room histories at the site makes this process unclear. Recent work in Room 62 suggests that by AD 1118 some wood elements, which may have come from the initial Chacoan roofs, perhaps from the nearby living rooms, were being reused for repairs. A precedent at Pueblo Alto for the short life of living rooms was established when most were converted to other uses within a decade or two of their initial construction (Windes 1987a, 1987b), a period that overlaps the initial construction at Salmon. At Salmon, too, some initial living rooms enjoyed only a brief period of occupation before being converted to refuse dumps (Reed, Chapter 8).

The period when structural deterioration and roof scavenging began to be a major factor at Salmon coincides with the change in ceramic traditions and design elements noted by Franklin (Chapter 19; Irwin-Williams, Chapter 16) and Washburn (2005), when McElmo-period pottery became prominent. At Salmon, many rooms were subdivided and made into smaller rooms or small kivas, a process seen at other great houses (e.g., Pueblo Bonito, Chetro Ketl,

and Aztec West) that appears to mark the presence of small habitation groups staking out claims within a larger architectural complex. At Aztec West, Pueblo Alto, and Pueblo Bonito, distinct architectural units—essentially small houses—were built in groups within the plaza or next to the great house (see Windes 1987a: Figures 10.12–10.15, 2003). Similar units existed at Salmon in the 1100s and 1200s.

The late 1080s building effort at Salmon was extraordinary, but subsequent remodeling and construction were small-unit building efforts, less formalized in the procurement of materials, not requiring a large labor force, and more leisurely in their progress. Although there are no tree-ring dates from this period, which spans the AD 1100s and early AD 1200s during the McElmo Phase, as it is known elsewhere, the extremely poor environmental times probably forced scaled-back efforts and adaptive measures to deal with the harsh circumstances. Large construction efforts were not attempted again at the site until the Great Kiva was rebuilt at about AD 1264, suggesting some organizational shift in the local society. Did the Great Kiva serve only residents of Salmon in the AD 1200s or was it built for a larger, dispersed community?

At Aztec during the same period, construction efforts were less intense, but the drive to maintain Chacoan standards is seen in the construction of Aztec East through the AD 1100s and into the AD 1200s, an effort not duplicated at Salmon. The lack of dates at Salmon in the AD 1100s may reflect a shift to local procurement for trees that grew poorly during the AD 1100s drought and thus failed to provide dates. But there is little question that Salmon in the AD 1100s represented a large resource center, full of usable cultural materials, including roofing, that could be recycled by residents who lived there but who failed to maintain the original standards imposed during the initial construction and subsequent use of the structure. There was habitation continuity at Salmon, but the use of space and the residential organization were very different in the AD 1100s than they were in the late AD 1000s, which is reminiscent of the changes observed for Pueblo Bonito during the same periods (Windes 2003).

When interior room areas are compared between the Chacoan and later San Juan constructions, the lengthy, perhaps episodic San Juan occupations in the AD 1100s at Salmon provide contrasting organizational and building efforts. The Secondary construction of smaller rooms, perhaps taking place over a century or more, provided approximately 16 percent of the total Chacoan floor area and about one-third to half of the required trees needed for construction. Rather than organizing for harvesting new wood, with the exception of the rebuilt Great Kiva, many of the Secondary occupants reused timbers already at Salmon—a considerable savings in labor and an apt response by groups not as tightly integrated as the original builders.

Salmon is unmistakably a Chacoan great house. In the subtleties and details of its construction we can see how the architects and builders closely adhered to the traditions, standards, and craftsmanship of the great houses built earlier in Chaco Canyon. Many aspects of great house construction would have been well known to those in the region without their having participated in the actual planning and labor. The selection of trees for structural elements, for instance, would have required considerable presence throughout the region and beyond as work groups sought suitable wood materials. The subsequent placement and arrangement of these timbers along with the stem preparation would not have been common knowledge. Compared to the large contemporary settlement on the bluffs behind the Aztec ruins, Salmon appears to lack a similar large potential labor pool, which may have affected decisions regarding wood procurement and other construction strategies. But someone gathered thousands of tree stems for the Salmon work, and we can only guess the impact of roving gangs of foresters as they cleared out trees in areas used by groups not invested in the same motives that created the great houses. The local area around Salmon must have suffered considerable devastation from the loss of thousands of junipers—a species that takes a long time to regenerate along the margins of a conifer habitat. If fire was used to increase beam production, then concerns from neighboring groups may have increased and impacted the social dynamics of the region. Clearly, the size and nature of the small-house occupation in the region is germane to understanding the complicated tapestry of human interactions along the Middle San Juan region just prior to and during the settlement of Salmon.

Construction wood sampled from prehistoric and protohistoric sites along the various drainages and high country within the Salmon region suggests that the most likely areas of procurement for the builders at Salmon would have been along the Los Piños and San Juan Rivers and the associated higher elevations northeast near the borders of New Mexico and Colorado, a distance of approximately 60–80 km or more. Although isolated stands of ponderosa pine and Douglas fir were located closer to the site, these would have been inadequate to supply the needed thousands of beams.

Before the final third stories were added at Salmon, by AD 1095, the construction of Aztec North and the planning for Aztec West risked rivalry and conflict between competing groups for limited timber and other regional resources. The Aztec builders would have sought timbers closest to the construction from trees mostly to the northeast between the Animas and Los Piños Rivers in similar if not the same areas used by the Salmon crews. Potential conflict may have been resolved by the Aztec architects by the selection of thousands of aspen latillas, instead of young ponderosa pine, for the Aztec West roofs. Aspen would have been harvested in areas farther north than the potential conflict areas. The shift to greater use of local tree resources at Salmon after AD 1095 may have been a response to conflicts with Aztec timber resources, although groups at Aztec and Salmon switched to mostly juniper elements after AD 1130. The potential for conflict may have affected not only the immediate areas around Salmon Ruin and Aztec, but also areas farther north along the lower margins of major conifer stands in the New Mexico–Colorado border area to the northeast. We must locate the extent of the potential forest resource areas along the Colorado border to ask whether they could have supplied all the timbers for great houses in the region without serious depletion before we derive models of conflict.

For the most part, long, large-diameter, straight beams were not necessary in the construction of Salmon except for the primary, load-bearing roof beams in the larger rooms and kivas. Local mountain juniper stems were probably sufficient for construction needs at both Salmon and Aztec. Juniper, tougher to cut and prepare than other conifers, provides only a single roofing element per stem. With local trees suitable for construction needs, the desire to import trees from long distances involves factors beyond mere practicality. The use of imported trees at Chaco Canyon was by necessity, but it probably was also imbued with symbolism that became embedded over time as one of the standards for great house construction. The logistics and effort to procure great numbers of nonlocal trees demanded massive organizational capabilities and human labor. The timing of the harvests must fit with other crucial demands imposed by a horticultural life. The different procurement strategies for Salmon and Aztec West reveal different variations on a Chacoan theme. These were carried out by groups skilled in the nuances of great house planning and construction.

The choice of wood distinguishes the Salmon and Aztec constructions. Both architects and builders could mostly rely on local tree resources, but planners and workers made choices that indicate different philosophies for procuring materials. Although the impact of a potential small labor force at Salmon compared to labor resources at Aztec may have forced different procurement strategies or the somewhat greater distances required to obtain wood for Salmon than for Aztec may have affected their strategies, these problems failed to deter procurement from at least 80 km away for building materials used in downtown Chaco. We know that much nonlocal timber was gathered for Salmon, although if the work force was small, they might have sought to reduce long-distance demands. A large settlement does not appear to have been present at Salmon prior to construction, leaving local tree resources relatively unimpaired by previous harvesting. We argue that the different emphasis at Salmon and Aztec West for the procurement of nonlocal trees (see Table 52.13) was invested in the leadership that designed and carried out the actual great house constructions. At both Salmon and Aztec West, the core units reflect knowledge and experience gained from work in Chaco Canyon of the proper standards for the use of structural wood, but its application differed between the two sites. After the core constructions, the greater use of local materials suggests that local labor forces were increasingly involved in the actual construction of both great houses and that less strict standards were applied.

Labor efforts between local and nonlocal preferences appear clearly differentiated between the Chacoan and later San Juan–Mesa Verdean construction episodes at Salmon and between the Aztec East and West Ruins. The late constructions employed almost exclusively juniper, which if procured locally would have dramatically decreased the labor efforts when compared to the initial construction. At Aztec, the overwhelming use of nonlocal species in the West Ruin is confirmation of the logistical capabilities and efforts sustained during the overall building enterprise, although some local materials were procured after the core units were completed. The dichotomy between local and nonlocal efforts is less clear at Salmon, although it parallels Aztec West in its adherence to the extensive labor investments for the core room units. Afterward, as the wing roomblocks were built, the extensive labor investments tapered off with an increased use of local wood.

Much of the evidence from Salmon suggests a progression of site use similar to that observed at Aztec Ruins (Brown et al. 2005). The initial construction was a massive effort, requiring a high level of organization and probably a substantial labor pool

that was mobilized for a relatively short period of time. Tree harvesting for roofing and wall apertures suggests that this mobilization took place between AD 1088 and 1090, with a secondary effort between AD 1094 and 1095 to place a third story above several rooms along the back room tiers to either side of the elevated kiva. It may have taken longer, of course, to lay out the general plan of the great house, to set foundations, and to build the lower masonry walls of the first-story rooms at least to the level of room-wide platforms or level with the tops of the doorways before any wooden structural elements were needed to be embedded within the masonry. Both sites contain small cobble rooms (along the south arc at Aztec West and in the Salmon plaza) that were late residences, but these units may have been builders' quarters during the initial great house constructions. A labor force had to be housed somewhere, and if there was little small-house development around Salmon, then identifying the potential workers' quarters would enhance our understanding of the size of the group mobilized for this massive construction effort.

Finally, although it is possible that small groups of residents from Salmon eventually migrated to found the Aztec West Ruin (Lekson 1999:137; Stein and McKenna 1988), or moved to Aztec West after AD 1115 and renovated it (Reed 2002:7), or built the Aztec East Ruin (Reed, Chapter 8), the timing and wood construction philosophies employed at the two great houses argue against it. If any of the three great houses had been planned and built by the same group, then we might expect a much higher degree of similarity in construction. It is important to note that the design and footings for Aztec West were probably prepared less than a half decade after the third-story additions made to Salmon in AD 1095 or slightly later—not much time for the same planners and builders to move on to Aztec to implement the construction of another great house. It is not clear, however, if those who designed and built the great houses were the same people who resided in or used them. The high degree of planning and craft specialization necessary to the task implies that they were not.

Acknowledgments

No research about Salmon can be conducted without giving special thanks to the efforts produced by the Salmon field staff. Several chapters in the final report to the funding agencies that are reproduced in this three volume new final report provided lengthy, detailed information about wood use at Salmon Ruin and other relevant data (see K. Adams, Chapter 40;

R. Adams 1980a; Shelley, Chapter 47) without which this report would not have been possible. It is our great honor to have followed in their ground-breaking footsteps. We especially appreciate the invitation by Paul Reed to participate in the Salmon Reinvestment Project and report, and to continue our wood studies at Salmon. I also wish to thank the several volunteers who helped document and sample the remaining wood in Salmon between 2002 and 2003. These are Jamie Schubert (CA), Margaret Kaiser (MD), Eileen Bacha (OH), and Gretchen Jordan (CO), who have helped with many a wood project and brought a wealth of experience and good humor to their tasks. Also our thanks to Nancy Espinosa, Salmon's curator, for her help at Salmon. My very special thanks, again, to Eileen Bacha, who compiled the wood data base for Salmon and ran all the statistics and graphs. Also thanks to Beth Bagwell, who lent much of her field equipment for the wood sampling and Paul Reed who has made this all happen and who answered many an inquiry regarding the field data. Larry Baker, director of the Salmon Ruins Museum, gave wholehearted permission for our field work and has also been a great friend and supporter of the project—our deepest thanks. Thanks to the Laboratory of Tree-ring Research staff for discussions and help about the Salmon wood, particularly Rex Adams, Richard Warren, and Ron Towner. Finally, our appreciation to Beth Bagwell and Chris Millington of the University of New Mexico for their graphics assistance.

REFERENCES CITED

Aasen, Diane K.
  1984   *Pollen, Macrofossil, and Charcoal Analyses of Basketmaker Coprolites from Turkey Pen Ruin, Cedar Mesa, Utah.* Master's thesis, Department of Anthropology, Washington State University, Pullman.

Adams, Charles E., and Charla Hedberg
  2002   Driftwood Use at Homol'ovi and Implications for Interpreting the Archaeological Record. *Kiva* 67(4):363–384.

Adams, Karen R.
  1976   Floristic Composition of the San Juan Drainage, Northwestern New Mexico. Ms. on file, Salmon Ruins Museum Library, Bloomfield, New Mexico.

  1979   Pines and Other Conifers from Salmon Ruin, Northwestern New Mexico: Their Identification and Former Role in the Lives of the Ancient People. Ms. on file, Salmon Ruins Museum Library, Bloomfield, New Mexico.

  1980   *Pollen, Parched Seeds, and Prehistory: A Pilot Investigation of Prehistoric Plant Remains from Salmon Ruin, a Chacoan Pueblo in Northwestern New Mexico.* Contributions in Anthropology 9. Eastern New Mexico University, Portales.

  1984   Evidence of Wood Dwelling Termites in Archaeological Sites in the Southwestern United States. *Journal of Ethnobiology* 4(1):29–43.

  2005   Subsistence and Plant Use Among the Chacoan and Secondary Occupations at Salmon Ruin. In *Salmon Ruins: Chacoan Outlier and Thirteenth-Century Pueblo in the Middle San Juan Region*, edited by P. F. Reed. Ms. in review, University of Utah Press, Salt Lake City.

Adams, K. R. and V. L. Bohrer
  1998   Archaeobotanical Indicators of Seasonality: Examples from Arid Southwestern United States. In *Seasonality and Sedentism: Archaeological Perspectives from Old and New World Sites*, edited by T. R. Rocek and O. Bar-Yosef, pp. 129–141. Peabody Museum Bulletin 6. Harvard University, Cambridge.

Adams, Karen R., and Vandy E. Bowyer
  2002   Sustainable Landscape: Thirteenth-Century Food and Fuel Use in the Sand Canyon Locality. In *Seeking the Center Place: Archaeology and Ancient Communities in the Mesa Verde Region*, edited by M. D. Varien and R. H. Wilshusen, pp. 123–142. University of Utah Press, Salt Lake City.

Adams, R. K.
  1976   Excavations at the Salmon Ruin: 1976. In *The San Juan Valley Archaeological Program, 1976*, edited by C. Irwin-Williams, pp. 41–86. Ms. on file, Salmon Ruins Library, Bloomfield, New Mexico.

  1980a   Salmon Ruin: Site Chronology and Formation Processes. In *Investigations at the Salmon Site: The Structure of Chacoan Society in the Northern Southwest*, vol. 1, edited by C. Irwin-Williams and P. Shelley, pp. 197–294. Unpublished report submitted to funding agencies. On file, Salmon Ruins Library, Bloomfield, New Mexico.

  1980b   *Debitage Analysis: Lithic Technology and Interpretations of an Archaic Base Camp Near Moquino, New Mexico.* Master's thesis, Department of Anthropology, Eastern New Mexico University, Portales.

Adovasio, J. M.
  1977   *Basketry Technology.* Aldine, Chicago.

Adovasio, J. M., and J. D. Gunn
  1986   The Antelope House Basketry Industry. In *Archeological Investigations at Antelope House*, compiled by D. P. Morris, pp. 306–397. National Park Service, Washington D.C.

Ahlstrom, Richard V.
  1985   *The Interpretation of Archaeological Tree-Ring Dates.* Ph.D. dissertation, Department of Anthropology, University of Arizona, Tucson. University Microfilms International, Ann Arbor.

Ahlstrom, Richard V. N., Jeffrey S. Dean, and William J. Robinson
  1978   *Tree-Ring Studies of Walpi Pueblo.* Final report prepared for the Heritage Conservation and Recreation Service, Interagency Archaeological Services, San Francisco, Contract CX-8880-7-0001. Laboratory of Tree-Ring Research, University of Arizona, Tucson.

Akins, Nancy J.
  1985   Prehistoric Faunal Utilization in Chaco Canyon: Basketmaker III Through Pueblo III. In *Environment and Subsistence of Chaco Canyon*, edited by F. J. Mathien, pp. 305–445. Publications in Archeology 18E. National Park Service, Santa Fe.

  1987   Faunal Remains from Pueblo Alto. In *Investigations at the Pueblo Alto Complex, Chaco Canyon*, vol. III (2), edited by F. J. Mathien and T. C. Windes, pp. 445–649. Publications in Archeology 18F. National Park Service, Santa Fe.

  2005   Human Remains Recovered from the Tower Kiva at Salmon Ruins. In *Salmon Ruins: Chacoan Outlier and Thirteenth-Century Pueblo in the Middle San Juan Region*, edited by P. F. Reed. Ms. in review, University of Utah Press, Salt Lake City.

Allen, T. F. H., and H. H. Iltis
	1980	Overconnected Collapse to Higher Levels: Urban and Agricultural Origins: A Case Study. In *Systems Science and Science*, edited by B.H. Banathy. Society for General Systems Research, Systems Science Institute, Louisville, Kentucky.

Altschul, Jeffrey. H.
	1978	The Development of the Chacoan Interaction Sphere. *Journal of Anthropological Research* 34:109–146.

Altschul, Siri von Reis
	1973	*Drugs and Foods from Little-Known Plants.* Notes in Harvard University Herbaria. Harvard University Press, Cambridge.

Appel, J.
	1979	Lithic Production in the Valley of Oaxaca, Mexico. Paper presented at the 44th annual meeting of the Society for American Archaeology, Vancouver, British Columbia, April 1979.

Armelagos, George J.
	1994	You Are What You Eat: Paleonutrition. In *The Diet and Health of Prehistoric Populations*, edited by K. D. Sobolik, pp. 232–241. Center for Archaeological Investigations Occasional Paper 22. Southern Illinois University, Carbondale.

Arno, S. F.
	1985	Ecological Effects and Management Implications of Indian Fires. *Proceedings of a Symposium and Workshop on Wilderness Fire*, 1983, Missoula, MO, pp. 81–86. General Technical Report INT-182. Intermountain Research Station, USDA, Forest Service, Ogden, Utah.

Aspinall, A., and S. W. Feather
	1972	Neutron Activation Analysis of Prehistoric Flint Mine Products. *Archaeometry* 58:453–455.

Atwood, W. W., and K. F. Mather
	1932	*Physiography and Quaternary Geology of the San Juan Mountains, Colorado.* USGS Professional Paper 166. U.S. Geological Survey, Washington D.C.

Ayers, H. G.
	1978	The Geology of Cherts: A Geoarchaeologist's View. Paper presented at the annual meeting of the Society for American Archaeology, Tucson, May 1978.

Bahre, Conrad J.
	1991	*A Legacy of Change: Historic Human Impact on Vegetation in the Arizona Borderlands.* University of Arizona Press, Tucson.

Bailey, F. L.
	1940	Navajo Foods and Cooking Methods. *American Anthropologist* 42(2):270–290.

Bailey, V.
	1932	*Mammals of New Mexico.* North American Fauna 53. USDA Division of Biological Survey, Washington D.C.

Baker, F.
	1968	*A Brief History of the Precambrian Rocks of the Needle Mountains, Southwestern Colorado.* New Mexico Geological Society Guidebook, Nineteenth Field Conference.

Baker, Larry L.
	2005	Salmon Ruins: Architecture and Development of a Chacoan Satellite on the San Juan River. In *Salmon Ruins: Chacoan Outlier and Thirteenth-Century Pueblo in the Middle San Juan Region*, edited by P. F. Reed. Ms. in review, University of Utah Press, Salt Lake City.

Baker, Larry L., and Kurt T. Mantonya
	2002	The Archaeoastronomy of Salmon Ruins. Paper presented at the 67th annual meeting of the Society for American Archaeology, Denver, Colorado.

Bandoian, C. A.
	1968	*Fluvioglacial Features of the Animas River Valley, Colorado and New Mexico.* New Mexico Geological Society Guidebook, Nineteenth Field Conference.

Bannister, B.
	1964	*Tree-Ring Dating of the Archaeological Sites in the Chaco Canyon Region, New Mexico.* Technical Series 6(2). Southwest Monuments Association, Globe, Arizona.

Barclay, A. D., and F. R. Earle
	1974	Chemical Analyses of Seeds III. Oil and Protein Content of 1253 Species. *Economic Bounty* 28(2):178–236.

Barnes, Burton V.
	1975	Phenotype Variation of Trembling Aspen in Western North America. *Forestry Science* 21:319–328.

Bartlett, K.
	1933	Pueblo Milling Stones of the Flagstaff Region and Their Relation to Others in the Southwest. *Museum of Northern Arizona Bulletin 3*. Flagstaff.

Basso, H. K.
	1969	*Western Apache Witchcraft.* University of Arizona Press, Tucson.

Bates and Lee
	1977	The Role of Exchange in Production Specialization. *American Anthropologist.* 79:824–841.

Beadle, G. W.
1939   Teosinte and the Origin of Maize. *Journal of Heredity* 30:245–257.

1972   The Mystery of Maize. *Field Museum of Natural History Bulletin* 43(10):2–11.

1980   The Ancestry of Corn. *Scientific American* 242(1):112–119.

Beaglehole, Ernest
1936   *Hopi Hunting and Hunting Ritual.* Publications in Anthropology 4. Yale University Press, New Haven, Connecticut.

Beaglehole, Pearl
1937   Foods and Their Preparation. In *Notes on Hopi Economic Life*, by E. Beaglehole, pp. 60–71. Publications in Anthropology 15. Yale University Press, New Haven, Connecticut.

Beezley, J. A.
1975   Faunal Analysis of the Salmon Site, LA 8846, San Juan Valley, New Mexico. Ms. on file, Salmon Ruins Library, Bloomfield, New Mexico.

Bell, W. H., and E. F. Castetter
1941   *The Utilization of Yucca, Sotol, and Beargrass by the Aborigines in the American Southwest.* UNM Bulletin Biological Series 5(5):1–74. University of New Mexico, Albuquerque.

Bennett, Joanne L.
1999   Thermal Alteration of Buried Bone. *Journal of Archaeological Science* 26:1–8.

Benson, L., and R. A. Darrow
1954   *The Trees and Shrubs of the Southwestern Deserts.* 2nd ed. University of New Mexico Press, Albuquerque.

Berry, Michael S.
1982   *Time, Space and Transition in Anasazi Prehistory* University of Utah Press, Salt Lake City.

Betancourt, Julio L.
1984   Late Quaternary Plant Zonation and Climate in Southeastern Utah. *The Great Basin Naturalist* 44(1):1–35.

Betancourt, J. L., and T. R. Van Devender
1981   Holocene Vegetation in Chaco Canyon, New Mexico. *Science* 214:656–658.

Bice, Richard A.
1983   The Sterling Site – An Initial Report. In *Collected Papers in Honor of Charlie R. Steen*, edited by N. L. Fox, pp. 49–86. Papers of the Archaeological Society of New Mexico 8. Albuquerque Archaeological Society Press.

Bird, R. McK.
1980   Maize Evolution from 500 BC to the Present. *Biotropica* 12(1):30–41.

Bird, R. McK., and J. B. Bird
1980   Gallinazo Maize from the Chicama Valley, Peru. *American Anthropologist* 45(2):325–332.

Biswell, Harold H., Harry K. Kallander, Roy Komarek, Richard J. Vogt, and Harold Weaver
1973   *Ponderosa Pine Fire Management.* Miscellaneous Publications 2. Tall Timbers Research Station, Tallahassee, Florida.

Bohrer, V. L.
1962   Nature and Interpretation of Ethnobotanical Materials from Tonto National Monument. In *Archaeological Studies At Tonto National Monument, Arizona*, by C. R. Steen, L. M. Pierson, V. L. Bohrer, and K. P. Kent, pp. 80–114. Technical Series 2. Southwest Monuments Association, Globe, Arizona.

1966   *Pollen Analysis of the Hay Hollow Site East of Snowflake, Arizona.* Interim Research Report 12. Geochronology Laboratories, University of Arizona, Tucson.

1970   Ethnobotanical Aspects of Snaketown, a Hohokam Village in Southern Arizona. *American Antiquity* 35:413–430.

1972a   *Paleoecology of the Hay Hollow Site, Arizona.* Fieldiana Anthropology 63(1). Field Museum of Natural History, Chicago.

1972b   The Diffusion and Utilization of Cotton North of Mexico. Ms. prepared for Handbook of North American Indiana, vol. 3, Environment, Origins, and Population, edited by R. I. Ford (book was never published).

1973a   Tularosa Valley Project: Tentative List of Utilized Plant Remains from Fresnal Shelter. In *Human Systems Research Technical Manual, 1973 Survey of the Tularosa Basin*, pp. 211–218. U.S. Department of the Army, White Sands Missile Range, New Mexico.

1973b   Ethnobotany of Point of Pines Ruin, Arizona, W:10:50. *Economic Botany* 27(4):423–437.

1975a   The Prehistoric and Historic Role of Cool-Season Grasses in the Southwest. *Economic Botany* 29(3):199–207.

1975b   The Role of Seasonality in the Annual Harvest of Native Food Plants in the Puerco Valley, Northwest of Albuquerque, New Mexico. Abstract. *New Mexico Academy of Science Bulletin* 15(2):3.

1978   Plants that Have Become Locally Extinct in the Southwest. *New Mexico Journal of Science* 18(2):10–19.

1981   Methods of Recognizing Cultural Activity from Pollen in Archaeological Sites. *Kiva* 46:135–142.

1986   The Ethnobotanical Pollen Record at Arroyo Hondo Pueblo, Additional Report I. In *Food, Diet, and Population at Prehistoric Arroyo Hondo Pueblo, New Mexico*, by W. Wetterstrom, pp. 187–250. School of American Research Press, Santa Fe.

Bohrer, V. L., and K. R. Adams
    1976   Guide to Learning Prehistoric Seed Remains from Salmon Ruin, Bloomfield, New Mexico. Ms. on file, Salmon Ruins Museum Library, Bloomfield, New Mexico.

    1977   *Ethnobotanical Techniques and Approaches at Salmon Ruin, New Mexico.* Contributions in Anthropology 8(1). Eastern New Mexico University, Portales.

Bohrer, V. L., H. C. Cutler, and J. D. Sauer
    1969   Carbonized Plant Remains from Two Hohokam Sites, Arizona BB:13:41 and Arizona BB:13:50. *The Kiva* 35:1–10.

Bradley, Bruce A.
    1988   Wallace Ruin Interim Report. *Southwestern Lore* 54(2):8–33.

    1996   Pitchers to Mugs: Chacoan Revival at Sand Canyon Pueblo. *Kiva* 61:241–256.

    2004   Wallace Ruin and Chacoan Missions. In *Chimney Rock: The Ultimate Outlier*, edited by J. M. Malville, pp. 115–112. Lexington Books, Lanham, Maryland.

Bradley, Z. A.
    1959   Site BC-236, Chaco Canyon. Ms. on file, National Park Service, Globe, Arizona.

Brand, Donald D., Florence Hawley Ellis, and Frank C. Hibben
    1937   *Tseh So, A Small House Ruin, Chaco Canyon, New Mexico.* UNM Bulletin 308, Anthropological Series 2(2). University of New Mexico Press, Albuquerque.

Breternitz, Cory D.
    1976   An analysis of axes and mauls from Chaco Canyon, New Mexico. Ms.on file, Chaco Center, National Park Service, Albuquerque, New Mexico.

    1997   An Analysis of Axes and Mauls from Chaco Canyon, New Mexico. In *Ceramics, Lithics, and Ornaments of Chaco Canyon: Analyses of Artifacts from the Chaco Project 1971–1978*, vol. II, edited by F. J. Mathien, pp. 977–996. Publications in Archeology 18G. National Park Service, Santa Fe.

Breternitz, D. A.
    1960   Orme Ranch Cave, NA6656. *Plateau* 33(2):25–39.

Breternitz, David A., Arthur H. Rohn, Jr., and Elizabeth A. Morris
    1974   *Prehistoric Ceramics of the Mesa Verde Region.* Museum of Northern Arizona Ceramic Series 5. Northern Arizona Society of Science and Art, Flagstaff.

Briuer, F. L.
    1976   New Clues to Stone Tool Functions: Plant and Animal Residues. *American Antiquity* 10:160–160.

Brown, Gary M., Thomas C. Windes, and Peter J. McKenna
    2005   Animas Anamnesis: Aztec Ruins, or Anasazi Capitol? In *Salmon Ruins: Chacoan Outlier and Thirteenth-Century Pueblo in the Middle San Juan Region*, edited by Paul F. Reed. Ms. in review, University of Utah Press, Salt Lake City.

Bryant, Vaughn M., Jr., and Don P. Morris
    1986   Uses of Ceramic Vessels and Grinding Implements: The Pollen Evidence. In *Archeological Investigations at Antelope House*, edited by D. P. Morris, pp. 489–500. National Park Service Publications in Archaeology 19. U.S. Government Printing Office, Washington D.C.

Bryson, R. A.
    1980   Ancient Climes on the Great Plains. *Natural History* 89:65–73, 87.

Bunzel, R. L.
    1929   *The Pueblo Potter: A Study of Creative Imagination in Primitive Art.* Columbia University Contributions to Anthropology 8. New York.

    1932   Introduction to Zuni Ceremonialism. In *Forty-Seventh Annual Report of the Bureau of American Ethnology, 1929–30*, pp. 467–544. Smithsonian Institution, Washington D.C.

Burgess-Terrel, M. E.
    1979   *A Study of Cucurbita Material from Salmon Ruin, New Mexico.* Master's thesis, Department of Anthropology, Eastern New Mexico University, Portales.

Cahen, D., L. H. Keeley, and F. L. Van Noten
    1979   Stone Tools, Toolkits, and Human Behavior in Prehistory. *Current Anthropology* 20(4):661–672.

Callahan, E.
    1976   *The Old Rag Report: A Practical Guide to Living Archaeology.* Department of Sociology and Anthropology, Virginia Commonwealth University, Richmond.

Cameron, Catherine M.
    2005   Exploring Archaeological Cultures in the Northern Southwest: What Were Chaco and Mesa Verde? *Kiva* 70:227–253.

Cameron, Catherine M., William E. Davis, and Stephen H. Lekson
    1997   1996 Excavations at the Buff Great House. University of Colorado, Boulder; and Southwest Heritage Foundation and Abajo Archaeology, Bluff, Utah. Ms. on file, Department of Anthropology, University of Colorado, Boulder.

Cameron, Judi L.
1995   *Sociopolitical and Economic Roles of Faunal Resources in the Prehistory of the Tonto Basin, Arizona.* Unpublished Ph.D. dissertation, Department of Anthropology, Arizona State University, Tempe.

Casteel, R. W.
1976   Comparison of Column and Whole Unit Samples for Recovering Fish Remains. *World Archaeology* 8:192–198.

Castetter, E. F.
1935   Ethnobiological studies in the American Southwest I: Uncultivated native plants used as sources of food. University of New Mexico Bulletin, Biological Series 4(1).

Castetter, E. F., and W. H. Bell
1942   *Pima and Papago Indian Agriculture.* University of New Mexico Press, Albuquerque.

1951   *Yuman Indian Agriculture.* University of New Mexico Press, Albuquerque.

Castetter, E. F., and M. E. Opler
1936   Ethnobiological Studies in the American Southwest III. "The Ethnobiology of the Chiricahua and Mescalero Apache." *University of New Mexico Bulletin* Whole Number 297, *Biological Series* 4(5).

Castetter, E. F., and R. M. Underhill
1935   The ethnobiology of the Papago Indians. *University of New Mexico Bulletin, Biological Series* 4(3):1–83.

Chamberlin, Ralph V.
1911   *The Ethno-Botany of the Gosiute Indians of Utah.* Memoirs of the American Anthropological Association 2(5):331–405.

Chang, Y. P.
1954   Bark structure of North American conifers. *U.S. Department of Agriculture Technical Bulletin*, No. 1095.

Chernela, Janet M., and Vernon E. Thatcher
1989   Comparison of Parasite Burden in Two Native Populations. *Medical Anthropology* 10:279–285.

Chisholm, M.
1968   *Rural Settlement and Land Use.* Hutchison, London.

Clark, J. R.
1979   Measuring the Flow of Goods with Archaeological Data. *Economic Geography* 55(1):1–17.

Claus, E. P., V. E. Tyler, and L. R.Brady
1970   Pharmacognosy, 6th ed. Lea and Febiger, Philadelphia.

Clouse, R. A.
1977   Wear Patterns, Scanning Electron Microscopy, X-rays, and Amino Acid Residue Analysis for Determining Tool Function. Paper presented at the Lithic Use-Wear Conference, March 1977, Burnaby, British Columbia.

Colton, Mary-Russell
1933   Hopi Courtship and Marriage. *Museum Notes* 5(9). Museum of Northern Arizona, Flagstaff.

Connelly, J. C.
1979   Hopi Social Organization. In *Handbook of North American Indians, the Southwest, Volume 9*, edited by A. Otiz, pp. 539–553. Smithsonian Institution, Washington, D.C.

Conover, W. J.
1971   *Practical Nonparametric Statistics.* Wiley, New York.

Cook, S. F.
1967   *Teitipac and Its Metateros: An Economic Anthropological Study of Production and Exchange in a "Peasant-Artisan" Economy in the Valley of Oaxaca, Mexico.* Ph.D. dissertation, University of Pittsburgh. University Microfilms, Ann Arbor.

Cook, Sarah Louise
1930   The Ethnobotany of Jemez Indians. Unpublished MA thesis, University of New Mexico, Albuquerque. 30 Pages.

Cordell, Linda S.
1975   Predicting Site Abandonment at Wetherill Mesa. *The Kiva* 40:189–202.

Correll, D. S., and M. C. Johnston
1969   *Manual of the Vascular Plants of Texas.* Texas Research Foundation

Cosgrove, C. Burton
1947   *Caves of the Upper Gila and Hueco Areas in New Mexico and Texas.* Papers of the Peabody Museum of American Archaeology and Ethnology 24(2). Harvard University, Cambridge.

Cowan, R. A.
1967   Lake-Margin Ecologic Exploitation in the Great Basin as Demonstrated by an Analysis of Coprolites from Lovelock Cave, Nevada. *Papers on Great Basin Archaeology, Reports of the University of California Archaeological Survey* 70:21–35.

Crabtree, D. E.
1972   *An Introduction to Flintworking.* Occasional Papers 28. Idaho State University Museum, Pocatello, Idaho.

Curtin, L. S. M.
1947   *Healing Herbs of the Upper Rio Grande.* Laboratory of Anthropology, Santa Fe.

Cushing, F. H.
    1886   A Study of Pueblo Pottery as Illustrative of Zuni Culture Growth. In *Fourth Annual Report of the Bureau of American Ethnology, 1882–83*, by J. W. Powell, pp. 467–521. Smithsonian Institution, Washington D.C.

    1920   *Zuni Breadstuff.* Indian Notes and Monographs 8. Museum of the American Indian, Heye Foundation, New York.

Cutler, H. C.
    1952   A Preliminary Survey of Plant Remains of Tularosa Cave. In *Mogollon Cultural Continuity and Change. The Stratigraphic Analysis of Tularosa and Cordova Caves*, by P. S. Martin, J. B. Rinaldo, E. Bluhm, H. C. Cutler, and R. Grange, Jr., pp. 461–479. Fieldiana: Anthropology 40. Field Museum of Natural History, Chicago.

    1956   The Plant Remains. In *Higgins Flat Pueblo, Western New Mexico*, by P. S. Martin, J. B. Rinaldo, E. Bluhm, and H. C. Cutler, pp. 174–183. Fieldiana: Anthropology 45(1). Field Museum of Natural History, Chicago.

    1964   Appendix A. Plant Remains from the Carter Ranch Site. In *Chapters in the Prehistory of Eastern Arizona II*, by P. S. Martin, J. B. Rinaldo, W. A. Longacre, L. G. Freeman, Jr., J. A. Brown, R. H. Hevly, and M. E. Cooley, pp. 227–234. Fieldiana: Anthropology 55. Field Museum of Natural History, Chicago.

    1966   *Corn, Cucurbits, and Cotton from Glen Canyon.* University of Utah Anthropological Papers 80. University of Utah Press, Salt Lake City.

Cutler, H. C., and W. Meyer
    1965   Corn and Cucurbits from Wetherill Mesa. *American Antiquity* 31(2):136–152

Cutler, H. C., and T. W. Whitaker
    1961   History and Distribution of the Cultivated Cucurbits in the Americas. *American Antiquity* 26(4):469–485.

Dalton, G.
    1975   Karl Polanyi's Analysis of Long-Distance Trade and His Wider Paradigm. In *Ancient Civilizations and Trade*, edited by J. A. Sabloff and C. C. Lamberg-Karlovsky, pp. 133–154. University of New Mexico Press, Albuquerque.

Daniels, Helen Sloan
    1940   *Durango Public Library Museum Project of the Archaeological Department.* Durango Public Library, Colorado.

Danielson, Dennis R.
    1993   *The Role of Phytoliths in Prehistoric Diet Reconstruction and Dental Attrition.* Master's thesis, Department of Anthropology, University of Nebraska–Lincoln.

Danielson Dennis R., and Karl J. Reinhard
    1998   Human Dental Microwear Caused by Calcium Oxalate Phytoliths in Prehistoric Diet of the Lower Pecos Region, Texas. *American Journal of Physical Anthropolology* 107:297–304.

Darlington, C. D.
    1956   *Chromosome Botany.* Allen and Unwin, London.

Daubenmire, R. F.
    1943   Vegetational Zonation in the Rocky Mountains. *Botanical Review* 9(6):325–393.

Dean, Jeffrey S., and Gary Funkhouser
    2002   Dendroclimatology and Fluvial Chronology in Chaco Canyon. In *Relation of "Bonito" Paleo-Channels and Base-Level Variations to Anasazi Occupation, Chaco Canyon, New Mexico*, by E. R. Force, R. G. Vivian, T. C. Windes, and J. S. Dean, pp. 39–41. Archaeological Series 194. Arizona State Museum, University of Arizona, Tucson.

Dean, Jeffrey S., and William J. Robinson
    1977   Dendroclimatic Variability in the American Southwest A.D. 680 to 1970. Laboratory of Tree–Ring Research, University of Arizona, Tucson. Final report to the National Park Service, Southwest Paleoclimate Contract CX–1595-5-0241.

Dean, Jeffrey S., and Richard Warren
    1983   Dendrochronology. In *The Architecture and Dendrochronology of Chetro Ketl, Chaco Canyon, New Mexico*, edited by S. H. Lekson, pp. 105–240. Reports of the Chaco Center 6. Division of Cultural Research, National Park Service, Albuquerque.

DeWet, J. M. J., and J. R. Harlan
    1972   Origin of Maize: The Tripartite Hypothesis. *Euphytica* 21:271–279.

Dittert, Alfred E. Jr., Jim J. Hester, and Frank W. Eddy
    1961   *An Archaeological Survey of the Navajo Reservoir District, Northwestern New Mexico.* Monograph 23. School of the American Research and the Museum of New Mexico, Santa Fe.

Dodd, W. A., Jr.
    1979   The Wear and Use of Battered Tools at Armijo Rockshelter. In *Lithic Use-Wear Analysis*, edited by B. Hayden, pp. 231–242. Academic Press, New York.

Doebley, J. F.
    1976   *A Preliminary Study of Wild Plant Remains Recovered by Flotation at Salmon Ruin, New Mexico.* Master's thesis, Department of Anthropology, Eastern New Mexico University, Portales.

    1981   Plant Remains Recovered by Flotation from Trash at Salmon Ruin, New Mexico. *The Kiva* 46(3):169–187.

Doebley, J. F., and V. L. Bohrer
    1983   Maize Variability and Cultural Selection at Salmon Ruin. *The Kiva* 49:19–37.

Doebley, J. F., and H. H. Iltis
1980   Taxonomy of *Zea* (Gramineae). I. A Subgeneric Classification with Key to Taxa. *American Journal of Botany* 67:982–993.

Dorsey-Vinton, Sheila
1997   *Dietary Analysis of Coprolites from the Lluta Valley of Arica, Chile.* Master's thesis, Department of Anthropology, University of Nebraska-Lincoln.

Douglass, William Boone
1917   Notes on the Shrines of the Tewa and Other Pueblo Indians of New Mexico. *Proceedings of the Nineteenth International Congress of Americanists*, by F. W. Hodge, pp. 344–378. Washington D.C.

Durand, Kathy R.
2003   Function of Chaco-Era Great Houses. *Kiva* 69:141–169.

Durand, Kathy R., and Stephen R. Durand
2002   A Closer Look at the Guadalupe Ruin Great House Community. Poster presented at the 67th annual meeting of the Society for American Archaeology, Denver, Colorado, March 2002.

2005   Faunal Exploitation in the Chacoan World. In *Salmon Ruins: Chacoan Outlier and Thirteenth-Century Pueblo in the Middle San Juan Region*, edited by P. F. Reed. Ms. in review, University of Utah Press, Salt Lake City.

Durand, Stephen R., Phillip H. Shelly, Ronald C. Antweiler, and Howard E. Taylor
1999   Trees, Chemistry, and Prehistory in the American Southwest. *Journal of Archaeological Science* 26:185–203.

Dutton, B. P.
1938   *Leyit Kin, A Small House Ruin, Chaco Canyon, New Mexico, Excavation Report.* UNM and School of American Research Monograph 1(6). University of New Mexico Press, Albuquerque.

1963   *Sun Father's Way: The Kiva Murals of Kuaua.* University of New Mexico Press, Albuquerque.

Eddy, Frank W.
1966   *Prehistory of the Navajo Reservoir District, Northwestern New Mexico.* Papers in Anthropology 15. Museum of New Mexico Press, Santa Fe.

1977   *Archaeological Investigations at Chimney Rock Mesa: 1970–1972.* Memoirs of the Colorado Archaeological Society 1. Colorado Archaeological Society, Boulder.

2004   Past and Present Research at Chimney Rock. In *Chimney Rock: The Ultimate Outlier*, edited by J. M. Malville, pp. 23–50. Lexington Books, Lanham, Maryland.

Ellis, F. H.
1959   An Outline of Laguna Pueblo History and Social Organization. *Southwestern Journal of Anthropology* 15(4):25–347.

1967   The Use and Significance of the Tcamahia. *El Palacio* 74:35–43.

Elmore, F. H.
1944   *Ethnobotany of the Navajo.* University of New Mexico and School of American Research Monograph 1(7). University of New Mexico Press, Albuquerque.

Emery, Irene
1966   *The Primary Structures of Fabrics.* Textile Museum, Washington D.C.

English, N. B., J. L. Betancourt, J. S. Dean, and J. Quade
2001   Strontium Isotopes Reveal Distant Sources of Architectural Timber in Chaco Canyon, New Mexico. *Proceedings of the National Academy of Sciences* 98:11891–11896.

Ericson, J. E.
1977   Egalitarian Exchange Systems in California: A Preliminary View. In *Exchange Systems in Prehistory*, edited by T. K. Earle and J. E. Ericson, pp. 127–139. Academic Press, New York.

Euler, R. C.
1954   Environmental Adaptation at Sia Pueblo. *Human Organization* 12(4):27–30.

Euler, R. C., G. J. Gumerman, T. N. V. Karlstrom, J. S. Dean, and R. H. Hevly
1979   The Colorado Plateaus: Cultural Dynamics and Paleoenvironment. *Science* 205:1089–1101.

Evans, R. K.
1973   *Craft Specialization in the Chalcolithic Period of the Eastern Portion of the Balkan Peninsula.* Ph.D. dissertation, University of California, Los Angeles. University Microfilms, Ann Arbor.

1978   Early Craft Specialization: An Example from the Balkan Chalcolithic. In *Social Archaeology*, edited by C. L. Redman, M. J. Berman, E. V. Curtin, W. T. Langhorne, Jr., N. M. Versaggi, and J. C. Wanser, pp. 113–129. Academic Press, New York.

Faulkner, A.
1972   *Mechanical Principles of Flintworking.* Ph.D. dissertation, Washington State University, Pullman. University Microfilms, Ann Arbor.

Faulkner, Charles T.
1991   Prehistoric Diet and Parasitic Infection in Tennessee: Evidence from the Analysis of Desiccated Human Paleo-Feces. *American Antiquity* 56:687–700.

Fenn, Forrest
    2004   *The Secrets of San Lazaro Pueblo*. One Horse Land and Cattle Company, Santa Fe.

Fewkes, J. W.
    1896   A Contribution to Ethnobotany. *American Anthropologist* 9(1):14–32.

Findley, J. S., A. H. Harris, D. E. Wilson, and C. Jones
    1975   *Mammals of New Mexico*. University of New Mexico Press, Albuquerque.

Fish, Suzanne K.
    1996   Modeling Human Impacts to the Borderlands Environment from a Fire Ecology Perspective. In *Effects of Fire on Madrean Province Ecosystems: A Symposium Proceedings*, by P. Folliott, L. DeBano, M. Baker, G. Gottfried, G. Solis-Garza, C. Edminster, D. Neary, L. Allen, and R. Hamre, pp. 125–134. General Technical Report RM-GTR-289. USDA Forest Service, Rocky Mountain Forest and Range Experiment Station, Ft. Collins, Colorado.

Flannery, K. V.
    1965   The Ecology of Early Food Production in Mesopotamia. *Science* 147:1247–1256.

    1973   The Origins of Agriculture. *Annual Review of Anthropology* 2:271–310.

Flannery, K. V., and M. D. Coe
    1968   Social and Economic Systems in Formative Mesoamerica. In *New Perspectives in Archeology*, edited by S. R. and L. R. Binford, pp. 267–284. Aldine, Chicago.

Flora, I. F., and Helen Sloan Daniels
    1940-41 *Sherds and Points, Vols. I–II*. Durango Amateur Archaeology Story. Durango News, Inc.

Floyd, M. Lisa, Marilyn Colyer, David D. Hannah, and William H. Romme
    2003   Gnarly Old Trees: Canopy Characteristics of Old-Growth Piñon-Juniper Woodlands. In *Ancient Piñon-Juniper Woodlands*, edited by M. Lisa Floyd, pp. 11–29. University Press of Colorado, Boulder.

Ford, R. I.
    1968a   Floral Remains. In *The Cochiti Dam Archaeological Salvage Project, Part I: Report of the 1963 Season*, assembled by C. H. Lange, pp. 236–261. Museum of New Mexico Research Records 6. Museum of New Mexico Press, Santa Fe.

    1968b   *An Ecological Analysis Involving the Population of San Juan Pueblo, New Mexico*. Unpublished Ph.D. dissertation, University of Michigan, Ann Arbor.

    1974   Appendix: Ethnobotanical Remains from Saltbush Pueblo. In *The Excavation of Saltbush Pueblo, Bandelier National Monument*, by D. H. Snow, pp. 75–80. Laboratory of Anthropology Notes 97. Museum of New Mexico, Santa Fe.

Forest Products Laboratory
    1974   *Wood Handbook: Wood as an Engineering Material* (revised). Forest Products Laboratory, Forest Research, Agriculture Handbook 72. U.S. Government Printing Office, Washington D.C.

Franklin, Hayward H.
    1975   Ceramic Analysis for the Salmon Site: 1974. In *The Structure of Chacoan Society in the Northern Southwest. Investigations at the Salmon Site, 1974–1975*, edited by C. Irwin-Williams, pp. 61–83. Ms. on file, Salmon Ruins Library, Bloomfield, New Mexico.

    1980   Salmon Ruin Ceramics Laboratory Report. In *Investigations at the Salmon Site: The Structure of Chacoan Society in the Northern Southwest*, vol. II, edited by C. Irwin-Williams and P. H. Shelley, part 5, pp. 1–583. Unpublished report submitted to funding agencies. On file, Salmon Ruins Library, Bloomfield, New Mexico.

Franklin, Hayward H., and Peter McKenna
    2004   Sterling Site Ceramics – A Progress Report. Paper presented at the Salmon Working Conference, Farmington, New Mexico, April 2004.

Fritts, H. C.
    1965   Tree-Ring Evidence for Climatic Changes in Western North America. *Monthly Weather Review* 93(7):421–443.

Fritts, H. C., D. G. Smith, and M. A. Stokes
    1965   The Biological Model for the Paleoclimatic Interpretation of Mesa Verde Tree-Ring Series. *Society for American Archaeology Memoir* 31(2):101–121.

Fry, Gary F.
    1977   *Analysis of Prehistoric Coprolites from Utah*. University of Utah Anthropological Papers 97. University of Utah Press, Salt Lake City.

Fry, Gary F., and Henry J. Hall
    1975   Human Coprolites from Antelope House: Preliminary Analysis. *The Kiva* 41:87–96.

    1986   Human Coprolites. In *Archeological Investigations at Antelope House*, edited by D. P. Morris, pp. 165–188. Publications in Archeology 19. National Park Service, Washington D.C.

Galinat, W. C.
    1970   The Cupule and its Role in the Origin and Evolution of Maize. *Massachusetts Agricultural Experiment Station Bulletin* 585:1–20.

    1971   The Origin of Maize. *Annual Review of Genetics* 5:447–478.

1988   The Origin of Corn. In *Corn and Corn Improvement*, edited by G. F. Sprague, and J. W. Dudley, pp. 1–31. 3rd ed. American Society of Agronomy, Madison, Wisconsin.

Galinat, W. C., and R. G. Campbell
1967   *The Diffusion of Eight-Rowed Maize From the Southwest to the Central Plains.* Massachusetts Agricultural Experiment Station Monograph Series 1. University of Massachusetts, Amherst.

Galinat, W. C., and J. H. Gunnerson
1963   Spread of Eight-Rowed Maize from the Prehistoric Southwest. *Harvard University Botanical Museum Leaflets* 20:117–160.

Galinat, W. C., T. R. Reinhart, and T. R. Frisbie
1970   Early Eight-Rowed Maize from the Middle Rio Grande Valley, New Mexico. *Harvard University Botanical Museum Leaflets* 22:313–331.

Gallagher, M. V.
1977   *Contemporary Ethnobotany Among the Apache of the Clarksdale, Arizona Area, Coconino and Prescott National Forests.* Archaeological Report 14. USDA Forest Service, Southwestern Region, Albuquerque.

Gallaher, Maggi, and Irene Vold (editors)
1993   *Epidemiology Report.* Department of Health, State of New Mexico, Santa Fe.

1994   *Epidemiology Report.* Department of Health, State of New Mexico, Santa Fe.

Gasser, R. E.
1979   The Cave Buttes Flotation Analysis: A Record of Noncultural Noise in the Prehistoric Context. Appendix D. In *Archaeological Investigations in the Cave Creek Area, Maricopa County, South-Central Arizona*, by T. K. Henderson and J. B. Rodgers. Anthropological Research Papers 17. Arizona State University, Tempe.

Gearing, F. O.
1958   The Structural Poses of the 18th Century Cherokee Villages. American Anthropologist 60 (pt 1):1148–1157.

Gifford, E. W.
1932   The Southeastern Yavapai. *University of California Publications in American Archaeology and Ethnology* 29(3):177–252.

1936   The Northeastern and Western Yavapai. *University of California Publications in American Archaeology and Ethnology* 34(4):247–354.

1940   *Apache-Pueblo:* Culture Element Distributions: XII. Anthropological Records 4(1). University of California, Berkeley.

Gillespie, William B.
1985   Holocene Climate and Environment of Chaco Canyon. In *Environment and Subsistence of Chaco Canyon, New Mexico*, edited by F. J. Mathien, pp. 13–45. Publications in Archeology 18E, National Park Service, Albuquerque.

1991   Faunal Remains from 29SJ 633. In *Excavations at 29SJ 633: The Eleventh Hour Site Chaco Canyon, New Mexico*, edited by F. J. Mathien, pp. 243–315. Reports of the Chaco Center 10. National Park Serivice, Albuquerque.

Gilmore, M. R.
1977   *Uses of Plants by the Indians of the Missouri River Region.* University of Nebraska Press, Lincoln.

Gish, J. W.
1976   *Palynology of the Robinson Site, North-Central Wisconsin.* Anthropological Research Paper 5. Arizona State University, Tempe.

Gnabasik, Virginia R.
1981   *Faunal Utilization by the Pueblo Indians.* Master's thesis, Eastern New Mexico University, Portales.

Goldfrank, E. S.
1927   The Social and Ceremonial Organization of Cochiti. *American Anthropological Association Memoir* 33:1–129.

Goodwin, G.
1942   *The Social Organization of the Western Apache.* University of Chicago Press, Chicago.

Graham, S.A.
1965   Entomology: An Aid in Archaeological Studies. In *Contributions of the Wetherill Mesa Archaeological Project*, assembled by D. Osborne, pp. 167–174. Memoirs of the Society for American Archaeology 19. Salt Lake City.

Grayson, Donald K.
1984   *Quantitative Zooarchaeology: Topics in the Analysis of Archaeological Faunas.* Academic Press, Orlando.

Grebinger, P.
1973   Prehistoric Social Organization in Chaco Canyon, New Mexico: An Alternative Reconstruction. *The Kiva* 39:3–23.

Gruell, G. E.
1985   Indian Fires in the Interior West: A Widespread Influence. *Proceedings of a Symposium and Workshop on Wilderness Fire*, edited by J. Lotan, pp. 15–18, Missoula, Montana, 1983. General Technical Report INT-182. USDA Forest Service, Intermountain Research Station, Ogden, Utah.

Guernsey, Samuel J.
1931   *Explorations in Northeastern Arizona.* Papers of the Peabody Museum of American Archaeology and Ethnology 12(1). Harvard University, Cambridge.

Hall, Edward T.
    1944   *Early Stockaded Settlements in the Gobernador, New Mexico: A Marginal Anasazi Development from Basket Maker III to Pueblo I times.* Columbia Studies in Archaeology and Ethnology II(1). Columbia University Press, New York.

Hantman, J., Kent Lightfoot, and Steadman Upham
    1979   The Implications of Changing Ceramic Production in the Prehistoric American Southwest. Paper presented at the 44th annual meeting of the Society for American Archaeology, Vancouver, British Columbia, April 1979.

Harding, J. W.
    1974   *Human Poisoning from Native Cultivated Plants.* Duke University Press, Durham, North Carolina.

Hargrave, Lyndon L.
    1939   Bird Bones from Abandoned Indian Dwellings in Arizona and Utah. *The Condor* 41:206–210.

    1970   *Mexican Macaws: Comparative Osteology and Survey of Remains from the Southwest.* Anthropological Papers of the University of Arizona 20. University of Arizona Press, Tucson.

Harlow, W. M.
    1931   *The Identification of the Pines of the United States, Native and Introduced, by Needle Structure.* Technical Publication 32, New York State College of Forestry at Syracuse.

Harrington, H. D.
    1964   *Manual of the Plants of Colorado.* Sage Books, Denver.

    1967   *Edible Native Plants of the Rocky Mountains.* University of New Mexico Press, Albuquerque.

Harrington, H. D., and Y. Matsumura (illustrator)
    1967   *Edible Native Plants of the Rocky Mountains.* University of New Mexico Press, Albuquerque.

Harris, A. H.
    1963a   *Vertebrate Remains and Past Environmental Reconstruction in the Navajo Reservoir District.* Museum of New Mexico Papers in Anthropology 11.

    1963b   *Ecological Distribution of Some Vertebrates in the San Juan Basin, New Mexico.* Museum of New Mexico Papers in Anthropology 8.

    1968   Faunal Remains from LA 6461, LA 6462, and LA 6455. In *The Cochiti Dam Archaeological Salvage Project. Part 1: Report on the 1963 Season,* assembled by C. H. Lange, pp. 198–235. Museum of New Mexico Research Records 6.

Harris, A., J. Schoenwetter, and A. H. Warren
    1967   *An Archaeological Survey of the Chuska Valley and the Chaco Plateau, New Mexico: Part 1.* Museum of New Mexico Research Records 4, pp. 120–121.

Harvey, B., III
    1970   *Ritual in Pueblo Art: Hopi Life in Hopi Painting.* Museum of the American Indian, Heye Foundation, New York.

Hatch, Sharon K.
    1994   *A Wood Sourcing Study at Chimney Rock Archaeological Area.* Master's thesis, Department of Anthropology, Northern Arizona University, Flagstaff.

Haury, Emil W.
    1950   *The Stratigraphy and Archaeology of Ventana Cave.* University of Arizona Press, Tucson.

Hayes, A. C.
    1964   *The Archaeological Survey of Wetherill Mesa, Mesa Verde National Park, Colorado.* Research Series 7A. National Park Service, Washington D.C.

    1976   A Cache of Gardening Tools: Chaco Canyon. In *Collected Papers in Honor of Marjorie Ferguson Lambert,* edited by A. H. Schroeder, pp. 73–84. Papers of the Archaeological Society of New Mexico 3. Albuquerque Archaeological Society.

Hayes, A. C., and J. A. Lancaster
    1975   *Badger House Community, Mesa Verde National Park.* Research Series 7E. National Park Service, Washington D.C.

Hays-Gilpin, Kelley Ann, Ann C. Deegan, and Elizabeth Ann Morris
    1998   *Prehistoric Sandals from Northeastern Arizona: The Earl H. Morris and Ann Axtell Morris Research.* Anthropological Papers of the University of Arizona 62. University of Arizona Press, Tucson.

Hefner, Ronald G.
    1985   *Excavations at Pump Mesa: Limited Testing of a Late Rose–Early Piedra Occupation in Northwestern New Mexico.* San Juan College Research Papers in Anthropology 1. Farmington, New Mexico.

    1987   *Excavations at Manzanares Mesa: Limited Data Recovery at Early Navajo and Baskermaker Sites on Manzanares Mesa in Northwest New Mexico.* San Juan College Research Papers in Anthropology 3. Farmington, New Mexico.

Heiser, C. B.
    1979   Origins of Some Cultivated New World Plants. *Annual Review of Ecology and Systematics* 10:309–326.

Heizer, R. F., and L. K. Napton
    1969   Biological and Cultural Evidence from Prehistoric Human Coprolites. *Science* 165(3893):563–568.

Heller, M. M.
1976　*Zooarchaeology of Tularosa Cave, Catron County, New Mexico.* Master's thesis, University of Texas, El Paso.

Hempel, C. G. (editor)
1965　Aspects of Scientific Explanation. In *Aspects of Scientific Explanation and Other Essays in the Philosophy of Science,* edited by C. G. Hemple, pp. 331–496. Free Press, New York.

Hensler, Kathy Niles
1999　Anasazi Ceramic Traditions: A View from the Cove. In *Anasazi Community Development in the CoveRedrock Valley: Archaeological Excavations Along the N33 Road in Apache County, Arizona,* edited by P. F. Reed and K. N. Hensler, pp. 551686. Navajo Nation Papers in Anthropology No. 33. Navajo Nation Archaeology Department, Window Rock, Arizona.

Hensler, Kathy Niles, and Joell Goff
2002　Ceramic Analysis. In *Two Millennia at Tocito: Archaeological and Ethnographic Investigations Along the N5000(2) Road, San Juan County, New Mexico,* edited by P. F. Reed and K. N. Hensler, pp. 197240. Navajo Papers in Anthropology No. 37. Navajo Nation Archaeology Department, Window Rock, Arizona.

Hensler, Kathy Niles, and Lori Stephens Reed
2005　Notes and Data on the Oxidation, Petrographic, and ICP Analysis of Salmon Ceramic and Raw Materials. Manuscript on file at Animas Ceramic Consulting, Inc., Farmington, New Mexico.

Hermann, F. J.
1970　*Manual of the Carices of the Rocky Mountains and Colorado Basin.* Agricultural Handbook 374. Forest Service, U.S. Department of Agriculture, Washington D.C.

Hevly, R. H., M. L. Heuett, and S. J. Olsen
1978　Paleoecological Reconstruction from an Upland Patayan Rock Shelter, Arizona. *Journal of the Arizona-Nevada Academy of Science* 13:67–78.

Hevly, R. H., P. J. Mehringer, Jr., and H. C. Yocum
1965　Modern Pollen Rain in the Sonoran Desert. *Journal of the Arizona Academy of Science* 3:123–135.

Hibben, Frank C.
1975　*Kiva Art of the Anasazi at Pottery Mound.* KC Publications, Las Vegas.

Hibben, Frank C., and Herbert W. Dick
1944　A Basketmaker III Site in Largo Canyon, New Mexico. *American Antiquity* 9(4):381–385.

Hill, J. N.
1970　*Broken K Pueblo: Prehistoric Social Organization in the American Southwest.* Anthropological Papers of the University of Arizona 18. University of Arizona Press, Tucson.

Hill, J. N., and R. H. Hevly
1968　Pollen at Broken K Pueblo: Some New Interpretations. *American Antiquity* 33(2):200–210.

Hill, W. W.
1938　*The Agricultural and Hunting Methods of the Navaho Indians.* Yale University Publications in Anthropology 18. New Haven, Connecticut.

Hobler, Philip M., and Audrey E. Hobler
1978　*An Archaeological Survey of the Upper White Canyon Area, Southeastern Utah.* Antiquities Section, Selected Papers V(13). Department of Development Services, Division of State History, Utah.

Hocking, G. M.
1956　Some Plant Materials Used Medicinally and Otherwise by the Navajo Indians in Chaco Canyon, New Mexico. *El Palacio* 63(5–6):146–165.

Hodder, I.
1974　Regression Analysis of Some Trade and Marketing Patterns. *World Archaeology* 6:172–189.

Hodder, I., and C. Orton
1976　*Spatial Analysis in Archaeology.* Cambridge University Press, New York.

Hogan, Patrick, and Lynne Sebastian
1991　*Archaeology of the San Juan Breaks: The Anasazi Occupation.* Office of Contract Archaeology, University of New Mexico, Albuquerque.

Holloway, R. G., and H. J. Shafer
1978　Organic Residue Analysis in Determining Stone Tool Function. In *Lithic Use-Wear Analysis,* edited by B. Hayden, pp. 385–399. Academic Press, New York.

Holmes, W. H.
1919　*Handbook of Aboriginal American Antiquities Part I, Introduction: The Lithic Industries.* Bureau of American Ethnology Bulletin 60. Smithsonian Institution, Washington D.C.

Hough, V. A.
1931　*The Bibliography of the Ethnobiology of the Southwest Indians.* Master's thesis, University of New Mexico, Albuquerque.

Hough, Walter
1914　*Culture of the Ancient Pueblos of the Upper Gila River Region, New Mexico and Arizona.* U.S. National Museum Bulletin 87. Washington D.C.

Hovezak, Mark J.
1992   *Construction Timber Economics at Sand Canyon Pueblo.* Master's thesis, Department of Anthropology, Northern Arizona University, Flagstaff.

Howell, J., Jr.
1941   Piñon and Juniper Woodlands of the Southwest. *Journal of Forestry* 39:342–345.

Hrdlicka, Alex
1908   *Physiological and Medical Observation Among the Indians of Southwestern United States and Northern Mexico.* Bureau of American Ethnology Bulletin 34. Smithsonian Institution, Washington D.C.

Hughes, P. (editor)
1972   *Pueblo Indian Cookbook.* Museum of New Mexico Press, Santa Fe.

Iltis, H. C.
1979   From Teosinte to Maize – The Incredible Transformation. *Summary, Missouri Botanical Garden 26th Annual Systematics Symposium, The Evolution and Systematics of Grasses,* pp. 7–12.

Irvine, F. R.
1961   *Woody Plants of Ghana.* Oxford University Press, London.

Irwin-Williams, C.
1972   *The Structure of Chacoan Society in the Northern Southwest: Excavations at the Salmon Site – 1972.* Contributions in Anthropology 4 (3). Eastern New Mexico University, Portales.

1973   A Manual for Lithic Analysis. Ms. on file, Salmon Ruins Library, Bloomfield, New Mexico.

1975   The San Juan Valley Archaeological Program: 1974–75. An Overview and Introduction. In *The Structure of Chacoan Society in the Northern Southwest: Investigations at the Salmon Site, 1974–1975,* edited by C. Irwin-Williams, pp. 1–22. Ms. on file, Salmon Ruins Library, Bloomfield, New Mexico.

1977   Investigations at the Salmon Site: The Structure of Chacoan Society in the Northern Southwest. Research proposal submitted to the National Science Foundation. Ms. on file, Salmon Ruins Library, Bloomfield, New Mexico.

Irwin-Williams, C., and N. Bronstein
1972   Lithic Analysis. In *The Structure of Chacoan Society in the Northern Southwest. Excavations at the Salmon Site – 1972,* edited by C. Irwin-Williams, pp. 57–64. Eastern New Mexico University Contributions in Anthropology 4(3).

Irwin-Williams, C., and H. J. Irwin
1966   *Excavations at Magic Mountain: A Diachronic Study of Plains–Southwest Relations.* Proceedings 12. Denver Museum of Natural History, Denver.

Irwin-Williams, Cynthia, and Phillip H. Shelley (editors)
1980   Investigations at the Salmon Site: The Structure of Chacoan Society in the Northern Southwest, 4 vols. Unpublished report submitted to funding agencies. Ms. on file, Salmon Ruins Library, Bloomfield, New Mexico.

Iverson, J.
1956   Forest Clearance in the Stone Age. *Scientific American* 194(3):36–41.

Jack, R. N.
1976   Prehistoric Obsidian in California I: Geochemical Aspects. In *Advances in Obsidian Glass Studies,* edited by R. E. Taylor, pp. 183–217. Noyes Press, Park Ridge, New Jersey.

James, John
1982   *Chartes, The Masons Who Built a Legend.* Routledge and Kegan Paul, London.

Johns, Timothy
1988   A Survey of Traditional Methods Employed for the Detoxification of Plant Foods. *Journal of Ethnobotany* 8(1):81–129.

Jones, Volney H.
1931   *The Ethnobotany of the Isleta Indians.* Master's thesis, Department of Biology, University of New Mexico, Albuquerque.

1938   An Ancient Food Plant of the Southwest and Plateau Regions. *El Palacio* 44(5–6):41–53.

1946   Appendix C. Plant Materials from Alkali Ridge Sites. In *Archaeology of Alkali Ridge, Southeast Utah,* by J. O. Brew, pp. 330–333. Papers of the Peabody Museum of American Archaeology and Ethnology Papers 21. Harvard University, Cambridge.

1955   Appendix V. Plant Materials from a Cave in Zion National Park (ZNP-21). In *Archaeology of Zion Park,* by A. H. Schroeder. University of Utah Anthropological Papers 22.

Jones, V. H., and R. L. Fonner
1954   [1931] Appendix C. Plant Materials from Sites in the Durango and La Plata Areas, Colorado. In *Basket Maker II Sites Near Durango, Colorado,* by E. H. Morris and R. F. Burgh, pp. 93–115. Carnegie Institute of Washington Publications 604.

Judd, Neil M.
1931   The Excavation and Repair of Betatakin. *Proceedings of the U.S. National Museum* 77 (Article 5).

1954   *The Material Culture of Pueblo Bonito.* Smithsonian Miscellaneous Collections 123, pp. 268–271. Smithsonian Institution, Washington D.C.

1959   *Pueblo del Arroyo, Chaco Canyon, New Mexico.* Smithsonian Miscellaneous Collections 133(1). Smithsonian Institution, Washington D.C.

1964   *The Architecture of Pueblo Bonito.* Smithsonian Miscellaneous Collections 147(1). Smithsonian Institution, Washington D.C.

Judge, W. James
1979   The Development of a Complex Ecosystem in the Chaco Basin, New Mexico. In *Proceedings of the First Conference on Scientific Research in the National Parks,* vol. II, edited by R. M. Linn, pp. 901–906. Transactions and Proceedings Series 5. National Park Service, Washington D.C.

Judge, W. J., W. B. Gillespie, S. H. Lekson, and H. W. Toll
1981   Tenth Century Developments in Chaco Canyon. In *Collected Papers in Honor of Erik Kellerman Reed,* edited by A. H. Schroeder, pp. 65–98. Papers of the Archaeological Society of New Mexico 6, Albuquerque.

Kane, Allen E.
1993   Settlement Analogues for Chimney Rock: A Model of 11th and 12th Century Northern Anasazi Society. In *The Chimney Rock Symposium,* edited by J. M. Malville and G. Matlock, pp. 43–60. General Technical Report RM-227. USDA Forest Service, Rocky Mountain Forest and Range Experiment Station, Fort Collins, Colorado.

2004   Chimney Rock: An Ancient Logging Town. In *Chimney Rock: The Ultimate Outlier,* edited by J. M. Malville, pp. 99–114. Lexington Books, Lanham, Maryland.

Kankainen, Kathy (editor)
1995   *Treading in the Past: Sandals of the Anasazi.* University of Utah Press, Salt Lake City.

Kaplan, L.
1956   The Cultivated Beans of the Prehistoric Southwest. *Annals of the Missouri Botanical Garden* 43:189–251.

1963   Archaeoethnobotany of Cordova Cave, New Mexico. *Economic Botany* 17(4):350–359.

Kato, T. A. K.
1975   *Cytological Studies of Maize.* Massachusetts Agricultural Experiment Station Research Bulletin 635. University of Massachusetts, Amherst.

Kearney, T. H., and R. H. Peebles
1960   *Arizona Flora.* 2nd ed. University of California Press, Berkeley.

Kelley, James E.
1975   Zooarchaeological Analysis at Antelope House: Behavioral Inferences from Distribution Data. *The Kiva* 41:81–86.

Kelley, J. E., V. Dirst, J. A. Beezley, and J. Bowen
1974   Faunal Analysis, Salmon Ruin, San Juan Valley, New Mexico, LA 8846. Ms. on file, Salmon Ruins Library, Bloomfield, New Mexico.

Kelly, George W.
1970   *A Guide to Woody Plants of Colorado.* Pruett, Boulder.

Kelly, I. T.
1932   Ethnography of the Surprise Valley Paiute. *Publications in American Archaeology and Ethnology* 31:67–210. University of California, Berkeley.

1964   *Southern Paiute Ethnography.* University of Utah Anthropological Papers 69. University of Utah Press, Salt Lake City.

Kennard, E.
1979   Hopi Economy and Subsistence. In *Southwest,* edited by A. Ortiz, pp. 554–563. Handbook of North American Indians 9. Smithsonian Institution, Washington D.C.

Kent, Kate Peck
1983   *Prehistoric Textiles of the Southwest.* School of American Research Press, Santa Fe.

Kent, Kate Peck, and Virginia Loehr
1974   Perishable Materials from Bc288, Chaco Canyon. Ms. on file (VA-2149) at the Chaco Center, University of New Mexico, Albuquerque.

Kidder, Alfred V., and Samuel J. Guernsey
1919   *Archeological Explorations in Northeastern Arizona.* Bureau of American Ethnology Bulletin 65. Smithsonian Institution, Washington D.C.

Kingsbury, J. M.
1964   *Poisonous Plants of the U.S. and Canada.* Prentice-Hall, Engelwood Cliffs, New Jersey.

Kirkpatrick, D. T., and R. I. Ford
1977   Basketmaker Food Plants from the Cimarron District, Northeast New Mexico. *The Kiva* 42:257–269.

Klecka, W. R.
1975   Discriminant Analysis. In *SPSS: Statistical Package for the Social Sciences,* edited by N. H. Nie et al., pp. 434–437. McGraw-Hill, New York.

Kluckhohn, C., and P. Reiter (editors)
　1939　Preliminary Report on the 1937 Excavations, BC 50–51, Chaco Canyon, New Mexico. University of New Mexico Anthropological Series 3(2).

Kohler, Timothy A., and Meredith H. Matthews
　1988　Long-Term Anasazi Land Use and Forest Reduction: A Case Study from Southwest Colorado. *American Antiquity* 53:537–564.

Kohler, Timothy A., George J. Gumerman, and Robert G. Reynolds
　2005　Simulating Ancient Societies. *Scientific American* 292:77–84.

Kohler, Timothy A., William D. Lipe, Mary E. Floyd, and Robert A. Bye, Jr.
　1984　Modeling Wood Resource Depletion in the Grass Mesa Vicinity. In *Dolores Archaeological Program: Synthetic Report 1978–1981*, pp. 99–105. Engineering and Research Center, Bureau of Reclamation, Denver.

Kowal, R. R.
　1980　CANCOV. Unpublished documentation. Department of Botany, University of Wisconsin, Madison.

Kroster, P.
　1979　Production and Distribution of San Martin Orange: An Example of Prehistoric Specialization and Distribution at Teotihuacan, Mexico. Paper presented at the 44th annual meeting of the Society for American Archaeology, Vancouver, British Columbia, April 1979.

Lamb, S. H.
　1971　*Woody Plants of New Mexico and Their Value to Wildlife*. New Mexico Department of Game and Fish Bulletin 14.

Lange, Charles H.
　1959　*Cochiti, A New Mexico Pueblo, Past and Present*. University of Texas Press, Austin.

Langham, D. G.
　1940　The Inheritance of Intergeneric Differences in *Zea-Euchlaena* Hybrids. *Genetics* 25:88–107.

Laski, V.
　1958　*Seeking Life*. American Folklore Society, Philadelphia.

Lees, S. H.
　1970　Socio-Political Aspects of Canal Irrigation in the Valley of Oaxaca, Mexico. Ph.D. dissertation, University of Michigan. University Microfilms, Ann Arbor.

Lekson, Stephen H.
　1984　*Great Pueblo Architecture of Chaco Canyon, New Mexico*. Publications in Archaeology 18B, Chaco Canyon Studies. National Park Service, Albuquerque.
　1991　Settlement Pattern and the Chaco Region. In *Chaco and Hohokam: Prehistoric Regional Systems in the American Southwest*, edited by Patricia L. Crown and W. James Judge, pp. 31–55. School of American Research Press, Santa Fe.
　1999　*The Chaco Meridian, Centers of Political Power in the Ancient Southwest*. AltaMira Press, Walnut Creek, California.

Lentz, David L.
　1978　The Selection of Reliable Strata Containing Maize from Salmon Ruin. Ms. on file, Department of Anthropology, Eastern New Mexico University, Portales.
　1979　*The Distribution Patterns and Fruit Productivity of Modern Junipers Growing in the Salmon Ruin Area and the Archaeological Interpretation of Juniper Seeds and Cones Found in Salmon Ruin, New Mexico*. Master's thesis, Department of Anthropology, Eastern New Mexico University, Portales.
　1984　Utah Juniper (*Juniperus osteosperma*) Cones and Seeds from Salmon Ruin, New Mexico. *Journal of Ethnobiology* 4(2):191–200.

Leopold, A. S.
　1959　*Wildlife of Mexico*. University of California Press, Berkeley.

Lightfoot, K. G.
　1979　Food Redistribution Among Prehistoric Pueblo Groups. *The Kiva* 44(4):319–339.

Lightfoot, Ricky R.
　1988　Roofing an Early Anasazi Great Kiva: Analysis of an Architectural Model. *The Kiva* 53(3):253–272.

Ligon, J. S.
　1961　*New Mexico Birds and Where to Find Them*. University of New Mexico Press, Albuquerque.

Lister, R. H.
　1965　*Contributions to Mesa Verde Archaeology: II, Site 870, Mesa Verde National Park, Colorado*. University of Colorado Studies, Series in Anthropology 11. University of Colorado Press, Boulder.
　1966　*Contributions to Mesa Verde Archaeology III: Site 866, and the Cultural Sequence at Four Villages in the Far View Group, Mesa Verde National Park, Colorado*. University of Colorado Studies, Series in Anthropology 12. University of Colorado Press, Boulder.

Lister, R. H., and F. Lister
　1964　*Contributions to Mesa Verde Archaeology I: Site 499, Mesa Verde National Park, Colorado*. University of Colorado Studies, Series in Anthropology 12. University of Colorado Press, Boulder.

Little, E. L., Jr.
   1950   *Southwestern Trees. A Guide to the Native Species of New Mexico and Arizona.* Agricultural Handbook 9. USDA Forest Service, Washington D.C.

Longley, A. E.
   1941   Knob Positions on Teosinte Chromosomes. *Journal of Agricultural Research* 62:401–413.

Lowie, R. H.
   1968   *Notes on Shoshonean Ethnography.* Anthropological Papers 20(3):187–314. American Museum of Natural History, New York.

Magers, Pamela C.
   1986   Weaving at Antelope House/Miscellaneous Wooden and Vegetal Artifacts. In *Archeological Investigations at Antelope House,* edited by D. P. Morris, pp. 224–305. National Park Service, Department of the Interior, Washington D.C.

Maher, L. J., Jr.
   1981   Statistics for Microfossil Concentration Measurements Employing Samples Spiked with Marker Grains. *Review of Palaeobotany and Palynology* 32:153–191.

Maker, H. J., C. W. Keetch, and J. U. Anderson
   1973   *Soil Associations and Land Classification for Irrigation, San Juan County.* Agricultural Experiment Station Research Report 257. New Mexico State University, Las Cruces.

Mangelsdorf, P. C.
   1974   *Corn: Its Origin, Evolution and Improvement.* Harvard University Press, Massachusetts.

Mangelsdorf, P. C., and R. G. Reeves
   1939   The Origin of Indian Corn and its Relatives. *Texas Agricultural Experiment Station Bulletin* 574:1–315.

Mangelsdorf, P. C., H. W. Dick, and J. Camara-Hernandez
   1967   Bat Cave revisited. *Harvard University Botanical Museum Leaflets* 22:1–31.

Marshall, M. P., J. R. Stein, R. W. Loose, and J .E. Novotny
   1979   *Anasazi Communities of the San Juan Basin.* Public Service Company of New Mexico and New Mexico Historic Preservation Bureau, Albuquerque.

Martin, A. F., and W. D. Barkley
   1961   *Seed Identification Manual.* University of California Press, Berkeley.

Martin, Paul S.
   1936   *Lowry Ruin in Southwestern Colorado.* Anthropological Series 23(1), Field Museum of Natural History, Chicago.

Martin, P. S., and F. Plog
   1973   *The Archaeology of Arizona: A Study of the Southwest Region.* Doubleday/Natural History Press, Garden City, New York.

Martin, Paul S., and Floyd W. Sharrock
   1964   Pollen Analysis of Prehistoric Human Feces, A New Approach to Ethnobotany. *American Antiquity* 30:168–180.

Mathews, Washington
   1887   The Mountain Chant: A Navajo Ceremony. In *Fifth Annual Report of the Bureau of American Ethnology,* 1883–84, by J. W. Powell, pp. 379–467. Smithsonian Institution, Washington D.C.

Mathien, Frances Joan
   2004   "A Cacique's Sanctum" or Road Ramp? Site 29SJ1924 in Chaco Canyon, New Mexico. In *Ever Westward: Papers in Honor of Elizabeth Kelley,* edited by R. N. Wiseman, T. C. O'Laughlin, and C. T. Snow, pp. 85–100. Papers of the Archaeological Society of New Mexico 30, Albuquerque.

Matson, R. G., and W. D. Lipe
   1977   Seriation of Pueblo Ceramic Assemblages from Cedar Mesa, Utah. Ms. on file, Department of Anthropology, Washington State University, Pullman.

McCormick, Timothy, and Catherine Cameron
   1974   Lithic Analysis. In *The San Juan Valley Archaeological Program: Investigations at the Salmon Site, 1974,* edited by C. Irwin-Williams, pp. 137–174. Ms. on file, Salmon Ruins Library, Bloomfield, New Mexico.

McGregor, J. C.
   1941   *Winona and Ridge Ruin, Part 1: Architecture and Material Culture.* Museum of Northern Arizona Bulletin 18, pp. 83–89.

McKenna, Peter J., and H. Wolcott Toll
   1992   Regional Patterns of Great House Development Among the Totah Anasazi, New Mexico. In *Anasazi Regional Organization and the Chaco System,* edited by D. E. Doyel, pp. 133–143. Maxwell Museum of Anthropology, Anthropological Papers 5. University of New Mexico, Albuquerque.

McNeil, Jimmy D.
   1986   Ornaments of Salmon Ruin San Juan County, New Mexico. Master's thesis, Department of Anthropology, Eastern New Mexico University, Portales.

MerIFluor
   1991   MerIFluor Package Insert for Cryptosporidium/Giardia Direct Immunofluorescent Detection Procedure. Meridian Diagnostics, Inc., Cincinnati.

Miller, David E. (editor)
   1976   *The Route of Dominguez-Escalante Expedition, 1776–77.* A Report of Trail Research Conducted Under the Auspices of the Dominguez-Escalante State/Federal Bicentennial Committee and the Four Corners Regional Commission. Report available in the Coronado Southwestern Collections, Zimmerman Library, University of New Mexico, Albuquerque.

Miller, James G.
   1965   Living Systems: Structure and Process. *Behavioral Science* 10:337–374.

Miller, Ronald K., and Steven K. Albert
   1993   Zuni Cultural Relationships to Piñon-Juniper Woodlands. In *Managing Piñon-Juniper Ecosystems for Sustainability and Social Needs,* coordinated by E. F. Aldon and D. W. Shaw, pp. 74–78. General Technical Report RM-236. USDA Forest Service, Rocky Mountain Forest and Range Experiment Station, Ft. Collins, Colorado.

Miller, S. F., F. Bordes, and J. L. Cotter
   1972   On Old and New Concepts of Typology. *Current Anthropology* 13:139–143.

Mindeleff, Cosmos
   1897   The Cliff Ruins of Canyon de Chelly, Arizona. In *Sixteenth Annual Report of the Bureau of American Ethnology, 1894–1895,* by J. W. Powell, pp. 73–198. Smithsonian Institution, Washington D.C.

Minnis, Paul E.
   1989   Prehistoric Diet in the Northern Southwest: Macroplant Remains from Four Corners Feces. *American Antiquity* 54:543–563.

   1991   Famine Foods of the North American Desert Borderlands in Historical Context. *Journal of Ethnobiology* 11:231–257.

Miranda Colin, S.
   1966   *Discussion Sobre el Origin y la Evolucion del Maiz.* Memorias del Segundl Congreso Nacional de Fitogenetica, A. C. La Escuela de Agricultura y Ganaderia del Instituto Technologico y de Estudios Superiores de Monterrey, Monterrey, N. L. Mexico.

Mobley-Tanaka, Jeannette L.
   1993   Intracommunity Interactions at Chimney Rock: The Inside View of the Outlier Problem. In *The Chimney Rock Archaeological Symposium,* edited by J. M. Malville and G. Matlock, pp. 37–42. General Technical Report RM-227, USDA Forest Service, Rocky Mountain Forest and Experiment Station, Fort Collins, Colorado.

Moerman, D. E.
   1977   *American Medical Ethnobotany: A Reference Dictionary.* Garland, New York.

Monroe, Lee S.
   1995   Gastrointestinal Parasites. In *Bockus Gastroenterology,* vol. 4, edited by W. S. Haubrich and F. Schaffnew, pp. 3140–3143. 5th ed. W. B. Saunders, Philadelphia.

Moore, Roger A., Jr.
   1981   *An Analytical Approach to Typology: The Projectile Point Sequence at Salmon Ruin, New Mexico.* Master's thesis, Department of Anthropology, Eastern New Mexico University, Portales.

Morain, S. A., T. K. Budge, and M. E. White
   1977   *Vegetation and Land Use in New Mexico.* New Mexico Bureau of Mines and Mineral Resources, Socorro.

Morenon, E. P.
   1975   Chacoan Roads and Adaptation: How a Prehistoric Population Can Define and Control its Social and Natural Environment. In *The Structure of Chacoan Society in the Northern Southwest, Investigations at the Salmon Site, 1974–1975,* edited by C. Irwin-Williams, pp. 187–200. Ms. on file, Salmon Ruins Museum, Bloomfield, New Mexico.

Morgan, L. H.
   1881   Houses and House-life of the American Aborigines. *Contributions to North American Ethnology* 2:536–556.

Morris, Don P (editor)
   1986   *Archeological Investigations at Antelope House.* Publications in Archeology 19. National Park Service, Washington D.C.

Morris, Earl H.
   1919   *The Aztec Ruin.* Anthropological Papers 26(1). American Museum of Natural History, New York.

   1921   *The House of the Great Kiva at the Aztec Ruin.* Anthropological Papers 26(2). American Museum of Natural History, New York.

   1924a   *Burials in the Aztec Ruin.* Anthropological Papers 26(3). American Museum of Natural History, New York.

   1924b   *The Aztec Ruin Annex.* Anthropological Papers 26(4). American Museum of Natural History, New York.

   1928   *Notes on Excavations in the Aztec Ruin.* Anthropological Papers 26(5). American Museum of Natural History, New York.

   1939   *Archaeological Studies in the La Plata District.* Publication 519. Carnegie Institution of Washington D.C.

Morris, Earl H., and Robert F. Burgh
   1941   *Anasazi Basketry: Basket Maker II Through Pueblo III.* Publication 533. Carnegie Institution of Washington, Washington D.C.

Morris, Elizabeth Ann
   1959   A Pueblo I Site near Bennett's Peak, Northwestern New Mexico. *El Palacio* 66(5):169–175.

Muenscher, W. C.
   1939   *Poisonous Plants of the United States.* MacMillan, New York.

Munro, Natalie D.
   1994   *An Investigation of Anasazi Turkey Production in Southwestern Colorado.* Master's thesis, Department of Archaeology, Simon Frasier University, Burnaby.

Musil, A. F.
   1963   *Identification of Crop and Weed Seeds.* Agricultural Handbook 219. Agricultural Marketing Service, U.S. Department of Agriculture, Washington D.C.

Muto, G. R.
   1979   Edge Damage: The Other Possible Causes. Paper presented in the Aspects of Lithic Technology symposium at the 44th annual meeting of the Society for American Archaeology, Vancouver, British Columbia, April 1979.

Nabokov, Peter, and R. Easton
   1989   *Native American Architecture.* Oxford University Press, Oxford, England.

Nash, Stephen Edward
   1999   *Time, Trees, and Prehistory: Tree-Ring Dating and the Development of North American Archaeology, 1914 to 1950.* University of Utah Press, Salt Lake City.

Neilson, Ronald P.
   1987   On the Interface Between Current Ecological Studies and the Paleobotany of Pinyon-Juniper Woodlands. In *Proceedings—Pinyon-Juniper Conference*, compiled by R. L. Everett, pp. 93–98. General Technical Report INT-215. USDA Forest Service, Intermountain Research Station, Ogden, Utah.

Nequatewa, E.
   1943   Some Hopi Recipes for the Preparation of Wild Food Plants. *Plateau* 16:18–20.

Newberry, John S.
   1876   Geologic Report. In *Report of the Exploring Expedition from Santa Fe, New Mexico, to the Junction of the Grand and Green Rivers of the Great Colorado of the West, in 1859*, by Capt. J. N. Macomb, pp. 12–118. U.S. Government Printing Office, Washington D.C.

Nicholson, Rebecca A.
   1992   Bone Survival: the Effects of Sedimentary Abrasion and Trampling on Fresh and Cooked Bone. *International Journal of Osteoarchaeology* 2:79–90.

   1996   Bone Degradation, Burial Medium and Species Representation: Debunking Myths, an Experiment-Based Approach. *Journal of Archaeological Science* 23:513–533.

Nickerson, N. H.
   1953   Variation in Cob Morphology Among Certain Archaeological and Ethnographical Races of Maize. *Annals of the Missouri Botanical Garden* 40:79–111.

Nie, N. H., and C. H. Hull
   1979   *SPSS Update: New Procedures and Facilities for Releases 7 and 8.* McGraw-Hill, New York.

Nordenskiöld, Gustav
   1893   *The Cliff Dwellers of the Mesa Verde, Southwestern Colorado.* P. A. Norstedt and Söner, Stockholm and Chicago.

Nusbaum, J. L.
   1922   *A Basket Maker Cave in Kane County, Utah.* Indian Notes and Monographs, Miscellaneous Series 29. Museum of the American Indian, New York.

Olsen, John W.
   1990   *Vertebrate Faunal Remains from Grasshopper Pueblo, Arizona.* Anthropological Papers 83. Museum of Anthropology, University of Michigan, Ann Arbor.

Ortiz, A.
   1969   *The Tewa World.* University of Chicago Press, Chicago.

   1979   San Juan Pueblo. In *Southwest*, edited by A. Ortiz, pp. 278–295. Handbook of North American Indians 9. Smithsonian Institution, Washington D.C.

Osborne, Carolyn M.
   1980   Objects of Perishable Materials. In *Long House, Mesa Verde National Park, Colorado*, edited by G. S. Cattanach, Jr., pp. 317–367. Research Series 7H. National Park Service, Washington D.C.

Owen, Robert L.
   1993   Parasitic Diseases. In *Gastrointestinal Disease*, vol. 2, edited by Marvin H. Sleisenger and John S. Fordtran, pp. 1190–1193. 5th ed. W. B. Saunders, Philadelphia.

Palmer, E.
   1871   *Food Products of the North American Indians.* USDA Report to the Commission on Agriculture, 1870, pp. 404–428. Washington D.C.

   1878   Plants Used by the Indians of the United States. *American Naturalist* 12:593–606.

Parsons, Elsie Clews
    1929   *The Social Organization of the Tewa of New Mexico.* American Anthropological Association Memoir 38.
            Menasha, Wisconsin.

    1939   *Pueblo Indian Religion,* vol. 1. University of Chicago Press, Chicago.

    1970   *Taos Pueblo.* New ed. Johnson Reprint, New York.

Parsons, Elsie Clews (editor)
    1936   *The Hopi Journal of Alexander M. Stephen.* Columbia University Contributions to Anthropology 23. Columbia
            University Press, New York.

Paytiamo, J.
    1932   *Flaming Arrow's People, by an Acoma Indian.* Duffield and Green, New York.

Pearson, G. A.
    1950   *Management of Ponderosa Pine in the Southwest, As Developed by Research and Experimental Practice.*
            Agriculture Monograph 6. U.S. Forest Service, U.S. Government Printing Office, Washington D.C.

Pepper, George H.
    1909   The Exploration of a Burial-Room in Pueblo Bonito, New Mexico. *Putnam Anniversary Volume,* pp. 196–252.
            Cedar Rapids, Iowa.

    1920   *Pueblo Bonito.* American Museum Natural History Monograph 27. New York.

Perkins, D., Jr., and P. Daly
    1968   A Hunter's Village in Neolithic Turkey. *Scientific American* 219(5):96–106.

Pippin, Lonnie C.
    1979   *The Prehistory and Paleoecology of Guadalupe Ruin, Sandoval County, New Mexico.* Ph.D. dissertation,
            Department of Anthropology, Washington State University, Pullman.

    1987   *The Archaeology and Paleoecology of Guadalupe Ruin.* University of Utah Anthropological Papers 107.
            University of Utah Press, Salt Lake City.

Pippin, L. C., and C. Irwin-Williams
    1972   Excavations at Salmon Ruin. In *The Structure of Chacoan Society in the Northern Southwest: Investigations at the
            Salmon Site – 1972,* edited by C. Irwin-Williams, pp. 15–25. Contributions in Anthropology 4(3). Eastern New
            Mexico University, Portales.

Poinar, Hendrik N., Melanie Kuch, Kristin D. Sobolik, Ian Barnes, Artur B. Stankiewicz, Tomasz Kuder, G. W. Spaulding,
            Vaughn Bryant, Jr. Alan Cooper, and Svante Pääbo
    2001   A Molecular Analysis of Dietary Diversity for Three Archaic Native Americans. *Proceedings of the National
            Academy of Sciences of the United States of America* 98:4317–4322.

Pond, A.
    1930   *Primitive Methods of Working Stone, Based on the Experiments of Halvor L. Skavlem.* Logan Museum Bulletin
            2(1). Beloit College, Beloit, Wisconsin.

Potter, Gayle
    1981   *Social Differentiation of Mesa Verdean Culture as Shown by the Examination of Manipulated Fiber Artifacts in
            Burials from Salmon Ruin, New Mexico.* Master's thesis, Department of Anthropology, New York University,
            New York.

Potter, L. D., and J. Rowley
    1960   Pollen Rain and Vegetation, San Augustine Plains, New Mexico. *Botanical Gazette* 122(1):1–25.

Powers, Robert P., William B. Gillespie, and Stephen H. Lekson
    1983   *The Outlier Survey: A Regional View of Settlement in the San Juan Basin.* Reports of the Chaco Center 3. National
            Park Service, Albuquerque.

Priesnitz, J.
    1979   *A Preliminary Investigation of Organizational Loci at Salmon Ruin, a Chacoan Outlier in Northwestern New
            Mexico.* Master's thesis, Department of Anthropology, Eastern New Mexico University, Portales, New Mexico.

Randles, Q.
    1949   *Pinyon Juniper in the Southwest.* USDA Yearbook of Argiculture, pp. 342–347. Washington D.C.

Randolph, L. R.
    1976   Contributions of Wild Relatives of Maize to the Evolutionary History of Domesticated Maize: A Synthesis of
            Divergent Hypotheses. I. *Economic Botany* 30:321–345.

Rapoport, Amos
    1969   *House Form and Culture.* Prentice-Hall, Englewood Cliffs, New Jersey.

Rattray, E.
    1979   Ceramic Production and Social Organization at Teotihuacan, Mexico. Paper presented at the 44th annual
            meeting of the Society for American Archaeology, Vancouver.

Reagan, A. B.
    1929   Plants Used by the White Mountain Apache Indians of Arizona. *Wisconsin Archaeology* 8:143–161.

Reed, E. K.
    1951   Turkeys in Southwestern Archaeology. *El Palacio* 58:195–205.

Reed, Paul F.
    2002   Salmon Ruins: From Cynthia Irwin-Williams's Vision to a Central Place in the Totah. *Archaeology Southwest* 16(2):7–9. Center for Desert Archaeology, Tucson.

    2005b   Salmon Pueblo as a Ritual and Residential Chacoan Great House. In *Salmon Pueblo: Chacoan Outlier and Thirteenth Century Pueblo in the Middle San Juan Region*, edited by P. F. Reed. Ms. in review, University of Utah Press, Salt Lake City.

Reed, Paul F. (editor)
    2000   *Foundations of Anasazi Culture: The Basketmaker-Pueblo Transition.* University of Utah Press, Salt Lake City.

    2005a   *Salmon Ruins: Chacoan Outlier and Thirteenth-Century Pueblo in the Middle San Juan Region.* Ms. in review, University of Utah Press, Salt Lake City.

Reinhard, Karl J.
    1985   *Cultural Ecology of Parasitism.* Master's thesis, Ecology and Evolution, Northern Arizona University, Flagstaff.

    1988a   *Diet, Parasitism, and Anemia in the Prehistoric Southwest.* Ph.D. dissertation, Anthropology, Texas A&M University, College Station.

    1988b   Cultural Ecology of Prehistoric Parasitism on the Colorado Plateau As Evidenced by Coprology. *American Journal of Physical Anthropology* 77:355–366.

    1990   Archaeoparasitology in North America. *American Journal of Physical Anthropology* 82:145–163.

    1992   Patterns of Diet, Parasitism, and Anemia in Prehistoric West North America. In *Diet, Demography, and Disease: Changing Perspectives on Anemia*, edited by P. Stuart-Macadam and S. Kent, pp. 219–258. Aldine de Gruyter, New York.

    1993   The Utility of Pollen Concentration in Coprolite Analysis: Expanding Upon Dean's Comments. *Journal of Ethnobiology* 9:31–44.

    1996   Parasite Ecology of Two Anasazi Villages. In *Case Studies in Environmental Archaeology*, edited by E. J. Reitz, L. A. Newson, and S. J. Scudder, pp. 175–189. Plenum Press, New York.

Reinhard, Karl J., and Dennis R. Danielson
    2005   Pervasiveness of Phytoliths in Prehistoric Southwestern Diet and Implications for Regional and Temporal Trends for Dental Microwear. *Journal of Archaeological Science* 32:981–988.

Reinhard, Karl J., and Sara LeRoy-Toren
    n.d.   Evaluating the Chinchorro Diet: Role of Plants and Diatoms. 2003 NSF proposal on file with authors.

Reinhard, Karl J., Robert H. Hevly, and Glenn A. Anderson
    1987   Helminth Remains from Prehistoric Indian Coprolites on the Colorado Plateau. *Journal of Parasitology* 73:630–639.

Reinhard, Karl J., Mark Daniels, Dennis R. Danielson, and Sergio M. Chaves
    2002   Multidisciplinary Coprolite Analysis. In *Bighorn Cave: Test Excavation of a Stratified Dry Shelter, Mojave County, Arizona*, edited by P. R. Geib and D. R. Keller, pp. 135–152. Bilby Research Center Occasional Papers 1. Northern Arizona University, Flagstaff.

Reinhard, Karl J., Sherrian Edwards, Teyana R. Damon, and Debra K. Meier
    2006   Pollen Concentration Analysis in Documenting Anasazi Dietary Variation. *Journal of Palaeogeography, Palaeoclimatology, and Palaeoecology* (in press).

Reiter, Winifred Stamm
    1931   *Personal Adornment of the Ancient Pueblo Indians.* Master's thesis, Department of Anthropology, University of New Mexico, Albuquerque.

Renfrew, C.
    1975   Trade As Action at a Distance: Questions of Integration and Communication. In *Ancient Civilization and Trade*, edited by J. A. Sabloff and C. C. Lamberg-Karlovsky, pp. 3–59. University of New Mexico Press, Albuquerque.

    1977   Alternative Models for Exchange and Spatial Distribution. In *Exchange Systems in Prehistory*, edited by T. K. Earle and J. E. Ericson, pp. 71–90. Academic Press, New York.

Reynolds, A. C., J. L. Betancourt, J. Quade, P. J. Patchett, J. S. Dean, and J. Stein
    2005   87Sr/86Sr Sourcing of Ponderosa Pine Used in Anasazi Great House Construction at Chaco Canyon, New Mexico. *Journal of Archaeological Science* 32:1061–1075.

Rice, Prudence
    1981   Evolution of Specialized Pottery Production: A Trial Model. *Current Anthropology* 22:219–240.

Richardson, J. W.
    1978   The Genus *Euphorbia* of the High Plains and Prairie Plains of Kansas, Nebraska, South and North Dakota. *University of Kansas Science Bulletin* 48:45–112.

Richert, Roland
    1964   *Excavation of a Portion of the East Ruin, Aztec Ruins National Monument, New Mexico.* Technical Series 4. Southwest Monuments Association, Globe, Arizona.

Ringrose, T. J.
    1993   Bone Counts and Statistics: A Critique. *Journal of Archaeological Science* 20:121–157.

Robbins, Wilfred W., John P. Harrington, and Barbara Freire-Marreco
    1916   *Ethnobotany of the Tewa Indians.* Bureau of American Ethnology Bulletin 55. Smithsonian Institution, Washington D.C.

Roberts, Frank H. H., Jr.
    1932   *The Village of the Great Kivas on the Zuni Reservation, New Mexico.* Bureau of American Ethnology Bulletin 111. Smithsonian Institution, Washington D.C.

Robinson, William J.
    1967   *Tree-Ring Materials as a Basis for Cultural Interpretations.* Unpublished Ph.D. dissertation, Department of Anthropology, University of Arizona, Tucson.

Robinson, W. J., B. G. Harrill, and R. L. Warren
    1974   *Tree-Ring Dates from New Mexico B: Chaco-Gobernador Area.* Laboratory of Tree-Ring Research, University of Arizona, Tucson.

Rodwell, Warwick J.
    1981   *The Archaeology of the English Church: The Study of Historic Churches and Churchyards.* B. T. Batsford, London.

Rohn, A. H.
    1963   An Ecological Approach to the Great Pueblo Occupation of the Mesa Verde, Colorado. *Plateau* 36:1–17.

    1971   *Mug House, Mesa Verde National Park, Colorado.* Research Series 7D. National Park Service, Washington D.C.

Roler, Kathy L.
    1999   *The Chaco Phenomenon: A Faunal Perspective from the Peripheries.* Unpublished Ph.D. dissertation, Department of Anthropology, Arizona State University, Tempe.

Roney, John R.
    2004   Bonito-Style Great Houses. In *Chimney Rock: The Ultimate Outlier,* edited by J. M. Malville, pp. 123–130. Lexington Books, Lanham, Maryland.

Rose, Janet C.
    1979a   A Palynological Study of Rooms 82W and 62W at Salmon Ruin, New Mexico. Ms. on file, Salmon Ruins Museum Library, Bloomfield, New Mexico.

    1979b   Data Table Concerning Ceramic Vessels from Which Pollen and/or Flotation Samples were Obtained, 1974–1977. Ms. on file, Salmon Ruins Museum Library, Bloomfield, New Mexico.

Rose, Martin C.
    1979   Report to Dr. C. Irwin-Williams, January 2,1979. Ms. on file, Salmon Ruins Museum Library, Bloomfield, New Mexico.

Rose, Martin C., J. Dean, and W. Robinson
    1981   *The Past Climate of Arroyo Hondo, Reconstructed from Tree Rings.* Arroyo Hondo Archaeological Series 4. School of American Research Press, Santa Fe.

Rossi, S.
    1977   Hearth Project —Salmon Ruin (LA 8846). Ms. on file, Salmon Ruins Museum Library, Bloomfield, New Mexico.

Russell, F.
    1975   *The Pima Indians.* University of Arizona Press, Tucson.

Samuels, M. L., and Julio L. Betancourt
    1982   Modeling the Long-Term Effects of Fuelwood Harvests on Piñon-Juniper Woodlands. *Environmental Management* 6:505–515.

San Juan Times
    1894a   The Land of Sunshine. June 8.

    1894b   Local Briefs. December 7.

San Miguel, George L., and Marilyn Colyer
    2003   Mesa Verde Country's Woodland Avian Community. In *Ancient Piñon-Juniper Woodlands,* edited by M. Lisa Floyd, pp. 89–110. University Press of Colorado, Boulder.

Savage, M., and Thomas W. Swetnam
    1990   Early 19th Century Fire Decline Following Sheep Pasturing in a Navajo Ponderosa Pine Forest. *Ecology* 71(6):2374–2378.

Schaafsma, Polly
    1980   Evidence for the Origins of the Pueblo Katchina Cult as Suggested by Southwestern Rock Art. *American Antiquity* 39:535–545.

Schafer, H. J., and R. G. Holloway
    1978   Organic Residue Analysis in Determining Stone Tool Function. In *Lithic Use-Wear Analysis,* edited by B. Hayden, pp. 385–399. Academic Press, New York.

Schiffer, M. B.
    1976   *Behavioral Archaeology.* Academic Press, New York.

Schlanger, Sarah H., and Richard H. Wilshusen
1993   Local Abandonments and Regional Conditions in the North American Southwest. In *Abandonment of Settlements and Regions*, edited by C. M. Cameron and S. A. Tomka, pp. 85–98. Cambridge University Press, Cambridge, England.

Schoener, T. W.
1971   Theory of Feeding Strategies. *Annual Review of Ecology and Systematics* 2:369–404.

Schoenwetter, J.
1974   Pollen Records of Guila Naquitz Cave. *American Antiquity* 39(2):292–303.

Schutt, J. A.
1978   Artifact Recovery Procedures and Microwear Patterns. Office of Contract Archaeology, Department of Anthropology, University of New Mexico. Paper presented at the 43rd annual meeting of the Society for American Archaeology, May 1978, Tucson, Arizona.

Sebastian, Lynne
1992   *The Chaco Anasazi: Sociopolitical Evolution in the Prehistoric Southwest*. Cambridge University Press, Cambridge, England.

Seme, M.
1980   *Analysis of Faunal Remains from Archaeological Sites, Black Mesa, Arizona*. Master's thesis, University of Texas at El Paso.

Shackley, M. Steven
2005   Source Provenance of Obsidian Artifacts from Salmon Ruins, Northwest New Mexico. Archaeological XRF Laboratory University of California, Berkeley. Report on file, Salmon Ruins Museum, Bloomfield, New Mexico.

Shaffer, Brian S.
1992   Quarter-Inch Screening: Understanding Biases in Recovery of Vertebrate Faunal Remains. *American Antiquity* 57:129–136.

Shaw, G. R.
1914   *The Genus Pinus. Publications of the Arnold Arboretum 5*. Riverside Press, Cambridge.

Sheets, Payson
1974   Variation in the Behavioral Structuring of Lithic Industries. Paper presented at the 73rd annual meeting of the American Anthropological Association, Mexico City, Mexico.

Shelley, Phillip H.
1980a   Lithic Appendices 6.1–6.2.13. In *Investigations at the Salmon Site: The Structure of Chacoan Society in the Northern Southwest*, vol. III, edited by C. Irwin-Williams and P. Shelley, pp. 563–760. Unpublished report submitted to funding agencies. Ms. on file, Salmon Ruins Library, Bloomfield, New Mexico.

1980b   Salmon Macaws: A Brief Report of Art Harris's and Brett Russell's Data from LA8846. Ms. on file, Salmon Ruins Library, Bloomfield, New Mexico.

1983   *Lithic Specialization at Salmon Ruin, San Juan County, New Mexico*. Ph.D. dissertation, Washington State University, Pullman. University Microfilms, Ann Arbor.

Silver, Constance S.
1980   The State of Preservation of Pueblo Indian Mural Paintings in the American Southwest. Ms. on file, International Center for the Study of the Preservation and Restoration of Cultural Property, Rome, Italy.

1951   Cretaceous Stratigraphy of the San Juan Basin. In *New Mexico Geological Society Guidebook of the South and West Sides of the San Juan Basin, New Mexico and Arizona*. Second Field Conference, October 12–14, 1951, pp. 104–118.

Smith, C. E., Jr.
1950   Prehistoric Plant Remains from Bat Cave. *Harvard University Botanical Museum Leaflets* 14(7):157–180.

Smith, C. G.
1973   Sele, a Major Vegetal Component of the Aboriginal Hualapai Diet. *Plateau* 45:102–110.

Smith, Howard N., Jr.
1974   *A Survey and Stylistic Analysis of Rock Art in the San Juan Basin, Northwestern New Mexico*. Master's thesis, Department of Anthropology, Eastern New Mexico University, Portales.

Smith, James W., and Yezid Gutierrez
1991   Medical Parasitology. In *Clinical Diagnosis and Management by Laboratory Methods*, edited by J. B. Henry, pp. 1185–1186. 18th ed. W. B. Saunders, Philadelphia.

Smith, Watson
1952   *Kiva Mural Decorations at Awatovi and Kawaik-a: With a Survey of Other Wall Paintings in the Pueblo Southwest*. Papers of the Peabody Museum of Archaeology and Ethnology 37. Harvard University, Cambridge.

1972   *Prehistoric Kivas of Antelope Mesa, Northeastern Arizona*: Papers of the Peabody Museum of Archaeology and Ethnology 39(1). Harvard University, Cambridge.

Sokal, R. R., and F. J. Rohlf
1969   *Biometry*. W. J. Freeman, San Francisco.

Spence, M., and J. Kimberlin
    1979   Obsidian Procurement Systems of Teotihuacan, Mexico. Paper presented at the 44th annual meeting of the Society for American Archaeology, Vancouver.

Speth, John D., and Susan L. Scott
    1989   Horticulture and Large-Mammal Hunting: The Role of Resource Depletion and the Constraints of Time and Labor. In *Farmers as Hunters: The Implications of Sedentism*, edited by S. Kent, pp. 71–79. Cambridge University Press, Cambridge.

Standley, P. C.
    1911   Some Useful Native Plants of New Mexico. *Smithsonian Institution Annual Report, 1911*. Washington D.C.

Stanislawski, Michael B.
    1963   *Wupatki Pueblo: A Study in Cultural Fusion and Change in Sinagua and Hopi Prehistory*. Unpublished Ph.D. dissertation, Department of Anthropology, University of Arizona, Tucson.

Steen, C. R., L. M. Pierson, V. L. Bohrer, and K. P. Kent
    1962   *Archaeological Studies at Tonto National Monument, Arizona*. Technical Series 2. Southwest Monuments Association, Globe, Arizona.

Stein, John R., and Peter J. McKenna
    1988   *An Archaeological Reconnaissance of a Late Bonito Phase Occupation Near Aztec Ruins National Monument, New Mexico*. Southwest Cultural Resources Center, National Park Service, Santa Fe.

Stevenson, Matilda Cox
    1894   The Sia. *11th Annual Report of the Bureau of American Ethnology* 1889–1890.

    1904   The Zuni Indians: Their Mythology, Esoteric Fraternities, and Ceremonies. In *Twenty-third Annual Report of the Bureau of American Ethnology, 1901–2*, by J. W. Powell, pp. 3–608. Smithsonian Institution, Washington D.C.

    1915   Ethnobotany of the Zuni Indians. In *Thirtieth Annual Report of the Bureau of American Ethnology, 1908–9*, by J. W. Powell, pp. 31–102. Smithsonian Institution, Washington D.C.

Steward, J. H.
    1933   Ethnography of the Owens Valley Paiute. *University of California Publications in American Archaeology and Ethnology* 33(3):233–350.

Stewart, O. C.
    1941   Northern Paiute Culture Element Distributions: XIV. *University of California Anthropological Records* 4(3):361–446.

Stiger, Mark A.
    1977   *Anasazi Diet: The Coprolite Evidence*. Master's thesis, Department of Anthropology, University of Colorado, Boulder.

    1979   Mesa Verde Subsistence Patterns from Basketmaker to Pueblo III. *The Kiva* 44:133–144.

Stokes, Marvin A., and Terah L. Smiley
    1968   *An Introduction to Tree-Ring Dating*. University of Arizona Press, Tucson.

Stone, J.
    1979   The Socio-Economic Implications of the Lithic Evidence from Huari, Peru. Paper presented at the 44th annual meeting of the Society for American Archaeology, Vancouver, British Columbia, April 1979.

Stone, William
    2003   *New Mexico Then & Now*. Westcliff, Englewood, New Jersey.

Street, David J.
    2001   How Fast is a Kiva: The Dendrochronology of Long House, Mesa Verde National Park, Colorado. *Kiva* 67(2):137–165.

Struever, M. B.
    1977   *Relation of Pollen and Flotation Analysis to Archaeological Excavations, Chaco Canyon, New Mexico (Flotation Component)*. Master's thesis, Department of Biology, University of New Mexico, Albuquerque.

Stuart, B. R.
    1945   Pug-A-Roo Picks Pine-Nuts. *The Masterkey* 19:155.

Sturtevant, E. L.
    1899   *Varieties of Corn*. Office of Experiment Stations Bulletin 57. U.S. Department of Agriculture, Washington D.C.

Swank, G. R.
    1932   *The Ethnobotany of the Acoma and Laguna Indians*. Master's thesis, Department of Botany, University of New Mexico, Albuquerque.

Swannack, J. D., Jr.
    1969   *Big Juniper House, Mesa Verde, Colorado*. Research Series 7C. National Park Service, Washington D.C.

Swetnam, Thomas W.
    1990   Fire History and Climate in the Southwestern United States. In *Effects of Fire Management of Southwestern Resources*, Technical Coordinator J. S. Krammes, pp. 6–17. General Technical Report RM-191. USDA Forest Service, Rocky Mountain Forest and Range Experiment Station, Ft. Collins, Colorado.

Swetnam, Thomas W., and Christopher H. Baisan
1996   Historical Fire Regime Patterns in the Southwestern United States Since AD 1700. In *Fire Effects in Southwestern Forests: Proceedings of the Second La Mesa Fire Symposium*, edited by C. D. Allen, pp. 11–32. General Technical Report RM-GTR-286. USDA Forest Service, Rocky Mountain Forest and Range Experiment Station, Ft. Collins, Colorado.

Syngg, John, and Tom Windes
1998   Long, Wide Roads and Great Kiva Roofs. *Kiva* 64:7–25.

Szuter, Christine R., and Frank E. Bayham
1989   Sedentism and Prehistoric Animal Procurement Among Desert Horticulturalists of the North American Southwest. In *Farmers as Hunters: The Implications of Sedentism*, edited by S. Kent, pp. 80–95. Cambridge University Press, Cambridge.

Teague, Lynn S.
1998   *Textiles in Southwestern Prehistory*. University of New Mexico Press, Albuquerque.

Tennessen, David, Robert A. Blanchette, and Thomas C. Windes
2002   Differentiating Aspen and Cottonwood in Prehistoric Wood from Chacoan Great House Ruins. *Journal of Archaeological Science* 29:521–527.

Terrel, M. E.
1979   *A Study of Cucurbita Material from Salmon Ruin, New Mexico*. Master's thesis, Department of Anthropology, Eastern New Mexico University, Portales.

Torrey, J.
1859   Botany of the Boundary. In *Report on the United States and Mexican Boundary Survey 2*, by W. H. Emory. Executive Document 135, 34th Congress, 1st Session, Washington D.C.

Touchan, Ramzi, Craig D. Allen, and Thomas W. Swetnam
1996   Fire History and Climatic Patterns in Ponderosa Pine and Mixed-Conifer Forests of the Jemez Mountains, Northern New Mexico. In *Fire Effects in Southwestern Forests: Proceedings of the Second La Mesa Fire Symposium*, edited by C. D. Allen, pp. 33–46. General Technical Report RM-GTR-286. USDA Forest Service, Rocky Mountain Forest and Range Experiment Station, Ft. Collins, Colorado.

Towner, Ronald H.
2003   *Defending the Dinétah: Pueblitos in the Ancestral Navajo Homeland*. University of Utah Press, Salt Lake City.

Train, P., J. R. Herrichs, and W. A. Acher
1941   *Medicinal Uses of Plants by Indian Tribes of Nevada*. U.S. Department of Agriculture Contributions to a Flora of Nevada 33 (cited by Moerman 1977).

Trigger, B.
1972   Determinates of Urban Growth in Pre-Industrial Society. In *Man, Settlement, and Urbanism*, edited by P.J. Ucko, R. Tringham, and G.W. Dimbleby, pp. 575–599. Schenkman Publishing Co., Cambridge.

Truell, Marcia L.
1972   *Archaeological Excavations at the Ravine Site, Chimney Rock, Colorado*. Master's thesis, Department of Anthropology, University of Colorado, Boulder.

Tyler, Hamilton A.
1991   *Pueblo Birds and Myths*. University of Oklahoma Press, Norman.

Underhill, R.
1954   *Workaday Life of the Pueblos*. Department of the Interior, Bureau of Indian Affairs, Indian Life and Customs 4.

U.S. Department of Agriculture
1974   *Seeds of Woody Plants in the United States*. Agricultural Handbook 450.

U.S. Department of Commerce, NOAA, Environmental Data Service
1976   *Climatological Data: Annual Summary, New Mexico 80(13)*. National Climatic Center, Asheville, NC.

1977   *Climatological Data: Annual Summary, New Mexico 81(13)*. National Climatic Center, Asheville, NC.

Van Dyke, Ruth
1999   The Chaco Connection: Evaluating Bonito Style Architecture in Outlier Communities. *Journal of Anthropological Archaeology* 18:471–506.

2004   Memory, Meaning, and Masonry: The Late Bonito Chacoan Landscape. *American Antiquity* 69(3):413–431.

Van West, C. R., and J. S. Dean
2000   Environmental Characteristics of the A.D. 900–1300 Period in the Central Mesa Verde Region. *Kiva* 66:19–44.

Varien, Mark D., Carla R. Van West, and G. Stuart Patterson
2000   *Competition, Cooperation, and Conflict: Agricultural Production and Community Catchments in the Central Mesa Verde Region*. Kiva 66:45–65.

Veblen, T. T., K. S. Hadley, E. M. Kel, T. Kitzberger, M. Reid, and R. Villalba
1994   Disturbance Regime and Disturbance Interaction in a Rocky Mountain Subalpine Forest. *Journal of Ecology* 82:125–135.

Vestal, P. A.
1952   Ethnobotany of the Ramah Navajo. *Papers of the Peabody Museum of American Archaeology and Ethnology* 40(4). Harvard University, Cambridge.

Vita-Finzi, G., and E. S. Higgs
  1970   Prehistoric Economy in the Mount Carmel Area of Palestine: Site Catchment Analysis. In *Proceedings of the Prehistoric Society*, pp. 1–37.

Vivian, Gordon
  1931   Basketry of Chetro Ketl. Ms. on file (VA2107c) at the Chaco Center, University of New Mexico, Albuquerque.

Vivian, Gordon, and T. W. Mathews
  1964   *Kin Kletso: A Pueblo III Community in Chaco Canyon, New Mexico*. Technical Series 6(1). Southwest Monuments Association, Globe, Arizona.

Vivian, Gordon, and P. Reiter
  1960   *The Great Kivas of Chaco Canyon and Their Relationships*. SAR Monograph 22. School of American Research, Santa Fe.

Vivian, R. Gwinn
  1970   *Aspects of Prehistoric Society in Chaco Canyon, New Mexico*. Ph.D. dissertation, University of Arizona, Tucson. University Microfilms, Ann Arbor.

  1972   Appendix II. Relict Ponderosa Pine Study. In *Prehistoric Water Conservation in Chaco Canyon*. Final technical letter report for NSF grant GS-3100. Submitted to the National Science Foundation, Washington D.C.

  1990   *The Chacoan Prehistory of the San Juan Basin*. Academic Press, New York.

Voll, C. B.
  1964   BC 362: A Small Late 11th and Early 12th Century Farming Village in Chaco Canyon, New Mexico. Archive 505, NPS Chaco Culture NHP Museum Archive, University of New Mexico, Albuquerque.

Wallen, D. R., and J. A. Ludwig
  1978   Energy Dynamics of Vegetative and Reproductive Growth in Spanish Bayonet (*Yucca baccata* Torr.). *The Southwestern Naturalist* 23(3):409–422.

Washburn, Dorothy K.
  2005   The Position of Salmon Ruins in the Middle San Juan AD 1000–1300: A Perspective from Ceramic Design Structure. In *Salmon Ruins: Chacoan Outlier and Thirteenth-Century Pueblo in the Middle San Juan Region*, edited by P. F. Reed. Ms. in review, University of Utah Press, Salt Lake City.

Watt, B. K., and A. L. Merrill
  1975   *Composition of Foods*. U.S. Department of Agriculture, Agricultural Handbook 8.

Weaver, H.
  1951   Fire As an Ecological Factor in the Southwestern Pine Forest. *Journal of Forestry* 49:93–98.

Webster, Laurie D.
  1997   *Effects of European Contact on Textile Production and Exchange in the North American Southwest: A Pueblo Case Study*. Ph.D. dissertation, Department of Anthropology, University of Arizona. University Microfilms, Ann Arbor.

  2000   The Economics of Pueblo Textile Production and Exchange in Colonial New Mexico. In *Beyond Cloth and Cordage: Archaeological Textile Research in the Americas*, edited by P. B. Drooker and L. D. Webster, pp. 179–204. University of Utah Press, Salt Lake City.

  2003   Unpublished survey of basketry collections made by Frederick W. Hodge at Hawikuh, New Mexico. National Museum of the American Indian, Smithsonian Institution, Washington D.C.

  2004   Unpublished survey of worked fiber collections made by Earl H. Morris at the West Ruin of Aztec, New Mexico, and George H. Pepper at Pueblo Bonito, New Mexico. American Museum of Natural History, New York.

Wellhausen, E. J., L. M. Roberts, and E. Hernandez X., and P. C. Mangelsdorf
  1952   *Races of Maize in Mexico*. Bussey Institute of Harvard University, Cambridge, Massachusetts.

Wetterstrom, Wilma E.
  1976   *The Effects of Nutrition on Population Size at Pueblo Arroyo Hondo, New Mexico*. Unpublished Ph.D. dissertation, University of Michigan, Ann Arbor.

  1986   *Food, Diet, and Population at Prehistoric Arroyo Hondo Pueblo, New Mexico*. School of American Research Press, Santa Fe.

Whalley, L. A.
  1980   *Chacoan Ceramic Exchange in the Middle San Juan Area, A. D. 900–1300*. Master's thesis, Department of Anthropology, Eastern New Mexico University, Portales.

White, Adrian S., and David A. Breternitz
  1976   *Stabilization of the Lowry Ruins*. Cultural Resources Series 1. Bureau of Land Management, Colorado State Office, Denver.

White, Leslie A.
  1932   The Acoma Indians. In *Forty-seventh Annual Report of the Bureau of American Ethnology, 1929–1930*, pp. 18–192. Smithsonian Institution, Washington D.C.

  1942   *The Pueblo of Santa Ana*. American Anthropological Association Memoirs 60. Collegiate Press, Menasha, Wisconsin.

  1945   Notes on the Ethnobotany of the Keres. *Papers of the Michigan Academy of Science* 30:557–568.

1962   *The Pueblo of Sia, New Mexico.* Bureau of American Ethnology Bulletin 184. Smithsonian Institution, Washington D.C.

1974   *Zia – The Sun Symbol Pueblo.* Calvin Horn, Albuquerque.

Whiting, Alfred F.
1939   *Ethnobotany of the Hopi.* Bulletin 15. Museum of Northern Arizona, Flagstaff.

1966   *Ethnobotany of the Hopi.* Northland Press, Flagstaff, Arizona.

Whitten, P.
1977a   93W, Floor Unit 1. Memorandum on file, Eastern New Mexico University, Portales.

1977b   93W, Floor Unit 2. Memorandum on file, Eastern New Mexico University, Portales.

1977c   93W, Floor Unit 5. Memorandum on file, Eastern New Mexico University, Portales.

Wilcox, David R.
1993   The Evolution of the Chacoan Polity. In *The Chimney Rock Archaeological Symposium,* edited by J. M. Malville and G. Matlock, pp. 76–90. General Technical Report RM-227, USDA Forest Service, Rocky Mountain Forest and Experiment Station, Fort Collins, Colorado.

2004   The Evolution of the Chacoan Polity. In *Chimney Rock: The Ultimate Outlier,* edited by Malville J. McKim, pp. 163–200. Lexington Books, Lanham, Maryland.

Wilcox, David R., and Lynette O. Shenk
1977   *The Architecture of the Casa Grande and its Interpretation.* Arizona State Museum, Archaeological Series 115. University of Arizona, Tucson.

Wilkes, Garrison
2004   Corn, Strange and Marvelous: But is a Definite Origin Known? In *Corn: Origin, History, Technology, and Production,* edited C. W. Smith, pp. 3–63. John Wiley and Sons, New York.

Williams-Dean, Glenna
1986   Pollen Analysis of Human Coprolites. In *Archeological Investigations at Antelope House,* edited by D. P. Morris, pp. 189–205. Publications in Archeology 19. National Park Service, Washington D.C.

Wilshusen, Richard H., and Eric Blinman
1992   Pueblo I Village Formation: A Reevaluation of Sites Recorded by Earl Morris on Ute Mountain Ute Tribal Lands. *Kiva* 57:251–269.

Wilshusen, Richard H., and Scott G. Ortman
1999   Rethinking the Pueblo I Period in the San Juan Drainage: Aggregation, Migration, and Cultural Diversity. *Kiva* 66:369–399.

Wilshusen, Richard H., and Ruth Van Dyke
2006   In Search of Chaco's Beginnings: The Collapse of Pueblo I Villages and the Origins of the Chaco System. In *The Archaeology of Chaco Canyon: An 11th Century Regional Center,* edited by S. H. Lekson, pp. 211–260. School of American Research Press, Santa Fe.

Wilshusen, Richard H., and C. Dean Wilson
1995   Reformatting the Social Landscape in the Late Pueblo I–Early Pueblo II Period: The Cedar Hill Data in Regional Context. In *The Cedar Hill Special Treatment Project: Late Pueblo I, early Navajo, and Historic Occupations in Northwestern New Mexico,* compiled by R. H. Wilshusen, pp. 43–80. La Plata Archaeological Consultants, Research Papers 1. Dolores, Colorado.

Windes, Thomas C.
1987a   *Investigations at the Pueblo Alto Complex, Chaco Canyon, New Mexico 1975–1979, Vol. I: Summary of Tests and Excavations at the Pueblo Alto Community.* Publications in Archaeology 18F. National Park Service, Santa Fe.

1987b   *Investigations at the Pueblo Alto Complex, Chaco Canyon, New Mexico 1975–1979, Vol. II: Architecture and Stratigraphy.* Publications in Archaeology 18F. National Park Service, Santa Fe.

1987c   Some Ground Stone Tools and Hammerstones from Pueblo Alto. In *Investigations at the Pueblo Alto Complex, Chaco Canyon,* vol. III, edited by F. J. Mathien and T. C. Windes, pp. 291–358. Publications in Archaeology 18F. National Park Service, Santa Fe.

1987d   The Use of Turkeys at Pueblo Alto Based on the Eggshell and Faunal Remains. In *Investigations at the Pueblo Alto Complex, Chaco Canyon,* vol. III, part 2, edited by F. J. Mathien and T. C. Windes, pp. 679–687. Publications in Archaeology 18F. National Park Service, Santa Fe.

2003   This Old House: Construction and Abandonment at Pueblo Bonito. In *Pueblo Bonito: Center of the Chacoan World,* edited by J. E. Neitzel, pp. 14–32. Smithsonian Books, Washington D.C.

2006   Gearing Up and Piling On: Early Great Houses in the Chaco Basin. In *Architecture of Chaco Canyon, New Mexico,* edited by S. H. Lekson, Chapter 3. University of Utah Press, Salt Lake City (in press).

Windes, Thomas C., and Dabney Ford
1996   The Chaco Wood Project: Chronometric Reappraisal of Pueblo Bonito. *American Antiquity* 61(2):295–310.

Windes, Thomas C., and Peter J. McKenna
2001   Going Against the Grain: Wood Production in Chacoan Society. *American Antiquity* 66:119–140.

Windes, Thomas C., Cheryl Ford, and Dabney Ford
    1994   The Chaco Wood Project: Reanalysis of Pueblo del Arroyo. Unpublished ms. submitted to the Southwestern
            Parks and Monuments Association, Tucson. Ms. on file, Salmon Ruins Library, Bloomfield, New Mexico.

Winter, J.
    1973   The Distribution and Development of Fremont Maize Agriculture: Some Preliminary Interpretations. *American
            Antiquity* 38(4):439–452.

Woodbury, A. M.
    1947   Distribution of Pigmy Conifers in Utah and Northeastern Arizona. *Ecology* 28:113–126.

Woodbury, R. B.
    1939   Ground and Pecked Stone Artifacts (Other than Arrow-Shaft Tools). In *Preliminary Report on the 1937
            Excavations, BC 50–51, Chaco Canyon, New Mexico*, edited by C. Kluckhohn and P. Reiter, pp. 58–79. Bulletin
            345, Anthropological Series 3(2). University of New Mexico, Albuquerque.

    1954   *Prehistoric Stone Implements of Northeastern Arizona*. Papers of the Peabody Museum of Archaeology and
            Ethnology 34(6). Harvard University, Cambridge.

Wright, H. E., Jr., Anne M. Bent, Barbara Spross Hansen, and L. J. Maher, Jr.
    1973   Present and Past Vegetation of the Chuska Mountains, Northwestern New Mexico. *Geological Society of America
            Bulletin* 84(4):1155–1179.

Wyman, L. C., and S. K. Harris
    1951   *The Ethnobotany of the Kayenta Navaho*. UNM Publications in Biology 5. University of New Mexico Press,
            Albuquerque.

Yanovsky, E., and R. M. Kingsbury
    1938   Analysis of Some Indian Food Plants. *Association of Analytical Chemistry* 21:648–655.

Zarn, M.
    1977   *Ecological Characteristics of Pinyon-Juniper Woodlands on the Colorado Plateau: A Literature Survey*. Technical
            Note 310. Bureau of Land Management, Denver.

Zedeño, Maria Nieves, James Busman, James Burton, and Barbara J. Mills
    1993   Ceramic Compositional Analyses. In *Interpretation of Ceramic Artifacts*, by B. J. Mills, C. E. Goetze, and M. N.
            Zedeño, pp. 187-234. Across the Colorado Plateau: Anthropological Studies for the Transwestern Pipeline
            Expansion Project, vol. XVI. UNM Project 185-461B. Office of Contract Archeology and Maxwell Museum of
            Anthropology, University of New Mexico, Albuquerque.

Zigmund, M.
    1981   *Kawaiisu Ethnobotany*. University of Utah Press, Salt Lake City.

Zwolinski, Malcolm J.
    1996   Effects of Fire on Montane Forest Ecosystems. In *Effects of Fire on Madrean Province Ecosystems: A Symposium
            Proceedings*, by P. Folliott, L. DeBano, M. Baker, G. Gottfried, G. Solis-Garza, C. Edminster, D. Neary, L. Allen,
            and R. Hamre, pp. 125–134. General Technical Report RM-GTR-289. USDA Forest Service, Rocky Mountain
            Forest and Range Experiment Station, Ft. Collins, Colorado.